Introductory
Textile
Science

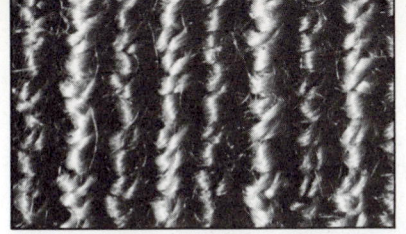

FIFTH EDITION

Introductory Textile Science

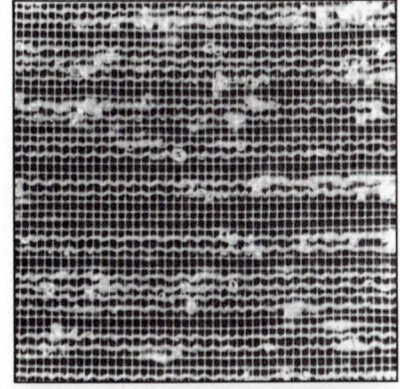

Marjory L. Joseph

California State University, Northridge

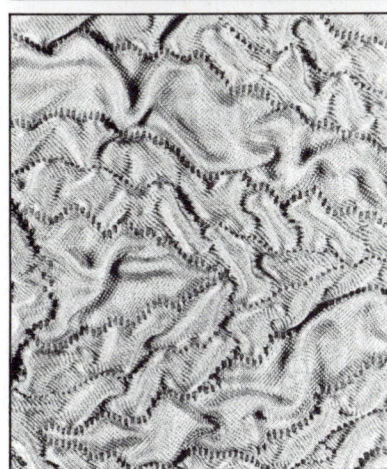

Holt, Rinehart and Winston

New York   Chicago   San Francisco   Philadelphia
Montreal   Toronto   London   Sydney   Tokyo
Mexico City   Rio de Janeiro   Madrid

Publisher   *Susan Katz*
Acquisitions Editor   *Karen Dubno*
Senior Project Editor   *Herman Makler*
Production Manager   *Nancy Myers*
Art Director   *Lou Scardino*
Text Design   *Caliber Design Planning, Inc.*

Library of Congress Cataloging-in-Publication Data

Joseph, Marjory L.
   Introductory textile science.

   Bibliography: p.
   Includes index.
   1. Textile fibers.   2. Textile fabrics.   I. Title.
TS1445.J64   1986   677   85-24726

ISBN 0-03-071484-2

Address correspondence to:
383 Madison Avenue
New York, N. Y. 10017

CBS COLLEGE PUBLISHING
Holt, Rinehart and Winston
The Dryden Press
Saunders College Publishing

To Ruth W. Ayres, my mentor

and

to my family: Nancy, Dave, and Bill

Preface

Introductory Textile Science is written to meet the major objectives identified in previous editions as well as several new objectives identified for this, the fifth edition. My major goal is to provide college and university students with a text that is interesting, pedagogically sound, and comprised of accurate and up-to-date information concerning textile fibers, yarns, and fabrics. Specifically, the book is designed to do the following:

Stimulate within each reader a desire to recognize and appreciate textile fabrics

Offer sound scientific theory concerning fibers, including their production, processing, and treatment, so that students may gain a scientifically sound base for decision making relative to the selection, use, and care of textiles

Identify guidelines based on the use of scientific data that may be used in the selection, use, and care of textile products

Provide the reader with the information that will lead to an understanding of the complex interrelationships among fibers, yarn structure or fiber arrangement, fabric structure, finishing, and coloring

Identify how these complex interrelationships can be used in the selection, use, and care of textile items

Help students become aware of the complexity of the textile industry and understand existing legal rules and regulations

Provide pedagogical aids to increase the ease of learning about textiles and making decisions concerning their selection, use, and care

Identify many of the new high-tech uses of textiles such as high performance fibers and fabrics and geotextiles.

In today's world, including space, no one is completely isolated from textile fabrics. They clothe, protect, decorate, and provide us with many hours of enjoyment. Fabrics cover furniture and floors of the home; they drape and curtain the windows. Textiles serve in kitchens, bathrooms, bedrooms, and living rooms. Fabrics make public buildings attractive and somewhat soundproof; specialized fabrics are found in a wide variety of industrial applications; and geotextiles are becoming extremely important. Every mode of transportation, including space vehicles, uses textiles in some form. Protective clothing serves industrial employees, firefighters, police officers, astronauts, race car drivers, and agricultural workers, to name only a few.

The years that have passed since the first edition of *Introductory Textile Science* have seen many developments in fiber science, in yarn processing, in fabric construction types and construction processes, and in finishing and coloring procedures. These developments have involved the production of new textile fibers, modifications of existing fibers, new ways to make yarns and fabrics, and new methods for finishing and dyeing fabrics. The past few years, in particular, have been characterized by tremendous developments in the technology of manufacturing yarns and fabrics and the finishing and coloration of fabrics. Some of the more important changes include developments in processing textiles that reduce energy requirements and conserve natural resources. Continuing developments in textiles for space exploration provide enhanced products for our own planet. Legislation continues to provide rules and regulations aimed at informing as well as protecting consumers.

In writing this new edition I have tried to prepare a text that is modern and accurate, and useful; to meet this goal, I have made many changes in this edition. Some will be obvious to the reader; others may not be quite so apparent. Therefore, it seems important to call attention to the changes that make this edition truly new.

First, and most important, throughout the text I have attempted to report the most recent developments. To that intent, I have provided current economic data and noted changes and trends in fiber use and consumption both over time and to the mid-1980s. I have integrated information into chapters on textile fibers concerning new fiber variants and modifications, yet retained basic information related to specific types of natural and manufactured fibers. Similarly, I have identified new methods of making yarn as well as changes in the traditional processes and have provided current information on methods and machinery used in fabric construction, noting processes that are gaining in use and that represent technological advances. Further, I have provided current information on legislation including labeling and protective regulations; identified voluntary guides for specifications used in preparing textiles that meet consumer needs and desires; and identified new technology and processes designed to conserve the nation's resources including energy utilization and ecological concerns.

Second, I have rearranged some of the chapters in order to provide clarity and to recognize a systematic sequence. In Part I, chapters have been put into a more logical order, in which fiber classification is followed by chapters on fiber theory and fiber identification. In Part II, a new chapter serves as a general introduction to the study of fibers. This chapter is followed by a description of the natural protein fibers and then the natural cellulosic fibers, making it possible to follow the natural cellulosic fibers with the chapters on the man-made cellulosic and modified cellulosic fiber chapters. Part III includes the chapter on stretch yarns and fabrics and on blends and combination yarns and fabrics, with the latter renamed "Blends and Combination Yarns and Fabrics." Parts IV and V on fabrics and on finish and color application have been left in the same order as in the fourth edition, but in Part VI on fabric end use the information on all textile legislation has been pulled together into one chapter, and this is followed by a chapter on fabric performance and testing. The text concludes with a new chapter that describes, in brief, specialized uses of textiles such as geotextile applications, high-performance fibers and fabrics, and applications in medicine.

Third, each chapter now begins with objectives which identify the important content of the chapter and the material considered essential to the reader. They are followed by a set of terms important to the concepts discussed in the chapter. At the conclusion of each chapter are sets of study questions and activities, which may be used as possible review exercises and learning experiences for students.

I have continued the effort to make this book meet the scientific standards required by many instructors by including relevant textile chemistry to simplify the understanding of fiber behavior and the chemical reactions related to finishing, dyeing, printing, and maintenance of fabrics. However, the chemistry has been confined to what is considered essential for this type of textbook. It is hoped that the chemistry is explained adequately and that it does support specific concepts involved in making and converting textile fibers into fabrics ready for consumer use.

The text has been arranged into parts that can stand independently. Thus, the instructor can select the order in which he or she wishes to present the material to students. For example, the instructor could start with fabric construction first and then move back to yarn and to fibers.

Although I believe that modern education should emphasize theoretical information, it is also important that theory be interpreted in a way that aids students and consumers. With this in mind, the audience for this text might include general home economics majors, merchandising majors, textile science majors, business majors, and others who have an interest in the production, processing, and maintenance of textile products.

No single text can be sufficient unto itself. The suggested references cited at the conclusion of the text are given in an effort to provide other interpretations and concepts in order to increase student knowledge and awareness concerning textiles. Whenever possible, an effort has been made to increase the reader's understanding of the knowledge needed for making sound decisions concerning the maintenance or care, durability, appearance, and comfort of textile products.

The field of textiles is a dynamic one. It combines natural science, social science, and art in a subject that is new every day. A large segment of the population derives economic security from various manufacturing and marketing processes associated with textiles. I will feel gratified, indeed, if this text enables the reader to develop some sense of the magnitude of the textile industry and acquire an interest in and respect for fabrics and the functions they perform.

Acknowledgments

Many persons, businesses, and organizations have helped in the preparation of the various editions of

Introductory Textile Science. I would like to express my appreciation for the contributions of the following individuals who provided careful scrutiny of the writing—content, sources, and teachability: Dr. Ruth L. Galbraith, Auburn University; Dr. J. W. Weaver, University of Delaware; Dr. Robert G. Steadman, Colorado State University; Dr. Ira Block, University of Maryland; Stasia Brokaw, Philadelphia College of Textiles and Science; Dr. Bonnita M. Farmer, California State Polytechnic University—Pomona; Susan S. Fiorito, The University of Iowa; Ruth E. Franzen, The University of Minnesota; Dr. Theresa A. Perenich, The University of Georgia; and Dr. Ardis M. Rewerts, The University of Texas at Austin, as well as the many other instructors and students who have provided helpful input.

For various editions I have had the help of the following for preparing the manuscript: Christine H. Smith, Dorothy Blackman, Doris Getsch, Barbara Coyle, and Nancy David. To each of these my sincerest thanks and deep appreciation.

Many in the various areas of the textile industry have provided valuable information; however, a few deserve special mention. Marshall Doswell of Springs Industries, Inc., provided the opportunity to see at first hand the various textile operations and to discuss questions with the technical staff of that organization. Through his interest, Springs Industries has provided a number of illustrations that add to the chapters on textile manufacturing. Others from Springs Industries who have been of great help are Dr. William H. Martin and Robert Slough.

For this edition I am especially grateful to Fisher Rhymes of the Man-Made Fiber Producers Association and to members of its technical committee, particularly Dr. B. V. Hettrick and Dr. Herbert Pratt. Their help and input regarding fiber theory and man-made fibers has been a tremendous aid and should ensure that the information about man-made fibers is accurate and represents the state of the art.

I would like to give a very special note of appreciation to my daughter, Nancy David, who assumed the responsibility for collecting illustrations, helped prepare new photographs that I took, and prepared the bibliography and index. Her help and cooperation are deeply appreciated.

In citing the help that friends and colleagues have extended to me, I wish at the same time to absolve them of, and assume full responsibility for, any errors or omissions the reader may discover.

As always, I acknowledge my dependence on the tolerance and help of my husband, William Joseph, and my daughter and son-in-law, Nancy and Dave. Without their support this work would not have been possible.

M.L.J.

Contents

PART V Finish and Color Application   279

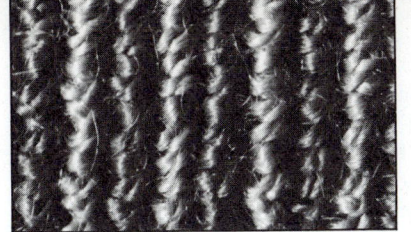

1

Introduction to Textiles

OBJECTIVES
◇ **To provide a general overview of the textile industry and its position in the national economy**
◇ **To establish basic historical background required for the understanding of the study of textiles**

KEY TERMS

careers in textile science
conservation

consumption and availability of fibers
pollution

production, world and national
safety
textile

Every person comes in contact with various textile products each day. Most of us must make decisions at some point concerning the selection of textile items. This process can be relatively easy if one has knowledge about the appearance, maintenance, durability, and comfort of textile products and the factors involved in making these decisions. However, as new developments occur in the field of textile science and technology, it becomes increasingly difficult to make intelligent selections because of the amount of information that must be processed. Knowledge of the chemical, physical, and microbiological properties of fibers and of the behavior that results from techniques used in creating fabrics guides the consumer in making wise selections in the marketplace. An attempt is made to provide key ideas and facts that help the student and/or the consumer become adequately informed concerning the selection, use, and care of textile products. Knowledge of proper maintenance procedures for the myriad textile products helps ensure continued satisfaction with a product after purchase. This book, then, attempts to provide key ideas and information that will aid readers in their efforts to become well-informed consumers.

Textile science covers a large area. To begin with, the word *textile* comes from the Latin *textilis,* "woven," which in turn comes from the Latin verb *textere,* "to weave." In textile science, however, a textile is freely defined as any product made from fibers; thus, the term refers not only to woven fabrics, but also to nonwoven fabrics, knitted fabrics, and special fabric constructions. The term *textile fiber* refers to *any product capable of being woven or otherwise made into fabrics.* These broad reciprocal definitions are now accepted and used by nearly everyone who works with fibers or fabrics at any step of manufacturing or processing.

Textile fibers and the fabrics made from them have almost limitless uses, and new applications are constantly being found. The uses of fibers in clothing, home furnishings, and other household textiles are familiar to everyone. But fibers are also used in the building trades, as insulation in appliances, and by industry for such products as filter clothes, pulley belts, and protective apparel; they are used in all forms of transportation including space vehicles; they are used in geoapplications to provide for such factors as drainage and stabilization. In fact, fibers and textile products play their essential roles in nearly every activity and situation conceivable, from playing in the sand to walking on the moon.

Historical Background

The immense scope of the textile industry makes it one of the largest in the world. It is also one of the oldest. Archeological evidence indicates that textiles of fine quality were made thousands of years before the oldest preserved written accounts refer to them. The early history of textile fibers and fabrics has been determined by such archeological discoveries as spinning whorls, distaffs, loom weights, and fragments of fabrics found in such places as the Swiss Lake regions and Egyptian tombs.

All early fabrics were composed of fibers from natural plant or animal sources. Wool, flax, cotton, and silk were the most important. Later, mineral matter in the form of rock asbestos was used. At first, plant and animal fibers apparently were subjected to a minimum of processing, and most early fabrics were probably made by a simple plain weave interlacing of groups of fibers and yarns or by knotting or plaiting fibers, grasses, or other raw materials. The ingenuity of human beings and their desire to enhance their own appearance, led, over the centuries, to the development of complicated fabrics and, within the past hundred years, to great technological expansion.

From ancient eras until the eighteenth century, all fabrics were constructed and decorated by hand. Weaving or felting took place in the home or in small workshops. Some artist-weavers of those past centuries achieved great skill, and many of their products have never been surpassed. Beautiful examples of old Oriental carpets and rugs, huge tapestries portraying intricate scenes, and early Coptic textiles hang in museums all over the world as treasured exhibits (Fig. 1.1).

The Industrial Revolution of the eighteenth and nineteenth centuries transferred the processing of fibers and the manufacture of fabrics from the home or small cottage shop to the factory. Mechanization gained importance, and the textile industry expanded. Cotton and wool were especially affected by the development of machine-powered equipment. The growth and production of these natural fibers became the concern of governments throughout the world. Tariffs were levied, wars fought, and regimes toppled because of the political, social, and economic pressures that accompanied industrial advances in textiles.

For most of recorded history, nature has been the only source of fibers for textiles. The first man-made fiber to become a reality was rayon, which appeared, commercially, early in the twentieth century. This was followed by cellulose acetate in the 1920s. Since the 1930s, scientists have produced many new fibers, fiber variants, and modifications of man-made fibers. In fact, there have been greater advances in fibers, fabrics, and wet processing techniques (finishing and dyeing) since 1900 than in the several thousand years before.

Since the 1960s, major changes in the production and manufacture of fibers, yarns, and fabrics have occurred. The development of second-, third-, and fourth-generation fibers, fiber variants and modifications, and new methods of processing fibers into ultimate end-use products has affected finishing and coloring of fabrics at the manufacturing level and behavior in use and care at the consumer level. New procedures and products used in finishing and coloring fabrics have provided consumers with a range of textile items that meets almost every possible need. Continued research and development will help the industry meet the needs of and challenges for the end of the twentieth and the early part of the twenty-first century. Of tremendous importance during the 1980s is the development of equipment used in processing fibers to ultimate end-use products that provide durability, reduce the use of valuable natural resources, and still provide top-quality products.

Factors Affecting the Textile Industry

The textile industry is large. Just how large? Actually, if all facets of the vast economic giant are taken into account, it will probably be found to involve more people and more money than any other industry. Even when we consider only the growth, production, manufacturing, and processing of fibers to fabrics, the textile industry still is very near the top among industries of the world in terms of both workers and dollar value.

The world of textiles is dependent upon many factors. The impact of fashion cannot be ignored. Fashion determines, for many consumers, what is bought, when it is bought, and how frequently it is replaced. Further, the dictates of fashion often determine whether durability is important, what type of care will meet consumer needs, and how frequently items will be discarded and replaced.

Of great concern to the future of textiles are considerations related to the production and care of textile products that permit conservation of energy and

1.1 Tapestry woven in wool and silk with metal threads; 12 feet 1 inch by 9 feet 9 inches (3.6 by 2.9 m). French or Flemish, late 15th century. (Metropolitan Museum of Art, Cloisters Collection; gift of John D. Rockefeller, Jr., 1937)

raw materials. In an era when the need to conserve energy and energy-rich resources is of great importance to the nation and the world, manufacturers must search for production methods that use a minimum amount of energy rich resources. Furthermore, products must be made available that require as little energy as possible for care.

Many of the manufactured noncellulosic fibers are derived from petroleum. With a limited supply of this raw material, and with the need to reduce imports of it, there may be a return to greater production of natural fibers. This could result in a concomitant reduction in the production of petroleum-based fibers. The same holds true for wet processing of textiles and the development of technology that reduces the use of energy. This in turn means a decrease in the use of energy-rich resources, a trend that is assuming great importance in the textile industry. It should be noted, however, that the use of natural resources, such as petroleum, in the care and maintenance of natural fibers matches or exceeds the use of such resources in producing man-made petroleum-based fibers. Thus, consumers must make informed choices in this regard.

As part of the trend toward conservation of energy and natural resources, another problem becomes apparent. The production of natural fibers, particularly cotton and wool, faces additional complications. As more land is taken over for commercial and residential use and as populations expand into rural areas, the amount of land available for agricultural use decreases. Thus, it becomes necessary to make do with less cotton or to increase the production per acre under cultivation and provide lush rangeland for sheep so that more sheep can be handled on less land. However, if production of man-made fibers must be reduced, consumers will ultimately have two choices: either help locate areas for the production of natural fibers or find ways to satisfy the needs for textiles with less available yardage of both natural and man-made fiber content.

The problem of conserving energy and natural resources cannot be solved easily. Furthermore, it is a problem that many consumers are neither aware of nor interested in. Students, however, should give thought to these issues and help seek solutions that will be desirable for both industry and consumers.

Environmental Concerns

There are other factors that the textile student should recognize. Among them are the dangers of pollution—noise, air, and water. The damage from noise pollution has long been a problem in the textile industry, particularly in fabric manufacture. Weaving rooms have been notorious for the loud sounds of the loom operation and the fly hitting the shuttle as well as other noisy operations. New types of looms using alternative methods for placing picks have reduced noise considerably in the weaving rooms. Other modifications of equipment aimed at reducing noise pollution are under development or have already been implemented. In addition, employees are asked to wear protective devices in areas where there is a high level of noise.

Pollution of the air and water has received considerable attention during the past decade and will continue to be a concern. To aid in reducing water pollution, manufacturers have installed costly water-purification equipment; they have turned to alternative methods of processing, including the use of solvents and foam technology. Solvents can be reclaimed and work effectively in several finishing and processing operations. Foams are designed to require a limited amount of liquid, which is mixed with air; this reduces the amount of liquid to be released, and it lowers energy requirements by reducing the amount needed in drying fabrics.

The pollution of outside air through exhaust of fumes and smoke has been controlled for some time in many areas and should be controlled in all parts of the United States within the near future. Pollution of inside air has, in the past, been responsible for a variety of illnesses among employees. Cleaning and filtering the air to reduce or eliminate this interior pollution has become a necessity for all plants today, owing, in part, to demands by various government agencies and employee groups.

Textile students and consumers in general should recognize that the installation of various controls required to reduce noise, air, and water pollution adds to the cost of production. These costs are usually passed on to the consumer of textile products.

The use of chemicals that are potential carcinogens or toxic in some other way has been discouraged or banned by the government and by special consumer advocate and medical groups. These concerns have resulted in the discontinuance of the use of certain products involved in finishing and dyeing fabrics. The problems with tris, a fire retardant, focused considerable public attention on the textile industry and problems with chemicals that are potential carcinogens. This product, which had

◇

TABLE 1.1 World Production of Man-Made Fibers, Cotton, Wool, and Silk (Data in Millions of Pounds and Percentages in Parentheses)

Year	Rayon and Acetate	Noncellulosic	Cotton	Wool	Silk*	Olefin	Glass	Total
1950	3,553 (17)	153 (1)	14,654 (71)	2,330 (11)	42	NA	NA	20,732
1960	5,749 (17)	1,548 (5)	22,295 (68)	3,225 (10)	68	NA	NA	32,885
1970	7,573 (16)	10,871 (23)	24,947 (53)	3,499 (8)	83	NA	NA	46,973
1976	7,076 (12)	18,963 (31)	27,513 (45)	3,278 (5)	106	2,335 (4)	1,486 (2)	60,757
1977	7,233 (11)	20,171 (31)	30,690 (47)	3,280 (5)	108	2,609 (4)	1,797 (3)	65,888
1978	7,314 (11)	22,121 (33)	28,600 (43)	3,369 (5)	112	2,833 (4)	2,002 (3)	66,351
1979	7,433 (10)	23,372 (33)	31,460 (44)	3,468 (5)	121	2,996 (4)	2,178 (3)	71,028
1980	7,148 (10)	23,094 (32)	31,451 (45)	3,485 (5)	123	2,964 (4)	1,991 (3)	70,256
1981	7,064 (10)	23,876 (32)	33,999 (46)	3,547 (5)	126	3,089 (4)	2,134 (3)	73,835
1982	6,497 (9)	22,358 (32)	32,357 (46)	3,563 (5)	121	2,987 (4)	1,987 (3)	69,870
1983	6,619 (9)	24,477 (34)	32,022 (45)	3,541 (5)	121	2,608 (4)	2,374 (3)	71,762

*Percentage for silk is below 1 percent.

seemed to be a successful way to treat fabrics for flame resistance, was banned late in the 1970s, and alternative methods for making fabrics flame resistant had to be found. Currently, the odor from formaldehyde is receiving the attention of industry as well as government agencies and consumer groups. This chemical is considered essential in certain finishing operations. Consequently, instead of finding alternative products, research has been directed at finding ways to reduce the release of free formaldehyde vapors into the air.

It is obvious to members of the textile industry as well as to teachers of textile science that consumer concerns become concerns of the industry. Protection from fire has become a requirement for children's sleepwear and many items used in home furnishings. Protection from injurious chemicals is another objective of textile manufacturers, consumer groups, and government agencies.

It must be noted, however, that the textile industry has not solved all of its problems related to environmental concerns and safety issues. There is still much to be done to ensure a relatively safe work environment.

Economic Factors

Statistical data help indicate the size and importance of the textile industry. More than 50 billion pounds of fiber were produced yearly between 1972 and 1976. Since 1976 over 60 billion pounds per year of fiber have been produced in the world (see Table 1.1). Each year has seen an increase, even in

periods of economic recession. In the United States, production of textile fibers has exceeded 10 billion pounds per year since the mid-1970s. Because of reporting procedures these figures do not always include olefin fibers, glass fibers, and the natural bast fibers. Therefore, fiber production figures appear lower than the actual amount produced and consumed.

Production of man-made fibers has increased, generally, each year. During the late 1970s, it rose to nearly 9 billion pounds per year. Owing to the economic recession of the early 1980s, man-made fiber production in the United States dropped slightly, but there was a noticeable increase in 1983.

Since the mid-1970s, over 30 billion pounds of man-made fiber have been produced yearly in the world. These figures include olefin and glass fiber, which accounted for between 4 and 5 billion pounds yearly. The report for 1982 indicated a drop in both fiber production and consumption. In the world market, fiber production dropped from a total for all fiber of nearly 74 billion pounds in 1981 to under 70 billion in 1982. An increase occurred in 1983 to approximately 72 billion pounds.

Per-capita consumption, now identified as average annual fiber available for consumption, shows rather dramatically what has happened to consumption of man-made fibers in the United States as compared with cotton and wool (Table 1.2). Since 1950 the consumption of cotton has dropped from over 29 pounds per capita to just over 15 pounds per capita in 1983. On the other hand, consumption of

◇ ─────────────────────────────

TABLE 1.2 Average Annual Fiber Consumption in the United States (Data in Pounds)

Year	Man-Made Fibers	Cotton	Wool	Total
1950	9.5	29.3	4.5	43.4
1955	11.0	25.4	3.3	39.7
1960	10.0	23.3	3.4	36.7
1965	18.3	23.9	2.9	48.0
1970	26.4	19.7	1.7	47.8
1975	32.8	14.9	0.7	48.4
1976	35.0	16.9	0.9	52.8
1977	38.1	15.8	0.9	54.8
1978	39.1	15.8	1.0	55.9
1979	38.3	14.8	0.9	54.0
1980	34.4	14.7	0.9	50.0
1981	34.2	14.5	1.0	49.7
1982	30.3	13.5	0.9	44.7
1983	36.6	15.8	1.2	53.6

man-made fibers has increased from less than 10 pounds per capita in 1950 to over 36.5 pounds in 1983. During the 1970s several years recorded consumption of man-made fibers similar to that for 1983. The peak year for man-made fibers to date is 1978, with over 39 pounds per capita. The peak year to date for total per-capita consumption of fiber was 1973, with 61 pounds per capita.

Tables 1.3 and 1.4 show the distribution of specific fiber consumption since 1970. It is clear that polyester has been the predominate fiber since 1977, when it surpassed cotton. It has retained that status since then. In general, since 1977 polyester has accounted for more poundage used than any other fiber; cotton has been second, followed by nylon. Man-made fibers have consistently exceeded natural fiber consumption since 1970.

Man-made fibers provide more yardage at less weight; therefore, the increase in the use of these fibers means that total yardage used has increased even in years when the total per-capita use by weight showed a slight overall drop. Furthermore, styles of the 1960s and early 1970s required less yardage than fashions of the 1950s. Styles of the 1970s and early 1980s varied widely in the amount of yardage required; thus, it is difficult to form conclusions about yardage used. It must be remembered, however, that per-capita consumption data include the use of textiles for home furnishings and domestics, for transportation, and for business and industry as well as for apparel.

It is apparent through studying these data that the use of man-made fibers has increased dramatically over the past 30 years, while the use of natural fibers has decreased.

World production of textile fibers increased through 1981 (Table 1.1). A slight drop has been noted between 1979 and 1980 and another drop of greater magnitude between 1981 and 1982. The world production pattern shows the same general pattern as the consumption data for the United States. The use of natural fibers has decreased, while the use of man-made fibers has increased. On the world market, however, the production of cotton continues to be greater than all noncellulosic man-made fibers together. However, if cellulosic man-mades and noncellulosic man-mades are added together, their production exceeded cotton by a slight amount in 1978 and again in 1979 and 1981.

Considerable data concerning fiber production and consumption are appearing in metric tons to be consistent with the metric system. However, as the United States still uses figures in pounds, data in pounds have been used in this text.

It has been noted that production of textile fibers has increased, in general, over the past decades, and particular increases have occurred in the production and consumption of man-made fibers. Increased production and consumption of textile products are due to a combination of factors; the increase in population and an increased level of consumption both play some part in the change. It is possible, however, that a reduction in consumption of textile products may be mandated in the future to ensure an adequate supply of textile end-use products to meet basic needs. How this can be accomplished will be another problem that present students of textiles will have to consider as future employees of the industry or as consumers of textile products.

Unions in the Textile Industry

Several unions are involved in various aspects of the textile industry. These unions provide a wide variety of services to their members. They relate well to manufacturers and to employees. In the United States it is generally acknowledged that unions have resulted in improved working conditions, higher wages, and increased benefits for all employees. Two of the most important unions in the textile industries are the Amalgamated Clothing and Textile Workers Union and the International Ladies Garment Workers Union.

TABLE 1.3   Estimated Per-Capita Consumption by Fiber in the United States (Data in Pounds)

Year	Rayon	Acetate	Nylon	Polyester	Acrylic	Olefin	Glass	Cotton	Wool	Total
1970	4.4	2.4	7.4	8.2	2.4	1.0	1.9	19.7	1.7	49.1
1971	4.8	2.4	8.9	10.6	2.4	1.4	2.4	20.4	1.3	54.6
1972	3.8	1.9	10.2	12.9	2.9	1.9	2.9	19.9	1.3	58.7
1973	4.7	1.9	11.0	15.1	3.3	2.4	3.3	18.3	1.0	61.0
1974	3.7	1.4	9.3	13.6	2.8	2.3	2.8	16.0	0.7	52.6
1975	2.3	1.4	9.5	14.6	2.3	2.3	2.3	14.9	0.7	50.3
1976	2.7	1.4	9.8	15.4	2.7	2.3	3.2	16.9	0.9	55.3
1977	2.7	1.4	10.8	16.7	3.2	2.7	3.6	15.8	0.9	57.8
1978	2.7	1.3	11.6	17.0	2.7	3.1	4.0	15.8	1.0	59.2
1979	2.1	1.2	12.0	16.7	2.6	3.0	4.0	14.8	0.9	57.3
1980	2.1	1.3	9.6	15.0	2.6	3.0	3.9	14.7	0.9	53.1
1981	2.2	0.9	9.6	15.1	2.2	3.5	4.3	11.9	0.7	50.4
1982	1.3	0.9	8.3	12.6	2.1	3.4	3.9	10.7	0.5	43.7
1983	1.7	0.9	10.3	14.9	2.1	3.8	4.0	11.9	0.9	50.5

TABLE 1.4   Mill Consumption of Fibers in the United States (Data in Billions of Pounds)

Year	Rayon	Acetate/Triacetate	Nylon	Polyester	Acrylic	Olefin	Glass	Cotton	Wool	Total
1970	0.9	0.5	1.3	1.6	0.5	0.2	0.4	3.8	0.3	9.5
1971	1.0	0.5	1.7	2.0	0.5	0.3	0.5	4.0	0.2	10.7
1972	1.0	0.4	2.1	2.5	0.6	0.4	0.6	3.9	0.2	11.7
1973	1.0	0.4	2.3	3.1	0.7	0.5	0.7	3.6	0.2	12.5
1974	0.8	0.3	2.0	2.9	0.6	0.5	0.6	3.3	0.1	11.1
1975	0.5	0.3	2.0	3.1	0.5	0.5	0.5	3.1	0.1	10.6
1976	0.6	0.3	2.1	3.3	0.6	0.5	0.7	3.4	0.1	11.6
1977	0.6	0.3	2.3	3.6	0.7	0.6	0.8	3.2	0.1	12.2
1978	0.6	0.3	2.5	3.7	0.6	0.7	0.9	3.0	0.1	12.4
1979	0.5	0.3	2.7	3.8	0.6	0.7	0.9	3.1	0.1	12.7
1980	0.5	0.3	2.3	3.5	0.6	0.7	0.9	3.1	0.1	12.0
1981	0.5	0.2	2.2	3.5	0.5	0.8	1.0	2.7	0.2	11.6
1982	0.3	0.2	1.9	2.9	0.5	0.8	0.9	2.5	0.1	10.1
1983	0.4	0.2	2.4	3.5	0.5	0.9	0.2	2.8	0.2	11.1

Aesthetic Concerns

In addition to their economic aspects, textile fibers and fabrics are important because of their aesthetic qualities and characteristics. The strong desire for attractive clothing and surroundings results in the constant search for new and different fashion fabrics for both apparel and home furnishings. As a result, there have been frequent new developments in fabric and yarn structure as well as in finishes and methods of color application.

Consumers want fabrics that not only are attractive but also are comfortable and durable and require a minimum amount of care. These somewhat conflicting desires have been satisfied to a large extent by tremendous scientific advances in finishing technology; thus consumers find fabrics in the form of easy-care, durable-press, no-iron products. Most textile products do give good service if selected wisely and if given proper care.

Textile Components

Fabrics are the primary concern of textile scientists. In this specialized context fabrics are characterized by certain definitive parts or components and certain properties. Not every fabric possesses all possible definitive parts, but many fabrics are produced by combining these definitive parts.

Fabrics are composed of *textile fibers*. These fibers may be short or long, fine or coarse, soft or stiff, smooth or rough. Fibers are the basic building blocks used in manufacturing fabric. In some fabrics—such as felts and other nonwoven cloth—fibers are arranged in some predetermined pattern and processed directly into a fabric. Frequently, however, fibers are first formed into *yarns*. These yarns may be simple or complex, single or ply, smooth or rough, highly twisted or loosely twisted. Yarns are then made into fabrics by one of the various methods used for *fabric construction*, such as knitting, weaving, knotting, or braiding.

After the manufacture of the actual fabric, selected finishing or "wet processing" procedures are applied in order to create the desired end product. Nearly every fabric receives at least one finish, and most receive several.

A final definitive part of a fabric is *color*. Some authors include color as a subdivision of wet processing or finishing, whereas others list color as an independent item. This book discussed finishes and color separately.

In summary, the definitive parts or components of a textile product include

fiber content—fiber or fibers used
yarn structure or arrangement of fibers
fabric structure—arrangement of yarns or
    fibers as they are bound together
finish—type, durability, method of application
color—type, durability, method of application

All fabrics have fiber content, some form of fiber arrangement, and fabric structure. The other definitive parts may not be involved in every fabric; however, most fabrics use yarn structure, and nearly all receive finishing treatments and color is some form.

Careers in Textiles

Opportunities for careers in textiles are almost endless in variety. The industry employs fiber producers (growers or manufacturers); yarn and fabric manufacturers; converters, who finish and color fabrics; designers, who design yarns, fabrics, and textile products; and marketing specialists for every possible level of the industry. Moving into the end-use area, there are product designers, who plan the designs for apparel, home furnishings, transportation vehicles, and industrial uses; garment manufacturers; manufacturers of domestics; industrial fabric manufacturers; marketing specialists for the wholesale trades; marketing organizations for the retail trade, which include buyers, fashion coordinators, salespeople, advertising agencies, and department managers; and all those involved in the transfer of the textile fibers through the various stages of manufacture to the final consumer.

There are opportunities in the textile industry for artists; scientists, especially in such fields as chemistry and home economics; business experts, advertising specialists; retailers; journalists; and educators.

Anyone who wishes to become a part of the textile industry should get information from such resources and individuals as instructors, professionals in the field, and various organizations or trade associations. The American Textile Manufacturers Institute (ATMI), the Fashion Group, the Home Fashions League, the Man-Made Fiber Producers Association, the National Cotton Council, Cotton Inc., and the Wool Bureau are a few of the groups that can provide helpful career information.

The Future

What does the future hold for consumers of textile products? It would be foolhardy to try to predict. Some general trends can be identified, but specific predictions seldom come easily and are seldom totally true. It would seem safe to say, however, that textiles will continue to be used for the next few decades; that many of the same fabrics will be available; that the selection, use, and care of textiles will not change drastically. However, it is equally important for consumers and students of textile science to recognize that some change will be inevitable and change may alter methods of use and care of textile items. The typical fabric available in the future may differ drastically from that available now in many ways, such as appearance, texture, and care procedures. The student of textile science should become involved in identifying changes that would be desirable, changes that might be demanded, and ways that consumers can respond to changes that occur. The textile specialist will be called upon to help identify patterns of change important to the production, selection, use, and care of textile products in the decades ahead.

Organization of the Text

An understanding of certain principles is necessary in studying any science. The principles that must be understood in studying textile science are emphasized throughout this text, which is organized as follows.

Part One discusses general fiber theory and classification. The rest of the book is arranged according to the order in which the definitive parts normally evolve in the manufacture of textile fabrics. Part Two is devoted to the chemical, physical, microscopic, and biological properties of textile fibers. It includes a summary of the history of natural fibers and a brief look at the background of man-made fibers. Production processes and guides to selection and care are included for each fiber type. Part Three is devoted to yarn structure. Part four covers fabric structure. Part Five deals with finishing procedures and color application. Part Six is devoted to the end use of fabrics, testing, and performance.

STUDY QUESTIONS

1. What are the definitive or component parts of a textile fabric?

2. Why should students study textiles?
3. Which fiber is the most used in the United States? Which is second?
4. What are some areas of conservation that are of concern to the textile industry?
5. How does production of textiles compare with consumption of textiles in both the world market and the United States?
6. This is the age of concern about exposure to chemicals in our daily lives. What are your views on this subject and how do they relate to textile science?
7. What environmental safeguards or health and safety regulations are in effect in your community? your state? the nation?

Activities

1. Clip advertisements for textile products. Underline all terms that appear to be descriptive of each item. How much information about the definitive parts of a textile product are identified? What information do you believe should be provided?
2. Study textile products, read attached labels, and note what type of information is provided to the consumer.

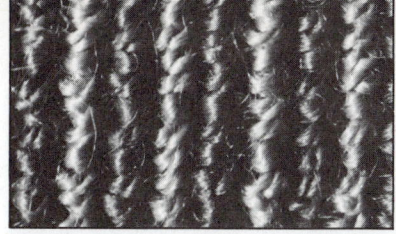

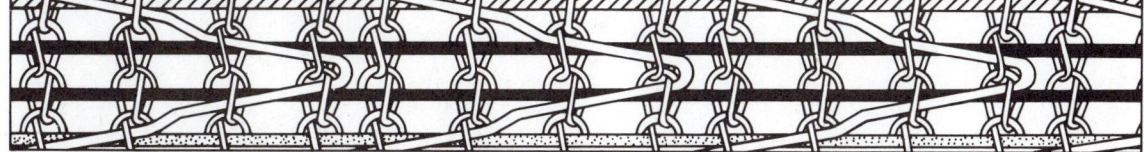

PART I

Fiber Theory and Classification

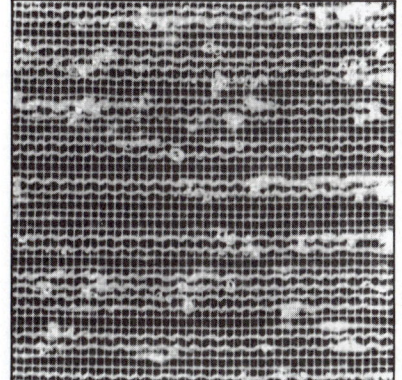

Textile science as it now exists has developed as a natural result of the tremendous expansion in textile science and technology that has occurred in the twentieth century. Major changes and developments have been identified in the decades since 1960. As the textile industry has grown, so has the need to refine definitions and classes—to sharpen the tools of the trade, in other words. Textile science, like any other discipline, has its own language, terminology, and methods of classification. These are the subject of the next three chapters, which explain many of the descriptive terms used in textile science and outline a basic system of classification that will help the student become familiar with the variety of textile fibers now available.

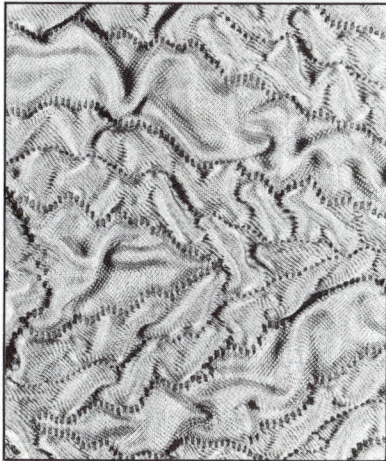

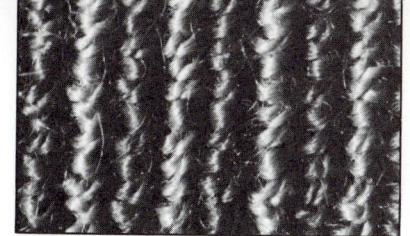

2

FIBER CLASSIFICATION

OBJECTIVES

◇ **To develop an organized set of categories for classification of all textile fibers, man-made and natural**

◇ **To identify clues relating to classification of fibers and related characteristics**

KEY TERMS

cellulosic
fiber classification
generic

man-made fiber
natural fiber

noncellulosic fiber
trade name

Systems of classification have been in use for hundreds, perhaps thousands of years. Human beings, as scientists, learned in the early stages of scientific development that placing like items together facilitated understanding.

When the study of textile fibers was new, a simple type of fiber classification, based on a systematic arrangement of fibers into categories of animal, vegetable, and mineral matter, sufficed. With the development of man-made fibers, this early classification was made obsolete, and new systems had to be devised.

Over the years, many systems of classification have been recommended. Some are no longer sufficiently discerning for the innumerable fibers on the market at the present time. Other systems formerly used are still helpful for major divisions, but because of the complexity of the fiber picture as it now exists, selected subclassifications were needed.

In 1960, the Textile Fiber Products Identification Act (TFPIA) became effective. This law requires most textile products sold at retail to have labels stating the textile fiber content. To reduce consumer confusion, the law established seventeen generic or family names that serve as classes for manufactured fibers. The original law also provided for the addition of other generic terms as justified and needed for fibers that might be developed after passage of the law. Since passage of the original law, four additional generic classes have been added. The original terms include the following: rayon,

acetate, triacetate, azlon, nylon, polyester, acrylic, modacrylic, nytril, olefin, saran, vinal, vinyon, spandex, rubber, glass, and metallic. The four generic terms added since 1962 are: aramid, anidex, novoloid, and lastrile. At present in several of the generic classes no fibers are being manufactured in the United States that fit the particular class. This group includes azlon, anidex, nytril, and lastrile. In general, fibers within a specific generic group or class possess the same basic properties and require the same basic care procedures. With this in mind, it should be apparent that any system of classification used for manufactured fibers should include the use of generic terms.

The system of classification used in this text provides for the division of fibers into two major types: natural and man-made or manufactured. Table 2.1 provides the classification system for natural fibers. Table 2.2 cites the system used for man-made fibers. In Table 2.2 the generic terms are identified with an asterisk and with lowercase letters, as designated by the TFPIA legislation. Trade names, when given, are capitalized.

Most generic groups do include trademarked fibers—those bearing a word, letter, device, or symbol that points distinctly to the origin or ownership of the particular fiber; the trade name may identify, as well, special variants or modifications of a basic fiber.

The use of the terms *animal, vegetable,* and *mineral* in fiber classification has been challenged because

◇ ───

TABLE 2.1   Natural Fibers

A. Cellulosic Fibers	c. agave	5) llama
1. seed hairs	1) sisal	6) mohair (Angora goat)
a. cotton	2) henequen	7) vicuña
b. milkweed	d. palm	c. fur fibers
c. kapok	e. New Zealand flax	1) mink
d. cattail	f. yucca	2) muskrat
2. bast fibers	g. palma istle	3) Angora rabbit
a. flax	4. nut husk fibers	2. animal secretion
b. ramie	a. coir (coconut)	a. silk
c. hemp	B. Protein Fibers	1) cultivated
d. jute	1. animal-hair fibers	2) dupioni
e. sunn	a. wool (sheep)	3) tussah, wild
f. kenaf	b. specialty hair fibers	b. spider silk
g. urena	1) alpaca	C. Mineral Fiber
3. leaf fibers	2) camel	1. asbestos (rock source)
a. abaca	3) cashmere	D. Natural Rubber
b. pineapple	4) guanaco	

there are differences between the behavior of vegetable cellulose used in the man-made cellulosic fibers and vegetable protein used in some of the man-made protein fibers. The latter are comparable to animal fibers rather than other vegetable fibers. Thus, a division of natural fibers into those of cellulosic, protein, and mineral type is preferred because this system does relate to the chemical behavior of the fibers.

The system of classification used in this text is based, then, on the following criteria:

1. The principal origin of the fiber. Fibers either occur as fibrous forms in nature or they are manufactured; thus, a major breakdown to indicate scientifically the origin of the fiber produces two major groups: natural fibers and man-made fibers.
2. The general chemical type. Fibers can be protein, cellulosic, mineral, or synthesized, also called noncellulosic man-made.
3. The generic term. The generic term or family name as specified in the Textile Fiber Products Identification Act provides scientifically cogent bases for grouping like fibers of the man-made variety.
4. The inclusion of common names of fibers and/or trade names. Many people are familiar with common names and trade names for fibers; therefore, examples of these should be included in any classification as a means of clarifying the group name for the student and consumer.

Table 2.1 provides a classification system for natural fibers and is based on the use of four categories that indicate the general chemical type or product: cellulosic, protein, mineral, and natural rubber.

The table of man-made fibers (Table 2.2) is based on a similar type of division: man-made cellulosic fibers, man-made modified cellulosic fibers, man-made protein fibers, man-made noncellulosic or synthetic fibers, man-made mineral fibers. The table also includes a section for fibers that have not been included in any generic class to date.

In using the tables it is important to remember that not all fibers are listed, only those considered of importance from either an economic or a historic point of view. Readers may wish to refer to various listings of fibers to obtain a more complete listing of trade names for man-made fibers.[1] A recent trend in the sale of textile products has been to emphasize the generic term for any man-made fiber involved and to omit trade names completely. This is due, in part, to the amount of fiber imported from other countries that does not carry a known trade name. Thus consumers are given the generic term with which they should be somewhat familiar. Students who are interested in studying other listings of

─────────────────────────────

[1]For a complete list of man-made fibers sold in the United States, see the *Man-Made Fiber Fact Book*, published by the Man-Made Fiber Producers Association, and the *Textile World Fiber Chart*, published every other year by *Textile World*.

TABLE 2.2 Man-Made or Manufactured Fibers

A. Man-Made Cellulosic Fibers
  1. rayon*
    a. cuprammonium (no longer made in the United States)
      Bemberg®
    b. viscose rayon
      1) regular and high tenacity
        Avtex®
        Absorb®
        Beau-Grip®
        Coloray®
        Durvil
        Enkaire®
        Enkrome®
        Fibro®
      2) high-wet-modulus rayon
        Avril®
        Avril Prima®
        Fiber 700
        Zantrel®
B. Man-Made Modified Cellulosic Fibers
  1. acetate*
    Avtex®
    Celanese®
    Chromspun®
    Estron®
  2. triacetate*
    Arnel®
C. Man-Made Protein Fibers
  1. azlon*
    No man-made protein fibers are currently manufactured in the United States.
D. Man-Made Noncellulosic Fibers
  1. nylon* (condensation polymer)
    a. type 6,6
      Actionwear®
      Ametek
      Antron®
      Blanc de Blanc
      Blue "C"®
      Cadon
      Cantrece
      Captiva®
      Cerex
      Cordura®
      Cumuloft
      DuPont
      Ultron®

    b. nylon, type 6
      Anso®
      Camalon
      Caprolan®
      Enka Sheer®
      Enkadrain®
      Enkaline®
      Shareen®
      Starbrite
      Static-Guard
      Zeftron®
    c. nylon, type 11
      Ametek
      Rilsan
    d. nylon, type 6,10
      Nylex
      Quill
    e. nylon (bicomponent)
      Cantrece®
  2. aramid* (condensation polymer)
    Kevlar®
    Nomex®
  3. polyester* (condensation polymer)
    Ametek
    Amtel
    Avlin®
    Dacron®
    Comfort Fiber
    Crepesoft®
    Encron®
    Estralyn
    Fortrel®
    Golden Glow®
    Golden Touch®
    Kodel®
    Polarguard®
    Sontara®
    Trevira®
    Ultra Touch®
  4. anidex* (discontinued)
  5. acrylic* (addition polymer)
    Acrilan®
    Bi-Loft®
    Creslan®
    Fi-Lana®
    Orlon®
    Pa-Qel® (bicomponent)
    Remember® (bicomponent)
    Zefran®
  6. modacrylic* (addition polymer)
    Acrilan®

      SEF®
      Verel®
      Zefran®
  7. novoloid*
    Kynol®
  8. nytril* (discontinued)
  9. olefin* (addition polymer)
    a. polyethylene
      Amco
      American
      Tyvek®
    b. polypropylene
      Alphabac
      Amco
      American
      Ametek
      Celestra®
      Duon
      Herculon®
      Marvess®
      Patlon®
      Typar®
  10. saran* (addition polymer)
    Ametek
    Saran
  11. vinal* (addition polymer)
    Kuralon (Japan); none made in the United States.
  12. vinyon* (addition polymer)
    Avtex
    Rhovyl
  13. spandex* (elastomeric)
    Cleerspan®
    Glospan®
    Lycra®
  14. rubber* (elastomeric)
    Contro®
    Softalastic
  15. lastrile* (elastomeric)
    None produced in the United States.
E. Man-Made Mineral Fibers
  1. glass*
    Beta®
    Chemglas®
    Fiberglas®
    Modiglas®
    PPG-Trianti®
  2. Metallic*
    Alistran
    Brunsmet®
    Chromflex®
    Lurex®

(continued on page 16)

TABLE 2.2 Man-Made or Manufactured Fibers

F. Other Man-Made Fibers	2. organic, not otherwise	Kynor
1. inorganic, not otherwise	classified	Teflon®
classified	polybenzimidazole	Tefzel®
alumina silica (e.g., Boron,	PBI	celiox
Fiberfrax)	polycarbonate	3. bigeneric
carbon (e.g., Panex)	Monobaste	Kermel: polyamide-imide
carbon silica (e.g., Avceram)	tetrafluoroethylene and/or	Mirafi 140: nylon and olefin
graphite	other fluorine polymers	Novolac/polyamide
quartz fiber	GFO fibers	polychal
sapphire whiskers	Gore-Tex®	promix

*Identifies generic name.

trade names and less familiar natural fibers should investigate references cited in the Bibliography.

The TFPIA does not provide names for natural fibers; except for hair fibers, natural fibers are listed and identified by their common name in the labeling of textile products. However, in the case of animal hair fibers, all such fibers may be identified by the term *wool* instead of identifying specific animal sources. Nonetheless, as consumers are willing to pay premium prices for selected types of animal fiber, retailers often use a specific animal name in order to identify these premium products. This is particularly true of fibers such as cashmere, vicuña, and llama.

There is and probably always will be some disagreement between fiber manufacturers and the Federal Trade Commission (FTC) regarding the group to which a fiber is assigned. This is especially so as new fibers are developed that seem not to fit into existing generic groups or that have sufficient variations that the manufacturers believe a new generic group is needed.

The TFPIA requires that most textile products aimed at the consumer market must be labeled to identify fiber content. The generic term must be used; a trade name may be used if the maker so desires. More specific information about this law and its application in the sale of merchandise is discussed in Chapter 32, "Textile Legislation."

The labeling required by the legislation is helpful, but it does not take the place of sound scientific knowledge. Consumers and technologists who can recognize fiber names and identify, classify, and evaluate fibers are qualified to make intelligent selections of fibers and fabrics and wise decisions concerning the care and handling of textile merchandise.

STUDY QUESTIONS

1. What is the TFPIA? Who is responsible for enforcing it?
2. What type of fibers are noncellulosic? man-made cellulosic? mineral?
3. How do natural and man-made fibers differ? How would they be similar?
4. What information would you need to categorize, or classify, a new fiber?
5. Of what value are trade names?
6. What generic groups of fibers are currently produced in the United States?
7. What generic groups of fibers are not currently produced in the United States? in the world?

Activity

Locate labels on different items on the market. What information is included? Do the labels contain information on fiber content? Do they have trademarks or trade names identified for the fibers used? Are these labels securely attached to the product?

Fiber Theory

OBJECTIVES

◇ **To describe the basic concepts relating to fiber structure and molecular arrangement**
◇ **To identify and describe the primary properties of fibers**
◇ **To identify and describe the secondary properties of fibers**
◇ **To provide tables of values for various fiber properties that will enable students and consumers to make comparison among fibers**

KEY TERMS

crystallinity
degree of orientation
degree of
  polymerization
denier
density
elastic recovery
elongation
flammability
flexibility (pliability)

fringed fibril theory
hydrogen bonding
length-to-width ratio
luster
moisture
  absorbency
moisture regain
morphology
physical shape
polymer

polymerization
resiliency
spinning quality/
  cohesiveness
tenacity
tex
thermal properties
uniformity
van der Waal's forces
  forces

Textile fibers are obtained from natural vegetable matter, animal hair or excrement, mineral matter, or manufacturing processes. Fibers from vegetable matter may be cellulosic or, in a few cases, protein in nature. The major sources of fibers from vegetable matter includes fibers from seed pods, such as cotton; from the stems of plants, such as flax, hemp, or jute; and from plant leaves, such as banana and agave. Animal fibers are primarily obtained from animal hair, except for silk, which is the product of excrement used by the silkworm in making its cocoon. Mineral fibers are obtained from such sources as rocks. Manufactured fibers can be made by using natural fibrous matter, or they can be synthesized from chemicals that bear no resemblance to fiber form. Regardless of the source, however, it is possible to identify certain qualities common to all fibers.

Textile fibers are made up of many polymolecules. A *polymolecule* is a molecule composed of more than one monomeric unit (single molecule) hooked together in some way. In textile science particularly, *polymers* or polymolecules are the long-chain molecules or macromolecules that are required to form fibers. These polymolecules are composed of many monomeric units, usually well over 100 and often between 200 and 15,000.

Polymerization is a chemical reaction in which monomers, small chemical compounds with low molecular weight, combine to form a polymer, a more complex molecule with a higher molecular weight and very different chemical and physical properties.

Polymers, or macromolecules, are built by repeating one monomeric unit or by repeating units composed of two or three different monomers in a systematic arrangement many times. This is polymerization. A simulation of the difference in length between a macromolecule and small molecules is shown in Figure 3.1.

To give some idea of how polymers differ from the basic units from which they are formed, consider polypropylene olefin fibers and the unit from which they are built, which is propylene, a gas. When propylene is polymerized using specified procedures, very large macromolecules that are fibrous in character are formed. These are the basis of polypropylene fibers.

It is helpful also to compare maltose sugar with cotton fibers. Both are composed of glucose units,

3.1 Model simulating difference in length between a macromolecule and a bimolecule or a four-unit molecule.

but the disaccharide, maltose, is built of only two glucose units, whereas the cellulose in cotton is composed of many thousands of glucose molecules joined by polymerization. As many as 12,000 to 15,000 glucose units are commonly found in each macromolecule of cellulose in cotton.

A polymer is described, in part, by its *degree of polymerization*, or *dp*, which identifies the number of molecular or monomer units joined together to form the polymolecule. Other characteristics of a polymer are great stability; a high degree of intramolecular force, which prevents easy destruction of the polymer; extremely high molecular weight; and physical properties that differ radically from the monomers from which it is formed.

Fiber Properties

A polymer must possess certain essential properties or characteristics if it is to qualify as a suitable substance for use in forming textile fibers. These pri-

mary properties include a high length-to-breadth, or width, ratio; tenacity or adequate strength; flexibility or pliability; cohesiveness or spinning quality; and uniformity. Secondary properties are those that are desirable; they may, and frequently do, improve consumer satisfaction with the textile made from the fiber. Characteristics in this group include physical shape, density or specific gravity, luster, moisture regain, elastic recovery, elongation, resiliency, thermal behavior, resistance to biological organisms, and resistance to chemical and other environmental conditions. The following discussion includes definitions and descriptions of these properties as they apply to textile fibers.

In order to qualify as a practical or economically viable fiber, a material must be available at a price that is competitive. In addition, the fiber supply should be consistent and in a quantity that meets demand at the competitive price established.

Primary Properties

HIGH LENGTH-TO-WIDTH RATIO Fibrous materials must possess adequate staple (fiber length), and the length must be considerably greater than the diameter. This is referred to as the *length-to-width* (or length-to-breadth) ratio. A minimum ratio of 100 is usually essential, and most fibers have ratios that are much higher. This means that a fiber is at least 100 times longer than it is wide.

Fibers shorter than ½ inch (1.27 cm) are seldom used in yarn manufacturing. Short fibers such as cotton measure from less than ½ inch (1.27 cm) to more than 2 inches (5.08 cm) in length. A cotton fiber 1 inch (2.54 cm) in length may have a diameter of 0.0007 inch (0.018 cm), which would give a length-to-width ratio of 1400. Typical ratios for several natural fibers are[1]

cotton	1400
flax	1200
ramie	3000
wool	3000
silk	33×10^6

The fiber molecules, as well as the fiber itself, are usually long and extremely thin or fine. The monomers that form the fiber molecules or fiber polymer produce linear chains, and these are all char-

[1] R. W. Moncrieff, *Man-Made Fibers*, 6th ed. (New York: Wiley, 1975), pp. 25–26.

acterized by extremely minute diameters compared with extremely long molecular or polymer length.

Short fibers, measured in centimeters or inches or fractions thereof, are called *staple fibers*. Long fibers, measured in terms of kilometers or miles, are called *filament fibers*. Because of their extreme length, filament fibers are not readily measured for length.

TENACITY A second property required for a product to become a satisfactory textile fiber is adequate strength. When discussing fibers, this property is defined as *tenacity*. Although strength varies considerably among the different fibers, it is important that a substance possess sufficient strength to be worked and processed by machinery, as well as to provide adequate durability in the end use to which it is allocated. *Tenacity* is the term applied to the strength of individual fibers. It is defined by the American Society for Testing and Materials (ASTM) as "the tensile stress expressed as force per unit linear density of the unstrained specimen."[2]

Tenacity is determined by mechanical devices and is interpreted using standard mathematical conversion formulas. Tenacities of selected fibers are cited in Table 3.1 and are expressed as grams of force per denier, g/d, gf/den., or gm/d. Other standard measures used to identify fiber tenacities include grams of force per tex, gf/tex; millinewtons per tex, mN/tex; millinewtons per denier, mN/den. *Denier* is a unit of fiber or yarn measurement equal to the weight in grams of 9000 meters of yarn or fiber. *Tex* is a unit of fiber or yarn measurement equal to the weight in grams of one kilometer of fiber or yarn.

Fiber strength can also be measured in pounds per square inch or newtons per square meter. This is called *tensile strength* and is obtained by determining the force required to break a fiber cross-sectional mass equivalent to one unit of the measure used. This measure is seldom used except for cotton, as it is easier and somewhat more accurate to test a mass of cotton fibers than a single fiber. Fiber tenacity varies, to some extent, depending on fiber size. Although tenacities are cited as a function of a fiber denier of 1, few fibers, if any, are only 1 denier in diameter; hence the variable tenacities.

It is important to note that fiber strength does not always indicate comparable yarn or fabric strength. For most fabrics a minimum fiber tenacity

[2] American Society for Testing Materials (ASTM), *Annual Book of ASTM Standards*, vol. 07.01 (1983), p. 63.

◊ ————————————————————————

TABLE 3.1   Fiber Tenacities (Data Obtained at 20°C (70°F), 65% Relative Humidity)

Fiber	Tenacity in Grams per Denier*
Asbestos	2.5–3.1
Cotton, raw	3.0–5.0
Flax, range	2.6–7.7
typical	5.5–6.5
Hemp	5.8–6.8
Jute	3.0–5.8
Ramie	5.3–7.4
Silk	2.4–5.1
Wool	1.0–1.7
Acrylic	2.0–3.6
Acetate	1.2–1.4
Triacetate	1.1–1.4
Glass	6.3–6.9
Modacrylic	2.0–3.1
Nylon 6,6, regular	4.3–9.0
6, regular	3.5–9.0
6,6, HT†	5.7–9.5
6, HT†	7.7–9.5
Polypropylene olefin	3.5–8.0
Polyester, regular	2.5–6.3
HT†	6.0–9.5
Saran	1.4–2.4
Spandex	0.5–1.5
Rayon, regular	2.4–3.0
HT†	3.8–4.4
HWM‡	4.0–5.0

*Range is from minimum to maximum.

†HT = high tenacity.

‡HWM = high wet modulus.

of about 2.5 grams per denier is usually considered essential. However, a number of relatively weak fibers—such as wool, with a strength considerably less than 2.5 g/d—are often used very successfully in making durable fabrics. This can be done because such fibers have other important properties, such as high elongation, superior elastic recovery, and resiliency, that compensate for the low tenacity and produce yarns and fabrics with characteristics that appeal to consumers and that provide adequate performance.

Fibers with high strength or tenacity are useful in sheer and lightweight fabrics, and they are of importance where the end-use product requires high strength. Fabrics used in work clothes and various industrial applications are better if made from fibers with high tenacity.

Fiber tenacity does not always reflect the actual

strength of a textile yarn and the resulting textile fabric. It is possible for yarns to be made so that fiber slippage occurs; this does not make optimum use of the actual fiber tenacity. This factor is important especially in the manufacture of yarns composed of staple-length fibers.

FLEXIBILITY *Flexibility or pliability*—the property of bending without breaking—is the third necessary characteristic or property of textile fibers. Fibers must be bendable, pliable, or flexible in order to form yarns and fabrics that can be creased, that have the quality of drapability and the ability to move with the body, that give when walked or sat upon, and, in general, that permit freedom of movement. Many substances in nature resemble fibrous forms, but because they are stiff or brittle, they do not make practical textile fibers.

It is further accepted that a fiber must flex or bend repeatedly in order to be classified as pliable or flexible. The degree of flexibility determines the ease with which fibers, yarns, and fabrics will bend and is important in fabric durability and general performance.

SPINNING QUALITY (COHESIVENESS) A fourth property required of textile fibers is that they have *spinning quality* or *cohesiveness.* This characteristic refers to the ability of fibers to stick together in yarn manufacturing processes. Cohesiveness indicates that fibers tend to hold together during yarn manufacturing as a result of the longitudinal contour of the fiber or the cross-section shape that enables the fibers to fit together and entangle sufficiently to adhere to one another. It may refer also to the surface or skin structure of the fiber, which causes fibers to stick together. When fiber shape and surface do not contribute to the cohesive quality of fibers, the same end result may be attained by using fibers of filament length that are easily twisted into yarn form. This latter characteristic is the equivalent of fiber cohesiveness and is generally referred to as *spinning quality.*

An alternative to natural cohesiveness that is commonly used in preparing filament fibers for yarnmaking is texturizing. This process introduces coils, crimp, zigzag shaping, or other configurations and surface modifications into the fiber to provide for cohesiveness or spinning quality. Man-made fibers that are cut into staple length for spinning frequently have had crimp added in order to provide adequate spinning quality.

The cohesiveness or spinning quality of a fiber manifests itself in such yarn characteristics as fineness and in such fabric characteristics as thickness or thinness, surface appearance, surface texture, and fabric durability.

UNIFORMITY To make yarns it is important that fibers be somewhat similar in length and width, in spinning quality or cohesiveness, and in flexibility. Man-made or manufactured fibers can be controlled during production so that a relatively high degree of uniformity is maintained and irregularities are held to a minimum. Furthermore, any man-made fiber can be produced to conform to existing fibers, whether natural or other man-made varieties. Yarns composed of fibers that are uniform are preferred because they are regular, they appear smooth or consistent in appearance, and they accept dyestuffs and finishing chemicals uniformly. Natural fibers are not so uniform as manufactured fibers, for it is difficult to control the various aspects of the environment. Therefore, to ensure an adequate degree of uniformity in yarn and fabric construction, it is necessary to blend natural fibers from many different batches in order to produce yarns that are uniform and provide desirable performance qualities. (See pages 174–175 for information about blending fibers in yarnmaking.)

Consumers of textile products frequently are not so aware of the presence or importance of primary properties as they are of secondary properties. Primary properties are essential, and therefore fibrous forms are not converted into yarns and fabrics for end-use products unless these properties are present at or above a minimum level.

Secondary Properties

Secondary properties possessed by textile fibers tend to vary among the many textile fibers. Not all fibers possess all secondary properties. Some secondary properties contribute to making an end product with superior characteristics, while others may detract from a textile product in end use. In addition, various finishing or wet processing operations may affect the secondary properties, either enhancing or detracting from them. When desirable properties or characteristics are absent, or present at only a very low level, selected finishing procedures can be applied to introduce desirable characteristics or increase those present at a low level. Further, various finishing processes can reduce or modify fiber characteristics that are undesirable because of the presence of certain secondary properties.

PHYSICAL SHAPE In addition to the high length-to-breadth ratio previously discussed, a fiber is described by noting such factors as average fiber length, cross-sectional shape, surface contour, and surface irregularities. These shape factors are the basis for the description of both the macroscopic and microscopic appearance of a fiber. Fiber shape is responsible for certain differences in yarn and fabric properties discussed in later chapters.

DENSITY Density is the mass per unit volume of a fiber expressed as grams per cubic centimeter or pounds per cubic foot.[3] Because density is commonly determined on balances or scales, it is frequently, but incorrectly, called weight. The correct expression for density is *mass per unit volume,* whereas *relative mass per unit volume* defines specific gravity. Comparisons of density values give the student a basis for identifying and describing the relative weight of a fiber based on volume or mass.

Glass fibers are compact and have a density value of 2.54, which is considerably higher than most fibers used in apparel and home furnishings. For example, nylon has a density of 1.14 and polyester has a density of approximately 1.3. If all other factors, such as yarn construction, fabric construction, and finishing operations, are held constant, fabrics made from fibers of low density will be lighter in weight than fabric made from fibers with a high density value. Table 3.2 gives the density values for many fibers available on today's market.

Fibers with different densities but of equal diameter will have different covering power, that is, the ability of the fiber to cover a surface. When fabrics are made with identical fabric count (the same number of ends and picks per inch) and the same fabric weight per square yard or meter, there will be a difference in fabric appearance, flexibility, air passage or permeability, and cover, depending on the density of the fiber or fibers used. For example, a fabric of an acrylic fiber with a density of 1.16 will have a significantly different appearance, flexibility, air permeability, and cover than a cotton fabric of identical fabric count and weight whose fiber density is 1.5. The acrylic fabric would have an appearance of bulkiness and fluffiness that would not be present in the cotton fabric.

LUSTER The term *luster* refers to the gloss, sheen, or shine that a fiber has. It is the result of the amount of light reflected by a fiber, and it determines the fiber's natural brightness or dullness.

[3] ASTM, *Annual Book of ASTM Standards* (1983), p. 26.

◊

TABLE 3.2 Densities of Selected Fibers

Fiber	Density in Grams per Cubic Centimeter
Natural Fibers	
Asbestos	2.10–2.80
Cotton	1.54–1.56
Flax	1.50
Hemp	1.48
Jute	1.50
Ramie	1.51
Silk	1.25–1.34
Wool	1.30–1.32
Man-Made Fibers	
Acetate	1.32
Triacetate	1.32
Acrylic	1.16–1.18
Aramid	1.38–1.44
Glass	2.54
Modacrylic	1.30–1.37
Nylon	1.14
Olefin, propylene	0.90–0.91
Polyester	1.23–1.38
Rayon	1.50–1.53
Saran	1.71
Spandex	1.20–1.25

Silk, a natural fiber, has a high luster, whereas cotton, also a natural fiber, has a very low luster in its natural state. The luster of man-made fibers is controlled. These fibers may have a very high luster, or the luster may be reduced as a part of the manufacturing process. The principal method of controlling the luster of man-made fibers is to add pigments such as titanium dioxide to the fiber solution prior to fiber formation. The availability of fibers with different levels of luster provides opportunities to market textile products that satisfy the various demands by consumers for a variety of choices based on appearance and aesthetic factors.

COLOR The natural color of fibers varies from pure white to deep gray, tan, or black. Natural fibers exhibit the greatest difference. Man-made fibers are usually white or off-white as they are manufactured; however, this is not always the case, and a few special types of man-made fibers may be naturally black.

MOISTURE REGAIN AND MOISTURE AB-SORPTION Textile fibers, in general, have a certain amount of water as an integral part of their

TABLE 3.3 Moisture Regain

Fiber	% of Regain*
Natural Fibers	
Cotton, raw	8.5
mercerized	8.5–10.3
Flax	12.0
Hemp	12.0
Jute	13.7
Ramie	6.0
Silk	11.0
Wool	13.6–16.0
Man-Made Fibers	
Acetate	6.5
Triacetate	3.2–3.5
Acrylic	1.5–2.5
Glass	0.0
Modacrylic	0.4–4.0
Nylon	3.5–5.0
Olefin	0.0–0.1
Polyester	0.4
Rayon	10.7–16.0
Saran	0.0–0.1
Spandex	0.3–1.2

*Data are cited in commercial terms for standard types of fibers and obtained at standard conditions of 20°C (70°F) and 65% relative humidity.

structure. Table 3.3 identifies the moisture regain of some textile fibers at standard or conditioned environments. ASTM defines *moisture regain* as "the moisture in a material determined under prescribed conditions and expressed as a percentage of the weight of the moisture-free specimen."[4]

Moisture regain or absorbency depends on the fiber morphology or molecular arrangement and the pore size in the outer layer of fiber skin. If a fiber has pore openings smaller than a molecule of water, the amount of moisture absorbed will be very minute. However, if the pore openings permit the passage of a molecule of water *and* if the molecular arrangement in the fiber is not highly oriented, considerable moisture can be absorbed. This is also true when the fiber molecules are not packed tightly, so that there is space between them. However, if the fiber molecules are closely packed, little moisture will enter the fiber even if openings in its outer layer are large enough to permit passage of the moisture or water molecules.

Moisture regain is determined using ASTM stan-

[4] ASTM, *Annual Book of ASTM Standards* (1983), p. 46.

dard procedures described as follows.[5] Fibers are conditioned thoroughly to air-dry weight at standard conditions of 65 percent relative humidity and 70° ± 2°F (20°C). The sample is weighed, dried to bone-dry state in a drying oven, reweighed, redried, and reweighed to constant weight. The regain is calculated according to the following formula:

percentage regain

$$= \frac{\text{conditioned weight} - \text{dry weight}}{\text{dry weight}} \times 100$$

Moisture content, although similar to regain, is determined under certain prescribed conditions and is usually expressed as a percentage of the mass of the moist material; that is, the original mass comprising the dry substance plus any water present. The procedure differs from the one used for regain; the sample is returned to a constant weight at standard conditions or other prescribed conditions and not to a dry weight. The formula is

percentage moisture

$$= \frac{\text{conditioned weight} - \text{dry weight}}{\text{conditioned weight}} \times 100$$

Moisture regain and *moisture absorption* are sometimes used synonymously. However, *moisture absorption* is frequently used to indicate the moisture content at either 95 or 100 percent relative humidity. This is more accurately referred to as *saturation regain.*

Fibers with good moisture regain will accept dyes and finishes more readily than fibers with low regain. A few fibers have no regain, and this creates problems in processing. The relation of fiber strength to moisture content is an important consideration in evaluating fiber behavior. Some fibers are stronger when wet than dry, others are weaker when wet, and still others exhibit no difference in strength between wet and dry states. These variations do mean that care must be taken in maintaining textile products. Fibers that are weaker when wet than dry require careful handling during maintenance in order to reduce the danger of damage. Therefore, it is important to plan care or maintenance procedures appropriate to the fibers involved. A typical example is the fiber rayon, which is considerably weaker when wet than dry. Because of this characteristic, gentle care is needed to prevent damage to the textile product, particularly to avoid stress on the product that could break the fibers.

[5] ASTM, *Annual Book of ASTM Standards* (1983), Test Method 2654-76, p. 490.

Cotton is stronger when wet than dry; thus, cotton can be laundered with ease since the potential for damage is reduced when it is wet. A fiber with little or no regain will wash and dry quickly, as little or no water is absorbed during laundering. Moisture regain also influences comfort. For a discussion of this factor, see Chapter 31.

ELASTIC RECOVERY AND ELONGATION The amount of stretch or extension that a fiber will accept is called *elongation*. The term *breaking elongation* refers to the amount of stretch that occurs to the point where the fiber breaks.

Elastic recovery designates the percentage of return from elongation or stretch toward the original length or measurement. If a fiber returns to its original length from a specified amount of attenuation, it is said to have 100 percent elastic recovery at *x* percent elongation (Table 3.4).

The elastic recovery of a fiber can be measured after applying stress for a short time, such as 30 seconds, then releasing the stress and determining the immediate elastic recovery, usually measured after a 1 minute recovery period. Table 3.4 includes data on immediate recovery after stress to elongate the fiber the specified amount.

Delayed recovery is determined by measuring the fiber length a specified amount of time after the removal of stress. The time of recovery may be minutes or hours. The longer the time during which stress is applied, the greater the tendency to have some permanent deformation or set that prevents complete elastic recovery.

The amount of elongation is an important factor in evaluating elastic recovery. Some fibers with low elongation have excellent elastic recovery; however, this property is of little value because of insignificant elongation. Thus, it becomes obvious that elongation and elasticity must be considered together in fiber evaluation. A fiber with extremely high elongation potential but with medium to low elastic recovery might be undesirable because the product could not return to size after extension.

RESILIENCY *Resiliency* is the ability of a fiber to return to shape following compression, bending, or similar deformation. It is important in determining the crease recovery of a fiber or fabric, and it plays a significant role in the rapidity with which flattened carpet pile will regain its shape and restore its appearance.

The property is evaluated on a comparative basis from excellent to poor. (See Table 3.5.) Elastic re-

◊ ─────────────────────────────

TABLE 3.4   Breaking Elongation and Elastic Recovery

Fiber	% Dry Elongation	% Recovery at *x*% Elongation*
Cotton	3–10	75 @ 2%†
Flax	2.7–3.3	65 @ 2%
Jute	1.7–1.9	74 @ 1%
Ramie	3.0–7.0	52 @ 2%
Silk	10–25	92 @ 2%
Wool	20–40	99 @ 2%
Acrylic	20–50	80–99 @ 2%
Acrilan	34–50	99 @ 2%
Creslan	34–46	80–99 @ 1%
Orlon	20–28	97 @ 2%
Zefran	35–40	99 @ 2%
Acetate	25–35	94 @ 2%
Triacetate	25–35	90–92 @ 2%
Glass	3–4	100 @ 2%
Modacrylic	35–48	79–99 @ 2%
SEF	48	86 @ 2%
Nylon, regular	19–40	100 @ 8%
high tenacity	16–24	100 @ 4%
Olefin	15–50	100 @ 2%
Polyester, regular	18–75	85–97 @ 2%
high tenacity	9.5–24	90–100 @ 2%
Spandex	500–700	100 @ 2%
Rayon, regular	19–24	82 @ 2%
high wet modulus	15–23	95+ @ 2%

*Data cite average range for immediate recovery.

†Results were obtained on electronic tensile apparatus using a load rate of 10 grams per denier per minute and a 30-second duration of load at 1 minute recovery.

◊ ─────────────────────────────

TABLE 3.5   Resiliency of Selected Fibers

Fiber	Resiliency Rating
Polyester	high
Wool	↑
Nylon	
Modacrylic	
Acrylic	
Olefin	
Triacetate	
Silk	
Acetate	
Cotton	
Rayon	↓
Flax	low

covery is a significant factor in the resiliency of a fiber, and usually good elastic recovery indicates good resiliency. For some fibers, a low resiliency has merit, as this helps to produce soft fibers that are desirable when soft fabrics are important.

TABLE 3.6 Ironing and Softening Temperatures for Selected Fibers

Fiber	Softens at °F	Suggested Ironing Temperature (°F)
Cotton		425°*
Flax		425
Silk		300
Wool		300
Acetate	380°	325
Triacetate	460	400
Acrylic	400	300
Modacrylic	300	215
Nylon 6	330	300
Nylon 6,6	425	350
Olefin	250	150
Polyester	450	325
Rayon		375
Spandex	340	300

*Recommendation applies to cotton with no special finish.

FLAMMABILITY AND OTHER THERMAL REACTIONS The chapters on specific fibers include paragraphs devoted to thermal reactions. These sections are primarily descriptive and indicate the behavior of the fiber at various temperatures. Burning characteristics of the fibers are important in determining care and use, and they serve as helpful guides in fiber identification. Table 3.6 identifies recommended temperatures to be used in ironing fabrics composed of different fibers and the temperature at which the fiber softens, when this applies, which aids in indicating processing temperatures. Thermal characteristics, such as reactions to wet and dry heat, must also be considered in the treatment of fibers.

Federal legislation on textile flammability is an important consumer issue, and a variety of types of textile end-use products must meet a specified resistance to flame. Discussion of such legislation is found in Chapter 32.

Additional Properties

In the chapters on various textile fibers, additional properties that affect fiber performance will be considered for each specific fiber or generic group of fibers. These properties are described in this book, and some fiber comparisons are made. For selected properties, comparative tables are given in this chapter. Table 3.7 provides a brief comparative picture of the abrasion resistance of selected fibers;

TABLE 3.7 Abrasion Resistance of Selected Fibers

Fiber	Abrasion Resistance
Nylon	high
Olefin	
Polyester	
Spandex	
Flax	
Acrylic	
Cotton	
Silk	
Wool	
Rayon	
Acetate	
Glass	low

TABLE 3.8 Sunlight Resistance of Selected Fibers

Fiber	Sunlight Resistance
Glass	high
Acrylic	
Modacrylic	
Polyester	
Flax	
Cotton	
Rayon	
Triacetate	
Acetate	
Olefin	
Nylon	
Wool	
Silk	low

Table 3.8 indicates the comparative resistance to sunlight of a selected group of fibers; and Table 3.9 shows how fiber groups react to acids, alkalies, and organic solvents.

In the fiber chapters, the various characteristics are discussed in relation to the way in which the property or characteristic influences the selection, use, comfort, appearance, durability, and maintenance of the item. These discussions include the way fibers react to selected chemicals, to environmental conditions such as sunlight and other climatic variables, to microorganisms such as bacteria and fungi, and to insects such as moths and carpet beetles.

As mentioned previously, it is essential to consider the cost of a fiber in determining its potential commercial success. The production or growth and processing of a fiber must be economical enough

TABLE 3.9 Reactions of Selected Fibers to Acids, Alkalies, and Organic Solvents

Fiber	Reaction to Acids	Reaction to Alkalies	Reaction to Organic Solvents
Cotton	harmed	resistant	resistant
Flax	harmed	resistant	resistant
Silk	harmed by mineral acids	harmed	resistant
Wool	resistant	harmed	resistant
Acetate	weakened	little effect	harmed by acetone, phenol, and chloroform; resistant to others
Acrylic	resistant to most	resistant to weak	resistant
Modacrylic	resistant to most	resistant	resistant to most
Nylon	harmed	resistant	harmed by phenol and formic acid; resistant to most others
Olefin	resistant	resistant	harmed by chlorinated hydrocarbons
Polyester	resistant	resistant	resistant
Rayon	harmed	resistant to weak	resistant
Spandex	resistant	resistant	resistant

that the final price of textile products does not exceed what the consumer is willing to pay. This does not rule out fibers that require vast sums of money for research and development, but it would probably eliminate fibers that are extremely costly to produce in quantity. One exception occurs in industrial uses where high cost may be necessary to provide the type of fiber required for highly specialized uses. On the other hand, fibers whose growth or manufacturing and processing require exorbitant sums would probably not be produced for typical consumer end uses.

Fiber Morphology

Morphology refers to the form and structure of a substance. In relation to fibers it applies to the biological structure of natural fibers, to the shape and cross section or appearance of all fibers, and to microscopic characteristics. The chapters on fibers consider morphology under the heading of microscopic appearance, shape, and structure of the fiber.

Molecular Arrangement

Textile fiber polymers have a high length-to-width ratio just as the actual fiber does. In comparative terms, if a typical fiber polymolecule were ⅛ inch (0.32 cm) in diameter, it would be 40 feet (12.2 m) long.[6] Actually, of course, the fiber molecule is ul-

[6] "The Solid State of Polyethylene," *Scientific American,* vol. 211, no. 5 (November 1964), p. 81.

3.2 Schematic diagram showing highly oriented molecules within a fiber.

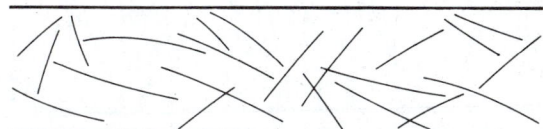

3.3 Schematic diagram showing molecules in random or amorphous arrangement with low orientation.

tramicroscopic, but this example suggests the relative length and width of a fiber molecule or polymolecule.

The pattern of molecular arrangement within the fiber varies widely. The molecules may be *highly oriented,* which means that they are parallel to each other and to the longitudinal axis of the fiber (Fig. 3.2); or they may exhibit *low orientation* and be at various angles to the fiber axis and may crisscross one another (Fig. 3.3). High orientation is associated with good fiber strength and low elongation, whereas low orientation tends to produce the reverse properties. Other characteristics that may be affected by the degree of orientation include moisture regain or absorbency and fiber flexibility.

Molecular orientation and crystallinity are properties that help define or describe the various pat-

3.4 Schematic diagram showing molecules in a crystalline arrangement, but not oriented.

oriented   amorphous

3.5 Oriented and amorphous areas within the same fiber. (Redrawn from *Encyclopedia of Polymer Science and Technology,* vol. 4, p. 456, by permission of Wiley-Interscience.)

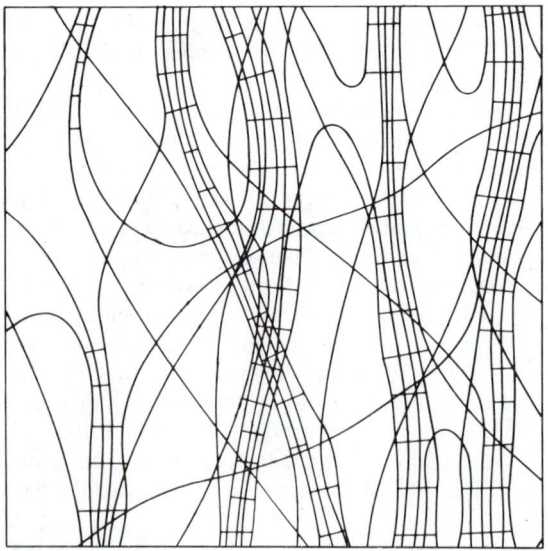

3.6 Modified fringed fibril structure.

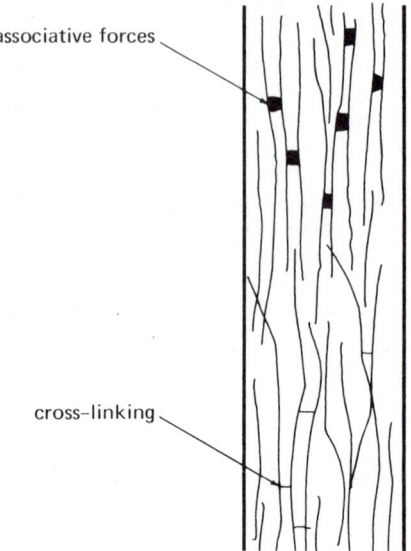

associative forces

cross-linking

3.7 Schematic diagram illustrating associative forces and cross-linking between molecules.

terns of molecular arrangement within the fiber. *Crystallinity* indicates that fiber molecules are parallel to one another, but they need not be parallel to the longitudinal fiber axis. Orientation of molecules describes a pattern in which molecules are arranged parallel to each other, they are in a crystalline form, and the molecules are parallel to the longitudinal axis of the fiber. Figure 3.2 is a graphic representation of fiber molecules that are highly oriented and therefore exhibit crystallinity. Figure 3.4 shows fiber molecules that are somewhat crystalline in arrangement but do not exhibit orientation to the longitudinal fiber axis.

When fiber molecules are arranged in random or amorphous groupings, as illustrated in Figure 3.3, they may lie apart, crisscross, or fall into other irregular arrangements. The extent to which amorphous areas occur is thought to vary widely from slight disorder to extreme disorder, depending upon the fiber and specific areas within the fiber.

Figure 3.5 illustrates a molecular arrangement in which both oriented and amorphous areas exist in the same fiber. This duality is common, particularly for natural fibers.

J. W. S. Hearle added a new concept to knowledge of arrangement of molecules within a fiber. His *fringed fibril theory* suggests that each macromolecule has the opportunity to pass through both highly oriented areas and amorphous or noncrystalline areas.[7] This concept had merit, as it provided a basis for fiber behavior in processing, use, and care.[8] In 1975, Morton and Hearle added modifications to the fringed fibril theory.[9] This concept admits to the presence of both the fringed fibril or micelle structure and a fibrillar form in the same fiber (Fig. 3.6). It has been accepted, further, that major structural differences occur among the various fibers. In particular, Morton and Hearle state that there will be differences between natural fibers, which grow very slowly, and man-made fibers, which are formed by high-speed extrusion and drawing.

Molecules may slip back and forth within a fiber, just as some fibers may slip within yarns. Molecular slippage is likely to be at a maximum in amorphous areas and lowest in crystalline areas. When a high degree of molecular slippage occurs, the fiber will have high elongation, but the molecules may not return to the optimum position, with the result that the fiber will be weak and have poor elastic recovery. In some fibers, molecules are joined to parallel molecules by cross-linking, which is brought about by chemical reactions (Fig. 3.7). On the other hand, in some types of fibers, molecules are held in place by associative forces. These forces can be broken easily, but they can be reestablished at the same or at new locations or sites.

An important type of associative force in textiles is *hydrogen bonding.* According to chemists, hydrogen bonding occurs between hydrogen atoms and small electronegative atoms such as fluorine, oxygen, and nitrogen. The hydrogen bond is present when a proton from the hydrogen atom is shared between two negative electrons from two different atoms. Hydrogen bonding is found in manufactured fibers that include hydrogen atoms and any one or more of the electronegative atoms mentioned above. It is important in fiber structure because it may aid in producing fibers that have desirable properties such as crease resistance and dimensional stability.

[7] J.W.S. Hearle and R. H. Peters, *Fiber Structure* (London: Butterworth & Co., 1963), p. 209.

[8] For more discussion on this and other related ideas, see Hearle and Peters, pp. 209–304; and H. F. Mark, N. G. Gaylord, and N. M. Bikales, eds., *Encyclopedia of Polymer Science and Technology,* vol. 4 (New York: Wiley-Interscience, 1966), p. 449ff.

[9] W. E. Morton and J.W.S. Hearle, *Physical Properties of Textile Fibers* (London: Butterworth & Co., 1975), pp. 27–33.

◇ ———————————————

TABLE 3.10 Fiber Properties Involved in the Performance of Fabrics

Appearance
   color
   luster
   abrasion resistance/pilling
   resiliency
   dye and finish affinity

Comfort
   density
   elongation/elastic recovery
   moisture regain and absorbency
   static charge
   flexibility or pliability
   resiliency

Maintenance
   strength or tenacity, wet and dry
   resiliency
   moisture absorbency
   abrasion resistance
   chemical resistance

Durability
   tenacity
   flexibility and pliability
   cohesiveness
   moisture regain and absorbency
   elastic recovery and elongation
   thermal reactions
   chemical reactions
   biological reactions

When molecules do not contain the polar groups necessary for hydrogen bonding, weaker associative forces can be established between molecules, provided the molecular segments lie very close together (4 Å to 5 Å). These forces depend on proximity and on positive and negative charges; they are usually referred to as *van der Waal's forces.*

Fiber Properties and Fabric Performance

Table 3.10 identifies the various fiber properties involved in determining appearance, maintenance, comfort, and durability of fabrics made from any specific textile fiber. Although fibers are only one aspect of fabric performance, this table should provide basic information for decision making in the selection, use, and care of a textile item.

STUDY QUESTIONS

1. What fiber properties would contribute to durability? to comfort?
2. Which natural fibers and which man-made fibers would tend to have properties that are very similar?
3. Why are the primary properties essential for an item to be a successful textile fiber?
4. What is the relation of fiber density to comfort?
5. Why is the property of moisture regain important to consumers?
6. Why should consumers be aware of thermal reactions in relation to the behavior of a textile fiber?
7. In what end uses would sunlight resistance be considered important?
8. What fiber properties are associated with high molecular orientation?
9. How does fiber tenacity affect the selection, use, and care of textile products?

Activity

If you have access to a textile testing laboratory, select several different kinds of textile fibers, yarns, or fabrics and test them for strength or tenacity, resiliency, elongation and elastic recovery, moisture regain or absorbency, and thermal properties.

4

FIBER IDENTIFICATION

OBJECTIVES
◇ **To develop a system for identifying textile fibers**
◇ **To provide simple directions and methods for testing fibers in the process of identification**
◇ **To identify fiber groups and some specific fibers**
◇ **To indicate situations where fibers might be damaged or destroyed by various products found and used in the normal care and operation of a home**

KEY TERMS

burning test
chemical solubilities
cross section, microscopic
disintegration
dissolving
longitudinal appearance,
  microscopic
melting

microscopic characteristics
residue
self-extinguishing
special instrument tests
staining tests
striations
thermal behavior

Qualitative identification of textile fibers can be difficult, and it may require several tests. Simple tests that can be used in identification are described in this chapter along with brief comments about their use and importance. In addition to their use in fiber identification, some tests yield insight into problems of processing and care of textile products.

Much of the information presented here is in chart or table form. The discussion indicates general procedures and only suggests interpretation. Reference is made to additional aids for fiber analysis. Further reactions and properties helpful in analyzing fibers and fiber behavior are found in the chapters on specific fibers or generic groups.

A consumer with a certain amount of training in textiles will find the ability to tentatively identify fibers extremely valuable. He or she may wish to verify label information and may need to know what fibers or fiber groups are in a fabric in order to care for it properly.

The major tests described include the burning test, which helps place a fiber into categories but seldom identifies a specific fiber; microscopic evaluation, which is a little more specific and in some cases may be accurate enough to identify individual fibers; and chemical solubility, which may be accu-

rate enough to categorize fibers into generic groups. Instruments used in more precise and accurate identification are mentioned. Readers who wish to be able not only to state what fiber type is involved but to identify a specific fiber would usually need instrumental evaluations as well as those described herein.

Tests for Fiber Identification

The Burning Test

The burning test is a good preliminary test. It provides valuable data regarding appropriate care and will help place a fiber into a specific category. It is not, however, a test that can be used alone to provide exact identification of specific fibers. In the case of yarns composed of two or more fibers, the test will usually give the reaction of the fiber that burns most easily; if a fiber is heat-sensitive, it will tend to melt or withdraw from the flame, leaving the flammable fiber to burn. Remember that the burning test is a preliminary test that indicates general grouping or categories only. The test is relatively simple but must be used with care to avoid

Fiber	Approaching Flame	In Flame	Removed from Flame	Odor	Residue
Natural Cellulosic cotton and flax	does not shrink away; ignites upon contact	burns quickly	continues burning; afterglow	similar to burning paper	light, feathery; light to charcoal gray in color
Man-Made Cellulosic rayon	does not shrink away; ignites upon contact	burns quickly	continues burning; afterglow	similar to burning paper	light, fluffy residue; very small amount
Man-Made Modified Cellulosic acetate	fuses and melts away from flame; ignites	burns quickly and evenly	continues to burn rapidly	acrid (hot vinegar)	irregular-shaped, hard black bead
Natural Protein wool	curls away from flame	burns slowly	self-extinguishing	similar to burning hair	brittle, small black bead
silk	curls away from flame	burns slowly and sputters	usually self-extinguishing	similar to burning hair	beadlike, crushable, black
weighted silk	curls away from flame	burns slowly and sputters	usually self-extinguishing	similar to burning hair	crushable, black the shape of fiber or fabric
Natural Mineral asbestos	does not melt (safe fiber)	glows red if heat is sufficient	returns to original form	none	same as original
Man-Made Mineral glass	will not burn	softens, glows red to orange, may change shape	hardens	none	hard, white bead
metallic	*pure* metal has no reaction *coated* metal melts, fuses, and shrinks	glows red burns according to behavior of coating	hardens	none	skeleton outline
					hard black bead
Man-Made Noncellulosic acrylic	melts and fuses away from flame; ignites readily	burns rapidly with hot flame and sputtering; drips, melts	continues to burn; hot molten polymer will drop off while burning	acrid	irregular, hard black bead

Fiber	Approaching flame	In flame	Removed from flame	Odor	Residue
modacrylic	fuses away from flame (considered safe)	burns slowly if at all; does not feed a flame	self-extinguishing	acrid, chemical odor	irregular, hard black bead
nylon	melts away from flame; shrinks, fuses	burns slowly with melting; drips	self-extinguishing	celery	hard, tough gray or tan bead
polyester	fuses; melts and shrinks away from flame	burns slowly and continues to melt; drips	self-extinguishing	chemical odor	hard, tough gray or tawny bead
olefin	fuses; shrinks, and curls away from flame	melts, burns slowly	continues to burn	chemical odor	hard, tough tan bead
saran	fuses, melts, and shrinks away from flame	yellow flame burns slowly, melts	self-extinguishing	chemical odor	irregular, crisp black bead
vinal	fuses, shrinks, curls away from flame.	burns with melting	continues to burn	chemical odor	hard, tough tan bead
vinyon	fuses and melts away from flame	burns slowly with melting	self-extinguishing	acrid	irregular, hard black bead
Elastomers					
spandex	fuses but does not shrink away from flame	burns with melting	continues to burn with melting	chemical odor	soft, sticky, gummy
rubber	shrinks away from flame	burns rapidly with melting	continues to burn	sulfur or chemical odor	tacky, soft black residue

injury and guard against fire. The procedure to follow in doing the burning test is as follows:

1. Select one or two yarns from the warp of the fabric (see page 213) or unravel a length of yarn from a knitted structure (see also step 9).
2. Untwist the yarn so that the fibers are in a loose mass.
3. Hold the loosely twisted yarn in forceps; move them toward the flame from the side. (That is, approach the flame from its own level, not by bringing the sample down into the flame.)
4. Observe the reaction as the yarn approaches the flame.
5. Move the yarn into the flame, and then pull it out of the flame and observe the reaction. Does the yarn start to burn as it nears the flame? Does it start to melt? Does it shrink away from the flame? Does it burn quickly or slowly? Does it have a sputtering flame, a steady flame, no flame at all? When removed, does it continue to burn? Is it bright red or colored to indicate that it has reached a high temperature? Does the flame go out when removed from the source? What type of ash or residue, if any, is formed?
6. Notice any odor given off by the fiber, both while it is in the flame and after it is removed.
7. Observe the ash or residue formed and what characteristics it has. Is it brittle? bead-shaped? fluffy? the shape of the yarn? Or is there nearly no residue?
8. Repeat for the filling yarn of woven fabrics (see page 213).
9. If the fabric does not have yarn structure, or if it is impossible to "deknit" a length of yarn from complex knitted structures, a small sliver of fabric can be cut and used in place of the yarn.

Typical reactions of selected fiber groups or types are given in Table 4.1. Several cautions should be noted regarding the burning test. Dyes and finishes may alter the flammability of fibers. Some finishes may reduce or prevent flaming, whereas others may increase the flammability. Both dyes and finishes can affect the color of the residue and, in some instances, the shape of the residue. For comparative results it is important to follow the procedure as outlined.

Microscopic Evaluation

It is possible to be quite definitive in the identification of some fibers through microscopic observa-

tions. Fibers are mounted to provide views of both their lengthwise and crosswise dimensions. Unfortunately, several of the man-made fibers are similar in their microscopic appearance; therefore, additional analysis is required for specific identification. Photomicrographs of selected fibers are included in the chapters devoted to fibers. When making microscopic evaluation, these illustrations plus the information in Table 4.2 should be used as guides.

Solubility

The solubility of a fiber in specific chemical reagents is frequently a definitive means of specific fiber identification. Frequently, however, this process identifies only generic groups or categories. If the student combines the results of the burning test, the microscopic evaluation, and the chemical solubility test, it is possible, in many cases, to positively identify specific fibers.

In addition to aiding in fiber identification, familiarity with fiber behavior in various chemicals provides helpful information concerning the processing and care of textile fibers. A few substances used in such procedures as stain removal, cleaning, and laundering may damage some fibers. Obviously, knowing what chemicals to avoid in care would extend the life of a textile product.

Table 4.3 provides an identification scheme that uses a system of elimination. It can be used for fabrics composed of one or more different fibers or fiber types. In support of Table 4.3, Table 4.4 indicates general fiber solubility in selected reagents. It is important that the student interested in determining fiber content by solubility follow the series of steps cited in Table 4.3 exactly as given. Any variation in the order of use of the chemicals may nullify the validity of the results.

When using the identification scheme cited, it is important to follow the procedure enumerated below very carefully.

1. Use the same sample of yarn or fabric until the total substrate, or sample, has been destroyed or put through every test.
2. Place the sample in the first reagent listed at the recommended temperature and leave the sample in the chemical for five minutes before continuing.
3. Remove any material that is left and rinse carefully in water.
4. Observe the amount of material left to deter-

◇ ───

TABLE 4.2 Microscopic Appearance of Textile Fibers

Fiber	Longitudinal Appearance	Cross-Sectional Shape
Man-Made		
acetate, triacetate	distinct lengthwise striations; no cross markings	irregular shape with crenulated or serrated outline
acrylic		
Acrilan, Courtelle, Creslan, Zefran	rodlike with smooth surface and profile	nearly round or bean shape
Orlon	broad and often indistinct length-wise striation; no cross markings	dog bone
bicomponent Orlon	lengthwise striations; no cross markings	irregular mushroom or acorn
modacrylic		
SEF	lengthwise striations	irregular round
Verel	broad and often indistinct lengthwise striation; no cross markings	dog bone
nylon		
nylon 6, nylon 6,6 regular	rodlike with smooth surface and profile	round or nearly round
Antron and Cadon	broad, sometimes indistinct lengthwise striations; no cross markings	trilobal
olefin		
polyethylene, polypropylene	rodlike with smooth surface and profile	round or nearly round
polyester		
Dacron, Fortrel, Kodel, and Vycron	rodlike with smooth surface and profile	round or nearly round
Dacron type 62	broad, sometimes indistinct lengthwise striations; no cross markings	trilobal
Trevira	broad, sometimes indistinct lengthwise striations; no cross markings	pentalobal
rayon		
viscose, regular	distinct lengthwise striations; no cross markings	irregluar shape with crenulated or serrated outline
high-tenacity viscose	rodlike with smooth surface; indistinct striations or none	slightly irregular shape with few serrations
high-wet-modulus viscose; Avril, Zantrel	rodlike, smooth surface	round or oval shaped
Cuprammonium	rodlike with smooth surface and profile	round or nearly round
saran		
Saran	rodlike with smooth surface and profile	round or nearly round
spandex Lycra	broad, often indistinct lengthwise striation; no cross markings	dog bone
Natural		
cotton, mercerized and not mercerized	ribbonlike convolutions (twists) sometimes change direction, and are less frequent in mercerized fibers; no significant lengthwise striations, but lumen may appear as striations in some fibers	tubular shape with tubes usually collapsed, and irregular in size
flax, bleached	bamboolike, pronounced crossmarking nodes; no significant lengthwise striations	very irregular in size as well as shape; round and oval are most prevalent
silk, boiled off	smooth surface and profile, but may contain nodes; no significant lengthwise striations	mostly triangular with point of triangle usually rounded off; irregular in size and shape
wool, cashmere, mohair, and regular (Merino)	rough surface, cross markings due to surface scales; medulla or central fiber core sometimes apparent in coarse grades	round or nearly round; medulla may appear shaded

TABLE 4.3 Scheme for Identification of Fiber Solubility (follow directions in text)

Chemical	Removes	Chemical	Removes
1. Glacial acetic acid, 25°C (75°F)	acetate, triacetate	6. Ammonium thiocyanate, at boil, 70% by weight	acrylics
2. Hydrochloric acid 1:1, 25°C (75°F)	nylon 6, and 6,6	7. Butyrolactone, 25°C (75°F)	modacrylics and nytriles
3. Sodium hypochlorite, 25°C (75°F) 5% available chlorine	silk, wool	8. Dimethyl formamide, 95°C (200°F)—not always effective	spandex
4. Dioxane, 100°C (212°F)	saran	9. Sulfuric acid, 75% by weight, 25% (75°C)	cellulosics
5. Meta xylene, at boil	olefins	10. Meta cresol, 95°C (200°C)	polyesters

TABLE 4.4 Solubilities of Fibers

Solution	Concentration	Temperature	Fibers Affected
acetone	100%	25°C (75°F)	acetate, Dynel modacrylic, triacetate
acetone	80%	25°C (75°F)	acetate
acetone	100%	50°C (120°F)	acetate, triacetate, modacrylics
acetic acid	glacial	25°C (75°F)	acetate, triacetate
acetic acid	glacial	95°C (200°F)	acetate, triacetate, nylon 6, nylon 6,6
meta cresol		25°C (75°F)	acetate, triacetate, nylon 6, nylon 6,6, silk, modacrylics, spandex
meta cresol		95°C (200°F)	acetate, triacetate, nylon 6, nylon 6,6, spandex, modacrylics, polyesters
phenol	90%	25°C (75°F)	acetate, triacetate, modacrylic, nylon 6, nylon 6,6, spandex
phenol	90%	95°C (200°F)	acetate, triacetate, modacrylic, nylon 6, nylon 6,6, polyester, spandex, acrylics (damaged)
NaOH	5%	boiling	acetate, triacetate, silk, wool
sodium hypochlorite	5% available Cl	25°C (75°F)	wool, silk
formic acid	90%	25°C (75°F)	acetate, triacetate, spandex, nylon 6, nylon 6,6, acrylics (weakened)
HCl	1:1	25°C (75°F)	nylon 6, nylon 6,6
HCl	concentrated	25°C (75°F)	acetate, triacetate, modacrylic, nylon 6, nylon 6,6, acrylics, spandex, rayon (with heat)
sulfuric acid	75% w/w	25°C (75°F)	acetate, triacetate, nylon 6, nylon 6,6, cellulosics, silk
dimethyl formamide		25°C (75°F)	acetate, triacetate, modacrylics, acrylics (Zefran requires heat), saran, spandex
xylene		boiling	olefins, rubber, saran

mine whether some fiber has been dissolved or altered in any way.

5. In some cases, it may be helpful to look at the remaining fibers under the microscope to determine whether they have been damaged or if some in the sample have been destroyed.

6. Record the results of each step carefully.

7. Place the remaining fibers in solution 2 and repeat the steps above.

8. Continue this procedure until all of the sample has been dissolved or the 10 steps have been completed.

In order to alert consumers to potential damage from chemical products found in the home, the following brief summary should be of interest. Acetone, which dissolves acetate and triacetate, is found in many fingernail polish removers and paint removers. Vinegar contains acetic acid; however, whereas glacial acetic acid is concentrated, vinegar is only 6 percent acid. It will not destroy fibers, but it may weaken those affected by the glacial acetic acid. Sodium hypochlorite, which has a pH of about 11, with 5 percent available chlorine is standard undiluted bleach sold for home laundering procedures. Cresol is frequently a component of household disinfectants and antiseptics. It is not strong enough in these products to destroy any fiber; however, fibers that are damaged by cresol will be weakened if such products are spilled onto the fabrics. Other chemical reagents used in fiber identification are not usually encountered in either laundering or dry cleaning procedures or in chemicals used in household activities. They are included in Table 4.3 as a part of the identification process and in Table 4.4 as information of scientific value in the study of textile science.

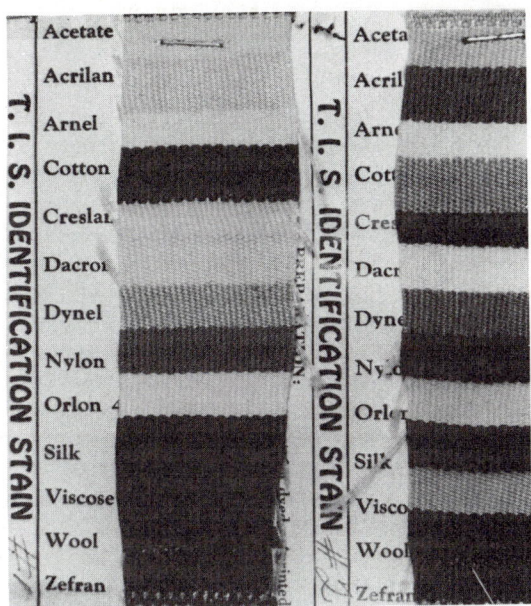

4.1 Multifiber testfabric stained with two different fiber identification dyes. Note differences among various fibers.

Staining Test

When fibers are white or off-white or when color can be stripped from fibers, staining techniques may be used as a part of identification. Specifically prepared mixtures of dyes are dissolved in water, or other chemicals if the specific stain mixture so specified, and the fibers are immersed in the solution and stained for a specified time and at a specified temperature. After staining, the fiber, yarn, or fabric pieces are dried and then compared with a known sample. Figure 4.1 shows an example of how different fibers react to a dye mixture used for fiber identification. Prepared stains are available from several sources, including Testfabrics, Inc.

Instrumental Analysis Procedures

Certain man-made fibers are not easily identified by any of the testing procedures cited. Positive verification of some fibers depends on the use of one or more sophisticated instrumental techniques. These include testing for density, melting point, refractive index, index of birefringence, the use of X-ray diffraction machines, infrared spectrophotometers, chromatographs of various types, electron scanning microscopes, and polarizing microscopes. These are standard equipment in many university laboratories, testing laboratories, and research laboratories. Although they may not be available in departments where textile science is taught, they may be available in chemistry departments.

Notes on Identification Procedures

The first step in identification should be the burning test, as this will indicate broad groupings of fibers. This should be followed by microscopic evaluation to establish more definitive groups. Solubilities will further classify the fibers, followed by staining techniques. However, if the laboratory has spectrophotometers, X-ray diffraction units, or other highly complex machines, their use may provide positive identification without the preliminary tests. They may always be used to further define the fiber under investigation and provide a positive identity.

STUDY QUESTIONS

1. Why is the chemical behavior of textile fibers important to the consumer and the person responsible for care of textile products?

2. Why is the knowledge of flammability of textile fibers of value to consumers?
3. Can the burning test be used to distinguish between cotton and rayon? Explain your answer.
4. Can the microscopic test be used for specific differentiation between nylon and polyester? Explain your answer.
5. How would you determine whether a fabric identified as a blend of cotton and polyester was actually composed of both cotton and polyester fibers?
6. Could you determine with only the burning test whether a fiber was silk?

Activities

1. Outline the procedures to be followed in fiber identification.
2. Select several fabrics or yarns of unknown fiber content, apply the various identification steps, and try to identify the fiber or fibers involved.
3. Collect a group of fabrics of unidentified fiber content. Using the procedures outlined, test each to determine fiber content, and prepare a scrapbook showing the results of each test and how you arrived at your conclusions.
4. Identify several fiber blends that could be distinguished by the use of the microscope.

PART II

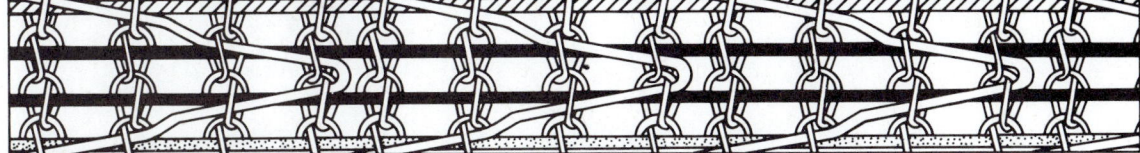

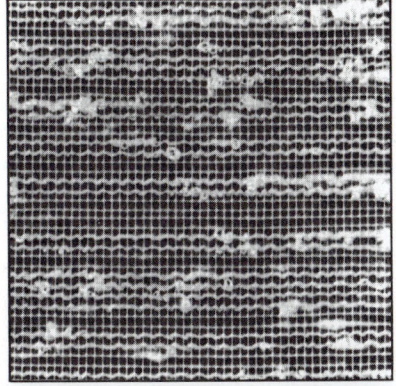

Textile Fibers

If Part II of this book had been written in 1900, it probably would have contained two chapters on fibers—one for the natural cellulose fibers and one for the natural protein fibers. Rayon, then identified as artificial silk, might have had a brief mention. Today, the fibers section is divided into 12 chapters, two of which are concerned with several different fiber groups.

Volumes have been written about many of the textile fibers described in subsequent chapters; some of these books are cited in the Bibliography. In this text, for each of the major fibers or fiber groups, there is a brief history, information on production and fiber properties, and discussion of selection, use, and care.

Chapter 5 provides an introduction to the study of fibers with special emphasis on the manufacture of man-made fibers. The next two chapters, 6 and 7, describe the natural protein fibers, then the natural cellulose fibers. Chapters 8 through 16 are devoted to the manufactured fibers, except for the reference to asbestos in the last chapter.

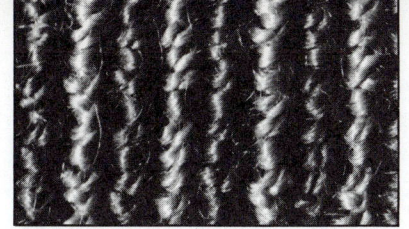

5

INTRODUCTION TO THE STUDY OF FIBERS

KEY TERMS

bicomponent	emulsion spinning	spinnerette
biconstituent	melt spinning	spinning processes
bigeneric	monofilament	staple fiber
delustering	multifilament	texturing
dry spinning	solution spinning	tow

Natural fibers are obtained from products produced by nature and in a form ready for conversion into yarns and fabrics. Manufactured or man-made fibers are produced from raw materials that may or may not resemble fibrous forms.

Natural fibers are obtained from various types of plant life (e.g., cotton, flax, jute, hemp); from animal life (e.g., wool, silk, mohair); and from mineral forms (e.g., asbestos). Considerable processing may be required to convert natural fibers into textile products, but the basic raw material is in a form that has the primary properties of a fiber. Growing, producing, or mining natural fibers is specific to each fiber type involved. Thus, discussion of natural fiber processing is included as a part of the specific fiber chapters.

The production of man-made fibers depends on several general principles and procedures. Thus, this chapter describes the basic history of man-made fibers, ways by which manufactured fibers are formed, physical forms in which they are available, and selected processes applicable to a variety of man-made textile fibers.

Early History of Man-Made Fibers

The first comment concerning the potential of creating man-made fibers is found in Robert Hooke's *Micrographia*, published in 1664. Hooke predicted that eventually there would be a way to duplicate the excrement of the silkworm. Reamur, in France, pursued Hooke's idea by suggesting that gums and resins then available, including the secretions from spiders, would be useful as a substitute for silk.

However, it was not until the nineteenth century that scientists actually made artificial fibers. Schwabe, in 1842, demonstrated that molten glass could be forced through fine openings to form fibers. In 1855, George Audemars made filaments from a solution of mulberry twigs in nitric acid. He pulled out a fine thread by inserting a needle in the solution and then removing it. The material adhering to the needle solidified in the air. E. J. Hughes, in 1857, created fibers from a solution in starch, glue, resins, and tannins.

The major breakthrough in the production of man-made fibers occurred in 1862 when Ozanam, a

5.1 Spinnerettes. The large spinnerette, with 3000 holes, is used for spinning fibers that will be cut into staple lengths; the smaller platinum spinnerette, with 350 holes, is of the type used for spinning continuous filaments that will remain in filament form. Some jets used in spinning fiber for cutting into staple length may have as many as 30,000 openings. (Avtex Fibers, Inc.)

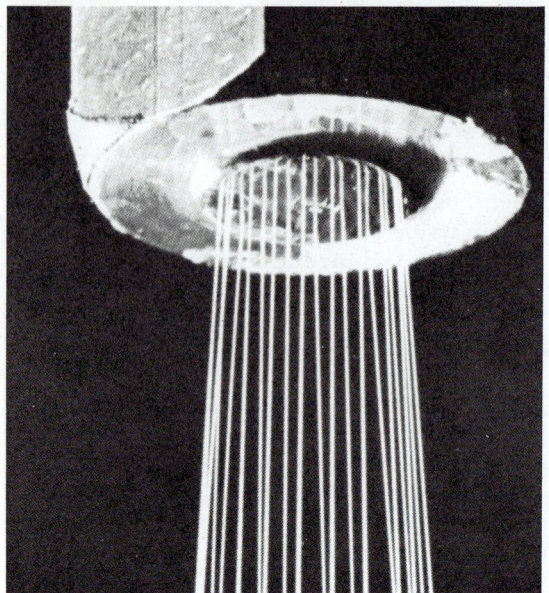

5.2 Spinning filament fibers through a spinnerette. (Avtex Fibers, Inc.)

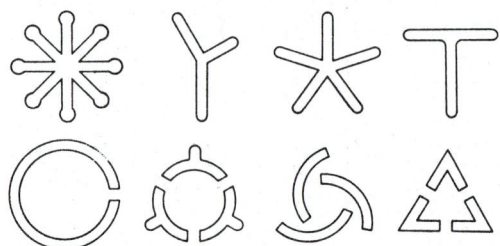

5.3 Various shapes available as openings for spinnerettes. (Adapted by permission of Fi-Tech, Inc.)

French scientist, invented the spinning jet, or spinnerette. This remarkable little device is the basis for all manufactured fiber production (see Fig. 5.1).

The pioneer work of Audemars, Ozanam, and others was combined to form the basis for the production of nitrocellulose rayon. In 1883, J. W. Swan produced nitrocellulose filaments by forcing a solution of cellulose nitrate in glacial acetic acid through a spinning jet. Swan used a denitration process to reduce the flammability of the fiber, then carbonized the filaments for use as the filament in the first electric light bulbs. Count Hilaire Chardonnet developed a usable rayon, which he introduced in 1889, and Cross and Bevan introduced the first viscose rayon in 1891. (See page 84.)

Fiber Forming and Spinning

Man-made fibers are polymeric forms that are produced by some type of chemical action or by the regeneration of natural polymers in a new physical form. The polymer is converted into some type of liquid or fluid state and forced through a spinnerette (Fig. 5.2). Although most spinnerettes are made with round openings, some may use orifices of other shapes in order to produce fibers with special characteristics (Fig. 5.3).

There are four basic processes involved in converting the polymeric form of a man-made fiber into an actual filament form: wet spinning, dry spinning, melt spinning, and emulsion spinning.

WET SPINNING The polymer or substance to be used in making the fiber is dissolved into some type of solution, then is forced through the spinning jet into another liquid, which reacts with the fiber solution. The process involves one of the following reactions: (a) The fiber polymer may have been chemically changed in order to make it soluble in the

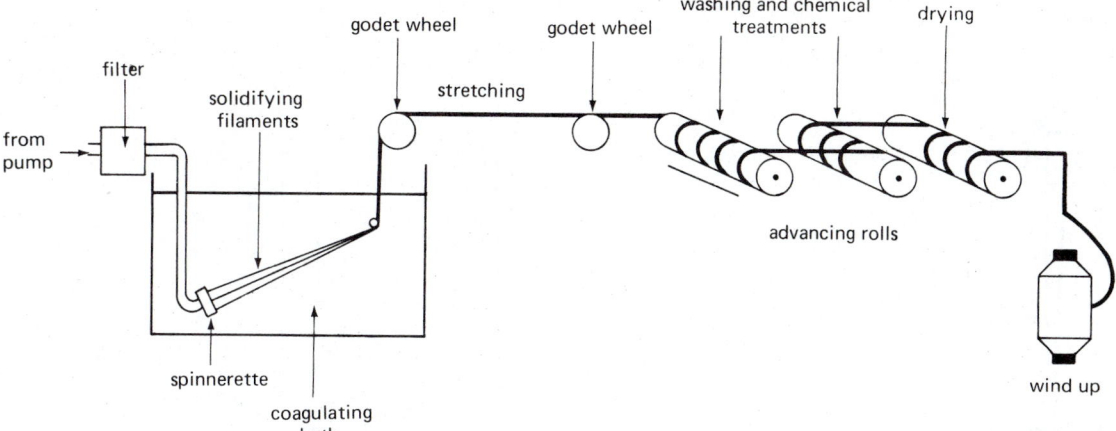

5.4 Diagram of wet spinning process.

solvent used; when this occurs, the fiber solution reacts with the receiving solution and reverses the chemical reaction so that the material is re-formed into a fiber shape. The difference is that in re-forming, a filament fiber shape has been made rather than a polymer in some other form, such as a fibrous mass, chip, or pellet. This process refers to the fiber solution as a derivative of the fiber form, the solution into which this passes is the coagulating bath, and the actual process is typically called regeneration. (b) Wet spinning may also be used when the fiber solution does not change the chemical form of the fiber. The solution is forced into a coagulating bath, which reduces the concentration of the fiber solution sufficiently to re-form the fiber, this time in a filament form. Figure 5.4 is a diagram of the wet spinning process. Fibers formed by the wet spinning process include rayon and some of the acrylic fibers.

DRY SPINNING In dry spinning the fiber solution is forced through the spinnerette into a warm air chamber. The warm air causes the solvent used to make the fiber solution evaporate, and the filament fibers are formed and harden. This process, too, may involve converting the fiber polymer into a different chemical form that is soluble in a suitable liquid. As the solvent evaporates, the fiber polymer is reconstituted and returns to its original chemical form, but now it is in a filament shape. Several fibers are made using the dry spinning technique (Fig. 5.5); acetate and triacetate, some types of acrylics and modacrylics, and some aramid fibers are dry-spun.

MELT SPINNING In melt spinning the fiber polymer is melted and the molten solution is forced through the spinnerette. As the soft filaments emerge from the spinnerette into the cooler environment, they harden into a standard filament form (Fig. 5.6). Melt spinning requires no chemical change of any kind in the polymeric material from which the fiber is formed. It does require that the fiber polymer can be melted without altering the chemical state of the material. Nylon, polyester, and glass are examples of melt-spun fibers.

EMULSION SPINNING Emulsion spinning is not used to a great extent, but it is important for selected types of specialty fibers. Some raw polymeric materials cannot be processed by the preceding methods because they either break down when heated to a melting temperature or are not soluble in solutions that can be used. For these substances the emulsion process is necessary. The polymer is dispersed or emulsified into a solution; the dispersion or emulsion is then forced through a spinnerette, and as the emulsion leaves the spinnerette, the fiber polymer forms into a fibrous shape. Depending on the type of fiber, the fibrous form produced by this method may be of staple or filament length. Teflon® is an example of a fiber spun by the emulsion process.

Fiber Modifications

Fiber manufacturers frequently create modifications or variants of the standard fiber polymers in

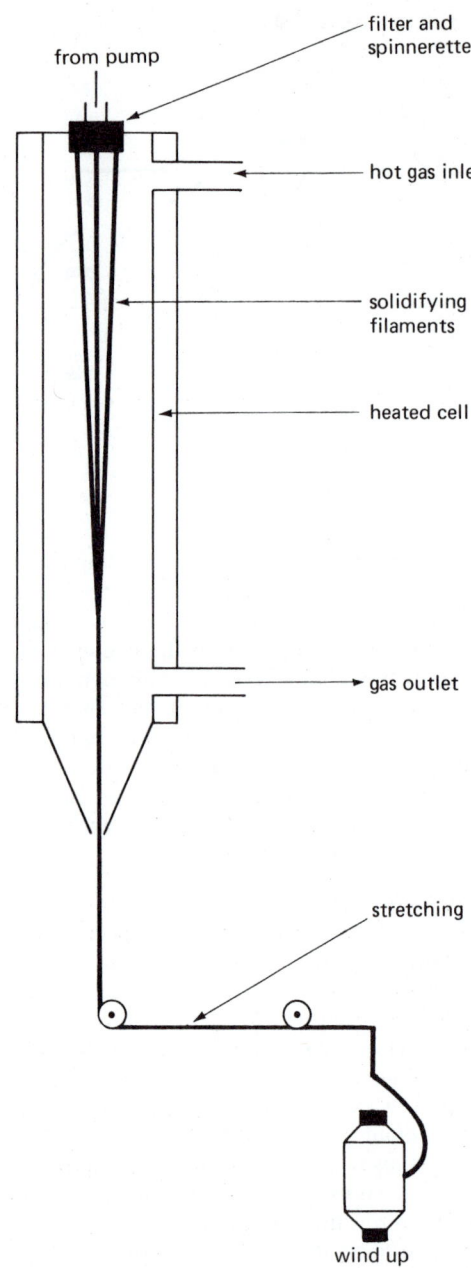

5.5 Diagram of the dry spinning process.

from pump

filter and spinnerette

hot gas inlet

solidifying filaments

heated cell

gas outlet

stretching

wind up

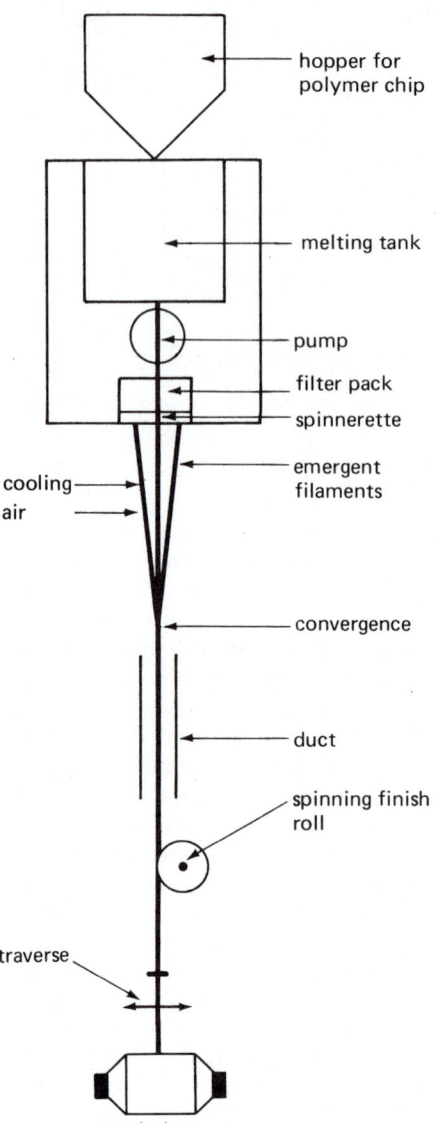

5.6 Diagram of the melt spinning process.

hopper for polymer chip

melting tank

pump

filter pack

spinnerette

emergent filaments

cooling

air

convergence

duct

spinning finish roll

traverse

wind up

order to produce fibers with special properties. These modifications or variants can be the result of adding small amounts of other chemicals to the fiber during the conversion to a fluid state, adding small amounts of chemicals during the actual polymerization process, modifying the shape and size of

the spinnerette's orifices or openings, or modifying the spinning process—particularly by changing the spinning bath composition or other processing steps. These modifications of the original fiber will frequently have characteristics that differ somewhat from the original fiber in such matters as reactions to dyes and finishing chemicals, amount of luster or sheen, fiber strength, and behavior in various environmental situations. Further, modifications may be made after the fiber is formed but prior to final stabilizing. The latter technique is used in producing some types of texturized fibers. A few of the modifications are cited below.

DELUSTERING Many man-made fibers are naturally very lustrous or bright. Since many customers do not want shiny fibers, manufacturers add delusterants to the solution before spinning the fiber. The delustering agents modify or alter the way light is reflected by the fiber so that the fibers can be made to appear somewhat matte or dull.

TEXTURIZING Texturizing involves modification of the shape of the fibers. This is discussed in detail in Chapter 19. The purpose of texturizing is to build into fibers various shapes that make filament fibers resemble yarns made of staple fibers. The resulting yarns may have built-in stretch and/or bulk.

FIBER VARIANTS Since the early developments in man-made fibers, manufacturers have continued to develop ways in which fibers would provide a variety of properties. Thus, fibers have been modified or altered to provide variants that would dye differently from others, that would have greater or lesser strength than others, that would perform somewhat differently, and that would have different modulus values. The manufacture of variants is accomplished by adding small amounts of different chemicals to the fiber formula, by modifying the polymeric compound used, or by creating types of cross-linking among molecules that result in different fiber behavior. Other types of modifications may be achieved by modifying the shape of the fiber that is formed; this can be done by using spinnerettes with different shapes or orifices, by using different chemicals in a coagulating bath, or by applying different speeds to the drawing and orientation operations for each specific fiber. The various fiber modifications have been identified in much research as third-, fourth-, or even fifth-generation fibers. Each major change developed for any of the man-made fibers, particularly the noncellulosic fibers, has been called a "new generation" of the fiber.

Fiber Forms

Man-made fibers are sold on the market in several different physical forms. They may be monofilament, multifilament, tow, or staple.

MONOFILAMENT In monofilaments, a single filament of a fiber is used as a yarn. Monofilaments tend to be somewhat stiff and lack the draping qual-

ities of multifilament yarns. Filaments for use in monofilament forms are extruded in extremely long lengths. Actual length is limited only by the amount of yardage that can be handled on the take-up package—the unit upon which the filament is wound as it comes from the forming processes. It is possible for a package of monofilament to be miles in length.

MULTIFILAMENT Multifilaments differ from monofilaments in that the final yarn is composed of several filaments combined into the single yarn unit. Multifilaments are formed by having sufficient number of holes in the spinnerette to result in a physical group that may be used as a yarn and that is composed of more than one filament. Most filament yarns involve many filaments. The process of making multifilament forms involves simultaneously forming the number of filaments to be combined into the single yarn. The multifilaments are held together by a slight amount of twist; in some cases a high amount of twist may be needed to maintain an uniform product. The ultimate size of a filament fiber depends on several factors: the size of the openings in the spinnerette, output and spinning speed, and draw ratio.

TOW A considerable amount of man-made fiber is marketed in a form called *tow*. This is composed of many hundreds or thousands of filaments that have been formed simultaneously by extrusion through special spinnerettes that have hundreds or thousands of orifices or openings. These many filaments are pulled together to form a large sliver of fibers.

Manufacturers can process tow into yarns by a direct process or by intermittent methods. The direct process takes the sliver to special machinery that converts the tow into yarn as it comes from the fiber-forming units. In the intermittent process the tow is cut into short lengths, called staple, and then processed into yarns like any staple fiber (see Chap. 17).

STAPLE FIBER Staple fibers are short fibers that resemble natural fibers, such as wool and cotton, in length. Man-made fibers may be cut into staple lengths for processing on the same type of machinery as that used in processing cotton or wool. The length of the cut—or staple fiber length—will be determined by the type of spinning equipment to be used. These cut fibers, varying in length from about 1 inch to 3 inches or more, are called staple fibers—just as natural fibers, except for silk, are identified as staple fibers. Man-made fibers are usually cut from tow, and the tow may be texturized before cutting in order to provide fibers that have cohesiveness or spinning quality sufficient for making into yarns that hold together well.

Staple fibers are packed into bales and shipped to manufacturers for conversion into yarns and then into fabrics. Some fibers may be made into fabrics directly, such as nonwoven structures. Man-made staple fibers may be blended with natural fibers during the yarn manufacturing process. When this is required for creating blended fiber yarns, the man-made fibers must be in staple form and in the same typical length as the natural fiber with which it is to be blended.

Bicomponent and Bigeneric Fibers

Extruding two filaments of different composition so that they coalesce as they coagulate or harden produces bicomponent or bigeneric (formerly called biconstituent) fibers. There are three basic methods for making these fibers: the side-by-side (S/S) type, the sheath/core (S/C) type, and the matrix/fibril (M/F) type. The side-by-side type (Fig. 5.7) is made

when two compatible polymer formulas are spun side by side and are sealed together as they emerge from the spinnerette. Special spinnerettes are required for all types of bicomponent or bigeneric fibers. In the sheath/core method, one component is

5.7 Photomicrograph of a side-by-side bicomponent.

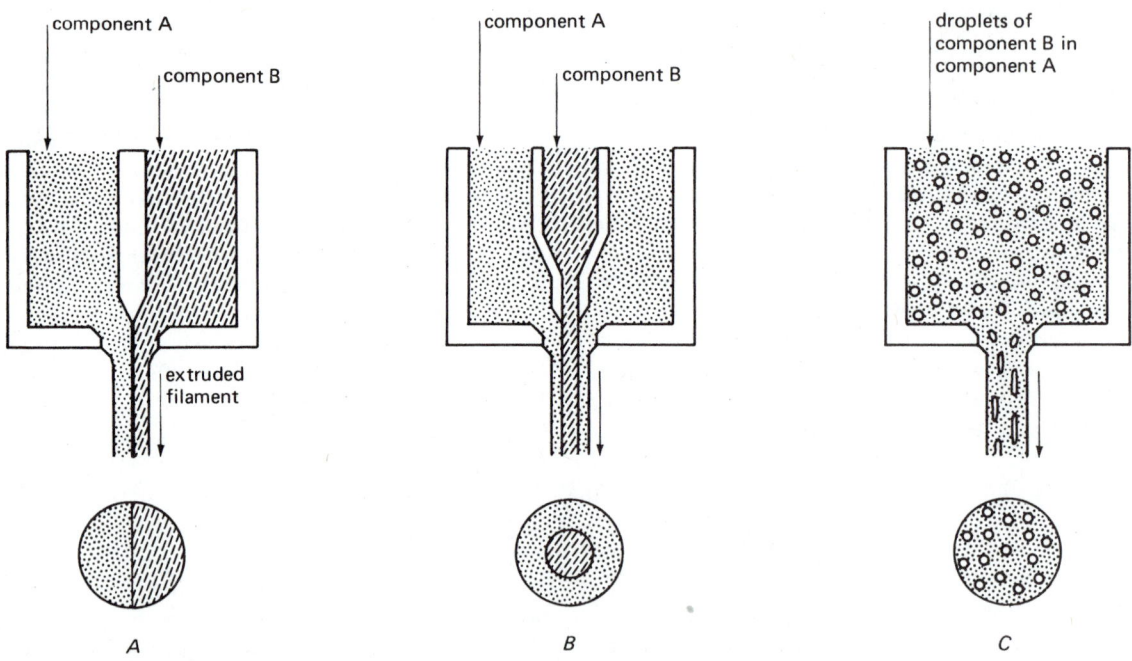

5.8 Diagram of three types of bicomponent, biconstituent, and/or bigeneric fibers. Extrusion techniques above, fiber cross section below. A: side by side (S/S). B: sheath/core (S/C). C: matrix- fibril (M/F).

extruded so that it forms a sheath around a second component, called the core. The matrix/fibril process involves the use of two mutually incompatible polymers that, when spun together in the same mix, form a filament in which one component forms fibrils within the other (Fig. 5.8).

Bicomponent fibers are usually made from two variants of the same generic fiber type. The two different variants exhibit different properties, such as different shrinkage levels, different thermal behavior, or different shapes, which result in filaments that coil. These differences enable yarn and fabric producers to introduce bulk, improved fit, retained sheerness, and/or attractive appearance into the end use item.

Bigeneric filament fibers are those in which the two different components are from two different generic groups. These two different generic polymers are mixed together just prior to extrusion. Such fibers have characteristics of both chemical polymers.

A change in terminology has been recently introduced, indicating that the term *biconstituent* is to be deleted from use. The term *bicomponent* is now to be used for any type of filament fiber in which two or more different fiber variants are used, while *bigeneric* can be used when two or more generic types are used. There may therefore be confusion in the use of these terms for the next few years. ASTM has accepted the use of *bicomponent* as the term for any fiber in which there are two or more different chemical polymers—it does not matter if these two are from the same generic class or not. However, it

has been suggested that fibers with different generic groups be modified, in name, to indicate that such a bicomponent fiber is a *bigeneric* fiber. The reader is cautioned that these terms are not clearly separated at the present time. However, it is important to be alerted to the fact that the term *bicomponent* is acceptable, and that the term *bigeneric* may be used when two different generic fiber types are employed in forming the filament.

STUDY QUESTIONS

1. Define the key terms listed at the beginning of this chapter.
2. Describe the various methods used in spinning man-made fibers.
3. What is a fiber variant?
4. Describe how tow is made and how it is usually used.
5. Discuss the early history of man-made fibers and consider reasons why they developed in the direction that they did.

Activities

1. Locate labels that might indicate that a product is composed of a bicomponent fiber. Determine what has been used and discuss what properties the product might have as a result.
2. Locate fabrics that are made of monofilament yarns and those that are made of multifilament yarns, and describe how they differ.

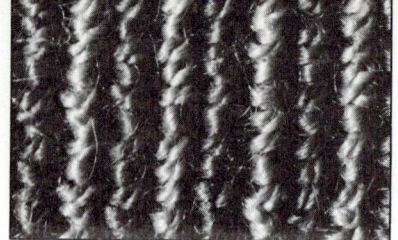

6

Natural Protein Fibers

OBJECTIVES

◇ **To list and describe the properties and characteristics of the various natural protein fibers**

◇ **To identify the differences between animal-hair protein fibers and animal-secretion protein fibers**

◇ **To describe recommended care procedures for protein fibers**

◇ **To identify the molecular structure of the protein fibers and discuss how the structures affect the properties and behavior of the fibers**

◇ **To identify legislation that applies to wool and silk**

◇ **To list and describe specialty fibers and note special properties of such fibers**

KEY TERMS

brins
crimp
degumming
fibroin
helical structure of wool
keratin
protein fibers
reeling

scale structure
serecin
silk and sericulture
specialty fibers
throwing
wool
Wool Products Labeling Act

Animal life is the source of natural protein fibers. Most of these fibers form the hair covering of certain animals; the remainder are the excrement of worms or insects in forming cocoons or webs. Animal-hair fibers are obtained from such animals as sheep, angora goat, cashmere goat, llama, Bactrian camel, alpaca, and vicuña. In addition, fibers from fur-bearing animals such as mink, rabbit, beaver, and muskrat may be used as fibers and converted into yarns rather than used as furs. Fibers from animal secretions are obtained from various types of silkworms and from such insects as spiders. The two major types of silkworms used are the *Bombyx mori,* the standard silkworm, and various types of *Antheraea* and *Attacus,* which are considered wild silkworms. All protein fibers have some properties in common. However, hair fibers and secretion fibers have some characteristics that are very different.

All protein fibers are composed of amino acids that have been formed into polypeptide chains hav-

ing large molecular weights. The number and arrangement of alpha-amino-acid residues vary among the fibers, and there is considerable difference between hair and secretion fibers.

Fibers in this group have excellent absorbency. Their standard moisture regain is high, and they absorb additional moisture when exposed to liquids or high humidity. Protein fibers tend to be warmer than most other fibers. The low degree of electrical conductance contributes to a buildup of static charges, so the resulting yarns and fabrics tend to release static, particularly when in a dry atmosphere. Moisture reduces the development of static charge on protein fibers.

Natural protein fibers have poor resistance to alkalies and can be dissolved in a 5 percent solution of sodium hydroxide at the boiling point. Most fibers in this group have good resistance to acids; the exception is silk, which is damaged or completely destroyed by concentrated mineral acids. These fibers are harmed by many oxidizing agents, particularly chlorine-type bleaches. Hydrogen peroxide bleach, however, also a type of oxidizing bleach, is used safely and successfully to bleach wool and silk. Sunlight causes white protein fiber fabrics to discolor slowly and turn yellow.

The density of fibers in this group is less than that of cellulosic fibers. As a group they have good resiliency and elasticity. All protein fibers except silk are comparatively weak and even weaker when wet, so care must be exercised during cleaning. The fibers burn slowly in flame, are considered self-extinguishing, leave a brittle, beadlike residue, and smell like burning hair or meat.

Since the mid-1950s protein fibers have faced serious threats to their status by the increasing use of man-made fibers. Before the introduction of noncellulosic man-made fibers, wool accounted for approximately 14 to 15 percent of the world's fiber production. Today, wool accounts for only 5 percent of the world's production. In the United States wool consumption is down to approximately 1 percent. Silk has never been a frequently used fiber, as it has usually represented luxury. Although the use of silk remains low, it has been increasing during the past few years. Despite the relatively low use of protein fibers, they have many fine properties and are highly desired for a variety of end uses.

WOOL

Historical Review

The early history of wool is lost in antiquity. Sheepskin, including the hair, was probably used long before it was discovered that the fibers could be spun into yarns or even felted into fabric. There is no evidence to support the theory that wool was the first fiber to be processed into fabric, but it seems certain that, as a part of the skin, wool was used for covering and protection by prehistoric peoples long before yarns and fabrics were made.

The earliest fragments of wool fabric have been found in Egypt, probably because of the preserving qualities of the climate. These have been dated from 4000 to 3500 B.C. There is indication, however, that wool fabrics were first made in Mesopotamia. Clay tablets from the Sumerian culture indicate that wool spinning was an important industry and the trading of sheep was a part of the economic life of Sumeria.

The earliest example of wool fabric found in Europe has been dated about 1500 B.C.; it was unearthed in archeological digs in Germany. Danish sites have yielded excellent fragments of early wool fabrics dated about 1300 to 1000 B.C. These fabrics are rough and coarse and contain considerable wild sheep hair.

Sheep were brought to the New World (America) by Columbus on his second voyage in 1493, and Cortez carried sheepherding to what are now the western United States and Mexico in 1521. Wool of high quality has been produced in the United States since George Washington encouraged the importation of fine Merino sheep from Spain in the late 1700s.

Production of wool in the United States has declined consistently for the past 40 years. In the early 1940s, the United States was producing approximately 11 percent of the world's total; currently the production is between 1 and 2 percent. Although the use of wool in the United States is low, fiber must be imported to meet the needs particularly for such uses as wool carpets.

Growth and Production

To provide the finest-quality wool, production is scientifically controlled. Sheep are inoculated against disease, dipped in chemicals to protect them against insects, and, unless on rangeland, fed diets designed to produce healthy animals.

Several breeds of sheep are raised primarily for their fiber. The best quality, in the United States, is obtained from the Merino, which produces fiber that is fine and exhibits good performance properties. The Delaine and Rambouillet breeds were developed from the Merino and produce wool slightly coarser than Merino but still of good quality and fineness. Coarse wools derive from the Navajo, Cotswold, Lincoln, and Romney breeds. Medium fibers are obtained from such breeds as the Cheviot, Columbia, Corriedale, Montadale, and Panama. In addition, a few breeds raised primarily for food value may produce acceptable wool for selected end uses.

Wool can be sheared from the living animal or pulled from the hide after the animal has been slaughtered for its meat. Sheared wool is called *fleece* or *clip wool* and is considered superior in quality to *pulled wool*, which is taken from the hides of slaughtered sheep.

Shearing is currently done very rapidly with

power shears. A good shearer can completely shear a sheep in less than one minute, sometimes as short a time as 20 seconds. Recent developments in Australia have led to a process called chemical or biological shearing. The animal is fed a chemical similar to that used in the treatment of cancer, which causes the hair to fall out within two weeks. Within a very short time following the loss of the hair, it starts to grow again, and the sheep suffer no damage. Fibers obtained in this way are slightly longer than those sheared from the animal, and there appears to be less physical damage to the fibers.

In the United States, shearing is done once a year in the early spring, and the fleece is removed in one piece, rolled, packed into bags, and shipped to the nearest processing center (Fig. 6.1). Pulled wool is removed from the hide by one of two methods. It may be treated with a dipilatory that loosens the fiber and permits it to be pulled away from the skin without damaging the hide, or it can be loosened by the action of bacteria on the root end of the fiber. Pulled wool is usually mixed with fleece or clip wool before processing into yarns and fabrics.

Preliminary grading of wool fibers is done while they are still in the fleece, because this step is important in determining cost. Factors used in determining the grade of wool include fiber fineness or diameter and length, the age of the animal, location of the fiber on the animal, the natural color, the breed of the sheep, and the condition under which the animal lived. After grading, fleeces are shipped to the mill, where they are prepared for further processing into yarns and fabrics.

Fiber Properties

Molecular Structure

Wool is a protein substance called *keratin* and is composed of 18 amino acid residues, of which 17 are present in measurable amounts. The amino acid residues join together, and the molecules are arranged in such a manner as to give the fiber many of its desirable properties, such as resiliency and elasticity. The molecular structure frequently given for wool is diagramed in Figure 6.2. This figure shows the folded characteristic of the *alpha* keratin molecule. When extended, it is referred to as *beta* keratin. As soon as the tension used to form beta keratin is removed, the molecule attempts to return to the alpha or folded form. This is partly responsi-

6.1 Shearing a sheep. (U.S. Dept. of Agriculture)

R = amino acid or other reactive groups

6.2 Diagram of the molecular structure of wool. (After Asbury)

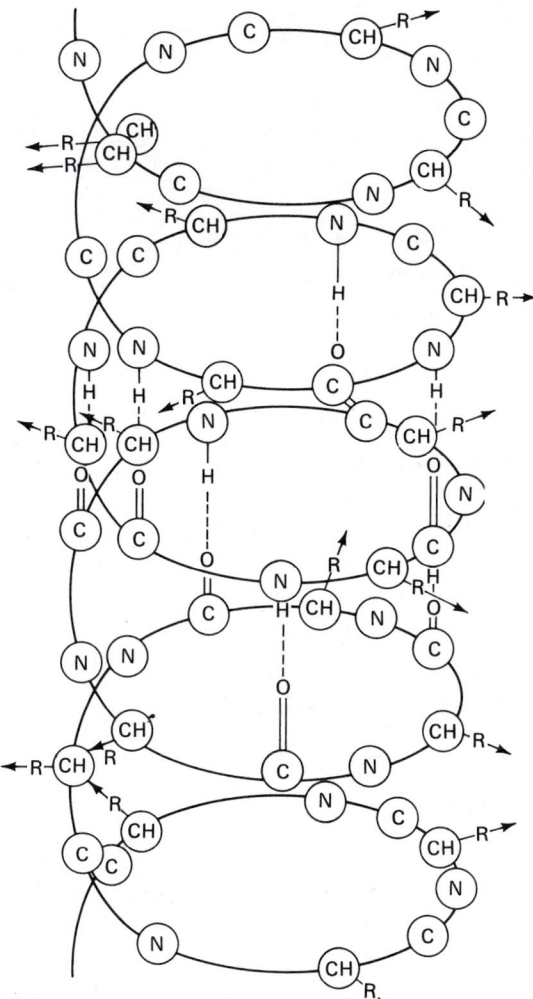

6.3 Diagram of the helical molecular arrangement of wool. (After Pauling and Corey)

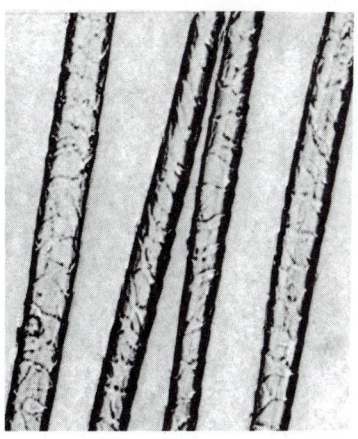

6.4 Photomicrograph of Merino wool, longitudinal view. (DuPont Company)

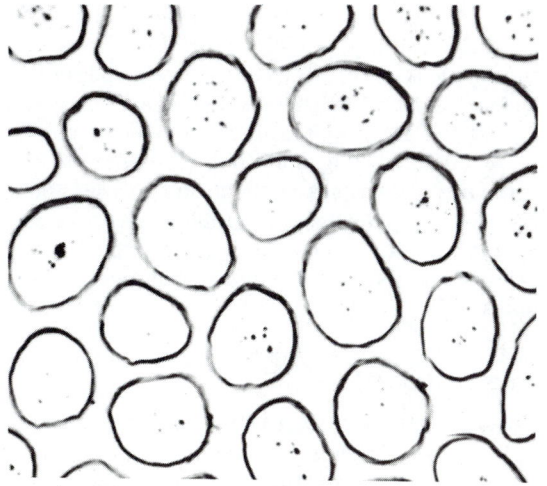

6.5 Photomicrograph of Merino wool, cross section. (DuPont Company)

ble for the ability of wool fiber to recover its shape after distortion.

Scientific analysis of wool completed during the middle of this century has provided evidence of a helical or spiral structure rather than a folded form for keratin. Figure 6.3 is a diagram of this helical structure. It is believed that the helical structure may be responsible for the high elongation property of wool fibers. Furthermore, additional research has suggested that the cystine linkage and the intramolecular hydrogen bonding are responsible for the shaping and setting characteristics of wool fibers and fabrics.

Microscopic Properties

Under microscopic observation, the length of the wool fiber clearly shows a scalelike structure (Fig. 6.4). The size of the scale varies from very small to comparatively broad and large. As many as 2000 scales are found in 1 inch of fine wool (700 per cm), whereas coarse wool may have as few as 700 per inch (275 per cm). Fine wool does not have as clear and distinct scales as coarse wool, but they can be identified under high magnification.

A cross section of wool shows three distinct parts to the fiber (Fig. 6.5). The outer layer, called *epider-*

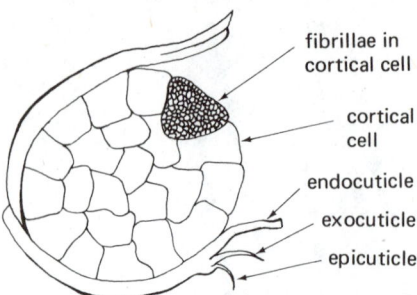

fibrillae in
cortical cell

cortical
cell

endocuticle

exocuticle

epicuticle

6.6 Diagram of wool fiber cross section, showing fiber morphology. Medulla not shown.

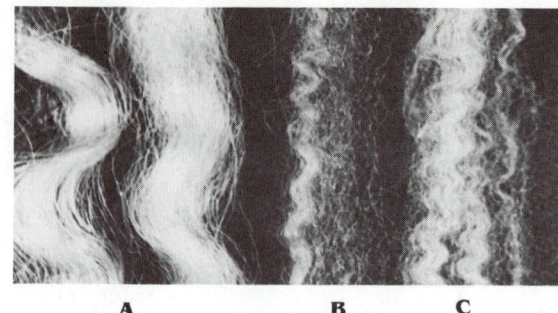

A   B   C

6.7 Wool fibers of different diameter and with different amounts of natural crimp. A: coarse. B: medium. C: fine.

mis or *cuticle,* is composed of the scales. These scales are somewhat horny and irregular in shape, and they overlap, with the top pointing toward the tip of the fiber; they are similar to fish scales. The major portion of the fiber is the *cortex* (composed of cortical cells); this extends toward the center from the cuticle layer. Cortical cells are long and spindle-shaped and provide fiber strength and elasticity. The cortex accounts for approximately 90 percent of the fiber mass (Fig. 6.6). In the center of the fiber is the *medulla.* The size of the medulla varies and in fine fibers may be nearly invisible. This is the area through which food reached the fiber during growth, and it contains pigment that gives color to fibers.

Physical Properties

SHAPE AND APPEARANCE Wool fibers vary in length from a short 1½ inches (3.8 cm) to about 15 inches (38 cm). Most authorities have determined that fine wools are usually from 1½ inches to 5 inches (3.8–12.7 cm) long; medium wools from 2½ to 6 inches (6.4–15.2 cm); and long (coarse) wools from 5 to 15 inches (12.7–38 cm) in length.

The width of wool also varies considerably. Fine fibers such as Merino have an average width of about 15 to 17 microns, whereas medium wool averages 24 to 34 microns and coarse wool about 40 microns. Some wool fibers are exceptionally stiff and coarse; these are called *kemp* and average about 70 microns in diameter.

The wool fiber cross section may be nearly circular, but most wool fibers tend to be slightly elliptical or oval in shape. Wool fibers have a natural crimp, a built-in waviness (Fig. 6.7). The crimp increases the elasticity and elongation properties of the fiber and also aids in yarn manufacturing. It is

three-dimensional in character; in other words, it not only moves above and below a central axis but also moves to the right and left of the axis. (See Table 6.1 for fiber property summary.)

LUSTER AND COLOR There is some luster to wool fibers. Fine and medium wool tends to have more luster than very coarse fibers. Fibers with a high degree of luster are silky in appearance.

The color of the natural wool fiber depends on the breed of sheep. Most wool, after scouring, is a yellowish-white or ivory color. Some fibers may be gray, black, tan, or brown.

TENACITY (STRENGTH) The tenacity of wool is 1.0 to 1.7 grams per denier (g/d) when dry; when wet, it drops to 0.7 to 1.5 g/d. Compared with many other fibers, wool is weak, and this weakness restricts the kinds of yarns and fabric constructions that can be used satisfactorily. However, if yarns and fabrics of optimum weight and type are produced, the end-use product will give commendable wear and retain shape and appearance. Fiber properties such as resiliency, elongation, and elastic recovery compensate for the low strength.

ELASTIC RECOVERY AND ELONGATION Wool has excellent elasticity and extensibility. At standard conditions the fiber will extend between 20 and 40 percent. It may extend more than 70 percent when wet. Recovery is superior. After a 2 percent extension the fiber has an immediate regain or recovery of 99 percent. Even at 10 percent extension, it has a recovery of well over 50 percent, which is higher than for any other fiber except nylon.

RESILIENCY The resiliency of wool is exceptionally good. It will readily spring back into shape after crushing or creasing. However, through the appli-

TABLE 6.1   Properties of Wool Fibers

Property	Evaluation
Shape	Fiber length varies from 1½ inches to about 15 inches; width varies from 15 to 70 microns. Fiber has a natural crimp or waviness.
Luster	medium
Tenacity (strength)	
dry	1.0–1.7 g/d
wet	0.8–1.6 g/d
Elastic recovery	99% recovery at 2% extension
Elongation	
dry	20–40%
wet	20–70%+
Resiliency	excellent
Density	1.30–1.32 g/ccm
Moisture absorption	
20°C/65% R.H.	13.6–16.0% of fiber weight
saturation	29%+
Dimensional stability	Subject to felting and relaxation shrinkage.
Resistance to	
acids	Good
alkalies	Low; many alkalies destroy the fiber.
sunlight	Prolonged exposure deteriorates fiber.
microorganisms	Generally good
insects	Damaged by moths and carpet beetles.
Thermal reactions	
to heat	Avoid prolonged exposure to temperatures over 140°C.
to flame	Burns slowly when in direct flame; is considered to be self-extinguishing.

cation of heat, moisture, and pressure, durable creases or pleats can be put into wool fabrics. This crease or press retention is the result of molecular adjustment and the formation of new cross-linkages in the polymer. Besides resistance to crushing and wrinkling, the excellent resilience of wool fiber gives the fabric its loft, which produces open, porous fabrics with good covering power, or thick, warm fabrics that are light in weight. Wool is very flexible and pliable, so it combines ease of handling and comfort with good shape retention.

MOISTURE REGAIN   The standard moisture regain of wool is 13.6 to 16.0 percent. Under saturation conditions, wool will absorb more than 29 percent of its weight in moisture. This ability to absorb is responsible for the comfort of wool in humid, cold atmospheres. As part of the moisture absorption function, wool produces or liberates heat. However, as wet wool begins to dry, the evaporation causes heat to be absorbed by the fiber, and "chilling" may be experienced, though the chilling factor is slowed down as the evaporation rate is reduced. Most subjects are not aware of this action of wool

fiber. The property of moisture absorption and desorption peculiar to wool and similar hair fibers is called *hygroscopic behavior*. Wool accepts colors and finishes easily because of its moisture absorption properties.

Despite the absorption properties of wool, it has an unusual property of exhibiting hydrophobic characteristics. That is, it tends to shed liquid easily and appears not to absorb moisture. The cause is a combination of factors: interfacial surface tension, uniform distribution of pores, and low bulk density. These moisture properties help make wool very desirable for use in a variety of situations where moisture can be a problem to comfort.

DIMENSIONAL STABILITY   Wool fibers are not dimensionally stable. The structure of the fiber contributes to a shrinking and felting reaction during processing, use, and care. This is due, in part, to the scale structure of the fiber. When subjected to heat, moisture, and agitation, the scales tend to pull together and move toward the fiber tip. This property is noticeable in yarns and fabrics and is responsible for both felting and relaxation shrinkage.

Felting shrinkage occurs as a result of mechanical action combined with heat and moisture. The scales on one fiber tend to interlock and hook together with contingent fibers, and they become entangled and matted. This causes yarns and fabrics to become matted if improperly handled. The felting behavior is used to advantage in certain types of finishing processes, as it makes the wool fabrics more compact, fuller, and more attractive. However, when not properly controlled, fabrics may become stiff and thick, shrink considerably, become matted in appearance, and generally look unattractive. Controlled handling of this property is used in making felt fabrics.

In addition to the shrinkage that occurs due to felting action, *relaxation* or *residual shrinkage* can occur as a result of the elongation and elasticity properties of the fiber. These latter properties may result in yarns being extended during conversion into fabrics; this extended state may be maintained during all manufacturing steps. However, when cared for or when exposed to moisture, the wool yarns tend to revert to their original length and the fabric shrinks. Wool tends to shrink and stretch so much that during use and care *progressive shrinkage* may occur. That is, the fabrics will continue to shrink each time the product is exposed to moisture during care. Finishing processes are used to prevent this as much as possible.

There are two major methods used in treating wool fibers, yarns, or fabrics in order to reduce or eliminate shrinkage: chemical attack, or polymer degradation, and polymer deposition. Degradative treatments destroy parts of the scales or cuticle of the fiber, which reduces the tendency to shrink during processing. The majority of the degradative treatments involve the use of chlorine in some form. Some of the typical degradative treatments include the following.

The Dylan process involves oxidation with permonosulfuric acid or alkaline wet chlorination with potassium permanganate pretreatment. The Sanforlan process, used in England, involves wet chlorination preceded by treatment with potassium permanganate. The Chloramine T process involves an acid wet chlorination using N-chloro-*p*-tolulosulfonamide. The Wira process involves gaseous chlorination followed by treatment with papain and bisulfite.

If properly done, these processes do not weaken the fiber sufficiently to affect use and care. However, the use of these methods is decreasing because of the development of polymer deposition treatments.

Polymer deposition treatments involve adding some type of polymer to the surface of the fibers, yarns, or fabrics so that the scales are coated and cannot move and become entangled. When properly done, this process does not reduce the flexibility or pliability of the fiber; it does not affect any property except that shrinkage is reduced. This process is sometimes called interfacial polymerization. It involves "fiber bonding," a treatment where fibers are "spot" welded together to reduce fiber movement. Typical polymers used in this process include polyamides, polymeric ethylene dichloride, and polyglycine. Acrylics and diisocyanates may be used in combination with other polymers such as polyamides (nylon).

Typical processes involving polymer deposition include the following. Bancor and Wurlan involve the use of nylon 6,10 (see Chap. 10). These processes are considerably less common than they were due to difficulty in obtaining the sebacyl chloride required for making nylon 6,10. Hercosett 57 uses polyamide with epichlorohydrin resin applied to a prechlorinated wool. Lanaset uses melamine formaldehyde resin. Resloom uses the same chemicals as the Lanaset process. Zeset TP uses a terpolymer from ethylene, vinyl acetate, and methacryloyl chloride. Dylan GRC uses a cationic polymer applied with a chlorinating agent.

Many of the polymer deposition processes depend on a preliminary chlorination treatment. However, the polymer coating maintains the strength and desirable characteristics of the wool and produces a product that can be washed, as long as the product is given careful handling.

Thermal Properties

Wool burns slowly in the presence of flame, with a slight sputtering. When bone-dry, the fiber burns relatively easily. If it has a normal moisture content it is considered nonpropagating, which means that the fiber will generally stop burning when the source of the flame is removed. A crisp, black, brittle bead-shaped residue is formed as wool burns; the odor given off may be compared to the smell of burning hair, meat, or feathers.

When wool is heated in boiling water for a long time, the fiber becomes weak and somewhat stiff. At dry temperatures above 130°C (266°F), it slowly decomposes and turns yellow; at temperatures greater than 300°C (572°F), wool chars and disintegrates.

Chemical Properties

EFFECT OF ALKALIES Wool protein, keratin, is highly susceptible to damage by alkalies. Solutions of 5 percent sodium hydroxide at room temperature and sodium hypochlorite bleach (full strength) will dissolve the fiber.

EFFECT OF ACIDS Wool is considered resistant to action by mild or dilute acids, but strong concentrated mineral acids, such as sulfuric and nitric, cause breakdown and decomposition of the fiber. Dilute solutions of sulfuric acid, however, are used in processing wool to ''burn out'' or *carbonize* vegetable matter adhering to the fibers prior to final wet processing.

EFFECT OF ORGANIC SOLVENTS Most organic solvents used in cleaning and stain removal are safe and do not damage wool fibers.

EFFECT OF SUNLIGHT, AGE, AND MISCELLANEOUS FACTORS The ultraviolet rays of the sun cause breakage of the disulfide bonds of cystine in the wool molecule, which results in photochemical oxidation. This causes fiber degradation and, if exposure is prolonged, eventual destruction. However, most uses are not under continued exposure to the sun's rays, so this problem is not so critical as it would be if end uses were primarily outdoors.

If wool is properly protected and stored, age has no destructive effect on the fiber. However, it is essential that wool items be stored clean to prevent damage from insects or microorganisms.

Static Charge

Wool is a poor conductor of electricity, and this contributes to the buildup of static electricity within wool yarns and fabrics. This manifests itself in static charges felt when one walks across wool carpeting or slides over wool upholstery when humidity is low.

Biological Properties

MICROORGANISMS Wool has some resistance to bacteria and mildew. However, both organisms may attack stains left on wool, and if it is stored in a damp area, mildew will form and eventually destroy the fiber. Rot-producing bacteria will bring about the destruction of wool that has been subjected to moisture and soil for long periods of time.

INSECTS Because wool is a protein and may be considered a modified food product, it becomes an appetizing meal for several types of insects. The larvae of varieties of clothes moths and carpet beetles are the most common predators on wool as a source of food. It has been estimated that these insects damage several million pounds of wool each year. Major damage occurs to wool fabrics. See Chapter 27 for a discussion of mothproofing finishes and treatments.

Use and Care of Wool

Woolen and worsted fabrics are used and prized throughout the world because of their outstanding properties. Wool fabrics are naturally crease-resistant, flexible, elastic, absorbent, warm, and comfortable. Wool fabrics tailor well, press easily, and can be shaped to conform to the body, provided they have not been finished to resist shaping. The major problem with wool over the years has been its tendency to shrink during care, but modern finishes have reduced shrinkage to a relatively low level.

Wool is considered to be a bicomponent fiber; the cortex is composed of two parts, *ortho* and *para*. These two parts react differently to certain stimuli and influence the crimp of the fiber, which in turn is related to its crease-resistance. Moisture affects the bicomponent property, so the crimp decreases when wet and increases when dry. This property aids in maintaining the elasticity and resiliency of wool, which in turn is important to the crease-resistance of wool fabrics.

Wool is rather demanding in terms of care. It can be dry-cleaned and pressed easily, but laundering is difficult unless the fiber or fabric has been treated to be washable; even then care must be used. It is important when washing wool that water temperatures be kept warm, not hot, and that temperatures be held constant throughout the entire washing and rinsing process. Agitation should be kept to a minimum to reduce the possiblity of felting. Chlorine bleaches must be avoided. If bleaching is necessary, hydrogen peroxide should be used. Mild, neutral detergents or soaps are recommended. It is important to make certain that wool fabric has been labeled as washable before laundering it at home. Wool fabrics or garments that have been clearly labeled as washable will usually have additional information about the specifics of care. It is important to read all labels and follow the directions carefully. Some wool fabrics have had nylon fiber blended with the wool in order to increase the ease of care and maintain fabric strength during the life of the product. The added nylon helps to render the fabric stable to home laundering. However, as with any wool fabric, gentle care is recommended.

Wool is easily dyed and has good colorfastness when proper dyestuffs are used. Acid and chrome mordant dyes are successful and are stable to most care procedures.

Following wear, woven wool garments should be placed on hangers and brushed carefully. This removes surface dust and soil and permits wrinkles to hang out. Knitted items, such as sweaters, should be aired and then folded and stored in drawers to prevent sagging and misshaping that could occur if placed on hangers. Frequent cleaning reduces insect damage, as dirty or soiled fabrics attract both insects and fungi.

The Wool Products Labeling Act (see Chap. 32) is a protection to the consumer against the purchase of fabrics designed to imitate wool in appearance but that do not possess the desirable qualities of a true wool product.

Woolen or worsted fabrics are available to consumers either in yardage or end-use items, particularly apparel. Woolen yarns are of low bulk density, usually made of the short wool fibers, and there is no second drafting or combing of the fibers. Fabrics made of woolen yarns are generally rougher, coarser, and thicker than worsted fabrics. Worsted fabrics are smooth, crisp, and frequently quite thin. Yarns used are smooth, compact, and made of relatively long, fine, and smooth wool fibers.

SPECIALTY AND FUR FIBERS

Fibers from animals other than sheep are often referred to as *specialty fibers.* These fibers, available in limited quantities, are desired for specialized uses where particular characteristics are important.

Mohair

Mohair is the fiber of the Angora goat. The major sources of mohair are the United States and South

6.8 Drapery fabric of 56 percent mohair wool. (Westgate: Mohair Council)

Africa. Angora goats are sheared twice a year. The fibers are fine and silky in appearance and measure 4 to 6 inches (10–15 cm) in length. Some animals are sheared only once a year if extremely long fibers are desired; these may be as long as 12 inches (30 cm). Mohair is similar to wool in both physical and chemical properties. Its major advantages include remarkable resistance to wear and abrasion, a high degree of luster, excellent resiliency, and adaptability to durable complex yarns and fancy weave fabrics. Typical end uses for mohair include suits, sportswear, upholstery, rugs or carpets, and draperies (Fig. 6.8). It may be blended with other fibers for selected uses.

Cashmere

Cashmere is the fiber from the cashmere (Kashmir) goat, which is raised in Asia. The fiber is combed from the animals rather than sheared, and the yield per goat averages about 4 ounces (114 g) of good fiber. The short fibers—1 to 3½ inches (2.5–8.9 cm)—are very soft and fine; longer fibers—2 to 5 inches (5–12.7 cm)—are somewhat coarse and stiff. Although similar to wool in most properties, cashmere does differ in that it is even more easily damaged by alkalies than sheep's wool.

The yearly production of true cashmere is very

small, so the fiber is expensive. However, consumers who wish a very soft and attractive textile product will pay the high price. Fabrics made of cashmere are warm, comfortable, and light in weight. The fiber is made into yarns of any type (see Part Three) and into fabrics that are thick, medium, or light in weight. Cashmere is found in apparel, primarily in such end-use items as suits, sweaters, and coats.

Camel Hair

The Bactrian, or two-humped, camel is the source of camel-hair fiber. The animal sheds about 5 pounds (2.7 kg) of fiber each year, which is used in textile products. The outer fibers are coarse and used mainly in low-quality merchandise; but the fine, short underhairs are as soft and fine as top-quality wool or mohair. Camel-hair fiber possesses thermal properties similar to those of wool or mohair, and garments of camel hair are usually noted for their warmth.

Fine camel-hair products require the same careful handling as cashmere or mohair. The major uses of the fiber for apparel is in coats, suits, and knitted sportswear. The natural tan to reddish-brown color is very attractive and frequently maintained as the fabric color.

Camel-hair fibers, particularly coarse fibers, are used in industry for special belting and ropes; they are also used in artist's brushes. In some countries camel hair is used for making coarse but very warm blankets.

Alpaca

The alpaca, a member of the camel family, is native to South America. It thrives in the Andes Mountain regions of Peru, Bolivia, Ecuador, and Argentina. The fiber is sheared from the animal once every two years. The fine fibers are separated from the coarse guard hairs and used in fabric manufacturing.

Alpaca is similar to camel hair and offers excellent warmth and insulation. The fibers are strong and glossy and make fabrics similar in appearance to mohair. Alpaca fabrics are used for suits, dresses, plush upholstery, and heavy linings. The natural range of fiber color, from white to brown or even black, produces a wide variety of attractive fabrics without the use of added dyestuffs.

Llama

The llama, also a member of the camel family, is found in the same geographic area as the alpaca and produces fabrics similar to those made from alpaca. Fibers are sheared from the animal once a year; they are soft, strong, and uniform in length and diameter. However, they are somewhat weaker than alpaca or camel hair. Most llama fabrics are produced by South American Indians. Some fiber may be sold to wool fabric manufacturers for blending with sheep's wool.

Musk Ox (Qiviut)

The musk ox, or qiviut, has been domesticated in Alaska. The animal sheds the fibers, they are collected, and the fine fibers are separated from the long guard hairs. The fine fibers are used for fabric, and they make a soft, fine yarn that can be made into soft, fine, warm, or even lacy fabrics. Much of the fiber is processed by Eskimos into fabrics that incorporate native designs.

Vicuña

The most valuable and most prized natural hair fiber is that taken from the vicuña. This small animal, about the size of a large dog, is found in the Andes Mountains at elevations of approximately 16,000 feet (4880 m). It is a member of the llama family and thus of the South American camel family. The vicuña is extremely wild, and attempts to domesticate it have been relatively unsuccessful. Thus, most fiber is collected from slain animals. The yearly kill is controlled and limited by the Peruvian government.

Vicuña is one of the softest fibers known to man. It is fine and lustrous, has a lovely cinnamon-brown or light tan color, and is strong enough to make very desirable fabrics. It is very light in weight and very warm. Choice uses of the fiber are for coats, suits, and soft shawls or capes. The fiber may be used in its natural colors or dyed.

Each vicuña yields about 4 ounces (114 g) of fine fiber plus 10 to 12 ounces (284–340 g) of shorter, less choice fiber. The total production is just a few thousand pounds per year, so garments of vicuña are comparable in price to costly fur products.

Fur Fibers

Fibers used in small amounts in blends with wool or other fibers are obtained from several animals more frequently used for fur pelts. These include mink, beaver, fox, chinchilla, muskrat, nutria, raccoon, and rabbit. They are used primarily to add softness, color interest, and prestige value to fabrics.

The angora fiber from the Angora rabbit is used in knitting yarns and in knitted fabrics to give a fluffy, silky white, appearance to products. The Angora rabbit is raised in the United States as well as in France, Italy, and Japan. The fur is combed and clipped from the animal every three months. Fibers are smooth, lustrous, fine, and resilient. As with any fine product, fabrics of the specialty and fur fibers require careful handling during maintenance procedures.

SILK

Historical Review

The history of silk is based on both fact and myth, and it is difficult to isolate truth from fiction. The legends concerning silk are romantic and interesting and do indicate the importance of the fiber in the development of countries.

The story told most frequently of the discovery of silk involves a Chinese empress. Emperor Huang Ti, who ruled China sometime between 2700 and 2600 B.C., assigned his empress, Hsi Ling Shi, the task of studying a blight that was damaging the imperial mulberry grove. Tiny white worms were devouring the leaves, then crawling from leaf to stem to spin shining, pale, almost white, cocoons. Hsi Ling Shi gathered a handful of cocoons and carried them into her apartment, where she accidently dropped one into a basin of hot water. The empress noticed that the cocoon separated into a delicate cobweblike tangle from which she could draw a slender, tiny filament into the air. She further observed that the filament was continuous, and the more she unwound, the smaller the cocoon became. This is how one legend records the discovery of silk fibers.

For approximately 3000 years China successfully held the secret of silk and sericulture and held a virtual monopoly on the silk industry. About A.D. 300

Japan learned the secret of raising silkworms and reeling the filaments from the cocoons.

Gradually silk production spread westward across Asia into India and eventually into Persia. Emperor Justinian of Constantinople was so enamored of silk that he persuaded two monks, who had lived in China and knew the techniques of sericulture, to bring silk cocoons and eggs back so that a silk industry could be started in his country.

During the late seventh century, sericulture was introduced into countries around the northern part of the Mediterranean Sea. Gradually cities in Italy and France became known for their beautiful silks. About 1480 silk weaving was started in Tours, France.

Shortly after the colonization of America, James I tried to establish a silk industry in the colonies. However, his attempts were not very successful, and by the nineteenth century it became obvious that sericulture could only be successful in countries where labor costs were low and labor was plentiful. Today, the major countries producing silk are Japan, Thailand, and China.

Throughout history, silk has maintained a position of great prestige and is considered a luxury fiber. It is often called the "queen of fibers." Perhaps one of the most important contributions silk has made in the history of textiles is that it was responsible for investigation into the possible production of man-made fibers. Scientists observed how the silkworm spun the fibers and believed that people could duplicate the art.

Sericulture

Silk fiber is produced by the larvae of a wide variety of moths, but the *Bombyx mori* is the major one raised under controlled conditions. These larvae live on mulberry leaves, and each tiny larva consumes an extremely large number of leaves. The present-day industry is carefully controlled to prevent disease, and modern silk "factories" are as clean and sterile as hospitals. Current research is directed toward developing other foods that the worms will eat or ways to preserve mulberry leaves in forms that will be appealing to the worms.

The female *Bombyx mori* lays as many as 700 eggs. Each egg is about the size of a pinhead, and each has a small dot on one end that is soft and permits the larvae to hatch easily. The eggs are carefully screened and tested to ensure freedom from disease. They can be kept for long periods in cold storage without damage. When a supply of fresh young mulberry leaves, or a substitute food, is ready, the eggs are warmed slightly, and three to seven days later the worm hatches and begins to feed on the tender leaves. The new larvae are about ¼ inch (0.64 cm) long.

During the growth cycle of the larva, it sheds its outer skin (molts) four times. Each time, it grows a new skin and increases in size. After the fourth molting, it eats for 10 more days, making a total eating period of about 35 days. At the end of the growing period the caterpillar has increased about 10,000 times over the weight of the newly hatched larva. It has grown to approximately 3 inches (7.6 cm) in length and is about ¼ to ½ inch (0.64–1.3 cm) in diameter. It is now ready to spin its cocoon, or chrysalis case.

The larva attaches itself to a specially constructed straw frame, rears its head, and begins to spew the silk liquid, which hardens upon contact with air. The larva spins by moving its head in a figure-eight motion and constructs the cocoon from the outside in (Fig. 6.9). As it spins, the larva decreases in size, and upon completion of the cocoon the caterpillar changes into the dormant chrysalis stage. Cocoons can be stored for long periods by killing the chrysalis. This is accomplished by heat and is called *stifling*. Cocoons not stifled are permitted to hatch, and the moths emerge, breed, and lay a new batch of eggs so that the cycle can start anew.

The silkworm extrudes the liquid from two tiny orifices or *spinnerets* in its head. The filaments, coated with a gummy substance called *sericin*, come from two glands within the worm.

In addition to the sericulture of *Bombyx mori*, several other moths produce larvae that spin cocoons composed of usable silk fiber. Of these, probably the most important are the moths that produce tussah (wild) silk, *Antheraea myllita* and *Antheraea pernyi*. These wild insects feed on oak leaves, and the cocoons are collected from trees and shrubs. The larvae of these species usually grow much larger than the cultivated silkworms, sometimes up to 6 inches (15 cm) in length; they are greener in color, and they are covered with short, fuzzy hair. The cocoons are frequently of irregular size and dark in color (Fig. 6.10). The fiber is therefore often tan or light brown and usually cannot be bleached white without incurring some damage.

6.9 Silkworms and cocoons. (International Silk Association)

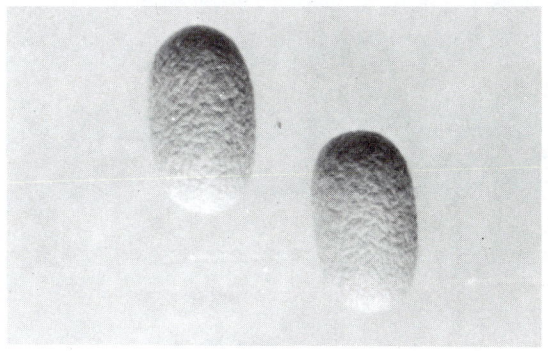

A

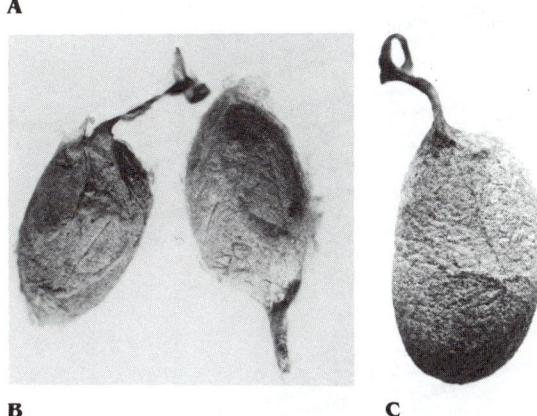

B   **C**

6.10 Varieties of cocoons from cultivated and wild silk worms. A: *Bombyx mori*. B: *Antheraea pernyi*. C: *Antheraea mylitta*. (Sericulture Experiment Station, Japan)

6.11 Reeling using motor-driven equipment as practiced in 1915–1955. (Sericulture Experiment Station, Japan)

6.12 Reeling as done with modern machinery, 1984. (Sericulture Experiment Station, Japan)

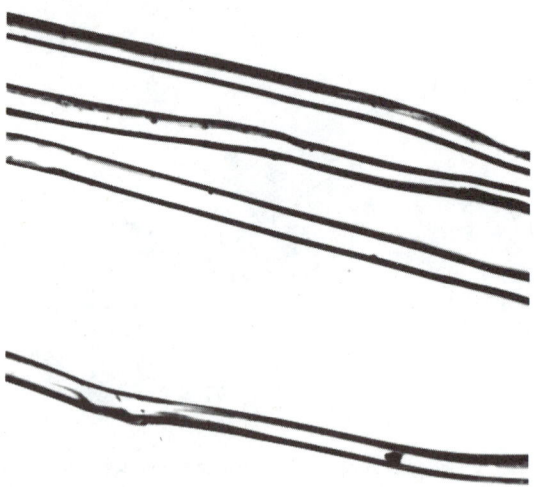

6.13 Photomicrograph of silk, longitudinal view. (DuPont Company)

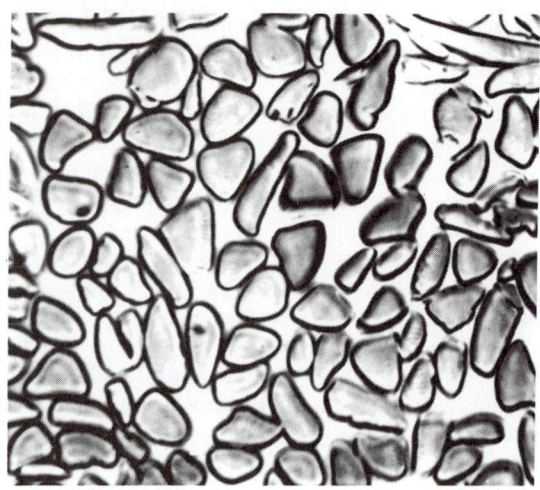

6.14 Photomicrograph of silk, cross section. (DuPont Company)

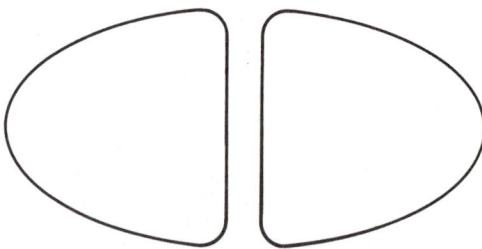

6.15 Diagram of silk filaments or brins.

6.16 Silk filaments: 1: raw silk. 2: dupioni silk. 3: wild silk. (Sericulture Experiment Station, Japan)

Sometimes two larvae will spin cocoons so that they become entangled. As the filaments are unwound from these tangled cocoons, it is impossible to separate them, so they form filaments with variations in diameter. These filaments are called *dupion.*

Processing

Reeling

Silk filaments are unwound from the cocoons in a manufacturing plant called a *filature*. Several cocoons are placed in hot water to soften the gum, and the surfaces are brushed lightly to make it possible to find the ends of the filaments. These ends are collected, threaded through a guide, and wound onto a wheel called a reel; hence the name *reeling.*

Reeling in modern filatures requires highly skilled operators as well as sophisticated machinery. Since the fibers are narrower at the beginnings and ends of the cocoons, the workers must join the cocoons so that the diameter of the reeled silk remains constant in size. Only uniform reeled silk sells for premium prices (Figs. 6.11 and 6.12).

Throwing

As the fibers are combined and pulled onto the reel, twist can be inserted to hold the filaments together. This is called *throwing,* and the resulting yarn is called *thrown yarn.* Several types of thrown yarn are available. They differ in the amount of twist and in methods of combining single yarns. They include the following:

Tram silk is a low-twist ply yarn formed by combining two or three single strands. It is moderately strong and is frequently used for filling yarns.

Organzine is a two or more ply yarn with a medium twist. It is very strong and is used for warp yarns. *Crepe organzine* is a very highly twisted yarn used in crepe fabrics and chiffons.

Singles is a strand of several filaments collected together and held by low, medium, or high twist. A *singles* yarn can be used for either warp or filling and in knitting.

Grenadine is a tightly twisted ply yarn composed of two or three singles. The ply twist is in the opposite direction from the twist of each single strand. For further discussion of yarns, see Part Three.

Degumming

Sericin remains on the fibers during reeling and throwing. Frequently it is left on through the fabric construction processes. Before final finishing, the gum is removed by boiling the fabric in soap and water. If stiffness is desired in the completed fabric, some of the sericin may be replaced, but this is not usually desirable since the presence of the sericin increases the tendency for silk to water-spot.

Fiber Properties

Molecular Structure

Silk is a protein fiber. The protein is called *fibroin;* as it is secreted, it is surrounded by the gummy protein substance called sericin. The sericin holds the fibroin filaments together. Fibroin is composed of about 15 amino acids, similar to wool, that form a polypeptide chain. Silk differs from wool in that the amino acids involved do not include cystine, which eliminates the possibility of sulfur or cystine linkages among the acids as they form the silk protein polymer. There is considerable difference of opinion among authorities about the arrangement of the acids; however, most agree that the simple amino acids such as glycine, alanine, serine, and tyrosine comprise the largest portion of the fiber. The molecular arrangement is highly oriented, which gives the fiber high strength.

Microscopic Properties

Cultivated degummed silk, viewed longitudinally under a microscope, resembles a smooth, transparent rod (Fig. 6.13). Silk with the sericin on it has rough, irregular surfaces. Wild silk tends to be quite even but somewhat darker than cultivated silk. Raw (tussah) silk may have longitudinal striations when viewed under the microscope.

Cross-sectional views of silk show triangular fibers with no inner markings (Fig. 6.14). Two filaments usually lie with their flat sides together; this is explained by the fact that two filaments are extruded by each silkworm and come together as diagramed in Figure 6.15. The two face-to-face filaments are often called *brins.*

Physical Properties

SHAPE AND APPEARANCE Silk filaments are very fine and long. They frequently measure about 1000 to 1300 yards (915–1190 m) and can be as long as 3000 yards (2750 m). The width of silk is from 9 to 11 microns, which means the fiber is fine. The fibers are smooth, they have a high natural luster or sheen, and they are off-white to cream in color; occasionally they may be yellow or light brown. Wild silk is uneven, has slightly less luster, and is tan to medium brown in color (see Table 6.2 and Fig. 6.16).

LUSTER Cultivated silk is a lustrous fiber; wild silk is somewhat dull.

◇ ─────────

TABLE 6.2 Properties of Silk Fibers

Property	Evaluation
Shape	The fiber is fine, 9–11 microns in diameter; it is long—from 1000 to 1300 yards; the filament is smooth, even, white to cream color. Wild silk is uneven and dark in color.
Luster	High
Tenacity (strength)	
dry	2.4–5.1 g/d
wet	2.0–4.3 g/d
Elastic recovery	92% recovery at 2% extension
Elongation	
dry	10–25%
wet	33–35%
Resiliency	Medium
Density	1.25–1.34 g/ccm
Moisture absorption	
20°C, 65% R.H.	11%
saturation	25–35%
Dimensional stability	Good
Resistance to	
acids	Low; dissolves or is damaged by most mineral acids; organic acids do not damage.
alkalies	Strong alkalies damage fiber; weak alkalies have little or no effect.
sunlight	Prolonged exposure causes fiber breakdown.
microorganisms	Good
insects	Destroyed by carpet beetles.
Thermal reactions	
to heat	Temperatures over 150°C result in yellowing and general discoloration.
to flame	Burns with a sputtering flame.

TENACITY (STRENGTH) Silk is one of the strongest natural fibers used in creating textile products. It has a tenacity of 2.4 to 5.1 grams per denier when dry. Wet strength is about 80 to 85 percent of the dry strength.

ELASTIC RECOVERY AND ELONGATION Silk has good elasticity and moderate elongation. When it is dry, the elongation varies from 10 to 25 percent; when wet, silk will elongate as much as 33 to 35 percent. At 2 percent elongation the fiber has a 92 percent elastic recovery.

RESILIENCY Silk has medium resiliency. Creases will hang out relatively well, but not so quickly or completely as for wool.

DENSITY The density or specific gravity of silk is cited as 1.25 to 1.34 grams per cubic centimeter, depending on the resource used. Because of the nature of silk, it is possible that the density varies among fibers as well as between the various types of moths that form the fiber. Another source of variation may be due to methods used in determining density. In any case, the density results in the formation of lightweight but strong filaments, yarns, and fabrics.

MOISTURE REGAIN Silk has a relatively high standard moisture regain of 11.0 percent. At saturation the regain is 25 to 35 percent. This relatively high absorption is helpful in applying dyes and finishes to silk; however, unlike many fibers, silk also absorbs impurities such as metal salts. These contaminants tend to damage silk by weakening the fiber or causing actual ruptures to occur when the fabric is not handled properly.

DIMENSIONAL STABILITY Silk fabrics have good resistance to stretch or shrinkage when laundered or dry-cleaned. Crepe fabrics will shrink when wet but can be steamed back into shape.

Thermal Properties

Silk will ignite and continue to burn when there is another source of flame. After removal from the source, it will sputter and eventually extinguish itself. It leaves a crisp, brittle ash and gives off an odor like that of burning hair or feathers. It burns similarly to wool.

Heated to about 135°C (275°F), silk will remain unaffected for long periods of time; however, if the temperature is raised to 177°C (350°F), rapid degradation occurs. Silk scorches easily if ironed with temperatures above 150°C (300°F), and white silk will turn yellow if pressed with an iron hotter than that.

Like other protein fibers, silk has a lower thermal or heat conductivity than cellulosic fibers. This factor, coupled with certain methods of construction, creates fabrics that tend to be warmer than comparable fabrics of cellulosic fibers.

Chemical Properties

EFFECT OF ALKALIES Silk is damaged by strong alkalies and will dissolve in heated caustic soda (NaOH); however, silk reacts more slowly than wool, and frequently the identity of the two fibers can be determined by the speed of solubility in NaOH. Weak alkalies such as soap, borax, and ammonia cause little or no damage to silk unless they remain in contact with the fiber for a long time.

EFFECT OF ACIDS   Silk protein, like wool, can be decomposed by strong mineral acids. Medium concentrations of hydrochloric acid (HCl) will dissolve silk, and moderate concentrations of other mineral acids cause fiber contraction and shrinkage. The molecular arrangement in silk permits rapid absorption of acids but tends to hold the acid molecules, so they are difficult to remove. This accounts for some of the acid damage to fibroin that does not occur to keratin. Organic acids do not damage silk and are used in some finishing processes. Some authorities maintain that the *scroop* of silk—a rustling or crunching sound—which used to be considered a natural characteristic, is actually developed by exposure to organic acids.

EFFECT OF ORGANIC SOLVENTS   Cleaning solvents and spot removers do not damage silk fibers.

EFFECT OF SUNLIGHT, AGE, AND MISCELLANEOUS FACTORS   Sunlight tends to accelerate the decomposition of silk. It increases oxidation and results in fiber degradation and eventual destruction.

Silk requires careful handling and adequate protection in storage to withstand the ravages of time. Oxygen in the atmosphere causes its gradual decompostion; thus, unless silk fabrics or textile products are stored carefully in sealed containers, the fiber will lose strength and eventually be destroyed. Silk that has been weighted (see Chap. 26) is destroyed more quickly than pure silk, and, if stored, tends to crack and split at fold lines.

Static Charge

Silk is a poor conductor of electricity, which results in the buildup of static charges on the fiber.

Biological Properties

Silk is resistant to attack by mildew and is relatively resistant to other bacteria and fungi. It is destroyed by rot-producing bacteria. Silk has good resistance to the clothes moth, but carpet beetles will eat it. Destruction attributed to moths has usually been caused by carpet beetles.

Use and Care of Silk

Silk has been the queen of fabrics for centuries. As in the past, it is still used for luxury fabrics and for high-fashion items. It is frequently considered a sensuous fabric because of its smooth and soft feel, or hand.

Dry cleaning is the preferred method of care for silk fabrics and products. If handled carefully, however, silk fabrics can be laundered. A mild soap or synthetic detergent in warm, not hot, water should be used, and minimal handling is recommended. Thorough rinsing is required, and the best method for extracting water is to roll the garment in a towel and then hang it in a cool place, out of the sun, to dry. Tumble drying should not be attempted unless a care label specifies that such procedures are acceptable. Silk should be ironed or pressed at medium to low temperatures; steam is acceptable.

When silk requires bleaching, hydrogen peroxide or perborate bleaches must be used, as chlorine bleaches may destroy the silk.

One problem with silk is that body perspiration tends to weaken the fibers and frequently will alter the color. Many deodorants and antiperspirants contain aluminum chloride, which damages silk. It is advisable to wear protective dress shields if perspiration is a serious problem.

Several factors are involved in the demand for silk. It offers an incredible variety in fabric and yarn structure. Through dyeing, many beautiful fabrics can be produced. Probably no other fiber is so widely accepted and suitable for various occasions. It is versatile and can be used in almost any type of apparel and in a wide variety of fabrics for home furnishings (Fig. 6.17).

Many silk fabrics cost considerably more than similar fabrics of man-made fibers. However, the consumer who has formed an attachment to silk is willing to pay the high price. Because silk combines strength, flexibility, good moisture absorbency, softness, warmth, luxurious appearance, and durability, choice products for the discerning consumer are made of this fiber. Its use, however, is limited primarily to apparel and home furnishings such as draperies and accessories.

STUDY QUESTIONS

1. What are the properties of wool that make it desirable for uses in both apparel and home furnishings?

6.17 A Japanese kimono of silk with some gold and silver threads.

2. What are the properties of silk that make it attractive to consumers?

3. What reasons can be cited for the use of specialty fibers? What care procedures are required for these products?

4. Why has the use of wool declined in the past four decades?

5. Discuss special processing techniques that help make wool easier to care for?

6. What are the differences in molecular construction between wool and silk?

7. How does the molecular arrangement of the amino acids in wool affect the behavior of wool fabrics?

8. How can you quickly identify some wool products or wool-blend products available on the market?

9. If a textile item were available in either wool or a blend of man-made fibers, which would you select and why?

10. What molecular structural differences make silk stronger than wool? gives wool a higher elasticity than silk?

11. Compare the comfort factors of wool and silk. Which would be better for humid days? for cold days? Why?

Activities

1. Survey various apparel and home-furnishing stores and determine what is available made from wool fibers or wool blends. How do they compare in price and appearance with similar products from man-made fibers? Do the same for silk.

2. Locate small samples of wool and of silk fabrics, place them in small glass containers, place pure, undiluted chlorine bleach on the fabrics, and observe what happens.

3. If there is a laboratory available for student use, complete a series of laboratory tests to determine the chemical behavior, physical properties, and thermal behavior of wool and silk. Compare your results with other fibers as they are studied.

4. Locate examples of items made of various specialty fibers. Compare their prices with those of items made of wool. Compare the appearance and hand of the fabrics with those of wool, silk, or man-made fibers.

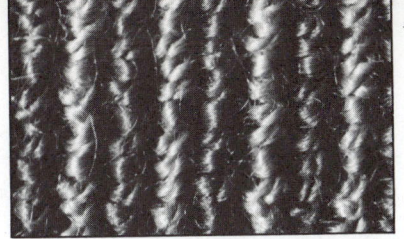

7

Natural Cellulosic Fibers

OBJECTIVES

◇ **To provide background on the historical development of natural cellulosic fibers**

◇ **To identify properties of natural cellulosic fibers and indicate how they influence selection, use, and care**

◇ **To describe the production, cultivation, and processing of natural cellulosic fibers, especially cotton**

◇ **To describe the molecular structure of cellulose, to indicate how various chemical actions can be used to alter fiber properties, and to describe what chemical reactions take place**

◇ **To identify various types of natural cellulosic fibers and describe how they are obtained from plant life**

KEY TERMS

bast fiber	hackling	ramie
cellulose molecules	hemp	retting
convolutions	jute	scutching
cotton	long staple	spinning
cross-linking	lumen	staple length
flax	natural cellulose	wickability (wicking)
glucose unit	nodes	

Plant fibers are composed of cellulose and therefore are classified as natural cellulosic fibers. The term *natural cellulosic* indicates the basic chemistry of the fiber and provides a scientific method for comparing natural cellulose with man-made cellulosic fibers.

Cellulose is a linear polymer or long chain molecule built by combining several thousand anhydroglucose units. Although glucose, a simple sugar, is soluble in water, cellulose is not because of the immense size of the polymolecule. Cellulose is a carbohydrate; it contains the elements carbon (44.4 percent), hydrogen (6.2 percent), and oxygen (49.4 percent). The repeating molecular unit is diagramed in Figure 7.1.

Two glucose units combine first to form cellobiose; than many cellubiose units combine to form cellulose. The number of anhydroglucose units in the cellulose molecule is referred to as the *degree of polymerization*. Each repeating unit equals *2n* or 2 anhydroglucose units. These units are flipped over as they join together. Thus, in order to diagram the method of joining, it is necessary to illustrate two units as in Figure 7.1.

Cellulose molecules form into fibrils or bundles of molecular chains that combine in groups to form the cellulose fibers. Each fiber is composed of many cellulose molecules. These are not arranged in a completely parallel manner; rather, certain portions of the fiber may have the molecules lying parallel, while other areas are characterized by a somewhat random molecular arrangement. As discussed in Chapter 3, the parts of the fiber where molecules lie side by side and are held together by many associative forces are called crystalline (see page 26). If the molecules, in addition to lying side by side, are parallel to the longitudinal axis, there is a high degree of molecular orientation. The cellulose fiber has areas where the molecules are not in complete crystalline arrangement; these areas of partial disorder approach an amorphous state. However, evidence from several cellulose scientists indicates there is no completely amorphous area in cellulose

7.1 Diagram of a cellulose molecule. Repeating unit is composed of two anhydroglucose units. A and C indicate terminal units of the molecule.

fibers. High orientation and crystallinity are usually accompanied by high strength, low elongation, and low pliability. Areas of molecular disorder slightly increase the elongation.

The strength of cellulose fibers is influenced by the degree of polymerization (dp) as well as by the molecular arrangement. The higher the dp, the stronger the fiber. A typical degree of polymerization for a native cellulose fiber is about 10,000; for regenerated cellulose, such as rayon, it is only about 500.

The molecules within the fiber tend to be held in place by hydrogen bonding (see page 27). When cellulose fibers are bent, the hydrogen bonds are broken and new ones form, causing creases or wrinkles that do not hang out.

The chemically reactive group in cellulose is the hydroxyl (OH) unit. This group may undergo substitution reactions in procedures designed to modify the cellulose fibers or in the application of some dyestuffs and finishes. Substitution occurs when one or more hydroxyl units are removed and other ions or radicals (atoms or groups of atoms) attach themselves to the carbon atom in place of the OH unit. Removal of the hydroxyl unit may also result in cross-linking of the cellulose molecules so that they are somewhat stabilized, which helps to form cellulose fibers that are highly resistant to creasing and recover from creasing easily.

Cellulose fibers have several properties in common. They burn easily and quickly with a yellow flame; they give off a smell like that of burning paper or leaves; they deposit a light, fluffy, grayish residue or ash. Cellulose is decomposed by acid solutions, especially strong mineral acids, but it possesses excellent resistance to alkaline solutions.

In general, cellulose is low in elasticity and resilience; consequently it wrinkles excessively unless treated. Cellulose fibers are soft and absorbent, so they usually make comfortable products. The fibers launder readily and can withstand strong detergents, high temperatures, and bleaches (if used properly). This group of fibers is seldom damaged by insects, but fungi, such as mildew, will destroy cellulose or at least stain it severely.

COTTON

Historical Review

The origin of cotton is unkown. Archeologists have contributed valuable information concerning the fiber's early use; but there is little evidence of when or where cotton first grew. Considerable evidence supports the theory that cotton was grown in Egypt about 12,000 B.C.; it was definitely grown in India about 3000 B.C. Most authorities agree that India was the principal country in which cotton was widely used before 2500 B.C.

For centuries it was believed that cotton was a product of the Old World and that it was brought to the shores of the Americas by early explorers. Today, scientists have produced reliable data to indicate that cotton was indigenous to the land that is now North and South America, as well as to Asia and Africa. Carbon 14 tests have produced evidence that cotton was grown and made into fabric in Peru as early as 2500 B.C. Thus, it would seem that cotton culture occurred simultaneously in several areas of the world. This supposition is further upheld by the fact that botanical differences are evident between Eastern and Western cotton, though it must be conceded that these differences could have evolved in adaptation to different environments.

The word *cotton* is derived from the Arabic *qoton* or *qutun,* which means a plant found in a conquered land. *Muslin,* also taken from the Arabic language, was applied to cotton fabrics woven in Mosul. Ancient writers describe this cloth as being so sheer that it was invisible when spread over the ground and saturated with dew.

When Columbus landed in the Bahamas in 1492, he was welcomed by natives who brought him cotton fibers, yarns, and fabrics. He found cotton growing on the islands (Sea Island variety), and he saw the various types of garments, nets, and hammocks *(hamacas)* made of cotton. It would seem logical to believe that if the natives thought cotton products were of sufficient importance to present to visitors, the plant must have been of value to them and, therefore, in use for some time.

There is evidence that cotton culture in what is now the United States dates back to about 500 B.C. The area in which cotton was first grown includes parts of the present states of Utah, Texas, and Arizona. Fragments of cotton fabrics have been found in dry caves and burial sites of the American Indians who inhabited the Southwest centuries ago. Anthropologists have interpreted this fact to indicate that cotton had an important place in early Indian culture. Scientific dating has placed these fabrics at about 500 B.C.

The first recorded planting of cotton in the United States occurred in Florida in 1536. Cultivation of the plant at that time was for its attractive blossom. It was not until the colony of Virginia was established that cotton was grown as a profit-making crop. Records show that it was cultivated throughout the Carolinas by 1665; by 1700 the cotton grown there furnished clothing to one-fifth of the population.

Early cotton raised as a commercial crop was of the Sea Island variety because the Churka or roller gin, which had been imported from India, could separate seeds and fiber in this type of cotton only. However, Sea Island cotton did not thrive away from the ocean. Upland varieties were adopted, but these were impossible to gin on the roller gin, so seed and fiber were separated by hand. This delayed considerably the establishment of a profitable cotton industry away from the ocean. Eli Whitney solved the problem by inventing the saw-type cotton gin in 1793. Following that invention the production of Upland cotton increased rapidly. In the ten-year period from 1793 to 1803 the cash value of cotton crops jumped from $150,000 to over $8 million.

Plants for manufacturing and processing cotton into yarns and fabrics were originally located in the New England states by virtue of the presence of both adequate waterpower to operate machinery and sufficient labor. After the Civil War, however, the manufacturing plants began to move south to be closer to the crop. At present, the production of cotton fabrics is concentrated in the Southeast, with some production in the mideastern states and the Southwest. Cotton cultivation, however, has spread across the entire southern tier of states. A large percentage of cotton is grown in California, Texas, and Mississippi.

Cotton is still the fiber used most in the world. About 46 percent of all fibers produced in the world is cotton. In the United States, however, the use of cotton has continued to decrease, and it now ranks second to polyester fiber in consumption.

Growth and Production

The cotton plant is a member of the Malvaceae, or mallow, family (Fig. 7.2). Several species are of the genus or class Gossypium. Cotton is cultivated best in warm, humid climates or in warm climates with adequate irrigation. A primary growing requirement is a long frost-free period of from 6 to 7 months with mild temperatures and about 12 hours of sunlight each day. During actual plant growth

7.2 Mature cotton bolls, open and closed, on plant. (National Cotton Council of America)

7.3 Mature cotton boll with fibers ready for picking. (National Cotton Council of America)

7.4 A modern four-row picker. (National Cotton Council of America)

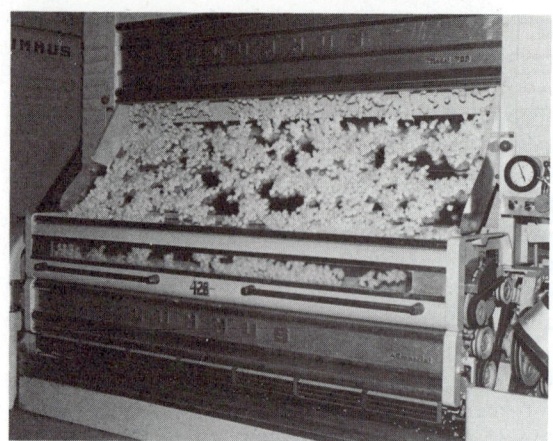

7.5 A modern cotton gin in operation. (National Cotton Council of America)

7.6 Newly ginned cotton is pressed into a bale. (National Cotton Council of America)

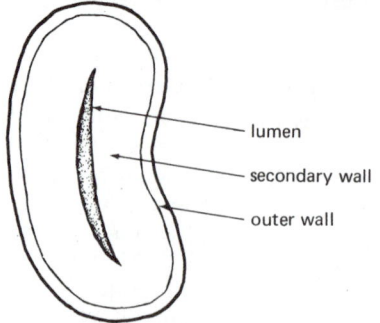

lumen
secondary wall
outer wall

7.7 Diagram of a cotton fiber, cross section.

either an average of 3 to 5 inches of rain a month or the equivalent through irrigation is required; this must be followed by a dry season for the fiber to mature.

The seeds are sown by machine in parallel rows 3 to 4 feet (0.9–1.2 m) apart. The blossom, which appears approximately 80 to 100 days after planting, is beautiful. When it opens, it is creamy white or light yellow in color; by the second morning the blossom has changed to pink, lavender, or red; and by the end of the second or third day the flower falls, leaving the young boll, or seed pod, in which the fibers form. About 50 to 80 days later the pod bursts open, and the fleecy cotton fibers are ready for picking (Fig. 7.3). The flowers appear over a long period of time; thus, the harvest period of mature cotton is of similar duration. However, because of the picking methods now used, it becomes necessary to pick fields once. Occasionally pickers may go over a field a second time. This means that some fibers may be in the field longer than others and may begin to degrade slightly or at least discolor. Picking is scheduled for the period when the most good-quality mature cotton can be picked. Before picking, plants are sprayed with a defoliant that causes the leaves to shrivel and fall off, leaving mostly the cotton bolls and fibers ready for picking.

Today, cotton is picked for the most part by mechanical devices. Current machines (Fig. 7.4) pick two or four rows of cotton simultaneously. Picking can be done using either strippers or pickers. The picker pulls the fibers from the cotton boll, while the stripper picks everything. Pickers work best on fields with lush growth and high fiber yield; strippers are more effective on fields of low yield. Both strippers and pickers pick multiple rows at the same time. If a second picking is to be done, the picker machines must be used.

Hand-picking of cotton would produce the best-quality fibers, for a field could be picked selectively as many times as needed and only the top-quality mature fibers would be picked at any one time. The obvious disadvantage to this system in industrialized countries is the cost of such labor. Consequently, hand-picking is not done commercially in the United States and is probably rare in other countries.

Processing

After cotton is picked, it is taken to the ginnery, where the fiber, called *cotton lint,* is separated from the seed (Fig. 7.5). In addition to separating lint and seed, the modern gin will remove some foreign matter, such as dirt, twigs, leaves, and parts of the bolls. The roller gin is still used for some long-staple fibers, but most cotton is ginned on the saw gin. The seeds are a valuable by-product of the cotton industry and produce cattle feed and cottonseed oil. The fiber, or cotton lint, is packed into large bales at the ginnery. Each bale weighs about 500 pounds (227 kg) gross (Fig. 7.6).

Samples of fibers are removed from the bales and used for determining the class. Factors in classification include the staple length, grade, and fineness of the fibers. *Staple length* refers to fiber length. *Grade* refers to color and brightness, the amount of foreign matter, and ginning preparation. Standards are established by the government.

Staple length may be divided into five groups: very short staple, fibers less than ¾ inch (1.9 cm); short staple, ¹³⁄₁₆ to ¹⁵⁄₁₆ inch (2.06–2.38 cm); medium staple, ¹⁵⁄₁₆ to 1⅛ inches (2.38–2.86 cm); ordinary long staple, 1⅛ to 1⅜ inches (2.86–3.5 cm); and extra long staple, 1⅜ inches (3.5 cm) or over.

Fibers stripped from the plant are usually dirtier than those picked; but if the plant has been properly treated prior to picking and if the weather has been cooperative, there tends to be little dirt and soil with the fibers.

The grade of cotton is determined by comparing samples with standards using such factors as color and waste content. Fiber length is determined using a digital fibrograph for short-, medium-, and long-staple Upland varieties. The array method is used for extra-long-staple Pima and Upland varieties.

The fineness and maturity of cotton fibers are not only important criteria in determining quality, but they also contribute to yarn strength and appearance. This measure is determined by several instruments that use the same scale; the results are reported as micronaire readings.

To maintain relatively even quality in cotton yarns and fabrics of similar type, cotton from various bales are blended together before being constructed into yarns or fabrics.

Fiber Properties

Microscopic Properties

Cotton fibers are composed of an outer cuticle (skin) and a primary wall, a secondary wall, and a central core, or *lumen* (Fig. 7.7). Immature fibers exhibit

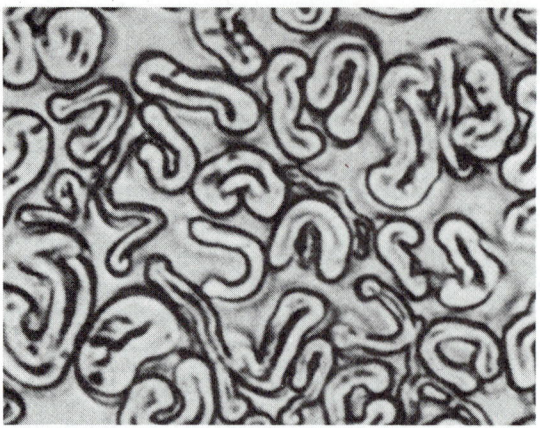

7.8 Photomicrograph of regular cotton, cross section.
(American Association of Textile Chemists and Colorists)

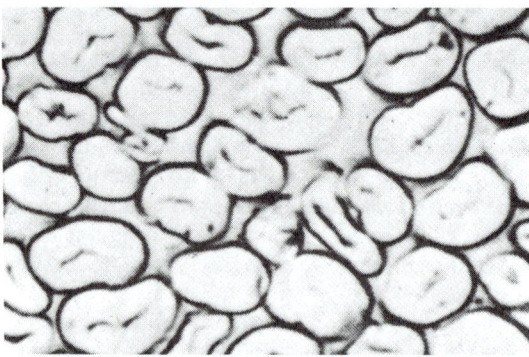

7.9 Photomicrograph of mercerized cotton, cross section.
(American Association of Textile Chemists and Colorists)

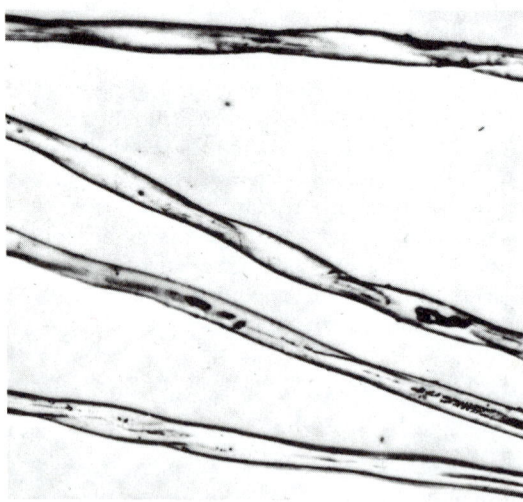

7.10 Photomicrograph of regular cotton, longitudinal view.
(DuPont Company)

thin wall structures and a large lumen, whereas mature fibers have thick walls and a small lumen that may not be continuous, because the wall closes the lumen in some sections (Fig. 7.8).

Fibers that have been swollen, as in mercerization (Fig. 7.9), do not show the twist as clearly as do untreated fibers, and the cross section tends to be smooth and round instead of flat and folded. Immature fibers may have an appearance similar to mercerized cotton.

The longitudinal view of regular cotton (Fig. 7.10) shows a ribbonlike shape with twist (convolutions) at irregular intervals. The diameter of the fiber narrows at the tip. The lumen may appear as a shaded area or as striations; this is more obvious in immature fibers. Some fibers are nearly circular, some are elliptical, and some are kidney-shaped. Immature fibers are generally more irregular than mature fibers.

Physical Properties

SHAPE AND APPEARANCE Cotton fibers are fairly uniform in width, which varies between 12 and 20 microns; the central portion of the fiber is wider than either end. Depending on variety and growing conditions, the length of the cotton fiber used in fabric manufacturing ranges from ½ inch to 2½ inches (1.27–6.35 cm), with most fibers in the ⅞- to 1¼-inch (2.22–3.18-cm) category. (See Table 7.1.)

The length, fineness, and uniformity of fibers aid in distinguishing the common varieties. American Upland has a diameter of approximately 18 microns, a length of less than 1⅛ inches (2.86 cm), and smooth, regular convolutions. The majority of cotton produced in the United States is Upland and includes such types as Acala SJ-2, Deltapine, Coker, Stoneville, McNair, and Des 56.

Long-staple cotton may be Upland or Pima varieties. The latter is usually considered extra-long staple and is grown, primarily, in the southwestern states. Long-staple cotton can be made into fine-quality and beautiful fabrics; some have a silklike appearance. However, it is more costly to process and more difficult to produce than Upland varieties of short or medium-length staple. While the production of American Pima extra-long staple has increased steadily since the 1950s, the amount produced each year is limited.

Egyptian cotton is imported in small amounts. It may be long in staple length, but it tends to be less uniform than American Pima.

◇ ───

Table 7.1 Properties of Cotton Fibers

Property	Evaluation
Shape	Fairly uniform in width, 12–20 microns; length varies from ½ to 2½ inches; typical length is ⅞ to 1¼ inches.
Luster	low
Tenacity (strength)	
dry	3.0–5.0 g/d
wet	3.3–6.0 g/d
Elastic recovery	low; 75% at 2% extension
Elongation	
dry	3–10%
wet	3–10%
Resiliency	low
Density	1.54–1.56 g/ccm
Moisture absorption	
raw: conditioned*	8.5%
saturation	15–25%
mercerized: conditioned*	8.5–10.3%
saturation	15–27%+
Dimensional stability	good
Resistance to	
acids	damage, weaken fibers
alkalies	resistant; no harmful effects
organic solvents	high resistance to most
sunlight	Prolonged exposure weakens fibers.
microorganisms	Mildew and rot-producing bacteria damage fibers.
insects	Silverfish damage fibers.
Thermal reactions	
to heat	Decomposes after prolonged exposure to temperatures of 150°C or over.
to flame	Burns readily.

*Standard conditioned environment = 65% relative humidity, 70°F ± 2°.

The color of cotton fibers may vary from almost pure white to a dirty gray. Part of the color may be due to impurities that can be removed during processing. Imported Egyptian cotton tends to be slightly yellow in color. High-quality cotton fiber is usually very light cream or almost white.

LUSTER The luster of cotton is low unless finishes have been added such as mercerization.

TENACITY (STRENGTH) Cotton has a tenacity of 3.0 to 5.0 grams per denier. This produces a fiber of moderate to above-average strength. When wet, cotton increases in strength, so it may have a wet strength equal to 110 to 120 percent of the dry strength. This means that fiber care and wet processing techniques do not require modification to compensate for reduced fiber strength when wet.

ELASTIC RECOVERY AND ELONGATION Cotton has an elongation of 3 to 7 percent at the breaking point. It may be as high as 10 percent under some conditions. It is relatively inelastic, with a recovery of only 75 percent at 2 percent extension. At 5 percent extension it exhibits less than 50 percent elastic recovery.

RESILIENCY The resiliency of cotton is low.

DENSITY Cotton is one of the most dense of all commonly used fibers, with a density of 1.54 to 1.56 grams per cubic centimeter, frequently reported as about 1.54.

MOISTURE REGAIN The moisture regain for cotton at standard conditions is 8.5 percent. Regain or absorbency at 95 percent relative humidity is approximately 15 percent, and at 100 percent relative humidity it may absorb 25 to 27 percent moisture. Wet cotton is not only stronger but also more pliable and less rigid than dry cotton.

Mercerized cotton fibers have been enlarged (swollen) and can absorb more moisture than non-mercerized fibers. Standard regain for the mercerized fiber varies from 8.5 to 10.3 percent; the latter figure is considered the more common.

DIMENSIONAL STABILITY Cotton fibers are relatively stable and do not stretch or shrink. Cotton fabrics, however, do tend to shrink as a result of tensions encountered during yarn and fabric manufacture. Consequently the fabrics require treatment to render them less susceptible to shrinkage.

Thermal Properties

Cotton burns readily and quickly, with a smell similar to burning paper. It leaves a small amount of fluffy gray ash. Long exposure to dry heat above 150°C (300°F) will cause the fiber to decompose gradually, and temperatures greater than 246°C (475°F) will cause rapid deterioration. Normal exposure to heat encountered in routine care and processing will not damage cotton, but it will scorch if ironed at too-high temperatures. Finishes, such as starch, increase the tendency to scorch.

Chemical Properties

EFFECT OF ALKALIES Cotton is highly resistant to alkalies. In fact, they are used in finishing and processing the fiber. Most detergents and laundry aids are alkaline, so cotton can be laundered in these solutions without damage.

EFFECT OF ACIDS Strong acids destroy cotton, and hot dilute acids cause disintegration. Cold dilute acids cause gradual fiber degradation, but the process is slow and may not be immediately evident.

EFFECT OF ORGANIC SOLVENTS Cotton is highly resistant to most organic solvents and to all those used in normal care and stain removal. It is, however, soluble in such compounds as cuprammonium hydroxide and cupriethylene diamine; these solvents, therefore, should be avoided except as they may be used in the chemical analysis and identification of cotton.

EFFECT OF SUNLIGHT, AGE, AND MISCELLANEOUS FACTORS Prolonged exposure to sunlight will cause the cotton fiber to become yellow and will gradually cause degradation. This damage is accentuated in the presence of moisture, some vat dyes, and some sulfur dyes.

If properly stored, cotton will retain most of its strength and appearance over a long period. Cotton fabric should be stored in dark, dry areas, and it should be clean before being stored. Storage in light areas may be helpful in avoiding damage from selected microorganisms. Storage in dry areas is a must.

Static Charges

Cotton does not build up static charges.

Biological Properties

MICROORGANISMS Cotton is damaged by fungi such as mildew and by bacteria. Mildew will produce a disagreeable odor and will result in rotting and degradation of cotton. Certain bacteria encountered in hot, moist, dirty conditions will cause the fiber to decay.

INSECTS Moths and beetles will not attack or damage cotton. Silverfish will eat cotton cellulose especially if it is heavily starched.

Use and Care of Cotton

Cotton is the second most widely used fiber in the United States. It may be used as the sole component, or fiber type, in fabrics, or it may be blended with man-made fibers such as polyester.

Fabrics of many different constructions, weights, and textures can be made from cotton fibers; thus, cotton has almost universal acceptance. It is used for apparel fabrics, for household or domestic goods, for home furnishings, and for industrial applications. It appears in high-fashion couture apparel as well as very low cost garments. The ability of cotton to accept color and finishes, combined with its comfort, makes it a desirable choice for the consumer. The comfort factor, particularly cotton's ability to absorb moisture and its softness, has made this fiber a favorite for modern apparel and for domestic items such as towels, sheets, and pillowcases. Furthermore, it is an ecologically sound choice, as it is biodegradable and a natural product. Many people consider it a wise choice because it does not require petroleum as a raw material. However, many products made of petroleum are used in cultivating the fiber and to prevent damage from insects and disease. In addition, considerable energy is used in the processing and finishing of cotton fabrics; some petroleum-based products are used in finishes and dyestuffs.

Cotton is frequently selected to blend with man-made fibers. In such blends the cotton fiber contributes comfort, while the man-made fibers add strength and easy care.

Much of the following discussion applies equally well to fabrics of 100 percent cotton and those in which cotton is blended with man-made fibers. Cotton fabrics have good wearing qualities, excellent launderability, good absorbency, good colorfastness when proper dyestuffs have been used, good pliability or flexibility, and good heat resistance. Adequate finishing processes must be applied to produce cotton fabrics that will not shrink as well as fabrics with crease resistance and durable-press characteristics. Cotton accepts finishes that produce resistance to shrinkage, water repellency, flame resistance, crease resistance, and minimum-care properties.

Comfort is one of the outstanding characteristics of cotton fabrics. The fiber has good strength and cohesiveness, so fine yarns can be constructed and fabrics can vary from sheer and lightweight to thick and heavy. This adaptability creates the comfort so prized for cotton fabrics or blends in which cotton is an important component.

Other factors that help in making comfortable fabrics include absorbency and *wickability*. A fiber is said to have wickability when moisture will move quickly along the surface of the fiber and through yarns and fabrics.

Care of cotton is not demanding. Most cotton fabrics can be laundered and dried with home laundering equipment. Most detergents have no negative effects on the fiber. However, some colors and some finishes may be damaged and even destroyed by some laundry aids. It is important, therefore, to read care labels carefully and adhere to recommended procedures. If cotton requires ironing, it may be ironed easily at medium to medium-high temperature settings.

Cotton may be sold directly from the farmer to the ginnery and then to yarn spinners at the current price on the spot market. Cotton also may be sold on the futures market, which depends on projected prices for cotton of middling quality at some date in the future. As more and more cotton farms become properties of large corporations, the sale of cotton by futures marketing has increased. This tends to hold the price of cotton at a stable price, which may be higher than what would occur on the spot market.

FLAX

Historical Review

Flax is considered by many to be the oldest fiber used in the Western world. Fragments of flax fabric (linen) have been found in excavations at the prehistoric lake regions of Switzerland, which date back to about 10,000 B.C.

The use of linen in Egypt between 3000 and 2500 B.C. has been verified. These early fabrics were of a fineness that has never been duplicated. Examples have been found that were spun so fine that more than 360 single threads joined together formed one warp thread. Other fabrics were made with more than 500 yarns per inch (197 yarns/cm).[1]

Belgium became an important center for growing flax because of the chemicals in the water of the River Lys. This water was found to be exceptional in retting flax, and it produced high-quality fibers. The town of Courtrai became a major center for the flax industry and remains an important center today. Linen fabric was introduced into Great Britain from Egypt about 1000 B.C., but actual use of flax probably did not occur until the first century A.D. During the same time, Ireland began to process flax into fabrics, and by A.D. 500 Irish linen was held in high esteem by rulers and nobility throughout Europe.

Flaxseed was brought to America by early colonists, who grew their own flax, spun their own yarn, and made their own fabrics. The production of flax fibers, however, never became a commercial success in the United States, and the production of the fiber and the making of linen fabrics remains centered in Europe and a few other countries such as New Zealand. That country is best known for New Zealand flax, a special variety; the country produces fiber but does not make any fabrics. The major growers of flax fiber are the Soviet Union, Belgium, Ireland, and New Zealand.

[1]*Ciba Review*, no. 49, p. 1766.

7.11 Pulling mature flax stalks. (International Linen Promotion Commission)

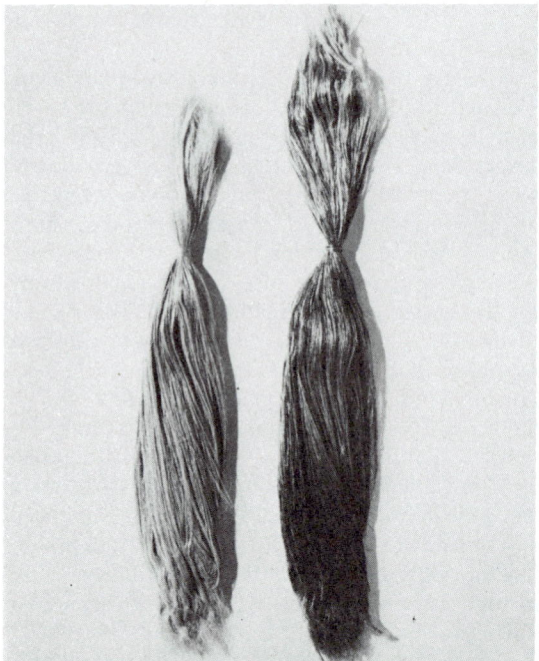

7.12 Retted flax. *Left:* Water or tank retted. *Right:* Dew retted. (International Linen Promotion Commission)

Growth and Production

Flax is a bast fiber—a woody fiber obtained from the phloem of plants. It derives from the stalk or stem of *Linum usitatissimum.* The flax plant requires a temperate climate with generally cloudy skies and adequate moisture. Bright sunlight and high temperatures are damaging unless alternated with abundant rainfall. Flaxseed is planted in April or May. When the crop is to be used for fiber, the seed is sown close together so that the plants will be

7.13 In hackling, or combing, flax is pulled over a series of pins, graduated in size, that separate waste from the fibers and clean and straighten them. The hackled flax is then ready to be fed into a drawing machine. (International Linen Promotion Commission)

7.14 Drawing of flax fiber to form sliver ready for spinning. (International Linen Promotion Commission)

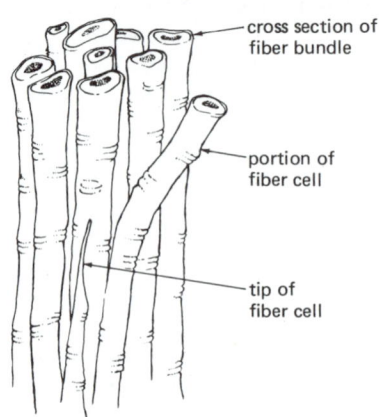

cross section of fiber bundle

portion of fiber cell

tip of fiber cell

7.15 Schematic diagram of fibrils in flax fibers.

closely packed and produce fine plants with long, thin stems. The plants grow to a height of 3 to 4 feet (0.9–1.2 m) for fiber use. The blossoms are a delicate pale blue, white, or pink. Flax for fiber is pulled before the seeds are ripe.

Processing

Pulling and Rippling

Flax for fiber is pulled by hand in some countries or by mechanical pullers (Fig. 7.11). It is important to keep the roots intact, as fibers extend below the ground surface. Harvesting occurs in late August when the plant is a rich brown color. After drying, the plant is *rippled;* that is, it is pulled through special threshing machines that remove the seed bolls or pods.

Retting

To obtain fibers from the stalk, the outer woody portion must be rotted away. This process, known as *retting,* can be accomplished by any of several procedures.

Dew retting involves the spreading of the flax on the ground, where it is exposed to the action of dew and sunlight. This natural method of retting gives uneven results but provides the strongest and most durable linen. It requires a period of 4 to 6 weeks.

Pool retting is a process whereby the flax is packed in sheaves and immersed in pools of stagnant water. Bacteria in the water rot away the outer stalk covering. The time required is 2 to 4 weeks.

Tank retting, similar to pool retting, utilizes large tanks in which the flax is stacked (Fig. 7.12). The tanks are filled with warm water, which increases the speed of bacterial action. Tank retting requires only a few days. Both pool and tank retting give good-quality flax that is uniform in strength and light in color.

Chemical retting is accomplished by stacking the flax in tanks, filling the tanks with water, and adding chemicals such as sodium hydroxide, sodium carbonate, or dilute sulfuric acid. Chemical retting can be completed in a matter of hours instead of days or weeks. However, it must be carefully controlled in order to prevent damage to the fiber.

Breaking and Scutching

After the retting is complete, the flax is rinsed and dried. The stalks are then bundled together and passed between fluted rollers that break the outer woody covering into small particles. It is then scutched to separate the outer covering from the usable fiber.

Hackling

After scutching, the flax fibers are *hackled,* or combed (Fig. 7.13). This operation separates the short fibers, called *tow,* from the long fibers, called *line.* This is accomplished by drawing the fibers between several sets of pins, each successive set finer than the preceding set. This process is similar to the carding and combing operation used for cotton (see Chap. 17) and prepares the flax fibers for the final steps in yarn manufacture. As the fibers are removed from the hackling machine, they are drawn out into a sliver (Fig. 7.14).

Spinning

The flax sliver is drawn out into yarn, and twist is imparted. Flax fibers are spun either dry or wet, but wet spinning is considered to give the best quality yarn. The final yarn processing is similar to that used for cotton fiber.

Fiber Properties

Microscopic Properties

Flax fiber is composed of bundles or fibrils of fiber cells held together by a bonding or gummy substance (Fig. 7.15). Under the microscope the longitudinal view of the fiber shows the width to be quite irregular (Fig. 7.16). the central canal, or lumen, casts a shadow, giving a slightly darker effect down the center. There are no convolutions as in cotton, but longitudinal lines or striations can be seen. The points at which the fiber width changes are marked by swellings and irregular joint formations called *nodes.* These are similar to the joints in bamboo.

The cross-sectional view of flax (Fig. 7.17) clearly shows the lumen, the thick outer wall, and a somewhat polygonal shape. Immature fibers may be oval in shape and have larger lumen than mature fibers.

Physical Properties

SHAPE AND APPEARANCE Flax fiber is not so fine as cotton; flax cells have an average diameter

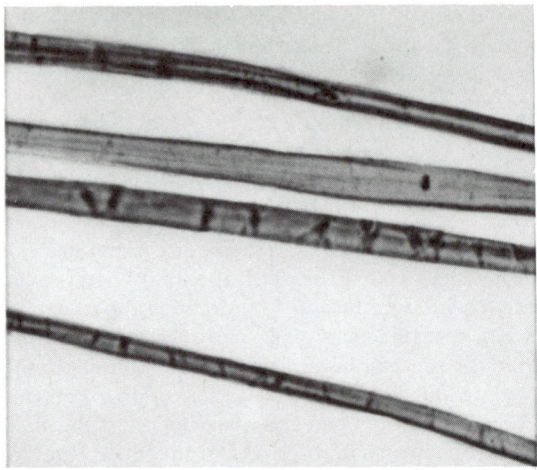

7.16 Photomicrograph of flax, longitudinal view. (DuPont Company)

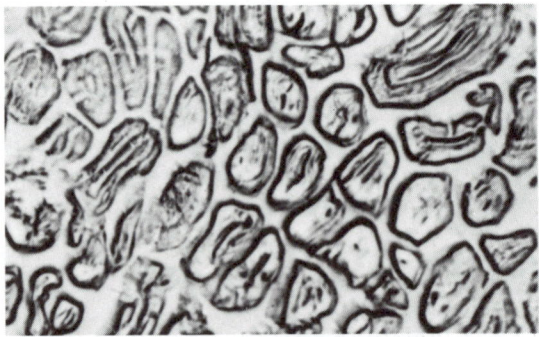

7.17 Photomicrograph of flax, cross section. (DuPont Company)

of 15 to 18 microns and vary in length from ¼ inch to 2½ inches (0.63–6.35 cm). Bundles of cells form the actual fiber as it is used in spinning into yarns, and these bundles may be anywhere from 5 to 20 inches (12.7–50.8 cm) long. Line fibers are usually more than 12 inches (30.5 cm) long; tow fibers are shorter.

The natural color of flax varies from light to ivory to gray. The choice fibers from Belgium are a pale sandy color and require little or no bleaching. (See Table 7.2.)

LUSTER   Flax fibers have a high natural luster with an attractive sheen.

TENACITY (STRENGTH)   Flax is a strong fiber; the normal tenacity ranges between 5.5 and 6.5 grams per denier. Some fiber of inferior quality may have a tenacity as low as 2.6 g/d, and some top-quality fiber may exhibit a tenacity as high as 7.7

g/d. Fabrics of flax are durable and easy to maintain because of the fiber strength. When wet, the fiber is about 20 percent stronger than when dry.

Most linen fabrics for apparel use have been given various resin finishes to provide consumers with easy-care performance. These finishes reduce the strength of flax so that these fabrics tend to give less durability.

Flax has low pliability or flexibility, which may result in reduced serviceability in uses where frequent bending is required.

ELASTIC RECOVERY AND ELONGATION   The amount of elongation that flax will undergo before breaking is very small. When dry, the fiber will extend only 2.7 to 3.3 percent. Within the limits of elongation the fiber has little elasticity. At a 2 percent extension it has an immediate elastic recovery of only 65 percent.

RESILIENCY   Linen fabrics are prone to crease and wrinkle badly. They are somewhat stiff and possess little resiliency. However, finishes can be applied that help offset this disadvantage to some degree.

DENSITY   The density of flax is 1.5 grams per cubic centimeter and is comparable to that of other cellulosic fibers.

MOISTURE REGAIN   Flax has a standard moisture regain of about 12 percent. The saturation regain is comparable to that of other cellulosic fibers. Flax has outstanding wicking properties, which makes it possible to move moisture along the fibers and yarns as well as to absorb moisture.

DIMENSIONAL STABILITY   Flax fibers do not shrink or stretch to any marked degree. However, as in the case of cotton, yarns and fabrics are subject to some relaxation shrinkage unless preshrunk during finishing operations. Ironing linen fabrics while damp will help stretch them back to their original size.

Thermal Properties

Like other cellulose fibers, flax burns quickly. It is highly resistant to decomposition or degradation by dry heat and will withstand temperatures to 150°C (300°F) for long periods with little or no change in properties. Prolonged exposure above 150°C (300°F) will result in gradual discoloration. Safe ironing temperatures may go as high as 260°C

TABLE 7.2   Properties of Flax Fibers

Property	Evaluation
Shape	Width varies; mean diameter is about $\frac{1}{1200}$ inch; length varies from a few inches to 22 inches or more; typical length is 10 to 15 inches.
Luster	medium to high
Tenacity (strength)	
range, dry	2.6 to 7.7 g/d
typical, dry	5.5 to 6.5 g/d
typical, wet	6.6 to 7.8 g/d
Elastic recovery	low; 65% recovery at 2% extension
Elongation	2.7–3.3%
Resiliency	poor
Density	1.5 g/ccm
*Moisture regain, standard conditioned**	12%
Dimensional stability	good
Resistance to	
acids	good to cool, dilute; low to hot, dilute; poor to concentrated, either hot or cold
alkalies	high resistance
organic solvents	good
sunlight	good
microorganisms	Mildew will damage the fiber.
insects	good
Thermal reactions	
to heat	gradual decomposition after prolonged exposure at 150°C
to flame	Burns readily.

*Standard conditioned environment = 65% relative humidity, 70°F ± 2°.

(500°F) as long as the fabric is not held at that high temperature for any length of time.

Chemical Properties

Flax is highly resistant to alkaline solutions; it is also resistant to dilute acids, but concentrated acids and hot dilute acids will cause deterioration. Flax has excellent resistance to dry-cleaning solvents and other organic compounds encountered in normal maintenance.

There is a gradual loss of strength when linen fabrics are exposed to sunlight, but this is not serious. Consequently, flax makes a good choice for curtain and drapery fabrics.

If stored properly, linen will age remarkably well. Table coverings and sheets packed away for many years have proved to be as strong as new linen fabrics.

Biological Properties

Dry linen has excellent resistance to mildew, but if the fabric is moist or stored in a humid atmosphere, mildew will grow rapidly and damage the fiber. Flax has good resistance to most household insects and pests; silverfish may damage the fiber if it has been starched.

Use and Care of Linen Fabrics

The strength of flax fibers makes it possible to manufacture a wide variety of yarns, from very fine to very heavy, which can be used to make a wide variety of fabrics, from sheer and loose to heavy and compact. Linen is a frequent choice for table coverings because it wears well, looks extremely attractive and elegant, and, when properly finished, lies flat on the table. To achieve this flat effect, a beetling finish is often used (see page 304).

The natural resistance of flax to chemicals, including detergents, bleaches, other laundry aids, and dry-cleaning solvents, provides a fabric that is easily maintained. Further, these properties, plus resistance to sunlight, inherent fiber strength, and resistance to aging, result in fabrics with a long life. The preferred method of care for linen fabrics is laundering. In general, linen fabrics do not soil quickly and, unless stained, do not require bleaching to remain white.

When selecting apparel items of linen, consumers prefer fabrics with crease-resistant or durable-press finishes. These may require special care instructions, which should be carefully followed.

JUTE

Jute is a bast fiber like flax. It has been used since the dawn of civilization; however, it did not attain economic importance until the latter part of the eighteenth century. Today, jute is one of the most widely used fibers in the world and is of special interest to countries with low economic standards, as it is a low-cost fiber. Jute is processed into fabrics in Asia, Scotland, and the United States.

Jute is obtained from the stem of the *Corchorus* plant, specifically *Corchorus capsularis* and *Corchorus olitorious*. The major growing areas are Bangladesh, India, and Thailand. In fabric form it is frequently called *burlap* or *hessian*.

The jute plant is cultivated in a manner similar to that used for flax. The seeds are planted close together and grow to a height of 15 to 20 feet (4.6 to 6.1 m). The fibers are extracted from the stem by retting followed by breaking and scutching.

Natural jute has a yellow to brown or grayish color and a silky luster. Fibers are irregular in diameter and vary from 5 to 10 feet (1.5–3 m) in length. The microscopic appearance is similar to flax except that there is less lumen in jute than flax. Fibers used in yarn construction are really bundles of fibrous material held together by a gummy substance of a pectinaceous character. It is difficult to bleach jute to a pure white; thus, many jute fabrics are naturally beige to brown in color.

The average strength of jute fiber is about 3.5 grams per denier; it has low elastic recovery, only 74 percent at 1 percent extension, and a low elongation—less than 2 percent. The resiliency is low, and yarns and fabrics that have been crushed or creased do not return to shape without treatment such as laundering and ironing.

The density of jute is about 1.5 grams per cubic centimeter; moisture regain is 13.7 percent at standard conditions. Jute will deteriorate, however, if held in moist areas for extended periods of time. Dry jute will last for a long time and retain much of

◊ ─────────────────────────

TABLE 7.3   Properties of Jute Fibers

Property	Evaluation
Shape	irregular in diameter and length, 5 to 20 feet long
Luster	silky
Tenacity (strength)	3.5 g/d
Elastic recovery	very low; 74% at 1% extension
Elongation	1.7–1.9%
Resiliency	low
Density	1.5 g/ccm
Moisture absorption	13.7% at standard conditions
Dimensional stability	good
Resistance to	
acids	good to dilute; poor to concentrated
alkalies	very good
sunlight	good
microorganisms	good
insects	good
Thermal reactions	
to heat	similar to those of flax
to flame	Burns readily.

its strength during that period. Dimensional stability is good. (See Table 7.3.)

Chemical reactions of jute are much like those of other cellulosic fibers. Resistance to alkalies is very good; to dilute acids, good. Concentrated acids do cause fiber breakdown. Sunlight does not damage jute.

Reactions to heat and flame are the same as for other cellulosic fibers. Jute has good resistance to microorganisms and insects, which contributes to its advantages in some end uses.

Major end uses of jute include bagging, carpet backing, and furniture construction. It is used for bagging because it permits stacking without slipping or shifting position. In the manufacture of furniture, jute is used as a base fabric and as taping before surface fabrics are applied. As a carpet backing, jute adds stability and reduces slippage. It also is used as a base for the manufacture of linoleum. The amount of jute used for carpets and linoleum is decreasing yearly as man-made fibers, particularly olefins, are taking the place of jute.

Care of jute is similar to that of flax except for the fact that colored jute may require dry cleaning. Jute is difficult to dye with colorfast properties. Jute is widely used in developing countries and others where labor is available at relatively low cost. It is a labor-intensive commodity and requires a high proportion of labor in processing.

RAMIE

China grass, or ramie, is a bast fiber that has been cultivated for hundreds of years in China, Taiwan, and to some extent in Egypt. In more recent times it has been of interest in many other countries, including the United States.

The ramie plant, a member of the nettle family, is a perennial shrub that can be cut several times a season after the necessary preliminary growth period. It can be started from seeds, which necessitates a development period of three years before fibers are formed; or it can be grown from root cuttings, which mature within two years.

After cutting, the ramie stalks are decorticated or retted to remove the outer woody covering and reveal the fine fibers within (Fig. 7.18). These are degummed in caustic soda to eliminate the pectins and waxes, then bleached and finally neutralized in a dilute acid bath. The fiber is then washed and dried.

Ramie fibers are long and very fine. They are white and lustrous and almost silklike in appearance. The strength of ramie is outstanding, from 5.3 to 7.4 grams per denier. Elastic recovery is low and elongation is poor. The fibers are somewhat brittle and stiff.

Ramie reacts chemically in the same manner as other cellulose fibers. The high degree of molecular crystallinity and low molecular accessibility reduce the rate of acid penetration and thus increase the time required for damage to occur as a result of strong acids.

Of special interest is the fact that ramie is highly resistant to microorganisms and insects. This is probably due to the presence of nonfibrous matter, which may contain material that is toxic to bacteria and fungi.

Ramie fabrics may resemble fine linen, or they can be heavy and coarse like canvas. Because the fiber tends to be stiff, ramie is usually blended with other fibers if it is to be used in apparel.

The use of ramie is increasing because of increased production of the fiber in Asia, particularly China. A fairly large amount of fabric in which ramie has been blended with silk, linen, cotton, and

7.18 Ramie stalks decorticated, showing fiber just under the bark. Stalk at right is partially degummed. (R. V. Allison, Everglades Experiment Station, Belle Glade, Florida)

some manufactured fibers is appearing on the market. Fabrics of 100 percent ramie appear to be popular for apparel and some home furnishings.

HEMP

Hemp is a bast fabric that was probably used first in Asia. Records indicate that it was cultivated in China before 2300 B.C. Sometime during the early Christian era, hemp was carried into Europe and became an important fiber.

Today, hemp is grown on every continent and in nearly every country. A tall herb of the mulberry family, it is a tough plant and will grow at altitudes to 8000 feet (2440 m) and in climates where temperatures are warm or hot. It can be replanted in the same fields without depleting soil nutrients.

The plants are cut by hand and then processed in a manner very much like that used for flax. It requires retting (Fig. 7.19), followed by stripping or scutching to obtain the fiber. Hackling, drawing, and spinning follow. The fiber is dark tan or brown and is difficult to bleach; however, it can be dyed bright and dark colors successfully.

Hemp fibers vary widely in length from 1 inch to several inches. Fibers used for industrial purposes

7.19 Retting hemp. The stalks are laid in rafts and submerged by stone weights. In the background, retted hemp has been stacked to dry. (Ciba Review)

7.20 Place mat of abaca fibers.

7.21 Evening bag of embroidered piña fiber.

may be several inches long, whereas fibers used for domestic textiles are about ¾ inch to 1 inch (1.9–2.54 cm) long. The density of hemp is 1.45 grams per cubic centimeter. Its strength varies between 5.8 and 6.8 grams per denier. Elongation and elasticity are both low. Standard moisture regain is 12 percent, and it can absorb moisture up to 30 percent of its weight.

Hot concentrated alkalies will dissolve hemp, but hot or cold dilute or cold concentrated alkalies will not damage the fiber. With the exception of cool weak acids, mineral acids will reduce the strength and eventually destroy the fiber completely. Organic solvents used in cleaning and bleaches, if handled properly, will not damage hemp.

The thermal properties and the effect of sunlight are the same as for cotton. Hemp is resistant to insects but is damaged by mildew.

Hemp fibers are used for cordage, rope, sacking, and heavy-duty covering fabrics. In some countries, hemp has been made into fine fabrics for use as wall coverings or draperies.

MISCELLANEOUS PLANT FIBERS

Other plant fibers discussed below include those that have limited use in the United States for specific products or those that have topical interest to the textile student.

KENAF   Kenaf, a fiber somewhat similar to jute, was widely used during World War II as a substitute for jute. Today, little kenaf is grown outside of India and Pakistan.

The fiber is obtained from the stalk of the plant, and methods of cultivation and processing are similar to those used for jute. The plant grows about 10 feet (3 m) tall, but the fibers are considerably shorter, as they break apart during processing. Kenaf is a light-colored fiber and is usually used in its natural state. It is not strong and has low elasticity. Water does not seem to have any effect on the fiber, and thus it finds widespread use in ropes, cordage, canvas, and other end uses where resistance to water is important.

URENA   Urena is another bast fiber that was developed as a result of shortage during World War II. It has been grown in South America for centuries, but present-day use seems to have started in the 1920s.

At present urena is used primarily in Africa. It grows to a height of more than 10 feet (3 m), and the processing is like that required for jute and hemp. When properly processed, the fiber is nearly white; it is soft and has a natural luster. Urena is used for sacking and in Africa for low-cost apparel and decorating fabrics.

SISAL   Sisal is one of a group of fibers obtained from the leaves of plants that belong to the agave family. It is raised in Mexico, especially in the Yucatan peninsula. The fiber is also cultivated in Africa, Java, and some areas of South America.

The leaves are cut when they are about 4 years old. The processing of the fibers involves separating them from the fleshy part of the leaf and removing the pectins, chlorophyll, and other noncellulosic substances. Sisal can be dyed bright colors by means of both direct and acid dyes. It is important in the manufacture of such items as matting, rough handbags, ropes and cordage, and carpeting.

HENEQUEN   Henequen is a leaf fiber from a member of the agave family. Its area of production is much the same as that of sisal, and it is processed similarly. The major application of this fiber is for agricultural twine.

ABACA   Abaca is obtained from the leaves of a plant that belongs to the banana family. In appearance it is often mistaken for the edible banana tree. The plant grows mainly in the Philippines, and most of the textile fiber is processed there, although some is found in Mexico. The leaf stalk from which the fiber is taken may reach a length of 25 feet (7.6 m). The fibers, therefore, are generally long; usable fibers may be up to 15 feet (4.6 m) in length. Good-quality abaca has a natural luster and is an off-white color. Poor grades are dark gray or brown.

Abaca is a strong fiber, flexible, and exceptionally good for making rope, cordage, place mats for either outdoor or indoor use, and selected items of apparel. The fabric is delicate and lightweight, yet strong (Fig. 7.20).

PIÑA   Piña fiber is obtained from the leaves of the pineapple plant. It is processed primarily in the Philippines. Piña is a white or light ivory fiber about 2 to 4 inches (5 to 10 cm) in length. The fiber is fine, lustrous, soft, flexible, and strong. It is highly resistant to water. Fabrics made of piña may be either soft and delicate or crisp. Considerable fiber is employed in making clothing and accessories with elaborate embroidery (Fig. 7.21). The fabrics are easily cleaned and will retain their appearance for long periods of time. Some rope and twine are also made from pineapple fiber.

If piña table coverings are used, it is extremely important to remove fruit stains from the fiber as soon as possible. Pectins and acids in some fruit juices can break down the fiber molecule, causing holes to appear. Prompt care usually prevents this from occurring.

COIR   Coir, a fiber from a seed source, is used for matting and cordage. It is obtained from the coconut and is the fibrous mass between the outer shell and the actual nut.

The natural color of coir is a rich cinnamon brown, and the fiber is frequently used in its natural color. It is used for outdoor floor mats and patio coverings. Because of a high degree of stiffness, it is wrinkle and crush resistant; it is strong and impervious to abrasive wear. In addition, coir can withstand exposure to weather of all kinds, so it proves to be a practical fiber for outdoor use. The fiber can be dyed dark colors, but it is difficult to bleach it sufficiently to produce pale hues.

KAPOK   Kapok is a seed hair fiber from the Java kapok tree. The tree grows to a height of 50 feet (15 m) or more. The seed pods are similar to the cotton boll. Ginning is not necessary, since the fibers can be dried, after which the seeds will easily shake away, leaving the soft fibers.

Kapok is extremely light, buoyant, and soft. Its major use has been for padding and stuffing, particularly in upholstered furniture, pillows, and some mattresses. Because it is nonallergenic, it makes an excellent filling for pillows. In recent years, however, foam rubber, polyurethane foam, and polyester fiberfill have replaced kapok as a filling fiber. The best-known use for kapok has been and continues to be as filler for life preservers. Kapok-filled preservers will support up to 30 times the weight of the preserver and will not become waterlogged. The fiber is difficult to spin into yarns, so it is employed primarily for these other end uses.

STUDY QUESTIONS

1. What geographical locations are best for raising cotton? Why?

2. Cite the properties of cotton and identify how they aid in providing products that please consumers.

3. What are the properties of flax that makes it desired for table coverings? for draperies? for dish towels?

4. Which retting process for flax is the most rapid? Which produces the best-quality fiber?

5. Describe the procedure for handling cotton fibers from the time the fiber is picked until it is ready to be made into yarns.

6. For each of the following fibers, cite the properties that make it desirable for textile use, and then give typical kinds of products in which it might be found: cotton, flax, jute, and hemp.

7. What problems are involved in the care of fabrics made of cellulosic fibers? What properties help to make care relatively easy?

8. Explain why cellulose fibers tend to have poor wrinkle resistance and recovery from wrinkling or creasing.

9. Why are linen fabrics more expensive than cotton?

10. What property of jute makes it good for sacks and for carpet backing?

Activities

1. Locate samples of natural cellulosic fibers in yarns or fabrics, and test them in the laboratory. If no laboratory is available, try to determine how crease resistant the fabrics may be, how strong, and how absorbent.

2. Sketch the cross sections of the cotton and flax fibers, and label their respective parts.

3. Shop various apparel and home furnishings stores, and determine what types of items and what price levels are prevalent for cotton, linen, and any other natural cellulosic fiber products available. Compare the amount of pure cotton fabrics with the number of fabrics made from blends including cotton.

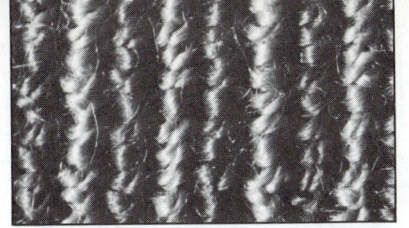

8

Man-Made Cellulosic Fibers: Rayon

OBJECTIVES

◊ **To describe the relationships between natural cellulose and man-made cellulosic fibers**

◊ **To provide specifics on the properties of man-made cellulosic fibers**

◊ **To identify the chemical reactions involved in forming rayon, especially viscose rayon**

◊ **To describe the modifications of viscose currently available**

◊ **To indicate recommended procedures for the use and care of rayon**

KEY TERMS

afterglow
cuprammonium process
hand
high-tenacity rayon
high-wet-modulus rayon

hollow or inflated fibers
man-made cellulosic
modulus
rayon
viscose process

Historical Review

Usually, Count Hilaire Chardonnet is given credit for the invention of a rayon fiber that could be manufactured in quantity. Chardonnet made a solution of cellulose nitrate, dissolved this in alcohol, and forced this solution through a spinnerette into water. The filaments hardened, were stretched to orient the molecules and introduce sufficient strength, and finally denitrated and purified to reduce flammability. By 1889, Chardonnet had exhibited fabric samples, and by 1895 his company, the Société Anonyme pour le Fabrication de la Soie de Chardonnet, was paying dividends. Today, the cellulose nitrate process is of historical interest only.

The viscose process was developed in 1891 by English scientists C. F. Cross and E. J. Bevan. Viscose manufacture has undergone considerable modification since those early years, but it basically is the same as the process Cross and Bevan developed. An important part of the development of rayon was the invention of the spinning box by C. F. Topham in 1905. This box caught the filaments and imparted sufficient twist to hold the filaments together to make a usable yarn.

The first company to make rayon in the United States, the American Viscose Company, opened in 1910. Following changes in ownership and management, the group producing rayon today operates under the name Avtex Fibers. Between 1916 and 1930 such companies as DuPont, Industrial Rayon, Celanese, American Enka, and North American Rayon joined the ranks of manufacturers of viscose rayon. The cuprammonium process for manufacturing "cupra" rayon was introduced in 1926.

The decades since 1950 have seen many improvements in rayon fibers, as well as the development of high-tenacity rayon, high-wet-modulus rayon, and other variants. However, during this period the use of rayon has gradually decreased. Manufacturers of rayon in the United States today are Avtex Fibers, Inc., American Enka Company, North American Rayon Company, and Courtaulds North America, Inc.

The Textile Fiber Products Identification Act (TFPIA) defines *rayon* as "a manufactured fiber composed of regenerated cellulose, as well as manufactured fibers composed of regenerated cellulose in which substituents have replaced not more than 15 percent of the hydrogens of the hydroxyl radicals."

8.1 Packing cellulose sheets into steeping tanks to form alkali cellulose. (Celanese Corporation)

8.2 Dumping alkali crumb from the shredder. (Avtex Fibers, Inc.)

1. cellulose   + caustic soda → soda cellulose + water
   $(C_6H_{10}O_5)_n$ + nNaOH   → $(C_6H_9O_5Na)_n$ + nH$_2$O

2. soda cellulose   + carbon disulfide → sodium cellulose xanthate
   $(C_6H_9O_4CS_2Na)_n$ + n/2 H$_2$SO$_4$ → $(C_6H_9O_4OCS_2Na)_2$

3. Aging period

4. sodium cellulose xanthate + sulfuric acid→ cellulose (viscose type)
   $(C_6H_9O_4OCS_2Na)_n$ + n/2 H$_2$SO$_4$ → $(C_6H_{10}O_5)_n$

   + carbon disulfide + sodium sulfate
   nCS$_2$ + n/2 Na$_2$SO$_4$

8.3 Chemical reactions in viscose manufacture. See Figure 7.1 for diagram of cellulose molecule.

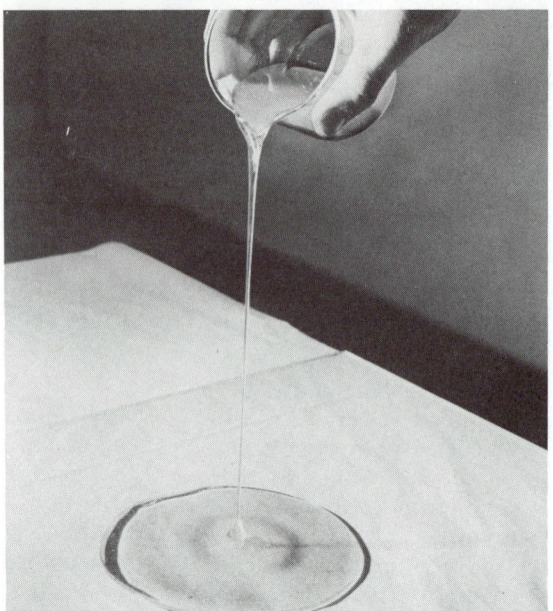

8.4 Viscose formed from xanthate crumb dissolved in sodium hydroxide. (Avtex Fibers, Inc.)

Manufacturing Processes

Viscose Process

The principal raw material for viscose rayon is a refined grade of pulp derived from wood. Cellulose is extracted from wood, purified, and formed into thin sheets that are about 2 feet (0.61 m) square. In the industry, such pulp is referred to as chemical pulp or dissolving pulp; the latter term is more common. It is important to note that cellulose pulp may be prepared for the rayon process in forms other than sheets of wood pulp.

Considered chemically, the raw material is similar to pure cotton cellulose and other celluloses of any of the natural cellulosic fibers.

The sheets of cellulose are steeped in a 17.5 percent solution of sodium hydroxide (NaOH) until the cellulose is converted to alkali cellulose (Fig. 8.1). After steeping, the alkalized pulp sheets are shredded into a crumb (Fig. 8.2). For selected types of rayon, the crumb is aged for varying periods of time. The aging process involves a chemical reaction between alkali cellulose and oxygen in the air. The oxygen acts as chemical "scissors" to shorten the cellulose polymer chain length from a high degree of polymerization (dp) to a lower dp suitable

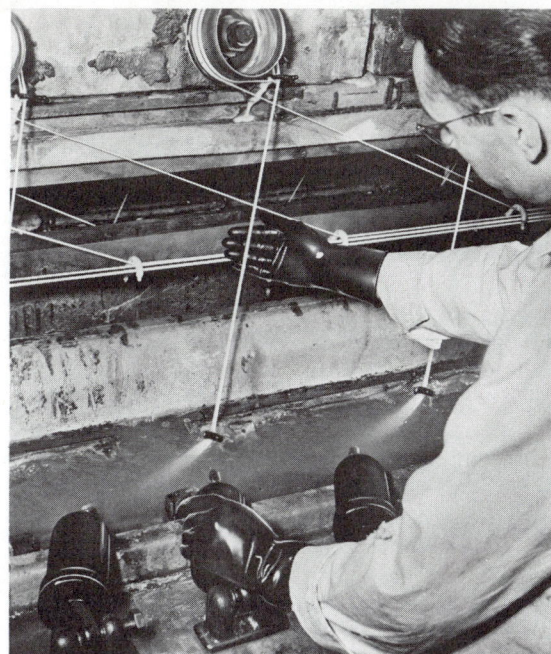

8.5 *Left:* Wet spinning. Collecting filaments into yarn as they emerge from the spin bath. *Right:* Take-up rolls on a continuous rayon filament machine showing filaments being wound onto a yarn package. (Avtex Fibers, Inc.)

for the desired type of rayon to be made. The reaction time in the aging process depends upon the starting dp of the pulp, the general chemical reactivity of the specific pulp used, the presence of a catalyst, and temperature.

After aging, the alkali cellulose crumbs are reacted with carbon disulfide. Up to this point the soda cellulose has been white, but the carbon disulfide changes it to a bright orange and chemically to a product called sodium cellulose xanthate. A summary of the reactions for these processes is given in Figure 8.3.

The xanthate crumb is dissolved in dilute sodium hyroxide (5% to 8% NaOH) and forms a honey-colored liquid. This solution is aged until it reaches the correct degree of coagulability with respect to its spinnability for specified spinning conditions. The degree of coagulability, taken in relation to spin bath conditions, influences the kind of product obtained and represents a key point in the ''art'' of manufacturing rayon fibers. Key factors in viscose production include concentration, the degree of polymerization of the cellulose, the presence of additives, temperature, and amount of reverse reaction of xanthate that has occurred prior to spinning (Fig.

8.4). The name *viscose* is taken from the viscous liquid solution formed in this manufacturing step.

The viscose is filtered and deaerated, delivered to the spinning machines, and forced by individual pumps for each spinnerette into an acid bath.

The spin bath for viscose rayon is composed of sulfuric acid (H_2SO_4), sodium sulfate (Na_2SO_4), water, and certain additives such as glucose and zinc sulfate. The composition and temperature of the spin bath influence the rates of coagulation of the cellulose xanthate and its subsequent regeneration to cellulose. These factors also influence the type of cross sections that may be obtained and whether or not a latent crimp can be imparted to the final fiber. Sodium sulfate is the primary coagulation medium. The acid neutralizes excess caustic of the viscose and effects regeneration of the cellulose from the xanthate. Zinc sulfate moderates the rate of regeneration by slowing the process. Filaments of cellulose xanthate are stretched during the regeneration step. The amount of stretch influences tenacity and modulus, with more stretch producing high-tenacity and high-wet-modulus types of rayon. Water is the basic solvent for the spin bath.

The acid bath interacts with the viscose and

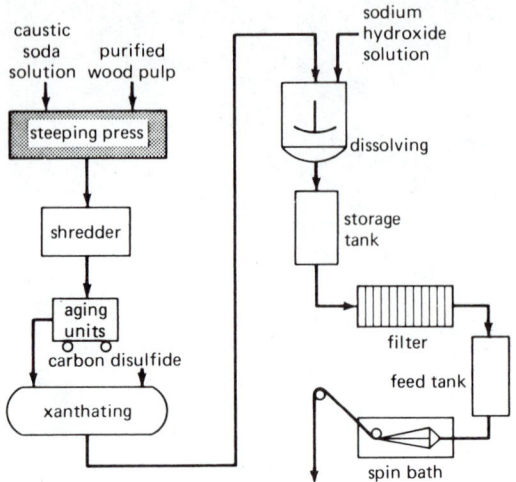

8.6 Flow chart for viscose rayon manufacture.

causes coagulation of the cellulose xanthate into filaments. Filaments are withdrawn continuously from the acid bath and are further treated with hot dilute acid to force regeneration of the cellulose xanthate back to pure cellulose with the release of carbon disulfide. These two steps of coagulation and regeneration comprise the wet spinning process for rayon (Fig. 8.5). The filaments are thoroughly washed after regeneration to remove any impurities that might adhere to the fibers. The final chemical reaction is diagramed in Figure 8.3.

The formed filaments are withdrawn from the spin bath and either combined directly into yarns or cut into short lengths for spinning into yarns by one of the methods typically used for cotton or wool fibers (see Chap. 17). The viscose process is diagramed in Figure 8.6.

The orifices in the spinnerette vary in size and number. Small orifices produce fine filaments, and the number of openings determine the number of filaments in the filament yarn form. For the manufacture of staple fibers, large spinnerettes with as many as 50,000 openings may be used. The filaments from such jets are collected with other filaments from many other such jets, all spinning at the same time. These filaments are then cut into the desired length for conversion by a yarn spinner into spun yarns.

If dull fibers are desired, a delustering agent, usually titanium dioxide, is added to the viscose before extrusion. The delustering agent breaks up the light rays and reduces the shine. The degree of brightness or dullness can be controlled by the amount of titanium dioxide added.

Since the early 1950s, viscose manufacturers have produced some fibers that have been dyed before extrusion. This process, called solution dyeing, uses either dyes soluble in a dye bath or pigments that disperse in the fiber.

Over the past 20 years significant advances have been made in the technology for producing viscose rayon. In years past, viscose manufacture was highly labor-intensive. The wood pulp was processed in relatively small batches through each of the processing steps. With the advent of new process equipment technology, including larger equipment, continuous processing equipment, and microprocessor technology, superior-quality viscose can be made with as much as one-tenth of the labor costs as required in the older technology.

The cellulose products industry, including rayon, have further benefited from modern technology associated with growing and harvesting wood resources, improved wood yields, and utilization of all products from wood, plus resolution of major environmental problems that heretofore have been troublesome for the pulp and paper manufacturer to control. Under today's conditions, and for the foreseeable future, cellulose as a polymer derived from nature is in abundant supply and can compete directly with other polymers derived from other resources such as oil and coal. In the last 25 years a significant number of patents have been issued on the technology for producing rayon and rayon variants. As a consequence, it is possible to produce a very broad range of rayon products having significantly different physical characteristics, especially in tenacity and elongation properties. Rayon manufacturers today are capable of producing "engineered" rayon product types that can be compatibly blended with virtually any other type of fiber, either natural or synthetic, to obtain optimum yarn-strength characteristics. This kind of versatility—in addition to ease of processability and the opportunities to utilize rayon's functional characteristics such as absorbency, comfort, and the broad range of aesthetic values such as color, hand, and appearance—gives rayon a unique place as a cellulosic fiber in the textile industry, for other types of cellulosic fibers, such as cotton, do not have that flexibility.

A unique characteristic that can be developed in

rayon is a chemical crimp, which becomes an inherent part of the rayon fibers. The latent crimp imparted at spinning is developed under wet relaxed conditions and can be maintained throughout the life of the textile product in which such fibers are used. These fibers have an imbalance in the structure of the skin and core, which causes the fiber to develop crimp. Chemical crimping is achieved by reducing the acid in the spin bath and increasing the bath temperature. These fibers have high bulk and fullness and improved cohesiveness if dried in a relaxed state. Rayon does not hold a mechanical crimp, as it would be lost the first time that such rayon was exposed to any wet relaxation processes.

Avtex Fibers, Inc., has announced a solvent spinning process for making rayon that reduces processing time and steps. Solvent spinning involves four steps instead of the eight in the traditional processing and reduces time required from three days to eight hours. Ammonia is the solvent used. Although the process is still experimental, Avtex hopes to use it commercially by 1987 or 1988.

Modified Viscose Rayon Fibers

HIGH-TENACITY VISCOSE The need for stronger rayon fibers became apparent in the early use of the fiber. By 1930, some medium-tenacity rayon was made by modifying the spinning or coagulating bath. High-tenacity rayon followed. To achieve high-tenacity viscose rayon, the concentration of zinc sulfate in the spin bath is increased from about 0.8 percent to 4–6 percent, and consequently the regeneration process is slowed down, producing fibers with a thicker skin and less core.

HIGH-WET-MODULUS RAYON High-wet-modulus viscose rayons differ from standard viscose in many ways. For example, there are "higher degree of polymerization" celluloses, richer viscoses—that is, higher ratios of caustic to cellulose and of carbon disulfide (CS_2) to cellulose—additional regeneration rate modifiers added to the viscose, lower spin bath temperature, lower salt concentration in the spin bath, higher zinc and lower acid concentrations in the spin bath, more immersion time in the spin bath, slower regeneration, and higher stretch. The resulting fibers have wet-modulus characteristics approaching that of cotton. Consequently, they are stronger and have better tensile stability than so-called regular viscose fibers. They resist elongation better than other viscose fibers; that is, elongation

at break is significantly lower at a much higher tenacity than regular rayon.

Modulus is a measure of resistance to stretch or elongation. A high modulus means that a high load has to be applied to achieve a small amount of extension or stretch. High-wet-modulus rayons are excellent in blends and produce good wash-and-wear properties because they accept "minimum care" finishes better and require less resin than do other viscose fibers. Further desirable properties of high-wet-modulus rayons are good stability to laundering and easy care; ability to be mercerized; and a crisp, lofty hand. (Hand is the "feel" of a fabric— the qualities that can be ascertained by touching.)

HOLLOW VISCOSE FIBER Hollow viscose, sometimes called inflated viscose, was developed to give more bulk for a given fiber weight, high moisture-absorption properties, a good covering factor, and hand similar to cotton's. These fibers are generally made by incorporating sodium carbonate in the spinning dope, thus generating carbon dioxide, which inflates the fiber.

FLAME-RESISTANT RAYON An important modification has been the development of flame-resistant rayon, frequently referred to as FR rayon. It was developed originally in response to legislation on flame-resistant textiles for consumer products.

Flame-resistant rayon today is not used in any consumer products. Because of its high cost, marketing attention has focused on governmental, institutional, and industrial applications, where the requirement to meet standards of flame resistance is a prerequisite in addition to the normal performance requirements of fabrics and garments. A wide range of products has been developed to meet the flame-resistance and thermal-bonding properties required to provide protection from identified and well-defined fire hazards. These are applications that are not legislated.

Flame resistance is achieved through the introduction of special chemicals, such as alkylphosphazene, into the viscose. The flame resistance of these fibers is permanent under normal use and care. As for all textile products, care instructions should be carefully followed.

The Cuprammonium Process

E. Schweitzer discovered in 1857 that cellulose would dissolve in a solution of ammonia and copper oxide. However, this reaction was not applied to the manufacture of fibers at that time. In 1891 cupra rayon was made in Germany by Max Fremery and Johann Urban, but it was not successful. In 1901, Edmund Thiele devised the stretch spinning process that made it practical to produce cupra rayon with good strength and fineness. Further improvements in the manufacture of cuprammonium fibers occurred in 1940 with the development of a continuous spinning process for these fibers. Cellulose from either wood pulp or cotton linters is purified and bleached to a pure white, then dissolved in a solution of ammonia, copper sulfate, and caustic soda. The solution is carefully controlled to maintain about 4 percent copper, 29 percent ammonia, and 10 percent cellulose. A clear blue liquid is formed that requires no aging before spinning, but it is not damaged if storage is necessary. If storage is required, however, it must be under an inert atmosphere such as nitrogen. Any undissolved cellulose and other impurities are filtered out of the solution before it is spun into fibers.

The cuprammonium solution is pumped through the spinnerette into a funnel through which soft water is running. The movement of the water stretches the newly formed filaments and introduces a small amount of molecular orientation. The fibers then move to the spinning machine, where they are washed, put through a mild acid bath to remove any adhering solution, rinsed, and then twisted the desired amount to form yarns.

Fiber Properties

Molecular Structure

Rayon is composed of cellulose. Like cotton, it is a polymer of anhydroglucose units (see Fig. 7.1). The average degree of polymerization for rayons is cited in Table 8.1; the degrees of polymerization of cotton and wool pulp are included for comparison. The difference in degree of polymerization between cotton and rayon accounts for some of the variance in physical properties between the two.

Other causes for the difference between rayon and cotton include the difference in the degree of crystallinity, 60 percent for cotton and 40 percent for rayon, and differences in hydrogen bonding as evidenced by the infrared spectra of native cellulose and regenerated cellulose.

Morphologically native celluloses, such as cotton and celluloses found in trees and other plants, are indeed different from coagulated and/or regener-

◇ ────────────────

TABLE 8.1 Average Degree of Polymerization (dp) for Cellulosic Fibers

Fiber	Degree of Polymerization
Cotton	9,000–15,000
Viscose rayon	
regular	250 –450
high tenacity	500 –650
high wet modulus	400 –550
Cupra rayon	400 –500
Wood pulp	
(native cellulose)	600 –1500

ated celluloses. The mechanisms of formation for natural celluloses are significantly different from man's ability to re-form cellulosic structures found in nature. The acts of depolymerizing native celluloses and the dissolving of cellulose alter the form of native cellulose. Rayon is structurally different from cotton molecularly, morphologically, and in relation to chain length. Contaminants of various types from the pulp and other materials used in the process introduce significant differences to rayon that are not present in cotton. These differences result in significant differences in properties between cotton and rayon. As a consequence of the technological developments for regeneration of cellulose by man, a much wider range of fiber properties is obtainable from the man-made regenerated cellulose fibers than is possible from native celluloses such as cotton.

To a significant extent, molecular orientation can be influenced by conditions used in the viscose rayon process. The current viscose process, however, in all of its variant modes to produce various rayon fibers, gives very little room for changing the crystallinity level of rayon fibers, which is approximately 40 percent, as compared with cotton, which is about 60 percent. Because of the relatively fixed degree of crystallinity in regenerated cellulose, the so-called amorphous areas are also rather constant.

The differences that are obtained in cross sections of rayon fibers and their dyeability are influenced entirely by the process technology for preparing viscose solutions and the manner in which they are spun and subsequently stretched. The degree of coagulability and the rate of coagulation are the essential dependent variables that need to be controlled to obtain desired fiber properties.

Along the length or longitudinal direction, regular viscose rayon has a relatively uniform diameter

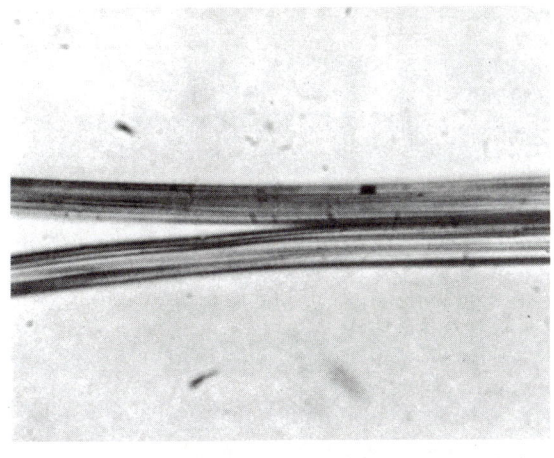

8.7 Photomicrograph 500× of regular rayon, longitudinal view. (Avtex Fibers, Inc.)

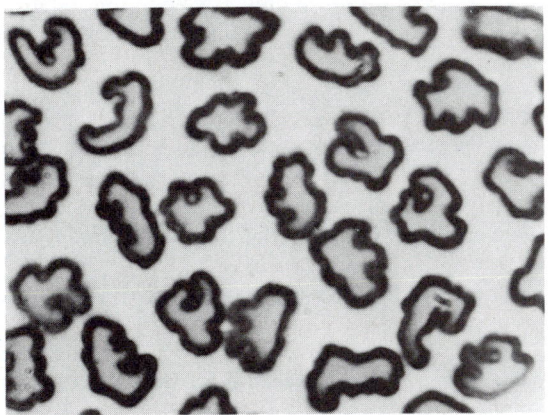

8.8 Photomicrograph 1075× of regular viscose fiber, cross section. (Avtex Fibers, Inc.)

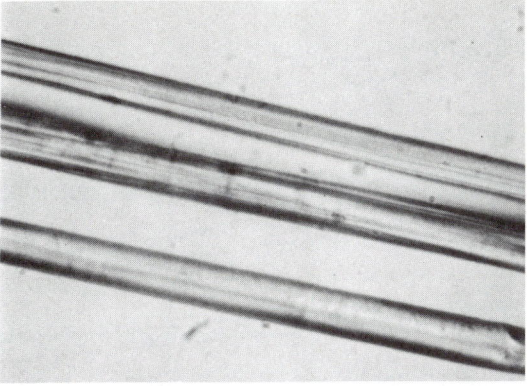

8.9 Photomicrograph 500× of high-wet-modulus rayon (Pivril IV), longitudinal view. (Avtex Fibers, Inc.)

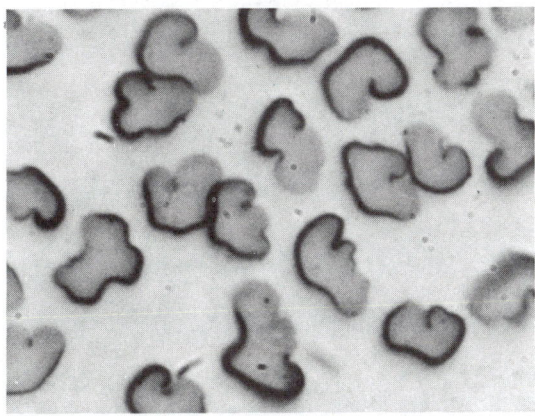

8.10 Photomicrograph 1075× of high-wet-modulus rayon (Avril IV), cross section. (Avtex Fibers, Inc.)

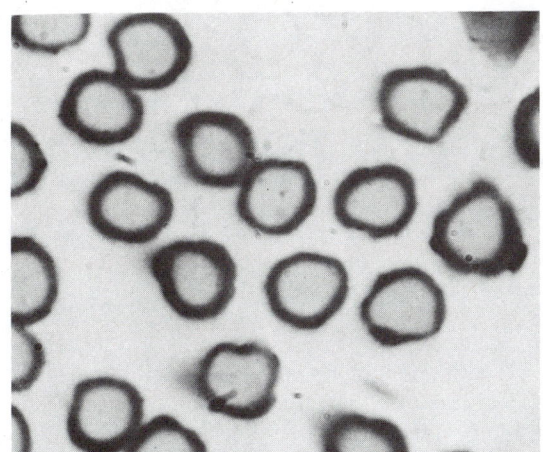

8.11 Photomicrograph of viscose showing skin and core formation. (Avtex Fibers, Inc.)

and may also appear to have *striations*. These striations are the result of light reflection by the irregular surface contour arising from the cross-sectional shape of the fibers (Figs. 8.7 and 8.8). A delustered fiber will have a grainy, pitted appearance, while bright fibers appear mainly transparent.

The cross sections of regular rayons are highly irregular and crenulated (Fig. 8.8) High-tenacity types, though irregular, have less pronounced crenulations; some may even have a bilobal appearance, a kidney bean shape. High-wet-modulus types come in several cross-sectional shapes—round, multilobal, and off round with a slight protrusion where the inside structure, or core, has penetrated the outside surface, or skin (Figs. 8.9 and 8.10). Figure 8.11 provides an example of the skin-and-core structure of viscose fiber.

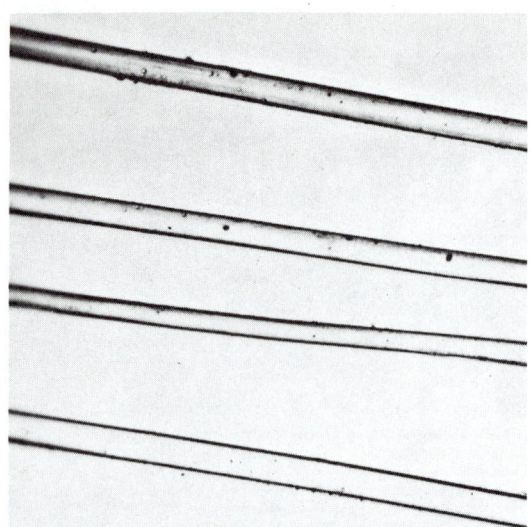

8.12 Photomicrograph of cuprammonium rayon, longitudinal view. (DuPont Company)

8.13 Photomicrograph of cuprammonium rayon, cross section. (DuPont Company).

Cuprammonium rayon, in the longitudinal view, appears uniform in width, has smooth surfaces, and exhibits no internal markings or striations (Fig. 8.12). The cross section is round or oval, it is relatively clear, and there are no irregularities in the contour (Fig. 8.13).

Physical Properties

SHAPE AND APPEARANCE Rayon fibers can be produced in any practical length desired. For continuous filament fiber, the length is determined or limited by the size of the package used to take up the newly formed filaments. Staple lengths are cut to lengths that can be practically processed. The apparent diameter is expressed as linear density in either denier or decitex. Commercially, rayon fibers with filament deniers in the range of 1 denier to as high as 1000 denier have been made, although there is very little rayon made where the per-filament denier exceeds 15. In terms of apparent denier, 1 denier is approximately 10 microns and 15 denier is approximately 40 microns.

LUSTER The luster of rayon can be controlled; it can vary from bright to dull. The addition of delusterants, mainly titanium dioxide, to the viscose solution provides the luster desired.

TENACITY (STRENGTH) Tenacity in grams per denier is given in Table 8.2 for the various types of rayon fibers. The dry strength of rayon indicates that it can be handled relatively easily; however, the wet strength denotes that care is required when working with fibers in the wet state.

The new high-tenacity and high-wet-modulus rayons are stronger than the regular viscose fibers and provide rayons with wet and conditioned tenacities that meet or exceed those of cotton.

ELASTIC RECOVERY AND ELONGATION The viscose process is modified to provide rayons that have low extensibility and high tenacity as well as rayons with high elongation and relatively low tenacity. These properties are incorporated into rayon by design and become inherent properties of each particular rayon type (see Table 8.2). Rayons can be engineered to provide characteristics concerning resistance to stress-strain, both conditioned and wet, that cover a broad range. The way in which yarns of staple fibers are formed and converted to fabrics, including treatment of fabrics, probably has more to do with the elastic properties of the fabric than do the elastic properties of the rayon fiber.

DENSITY The density of rayon fiber is about 1.5 grams per cubic centimeter. This is similar to natural cellulose and means that fabrics of rayon, when made exactly the same as fabrics of cotton, will be similar in weight.

TABLE 8.2 Properties of Rayon Fibers

Property	VISCOSE					Cuprammonium
	Staple Fibers				Filament	
	Regular	Intermediate Tenacity	High Performance	High Wet Modulus	High Tenacity	
Shape	Shape can be controlled by the manufacturer. Therefore, it is uniform in appearance. Length and denier are determined by the manufacturer for the desired end use. Available in both filament and staple. Diameter varies from 12 to 40 microns.					
Luster	Controlled by manufacturer. Can vary from dull to bright.					
Tenacity (g/d)						
conditioned*	2.4–3.0	3.1–3.4	3.8–4.4	4.0–5.0	4.0–6.5	1.7–2.3
wet	1.1–1.5	1.5–1.8	1.9–2.8	2.2–3.0	3.5–4.3	0.9–1.4
% Elastic recovery at 2%						
stretch	82	97		95		75
Wet modulus at 5%	2.3–2.0	2.3–3.0	4.0–5.5	6.0–9.5		
% Elongation at break						
conditioned*	19–24	20–23	24–27	15–23	9–26	10–17
wet	21–28	21–28	20–26	21–28	14–30	17–33
Resiliency	low	low	low	low	low–medium	low
Density (g/ccm)	About 1.5 for all types of rayon					
% Moisture regain						
conditioned*	10.7–16 for all viscose types					12.5
saturation	25–27 for all viscose types					27.0
Resistance to						
acids	Generally not good, but under some circumstances it may be acceptable.					
alkalies	Generally not good, but under some circumstances it may be acceptable.					
sunlight	average	average	average	good	good	good
microorganisms	Mildew will destroy all types of cellulosic fibers.					
insects	Silverfish will damage all types of cellulose fibers.					
Thermal reactions						
to heat	Extended exposure to high temperatures will eventually degrade the fiber.					
to flame	Flame-resistant rayon resists burning. Other rayons burn.					

*Conditioned environment = 65 percent relative humidity, 70°F ± 2°.

RESILIENCY The resiliency of rayon is relatively low, so rayon fabrics are soft, and, like cotton, require finishes if they are to provide adequate recovery from wrinkling, crushing, or creasing. High-wet-modulus rayon has better resiliency than regular rayon.

MOISTURE REGAIN The moisture absorption of rayon fibers at standard regain and saturation are given in Table 8.2 for the different types. The moisture regain for rayon is slightly higher than for natural cellulosic fibers. Because of this higher absorbency, rayon fibers tend to dye and to finish more readily than cotton. The higher absorption is due in part to the lower degree of polymerization; that is, there are more amorphous areas into which water, dyes, and/or finishes can be absorbed.

DIMENSIONAL STABILITY Regular rayons are subject to easy stretching during yarn and fabric manufacture, followed by relaxation shrinkage after laundering. High-wet-modulus viscose fibers have been designed so as not to stretch as easily and thus are less likely to suffer relaxation shrinkage.

The degree of relaxation shrinkage that occurs in rayon fabrics is the result of fabric construction more than of fiber characteristics. Tightly woven fabrics will exhibit less size change because of the compact arrangement of yarns and fabrics. Finishes are used on most rayon fabrics to control dimensional stability.

Thermal Properties

Rayon fibers burn like other cellulosic fibers, with a yellow flame and relatively rapidly. A small amount of light gray or off-white fluffy residue is left. When the flame is extinguished, there may be an *afterglow,* a tendency to glow or remain hot after the flame is extinguished.

Some new types of rayon contain flame retardants that are quite effective in creating desirable flame-resistant characteristics. Rayon fabrics, like other celluloses, may be scorched in ironing if the temperature is too high for too long a time. Ironing temperatures similar to those used for cotton are acceptable. Laundering temperatures should generally not exceed 140°F. High laundering temperatures are permissible, but manufacturer's label instructions should be followed.

Chemical Properties

EFFECT OF ALKALIES Since rayons are chemically similar to cotton, both types of fibers respond in somewhat the same manner to various chemical stimuli; however, rayon is perhaps more affected by chemical treatments than cotton because of the morphological properties, which are a result of the way in which the molecules are associated with each other. The hydroxyls from the cellulose in rayon are much more readily accessible to reaction than are those in cotton. Consequently, the chemical effects occur at a faster rate than they would with cotton.

EFFECT OF ACIDS Hot and cold concentrated inorganic acids cause rayon fibers to disintegrate. Hot dilute acids result in fiber breakdown, but cold dilute acids have little or no effect.

EFFECT OF ORGANIC SOLVENTS Rayon fibers have good resistance to dry-cleaning solvents and stain removal agents. Many other organic compounds appear to have little or no harmful effect on the fiber.

EFFECT OF SUNLIGHT, AGE, AND MISCELLANEOUS FACTORS Rayon fibers undergo deterioration when exposed to the ultraviolet rays of the sun for long periods of time. This is especially true for regular rayon, which is comparatively low in strength and tends to exhibit a shorter life when exposed directly to light. However, normal apparel and home furnishings, including draperies, have good resistance to ultraviolet light and provide satisfactory durability. All rayons have good resistance to aging and last for many years when properly

stored. They should be stored clean in dry, relatively dark areas.

Strong oxidizing agents attack and damage most rayon fibers, as they do other cellulose. Weak oxidizing chemicals, such as hypochlorite and peroxide bleaches, can be used safely on most rayons. The manufacturers of Zantrel® advise consumers to avoid peroxide bleach. It is essential that any bleach be properly diluted and used according to directions.

Static Charge

Rayon fibers do not build up static charges.

Biological Properties

Viscose and cuprammonium rayons are resistant to all insects. Silverfish, which may attack cellulose, may damage fabrics of rayon.

Mildew will destroy rayons of all types; soil increases the ease with which mildew forms on yarns and fabrics, thus accelerating the rate of damage. Cellulose, including rayon, is biodegradable; thus certain rot-producing bacteria will damage the fiber. Special finishes increase the resistance of rayon fibers to such organisms.

Use and Care of Rayon Fibers

Rayon fibers are used in apparel and home furnishings fabrics; for industrial use such as reinforcing yarns, tires, and various types of reinforced rubber products such as brake hose or radiator hose; and for a wide range of nonwoven products, including personal care products, medical and surgical products, and a wide variety of wipes.

Rayon as a reinforcing medium for automotive tires is a premium performing material. It has an important place in the market as a reinforcing fiber, mostly in rubber products. The area of nonwoven applications is a major one for rayon in all developed parts of the world. It is estimated that as much as 40 percent of all the rayon produced today in the United States is consumed by the industry's customers who are engaged in the manufacture and sale of nonwoven products.

Because it can be processed into either filament or staple form (Fig. 8.14), rayon offers more variety in fabric and yarn construction than do the natural cellulose fibers. Through control of fiber size, yarn number, fabric construction techniques, dyes, and

A

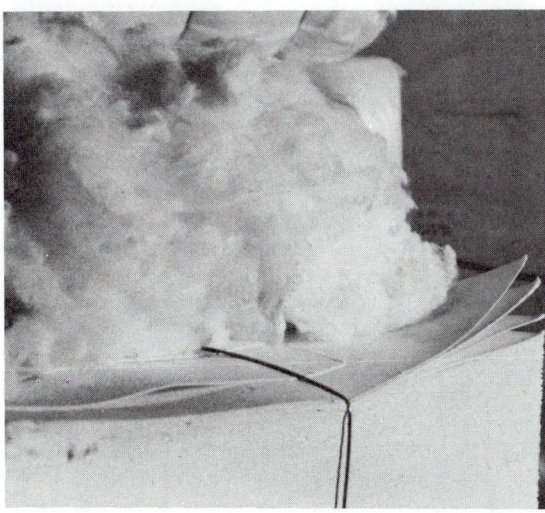

B

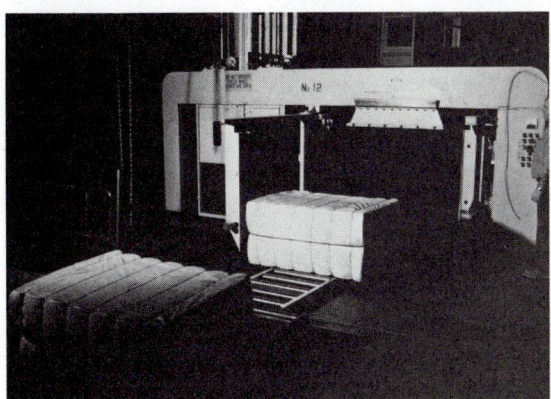

C

8.14 A: Filament viscose. B: Staple viscose. C: Packing fibers into bales. (Avtex Fibers, Inc.)

finishes, fabrics can be produced that are sheer to heavy, soft to firm, stiff to limp, in all colors including white. Simple, complex, or textured yarns can be made (see Parts Three and Four).

Blends or combination fabrics available to the consumer in 1984 included rayon and polyester; rayon and acrylic; rayon and cotton; rayon and flax; rayon, polyester, and acrylic; rayon and nylon; rayon and acetate; and rayon and wool. Rayon contributes absorbency and comfort when blended with other fibers; it also contributes styling, ease of dyeing, and softness. Rayon fabrics tend to stretch when wet and shrink upon drying. High-wet-modulus rayons have less potential for this than other rayon fibers. Rayon fabrics are stabilized against shrinkage by the use of chemical reactant finishes, or a combination of chemical reactant finishes and mechanical techniques such as Sanforizing®.

Although laundry treatment and handling are dependent on yarn and fabric construction, finish and color application, and fiber content, rayon is not damaged by detergents and other laundry aids such as starches, fabric softeners, and water softeners. When it is essential for appearance, rayons can be bleached with hypochlorite or peroxide bleaches. However, it is essential that any bleach be properly diluted prior to the addition of fabrics.

Flame-resistant fabrics may require special care. Labels should be provided, and the directions given should be followed carefully in order to maintain the flame-resistant property.

Although rayon fabrics can be ironed at medium to high temperatures, finishes used on the fiber may require medium to medium-low temperatures. In fact, since rayon is cellulose, it can tolerate the same general care given to cotton fabrics of the same type and with the same finishes and dyestuffs.

STUDY QUESTIONS

1. Cite the properties of viscose and cuprammonium rayon. How do they differ? In what way are they alike?
2. What are the modifications of viscose rayon that are available on the market at present? What are their characteristics? In what types of items would these fibers be used?
3. What are the advantages of rayon? the disadvantages?
4. How does high-wet-modulus rayon differ from regular rayon? What is meant by the term *high wet modulus*?

5. What considerations for care are necessary for handling rayon fabrics?
6. What is the chemical composition of rayon? How is it like or unlike natural cellulose fibers?
7. Compare the properties of rayon and cotton. Why do they differ despite the fact that they are both cellulose?
8. In what types of end uses are rayon fibers or rayon blends found?

Activities

1. Look at rayon fabrics and garments in apparel and home furnishings; determine what types of labels are given and care methods recommended. What particular end uses would be appropriate for fabrics of rayon?
2. Find various rayon fabrics on the market; study the labels, and cite the information given and the care procedures recommended.
3. What fiber blends can you find on the market that include various types of rayon?
4. Collect samples of various types of rayon fabrics and perform various tests in the laboratory to determine how they compare with standard values for physical and chemical behavior.

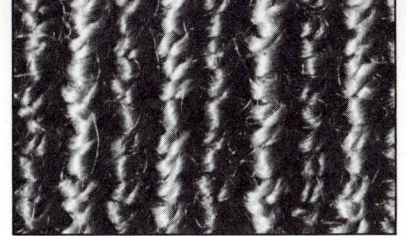

9

Modified Cellulosic Fibers: Acetate and Triacetate

KEY TERMS

acetate	dry spinning	spinning dope
acetylators	hydrolysis of acetate	triacetate
acid dope	secondary acetate	

Historical Review

Cellulose acetate, an ester of cellulose and acetic acid, was first produced in 1869 by Paul Schutzenberger. However, 35 years passed before a practical, safe, and a relatively inexpensive technique for producing the product was developed by Henri and Camille Dreyfus. At that time the primary use of cellulose acetate was in the form of lacquers, plastic film, and ''dope'' for use on early airplane fabrics. The first acetate fibers were produced in 1921 by the Dreyfus firm. In 1924, an allied organization began to produce acetate in the United States. Today, acetate is produced in the United States by Celanese Corporation, Avtex Fibers, Inc., and Eastman Fibers.

Triacetate fibers were developed along with regular secondary acetate. However, commercial manufacture of triacetate was delayed until the mid-twentieth century, at which time scientists found satisfactory and relatively safe solvents that were available in sufficient quantity to make production economically profitable. Another problem that had plagued the production of triacetate had been to locate dyes that would work on the fiber; this, too, was solved by the 1950s. The only triacetate fiber produced in the United States is Arnel®, produced by Celanese Corporation, which introduced it in 1952.

The nomenclature used for rayon, acetate, and triacetate fibers has been a problem. All through the first half of the twentieth century, both cellulose acetate fibers and rayon (regenerated cellulose fiber) were identified first as ''artificial silk'' and then as ''rayon.'' As the fibers are quite different in behavior, these names were misleading and frequently led to consumer dissatisfaction. With the passage of the Textile Fiber Products Identification Act, the problem of names has been alleviated to a great degree. In the United States, correct use of the terms is the normal practice; however, some foreign countries still tend to use the term *rayon* for both man-made cellulose fibers and modified cellulose fibers. For countries exporting to the United States, this practice is disappearing, and proper technology is commonly used.

Acetate is defined by the TFPIA as ''a manufactured fiber in which the fiber-forming substance is cellulose acetate. Where not less than 92 percent of the hydroxyl groups are acetylated, the term *triacetate* may be used as a generic description of the fiber.''

9.1 Feeding cellulose to a shredder. (Celanese Corporation)

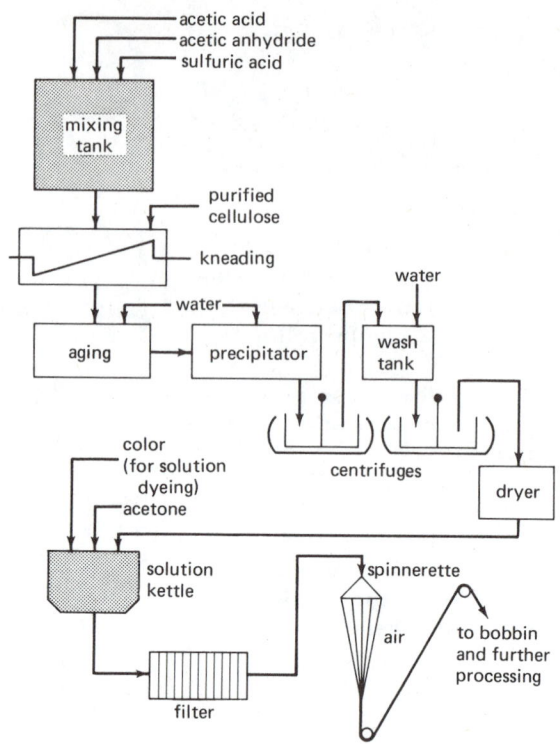

9.2 Flow chart showing process in acetate manufacture. (Celanese Corporation)

1. cellulose   +   acetic anhydride $\longrightarrow$ cellulose triacetate

2 anhydroglucose units $n*$

1 acetylated anhydroglucose unit

2. cellulose triacetate   +   water $\longrightarrow$ secondary acetate:

A ratio of 0.5 to 1.0 acetyl radical ($OOCCH_3$) per anhydroglucose unit is replaced by hydroxyl (OH) radicals. Exact order is unknown.

9.3 Chemical reactions in acetate manufacture.

94   Textile Fibers

Manufacture of Regular Acetate

The raw materials for manufacturing regular, or secondary, acetate include cellulose, acetic acid, and acetic anhydride, plus sulfuric acid as a catalyst. Cellulose from either wood pulp or cotton linters may be used, but wood pulp is the more common source. The cellulose is purified, bleached, and shredded (Fig. 9.1). Shredded cellulose is fed into pretreatment tanks, where it is thoroughly mixed with glacial acetic acid—35 percent based on weight of cellulose—and held for a specified time. A flow chart for the production of acetate is shown in Figure 9.2. Pretreated cellulose is transferred to kneading machines called *acetylators,* where acetic anhydride is added. During this step the pretreated cellulose assumes a liquid form as a new chemical compound, cellulose acetate. The chemical reaction is diagramed in Figure 9.3. At this point the cellulose acetate is a clear liquid called *acid dope.* It is emptied into special storage tanks, where it is aged or ripened. Water is added to the solution to reduce the acid concentration from 100 to 95 percent. During the ripening, hydrolysis occurs, which removes some of the acetyl groups from various parts of the cellulose molecule, replacing them with a hydroxyl radical and producing regular acetate (acetyl radical = $OOCCH_3$; hydroxyl radical = OH).

Upon completion of ripening, the secondary acetate is mixed with water, and the acetate precipitates out in the form of small flakes. The flakes are washed free of excess acid and dried. During the precipitation and washing, the excess acetic acid and the sulfuric acid are recovered for reuse, which helps reduce the cost of manufacture as well as pollution of the environment.

The cellulose acetate flake is dissolved in acetone to form the *spinning dope.* The dope is forced through filters to remove any undissolved acetate and impurities, then forced through a spinnerette into a warm-air chamber (Fig. 9.4). The acetone evaporates and is recovered; the acetate coagulates as it falls through the warm-air chamber. As the filaments travel downward, pulled by gravity, they are twisted together to form yarn (Fig. 9.5). The method of spinning acetate is *dry spinning.*

Manufacture of Triacetate (Arnel)

Triacetate is manufactured from the same raw materials as secondary or regular acetate. The process is identical with that used for regular acetate up to

9.4 Dry spinning of acetate fibers. The solution is forced through the spinnerette into an air chamber, where fibers are formed as the solvent evaporates in a heated environment. (Celanese Corporation)

9.5 Spinning filament. Using a vacuum device, the operator pulls filaments from the spinnerette to start winding a new bobbin, shown at bottom of photograph. (Celanese Corporation)

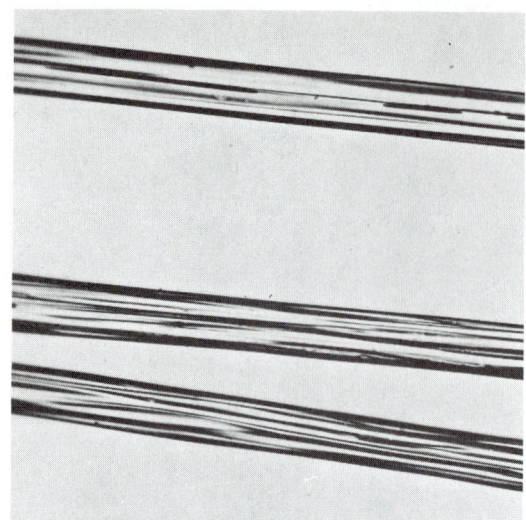

9.6 Photomicrograph of acetete, longitudinal view. (DuPont Company)

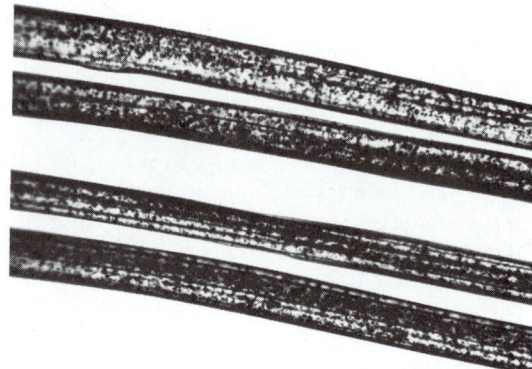

9.8 Photomicrograph of triacetate, longitudinal view. (DuPont Company)

9.7 Photomicrograph of acetate, cross section. (DuPont Company)

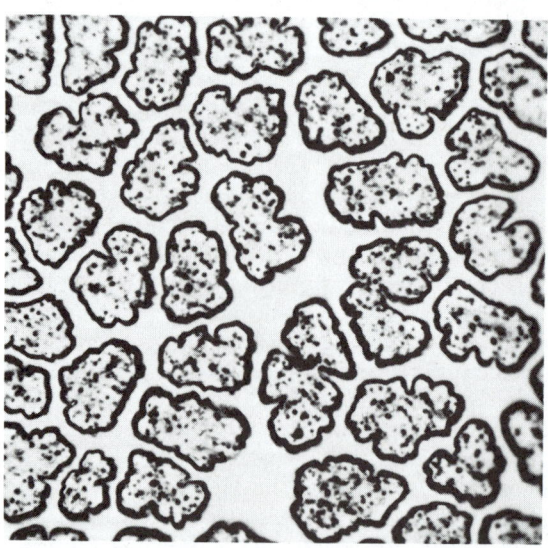

9.9 Photomicrograph of triacetate, cross section. (DuPont Company)

the ripening or aging step, which is omitted for triacetate. This eliminates any hydrolysis action and leaves the triacetate flake. The flake is dried, then dissolved in methylene chloride instead of acetone. Spinning is the same as for regular acetate: the solution is forced through the spinnerette into a warm-air chamber.

To produce triacetate fibers that have high crystallinity and stability, a heat treatment is applied. This causes the fibers to retain the form and shape they had at the time of the heat treatment. Either wet or dry heat may be used; safe drying temperatures are approximately 215°C, wet or steam temperatures are about 130°C.

Fiber Properties

Molecular Structure

Acetate is a polymer composed of units of cellulose acetate in which an average of 2 to 2.5 of the three OH units per glucose residue have been replaced by the acetyl radical, $OOCCH_3$. The degree of polymerization of acetate is between 350 and 400. Triacetate differs from acetate only in that more than 92 percent of the hydroxyl radicals have been replaced by acetyl groups. The degree of polymerization is similar for both secondary acetate and triacetate. The diagram of acetylated cellulose is given in Figure 9.3.

Microscopic Properties

In the longitudinal view, acetate can be seen as uniform in width, with several lines parallel to the length of the fiber (Fig. 9.6). These striations are farther apart in general than the striations in viscose rayon. Bright acetate is clear, whereas dull or pigmented acetate appears speckled or pitted. The cross section of acetate shows that the fibers are lobed in outline, with irregular curves, but there are no sharp points such as sometimes appear in viscose (Fig. 9.7).

Triacetate is very similar in microscopic appearance to acetate. Figure 9.8 shows a delustered triacetate filament, where in addition to the striations there is the speckled or pitted look associated with delustering. The cross section is lobed and similar to acetate (Fig. 9.9). A positive distinction between triacetate and regular acetate cannot be made by microscopic examination.

Physical Properties

SHAPE AND APPEARANCE Acetate and triacetate are man-made fibers and have the flexibility of such products—they can be made to any length and in a variety of diameters, from very fine to relatively heavy fibers. Spinnerettes can be made with orifices shaped other than round; this makes possible the production of a variety of different-shaped acetate and triacetate fibers. One of the better known is *crystal acetate,* a flat filament that has considerable sheen and crispness. The filaments, whether they are fine, medium, or heavy, can be combined in many ways to produce a wide variety of yarns (see Table 9.1).

LUSTER The luster of acetate and triacetate can be controlled as mentioned previously; thus, fibers can be obtained that are very dull, very bright and shiny, or at any stage between.

TENACITY (STRENGTH) Acetate has a dry tenacity of 1.2 to 1.4 grams per denier; when it is wet, the strength drops to 0.8 to 1.0 g/d. Triacetate (Arnel) possesses a dry tenacity of 1.1 to 1.4 g/d and a wet strength of 0.8 to 1.0 g/d. The strength of both acetate and triacetate fibers is relatively low when compared with that of many other fibers. However, the fibers have some desirable properties that make it attractive for use in selected types of apparel and home furnishings. These other properties may outweigh the low strength.

ELONGATION AND ELASTIC RECOVERY Acetate and triacetate have good elastic recovery and elongation. (Figures are cited in Table 9.1.) If stretched more than 1 percent, acetate undergoes some permanent deformation and will not return to its original size, but it still is adequate for many uses. Triacetate has slightly less recovery at 2 percent extension: 92 percent recovery, as compared with acetate at 94 percent. At 4 percent extension, however, triacetate is considerably better than acetate.

RESILIENCY Regular acetate does not have good recovery from crushing or wrinkling; its resiliency is low. Triacetate possesses good resiliency, and if it is properly heat-treated, wrinkles hang out quickly and relatively completely.

DENSITY The density of both secondary acetate and triacetate is 1.32. Both are lighter than regular cellulose, making it possible to construct some fabrics that are light in weight.

MOISTURE REGAIN Standard moisture regain for acetate is 6.5 percent, and for triacetate (Arnel) it is 3.2 to 3.5 percent. At saturation, acetate will absorb up to 14 percent moisture, whereas triacetate will absorb about 9 percent. When heat-treated, the standard regain for triacetate may be reduced to 2.5 to 3.0 percent.

DIMENSIONAL STABILITY Both acetate and triacetate fibers are comparatively resistant to stretch or shrinkage, except when relaxation shrinkage might occur because of tensions applied when constructing fabrics. The fiber may shrink when exposed to high temperatures. Triacetate is specially resistant to stretch or shrinkage.

TABLE 9.1 Properties of Acetate and Triacetate Fiber

Property	Acetate	Triacetate
Shape	Shape can be controlled by the manufacturer; therefore, it is uniform in observed appearance. Length and denier are determined by manufacturer for end use.	
Luster	Controlled for both. Can vary from dull to bright.	
Tenacity (g/d)		
dry	1.2–1.4	1.1–1.4
wet	0.9–1.0	0.8–1.0
Elastic recovery	100% at 1% extension	90–100% at 1–2% extension
	48–75% at 4% extension	80–84% at 4% extension
Elongation		
dry	25–35%	25–35%
wet	35–45%	30–40%
Resiliency	low	good
Density (g/ccm)	1.32	1.32
Moisture absorption		
20°C/65% R.H.	6.5%	3.2–3.5%
saturation	14.0%	9.0%
Dimensional stability	good	good
Resistance to		
acids	Both fibers have fair resistance to dilute acids and poor to concentrated acids.	
alkalies	Both fibers have good resistance to dilute alkalies; both are eventually destroyed in concentrated alkalies.	
sunlight	Loss of strength for acetate; triacetate has superior resistance.	
microorganisms	Both discolor; acetate will lose strength, but triacetate retains strength.	
insects	Silverfish will eat sized acetate or triacetate.	
Thermal reactions		
to heat	Softens and melts at temperature over 175°C.	Softens at temperature over 235°C; non-heat-treated at 170°C.
to flame	Both fibers burn easily and quickly.	

Thermal Properties

ACETATE Regular cellulose acetate is easily soft-ened by temperatures above 177°C (350°F). The fiber melts and burns evenly, forming a hard black bead ash or residue. It gives off a chemical odor or an odor similar to that of hot vinegar. Because of its sensitivity to high temperatures, the fiber should be ironed at low to medium settings with steam. If properly handled, permanent flattening of yarn and fibers for design effects—such as moiré taffeta—can be achieved by the use of controlled temperatures.

TRIACETATE (ARNEL) Triacetate melts and burns in the same manner as regular acetate. How-ever, triacetate can be heat-treated so that it will withstand temperatures near 212°C (450°F) with-out damage. The thermoplasticity of triacetate, cou-pled with the potential to heat-treat or heat-set the fiber, makes it possible to set permanent pleats and other shapes into triacetate fabrics.

Chemical Properties

EFFECT OF ALKALIES Dilute alkalies have little effect on either acetate or triacetate. Concentrated alkalies cause saponification of both and eventual loss in fiber weight and a reduction in the soft hand of fabrics.

EFFECT OF ACIDS Concentrated acids, both or-ganic and inorganic, weaken the fibers and in most instances cause complete fiber degradation. Hot acids, both dilute and concentrated, may cause decomposition or, at least, a loss of strength. Cold dilute acids may weaken the fiber if exposure is prolonged.

EFFECT OF ORGANIC SOLVENTS Most petroleum solvents used in dry cleaning do not damage acetate fibers. However, such solvents as acetone, phenol, and chloroform will destroy the fibers; trichloroethylene will swell them. One should be cautious when using fingernail polish remover near acetate, as it often contains acetone. Acetate should be handled carefully when removing stains, as some stain removers include chemicals that might damage the fibers.

EFFECT OF SUNLIGHT, AGE, AND MISCELLANEOUS FACTORS Acetate loses strength and may develop splits after prolonged exposure to sunlight. Over time, acetate will become weaker from aging, although storage away from light and circulating air will delay the process. Triacetate has excellent stability to aging and is more resistant to sunlight than acetate, silk, or nylon. Bright fibers of both secondary acetate and triacetate generally have better resistance to sunlight than delustered fibers. Special dull acetate variants have been developed for use in draperies.

Static Charges

All acetates, both regular and triacetate, develop static charges, especially when the air is very dry. The fibers are poor conductors of electricity, which contributes to the development of static.

Biological Properties

MICROORGANISMS Fungi such as mildew and bacteria may discolor acetate and triacetate. Some weakening of acetate may occur, but triacetate retains its strength.

INSECTS Moths and other household pests do not damage acetate fibers. However, silverfish may attack any sizing on acetates or triacetates.

Use and Care of Acetate and Triacetate

Regular acetate is used by many designers for its outstanding drapability and its desirable hand. Acetate can be made into fabrics of varying weight, thickness, degree of softness or stiffness, and appearance. Because of its thermoplastic property, one should make sure that laundering or dry cleaning is carried out at temperatures below those that might cause damage. Low temperature settings on irons and warm, not hot, water should be used. The relatively low moisture regain of acetate renders fibers resistance to damage by staining and to size change due to fiber shrinkage or stretch. Acetate fabrics should not be wrung or twisted when wet, for they retain wrinkles and creases and would require considerable ironing or steam pressing.

The fiber accepts special dyestuffs satisfactorily, and white acetate retains its whiteness without bleaching when laundered according to care instructions. If bleaching should be required, a minimum of mild bleach should be used. Acetate finds widespread use in such applications as outer apparel, including suits and dresses, jacket and coat linings, draperies, upholstery, and pillow covers. Considerable loungewear may be made of acetate.

Triacetate has the versatility and desirable properties of regular acetate, plus additional characteristics that influence its use and care. It is capable of receiving permanent pleats and creases that will withstand wear and maintenance through the use of heat-setting techniques. Triacetate is dimensionally stable and can be handled and maintained at higher temperatures than regular acetate. It is a little crisper than acetate but still has adequate softness and pliability for use in a wide variety of knitted and woven fabrics.

Fabrics of heat-treated triacetate are less thermoplastic and more hydrophobic; thus, they withstand high ironing temperatures, if needed, and dry in less time than non-heat-set acetate. Dimensional stability and easy-care performance during laundering are imparted to the fiber by the heat-setting techniques.

Triacetate is outstanding in knits, as these fabrics will hold their shape, retain permanent pleats, and pack well for travel. Celanese, the manufacturer of Arnel, maintains a trademark licensing program for the fiber. This means that any textile product to be labeled with the Arnel trade name must meet minimum specifications established by Celanese. Triacetate is available in filament form only.

Triacetate is more expensive than acetate and several other man-made fibers currently on the market. Solution-dyed acetate brings premium prices because of its special characteristics. Both triacetate and acetate are used in a variety of home furnishings, domestics, and apparel fabrics. Acetate fibers are used in various industrial applications; one of the most important is the use of acetate fiber as the filter media for cigarettes.

STUDY QUESTIONS

1. Compare the properties of acetate and triacetate. How do they differ? How are they alike?
2. Compare the properties of acetate and triacetate with pure cellulose fibers, both natural and man-made. How are they alike? How do they differ?
3. Why was the introduction of triacetate to the market delayed so long after the introduction of acetate and the actual discovery of triacetate?
4. What is the major difference in the manufacturing steps between acetate and triacetate?
5. What cautions must be exercised in the care of acetate and triacetate fabrics?
6. If you had a choice between acetate curtains and polyester curtains, which would you choose? When you have read the polyester chapter, return to this question and determine which choice would be best and why.

Activities

1. Visit apparel stores and find items that include either acetate or triacetate fibers. What types of apparel items are typical for these fibers? What price levels? Can you determine whether similar products are made from other man-made fibers? If so, how do prices compare? Repeat this activity for home furnishings made of acetate or triacetate.
2. Take samples of acetate and triacetate fabrics, and apply typical home spot removers, agents such as nail polish remover, and vinegar. See what happens when these products are placed on samples of these fabrics.
3. Take samples of acetate and triacetate, wash them by hand, and *wring* them to remove excess water. What happens to the fabrics?
4. Repeat activity 3 using fabrics of rayon. Compare the results with those you got for acetate and triacetate. Repeat with nylon and polyester fabrics.

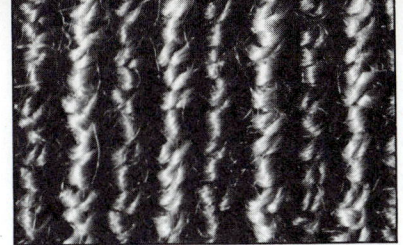

10

Polyamide Fibers: Nylon and Aramid

OBJECTIVES

◊ **To provide information concerning the manufacture of nylon and aramid fibers**

◊ **To describe the properties of the polyamide, nylon, and aramid fibers**

◊ **To identify typical end uses for nylon and aramid fibers**

◊ **To describe the interrelationships between the properties of nylon and aramid fibers and the typical end uses for these fibers**

◊ **To provide information concerning the less common variants and modifications of nylon fibers**

KEY TERMS

aramid
condensation polymerization
noncellulosic fiber

nylon
polyamide
synthetic fiber

NYLON

Historical Review

The history of nylon is a story of fundamental research. In 1927, E. I. DuPont de Nemours and Company decided to give a small group of scientists unrestricted funds to do research on macromolecular materials. Wallace Carothers was selected to head this unusual research team. The group was organized and started its investigation in 1928. One of the areas selected for study was giant molecules, called macromolecules, polymolecules, or polymers, that resembled the polymers found in natural fibers and existing plastic products. Scientific data accumulated, including the know-how to manufacture controlled linear polymers—giant molecules composed of relatively small molecules linked end to end (see Fig. 3.1).

In 1930 the chemists discovered an unusual characteristic in one of the polymers under investigation. It was found that when a glass rod in contact with molten polymer was pulled away slowly, a fine filament that hardened when exposed to cool

air was formed. Furthermore, it was observed that the cold filaments could be stretched several times their extruded length to produce a flexible, strong, and attractive fiber.

The next few years were devoted to improving the polymer, finding efficient methods for manufacturing it, developing necessary mechanical equipment for its production, and, perhaps most important, finding possible uses for the new fiber. In 1938 a pilot plant commenced operations, and in 1939 a large-scale plant was put "on stream" by DuPont at Seaford, Delaware.

Nylon, in the form of knitted hosiery, was test-marketed in various parts of the United States in late 1939 and early 1940. Introduction of the fiber to the general public was well planned and coordinated; it was a classic example of the successful mass marketing of a new product. Throughout the nation, heralded by well-planned advertising campaigns, nylon stockings were launched on May 15, 1940. They were a tremendous and immediate success. So much so, in fact, that people now use the term *nylons* to mean "hosiery."

The first nylon developed was type 6,6. The numbers derive from the fact that there are six car-

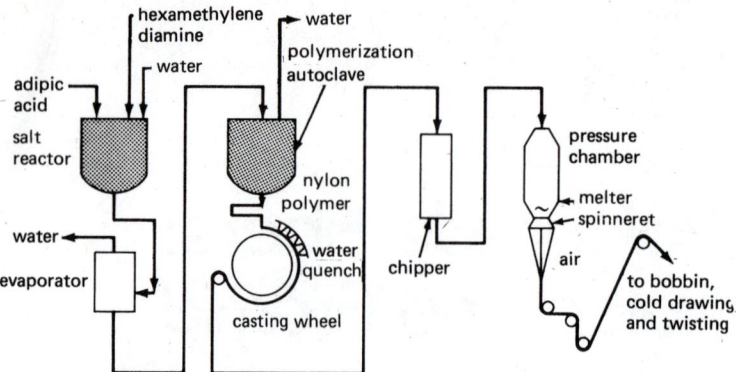

10.1 Flow diagram showing steps in manufacture of nylon 6,6.

$$HOOC(CH_2)_4COOH + NH_2(CH_2)_6NH_2 \rightarrow H_2O + HOOC(CH_2)_4CONH(CH_2)_6NH_2$$

adipic acid + hexamethylene → water + hexamethylenediamine
                diamine   adipamide

The polymer repeat is

10.2 Chemical reactions in nylon 6,6 manufacture.

n = times repeated in final molecule = 50–80+

bon atoms in each of the two chemicals used in making this product. Nylon type 6,10—composed of one chemical with six carbon atoms and one with ten—was developed simultaneously. Nylon 6,10 was used primarily for making bristles for toothbrushes, paintbrushes, and similar products. Since the mid-1940s many other types of nylon have been produced.

The original Textile Fiber Products Identification Act included *nylon* as one of the generic terms. Some of the nylons developed during the 1950s and 1960s did not conform to the definition of nylon as well as manufacturers wished; thus, they requested an additional generic term, and in 1973 the Federal Trade Commission added the generic term *aramid* to identify aromatic polyamides.

DuPont has stated that the real importance of nylon lay in the fact that, for the first time, science had returned to basic elements to create molecules tailored specifically for use as a textile fiber. Scientists had stopped trying to imitate the silkworm and had struck out on their own to create a fiber. These fibers, often called *synthetic fibers,* are made from raw materials that bear no resemblance to any type of textile fiber obtained from natural sources.

For some time nylon was the most used synthetic fiber. It has been exceeded by polyester since the late 1960s. Currently, it ranks third in amount of individual fiber used in the United States. Only polyester and cotton are used in greater quantities than nylon.

The TFPIA defines nylon as "a manufactured fiber in which the fiber-forming substance is a long-chain synthetic polymer in which less than 85 percent of the amide

$$\left(\begin{array}{c} -C-NH- \\ \parallel \\ O \end{array} \right)$$

linkages attach directly to two aromatic rings."

Manufacturing and Molecular Structure

Nylon 6,6

Nylon 6,6 is made of two basic chemicals, hexamethylene diamine and adipic acid, each containing six carbon atoms per individual molecule. The nylon is made by the linear condensation polymerization process (Fig. 10.1). This means that as a molecule of the acid and a molecule of the diamine join together, a small molecule—in the case of these two chemicals, water—is given off as a by-product of the reaction. Modern methods of manufacture involve the production of adipic acid from cyclohexane and hexamethylene diamine from benzene. The cyclohexane is usually derived from the distillation of petroleum.

Specific amounts of the acid and the diamine are combined in solution to form a salt called 1-aminohexamethylene adipamide, or nylon salt. This nylon salt is purified and then polymerized in an autoclave under an atmosphere of nitrogen. It is extruded in a ribbon form and chipped into small flakes or pellets. The polymer then is remelted and extruded through a spinnerette into cool air, where the nylon filament is formed. After cooling, the filaments are stretched or cold-drawn to orient the molecules in the fibers and develop fiber strength and fineness. According to data from some manufacturers, nylon fibers may be heated slightly to increase the ease and speed of drawing. Alternatively, the polymer may be produced continuously and pumped directly to the spinnerette instead of being made into flake or pellet form first.

The 6,6 polymer is composed of hundreds of molecules of adipic acid and hexamethylene diamine hooked together end to end to form the macromolecule. Nylon 6,6 has a molecular weight of 12,000 to 20,000. The degree of polymerization for this type of nylon varies from about 50 to more than 80. The chemical reactions involved in producing nylon 6,6 are given in Figure 10.2.

Nylon 6

Nylon 6 is manufactured by polymerization of caprolactam, a cyclic form of omega caproic acid having the formula $NH_2(CH_2)_5COOH$. The structure of caprolactam is diagramed as follows:

$$CH_2(CH_2)_4CONH$$

Or it can be structured as follows:

$$
\begin{array}{ccc}
 & CH_2 & \\
H_2C & & CH_2 \\
| & & | \\
H_2C & & CH_2 \\
| & & | \\
OC & - & NH
\end{array}
$$

The unit forming the nylon polymer repeat is indicated thus:

$$
\left(
\begin{array}{ccccccc}
H & H & H & H & H & & H \\
| & | & | & | & | & & | \\
-C & -C & -C & -C & -C & -C & -N- \\
| & | & | & | & | & & \| \\
H & H & H & H & H & & O
\end{array}
\right)_n \quad n = 200 \pm
$$

Like nylon 6,6, the nylon 6 polymer is formed under pressure in an autoclave. It is extruded and chipped into pellet or flake form, washed, dried, then melt-spun through the spinnerette. The filaments, like nylon 6,6, are cold-drawn.

Fiber Properties of Nylon 6,6 and Nylon 6

Microscopic Properties

Nylon filaments are smooth and shiny. When viewed in cross section, nylon can be round, trilobal, or square. Longitudinal magnification shows relatively transparent fibers of uniform diameter, with a slightly speckled appearance (Figs. 10.3–10.8).

Physical Properties

SHAPE AND APPEARANCE Nylon is a manmade fiber, so the diameter and length of the filaments are determined by the manufacturer. Very fine or relatively coarse fibers can be made, depending on the intended use. Fibers can be extruded for multifilament or monofilament yarns, or they can be formed as tow and cut for staple fiber use. A majority of the nylon fiber production is used in filament form.

LUSTER The luster of nylon can be controlled by the addition of titanium dioxide (TiO_2) and may vary from dull to very bright.

TENACITY (STRENGTH) One of the major advantages of nylon fibers is their strength. Regular nylon is stronger than most natural fibers, and manufacturers produce nylon in medium to high tenacities. Nylon 6,6 has a tenacity of 4.6 to 5.8 grams per denier for regular strength and 5.8 to 9.0 g/d for high-tenacity fiber. When it is wet, the strength may drop by 10 to 20 percent. Nylon 6 is made in three tenacities: regular, medium and high. Tenacity for regular is 3.5 to 5.8 g/d; for medium tenacity it is 6.0 to 7.0 g/d; and for high tenacity it is 7.7 to

10.3 Photomicrograph of delustered nylon 6,6, longitudinal view. (DuPont Company)

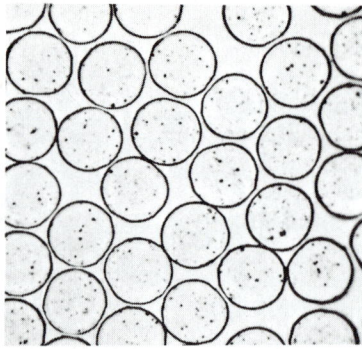

10.4 Photomicrograph of delustered nylon 6,6, cross section. (DuPont Company)

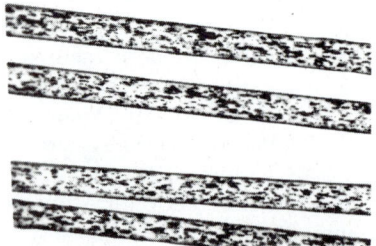

10.5 Photomicrograph of delustered nylon 6, longitudinal view. (DuPont Company)

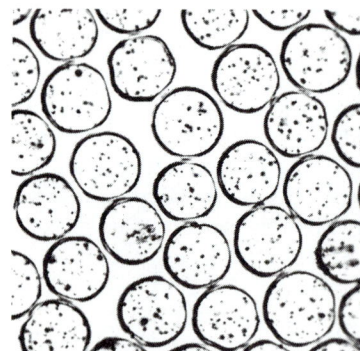

10.6 Photomicrograph of delustered nylon 6, cross section. (DuPont Company)

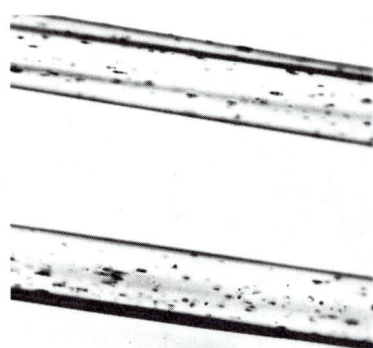

10.7 Photomicrograph of trilobal nylon 6,6, longitudinal view. (DuPont Company)

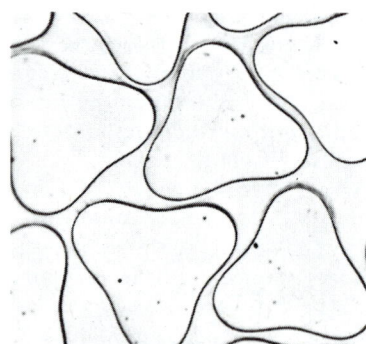

10.8 Photomicrograph of trilobal nylon 6,6, cross section. (DuPont Company)

9.0 g/d. When wet, nylon 6 loses between 10 and 15 percent of its strength (see Table 10.1).

ELASTIC RECOVERY AND ELONGATION
Nylon is a highly elastic fiber with good elongation properties. Recovery from a 4 percent extension is 100 percent. This contributes to outstanding shape retention for nylon fabrics. The return to shape and size, however, is not instantaneous; it may take several minutes before the product has completely returned to its original size. The use of elevated temperatures and moisture increases the rate and completeness of recovery from extension or stretch.

RESILIENCY Nylon has good to very good recovery from creasing, wrinkling, or crushing.

DENSITY The density of nylon 6,6 and nylon 6 is 1.14 grams per cubic centimeter. If nylon and cotton yarns of identical diameter were made into two identical fabric constructions, the nylon fabric would be considerably lighter than the cotton because of the lower fiber density for the nylon.

MOISTURE REGAIN Compared with natural fibers, nylon has rather low moisture absorbency. Nylon 6,6 has a 3.8 to 4.5 percent moisture regain at standard conditions; for nylon 6 the range is 3.5 to 5.0 percent. At conditions of 95 percent relative humidity, nylon fibers will absorb approximately 8 percent moisture. Nylon 6 has a slightly higher absorbency than nylon 6,6. The low moisture regain, plus poor electric conductivity, may cause an accumulation of static electric charges on nylon fabrics.

DIMENSIONAL STABILITY Because nylon is heat-sensitive, or thermoplastic, it can be heat-set during processing so that it will retain its shape during use and care. The fiber will stretch under stress but will return to its original size following release of the stress. (For details about heat setting, see

TABLE 10.1 Properties of Nylon 6,6 and Nylon 6

Property	Nylon 6,6	Nylon 6
Shape	Shape is controlled by the manufacturer. Filaments are uniform; length and diameter are determined by the manufacturer for specified types. Available in filament or staple; bright, semidull, or dull.	
Luster	Controlled from bright to dull.	
Tenacity (strength)		
dry	4.3–9.0 g/d	3.5–9.0 g/d
wet	4.0–7.6 g/d	3.2–8.0 g/d
Elastic recovery	100% recovery at 4% extension	
Elongation		
conditioned*	19–40%	16–50%
wet	20–46%	18–55%
Resiliency	good	good
Density	1.14 g/ccm	1.14 g/ccm
Moisture regain		
conditioned	3.8–4.5%	3.5–5.0%
wet	8.0%	8.5%
Dimensional stability	excellent	excellent
Resistance to		
acids	All nylon has poor resistance to acids. Some mineral acids and some organic acids dissolve nylon fiber.	
alkalies	All nylon has good resistance.	
organic solvents	Generally good for both types.	
sunlight	Sunlight is generally destructive unless special finishes have been added.	
microorganisms	high	high
insects	Resistant to most; may be damaged by ants, crickets, and roaches.	
Thermal resistance		
to heat	All nylon softens and melts if temperatures are above 250°C	210°C
ironing temperature	150°C	150°C
to flame	Heat-sensitive; shrinks from flame, melts, drips, burns in open flame; frequently self-extinguishing. Some finishes and dyestuffs may alter behavior in flame.	

*Conditioned environment = 65% relative humidity, 70°F ± 2°.

page 292.) Application of temperatures higher than those used for heat setting may cause fiber deformation and shrinkage. Therefore, in order to maintain dimensional stability, it is important to avoid high temperatures for most nylon products.

Thermal Properties

Nylon 6,6 melts at approximately 250°C (480°F) and nylon 6 at 210°C (400°F). All nylon can withstand temperatures to about 150°C (300°F) without damage, but when temperatures exceed 150°C for a few hours, the fibers will discolor. If temperatures approach 177°–205°C (350°–400°F), the fiber softens, discolors, and loses strength quickly. Low temperatures have no adverse effect on nylon.

Safe ironing temperatures for nylon 6,6 are considered to be between 150°C and 175°C (approximately 300°–350°F). Temperatures above 175°C should be used carefully to avoid glazing of fibers and yarns. Nylon 6 should be ironed, when necessary, at 150°C or less.

Nylon melts and tends to shrink away from a flame, forming a fine gray or tan residue that hardens as it cools. Fabrics of nylon are relatively flame-resistant since they are usually self-extinguishing after the source of flame is removed. The ignition temperature of nylon is about 530°C (980°F). The smoke is white or grayish in color.

Chemical Properties

EFFECT OF ALKALIES Nylon is substantially inert to alkalies.

EFFECT OF ACIDS Mineral acids, such as hydrochloric, nitric, and sulfuric, cause nylon to disintegrate or dissolve almost immediately. Even solutions of 3 percent at room temperature cause a noticeable loss in strength, and dilute solutions of hydrochloric acid will destroy the fiber. Formic acid at concentrations of 90 percent at room temperature will dissolve nylon 6,6; concentrations above 50 percent will attach nylon 6.

EFFECT OF ORGANIC SOLVENTS Most organic solvents have little or no effect on nylon. There are a few organic chemicals that do damage the fiber. Included in this group are various phenols frequently found in household disinfectants. Care should be observed when using these substances to prevent contact with nylon carpeting, nylon hosiery or other items of apparel, and nylon bristles.

Organic chemicals used for stain removal and dry cleaning, such as perchloroethylene, do not damage nylon.

EFFECT OF SUNLIGHT, AGE, AND MISCELLANEOUS FACTORS Sunlight has a destructive effect on nylon, and there is a marked loss of strength after extended exposure. If nylon is left in direct sunlight for several weeks, it may actually decompose. Bright nylon has better resistance to sunlight than delustered fiber. Special dyes have been developed for nylon that inhibit sunlight damage. These are important when the fiber must be subjected to sun for long periods of time.

Age appears to have little or no effect on the fiber. If stored away from light and other deleterious influences, nylon will last for many years.

Nylon is a very tough and very flexible fiber. In addition, it has excellent resistance to abrasion. However, the product itself may be abrasive and wear other fibers, fabrics, or surfaces.

Soaps and synthetic detergents do not damage nylon fibers. Most manufacturers state that bleaches, if properly diluted, can be used safely on all nylons unless the dyes are affected.

Static Charge

Nylon is not a good electrical conductor, and it will hold static charge until it can discharge it to a good conductor, such as the human body.

Biological Properties

Nylon is highly resistant to attack by most insects and microorganisms. However, some insects normally found outdoors, including ants, crickets, and roaches, will eat nylon if they are trapped in folds or creases. Microorganisms that produce mildew may attack finishes used on nylon but do not damage the fiber itself. Bacteria have no effect on nylon.

Other Nylons

Many other nylons are being manufactured in the United States as well as in other countries. Although nylon 6,6 and nylon 6 account for most of the nylon fiber used in the United States, these other, less common, nylons do have some interesting characteristics and are considered sufficiently important to be mentioned. These nylons are identified by either the same numbering system used for types 6,6 and 6 or by a combination of numbers and letters. The numbers, when used, identify the number of carbon atoms in the chemicals used in forming the polymer.

Nylon PACM-12

PACM-12 is prepared by polymerizing bis(*p*-aminocyclohexyl) methane with dodecanedioic acid

$$\left[\begin{matrix} H & & H & & & H & O & & O \\ | & & | & & & | & \| & & \| \\ N & \langle S \rangle & C & \langle S \rangle & N & C & (CH_2)_{10} & C \\ & & | & & & & & & \\ & & H & & & & & \end{matrix} \right]_n$$

This fiber was formerly produced under the tradename Qiana®. The fiber is no longer in production. Its properties were highly prized in luxury fabrics and included the following:

tenacity: about 3.5 g/d
elastic recovery: excellent
elongation: a potential to 35%
resiliency: excellent
density: 1.03 g/ccm
moisture regain: about 2%
dimensional stability: excellent
wash-and-wear properties: excellent

Qiana

The name Qiana is no longer applied to PACM-12 nylon. It is now a certification mark of E. I. DuPont de Nemours and Company for fabrics that are constructed to certain strict standards set by the company. The name Qiana is *not* restricted to a single fiber or generic group.

Nylon 11

Nylon 11 was developed in France, where it is trademarked Rilsan. The fiber has been widely marketed in Europe and in some areas of South America. Recently it has been produced in the United States in a monofilament form by Rilsan Corporation, a subsidiary of the French company.

Nylon 11 is a polymer of aminoundecanoic acid, which has the formula $NH_2(CH_2)_{10}COOH$. The product is polymerized through a series of steps and is melt-spun. The polymer repeat is

$$\left(-HN(CH_2)_{10}CO-\right)_n \text{ or } \left[-N-\left(\begin{matrix} H \\ | \\ C \\ | \\ H \end{matrix}\right)_{10} -C- \atop \| \atop O \right]_n$$

The fiber properties are similar to those of nylon 6 and 6,6, except that nylon 11 has a lower moisture regain, 1.8 percent; lower density, 1.04 g/ccm; and a lower melting point, 189°C (374°F). It has been stated that nylon 11 does not discolor or turn yellow or gray as quickly as do types 6,6 and 6. The low density makes it adaptable for making into bulked yarns.

Nylon 4

Nylon 4 is made by polymerizing 2-pyrrolidone to form polypyrrolidone. The polymer repeat is

$$\left[-\left(\begin{matrix} H \\ | \\ C \\ | \\ H \end{matrix}\right)_3 -C-N \atop \| \quad | \atop O \quad H \right]_n$$

It has been compared with natural fibers in terms of moisture regain or absorbency, which is higher for nylon 4 than for cotton. Other properties are similar to nylon 6 and 6,6. Commercial development has been slow because of difficulties encountered during spinning and economic problems.

Nylon 3 and Dimethyl Nylon 3

Nylon 3 is made by polymerizing acrylamide to form poly b-alanine, that is,

$$\left(\begin{matrix} H & H & & H \\ | & | & & | \\ -C & -C & -C & -N \\ | & | & \| & \\ H & H & O & \end{matrix}\right)_n$$

As yet this has not been produced commercially, but the fiber exhibits useful properties, including a high degree of stability to light, a characteristic not found in the more common nylons. The literature still identifies nylon 3 as being under consideration as an economically viable fiber.

Dimethyl nylon 3 is made by polymerizing 4,4-dimethyl azetidin-2-one to form the polymer repeat

$$\left(\begin{matrix} H & CH_3 & H \\ | & | & | \\ -N-C- & & C-C \\ | & | & \| \\ & CH_3 & H & O \end{matrix}\right)_n$$

The manufacturing procedure is similar to that used to make nylon 6. Unlike nylon 6, however, the fiber is solution-spun, since it would decompose during melt spinning. Properties include a tenacity of about 3 grams per denier, an elongation of about 40 percent, and a moisture regain of 4.5 percent.

Nylon 7

Polyheptanoamide, nylon 7, is made in the Soviet Union under the name Enant. The polymer repeat is

$$\left(\begin{matrix} H & H & H & H & H & H & H \\ | & | & | & | & | & | & | \\ -N-C-C-C-C-C-C- \\ | & | & | & | & | & | & \| \\ H & H & H & H & H & H & O \end{matrix}\right)_n$$

The fiber is similar to nylon 6,6 and nylon 6, but nylon 7 has great stability to heat and ultraviolet light. The moisture regain is slightly lower than that of nylon 6.

Nylon 12

Nylon 12 is polymerized from dodecalactam. The repeat is

$$\left(\begin{matrix} H & H & H & H & H & H & H & H & H & H & H \\ | & | & | & | & | & | & | & | & | & | & | \\ -N-C-C-C-C-C-C-C-C-C-C-C- \\ | & | & | & | & | & | & | & | & | & | & \| \\ H & H & H & H & H & H & H & H & H & H & O \end{matrix}\right)_n$$

The fiber has a low moisture regain, superior stretch properties and elastic recovery when wet, greater resilience than regular nylons, and a silklike hand. Other properties are similar to nylons 6,6 and 6. Some nylon 12 is being made in the United States in monofilament form.

Nylon 6T

Nylon 6T is made by polymerizing hexamethylene diamine with terephthalic acid. The polymer repeat is

$$\left(-N - \underset{\underset{H}{|}}{\overset{\overset{H}{|}}{C}} - \underset{\underset{H}{|}}{\overset{\overset{H}{|}}{C}} - \underset{\underset{H}{|}}{\overset{\overset{H}{|}}{C}} - \underset{\underset{H}{|}}{\overset{\overset{H}{|}}{C}} - \underset{\underset{H}{|}}{\overset{\overset{H}{|}}{C}} - \underset{\underset{H}{|}}{\overset{\overset{H}{|}}{C}} - \underset{H}{\overset{H}{N}} - \underset{O}{\overset{}{C}} - \langle\!\!\!\bigcirc\!\!\!\rangle - \underset{O}{\overset{}{C}} - \right)_n$$

Properties of nylon 6T include a high melting point of 370°C (700°F); density of 1.21 g/ccm; moisture regain of 4.5 percent; tenacity slightly lower than nylon 6,6; and elastic properties slightly higher than nylon 6,6.

The fiber has superior thermal properties. It retains all of its strength after exposure to 185°C (365°F) for 5 hours and 60 percent after exposure at 220°C (438°F) after 5 hours. Regular nylon has no strength after exposure at 220°C and less than half after exposure at 185°C for several hours. Nylon 6T has been a precursor to the development of aramid fibers such as Nomex.

Nylon 6,10

This nylon is made from hexamethylene diamine and sebacic acid. The polymer repeat is

$$\left(-N - (CH_2)_6 - \underset{\underset{O}{\|}}{\overset{\overset{H}{|}}{N}} - \underset{}{\overset{}{C}} - (CH_2)_8 - \underset{O}{\overset{\|}{C}} - \right)_n$$

This nylon has a melting point of 214°C (417°F), which is much lower than that of nylon 6,6; a moisture regain of 2.6 percent; and outstanding resilience. The most common uses for nylon 6,10 are for bristles in a variety of types of brushes and for various plastic forms. It is seldom used for multifilament yarns for conversion into textile fabrics.

Nylon 46

A new nylon fiber, nylon 46, was introduced in the spring of 1984. It is claimed to have characteristics superior to conventional nylons for engineering and industrial use. Trademarked Stanyl®, the fiber is made by interacting 1,4-diaminobutane (DAB) and adipic acid.

$$H_2N - (CH_2)_4 - NH_2 + HOOC - (CH_2)_4 - COOH \rightarrow$$
$$H[-HN - (CH_2)_4 - NH - CO - (CH_2)_4 - CO -]_nOH$$

Fiber properties include a density of 1.18; melting temperature of 300°C; superior dimensional stability; a modulus of 20 grams per denier; and tenacity of 9.5 grams per denier. It is aimed at industrial uses.

Nylon Modifications

In addition to developing nylon fibers from new chemicals, fiber scientists have been actively involved in modifying the common forms of nylon 6,6 and 6 to provide variants with special characteristics.

CROSS-SECTIONAL CHANGES Original nylon fibers were round in cross section; modified cross sections include hollow filaments, triangular, irregular, trilobal, and other multilobal shapes. These changes are made possible by altering the shapes, arrangements, and number of orifices in the spinning jet and by incorporating various additives in the spinning melt.

Modified cross sections can produce many desirable qualities, such as increased cover; a crisp, silklike, firm hand; reduced pilling; increased bulk; sparkle effects; and heightened resistance to soil. Trilobal nylon is available in various fiber deniers or diameters and is widely used in apparel, floor coverings, and other home furnishing fabrics.

TEXTURED NYLON Nylon filaments can be texturized to add bulk and/or stretch (see Chapter 19). In addition, special manufacturing processes produce filaments that will develop crimp during finishing operations. These producer-textured fibers require careful handling during fabric making, but the end product has characteristics appealing to consumers, such as good elongation and outstanding recovery from stretch. The fiber also exhibits good cover, is opaque, and makes lightweight fabrics.

BICOMPONENT FIBERS   Several examples of bicomponent polyamide fibers have been on the market at various times. The major bicomponent is composed of two nylon variants with different shrinkage potentials. Upon exposure to heat, a latent crimp is developed, as one component shrinks more than the other. The fiber has superior fit retention and resilience, which makes it highly desirable for women's hosiery. Other bicomponent nylons include a sheath-core type made in England and a side-by-side type made in Japan. The former is used in carpets and bonded fiber fabrics, whereas the latter is used primarily for stretch underwear and hosiery.

BIGENERIC FIBERS INCLUDING NYLON   Several bigeneric filaments have been made of nylon plus some other fiber from a different generic group. These can be made using different techniques, but the matrix form is most common. A new bigeneric that has recently been announced is No Schock® nylon. This is considered bigeneric, although it is 98.2 percent nylon; the remaining portion of the fiber is carbon. Others include a stretch fiber of nylon and spandex and a fiber of nylon and olefin used in melded fabrics for highly specialized uses.

A bigeneric yarn identified as T-278 has recently been introduced. This is a cospun yarn composed of 60 percent polyester by weight and 40 percent nylon. The filament count is actually 50/50. It is used in certain certified fabrics and has been identified by various names, including Monece® and Bitrece®. Properties cited for Monece® include a glowing luster, satiny surface, durable pleating potential, wrinkle resistance, antistatic, good covering power, and good drapability. It has been promoted for sleepwear, loungewear, and lingerie.

CROSS-LINKED NYLON   Nylon molecules can be cross-linked by adding chemicals characterized by reactive groups at both ends of the molecule. This chemical reacts with either the terminal amine group or the terminal carboxyl group on the nylon molecules, and adjacent molecules within the fiber hook together to provide greater stability. These fibers are especially useful in tires, where an increase in modulus is desired.

GRAFT POLYMERIZATION   Nylon fibers can be modified by grafting other chemicals onto the fiber molecules. One important property that may be altered in this way is moisture absorbency. It can be increased sufficiently to make a relatively comfortable fabric; in addition, as the moisture regain is increased, the buildup of static charges decreases.

ANTISTATIC NYLON   Several nylons have been introduced that are characterized by reduced static buildup. This may be accomplished by several processes, but the most common involves the addition of a small amount of a conducting polymeric substance to the melt solution before filaments are spun. These fibers have a silklike luster, good covering power, resistance to soiling, and superior whiteness retention.

Another approach is to coat nylon filaments with a microscopic layer of metallic substances. Antistatic nylons may be made also by finishing processes (see page 306).

Anso-X® is a durable static-controlled fiber developed primarily for carpets and other home furnishing fabrics; other fibers from the same manufacturer with static control include Anso IV®, Anso IV HP® (which has a modified cross section and a soil- and stain-resistant modifier), Anso IV® with Halofresh® (which has a modified cross section, soil resistance, durable static control, and antimicrobial protection). Natural Touch® is available as a staple fiber with soil-hiding properties and antistatic characteristics. Static-Guard® nylon has an antistatic filament added to a base yarn of nylon. It is used primarily for carpeting and other home furnishings.

MODIFICATION OF DYEING BEHAVIOR   Nylons that accept different types of dyestuffs are produced by incorporating small amounts of special chemicals into the polymer. Nylon with different dye affinities are combined in some carpets to produce special color patterns.

REDUCTION OF DAMAGE BY LIGHT   Antioxidants and light-absorbing chemical substances can be added to the melt before spinning to reduce damage from exposure to light and ultraviolet rays. In addition to reducing damage from light, they reduce discoloration. They also reduce strength somewhat.

Use and Care of Nylon

Nylon is widely used in fabric for apparel, home furnishings, industrial applications, and geotextiles. It has proved to be the leading fiber in the manufacture of women's hosiery and lingerie. For outerwear, it is used in woven and knitted fabrics; in addition, it is often used with other fibers in blends to provide fabrics with good dimensional stability, elastic recovery, shape retention, and abrasion resistance.

Many carpeting materials and upholstery fabrics are made of nylon because it wears well, is easy to clean, and does not require special protection against moths and carpet beetles. Trilobal and hollow filament nylons are popular in carpetings because they resist crushing, do not show soil quickly, and retain an attractive appearance.

Nylon is easy to launder. It can be washed safely at all laundry temperatures and drip-dried or tumble-dried. However, it is best to launder at medium to low temperatures and iron at low temperatures when necessary, in order to reduce unnecessary wrinkling or imparting wrinkles that cannot be removed by normal home care. Frequently, nylon fabrics do not require ironing. When tumble-drying nylon items, it is important to remove them as soon as the tumbling action stops to prevent new wrinkles from being set into the fabric.

Most manufacturers of nylon state that any type of soap or synthetic detergent may be used. Most stain removal agents will not damage the fiber. Although many bleach labels indicate that the product can be used safely on nylon, fiber manufacturers suggest that bleach be used as seldom as possible.

A major problem encountered in laundering nylon items is that they tend to scavenge color and soil from other items during the washing. This results in gray or discolored articles that may be difficult, if not impossible, to restore to their original appearance. White nylon fabrics are particularly vulnerable to such behavior and therefore should be washed alone or with other white items only. It is important to rinse nylon articles thoroughly; sometimes colored detergents, if not completely removed by rinsing, may leave color in white nylon fabrics.

Several special nylons have had a fluorescent whitening agent added to the spinning melt to retard discoloration of white nylon during normal use and care. The use of whitening and brightening agents in the laundering process should also help to retain fabric whiteness.

Modern dyestuffs, if selected wisely and applied properly, produce fast colors on nylon fabrics. However, it is essential that all excess dye be removed. Care must be used to avoid streaky and uneven dyeing.

Pilling, the formation of tiny balls of fiber on the surface of the fabric, is a severe problem with fabrics made of spun nylon yarns. Pills form quickly on yarns of staple fibers, since the nylon fibers are extremely strong and the pills are not rubbed off after they form, as would occur on fabrics made from fibers with less strength.

If nylon fabrics are to be comfortable in apparel, it is important to provide adequate air spaces, or interstices, between yarns to permit the passage of water vapor. Some finishing processes have improved the wicking property of nylon, while others can improve its absorbency. Such finishes or fabric constructions increase wearer comfort by aiding in drawing moisture away from the body.

The ability to heat-set nylon makes it possible to build in various surface designs such as embossed effects. Puckered or crinkled nylon can be made by using chemical finishing (see Chapter 27).

ARAMID FIBERS

The definition of aramid fibers as stated in the amendment to the Textile Fiber Products Identification Act is

a manufactured fiber in which the fiber-forming substance is a long-chain synthetic polyamide in which at least 85 percent of the amide

$$
\left(
\begin{array}{c}
\quad\quad H \\
\quad\quad | \\
-C-N- \\
\;\parallel \\
\;O
\end{array}
\right)
$$

linkages are attached directly to two aromatic rings.

Aramid fibers on the world market include Nomex®, Kevlar®, Conex, Fenilon, Arenka, and Kermel. Of these, Nomex and Kevlar from DuPont are the most important to the United States market. Aramid fibers were developed primarily for their inherent heat resistance and high strength.

The aramids are wet- or dry-spun from a solution. Nomex, poly (*m*-phenylene isophthalamide), is made by reacting metaphenylene diamine with isophthalic acid; it is dissolved in a solvent and extruded into hot air. The fiber is drawn to develop fiber properties. The formula repeat for Nomex is

$$\left(-\overset{\overset{\displaystyle H}{|}}{N}-\underset{}{\bigcirc}-\overset{\overset{\displaystyle H}{|}}{N}-\underset{\underset{\displaystyle O}{\|}}{C}-\underset{}{\bigcirc}-\underset{\underset{\displaystyle O}{\|}}{C}-\right)_n$$

Kevlar, poly (*p*-phenylene terephthalamide), is made from paraphenylene diamine and terephthaloyl chloride. They are first dissolved in a solvent, which is then added to a strong mineral acid such as sulfuric acid. Filaments are extruded into a short air space and then into water or dilute sulfuric acid. Drawing is not required to develop fiber properties, but fibers are heat-treated to increase the modulus of the fiber. The repeat is

$$\left(-\overset{\overset{\displaystyle H}{|}}{N}-\underset{}{\bigcirc}-\overset{\overset{\displaystyle H}{|}}{N}-\underset{\underset{\displaystyle O}{\|}}{C}-\underset{}{\bigcirc}-\underset{\underset{\displaystyle O}{\|}}{C}-\right)_n$$

Fiber Properties

NOMEX® Nomex is somewhat dog-bone-shaped in cross section and smooth in longitudinal view. It is available in filament, staple, or paper forms. The tenacity of filament Nomex is 5.3 grams per denier when dry and 4.1 g/d when wet. Elongation is 22 percent at standard conditions and 16 percent when wet. The density is 1.38 g/ccm. Moisture regain is 3.5 percent, but as relative humidity increases, moisture regain increases to nearly 8 percent at the saturation point.

Dimensional stability is excellent at normal conditions. In boiling water Nomex will shrink about 1 percent, and if exposed repeatedly to water at the boiling point it will shrink slightly over 3 percent. In dry heat no change occurs until temperatures above 260°C (500°F) are reached, at which point about a 1 percent shrinkage may occur.

The most important property of Nomex is its resistance to temperature and flame. The fiber retains useful properties at temperatures up to 370°C (700°F); however, temperatures above that cause rapid degradation. At the temperature where nylon 6,6 will melt, Nomex aramid retains at least 60 percent of its strength. The initial modulus of Nomex, the resistance to initial pull or stretch, is four times greater than that of nylon 6,6. The fiber has low flammability and is self-extinguishing when removed from a flame source. Various finishing and processing agents may reduce flame resistance.

Resistance of Nomex to alkalies is good to all but sodium hydroxide at elevated temperatures and in concentrations of 50 percent or more. Acid resistance is better than for nylon 6,6, but acids still affect this aramid fiber and are particularly damaging if concentrated and warm or hot.

Most organic compounds have little or no damaging effect on Nomex. Bleaching agents are safe except for sodium chlorite at warm temperatures. Sunlight and ultraviolet rays degrade Nomex and bring about a color change. If the fiber is to be used in outdoor applications, it should be protected from ultraviolet light.

Nomex is difficult to dye, but can be colored in a limited range of medium to dark shades. It is also available in color-sealed yarns in several shades.

KEVLAR®, KEVLAR 29, AND KEVLAR 49 Kevlar and Kevlar 29 are similar and will be discussed together under the single term *Kevlar*. This aramid fiber has an extremely high tenacity, approximately 22 grams per denier, which is more than five times the strength of a steel wire of the same weight and more than twice the strength of high-tenacity industrial nylon, polyester, or fiberglass. It has an unusually high initial modulus of 476 grams per denier. This is about two times greater than fiberglass or steel, four times greater than industrial polyester, and nine times greater than industrial nylon. Moisture regain is about 7 percent. Elongation is low, only about 4 percent.

Thermal properties of Kevlar are superior. It has outstanding stability to heat, retaining a high percentage of strength after exposure to temperatures to 260°C (500°F). Kevlar has superior resistance to most chemical reagents. Acids do cause a loss in strength, and hydrochloric acid and nitric acids completely degrade the fiber. Concentrated alkalies at elevated temperatures attack the fiber and damage it.

Kevlar 49 has a strength similar to regular Kevlar, but the modulus of Kevlar 49 is nearly twice that of regular Kevlar. Elongation is 2.5 percent, density is 1.44, the fiber is round, and moisture regain is 3.5 to 4.5 percent at standard conditions.

Thermal properties of Kevlar 49 are similar to those of other Kevlar fibers, with a superior stability to temperatures up to 700°F and good stability to temperatures above that level.

Chemical resistance of Kevlar 49 is excellent except for a loss of strength when exposed to hydrofluoric, nitric, or sulfuric acid in concentrated form.

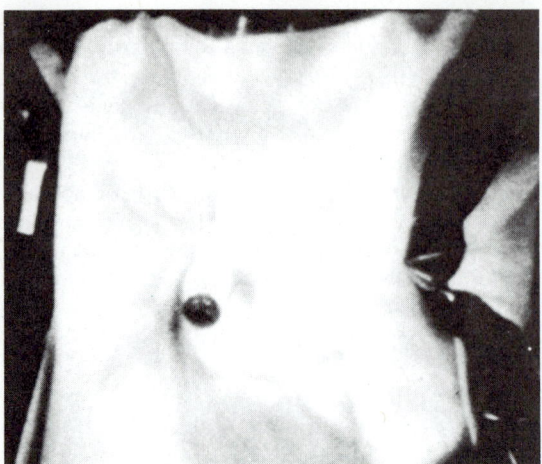

10.9 Kevlar as armor fabric. In a test conducted at the U.S. Army's Edgewood Arsenal, a bullet fired at Kevlar fabric from a .38 caliber handgun at a range of 10 feet (3 m) rebounds without penetration. (DuPont Company and U.S. Army photo)

Uses of Aramid Fibers

A popular use of Kevlar aramid fibers is in the manufacture of tire cord. The advantages of aramid-reinforced tires are that they are lighter in weight than those using glass or steel fiber, they give good performance at sustained high speeds, and they have a lower resistance to running and therefore save on fuel consumption. They run cooler than other tires. They are made on existing equipment, they cost less than steel-reinforced tires, and they have outstanding durability.

Nomex aramid fibers have two main types of uses: where resistance to combustion and low smoke generation are required, and where chemical stability and durability and high temperatures are needed. Typical uses for Nomex include protective suits for fire fighters, race car drivers, and employees in plants where heat and fire pose a hazard; aircraft furnishings; hot gas filtration fabrics; electrical insulation; covers for laundry presses and ironing boards; selected components of space vehicles; and portions of apparel for space personnel.

Kevlar is used in a variety of applications. One of the most interesting and important uses is in body armor or bulletproof vests, and it is credited with saving numerous lives of police officers. This use depends on the high strength of the fiber and, most

important, the high modulus (Fig. 10.9). It was also used as structural reinforcement for the *Gossamer Albatross,* the first man-powered aircraft to fly the English Channel. Other uses for the fiber include:

> bracing belts in high performance radial tires, where Kevlar gives improved durability and good ride characteristics
>
> high-pressure hoses
>
> conveyor belts
>
> ropes and cables used as antennae supports, oceanographic cables, crane ropes, boat rigging, helicopter hoist cables, special cables for deep-sea workstations
>
> a reinforcement for concrete in various types of construction processes.
>
> making booms to control oil spills and aid in mop-up operations
>
> many parts of the space shuttle *Columbia*
>
> fiber reinforcement for resins, which in turn are used in space vehicles, body panels for Formula I race cars, boats of various types, and some sports car bodies

Care of aramid fibers may not be encountered by the typical consumer. However, if care is required, the fiber may be laundered and dried much like nylon products.

STUDY QUESTIONS

1. What contribution to textiles was made by the discovery of nylon?
2. Identify the differences in properties between nylon 6,6 and nylon 6. How do these differences influence use and care?
3. How do the general properties of nylon influence use and care?
4. Cite typical end uses for nylon fibers, and discuss why nylon is appropriate to such uses.
5. How do nylon and aramid fibers differ? How are they alike?
6. What are the major properties of the aramid fibers?
7. The aramid fibers are generally found in what types of end-use products? Why?
8. Why has nylon been the major fiber used for hosiery?
9. Nylon can be used in blends with wool. What characteristics would the nylon provide and why is it a good fiber to blend with wool?

Activities

1. Locate resources that will provide information on the special uses for aramid fibers, and describe why this type of fiber is suitable to those uses. Do the same for nylon, particularly new nylon variants or modifications.
2. Visit stores and determine what types of products are made of nylon.
3. Visit police stations and determine whether they use Kevlar aramid bulletproof vests or other items of apparel. If so, have they observed many cases where the aramid fiber has saved lives?
4. The hydrophilic, hydrophobic, and oleophilic properties of fibers are important in care and comfort. The following activity can provide some idea of these properties in relation to fibers. It can be applied to any of the fibers, and comparisons could be made among them as well as with nylon fibers alone.

   Pour a small amount of water or a small amount of oil into a shallow container. Place small tufts of fiber on the surface of the liquid. Do not mix fibers. Measure the time required for the tufts to absorb enough liquid to cause them to sink. Classify the fibers as to whether they absorb water or oil or both. Explain your results in terms of fiber properties and then indicate how this information would influence use and care of the fiber.
5. Visit fire stations or industries where aramid fibers may be used for protection. Determine what the reaction to the use of aramid fibers has been at the various locations.

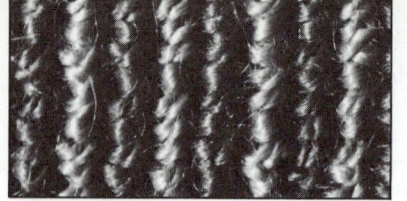

11

Polyester Fibers

KEY TERMS

benzoate polyester
hydrolyzed polyester
polyester
POY polyester

Historical Review

Polyester fibers were first identified by Carothers and his team of scientists at DuPont during the early years of their fundamental research. However, when polyamide fibers (nylon) appeared to show promise, they were selected for development, and research on polyester fibers was temporarily set aside.

While Carothers and his team directed their emphasis to the polyamides, chemists in Great Britain began experimenting with long-chain linear polyester polymers. In 1941, J. R. Whinfield and J. T. Dickson of Calico Printers Association introduced a successful polyester fiber. Its development was delayed by World War II, and public announcements of the discovery were withheld until 1946. Imperial Chemical Industries (ICI) purchased the rights to manufacture the fiber for all countries except the United States, where DuPont obtained the manufacturing privilege.

DuPont's polyester fiber was made available to U.S. consumers in 1951 under the trademark Dacron® (pronounced day'-kron). A large manufacturing plant was completed in 1953, and since that time Dacron polyester and the many other polyester fibers together have become the most widely used man-made fiber. In fact, since the late 1970s, polyester fiber is the single most used fiber in the United States, exceeding cotton as well as other fibers.

Fabrics of polyester fibers or blends with polyester found immediate consumer acceptance because of their ease of maintenance and excellent wrinkle resistance and recovery.

The Textile Fiber Products Identification Act defines a polyester fiber as

a manufactured fiber in which the fiber-forming substance is any long-chain synthetic polymer composed of at least 85 percent by weight of an ester of a substituted aromatic carboxylic acid, including but not restricted to substituted terephthalic units

$$\rho \left(-R-O-\underset{\underset{O}{\|}}{C}-C_6H_4-\underset{\underset{O}{\|}}{C}- \right)$$

and parasubstituted hydroxybenzoate units,

$$\rho \left(-R-O-C_6H_4-\underset{\underset{O}{\|}}{C}-O- \right).$$

This definition, as amended in September 1973, provides for inclusion in the polyester category of benzoate polyesters such as A-Tell, manufactured in Japan.

ethylene glycol + terephthalic acid ⟶

$$HOC_2H_4OH + HOOC - \langle \rangle - COOH \longrightarrow$$

$$(HOOC - C_6H_4 - COOH)$$

polyester, ethylene terephthalate + water
$$HO[OC-C_6H_4-COOCH_2CH_2O]_nH + H_2O$$

11.1 Chemical reactions in polyester formation.

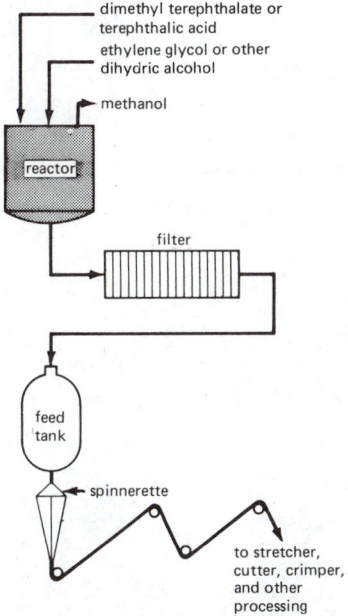

dimethyl terephthalate or terephthalic acid

ethylene glycol or other dihydric alcohol

methanol

reactor

filter

feed tank

spinnerette

to stretcher, cutter, crimper, and other processing

11.2 Flow diagram showing steps in polyester manufacture.

Production and Molecular Structure

Polyesters are the product of reactions between a dihydric alcohol and dicarboxylic acid. They may be formed from substitute products as long as the end product is an ester. The current generic definition of polyester fibers specifies the use of an aromatic carboxylic acid *or* a substituted product. In the manufacture of most polyester fibers, ethylene glycol is used as the dihydric alcohol. One exception was noted in the manufacture of the Kodel® 200 series, a carpet fiber manufactured by Eastman Fibers. This polyester used cyclohexane dimethanol.

The reaction of the ethylene glycol and terephthalic acid is shown in Figure 11.1. Dimethyl terephthalate has been used more frequently than terephthalic acid because it is more readily available in pure form. The reaction that occurs when dimethyl terephthalate is used is similar to that shown in Fig-

ure 11.1, except that methanol (methyl alcohol, CH_3OH) rather than water is a by-product of the reaction.

Terephthalic acid or dimethyl terephthalate and ethylene glycol polymerize by condensation reaction to form the polyester polymer. The repeat unit for this polyethylene terephthalate (PET) may be represented thus:

$$n = 80-100$$

Each fiber molecule or polymer contains about 80 to 100 repeat units. The manufacture of polyester is diagramed in the flow chart, Figure 11.2. These reactions, with some modifications for certain fiber variants, are used to produce most polyester fibers. One major exception was the Kodel 200 series, which employed a different dihydric alcohol, as stated previously, and formed the following repeat unit

The two substances are polymerized by condensation at a high temperature. As the resulting polyester leaves the polymerization vessel, it enters a cool area, where the strands solidify. These strands, which are about as thick as spaghetti, are cut into small pellets or chips, dried, and stored until needed for filament formation (Fig. 11.3). The actual formation of the fiber filaments may occur at the same plant, or the polyester pellets or chips may be transferred to other locations. Subsequently, the pellets or chips are melted and forced through the fiber spinnerettes. The filaments solidify in cooling air (Fig. 11.4) and are then taken up on containers resembling large spools. Before the filaments can be used, they must be drawn and stretched to impart strength and control elongation. The drawing process can be done partially as the filaments are extruded. These partially oriented yarns (POY) are used for making textured yarns.

Drawing units may be attached directly to the spinning unit so that the final yarn can be made in a continuous operation. However, the usual process, particularly for filament yarn, is to make the

11.3 Storage facilities for DMT pellets. (Hoechst Fibers)

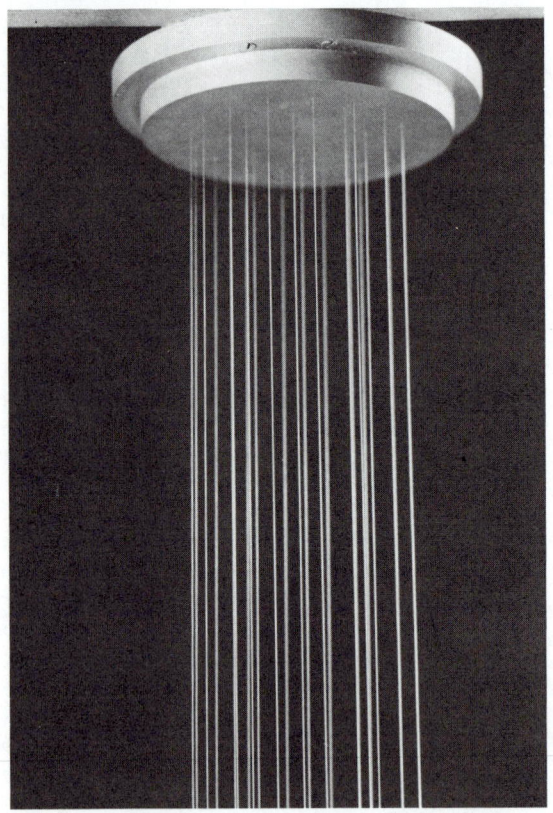

11.4 Melt spinning polyester filaments. (Hoechst Fibers)

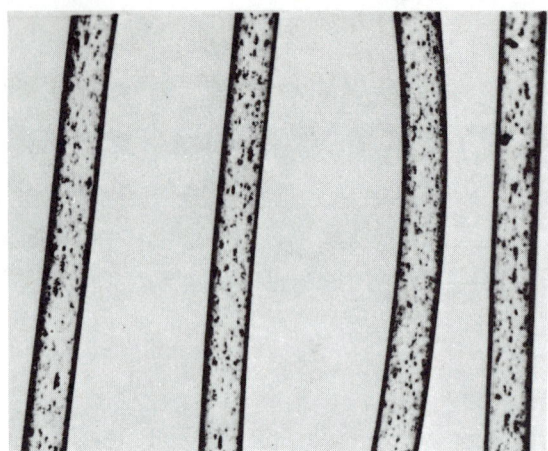

11.5 Photomicrograph of regular polyester, longitudinal view. (DuPont Company)

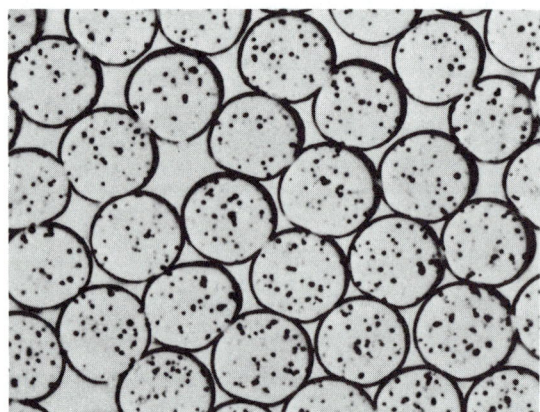

11.6 Photomicrograph of regular polyester, cross section. (DuPont Company)

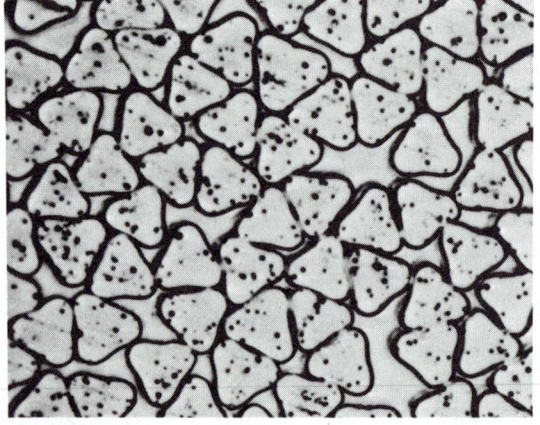

11.7 Photomicrograph of trilobal polyester, cross section. (DuPont Comapny)

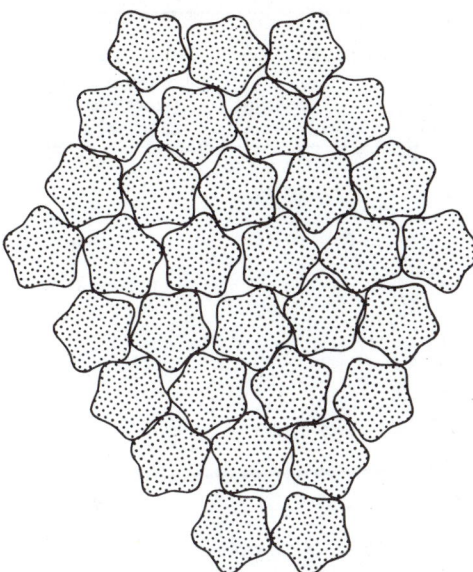

11.8 Cross section of pentalobal polyester, Trevira.

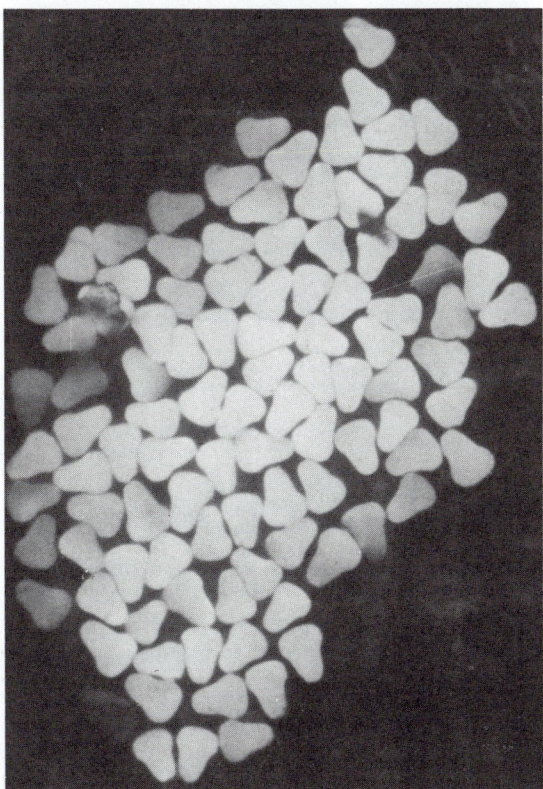

11.9 Photomicrograph of T-shape polyester. (DuPont Company)

filaments and take them up on a supply package. When needed, these are drawn on a draw stretch unit. Most filament polyester is textured. This usually is a third distinct operation, performed by either the fiber producer or the textured yarn manufacturer.

It should be noted that most manufacturers make polyester fibers by using a direct polymerization to spin process and omit the pellet or chip stage. This is a continuous process from raw materials to fiber.

A large proportion of polyester fiber used today is in the staple form, that is, cut to lengths of about 1½ inches after the fiber has been crimped following the required drawing. Staple fibers are frequently blended with cotton or other fibers and spun into yarns using a standard yarn manufacturing process (see Chap. 17).

Polyester is the most used single fiber in the United States today. Three and one-half billion pounds of polyester fiber were used by mills in the United States in 1983, as compared with the nearest competitor, cotton, at 2.8 billion and with nylon at 2.4 billion pounds. To meet the demand by textured yarn and fabric manufacturers, there are many variants of polyester available. These include variants identified as second-, third-, fourth-, and even fifth-generation modifications. In early 1984 data indicated that eleven manufacturers in the United States were producing polyester fiber, and many of these produced a variety of types. Each type has at least one specific characteristic that makes it perform slightly differently from other types. The variability may be in the crimp, the strength, the dyeing characteristics, the softening and melting temperatures, the cross-sectional shape, the whiteness, or some other property that might influence processing into yarn or behavior in the end-use product.

Fiber Properties

Microscopic Appearance

The longitudinal view of polyester with a round cross section exhibits uniform diameter, smooth surface, and a rodlike appearance (Fig. 11.5). The surface may appear grainy, spotted, or pitted.

The cross section of regular polyester is round (Fig. 11.6). In addition, there are several variants in cross-sectional shape. The most common are trilobal (Fig. 11.7), T-shape, pentalobal (Fig. 11.8), eight-sided star, and trilateral variants (Fig. 11.9).

TABLE 11.1 Properties of Polyester Fibers from Various Producers

Fiber Producer	Tenacity (g/d)	% Elongation	% Elastic Recovery at 2% Extension	Density (g/ccm)	% Moisture Regain (standard conditions)*
DuPont					
regular	2.8–5.2	19–30	97	1.38	0.4
high tenacity	6.0–9.5	10–14	100	1.38	0.4
Eastman					
200 series	2.5–3.0	24–34	85–95	1.23	0.4
400 series	4.5–5.5	35–45	75–85	1.38	0.4
Celanese					
regular	3.0–6.3	24–50	100	1.38	0.4
high tenacity	7.1–9.0	9.5–24	100	1.38	0.4
Avtex	3.0–4.6	18–22	90–97	1.38	0.4
American Enka					
regular	4.4–5.0	20–35	95–97	1.38	0.4
high tenacity	8.5–8.9	11.5–13.0	100	1.38	0.4
Hoechst Fibers Industries	3.2–6.3	27–75	95–97	1.38	0.4

*Standard conditions = 65 relative humidity, 70°F ± 2°.

TABLE 11.2 Selected Other Properties of Polyester Fibers

Property	Evaluation
Shape	Shape for polyester fibers is controlled by manufacturers; it may be of a wide choice of diameters and either round or multilobal in cross section.
Luster	Controlled from bright to dull.
Resiliency	excellent
Dimensional stability	excellent
Resistance to	
acids	Strong acids destroy fibers; weak acids have little or no effect.
alkalies	Resistance is good to weak alkalies and moderate to strong alkalies at room temperature.
sunlight	Behind glass, resistance is excellent; in direct sun, resistance is better than that of nylon.
microorganisms	excellent
insects	excellent
Thermal reactions	
to heat	Will melt at temperatures from 238°C to 290°C.
to flame	Will burn slowly, and melting fibers tend to drop off, preventing further burning. Can be finished to have superior flame resistance.

Physical Properties

SHAPE AND APPEARANCE Except for the multilobal varieties, polyester fibers are generally round. They are uniform in size and can be of any practical length and of any diameter required by the ultimate user. The fiber is partially transparent and white or slightly off-white in color. Optical bright- eners are frequently added to produce very white polyester fibers. Crimping is a normal part of the manufacture of staple polyester fibers.

LUSTER The inclusion of pigment in the melt solution causes changes in the light reflection and thereby produces fibers that may be dull or semidull in appearance. It is the presence of these delusterants that causes the grainy or pitted look under the microscope.

TENACITY (STRENGTH) Several physical properties of polyester fibers are cited in Table 11.1, including fiber tenacity or strength. Regular and high-tenacity fibers are produced by several manufacturers, and strength varies from a low of 2.5 grams per denier to a high of 9.5 g/d. There is no loss of strength when polyester fibers are wet. Variation in tenacity is due to differences in the formulation of the polymer and differences in molecular orientation imparted during the drawing process and subsequent heat stabilization. Weaker fibers, having tenacities of 2.5 to 3.5 g/d, are usually reserved for apparel uses. Tenacities of 7.0 or greater are sold primarily for industrial applications.

ELASTIC RECOVERY AND ELONGATION Table 11.1 indicates elastic recovery and elongation for a selected group of polyester fibers. The amount of extension or elongation for polyester varies inversely with tenacity. As elongation decreases, strength increases. Elastic recovery of high-tenacity polyester is good to excellent. Regular-tenacity polyester exhibits some variation in elastic recovery, but it is superior to cellulosic fibers and only slightly inferior to nylon.

RESILIENCY The property of resilience and recovery from creasing and wrinkling is excellent for polyester fibers. Furthermore, heat setting can stabilize yarns and fabrics so that they need little or no pressing to retain a smooth appearance. Even if caught in a rainstorm, fabrics of polyester will usually dry without noticeable wrinkles. Pleats or creases heat-set into fabric during finishing will remain neat and distinct over a long wearing or use period. See Table 11.2 for data concerning selected properties of polyester fibers.

DENSITY The density of most polyester fibers is 1.38. Kodel 200 series was a noticeable exception, with a density of 1.23. One series of fibers from Hoechst is cited by that company as having a density of 1.34.

MOISTURE REGAIN Polyester fibers have low moisture regain of 0.4 percent at standard conditions. Even at 95 to 100 percent relative humidity the moisture content is only 0.6 to 0.8 percent. Because of this low regain, moisture has little effect on the strength or elongation of the fiber, and static electric charges may be accentuated. Furthermore, the low moisture absorption requires special techniques in dyeing and finishing.

WICKING Polyester fibers typically have a low level of wicking. The level can be raised through certain yarn and fabric constructions and finishes producing products that carry moisture from the outside environment through to the inside, or body perspiration through to the outside. However, when this is undesirable, other yarn and fabric constructions and finishes can be substituted to inhibit the movement of moisture through the fabric.

DIMENSIONAL STABILITY If polyester fiber is properly heat-set, it will neither shrink nor stretch when subjected to washing, dry cleaning, or ironing temperatures that are lower than the heat-setting temperature, which is usually above 195°C (385°F) and may be as high as 220°C (425°F) for some products. If polyester is subjected to boiling water for one hour, the fiber will shrink 11 to 12 percent. For satisfactory end use, heat setting is essential.

Heat setting is required if yarns and fabrics are to possess the easy-care, wrinkle-free properties associated with polyester. Permanent pleats in polyester fabrics or smooth, flat surfaces, once heat-set, will hold as long as processing or maintenance temperatures do not exceed the heat-setting temperatures.

Thermal Properties

Polyester fibers melt at temperatures from 238°C to 290°C (460°–554°F), depending on type or variant of fiber. As the fiber melts, it forms a gray or tawny-colored bead that is hard and noncrushable. Polyesters will burn and produce a dark smoke and an acrid odor. However, they do not burn as rapidly as most other fibers. In many fabric constructions the fibers melt and drip away from the source of igniton, preventing the propagation of flame.

Moderate heat does not discolor polyester. Polyester fiber fabrics can be ironed at temperatures between 120° and 150°C (250°–300°F). The lower temperatures are suggested particularly for lightweight fabrics.

Polyesters retain 70 to 80 percent of their strength following prolonged exposure to 150°C (300°F); at lower temperatures there is minimal or no loss of strength. At temperatures above 150°C, strength loss occurs rapidly. Fibers held at 176°C (350°F) for 11 days lost 75 percent of their strength; however, after 30 days at 150°C, 75 percent of their strength had been retained. Eastman notes that the Kodel 200 series had superior resistance to high temperatures.

Chemical Properties

EFFECT OF ALKALIES   Polyester has good resistance to weak alkalies even at high temperatures. It exhibits only moderate resistance to strong alkalies at room temperature and is degraded quickly at elevated temperatures. Resistance is reduced as exposure time is increased.

EFFECT OF ACIDS   Weak acids, even at the boiling point, have no effect on polyester unless the fiber is exposed for several days. Polyesters have good resistance to strong acids at room temperature. Prolonged exposure to boiling hydrochloric acid destroys the fibers, and 96 percent sulfuric acid causes disintegration. Kodel 200 series fibers are more resistant to this environment than other polyesters.

EFFECT OF ORGANIC SOLVENTS   Polyester fiber is generally resistant to organic solvents. Chemicals used in cleaning and stain removal will not damage it, but hot meta-cresol will destroy the fiber, and certain mixtures of phenol with trichlorophenol or tetrachloroethane will dissolve polyesters. Oxidizing agents and bleaches do not damage polyester fibers, but the use of chlorine bleach may cause some discoloration.

EFFECT OF SUNLIGHT, AGE, AND MISCELLANEOUS FACTORS   Polyester exhibits good resistance to sunlight when behind glass, so it is satisfactory for window coverings, but prolonged exposure to direct sunlight weakens the fiber. The strength of polyester fibers is not affected by aging. The fiber resists abrasion damage very well.

Soaps and synthetic detergents and other laundry aids do not damage the fiber. It can be easily and safely laundered in automatic washers and dried in controlled-temperature dryers. Control of both laundering and drying temperatures is essential, however, to prevent the formation of undesirable wrinkles and creases.

One of the most serious faults of polyester is its *oleophilic* property. It absorbs oily substances easily and holds the oil tenaciously. Visa® finish by Milliken is a successful soil-release finish for polyester fabrics. Also, improved detergent systems and prewash sprays have greatly reduced this problem.

Static Charge

Polyesters do build up static charge; they have low electrical conductivity.

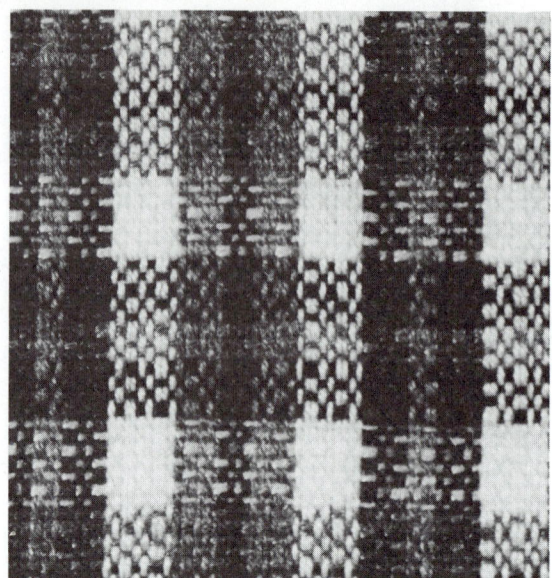

11.10 *Cross-dyed polyester fabrics. Modifications of polyester fibers can control dye acceptance to permit formation of checks and plaids after fabric is woven.* (DuPont Company)

Biological Properties

Insects will not destroy polyesters if there is other food available. However, if trapped, beetles and other insects will cut their way through the fabric as a means of escape.

Although microorganisms will not harm the fiber, they may attack finishes. Usually, any discoloration is easily removed since it does not penetrate the fiber. In yarns and fabrics where polyester has been blended with cellulosic fibers, some damage may occur to the cellulose fibers.

Modified Polyester Fibers

Special modifications in polyesters introduce a variety of altered properties. Changes that alter the cross section produce fibers with different hand and appearance. Chemical modifications result in fibers that may be flame-resistant or that differ in strength, which will alter pilling properties, increase crush resistance, alter dye receptivity (Fig. 11.10), and change the hand of fabrics.

Modified Cross Sections

Cross-sectional shape is changed by altering the shape of the openings in the spinnerette. Fibers with cross sections that are trilobal, pentalobal, heptalobal, and octalobal have different characteristics related to hand, drape, and appearance than round fibers. Fabrics made from polyester fibers with trilobal and pentalobal cross sections are characterized by a silklike hand and appearance. Fabrics made from heptalobal and octalobal fibers have little or none of the glitter that may be characteristic of other shaped fibers. Fibers of different shapes are often used in carpet yarns in order to give good appearance; these fibers also tend to show soil much less quickly. This latter characteristic is due to light scattering by the projecting lobes of the fiber, while the soil tends to lodge in the valleys between the lobes. Other properties given by the various lobal shapes include a pleasing luster and surface sheen and an improved covering power.

Chemical and Physical Modifications

Performance characteristics such as dyeing behavior, strength, pilling, texture, bulk, and thermal properties can be modified. Fiber dyeability is altered by the introduction of chemicals that add sulfonic groups to the molecule and by the substitution of isophthalic acid for a small portion of the terephthalic acid. These changes create fibers that can be dyed by cationic dyes as well as disperse dyes, which are the type of dye most frequently used for polyester.

Polyester can be given different strengths and pilling behavior through such techniques as modifying the spinning speed and the degree of molecular orientation, or through the use of lower-molecular-weight polymolecules.

A problem with polyester fibers is the oleophilic property noted previously. Research continues on systems to modify the fiber as a method of reducing this characteristic.

Several research studies have been reported in the technical literature during the past few years concerning another chemical modification of polyester—the hydrolysis or caustic reduction of the fiber. This process is used to etch away the outer layer of the polyester filament to reduce the diameter of the fibers, thus reducing the denier. The action involves the saponification of the polyester and is not reversible. Careful control of temperatures, the percentage of sodium hydroxide, and time are required to provide the amount of etching desired and to prevent excess damage to the filaments. Further, the action differs with different types of polyester fibers. Fibers of bright, round cross section are more resistant to caustic reduction than delustered, multilobal filaments. Textured yarns react faster than nontextured yarns. The process is used as one method for developing a fabric with improved aesthetic and tactile properties. The fibers are said to have improved hand, a hydrophilic surface, improved wicking and wetting properties, a soft and silky hand, and improved dyeability.

Other changes of a physical nature have produced fibers with increased loft and bulk for use as fiberfill. Such fibers have various cross-sectional shapes, but one has air shafts built into the fiber in order to provide a fiber that has outstanding loft, is good insulation, and is comfortable. This fiber, called Quallofil®, is used as a filler for pillows, upholstery, and selected items of apparel.

Another variant, called a comfort fiber, has been introduced by Celanese. The fiber is described as being chemically and physically modified. The properties include good bulk, loft, and cover; excellent comfort and dyeability; shrinkage resistance; durability; and sufficient flame resistance to meet legislation requirements.

Polyester fibers do not absorb odors and they are considered nonallergenic. Because polyester is widely used in blends with cotton, some manufacturers make a modified fiber with an initial modulus similar to that of cotton. This provides consistency for processing on cotton system spinning machines.

Flame-Resistant Polyesters

Inherently flame-resistant polyester is desired because the property is an integral part of the fiber, whereas topical finishes may be removed during use and care. One process used for producing inherently flame-resistant polyester involves copolymerization of a derivative of phosphinic acid with the polyethylene terephthalate. Some of the flame-resistant polyester fibers are Tetoron®, Extra®, Trevira® 271, Toyobo GH, and Heim. Trevira 271 is currently (1984) the only domestically produced flame-resistant polyester.

POY Polyester

Partially oriented polyester (POY) is only partially drawn during manufacture. The remaining orientation is achieved as part of a texturizing process. Previously, polyester was completely oriented prior to texturizing. Some manufacturers maintain that POY processing provides yarns with less sensitivity to atmospheric conditions and better thermal stability. POY-textured polyester has superior dyeability, a crisp hand, superior bulk, and reduced kinking problems.

Polypivalolactone Polyester

Another polyester that has been announced but not developed to any great amount is polypivalolactone. The fiber is a polyester polymerized from the beta lactone of pivalic acid.

Characteristics cited for this polyester include excellent recovery from stress or elongation, which imparts good crease recovery, and excellent resistance to ultraviolet light. Good wash-and-wear characteristics are apparent in fabrics made of this polyester. As yet, no commercial quantities of the fiber are available.

Other Modifications

Two modifications of polyester were announced early in 1984 by a Japanese company. One, called Mawus-M, has a high bacteriostatic performance that is durable; it has good moisture absorbency characteristics as well. A second modification, Mawus-R, is a heat-resistant polymer that remains free from holes even if a lighted cigarette is held against the fabric for 3 minutes. The substances incorporated into the polyester molecular structure have not been identified.

Benzoate Polyesters

As a result of the change in the TFPIA definition of polyester, fibers previously considered polyester-ethers are now categorized as polyesters. The only fiber of importance, to date, in this category is a fiber trademarked A-Tell, made in Japan. This benzoate polyester is made by reacting parahydroxybenzoic acid and ethylene oxide, which gives para-oxyethylenebenzoic acid. This chemical is polymerized to form polyethylenebenzoate (PEB) with the following repeat:

$$\left(-O-\overset{\overset{O}{\|}}{C}-\underset{}{\bigcirc}-O-\overset{\overset{H}{|}}{\underset{\underset{H}{|}}{C}}-\overset{\overset{H}{|}}{\underset{\underset{H}{|}}{C}}-\right)_n$$

The molecular repeat is noncentrosymmetrical. This is quite different from most manufactured fibers but very similar to natural fibers. The PEB tends to have properties that resemble natural fibers, especially silk.

The general physical properties of the benzoate polyesters are as follows:

tenacity: 4.0–5.3 g/d
elongation: 15–25%
elastic recovery: 95–100% at 3% extension
density: 1.34 g/ccm
moisture regain: 0.4%

Microscopic properties have not been well publicized, but A-Tell has been described as a trilobal fiber.

The fiber has good to excellent resistance to acids, alkalies, and organic solvents. It can be dyed with disperse or azoic dyestuffs to deep and vivid shades. It resists microorganisms and insects.

Thermal reactions are similar to those of other polyester fibers. It softens at about 200°C (390°F) and melts at about 225°C (435°F). It can be heat-set for permanent pleats and appearance retention. Recommended ironing temperature is 160°C (320°F), which is higher than that recommended for PET polyester.

The fiber has a silklike hand and drape, good wrinkle resistance, easy-care properties, and an attractive appearance. It has many of the visual and tactile properties of silk plus the easy care and wrinkle-free characteristics associated with polyester.

Use and Care of Polyester Fiber Fabrics

The most important characteristics of polyester fabrics are their wrinkle-free appearance and ease of care. These fabrics require little or no ironing; they are easy to launder and quick to dry; they can be dry-cleaned safely when necessary. Fabrics of 100 percent polyester are usually made from filament fibers, typically textured fibers. These fabrics are widely used in apparel, home furnishings, and various commercial and industrial applications.

Blends of polyester with wool, cotton, rayon, or flax fibers are popular and found in many different end-use products. In blended fabrics the polyester fibers contribute easy maintenance, strength and durability, abrasion resistance, wrinkle-free appearance, and shape and size retention. Protein or cellulosic fibers in the blend enhance dyeability, comfort, and absorbency, and reduce static charges.

Like many other types of fabrics, polyester staple fiber fabrics are subject to pilling. However, some of the newer polyesters exhibit less pilling than older varieties, because their tenacity has been decreased somewhat (with little or very little increase in elongation), and this drop reduces abrasion resistance, which means that pills tend to break off the fabric as they are formed.

Polyesters are used in industry for such items as laundry bags, calender sheeting, press covers, conveyor belts, fish netting, and selected types of protective clothing. Other uses include fire hoses, sailcloth, rope, and tire cord.

Consumer use of polyester fabrics has increased rapidly over the past 10 years. Per-capita consumption of polyester fiber in the early 1970s was about 8 pounds; by 1983 it had increased to nearly 15 pounds per year. These fibers are used for almost every type of wearing apparel and home furnishing.

An interesting and important use of polyester yarns and fabrics is for surgical implants, where its advantage is that it does not cause physiological reactions. However, in the more typical uses of polyester, finishes and dyestuffs may produce allergenic reactions for some individuals, just as they do in many other fibers.

Despite the easy-care properties of polyester fabrics, some consumers have experienced problems with shrinkage of polyester knits. These problems are probably due to the use of polyester that has not been properly heat-set. Users of knit polyester fabric may wish to wash the yardage before use in order to minimize any shrinkage that might occur after it is made into end-use items such as apparel. Another step to reduce shrinkage of polyester is to avoid high temperatures as part of care operations. Although this problem does not occur as frequently with woven fabrics, it can arise if the fabric has not been finished and heat-set correctly. In general, polyester is considered a stable fiber, and polyester fabrics are considered dimensionally stable.

The care of 100 percent polyester fabrics is minimal. It is advisable to treat heavily soiled areas with a lubricating detergent and then wash by machine or by hand, using warm water and a good soap or synthetic detergent. Most items can be drip-dried or tumble-dried if removed from the dryer before wrinkles can be set. That means removing as soon as the dryer stops rotating. White polyester fabrics should be washed separately. For best results, label information should always be followed.

When polyester fiber has been blended with other fibers, it is essential for consumers to adhere to any care directions given on attached labels. The method of care may be determined to some degree by other fibers in the blend, although the use of polyester fiber typically makes care of blends an easy task. Bleaches can be used on 100 percent polyester and on blends, except when the other fiber(s) or the finishes might be damaged.

Because of the oleophilic property of polyesters, oil-borne spots and stains may be difficult to remove. One treatment for oily stains involves applying a liquid detergent such as a clear liquid hair shampoo or a prewash spray to the stain before laundering. This usually will lift off oil and grease. Spray-type spot removers and heavy-duty liquid detergents may be effective on tenacious stains. When they are used, it is helpful to rub the compound thoroughly into the stained areas before laundering.

Polyester fabrics are extremely popular. They provide good appearance, comfort, easy maintenance, and durability. Blends with cellulosic fibers that have been given durable-press finishes are easy-care, wrinkle-free, and durable. Woven, knitted, and nonwoven fabrics of polyester or blends including polyester are available in a wide selection.

STUDY QUESTIONS

1. Describe the manufacturing process involved in making polyester fibers.
2. What are the properties of the various polyester fibers?
3. What modifications are available that alter polyester properties for selected end uses?
4. Why do you think polyester fiber is the most used single fiber?
5. Compare the properties of nylon and polyester fibers, and indicate how they influence end uses for fabrics made of these fibers. Can this explain the difference in typical consumer products made of the two different generic fiber types?
6. Why are cotton/polyester blends so popular with consumers?
7. What other fibers are frequently blended with polyester? Why?

Activities

1. Visit various types of stores and determine how many different types of end-use products are available made from polyester fibers or from blends including polyester fibers.
2. Study current technical literature and discover what new developments have been announced concerning polyester.
3. Shop in various stores and observe how many labels on polyester fabrics include a trade name for the polyester content.

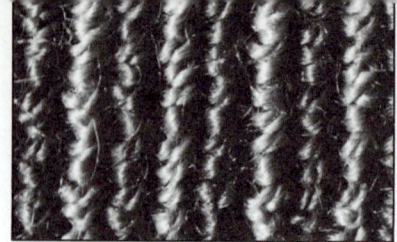

12

Acrylic and Modacrylic Fibers

KEY TERMS

acrylic fibers
addition polymerization

bicomponent fibers
modacrylic fibers

ACRYLIC FIBERS

Historical Review

The success of nylon was so extraordinary that many manufacturers began experimenting with other chemicals in attempts to find other fiber-forming polymers. Early in World War II, DuPont developed an acrylic fiber, Fiber A. This fiber, which evolved partly from the fundamental research done earlier by Carothers, showed potential as a substitute for either wool or silk. In the staple form the fiber resembled wool; in filament form it resembled silk in both texture and appearance. During the late 1940s the DuPont organization completed development of Orlon®, introduced pilot plant quantities to a test market, and evaluated the results. Interest was of sufficient magnitude that DuPont built a full-scale plant in Camden, South Carolina; production began at the facility in 1950.

The increased public acceptance of man-made fibers encouraged other companies to enter the industry. Monsanto Chemical Company and Ameri-

can Viscose Corporation joined forces and formed, in 1949, the Chemstrand Corporation with the objective of producing an acrylic fiber that they named Acrilan®. The first fibers were somewhat inferior in properties, so the company made minor changes in formulations and manufacturing techniques and introduced a modified product in 1954 that has been extremely successful. The current company producing Acrilan is Monsanto Fibers.

American Cyanamid Corporation introduced commercial quantities of their acrylic fiber, Creslan®, in 1958; during the same year Dow Chemical (now Badische Corporation) introduced a new fiber called Zefran®. Although this was basically an acrylic fiber, the Dow chemists preferred to call it an acrylic-alloy fiber.

Since 1958 very few new acrylic fibers have been introduced by American firms. However, there has been extensive research and development in modifying acrylic fibers to produce special fibers with special characteristics. These modifications include changes in dyeing behavior, the introduction of bicomponent fibers with special crimping and texturing properties, and changes in behavior of the fibers in flame and extreme heat.

The Textile Fiber Products Identification Act defines an acrylic as

a manufactured fiber in which the fiber-forming substance is any long-chain synthetic polymer composed of at least 85 percent by weight of acrylonitrile units.

$$\left(\begin{array}{c} -CH_2- \ CH- \\ | \\ CN \end{array} \right)$$

Production and Molecular Structure

Acrylic fibers are polymers formed by addition polymerization. At least 85 percent by weight of the chemical acrylonitrile or vinyl cyanide is required. The remaining portion can be any organic chemical similar in structure and containing a double bond between two carbon atoms. The formula for acrylonitrile is $H_2C=CHCN$, diagramed as:

$$\begin{array}{ccc} H & H \\ | & | \\ H- \ C & = \ C-CN \end{array}$$

To polymerize the acrylonitrile, the double bond (=) between two carbon atoms must be broken. As this occurs, molecules attach themselves or add together to form a linear chain with many molecular segments, a process called addition polymerization. The average number of molecules in a polymolecule of acrylic fiber is about 2000. The structural formula of acrylic polymer is

$$\begin{array}{ccccccccc} H & H & H & H & H & H & & H & H \\ | & | & | & | & | & | & & | & | \\ -C & -C- & C- & C- & C- & C & \cdots\cdots & C & C- \\ | & | & | & | & | & | & & | & | \\ H & CN & H & CN & H & CN & & H & CN \end{array}$$

The repeat unit is

$$\left(\begin{array}{cc} H & H \\ | & | \\ -C- & C- \\ | & | \\ H & CN \end{array} \right)_n \qquad n = c.\ 2000$$

It had been known for many years that acrylonitrile would polymerize to form a high-molecular-weight polymer, but the resulting fiber was characterized by insolubility and degradation at relatively low melting temperatures. Chemists finally discovered solvents that would dissolve the poly-

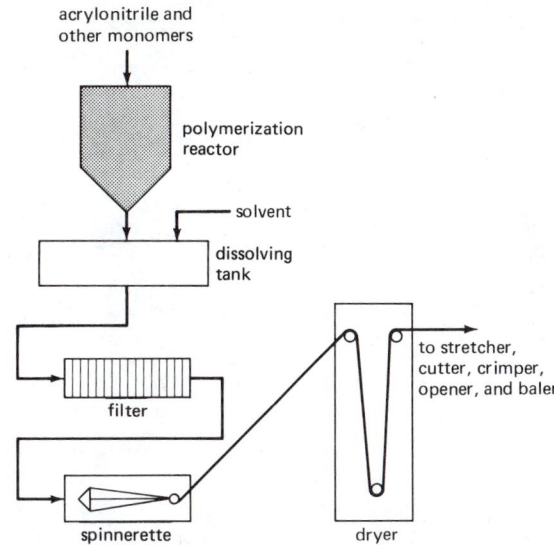

12.1 Flow diagram showing processes in acrylic fiber manufacture.

mer; two of those that are satisfactory are dimethyl formamide and dimethyl acetamide. The dissolved polymer is extruded through spinnerettes into a heated spinning container where the filaments solidify, the solvent is recovered, and the solid filaments, while still hot, are stretched to introduce molecular orientation and fiber fineness (Fig. 12.1). In addition to this dry-spinning process, wet-spun fibers are also produced commercially.

Orlon, manufactured by DuPont, was originally a pure polymer of acrylonitrile, but today most types of Orlon are modified by the addition of up to 14 percent of a second component. It is known that this second chemical produces the property differences of the various fibers. Although the patent literature indicates several possible chemicals, it does not specify which are used in which types of Orlon.

Acrilan acrylic, a product of Monsanto Fibers, is composed of 85 percent acrylonitrile, plus other compounds, depending on the type of Acrilan. A study of the patent literature indicates that one type is made from acrylonitrile and vinyl acetate ($CH_3-COOCH=CH_2$), and the evidence also suggests that one other variety derives from acrylonitrile and vinyl pyridine. All compounds used possess the double bond, which permits addition polymerization by cleavage of those double bonds.

The manufacture of Acrilan is similar to that of Orlon, except for the probable use of dimethyl acetamide as the solvent, and it appears that the fila-

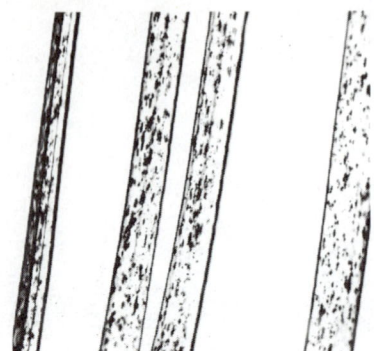

12.2 Photomicrograph of Orlon® acrylic, longitudinal view. (DuPont Company)

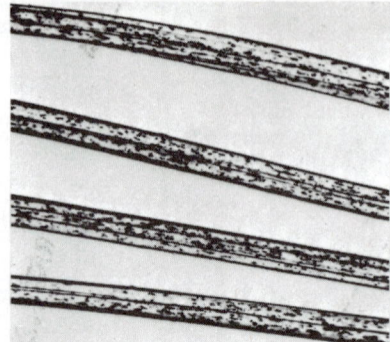

12.3 Photomicrograph of bicomponent acrylic fiber. (DuPont Company)

12.4 Photomicrograph of Acrilan® acrylic, longitudinal view. (DuPont Company)

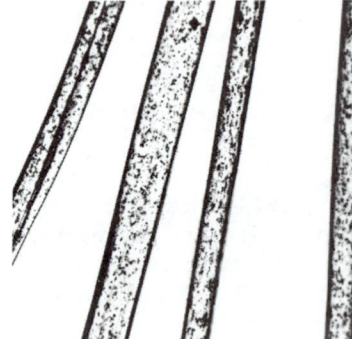

12.5 Photomicrograph of Creslan® acrylic, longitudinal view. (DuPont Company)

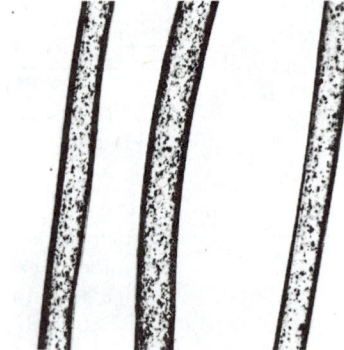

12.6 Photomicrograph of Zefran® acrylic, longitudinal view. (DuPont Company)

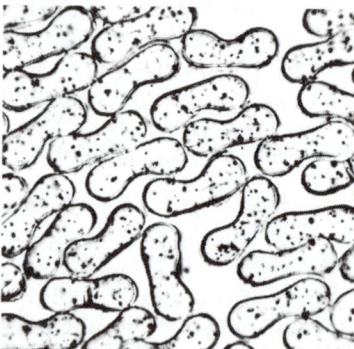

12.7 Photomicrograph of Orlon® acrylic, cross section. (DuPont Company)

12.8 Photomicrograph of bicomponent acrylic, cross section. (DuPont Company)

12.9 Photomicrograph of Acrilan® acrylic, cross section. (DuPont Company)

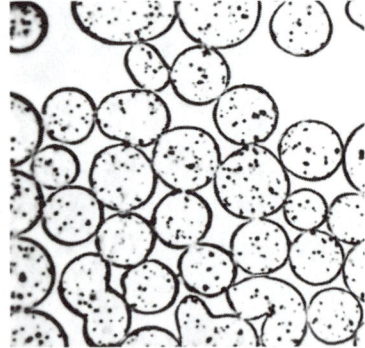

12.10 Photomicrograph of Creslan® acrylic, cross section. (DuPont Company)

ments are spun into a bath rather than dry-spun. After coagulation, the fibers are stretched and crimped.

Creslan acrylic is manufactured by the American Cyanamid Company. Although information concerning its production is not available, it is believed that Creslan is a copolymer. It has been suggested that the fiber is wet-spun using a cold coagulating bath.

Badische Corporation manufactures Zefran acrylic, which is composed of acrylonitrile and a second compound believed to be vinyl pyridine.

TABLE 12.1 Selected Physical Properties of Trademarked Acrylic Fibers

Property	Orlon®	Acrilan®	Zefran®	Creslan®
Tenacity (g/d)				
dry	2.2–2.6	2.0–2.7	2.9–3.6	2.4–3.2
wet	1.8–2.1	1.6–2.2	2.3–2.9	1.8–2.7
Elongation				
conditioned*	20–28%	34–50%	35–40%	34–46%
wet	26–34%	34–60%	38–46%	34–46%
Elastic recovery at				
2% extension	97%	99%	99%	99%
Density (g/ccm)	1.16	1.17	1.18	1.17
Moisture regain	1.5%	1.5%	1.5–2.5%	1.5%

*Conditioned environment = 65%; relative humidity, 70°F ± 2°.

This supposition is neither affirmed nor denied by the manufacturer.

Manufacturers of acrylic fibers market a variety of fiber modifications. Various types have been developed that accept either acid or cationic dyes and have outstanding bulking properties. Bicomponent acrylics exhibit improved bulk and resilience. Some manufacturers market ''producer-dyed'' acrylics that are pigmented and/or ''producer-colored'' fibers that utilize other techniques of coloration.

Fiber Properties

Microscopic Properties

Acrylic fibers, viewed longitudinally, show uniform diameters, a rodlike appearance, and some irregularly spaced striations or parallel lines (Figs. 12.2–12.6). Cross-section microscopic views exhibit minor differences among the various kinds. Orlon possesses a dumbbell shape for most types (Fig. 12.7), whereas the bicomponent varieties, 21 and 24, have cross sections that are mushroom- or acorn-shaped (Fig. 12.8). Fine Acrilan fibers have nearly round cross sections (Fig. 12.9), whereas fibers of high denier tend to be somewhat bean-shaped. The cross sections of Creslan and Zefran are round (Fig. 12.10). In general, acrylic fibers that have been delustered show the characteristic spotted effect caused by the pigment breaking up or reflecting light rays.

Physical Properties

SHAPE AND APPEARANCE Like all man-made fibers, acrylics can be controlled in terms of length and diameter or denier. In general, the fiber is marketed in staple or tow form.

The first acrylics ranged from creamy to deep yellow, but production improvements have resulted in a whiter product. The natural color of acrylics today range from white to cream. The introduction of Zefkrome marked the first appearance of producer-dyed acrylic fibers. Now there are producer-dyed and/or producer-colored Acrilan and Zefran.

LUSTER Acrylic fibers are available in bright, semidull, and dull lusters.

TENACITY (STRENGTH) The tenacities of acrylic fibers, when dry and when wet, are cited in Table 12.1. Although the tenacity of acrylic fibers is not high, it is adequate for a variety of end-uses.

ELONGATION AND ELASTIC RECOVERY The elongation of acrylic fibers varies from 20 to 50 percent (see Table 12.1). When fibers are wet, the elongation increases for all acrylics.

The elastic recovery of acrylic fibers is medium to high. At 2 percent extension, the immediate elastic recovery for Orlon is 97 percent. Acrilan, Creslan, and Zefran recover 99 percent. Recovery drops rather sharply as elongation is increased. In general, acrylics have poorer recovery than many other fibers.

Bicomponent acrylics are available in the Orlon types Wintuk and Sayelle, Acrilan type T57, and Creslan type T68. Bicomponents are characterized by good bulking and elastic recovery properties (Fig. 12.11).

RESILIENCY Acrylic fibers have good resiliency. They resist wrinkling, and undesired creases hang out quickly. In bulky fabrics acrylic fibers are espe-

TABLE 12.2   Other Selected Properties of Acrylic Fibers

Property	Evaluation
Shape	Controlled by manufacturer; may be filament or staple in length; round, dog bone, or other irregular shape in cross section.
Luster	Ranges from bright to dull, depending on planned end use.
Elastic recovery	good at low levels of elongation
Elongation, dry	20–50%
Resiliency	good
Density	1.16–1.18 g/ccm
Moisture absorbency	1.0–2.5%
Dimensional stability	good with correct care procedures
Resistance to	
acids	good resistance to weak acids; fair to strong acids
alkalies	good resistance to weak alkalies; poor to strong alkalies
sunlight	excellent
microorganisms	excellent
insects	excellent
Thermal reactions	
to heat	Maintain at temperatures below 160°C; do not subject to boiling water.
to flame	Burn readily unless specially treated.

cially resilient and lofty. These fibers retain their shape well (see Table 12.2).

DENSITY   Acrylic fibers have a low density that varies from 1.16 to 1.18 g/ccm (see Table 12.1). This low density results in a fiber that has excellent covering power and bulk with low weight.

MOISTURE REGAIN   The standard moisture regain of acrylic fibers varies from 1.0 to 2.5 percent. The saturation regain is also low; it increases only 1 to 2 percent over the standard regain.

DIMENSIONAL STABILITY   With proper care, acrylic fibers show little dimensional change. High temperatures and excess steam should be avoided. Bicomponent acrylic fibers retain crimp to a high degree and, thus, their shape and size. If stretch occurs, proper laundering and tumble-drying will usually return the fabric to its original size and shape.

Thermal Properties

Acrylic fibers have adequate resistance to heat. Degradation or decomposition of the fiber occurs before true melting, although when held near a flame the fibers will shrink or appear to melt and pull away. Sticking temperatures are given as between 232° and 255°C (450°–490°F). Iron settings should be kept below 160°C (320°F); higher temperatures may cause yellowing and discoloration.

Upon exposure to fire, acrylic fibers burn with a yellow flame and form a gummy, hot residue that drips away from the burning fiber. When cold, the residue is hard, black, and irregular in shape.

Acrylics can be tumble-dried if the drying temperatures do not exceed 150°C (300°F). It is recommended that these fibers not be subjected to boiling water, because the combination of heat and moisture results in some shrinkage.

Chemical Properties

EFFECT OF ALKALIES   Acrylic fibers have good resistance to weak alkalies, but concentrated alkalies generally cause rapid degradation. Zefran is moderately resistant to alkalies, but it tends to yellow at high temperatures when in an alkaline environment. Though less susceptible than other acrylics, Acrilan will exhibit evidence of damage from concentrated alkaline substances.

EFFECT OF ACIDS   Acrylics have good resistance to most mineral acids and organic acids. Weak or dilute acids appear to have no destructive effect, but strong or concentrated acids cause a loss in fiber strength, and cold concentrated nitric acid dissolves acrylic fibers.

EFFECT OF ORGANIC SOLVENTS   Solvents used in cleaning and stain removal have no effect on acrylic fibers, and bleaches can be used if directions are followed. Oxidizing agents other than bleaches used in processing do not destroy acrylic fibers.

EFFECT OF SUNLIGHT, AGE, AND MISCELLANEOUS FACTORS Acrylic fibers have excellent resistance to sunlight and other climatic elements. Age does not appear to affect acrylics; after prolonged storage there is no noticeable change in fiber properties. Detergents and soaps have no deleterious effect.

Static Charge

Static electricity will build up on acrylic fibers, particularly if the humidity is low.

Biological Properties

Mildew and bacteria do not attack acrylic fibers, and none of the common household pests, such as moths and carpet beetles, will eat or damage these fibers.

Acrylics: Types and Modifications

Acrylic fibers currently produced in the United States are identified in Table 12.1. Although various acrylic fibers have many properties in common, they do differ in such characteristics as cross-sectional shape, dyeing behavior, and appearance and hand. Such differences are due to the properties of the chemicals used to modify the polymer as well as to the type of spinning technique used.

Various types of acrylics are available with special dyeing characteristics. Most are cationic- and disperse-dyeable; some, such as Orlon types 33, 49, and 79, are acid-dyeable. Acrylic fibers vary in dye receptivity as well as in dye affinity. Differences are evident in bulkiness and in properties related to spinning and crimping behavior.

Among the most important additions to the acrylic family are bicomponent fibers. Bicomponent acrylics are made of two different chemical formulations extruded simultaneously. Each component differs in properties. When dry, one component curls and gives a spiral crimp to the fiber. The other may have a higher moisture regain and may accept a deeper shade of color because of easier dye penetration. It is essential that the fibers be dried without any tension so that the spiral crimp develops properly and the yarn returns to its original size.

Another type of bicomponent develops helical, nonreversible crimp during dyeing or hot, wet treatment.

Orlon type 43 has been designed to have a soft, luxurious hand similar to that of cashmere. This fiber is used in fine-gauge or semibulky knits and is pill-resistant. In certified products it is labeled Nomelle.

Acrylic fibers manufactured by Monsanto are trademarked Acrilan when the products meet quality standards. Monsanto acrylic fibers include bright fibers, semidull fibers, bicomponent fibers, fire-resistant fibers for carpets, and special fibers for indoor-outdoor carpeting.

American Cyanamid permits products to be trademarked Creslan if the end use conforms to company performance standards. In general, the types of Creslan available are similar to fibers made by other companies. Creslan will accept disperse dyes as well as basic or cationic dyes.

Of the Zefran acrylic fibers, manufactured by Badische Corporation, Type 201 is basic or cationic-dyeable, can be bright or semidull, and is usually recommended for floor coverings. Type 101 has special dyeing characteristics, is usually bright, and is intended for apparel. Type 405 is producer-dyed in a manner similar to mass pigmentation.

Use and Care of Acrylic Fibers

Acrylic fibers respond well to handling and are considered easy-care fibers. All types are used in knitted and woven fabrics. Blends of acrylic fibers with wool, cotton, other cellulose fibers such as rayon, and man-made noncellulosic fibers such as modacrylics and nylon are common in consumer goods. Acrylic fibers have low density and are soft; both of these properties contribute to producing fabrics that are bulky, soft, and light in weight compared with fabrics of similar construction made of natural fibers.

With concern for flame-resistant fibers, acrylic fiber manufacturers have developed modifications that have inherent flame resistance. One type of Acrilan, type B96, is one acrylic fiber with flame-resistant properties.

Acrylic fibers are highly suitable for blankets, carpeting, upholstery, and special floor coverings

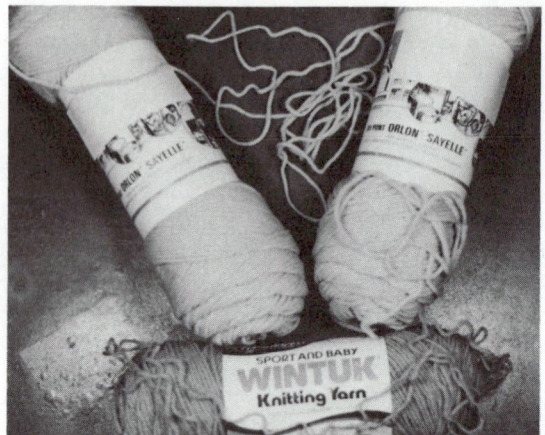

12.11 Knitting yrans of bicomponent acrylic fibers.

for such end uses as tennis courts and other sports surfaces. Properties that make them appropriate for such applications are rapid recovery from deformation, light weight, good covering power, and ease of maintenance.

Acrylic fibers are found in many items of apparel where shape retention and easy care are important considerations. Their light, bulky, soft properties make them prized choices for sportswear, sweaters, hosiery, and fleecewear.

Many acrylic fabrics can be safely washed in home laundry equipment and dried in home dryers that have variable temperature controls. Products bearing the certified trademarks of Sayelle or Wintuk (see Table 12.3) should be laundered in automatic washers and dried in automatic dryers; the tumbling action of the dryer is essential as part of the process needed to restore these fabrics to proper size and shape. It is important for the consumer to follow directions given on care labels for all acrylic fiber fabrics.

Deep-pile fabrics frequently have acrylic fibers in their construction. Acrylics are also used in a number of industrial applications. Many crochet and knitting yarns are made of acrylic fibers. These are easy to use, provide attractive finished products, retain their shape, and are easy to maintain.

MODACRYLIC FIBERS

Historical Review

The first modacrylic fiber, Dynel, was introduced to the public in 1949–1950 by Union Carbide Corpo-

ration. This was followed in 1956 by Verel®, a modacrylic fiber produced by Tennessee Eastman. SEF® and Elura®, made by Monsanto Fibers, were first marketed in 1972. A few foreign manufacturers are making modacrylic fibers, but the only modacrylic currently in production in the United States is made by Monsanto, SEF.

The TFPIA defines modacrylic as

a manufactured fiber in which the fiber-forming substance is any long-chain synthetic polymer comprised of less than 85 percent but at least 35 percent by weight of acrylonitrile units:

$$\left(CH_2 - CH - \atop \quad\quad\ \ |\ \atop \quad\quad\ CN \right)$$

except fibers qualifying under subparagraphs 2 of paragraph j (rubber) and fiber qualifying under paragraph g (anidex).

Production and Molecular Structure

Modacrylics are addition polymers composed of acrylonitrile (vinyl cyanide) and a second comonomer. The acrylonitrile accounts for at least 35 percent by weight but less than 85 percent of the polymer. The comonomer varies depending on the specific fiber producer. Dynel, the first modacrylic, was made from 60 percent vinyl chloride and 40 percent vinyl cyanide (acrylonitrile). A possible repeat is

$$\left(\begin{array}{cccc} H & H & H & H \\ | & | & | & | \\ -C- & C- & C & -C- \\ | & | & | & | \\ H & CN & H & Cl \end{array} \right)_n$$

Each of these chemicals has a double bond in the monomer; these are broken to permit the molecules to add together to form the polymolecule. The structural formula for acrylonitrile or vinyl cyanide is

$$\begin{array}{cc} H & H \\ | & | \\ H-C & = C-CN \end{array}$$

and for vinyl chloride it is

$$\begin{array}{cc} H & H \\ | & | \\ H-C & = C-Cl \end{array}$$

TABLE 12.3   Selected Properties of Modacrylic Fibers

Property	Evaluation
Shape	Controlled by manufacturer; irregular cross sections for all types.
Luster	Controlled from bright to dull.
Tenacity (strength)	2.0–3.1, g/d, same wet and dry
Elastic recovery	79–99% at 2% elongation
Elongation	35–48%
Resiliency	very good
Density	1.30–1.37 g/ccm
Moisture absorption	0.4–4.0% at standard conditions
Dimensional stability	good
Resistance to	
acids	good to excellent
alkalies	good to weak alkalies, moderate to strong alkalies
sunlight	excellent
microorganisms	excellent
insects	excellent
Thermal reactions	
to heat	Soften and shrink at temperatures from 150° to 190°C.
to flame	Shrink away from flame; do not support combustion; difficult to ignite; self-extinguishing and dripless.

Various methods are used to break the double bond so that addition polymerization can occur. The two chemicals are polymerized in an autoclave, where the polymer, in the form of a white powder, is made. The polymer is dissolved in acetone, filtered to remove impurities and undissolved polymer, and then extruded into a water bath, where it coagulates to form filaments. After spinning, the filaments are stretched while hot, annealed by heat to stabilize, and crimped. The heat treatment is essential to provide characteristics found desirable for end-use products.

Manufacturers of yarn and fabric may obtain the fiber in staple or in tow form. SEF, available from Monsanto, is used in several types of products. Information on the current status of Elura is unavailable.

Fiber Properties

Microscopic Properties

The longitudinal view of modacrylic fiber varies from a somewhat clear, uniform fiber to one with a grainy surface with faint striations. The cross section varies from one that is nearly round to a peanut shape. SEF modacrylic has an irregular cross section.

Physical Properties

SHAPE AND APPEARANCE   SEF is a white fiber with a slightly yellowish tone. It is easily bleached to a good white. It is available in its natural color or producer-dyed colors. Some modacrylics have built-in crimp. SEF is available in staple form only.

LUSTER   Modacrylic fibers are available in various lusters from bright to dull.

TENACITY (STRENGTH)   The tenacities of SEF and Verel are cited as 2.2 for SEF and 2.0 to 3.1 for Verel. Although the modacrylic fibers may be lower in strength than many other fibers, the tenacity is within satisfactory limits for the typical end uses. (See Table 12.3.)

ELONGATION AND ELASTIC RECOVERY   Modacrylic fibers have elongations of 48 percent for SEF and 35 percent for Verel. Verel has an immediate elastic recovery of only 79 percent, while the recovery for SEF is 86 percent. After a period of time under stress, SEF recovers all but 0.5 percent of the elongation, whereas Verel recovers all but 1 percent.

RESILIENCE   The resiliency of the modacrylics is good to very good. In pile fabrics modacrylics will return to shape after crushing in a very short time.

DENSITY The density of SEF is 1.35 g/ccm and of Verel, 1.37. Some other modacrylic fibers have been described as having densities as low as 1.30. The densities of modacrylic fibers compare with that of silk, wool, and acetate and contribute to the high bulk and lightweight characteristics of fabrics made of modacrylic fiber.

MOISTURE REGAIN The amount of moisture modacrylic fibers have at standard conditions varies from 0.4 to 4.0 percent. SEF is the most commonly used modacrylic fiber for apparel, and it has a moisture regain of 2.5 percent. There is little or no change in moisture regain when the fiber is subjected to high humidity.

DIMENSIONAL STABILITY Modacrylic fibers can be engineered so that there is little or no fiber shrinkage when they are exposed to hot water or temperatures below 170°C (375°F). Some modacrylics can be designed to shrink a predetermined amount when treated by boiling water or steam. Fibers with different levels of shrinkage are available for use in making fabrics with interesting and varied textures, such as pile fabrics with different heights of pile and "fake fur" fabrics. If modacrylic fiber fabrics have been properly stabilized after the fabrics are made, consumers should not encounter any undesirable dimensional change if proper care is given (see Table 12.3).

Thermal Properties

One of the most important properties of modacrylic fibers is their behavior when exposed to flame. Modacrylics do not support combustion. They are very difficult to ignite and are self-extinguishing. A hard black char is left, and no dripping occurs.

Verel resisted temperatures to 150°C (300°F); however, it began to stick at 180°C (356°F). If exposed to 180°C for extended periods, the fiber became discolored and stiff.

SEF modacrylic will resist temperatures to 190°C (375°F). Exposure to boiling water may cause from 1 to 6 percent shrinkage. Modacrylics can be laundered in home equipment with warm water, and fabrics can be dried in home tumble dryers if temperatures can be controlled.

Chemical Properties

EFFECT OF ALKALIES Modacrylic fibers possess good resistance to most alkalies. Prolonged exposure in some concentrated alkaline solutions results in fiber discoloration but little or no reduction in strength.

EFFECT OF ACIDS Modacrylics have good to excellent resistance to acids. At elevated temperatures, SEF may lose 5 to 10 percent of its normal strength following exposure to acids. Other modacrylics, in general, show little or no damage from acids at any concentration.

EFFECT OF ORGANIC SOLVENTS Most organic solvents have no deleterious effect on modacrylics. Acetone causes gradual disintegration of many modacrylic fibers, but SEF has good resistance. A 90 percent solution of formic acid will damage all modacrylics. Some solvents used in paint removers will stiffen, shrink, and weaken some modacrylics. Tests have shown that SEF has good resistance to most such solvents. Organic solvents used in home cleaning and stain removal can be used safely on modacrylic fibers.

EFFECT OF SUNLIGHT, AGE, AND MISCELLANEOUS FACTORS Modacrylics have excellent resistance to sunlight. Age appears to have no effect. The fibers are not damaged by bleaches, if properly used, nor by any type of detergent. The fibers are considered nonallergenic and nontoxic.

Static Charge

Modacrylics have high electrical resistivity and build up static charges.

Biological Properties

Modacrylic fibers exhibit excellent resistance to microorganisms and insects. However, as with many fibers, the presence of some finishes and soil may attract molds, mildew, and insects.

Types of Modacrylic Fibers

Tennessee Eastman manufactured Verel modacrylic, and it was available in several different types. Currently, production of this fiber has been discontinued.

Monsanto Fibers, manufacturers of SEF and Elura, promote these fibers for a variety of end uses. Elura has been identified as the modacrylic designed for wigs and hairpieces; SEF is made primarily for specialized types of apparel and selected special furnishings. SEF is available in various types

12.12 Children's sleepwear of type S-06 SEF® modacrylic fibers. (Monsanto Fibers)

12.13 Speaker grille of molded SEF® modacrylic fibers. (Monsanto Fibers)

characterized by differences in luster, amount and type of crimp, and shrinkage potential. Producer-dyed SEF is marketed, and a bigeneric yarn of modacrylic and polyester has been promoted for knit sleepwear.

A special modacrylic staple fiber is being made in Japan especially for use in children's stuffed toys. It has excellent flame resistance and gives a high shine or "mirror" surface to the item.

Use and Care of Modacrylic Products

The future of modacrylic fiber expansion is uncertain. The current market and existing federal standards concerning flame resistance established a firm market for current production. However, the general deemphasis on additional flammability legislation makes market expansion questionable at this time.

The major end uses for modacrylic fibers are draperies, casement curtains, children's sleepwear (Fig. 12.12), "fake" furs, blankets, knitted goods, wigs and other hairpieces, transportation fabrics, and industrial materials. All of these uses depend to a certain degree on the flame resistance of the fiber.

Fabrics made of modacrylic fibers are soft, resilient, stable in size, easily laundered, safely drycleanable, low in pilling, resistant to sunlight, and resistant to flame. This last factor is of great importance in this era of consumer concern about flame-resistant fabrics, as well as government and consumer advocates' demands for flame-resistant items.

Modacrylic fibers are frequently used in blends with other fibers, especially acrylic fibers. Special fabrics of modacrylic and acrylic fibers are used for coating fabrics (especially high-pile types), for knitting yarns, and for carpeting. In blends with polyester, fabrics are produced for apparel, carpeting, area floor coverings, knitting yarns, and draperies.

Pleats, creases, and even molded shapes (Fig. 12.13) can be heat-set in modacrylic fabrics. This process can build in permanent design lines and produce molded shapes for such home and industrial uses as chair seats, speaker grilles, and aircraft furnishings.

Modacrylic fibers have easy-care characteristics. They can be laundered easily and safely in home equipment, and they can be dry-cleaned if desired. The only caution is to avoid high temperatures at all stages of care. Stains are easily removed by normal care procedures.

One other caution should be noted. The use of acetone should be avoided or at least checked prior to use, as some modacrylics are softened and strength is reduced after exposure to acetone. Thus, it is important to avoid spilling acetone-containing solvents, such as nail polish removers and paint thinners, on modacrylic fibers. As for any fabric, care directions provided on labels should be followed in the maintenance process.

STUDY QUESTIONS

1. List and describe the properties of acrylic fibers.
2. Why are acrylic fibers popular with consumers? In what types of end-use items are these fibers generally found?
3. Why might consumers become dissatisfied with acrylic fiber fabrics?
4. What are the properties of modacrylic fibers? How do they differ from acrylic fibers?
5. How are the acrylic and modacrylic fibers alike?
6. In what type of end-use items would the typical consumer tend to find modacrylic fibers?
7. Why are acrylic bicomponent fibers popular?

Activities

1. Locate fabrics and end-use items available on the market made of acrylic and/or modacrylic fibers either alone or in blends. Obtain samples, if possible, and test them in the laboratory. If samples are not available, describe the type of product in which the fibers have been found, and state why they are or are not appropriate to the specific end use.
2. Interview owners and managers of fabric stores, and determine the prevalence of acrylic and/or modacrylic fiber fabrics on the current market. Explain the information you obtain.

13

Olefin Fibers

KEY TERMS

atatic   polyethylene
isotatic   polypropylene
olefin

Olefin fibers are manufactured by a great many companies. A majority of the companies are small and produce limited amounts of the fiber. Polyethylene fibers were first developed by Imperial Chemical Industries in England, and the first polypropylene fibers were made by Montecatini in Italy in 1952. Since that time various olefin fibers have been made by a variety of manufacturers in the United States and in many foreign countries. There are currently (1984) over 60 companies producing olefin fibers in the United States.

The Textile Fiber Products Identification Act defines olefin as "a manufactured fiber in which the fiber-forming substance is any long-chain synthetic polymer composed of at least 85 percent by weight of ethylene, propylene, or other olefin units, except amorphous (noncrystalline) polyolefins qualifying under category 1 of paragraph j (rubber) of Rule 7." Such a definition gives scientists considerable leeway, for they can manufacture olefin fibers from any of the hydrocarbons of the alkene group—those hydrocarbons that have a double bond in the basic chemical component. At the present time, the fiber industry is concentrating its efforts on polymers from ethylene ($CH_2 = CH_2$) and propylene ($CH_3CH = CH_2$).

Production

Two general processes are used in manufacturing polyethylene: the high-pressure system and the low-pressure method. The high-pressure system polyermizes the ethylene gas in autoclaves at 200°C (392°F) under pressure equal to 10 tons per square inch (1.4 metric tons/cm^2). The low-pressure method polymerizes the gas at temperatures of 55°–65°C (130°–150°F) by using pressure of only 450 pounds per square inch (32 kg/cm^2), with a catalyst and a hydrocarbon solvent. This process is less expensive and results in polymers more suitable for textile fibers than those created by the high-pressure process.

To produce olefin fibers the polymer is melt-spun at temperatures of 300°C (570°F) into water or a current of cooling air. The filaments are cooled and then "cold-drawn" or stretched to six times the spun length. This drawing process introduces molecular orientation and makes the fiber fine and pliable.

The molecular structure of polyethylene is a linear polymer of ethylene units:

$$-CH_2CH_2CH_2CH_2CH_2CH_2 \ldots CH_2-$$

TABLE 13.1 Properties of Olefin Fibers

Property	Polyethylene	Polypropylene
Shape	Controlled during manufacture, but usually olefin fibers are round.	
Luster	Controlled; may be bright to dull.	
Tenacity (strength)	1.5–3.0 g/d for high pressure	3.5–8.0 g/d
	4.0–7.0 g/d for low pressure	
Elastic recovery	100% at 2% extension for both	
Elongation	20–80%	15–50%
Resiliency	good	good
Density	0.92–0.96 g/ccm	0.90–0.91 g/ccm
Moisture absorbency	less than 1% for both	
Dimensional stability	If stabilized, good resistance unless subjected to temperatures above 120°C.	
Resistance to		
acids	excellent	excellent
alkalies	excellent	excellent
organic solvents	medium	medium
sunlight	slowly degrades	slowly degrades
microorganisms	good	good
insects	good	good
Thermal reactions		
to heat	Shrink at 75°C.	Shrink at 120°C.
	Melt at low temperature.	Melt at 170°C.
to flame	Both fibers burn and emit heavy, sooty, waxy smoke.	

The repeat unit is

$$
\left(
\begin{array}{c}
\ \ \text{H} \quad \text{H} \\
\ \ | \qquad | \\
-\text{C}-\text{C}- \\
\ \ | \qquad | \\
\ \ \text{H} \quad \text{H}
\end{array}
\right)_n \qquad n = \text{c. }550
$$

The manufacture of polypropylene requires special procedures because of the characteristics of the monomer. The structural formula for propylene is

$$
\begin{array}{c}
\qquad \text{H} \\
\qquad | \\
\text{H}-\text{C}=\text{C}-\text{H} \\
\qquad | \\
\qquad \text{CH}_3
\end{array}
$$

When this monomer polymerizes, the pendant CH_3 can lie in either direction. This polymer form, called *atatic,* has little molecular packing or crystallinity and does not form a good fiber. To make a satisfactory fiber, propylene must be polymerized into the *isotatic* form, where the methyl side chain, the —CH₃— group, is always on the same side of the backbone carbon chain, that is:

$$
\left(
\begin{array}{c}
\text{H} \ \ \text{H} \ \ \text{H} \ \ \text{H} \ \ \text{H} \ \ \text{H} \ \ \text{H} \ \ \text{H} \qquad\qquad \text{H} \ \ \text{H} \\
|\ \ |\ \ |\ \ |\ \ |\ \ |\ \ |\ \ | \qquad\qquad |\ \ | \\
-\text{C}-\text{C}-\text{C}-\text{C}-\text{C}-\text{C}-\text{C}-\text{C}-\ \cdots\ -\text{C}-\text{C}- \\
|\ \ |\ \ |\ \ |\ \ |\ \ |\ \ |\ \ | \qquad\qquad |\ \ | \\
\text{CH}_3\,\text{H} \ \ \text{CH}_3\,\text{H} \ \ \text{CH}_3\,\text{H} \ \ \text{CH}_3\text{H} \qquad \text{CH}_3\text{H}
\end{array}
\right)
$$

To produce this form of polypropylene, special catalysts must be used. These catalysts control the polymerization so that the isotatic form is produced. The polymerization process involved is addition; as the double bond is broken in the propylene molecule, the monomer or single molecules join or add together.

As an alternative to the formation of fibers by melt spinning, some olefin fibers are made from film. The polymer is extruded in a sheet form, the sheet is cut into narrow tapes or strips, and the tape is fibrillated using special mechanical devices. The fibrillated tape is twisted to form yarn that is similar to extruded filaments.

The repeat unit for polypropylene is

$$(-\text{CHCH}_3\text{CH}_2-)_n \qquad n = 7,000+$$

This can be structured as follows:

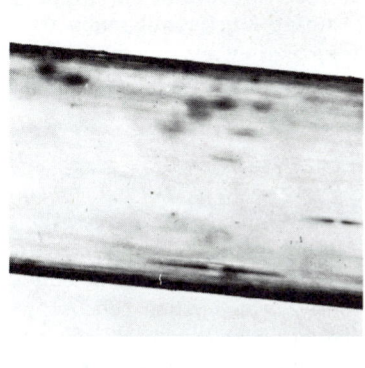
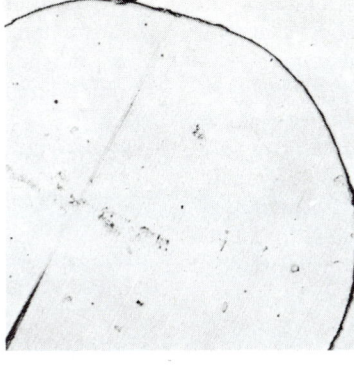

13.1 (*Left*) Photomicrograph of polyethylene, longitudinal view. (DuPont Company)

13.2 (*Right*) Photomicrograph of polyethylene, cross section. (DuPont Company)

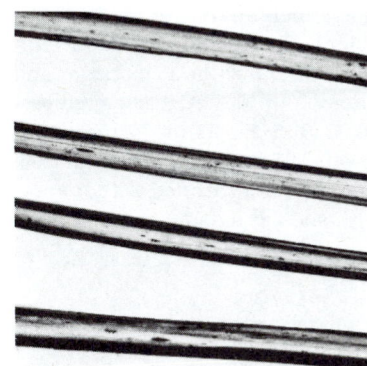
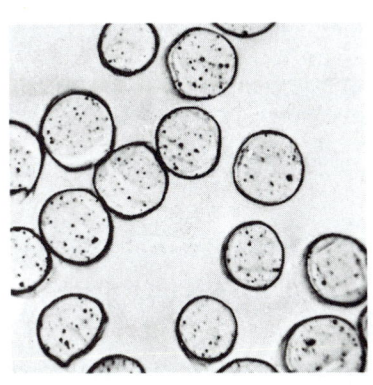

13.3 (*Left*) Photomicrograph of polypropylene, longitudinal view. (DuPont Company)

13.4 (*Right*) Photomicrograph of polypropylene, cross section. (DuPont Company)

$$\begin{pmatrix} \begin{array}{cc} H & H \\ | & | \\ -C & C- \\ | & | \\ H-C-H & H \\ | \\ H \end{array} \end{pmatrix}$$

The typical molecular weight for olefin fiber is usually 250,000 or more.

Fiber Properties

Microscopic Properties

Both polyethylene and polypropylene fibers resemble glass rods in longitudinal and cross-sectional views (Figs. 13.1–13.4). They are even, clear, and usually round or elliptical. Some polypropylene fibers are given various forms for special end uses; these have irregular cross sections.

Physical Properties

SHAPE AND APPEARANCE The ethylene polymers are smooth, white, and waxy in both appearance and feel. The low-pressure type is somewhat less waxy than the high-pressure fiber. The polypropylene polymer is less waxy than polyethylene, but it, too, is smooth and white. The multifilament yarns are soft and have a pleasant hand (see Table 13.1).

LUSTER Olefin fibers vary in luster from bright to dull. The majority of olefin fibers used for textiles have a medium luster.

TENACITY (STRENGTH) The high-pressure polyethylene fibers have comparatively low tenacity, only 1.5 to 3 grams per denier. There is no difference between wet and dry strength. Low-pressure fibers are stronger; their tenacity varies with the degree of polymerization from about 4 to 7 grams per denier, either wet or dry.

The tenacity of polypropylene fibers also varies with the degree of polymerization from about 3.5 to 8.0 grams per denier. In both instances the stronger fibers have a higher degree of polymerization and greater molecular orientation.

ELASTIC RECOVERY AND ELONGATION The elongation of the low-density ethylene has a wide variation from 20 to 80 percent. This type has excellent elastic recovery: 100 percent at 2 percent extension, 95 percent at 5 percent extension, and 88 percent at 10 percent extension. High-density polyethylene has an elongation from 10 to 45 percent, and elastic recovery is also excellent, with 100 percent recovery up to 10 percent elongation. Both types develop permanent deformation if stretched more than 10 percent.

The elongation of polypropylene fibers may be influenced also by the degree of polymerization and molecular orientation. The denier of the fiber further influences the elongation, fine fibers tending to have higher degrees of stretch. The elastic recovery of polypropylene is excellent. At up to 5 percent extension the fibers have 100 percent recovery; at 10 percent extension the recovery is from 95 to 100 percent; and at 15 percent extension the recovery is about 90 percent.

RESILIENCY Both polyethylene and polypropylene have good resistance to crushing. Evidence indicates that polypropylene fibers give good service in floor coverings. However, to obtain optimum performance from polypropylene carpeting, the structure should be characterized by low, uncut pile and tightly twisted yarns.

DENSITY Olefin fibers are lighter than water and will float. The density of polyethylene varies from 0.92 to 0.96 grams per cubic centimeter; polypropylene fibers have a density between 0.90 and 0.91 g/ccm. With such a low density, the fibers can be used to make various lightweight fabrics.

MOISTURE REGAIN Both types of olefin fibers have practically no moisture absorbency or regain. The producers of Meraklon® polypropylene state that their fiber will absorb up to 0.1 percent moisture when thoroughly wet. Other manufacturers give from 0 to 1 percent as saturation regain.

DIMENSIONAL STABILITY Unless the olefin fibers are properly heat-set, they will shrink when exposed to warm temperatures. This fact has been used to advantage by some manufacturers as a means of producing interesting designs in fabrics. A fabric called Trilok is a good example. It is highly textured because of the shrinkage of olefin yarns and is an excellent fabric for insulation, for sound baffles, and for special protective clothing.

When olefin yarns are preshrunk and properly heat-treated, the resulting fabrics will retain their size and shape as long as they are not subjected to temperatures greater than about 120°C (250°F).

Thermal Properties

Olefin fibers burn slowly. A hard tan or fawn-colored residue is formed. Probably the most serious disadvantage of olefin fibers is their heat sensitivity. They will shrink at temperatures as low as 100°C (212°F) if not properly treated. They can be preshrunk and stabilized, but even then the fibers may soften and melt at relatively low temperatures.

Polyethylene fibers melt at 105°–125°C (220°–255°F). Polypropylene fibers will withstand temperatures to 138°C (280°F) without damage, and they do not actually melt until they reach a temperature of about 170°C (335°F). As many irons cannot be set below about 185°F, and few go that low, most olefin fibers should not be ironed without protection of some type, such as a damp press cloth.

Chemical Properties

EFFECT OF ALKALIES Olefin fibers are highly resistant to alkaline substances.

EFFECT OF ACIDS The polyethylene fibers have excellent resistance to acids, except for strong oxidizing acids, which cause a loss of strength and, after prolonged exposure, complete disintegration. Polypropylene has the same general resistance to acids as polyethylene, although some of the polypropylene fibers appear to be weakened by chlorosulfonic acid.

EFFECT OF ORGANIC SOLVENTS Chlorinated hydrocarbons cause swelling and may result in degradation of all olefin fibers. The fibers should not be dry-cleaned if perchloroethylene is the cleaning solvent used; however, trichloroethylene may be used on the fiber.

EFFECT OF SUNLIGHT, AGE, AND MISCELLANEOUS FACTORS Both polyethylene and polypropylene lose strength and slowly degrade after exposure to sunlight. To make these fibers usable for the many outdoor and other applications that expose them to sunlight, stabilizing and inhibiting chemicals that increase resistance to damage from sunlight are added during manufacture. Age, however, has no effect on olefin fibers. Soaps and synthetic detergents do not appear to be harmful, and bleaches, if properly diluted, can be used safely.

The olefins are subject to staining and spotting by oils and greases, and polyethylene stains more quickly than polypropylene. However, the stains usually can be removed if prompt action is taken.

These fibers are nonallergenic. Manufacturers claim that olefins do not pill badly. They have a high degree of cohesiveness, which results in their holding together exceptionally well in yarns.

Static Charge

Olefin fibers do have static electric buildup, but it is considered to be less than that of nylon or polyester fiber fabrics.

Biological Properties

Olefin fibers have good resistance to microorganisms such as mildew and bacteria and to insects such as moths, beetles, and other household pests.

Use and Care of Olefin Fibers

Polyethylene fibers are widely used in industrial fabrics, but they have not been well accepted for apparel or home furnishings. One reason for this is the fact that polyethylene fibers cannot be dyed by normal techniques, although pigments can be added to the molten polymer before extrusion. However, the primary use for polyethylene fibers during the past decade has not required coloration.

Polypropylene fibers have a variety of industrial applications and have also attained widespread acceptance in home furnishings and some apparel fabrics. Several manufacturers have made fabrics for suits and dresses, and blends of polypropylene with wool, cotton, and rayon are used in knitted fabrics for sportswear.

Depending on yarn and fabric construction and finishing, the hand of polypropylene fabrics will vary greatly. The fabric has been used in coating fabrics, blanket fabrics, and knitted fabrics for sportswear.

The best-known domestic and commercial uses for polypropylene fibers are in carpeting, drapery fabrics, upholstery fabric, and carpet tiles (Fig. 13.5). The fiber has been employed in needle-punched indoor-outdoor carpeting with great suc-

13.5 Herculon® olefin upholstery fabric. (Hercules, Inc.)

13.6 Herculon® olefin commercial carpeting (Hercules, Inc.)

cess. Indoor tufted carpeting of polypropylene is also very popular, very successful, and durable (Fig. 13.6). Industrial uses for polypropylene include civil engineering fabrics and geotextile applications.

The fiber is easily cleaned and resists crushing, two factors that increase its popularity for floor coverings. The introduction of the polypropylene fibers to indoor-outdoor carpeting and carpet tiles has led to a tremendous increase in the amount of carpet to be found in kitchens, work areas, patios, and around swimming pools. With the introduction of Marvess® Sunlight Resistant olefin, tufted carpet can now be designed with extremely high resistance to color fading for both commercial and residential applications including swimming pool areas, decks, miniature golf courses, balconies, sidewalks, walkways, patios, and breezeways.

Polypropylene and some polyethylene are used as a base for tufted carpeting in both woven and nonwoven fabric constructions. These base fabrics hold their shape and aid in retaining the tufted pile yarns in an upright position.

Some of the other end uses for olefin fibers include the following. Polypropylene represents a large market for cover stock for diapers and other disposable items. Solution-dyed polypropylene, needle-punched and tufted, is widely used in automotive interiors for economy, low weight, good color retention, and heat stability. Other applications are flooring, panels, shelves, liners, and loading decks.

Because of its excellent resistance to chemicals, polypropylene can be used in woven, knitted, or nonwoven form for filters for chemicals, air, and various liquids. Industrial applications for polypropylene include rope, bagging, nets, sewing threads, felts, channel fabrics, and liner fabrics where strength, elongation, toughness, and light weight are desirable. Nonwoven applications for polypropylene have increased tremendously in the last few years because of the fiber's unique combination of properties, including durability, economy, low density (which provides increased bulk and cover), wicking properties, and thermal bonding. Major markets today include furniture and bedding construction fabrics, laminates for vinyl "artifical leather" goods, carpet backing, pavement repair,

roofing felts, geotextile fabrics (especially for subsoil use), and many others.

Olefin fibers are relatively low in cost. The increase in production since 1965 has been considerably greater than expected. Many polypropylene and polyethylene manufacturers do not trademark their fibers. However, a few trademarks used for these fibers are cited in Table 2.2, page 15.

One unusual application of olefin fibers is particularly interesting to skiers. Specially shaped filaments locked into a durable but flexible base are used to form artificial ski slopes.

Olefin fibers and fabrics launder well, dry quickly, and require little or no ironing. Floor coverings are easily cleaned, and stains wipe off with a sponge or cloth and water. Detergents can be used for stubborn stains. The olefins respond to laundering better than to dry cleaning; in fact, dry cleaning is seldom recommended.

STUDY QUESTIONS

1. What care procedures would be recommended for products made of olefin fibers?
2. Why is olefin a good choice for carpeting for indoor-outdoor use?
3. What type of apparel items lend themselves to fabrics made of olefin fibers?
4. What might cause consumer dissatisfaction with products made of olefin fibers?
5. How are olefin fibers usually colored? Why?
6. What is the relation between the chemical properties of olefin fibers and selected end uses for the fibers?

Activities

1. Visit the marketplace and identify various products made with olefin fibers. What types of products do you find? Why might they be made of olefin fibers?
2. List the properties of polyethylene and polypropylene fibers. Compare the two and identify similarities and differences.

14

Elastomeric Fibers

OBJECTIVES

◊ **To describe the properties of natural and synthetic rubber fibers**

◊ **To describe processes used in producing man-made elastomeric fibers such as spandex**

◊ **To describe the properties of elastomeric fibers, especially spandex**

◊ **To identify typical end uses and care procedures for elastomeric fibers**

KEY TERMS

anidex
elastomers
lastrile

rubber, man-made
rubber, natural
spandex

Elastomers are elastic, rubberlike substances. They can be prepared in various forms, but discussion here is limited to fibrous forms used in textile products. All elastomers are characterized by extremely high elongation—at least 200 percent, and frequently between 500 and 800 percent—and excellent elastic recovery.

RUBBER

The Textile Fiber Products Identification Act defines rubber as

a manufactured fiber in which the fiber-forming substance is comprised of natural or synthetic rubber, including the following categories:

1. a manufactured fiber in which the fiber-forming substance is a hydrocarbon such as natural rubber, polyisoprene, polybutadiene, copolymers of dienes and hydrocarbons, or amorphous (noncrystalline) polyolefins.
2. a manufactured fiber in which the fiber-forming substance is a copolymer of acrylonitrile and a diene (such as butadiene) composed of not more than 50 percent but at least 10 percent by weight of acrylonitrile units

$$\left(\begin{array}{c} CH_2 - CH - \\ | \\ CN \end{array} \right)$$

The term *lastrile* may be used as a generic description for fibers falling in this category.

3. a manufactured fiber in which the fiber-forming substance is a polychloroprene or a copolymer of chloroprene in which at least 35 percent by weight of the fiber-forming substance is composed of chloroprene units

$$\left(\begin{array}{c} -CH_2 - C = CH - CH_2 - \\ | \\ Cl \end{array} \right)$$

The thick, gummy liquid obtained from trees of the *Hevea* species has been used for many hundreds of years. In 1839 Charles Goodyear discovered that the properties of rubber were greatly changed when it was heated with sulfur. Strength and elasticity were increased, and cold temperatures no longer hardened it or made it brittle. Goodyear's process is known as *vulcanizing;* it set the scene for the development of rubber in many forms.

Rubber in fiber form originated in the 1920s as a result of research by U.S. Rubber Company. Scientists discovered that liquid rubber (latex) could be extruded in fiber form, which has high elongation and elastic recovery. These early fibers were not used alone but served as a central core for other fibers, such as cotton, which were wrapped around them. To some extent this is still used today.

Synthetic rubbers were first developed in the early 1930s. Today, both natural and synthetic rubber have wide markets; they are used for many different types of products.

The properties that make rubber desirable in selected end uses include a high degree of elasticity, flexibility and pliability, strength, toughness, impermeability to water and air, resistance to cutting and tearing, resistance to many chemicals, and a density of about 1.0 g/ccm.

The properties that introduce problems in end use include sensitivity to temperatures greater than 93°C (200°F), which cause deterioration and loss of pliability; deterioration by sunlight; loss of strength and elasticity through aging; damage from body oils; and damage caused by petroleum solvents. In general, synthetic rubbers have fewer of these drawbacks than natural rubber.

To prepare latex for fiber, the manufacturer mixes it with certain ingredients (classified information) to reduce air and light deterioration; it is then vulcanized. The fine rubber filaments are covered with some other textile fiber, such as cotton, rayon, or nylon. The technique used in covering a rubber core controls the degree of elongation and elastic recovery of the final yarn. The fiber used in covering the rubber is important, for it influences the comfort, absorbency, hand, and appearance of the end product.

Rubber yarns contribute support and improved fit to end-use products. Fabrics with rubber are comparatively crease-resistant and require a minimum of ironing.

Rubber can be laundered if the water temperature does not exceed 60°C (140°F). Built soaps or synthetic detergents can be used, and they remove oily soil better than unbuilt detergents. Drying in an automatic dryer at medium temperature settings is considered safe, but the dryer must have temperature controls to prevent excessive heat. Many authorities, however, recommend air drying for any product in which rubber is a component. It is very important to clean fabrics containing rubber frequently; in fact, cleaning after each wearing will reduce damage from body oils and extend the life of the product. Dry cleaning of fabrics with rubber should be avoided.

Rubber yarns are used in foundation garments, swimwear, surgical fabrics (such as elastic bandages and support hose), underwear for both sexes, elastic yarns for decorative stitching; shoe fabrics; tops of men's and children's socks, and elastic tape. Various forms of natural and synthetic rubber are used in textile finishing.

Foam latex, though not a true textile, requires the same careful handling as textile fibers. It is used for upholstery filler, mattresses, pillow forms, and similar products. Polyurethane has replaced latex foam in many end uses. It is less subject to deterioration by factors that damage other rubbers, such as light, dry-cleaning solvents, and age. Polyurethane foams are manufactured from the same chemicals used to produce spandex fibers.

During the 1960s one chemical company sought to establish a new generic term for an elastomeric fiber. As a result, the FTC redefined rubber and specified the name *lastrile* as a substitute generic term for one special group of rubber fibers (as indicated in the definition cited earlier). To date there has been no commercial development or production of lastrile fibers.

SPANDEX

The Textile Fiber Products Identification Act defines spandex as ''a manufactured fiber in which the fiber-forming substance is a long-chain synthetic polymer comprised of at least 85 percent of a segmented polyurethane.''

Spandex was introduced by the DuPont Company in 1958. Plans for volume production and the trade name Lycra® were announced in late 1959. U.S. Rubber introduced a spandex elastomer trademarked Vyrene® the same year. Since the mid-1970s, however, there has been no production of this elastomeric fiber. During the 1960s several new spandex fibers were released in limited quantities. However, at present (1984) only Lycra, Cleerspan®, and Glospan® are available from manufacturers in the United States.

Various textile authorities have predicted the ultimate inclusion of spandex fibers in a large percentage of all fabrics manufactured. This effort to build stretch into consumer products has occurred to some extent, but there has not been the amount of use that was predicted in the early 1970s. Further, comfort stretch (see Chap. 20) can be achieved by a variety of methods, not all of which include the use of spandex fibers.

$$\text{HO} - \text{R} - \text{OH} \ + \ \text{OCN} - \langle \ \rangle - \text{CH}_2 - \langle \ \rangle - \text{NCO} \longrightarrow$$

macropolyester + diphenyl methane diisocyanate

$$\text{OCN} - \langle \ \rangle - \text{CH}_2 - \langle \ \rangle - \text{NHCOO} - \text{R} - \text{OCONH} - \langle \ \rangle - \text{CH}_2 - \langle \ \rangle - \text{NCO}$$

macrodiisocyanate intermediate

Production

Spandex fibers are composed of segmented polyurethane. The structure is achieved by a chemical reaction between a diisocyanate and a second monomer with the formation of a block polymer, in which long chains of a flexible structure are joined to short chains of a stiff structure through urethane linkages. The fact that these linkages are stable to acids and alkalies permits dyeing, finishing, and laundering. The block-type polymer provides both elasticity and stability to fabrics.

The chemical reaction is complex. Furthermore, it would appear that manufacturers of spandex fibers use different processes to form the polyurethane. One process includes three steps. First, ethylene glycol, propylene glycol, and adipic acid are combined to form a macropolyester with a molecular weight of about 2000. The second step combines this macropolyester with diphenyl methane diisocyanate to form an intermediate polymer. A diagram for this process is shown at the top of the page.

The intermediate is next extended to a high polymer by condensation with an aliphatic diamine such as ethylene diamine. The structural formula for the repeat unit is at the bottom of the page.

Some of the spandex fibers are processed to develop cross-links between molecules, and better stability is thereby created.

Little technical information is available on the production of most spandex fibers. However, it may be safely conjectured that a diisocyanate is combined with a substance containing terminal hydroxyl groups and then with a diamine. The base compounds may vary widely.

14.1 Photomicrograph of Lycra spandex, longitudinal view. (DuPont Company)

Fiber Properties

Microscopic Appearance

Spandex fibers vary in microscopic appearance, but there are some similarities (Figs. 14.1 and 14.2). As for many man-made fibers, the longitudinal view shows fibers of even diameter. Spandex typically appears spotted or grainy. The cross sections exhibit differences in the shape of the primary filaments, but the way they coalesce into yarns is similar for most spandex fibers. Lycra filaments are smooth, with essentially round cross sections that fuse to-

$$- \langle \ \rangle - \text{CH}_2 - \langle \ \rangle - \text{NHCNH} - \text{CH}_2\text{CH}_2 - \text{NHCNH} - \langle \ \rangle - \text{CH}_2 - \langle \ \rangle - \text{NHC} - \text{O} - \text{R} - \text{O} - \text{CNH} -$$

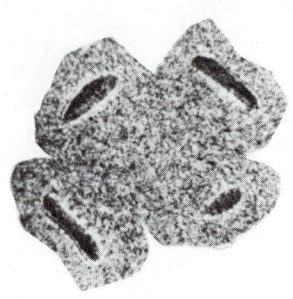

14.2 Photomicrograph of Glospan spandex, cross section, 280 denier. (Globe Manufacturing Company)

Chemical Properties

Spandex filaments have good resistance to most chemicals. Concentrated alkalies at elevated temperatures cause loss of strength and eventual degradation. Strong hypochlorite bleaches may affect spandex by causing a yellowing and a loss of strength. Strong oxidizing compounds such as nitrous acid may produce a change in color and loss of strength in certain spandex products.

Comparisons with Rubber

Major advantages of spandex over rubber include resistance to degradation by ultraviolet light (sunlight); by weathering, especially smog; and by oil, particularly body oils. Spandex has a higher modulus of elasticity than rubber and can give garments that are lighter in weight but still provide the same degree of figure control. Spandex fibers are superior to rubber in their flex life and dyeability, as well as in their resistance to oxidation, to abrasion, to damage by dry-cleaning solvents, and to damage in machine laundering and drying.

Use and Care of Spandex Fibers

Spandex fibers can be laundered by hand or machine and dried in the air or in a dryer at medium to low temperatures. Any type of good detergent can be used. DuPont recommends perborate bleaches rather than chlorine-containing bleaches for Lycra spandex. Normal concentrations of chlorine in swimming pools may cause long-term damage to spandex. In addition to discoloration from chlorine compounds, white spandex may yellow as a result of acid fumes, smog, body oils, and perspiration. However, this does not affect stretch properties to any noticeable degree. Frequent laundering may reduce the discoloration. Colored fabrics show very little, if any, color change with proper care.

Spandex is utilized in the bare filament or uncovered form; in yarn constructions where spandex is wrapped spirally with yarns of other fibers to produce a covered yarn; and in core-spun yarns. The amount of stretch can be predetermined and controlled by yarn-spinning machine adjustments. Spandex provides a high flex life and can be used in varying amounts to provide comfort or power stretch (see Chap. 20). Spandex combines high holding power with light weight.

End-use items that contain spandex fibers in-

gether at random points. Globe's spandex fiber, Glospan, has serrated edges, which are fused rather heavily to form crenulated or coalesced multifilament yarns. The fusion of filaments serves a twofold purpose. It prevents filaments from stripping out of the yarn, and it minimizes damage if the yarn is pierced by a sewing machine needle.

Physical Properties

The tenacity of spandex fibers varies from about 0.5 to 1.5 grams per denier. The fibers generally have an elongation of 500 to 700 percent or greater. This elongation provides an actual strength in use that is considerably higher than indicated by tenacity values. Elastic recovery is excellent. Immediate recovery from 200 percent elongation is 97 percent, and from 50 percent elongation the recovery is more than 99 percent. The fiber exhibits minor differences in density, ranging from 1.2 to 1.25 grams per cubic centimeter. This is due to the difference in the actual formulations and proportions of flexible to hard segments.

Moisture regain is low and varies from 0.3 to 1.2 percent for different fibers.

Spandex fibers are available in fine to heavy denier or diameter. They are normally left undyed, but they accept selected dyes easily and evenly.

Thermal Properties

Spandex fibers will burn and form a gummy residue. They can be ironed safely at temperatures below 150°C (300°F) and can be tumble-dried without damage, provided the dryer has temperature controls. Most spandex fibers are not damaged by temperatures used in either dry cleaning or laundering operations. Low ironing temperatures are recommended. Most spandex fibers are not damaged by short exposure to temperature between 95° and 150°C (200°–300°F).

clude swimsuits, foundation garments, bras, straps for lingerie, sock tops, hosiery, medical products requiring elasticity, outerwear apparel, home furnishings such as slipcovers, and domestic materials such as fitted sheets.

ANIDEX

A generic term, *anidex* was added to the Textile Fiber Products Identification Act in 1969. This term is defined as "a manufactured fiber in which the fiber-forming substance is any long-chain synthetic polymer composed of at least 50 percent by weight of one or more esters of a monohydric alcohol and acrylic acid ($CH_2=CH-COOH$)."

The only anidex fiber developed was ANIM/8, announced by Rohm and Haas in 1970. The fiber was never marketed commercially. However, it was described as an elastomeric fiber that could be bleached with chlorine; was adaptable to various types of yarnmaking processes, such as core spinning and bare constructions; could be given a wide selection of dyes in either solid colors or prints; and could take permanent-press and soil-release finishes without loss of elasticity.

1. Describe the properties of rubber fibers. How do natural and man-made rubber fibers differ? How are they similar?
2. Describe spandex fibers and cite their properties.
3. What are typical end uses for rubber and for spandex fibers?
4. Why is spandex recommended over rubber for many end uses?
5. In what end uses might rubber fibers be a better choice?
6. Why is spandex a good choice for fabrics to be made into swimwear?
7. What other types of sportswear usually include some spandex fiber? Why?

Activities

1. What type of products with spandex fibers included in the fabric are available on the consumer market? Locate special products with spandex as well as typical consumer products.
2. Locate fabrics in which spandex has been used, and test with varying levels of chlorine to determine what would happen to swimsuits worn in swimming pools.

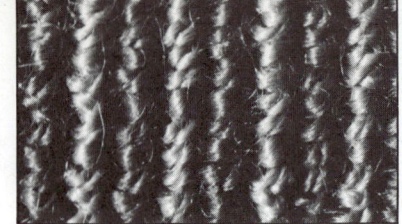

15

Other Man-Made Noncellulosic Fibers

OBJECTIVES

◊ **To describe the general properties of the man-made noncellulosic fibers in limited use**

◊ **To identify special fibers that provide special high-performance properties**

◊ **To identify the properties of high-performance fibers that make them applicable for specialized end uses**

◊ **To provide information concerning generic groups of fibers not produced in the United States at present but that have been identified in the TFPIA**

KEY TERMS

azlon	polychal	saran
novoloid	polyformaldehyde fiber	teflon
nytril	polyurea fiber	vinal
PBI fiber	promix	vinyon

Generic groups of fibers identified by the Textile Fiber Products Identification Act as well as individual fiber types not listed in the TFPIA that are of limited importance or of limited use are discussed in this chapter. Because of specific characteristics, these fibers are of sufficient importance that students should be aware of them. Fibers in a few of the generic groups are not being produced at the present time, but they offer properties that may bring about their return, or the fiber may be of historical value. Several of the fibers are of considerable importance in industrial products, and a few find limited use in specialized types of apparel and home furnishings.

SARAN

The first saran fiber appeared on the market in 1940. The TFPIA defines saran as "a manufactured fiber in which the fiber-forming substance is any long-chain synthetic polymer composed of at least 80 percent by weight of vinylidene chloride units ($-CH_2-CCl_2-$)."

Dow Chemical Corporation introduced saran fiber, and it has been spun, under license, by several other companies. According to information available in early 1984, saran is being produced by Ametek Company. The world production, as well as United States production, of saran is low. Most manufacturers that did produce a saran fiber have discontinued it in favor of olefin fibers, which are considerably less expensive.

Production

Saran is manufactured by polymerizing 80 percent or more of vinylidene chloride and 20 percent or less of vinyl chloride or vinyl cyanide, in the presence of heat and a catalyst. The chemical action and the molecular repeat diagram are as follows:

$$
\begin{array}{cccc}
\text{H} & \text{Cl} & & \text{H} \quad \text{H} \\
| & | & & | \quad\quad | \\
\text{H}-\text{C}=\text{C}-\text{Cl} & + & \text{H}-\text{C}=\text{C}-\text{Cl} \rightarrow
\end{array}
$$

vinylidene chloride   vinyl chloride

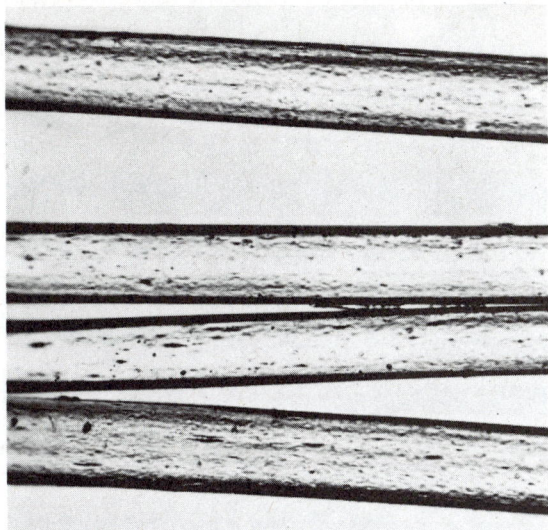

15.1 Photomicrograph of saran, longitudinal view. (DuPont Company)

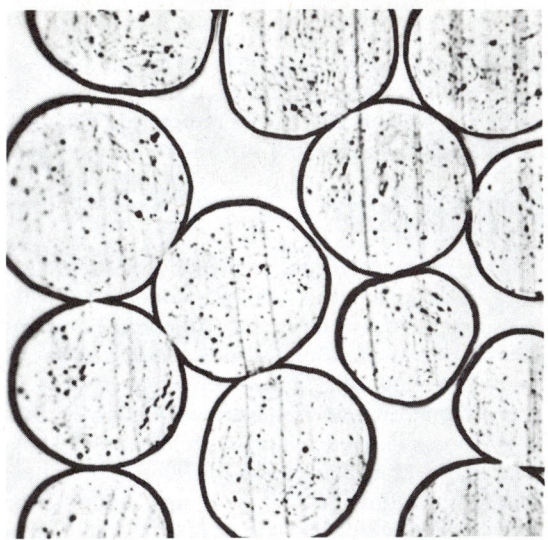

15.2 Photomicrograph of saran, cross section. (DuPont Company)

$$\left(\begin{matrix} H & Cl & H & H & H & Cl & H & Cl \\ | & | & | & | & | & | & | & | \\ -C- & C- & C- & C- & C- & C- & C- & C- \\ | & | & | & | & | & | & | & | \\ H & Cl & H & Cl & H & Cl & H & Cl \end{matrix} \right)_n \quad n = 80+$$

saran polymer

The polymer is melt-spun into cool air and quenched in water to solidify the fibers rapidly. The filaments are cold-drawn or stretched.[1] Although there are dyestuffs on the market that can be used with satisfactory results on saran fibers, yarns, or fabrics, the preferred method for coloring is to add pigments to the melted polymer before extrusion.

Fiber Properties

Microscopic Properties

Regular saran fibers are transparent, even, smooth, and almost perfectly round in cross section (Figs. 15.1 and 15.2).

Physical Properties

SHAPE AND APPEARANCE Regular saran fibers are even and somewhat silky in appearance. They are off-white, with a faint yellow tint. Fila-

[1]The familiar transparent Saran-Wrap® used in kitchens is made by extruding the polymer into sheets instead of drawing it into filament form.

ment fibers are smooth and highly lustrous; staple fibers are somewhat lustrous and have a built-in crimp that becomes an inherent part of the fiber. This crimp closely resembles the natural crimp of wool in both appearance and performance; it enables the fibers to cling together in yarn manufacture.

TENACITY (STRENGTH) The tenacity of saran, wet or dry, varies from 1.4 to 2.4 grams per denier.

ELASTIC RECOVERY AND ELONGATION The elongation of saran ranges from 15 to 30 percent, wet or dry, and the fiber has excellent recovery. At 1 percent elongation, recovery is 100 percent; at 3 percent elongation, the recovery is 98.5 percent; and at 10 percent elongation, recovery is 95 percent.

RESILIENCY Saran fibers have good resiliency, a property that has made them successful in carpeting.

DENSITY The density of saran is 1.7 grams per cubic centimeter. Because of this comparatively high density, the fibers produce fabrics that may be uncomfortable in apparel, but they are very effective in home furnishing fabrics.

MOISTURE REGAIN Saran fibers have less than 0.1 percent moisture absorption even after 24 hours of immersion in water. This makes dyeing difficult and explains why solution or mass pigmentation is preferred.

DIMENSIONAL STABILITY   If they are properly processed and if high temperatures are avoided, saran fibers have excellent size and shape retention.

Thermal Properties

Saran is practically nonflammable. The fibers will melt and burn slowly if held in a flame, but they do not support combustion, and as soon as the fibers or fabrics are removed from a direct source of flame, they self-extinguish. This property makes saran fibers desirable in drapery fabrics for public buildings where nonflammable materials are required by law.

A major disadvantage of saran fibers is their heat sensitivity. Although they have outstanding flame resistance, they soften at 115°C (240°F) and melt at about 177°C (350°F). The low softening point indicates that ironing is not advisable unless iron temperatures can be kept low. Warm water can safely be used in care.

Chemical Properties

EFFECT OF ALKALIES   Saran fibers are resistant to most alkaline substances. However, sodium hydroxide causes rapid deterioration, and ammonium compounds may cause discoloration. Other alkalies do not damage the fiber.

EFFECT OF ACIDS   Saran fibers are highly resistant to all acids at all levels of concentration and at both hot and cold temperatures.

EFFECT OF ORGANIC SOLVENTS   Saran has good resistance to organic solvents at room temperature. Substances such as acetone, carbon tetrachloride, and alcohol may cause a loss in fiber strength at temperatures over 65°C (150°F). Most cleaning solvents and stain-removal agents can be used safely at room temperature; however, the use of perchloroethylene, a common dry-cleaning solvent, should be avoided.

EFFECT OF SUNLIGHT, AGE, AND MISCELLANEOUS FACTORS   Sunlight causes white or light-colored saran fabrics to darken, but there is no reduction in strength. The fibers appear to be impervious to age. Saran upholstery used on outdoor furniture, while expensive, will last for several years in tropical conditions.

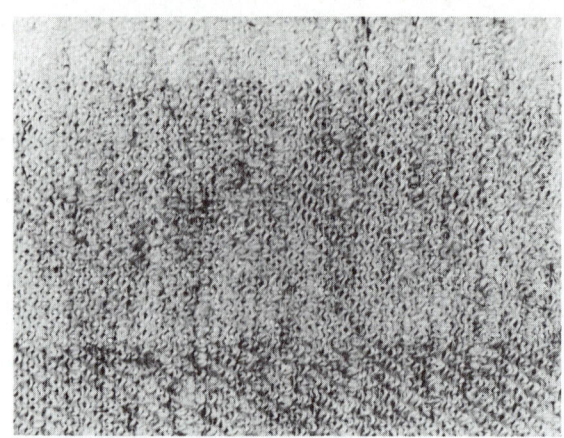

15.3   Drapery fabric using saran fibers.

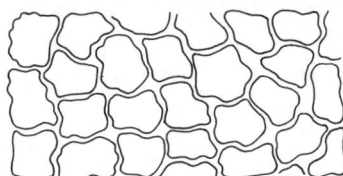

15.4   Sketch from photomicrograph of vinyon, cross section.

Static Charge

Saran does not develop static electric charges.

Biological Properties

Saran fibers are immune to attack by moths, other household insects, mildew, and bacteria.

Use and Care of Saran Fibers

Although saran fibers are rather dense, and therefore undesirable for apparel, they are outstanding for a variety of home furnishings, including upholstery, drapery fabric, and outdoor furniture (Fig. 15.3). Saran has been used in automobile upholstery, but that use has decreased because of the scarcity of the fiber and its high cost. Staple saran fibers are more often used for drapery fabrics, while filament fibers tend to be selected for upholstery. The filaments pack closer together in both the yarn and in the fabric, reducing the space in the interstices, which reduces the amount of soil and stain that can penetrate through the fabric. Both types of fiber are easy to clean. They require low washing and drying temperatures, and any type of soap or detergent can be used safely.

Saran fibers have been used for special-performance fabrics and in some industrial fabrics. However, this use is decreasing, and newer high-performance fabrics as well as olefin fibers are replacing saran.

VINYON

The first vinyon fibers were made experimentally in 1933, but commercial production did not occur until 1939. Vinyon was, in fact, introduced the same year as nylon. Because of the difference in properties and the application of nylon to hosiery and other apparel, nylon received the publicity as the "new" fiber rather than vinyon. Today, vinyon is produced by Avtex Fibers, Inc., in the United States. The fiber is also produced in several foreign countries under such trade names as Clevyl, Leavil, Rhovyl, Teviron, Thermovyl, Valren, and Viclon. However, it is said that there is considerable difference in the fiber produced in the United States and those produced in foreign countries.

Vinyon is defined by the TFPIA as "a manufactured fiber in which the fiber-forming substance is any long-chain synthetic polymer composed of at least 85 percent by weight of vinyl chloride units $(-CH_2CHCl-)$."

Production

Vinyon fibers are either polymers of vinyl chloride or copolymers of vinyl chloride and a second vinyl compound, usually vinyl acetate. These chemicals are polymerized under pressure or by means of a catalyst; the process is addition polymerization. The polymer is dissolved in an appropriate solvent and spun into a coagulating medium—water, warm air, or other acceptable environment.

Procedures for polymerization of vinyl chloride are best if the polymerizing is done in temperatures about $-30°C$ ($-22°F$). This results in fibers with satisfactory strength and stability and forms a syndiotatic polymer, in which the chlorine atoms are found in the same position relative to the backbone of the polymer:

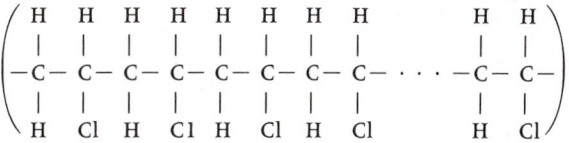

Fiber Properties

Vinyon is a long chain of vinyl chloride units. If the polymer is composed of two compounds, the second one occurs periodically in the linear chain. The fiber has irregular, round, dog bone, or dumbbell-shaped cross sections (Fig. 15.4) and smooth, even, relatively clear longitudinal views. Some types of vinyon show faint striations.

Vinyon is white and somewhat translucent. Tenacity varies from 0.7 to 3.8 grams per denier; there is no difference between wet and dry fibers. The range of tenacity is caused by various differences in molecular arrangement and polymerization processes.

There is a tremendous spectrum of elongation values, from a low of 12 percent for strong fibers to a high of 125 percent for weak fibers. The fibers have a density of 1.34 to 1.43 grams per cubic centimeter. They absorb very little moisture, only about 0.1 percent.

Vinyon does not support combustion but will burn in a direct flame and melt easily. Syndiotatic vinyon polymers are characterized by good tensile strength, good to high tearing resistance, excellent dimensional stability, low elongation, and good resistance to temperature change.

Vinyon fibers have excellent chemical resistance. Acids and alkalies have almost no effect, and most solvents used in cleaning do not damage the fiber. Acetone and other ketones, aromatic hydrocarbons, and ethers are harmful. Soaps and synthetic detergents have no undesirable effect on the fibers.

Use and Care of Vinyon Fibers

Vinyon fibers are widely used in industry. Because of their low softening and melting temperatures, copolymer types find application in heat sealing and bonding of fiber mats to form bonded, melded, and needled fabrics. The fibers are combined with other fibers to create molded, embossed, and bulked effects. In a film form, vinyon is used in making heat-sealable paper.

Vinyon fiber is not made in large quantities. Use in the United States has been primarily industrial. However, in several foreign countries, vinyon is promoted as a flame-retardant fiber and used for selected items of apparel. These fibers differ from the vinyon made in the United States as a result of different monomers used along with the vinyl chloride. Leavil, made in Italy, and Teviron, made in Japan, have been promoted for use in apparel that must meet flame-resistant specifications. Leavil has a tenacity of 4.0 grams per denier, good elongation, superior resistance to dry-cleaning solvents, and outstanding flame-resistant properties. Because of its flame resistance, the fiber has been used for children's sleepwear, draperies, blankets, bedspreads, and carpeting.

Other developments in the application and use of vinyon fibers as a flame•resistant fiber have occurred in Japan with the promotion of Teviron, Envilon, and Viclon fibers.

The fiber can be laundered or dry-cleaned. Any type of laundry detergent or soap may be used; bleaches can be used if necessary. Because of the low softening temperatures, drying in a dryer is not recommended unless the lowest temperature setting is used. Air drying is recommended. It is this latter caution that may discourage the use of the fiber in apparel in the United States.

VINAL

The TFPIA defines vinal as ''a manufactured fiber in which the fiber-forming substance is any long chain synthetic polymer composed of at least 50 percent by weight of vinyl alcohol units $(-CH_2-CHOH-)$ and in which the total of the vinyl alcohol units and any one or more of the various acetal units is at least 85 percent by weight of the fiber.''

Vinal fibers are manufactured in foreign countries. Although no vinal fibers are made in the United States, a few vinal fiber products are marketed in this country. Trade names for vinal include Kuralon, Mewlon, Solvron, Vilon, Vinol, and Vinylal. The major producing countries are Japan and Germany.

The polymer is made from vinyl alcohol. As vinyl alcohol is unstable, the fiber polymer is made indirectly by hydrolysis of polyvinyl acetate. The

polyvinyl solution is spun to form fibers with a molecular repeat of

$$\begin{pmatrix} & H & H & H & H & \\ & | & | & | & | & \\ -C- & C- & C- & C- \\ & | & | & | & | & \\ & H & OH & H & OH & \end{pmatrix}$$

As extruded, the fibers are water-soluble and must be treated with formaldehyde to make them insoluble. The treatment develops cross-links in the fiber polymer, which increases stability. After the formaldehyde treatment intramolecular and intermolecular cross-linkages occur to stabilize the polymer. The following is a typical structural formula for the cross-linked polymer.

Under magnification vinal fibers are smooth, somewhat grainy, and characterized by faint striations. The cross section may be bean-shaped, U-shaped, or nearly round. A somewhat flat U is the most common (Fig. 15.5).

Vinal fibers vary in tenacity from 3.5 to 6.5 grams per denier; in elongation they range from 15 to 30 percent. The stronger fibers have low elongation and a high degree of molecular orientation. Vinal fibers are about 25 percent weaker when wet than when dry. Modifications in the spinning process, using a wet spinning operation, have produced a vinal fiber with a strength of 7.5 grams per denier, excellent modulus, and superior resistance to dimensional change.

The density of vinal is about 1.26 grams per cubic centimeter. The fiber has a standard moisture regain of 5 percent and, when saturated, will absorb up to 12 percent moisture. The Japanese fiber Mewlon is being recommended as a substitute for asbestos. It has a very high modulus, high tenacity of

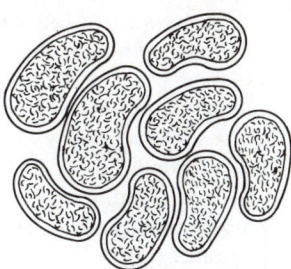

15.5 Sketch from photomicrograph of vinal, cross section.

about 10 g/d, low elongation of less than 8 percent, excellent impact resistance or modulus, a density of 1.3, a moisture regain of only 3 percent, and a maximum temperature for continued use of 120°C (250°F).

Vinal does not support combustion but melts at about 220°C (425°F). It softens at 200°C (390°F). Although this is somewhat lower than the softening point of some fibers, it is higher than that of many other vinyl type fibers and is adequate for a number of end-use requirements.

Vinal has good chemical resistance. Alkalies have little or no effect, and commonly encountered solvents do very little damage. Weak acids do not harm the fiber, but concentrated acids do cause disintegration. Formic acid, phenol, cresol, and hydrogen peroxide are particularly hazardous and completely dissolve the fibers at room temperature.

Chlorine bleaches can be used safely if diluted according to directions. Vinal has a high tolerance for sea or salt water when cross-linked. Coloring is difficult, so much, if not all, vinal is colored using pigments and mass pigmentation processes.

The fiber has excellent resistance to microorganisms and insects; it is especially resistant to rot-producing bacteria.

Except for limited industrial applications, the fiber has not been used in the United States to any great extent. In Japan and some other countries, it is used in protective apparel such as raincoats, jackets, umbrella fabrics, socks, and gloves. It has been combined with cotton or rayon in blends that are said to be very attractive and silky in appearance. Industrial uses include fishing nets, filter fabrics, tarpaulins, and bristles for certain types of brushes.

An important industrial use of vinal involves the water-soluble form of the fiber. Some of these specialized uses include the following:

Using the vinal fiber as a ground cloth for elaborate embroideries. After embroidering, the ground or base cloth is dissolved away, leaving a cut-out pattern that is lacy and delicate.

Using yarns of soluble vinal as connecting yarns between socks during knitting. The vinal is dissolved during finishing, and the socks separate for final processing. This is an important economic feature.

Using soluble fibers of vinal in yarns with other fibers in the knitting of sheer fabrics. The yarns can be knit on regular equipment; following knitting, the vinal portion of the yarn is dissolved away in the washing process, leaving a very sheer knit fabric.

NOVOLOID

The Federal Trade Commission added a new generic term in 1973 for fibers developed from novolac materials. The term *novolac* is defined as "a manufactured fiber containing at least 85 percent by weight of a cross-linked novolac."

The only novoloid fiber on the market is Kynol®, which is marketed by American Kynol, Inc. Kynol is made from phenol formaldehyde that is converted to a cross-linked novolac. The actual formulas are not available, but one typical repeat that has been suggested is

Manufacturing procedures are not available.

Physical properties of Kynol novoloid include the following: a tenacity of 1.7 to 2.0 grams per denier, elongation of 35 percent, density of 1.25 grams per cubic centimeter, and moisture regain of 6 percent. Fibers are normally ellipsoid in cross section, but they can be modified to be trilobal, ribbon, or Y-shaped. The fiber has excellent resistance to organic solvents and nonoxidizing acids, fair resistance to dilute acids and alkalies; poor resistance to concentrated acids and alkalies. Novoloid fiber is highly resistant to mildew and to aging and has good resistance to sunlight.

The characteristic that makes Kynol most desirable is its reaction to flame. It resists flame temperatures to 2500°C (4500°F) and does not melt. Char

15.6 Balaclava of Kynol novoloid fiber for workers in steel mills, foundries, and petrochemical plants. (American Kynol, Inc.)

silk. During the early part of the twentieth century their use was encouraged as one method of duplicating wool that would be less expensive than actual wool fiber. The first commercial azlon fiber was Lanital, made in Italy. This was followed by a variety of fibers: Ardil in England, Aralac and Vicara in the United States, Fibrolane in England, and Merinova in Italy. Apparently no azlon fibers are currently in production in any country.

A brief comment concerning their properties is of interest historically. The fibers are relatively weak, 0.9 to 1.5 grams per denier in tenacity. Density varied from 1.25 to 1.3. The fiber had good elastic recovery and elongation, high moisture absorbency or regain, and excellent resistance to microorganisms and insects. The fiber was exceptionally soft and made fabrics that closely resembled fine wool or cashmere. However, one serious negative aspect was probably responsible for its discontinuance: when wet, the fibers had a very unpleasant odor and required careful handling because of a very low wet strength.

Azlon fibers were used as a replacement for wool during and immediately following World War II, when wool was at a premium. Fabrics were soft and had a pleasant hand, and were dimensionally stable.

NYTRIL

Nytril fiber is defined by the TFPIA as "a manufactured fiber containing at least 85 percent of a long-chain polymer of vinylidene dinitrile [$-CH_2-C(CN)_2-$], where the vinylidene dinitrile content is no less than every other unit in the polymer chain."

Nytril fibers were introduced in 1955. The fiber had several trade names, including Darvan and Travis. Production of the fiber was discontinued in the United States in the early 1970s; it appears that the fiber is no longer made anywhere in the world as of 1984.

Nytril fibers had the following properties: a tenacity of 1.75 grams per denier; elongation of 30 percent; elastic recovery of 70 percent at 3 percent extension; moisture regain of 2.2 percent at standard conditions; a density of 1.18; high resiliency; easy-care properties; good resistance to dilute acids and alkalies but not to concentrated; good resistance to organic solvents; excellent resistance to sunlight and age; and excellent resistance to microorganisms and insects.

forms, but the fiber integrity is retained. Whereas other fibers melt, shrink, drip, and curl, Kynol novoloid converts to a carbon textile and retains much of its original strength and flexibility. It remains intact to protect against flame and acts as a heat barrier. During the change to carbon, the amount of smoke generated is very low.

The fiber is available in woven and knitted fabrics suitable for apparel, draperies, blankets, and protective coverings. Blends of Kynol novoloid and aramid fibers are flame-resistant and abrasion-resistant; mixtures of novoloid and polyester have superior chemical resistance.

Novoloid can be dyed with disperse and cationic dyes to give a good selection of colors. Because of its flame resistance, the fiber is marketed for its protective properties. It is used for protective apparel for fire fighters, race car drivers, and employees in high-risk occupations (Fig. 15.6).

AZLON

Azlon is defined by the TFPIA as "a manufactured fiber in which the fiber-forming substance is composed of regenerated naturally occurring protein."

Man-made protein fibers were developed in the late nineteenth century in an attempt to duplicate

Nytril fibers were made into a variety of experimental fabrics, but despite their many positive properties, they were never successfully commercialized because they were difficult to dye.

MISCELLANEOUS FIBERS

The following fibers are included because of special properties and characteristics that make them important in various end uses. Some of these are considered high-performance fibers, and most of them are used primarily in industrial applications.

Teflon®

Teflon is familiar to many as the coating for cooking utensils or in plastic forms, but the product also is made into fibers that offer several attractive properties for selected end uses. Because of the specialized nature of the fiber, it was not included in the Textile Fiber Products Identification Act. Thus, there is no generic definition.

Teflon is made of tetrafluoroethylene ($CF_2=CF_2$), which polymerizes under pressure and heat in the presence of a catalyst. Because of the inertness and high melting point, the fiber is formed by carefully controlling the polymerization process so that the polymer itself is ribbonlike in shape with a high length-to-breadth ratio. The process is a type of emulsion spinning. These polymer particles can be handled as a fiber without further processing. In actual production it appears that the polymerization and spinning of filaments can occur simultaneously. The repeat unit for Teflon is

$$\left(\begin{array}{cc} F & F \\ | & | \\ -C- & C- \\ | & | \\ F & F \end{array} \right)_n$$

Teflon is of medium strength, 1.6 grams per denier. It has low elongation and good pliability. It has a higher density than most fibers, 2.3 g/ccm, and it has no moisture regain. Teflon fibers will not burn and will withstand temperatures to 260°C (500°F) without damage. They are chemically inert and therefore unaffected by acids, alkalies, or organic solvents. Microorganisms and insects have no destructive effect.

Teflon is naturally tan in color when made, but it can be bleached to a white by treatment in boiling concentrated sulfuric acid in which minute amounts of nitric acid are added slowly.

The fiber is not used in apparel or home furnishing fabrics to any great extent (see page 399). It is used for industrial and commercial products such as industrial felts, filter fabrics to reduce smokestack emissions, gaskets, packing fabrics, covers for press units in commercial laundries, and electric tapes. A textured Teflon has been made using the air texturizing process. Yarns of the fiber can be woven, knitted, felted, or braided.

Teflon has extreme resistance to chemicals, sunlight, weather, and aging. It does develop high electrical or static charges. This latter problem can be reduced by adding electrically conductive pigment to the spinning solution.

It is probable that the use of Teflon will continue to be limited to specialized applications in industry and for certain types of geotextiles. See also the discussion of Gore-Tex®, page 399.

Polybenzimidazole (PBI)

Polybenzimidazole has a repeat unit of

Properties of the fiber include the following: density is 1.43 g/ccm; tenacity is 2.7 g/d, while initial modulus is 32 g/d; breaking elongation is 27 percent; moisture regain is 15 percent; heat resistance is high; and resistance to chemicals is excellent.

The fiber is made by reacting tetraaminobiphenyl and diphenyl isophthalate. The fiber is dry-spun from a dimethylacetamide solution.

PBI does not burn in air, remains dimensionally stable at high temperatures, and emits little or no smoke when in a flame. The fiber does not melt. It can be made into fabrics for apparel that is comfortable and attractive. PBI does lose some strength after extended exposure to ultraviolet light. It has good abrasion resistance. Strength retained after exposure to temperatures of 570°F for 168 hours is 100 percent; after exposure for 60 minutes at 750°F, 80 percent of the strength is retained.

PBI is used as a substitute for asbestos in applications requiring high thermal stability, chemical resistance, and flame resistance. Thermal protective clothing made of PBI provides good comfort, outstanding thermal protection, abrasion resistance, and good flexibility without embrittlement after exposure to flame. PBI is used in fire fighters' turnout coats, proximity clothing, industrial protective apparel, high-temperature protective gloves, welders' apparel, aircraft seat encapsulates, and various types of industrial situations. It has been used where high temperatures can be expected, as in conveyor belts for glass handling. The fiber is expensive, so its use will probably continue to be limited to specialized applications where its performance justifies the cost.

Polycarbonate Fibers

Although polycarbonates are a type of polyester, they are mentioned here because of their limited availability and specialized uses. The repeat unit is

$$\left(-O-\bigcirc-\overset{\overset{CH_3}{|}}{\underset{\underset{CH_3}{|}}{C}}-\bigcirc-O-\overset{\overset{O}{\|}}{C}-\right)$$

Density for polycarbonates is given as 1.23 g/ccm; moisture regain is less than 1 percent; elongation is 20 to 45 percent; tenacity is approximately 4.5 g/d; elastic recovery is high; and resistance to heat and weather is excellent. Fabrics of the fiber have good crease recovery.

A special type of polycarbonate fiber, Solvex®, has been developed and marketed for a very specialized use. The fiber disintegrates in dry-cleaning solvents; thus, it is used as basting for tailored garments during construction. The operation of pulling the basting threads is unnecessary because the thread becomes brittle in cleaning solvent and breaks into small pieces that are rinsed away. A saving of more than 50 percent in labor costs for this part of the tailoring operation occurs as a result of using this thread.

Polyurea Fibers

Polyurea fibers are based on poly(4,4-methylene dicyclohexylene)urea and have a repeating unit similar to

$$\left(\begin{array}{c}\underset{|}{\overset{|}{H}}\;\underset{|}{\overset{|}{H}}\;\underset{|}{\overset{|}{H}}\;\underset{|}{\overset{|}{H}}\;\underset{|}{\overset{|}{H}}\;\underset{|}{\overset{|}{H}}\;\underset{|}{\overset{|}{H}}\;\underset{|}{\overset{|}{H}}\;\underset{|}{\overset{|}{H}}\;\underset{|}{\overset{|}{H}}\qquad\underset{}{\overset{|}{H}}\\ -C-C-C-C-C-C-C-C-C-N-\;C-N-\\ \underset{}{\overset{|}{H}}\;\underset{}{\overset{|}{H}}\;\underset{}{\overset{|}{H}}\;\underset{}{\overset{|}{H}}\;\underset{}{\overset{|}{H}}\;\underset{}{\overset{|}{H}}\;\underset{}{\overset{|}{H}}\;\underset{}{\overset{|}{H}}\;\underset{}{\overset{|}{H}}\qquad\underset{}{\overset{\|}{O}}\end{array}\right)$$

These fibers are strong; they have a low density, low moisture regain, good resistance to chemicals, and average resistance to heat. Polyurea fibers resemble silk in texture and hand, and they are similar to nylon in physical properties. Fabrics of these fibers are used in industrial applications. They have some potential for apparel fabrics, but no use in that area has occurred to date.

Polyphenylene Sulfide

Polyphenylene sulfide fibers have the following properties: a tenacity of approximately 3 g/d; elongation of 25–35 percent; an elastic recovery of 100 percent at 2 percent extension and of 86 percent at 10 percent extension; a moisture regain of only 0.6 percent; a density of 1.38 g/ccm; a melting point of 185°C (365°F).

The fiber is made by reacting paradichlorobenzene and sodium sulfide in a polar solvent at high temperature. The fiber has excellent chemical resistance except to nitric acid, sulfuric acid, phosphoric acid, chromic acid, and sodium hypochlorite.

Celiox® Fibers

Celiox fibers are heat-stabilized polyacrylonitrile that has been subjected to a treatment that results in the development of a cyclic structure with cross-linking and the addition of oxygen. The treatment creates a ladderlike molecular structure that makes the fiber highly heat-resistant and nonmelting. It is a nonmineral fiber with the exceptional heat resistance of a ceramic fiber but with the hand of normal textile fibers. Specific properties include a density of 1.4 g/ccm; moisture regain of 10 percent at standard conditions; tenacity of 1.5 g/d; initial modulus of 40 g/d; elongation of 10 percent.

The important property of Celiox is its resistance to heat and flame. It can be used as a substitute for asbestos. It can be made into fabrics considerably more easily than asbestos and provides a pleasant hand, comfort owing to the lower density, and high elongation. It is considered nonflammable. It sublimes at 3650°C (6000°F). It does not ignite and has no afterglow. It retains full strength after 24 hours' exposure to temperatures of 204°–232°C (400°–450°F).

The fiber is recommended for use in protective apparel such as uniforms for those working in high-temperature situations such as the steel industry or industries where workers are exposed to molten metal splash.

Polyacrylate Fiber

A cross-linked polyacrylate fiber has been introduced by Courtaulds. The brand name is Inidex®. It is promoted as a nonflammable fiber with very low smoke generation when involved in a fire. Inidex has considerable resistance to heat and chemicals, except for strong oxidizing agents such as nitric acid, sulfuric acid, and strong sodium hypochlorite. In resistance to ultraviolet light it is superior to aramid fibers. Currently Inidex is being used in industrial fabrics and as a possible upholstery filler. Because of the nonflammability it is suggested for use as a barrier fabric in bedding.

EXPERIMENTAL FIBERS

Chameleon Fibers

Fibers that change color with the surroundings have been developed for selected uses. These incorporate dye molecules that are sensitive to light and heat and that change color as the amount and type of light changes and/or as the amount of heat varies.

Polychromatic Fibers

Polychromatic fibers have a transparent outer surface and an internal cavity that extends longitudinally the length of the fiber. This space is filled with liquid microcrystals that change color as the temperature changes. They have been used in a variety of accessories and have potential in fabrics for apparel, home furnishings, and theatrical costumes.

Polybutylene Terephthalate (PBT)

PBT is a new fiber with a molecular structure similar to but different from that of nylon or polyester.

In the United States it is identified as a type of polyester. The molecular repeat is

$$\left(\begin{array}{c} -\underset{\underset{O}{\|}}{C} -O-CH_2-CH_2-CH_2-CH_2-O-\underset{\underset{O}{\|}}{C} - \end{array} \right)_n$$

The properties of PBT have been described as an elegant touch or hand, initial modulus similar to nylon 6; an elastic recovery and elongation higher than nylon 6 or polyester; excellent physical and chemical properties; a low moisture regain of 0.4 percent. The fiber is being recommended for use in sportswear, casual shirts and pants, linings, and accessories. Celanese produces PBT in the United States. Type 661 PBT polyester is a draw texturizing yarn for stretch applications. ESP® of Fortrel polyester is a licensed trademark to identify PBT yarn in fabrics that conform to Celanese's performance requirements. The yarn is used in stretch denim, corduroy, swimwear, and other body-suit fabrics. PBT is made also in Japan.

Dexon

Dexon is a polyglycollide fiber. It has good strength and adequate resistance to heat. A problem with the fiber as originally developed has been turned into an asset. The fiber does not have good stability to moisture and hydrolysis. Thus, it has been developed for use in the medical profession for internal sutures. The fiber dissolves away, leaving no trace. It does last sufficiently for good healing, and it has been found to be nonallergenic.

Bigeneric and Bicomponent Fibers

The techniques for spinning bicomponent and bigeneric fibers, as well as the problems of terminology, have been discussed in Chapter 5. A few of the more notable bicomponent and bigeneric fibers are now described in brief. It may be of interest to note that very few bigeneric fibers are being produced in the United States at present; most available fibers of this type are from foreign countries. Bicomponent fibers, those composed of the same generic product, are often identified only by the generic term and not by the fact that they are bicomponent. This area of fiber technology should be watched over the next few years, as changes are evidently occurring both in terminology and in production and uses.

Polychal

A fiber identified as a polychal fiber has been marketed for a number of years. This fiber, Cordelan, is made in Japan. The fiber is a matrix fiber composed of 50 percent polyvinyl chloride, or vinyon, and 50 percent polyvinyl alcohol, or vinal. It is spun by an emulsion process that resembles wet spinning but differs in the fiber formation. The emulsion is composed of a mixture of the two fiber-forming components and is extruded through the spinnerette in this mixed or emulsified form. The fiber cross section exhibits a kidney shape, and under extremely high magnification small dark dots that indicate one fiber type in a white fiber matrix can be observed.

Physical properties of the fiber are as follows: density, 1.32 g/ccm; moisture regain, 3.2 percent; tenacity, 3.02 g/d; elongation, 18.4 percent. The fiber has good resistance to chemicals, except for sodium hypochlorite, which degrades the fiber and should therefore not be used as a bleach. The fiber does not absorb stains.

The most important property of Cordelan is its thermal behavior. Although it will soften at temperatures greater than 130°C (266°F) and will gradually degrade, it does not actually melt and does not support combustion. Therefore, it is considered a safe flame-resistant fiber. It will burn in the presence of fire, but it does not emit toxic fumes as some of the other flame-resistant fibers and finishes do.

Cordelan is easily laundered and can be tumble-dried as long as there is a low temperature setting for the dryer. The fiber has a pleasing hand and produces soft and aesthetically pleasing fabrics.

Major uses for the fiber include children's sleepwear (Fig. 15.7); work or career apparel; home furnishings such as draperies, upholstery, bedspreads, and blankets; wigs; and industrial fabrics. Cordelan may be used in blends with other fibers such as polyester and wool.

Because of the nature of this polychal fiber, it must be labeled as a matrix fiber with the respective percentages of the two generic fiber types. Thus a typical label might state: Cordelan matrix fiber: 50 percent vinal, 50 percent vinyon.

Chinon

Chinon has been identified as a promix fiber composed of 70 percent acrylonitrile and 30 percent azlon. It is made by a graft process. Although information concerning the manufacture is not available, data concerning properties indicate that the fiber has a density of 1.22 g/ccm, a moisture regain of 4.5 to 5.5 percent, and a tenacity of 3.5 to 4.5 g/d.

Fabrics of this fiber are said to have a silky texture and silky scroop or sound, excellent drapability, deep luster, good colorfastness, and little or no static charge.

Fabrics can be dyed by a wide variety of dyestuffs. They are light in weight, and they are considered easy-care and can be laundered or dry-cleaned with normal procedures except that chlorine bleaches should *not* be used. When ironing is required, it should be done at medium or low temperature settings.

Mirafi

Mirafi has been identified as composed of polypropylene and nylon. The fibers are formed into a non-woven fabric and used primarily in geotechnical applications. These uses include ground stabilization in road building, erosion control, land reclamation, drainage, and irrigation applications.

15.7 Child's sleepwear of Cordelan matrix (vinyon/vinal polychal) fiber. (Macy's)

A recent announcement identifies a fiber called Miradrain, which is made into fabrics that have a wafflelike appearance and is used to prevent soil from entering and clogging drain systems. The fabric is very light in weight but resists earth pressures in excess of 4000 pounds per square foot without impaired performance.

Novolac/Polyamide

This bicomponent or bigeneric fiber is composed of 60 to 90 percent novoloid and 40 to 10 percent polyamide. The fiber has good flame resistance, is easily dyed, and exhibits good properties for apparel and home furnishings.

Kermel

Kermel is a polyamide-imide fiber made from trimellitic anhydride chloride and either a diamine or a diisocyanate. The fiber molecular repeat is said to be

Kermel can either be dry- or wet-spun. Its outstanding property is excellent resistance to flame and heat. It has good hand and drapes well; thus, it is suitable for a variety of household textiles, protective clothing where heat and flame resistance is important, and industrial uses.

DuPont 278

Some filament yarns are formed so that different filaments are of one fiber and other filaments are of a different type of fiber. While each fiber remains a single filament of one fiber type, the combination of two or more different types of chemicals results in a blend yarn that performs similarly to bicomponent or bigeneric fibers. One example of such a product is DuPont 278. This multifilament yarn is composed of 60 percent polyester and 40 percent nylon. As yet, the product has been primarily experimental, but it appears to have considerable importance for apparel or home furnishing products.

The amount of polyester and nylon is the same as that reported to be in the new Qiana yarn, Type 483. However, this seems to be a combination of filaments where each filament is a single component of individual type of fiber, whereas T-483 is reported to be a bicomponent of some type.

Belleseime

A bigeneric fiber developed in Japan, Belleseime is promoted for upholstery and resembles suede. It is made of 68 percent polyester, 20 percent nylon, and 12 percent polyurethane. The product is reported to have outstanding drapability, a silky luster, good dimensional stability, high resistance to flame, and extremely easy care.

STUDY QUESTIONS

1. Describe saran fibers and identify uses for them. Why has saran not been as popular as olefin, nylon, or polyester?
2. What are the properties of vinyon fibers? Where are they used?
3. What are characteristics of vinal fibers? What special characteristic of this fiber makes it different from other fibers and influences certain types of end uses?
4. What are novoloid fibers? Where are they used?
5. What single property do azlon and nytril fibers have in common? What are the characteristics of these two generic groups?
6. List several of the fibers discussed in this chapter, describe them, and note typical end uses.
7. What single characteristic appears to be important in the development and use of many of the special man-made fibers?
8. What are special uses for Solvex fibers?
9. What property of chameleon fibers might make them a favorite with young people for special apparel items?

Activities

1. Locate current readings concerning special man-made fibers, and determine the current status of such fibers.
2. Seek information and/or items that might be made of some of the special fibers discussed in this chapter. Indicate what these uses are and why the fibers are appropriate.

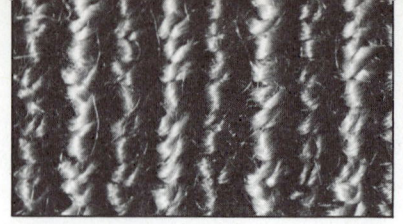

16

Mineral and Miscellaneous Inorganic Fibers and Yarns

KEY TERMS

aluminum fibers
asbestos
carbon fibers
continuous filament process

cullet
glass fiber
metallic fibers
staple fiber process

NATURAL MINERAL FIBER

Asbestos

Asbestos is the only mineral substance used as a textile fiber in the form in which it is mined. Its use has decreased rapidly because of health problems related to its mining, processing, and use. Nevertheless, the fiber is discussed here in order to provide insight into its properties both good and bad.

The substance is found in fibrous veins of serpentine or amphibole rock (Fig. 16.1). It has been known since the days of early Greek and Roman civilizations. The use of asbestos was recorded by Pliny the Elder in the first century A.D. Legends concerning this fiber have been told for centuries. It is said that Emperor Charlemagne delighted in mystifying guests by throwing a tablecloth of asbestos into a roaring fire and then removing it, unharmed and clean, from the flames. Marco Polo told friends

about a substance he had observed in Siberia that could be woven into attractive textiles that would not burn, even in direct flame. These stories all identify the most important property of asbestos: it is completely fireproof.

Commercial development of the fiber began in the nineteenth century after the discovery of large deposits of asbestos in Canada and South Africa. There are many varieties in the asbestiform group of minerals, but only six are of economic importance, and only one has had real value for use as a textile fiber—chrysotile.

According to data from the U.S. Department of Interior, chrysotile accounted for 95 percent of all textile asbestos in 1959. Chrysotile is a fibrous form of serpentine rock and is composed of hydrated magnesium silicate [$Mg_3Si_2O_5(OH)_4$].

Several properties combine to make this type of asbestos especially adaptable to textiles. The fibers have good strength, flexibility, toughness, low conductivity, and adequate length for spinning into

16.1 Asbestos rock showing both rock and fiber form. (Manville Products Corporation)

yarns. The tenacity of chrysotile varies from 2.5 to 3.1 grams per denier. The fiber has a silky texture, a soft to harsh hand, and a white, amber, gray, or green color. Asbestos withstands extremely high temperatures. The water bound within the molecular structure of the fiber is lost at 593°C (1100°F), and the fiber will fuse at 1520°C (2770°F) if held at that temperature. Brief exposure to temperatures as high as 3315°C (6000°F) can occur without fiber destruction. The chemical resistance of asbestos is good and permits the use of the fiber in various chemical manufacturing processes.

During the late 1970s, considerable evidence was collected that marked asbestos as a serious health hazard. It has been identified as a potential carcinogen and has been cited as causing a variety of lung diseases. It appears to be relatively easy to inhale or ingest small particles of asbestos as they break away from the rock and fiber forms. Thus, special health precautions must be taken by both workers with and users of the product.

During the past few years the federal government, in an attempt to eliminate asbestos as a health hazard, has required that many asbestos installations be removed and replaced with safe fibers or insulating materials.

As a result of this concern and the mounting case against asbestos, considerable research has been devoted to identifying alternative types of fibers that could replace asbestos. Some of the alternatives are

mentioned later in this chapter, others have been identified in the previous chapter.

MAN-MADE MINERAL FIBERS

Glass Fiber

The origin of glass and glass fibers is uncertain. One legend credits Phoenician fishermen with the discovery of glass fiber. It is said that they noticed pools of a molten substance under fires they built on a sandy beach of the Aegean Sea. Heat from the fire had caused the silica in the sand to fuse with the alkali of the wood ash from the fire. Natural curiosity caused them to poke at the molten material, and as they withdrew their sticks, they pulled out long, stringlike forms. These were probably the first glass fibers.

Serious efforts to create textiles from glass fibers began in the late nineteenth century. Edward D. Libbey succeeded in attenuating glass into fiber and made sufficient yarn to manufacture fabric for a dress, which was displayed at the Columbia Exposition of 1893. The garment was attractive and not transparent as the public had anticipated. However, the fibers were coarse and low in strength and pliability. It seemed there would be no future for glass fibers.

Fortunately, that was not the case as uses, other than apparel, became apparent. Further, researchers continued to work on developing a fiber that would give adequate strength and flexibility in selected end uses. Owens-Corning Fiberglas Corporation produced the first glass fiber in commercial quantities in the early 1930s. They called their product Fiberglas.

Today, glass fibers are manufactured by several corporations and sold under various trade names such as Fiberglas®, Beta®, Chemglass®, and Modiglass®. The TFPIA defines glass as "a manufactured fiber in which the fiber-forming substance is glass."

Production

The raw materials for glass are primarily silica, sand, and limestone, with small amounts of other compounds such as aluminum hydroxide, sodium carbonate (soda ash), and borax. The formulation of the glass depends on the desired end use. For ex-

ample, fibers for electrical applications differ in composition from those used in chemical industries. Most textile glass fiber is made from the formulations developed for electrical end uses.

The selected raw materials are melted in a furnace at temperatures of about 1650°C (3000°F). The compounds combine to form a clear melt, which is shaped into marble form about ⅝ inch (1.6 cm) in diameter. As the marbles cool, they are inspected, and any with imperfections, such as bubbles of air, are sorted out to prevent flaws in the final filaments. The perfect marbles are fed into a small furnace and remelted; the molten glass falls, by gravity, through a platinum bushing (similar to a spinnerette) with 400 to 1600 orifices (Fig. 16.2). As the melted glass leaves the bushing, it solidifies. For filament yarns the fibers are pulled together, lubricated for ease in handling, and wound on tubes in strand or filament form for use in fabric manufacture (Fig. 16.3). Each marble produces about 100 miles (160 km) of filament; the marble weighs less than 1 ounce (less that 28 grams) and is called *cullett.*

Several manufacturers are now making glass fibers from a direct melt process. In this technique the molten glass is fed directly from the furnance to

16.2   Molten glass flows from tiny orifices in rectangular bushings. (PPG Industries)

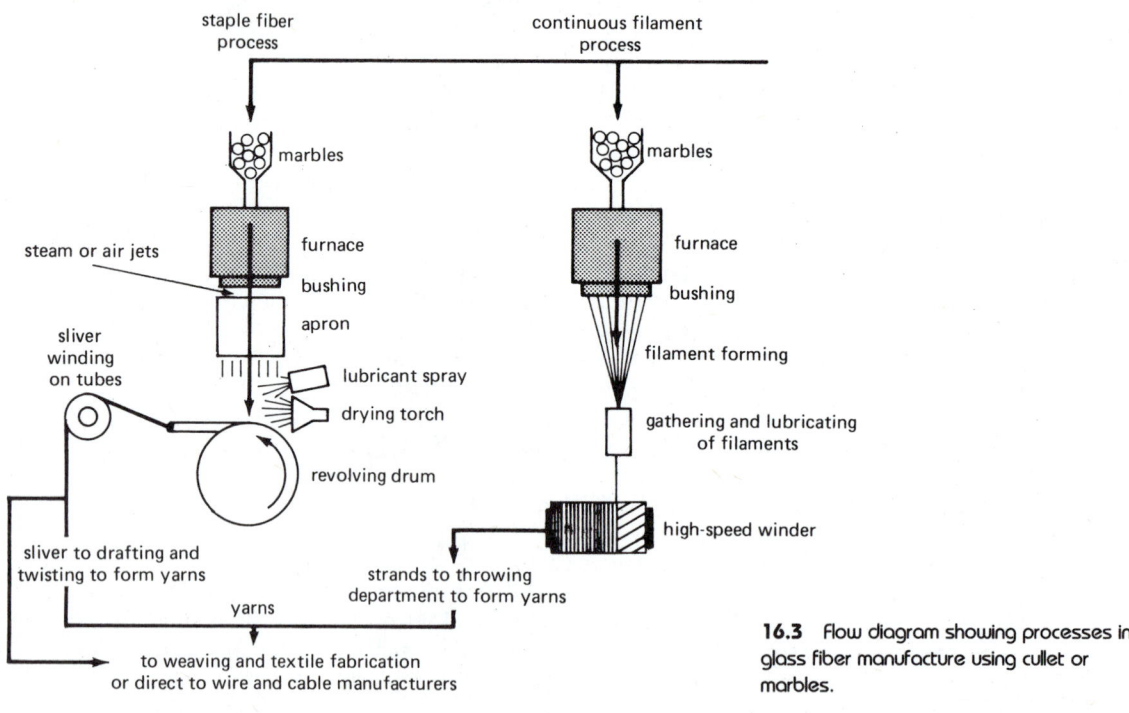

16.3   Flow diagram showing processes in glass fiber manufacture using cullet or marbles.

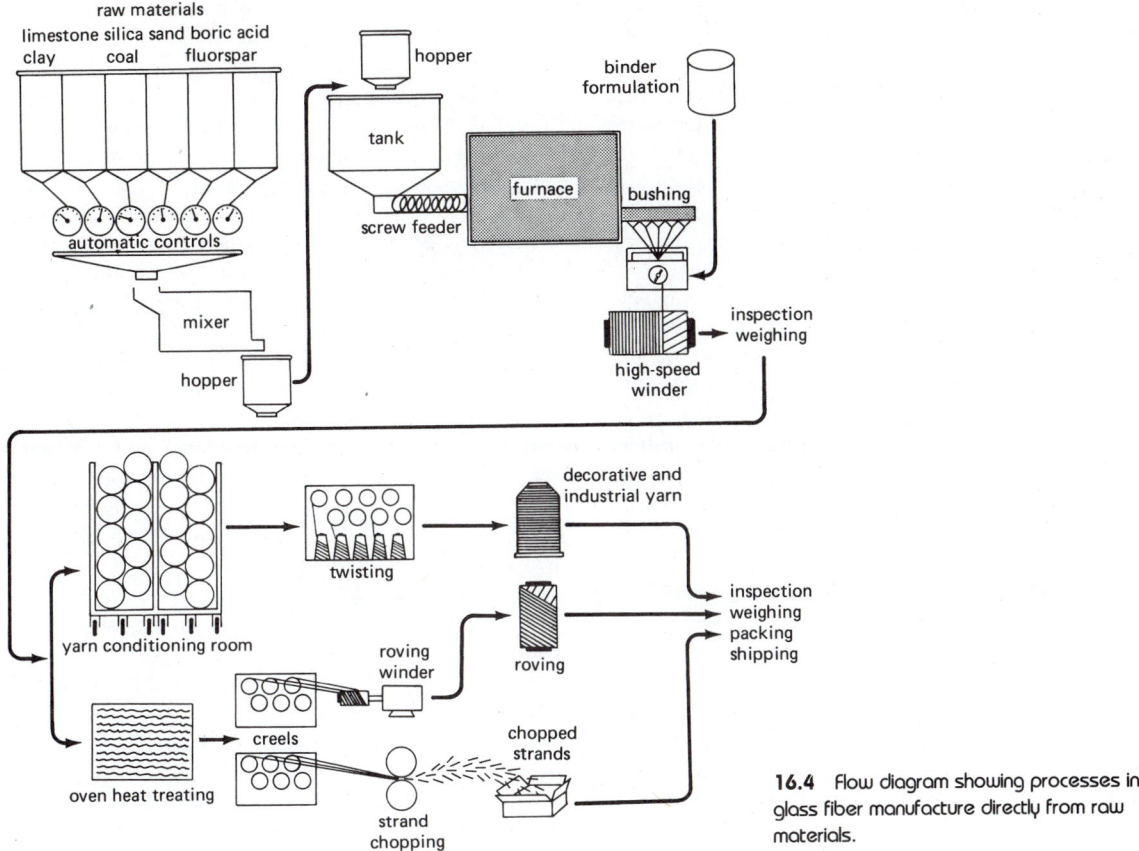

raw materials
limestone silica sand boric acid
clay   coal   fluorspar

hopper

binder
formulation

tank

furnace

bushing

screw feeder

automatic controls

mixer

hopper

inspection
weighing

high-speed
winder

yarn conditioning room

twisting

decorative and
industrial yarn

roving
winder

roving

inspection
weighing
packing
shipping

oven heat treating

creels

strand
chopping

chopped
strands

16.4 Flow diagram showing processes in glass fiber manufacture directly from raw materials.

the bushing where the filaments are formed (Figure 16.4). This procedure has considerable economic advantage, as the process of forming the marble and cooling and inspecting it has been deleted.

Staple fibers, used more often as reinforcement for plastic or as insulation mats, can be spun into yarns following the same general procedure used for cotton or wool (see Chap. 17). The staple fibers, however, are produced in a different manner than filament yarns. The fibers are hit by a jet of steam under high pressure as they leave the platinum bushing, or spinnerette. This breaks the filaments into short lengths between 5 and 15 inches (12.7–38 cm). These fibers are collected on a drum and carded, then pulled into a sliver and roving (see Fig. 16.3). When the glass fibers are to be used as reinforcement for plastic, the fibers are gathered in a thick batt or mat instead of being pulled into a sliver form. Recently manufacturers have developed *foamed* glass for use as a plastic reinforcement.

Fiber Properties

Glass fiber has high strength, a tenacity of 6.3 to 6.9 grams per denier. Elongation is only 3 to 4 percent, but elastic recovery is 100 percent. The fiber has outstanding dimensional stability, and it can absorb extreme stress without permanent deformation. Density is 2.54 grams per cubic centimeter, which is too dense for general apparel use but quite satisfactory for various types of home furnishings and commercial and industrial uses. The fibers do not absorb measurable amounts of moisture, and they have good resistance to creasing and wrinkling. Glass fiber is smooth, even, transparent, and circular in cross section.

Fibers of glass will not burn. However, they soften at about 815°C (1500°F), and strength begins to decline at temperatures above 315°C (600°F). After brief exposure to heat, fiber strength returns, and this property is used in some finishing processes. However, if the glass is heated sufficiently to melt, the configuration of the filaments is lost.

Hydrofluoric and hot phosphoric are the only acids that attack glass fibers. However, the fibers are damaged by strong alkalies at both cold and warm temperatures and by hot weak alkalies. Organic solvents have no effect. Glass fibers can be laundered easily and dry quickly, usually by simply wiping with a cloth.

Glass fibers exhibit excellent resistance to age, sunlight, and weather. Microorganisms and insects will not damage them.

A major problem with glass fibers is their inability to resist abrasion. When folded, as for hems in draperies, the edge will tend to crack if it is subjected to rubbing against other surfaces such as the floor, windowsills, or furniture. Although glass fibers do have flexibility, it is somewhat lower than that of most fibers used in consumer goods.

The dyeing and printing of glass were a real challenge to the textile technologist. A process called Coronizing, by which either solid colors or prints can be applied, proved to be an adequate solution to the problem. The fabric is padded with a colloidal dispersion of silica and heat-set. After heat setting, pigment is applied with a resin solution and the fabric is dried, treated with a final compound to produce colorfastness, and given a final drying. The Coronizing process also softens the yarns so that they flatten and prevent yarn slippage in fabrics.

A superfine glass filament, called Beta, was introduced in the late 1960s. This fiber has been used in draperies, bedspreads, and table coverings. Glass has been tried for upholstery fabric because of its flame-resistance properties, but neither furniture makers nor consumers have widely accepted its use.

Use and Care of Glass Fibers

Glass fiber is widely used in industrial textiles for such applications as filter cloths, fire blankets, insulating fabrics and filler, special mail bags, and heat- and electrical-resistance tapes and braids. The fiber is widely used as a reinforcement for plastic forms such as sports car bodies, dune buggies, boat hulls, furniture, and sports equipment.

Glass is not used in apparel because the sharp fiber ends that are found at cut edges frequently case skin irritation. The fiber is used for a variety of home furnishings such as draperies, glass curtains, lampshades, awnings, ironing board covers, and ta-

blecloths. Industrial uses are numerous, and it is one of the fibers used in geotextiles.

Laundering is the preferred method of care for glass fiber fabrics. Dry cleaning is not recommended. The fabrics should be handled carefully to prevent excess abrasion, crushing, or wrinkling. Mild soaps and detergents should be used and alkaline substances avoided. Bleach may be used when needed; a week solution of a hypochlorite bleach is safe. Glass fabrics should be laundered separately, as tiny residues of fiber may be deposited into the washing vessel. The use of sinks or large containers is recommended. Laundry equipment is not recommended for care, as the fabrics can deposit small bits of fiber into the machine that are picked up by fabrics washed in a later load. This can result in serious skin irritations and dermatitis. If a washing machine must be used for the care of glass fiber fabrics, wash the machine out thoroughly afterward and put the unit through a standard wash cycle without any fabrics in it.

After washing, glass fabrics should be rinsed thoroughly, then rolled in or wiped with a towel. Window coverings can be rehung immediately; other fabrics may be laid on a smooth surface or hung over padded lines. Do not use a dryer. Other prohibitions relating to the care of glass fiber fabrics include the following: never spin-dry, never wring, do not rub, and do not use strong alkaline detergents. Ironing is not recommended, but as it is seldom needed this does not cause serious problems.

Metallic Fibers and Yarns

Metallic threads or yarns are the oldest form of man-made fiber, dating back to ancient Persia and Assyria. These early metallic fibers, more accurately a monofilament type of yarn, were the result of slitting very thin sheets of metal into narrow, ribbon-like forms. Some metallic yarns are made using variations of this very early process.

The TFPIA defines metallic fibers as "a manufactured fiber composed of metal, plastic-coated metal, metal-coated plastic, or a core completely covered by metal."

Gold, silver, and aluminum are the metals most often used in textile products. Gold and silver yarns are extremely costly, but they are found in some expensive items such as imported brocades. Although these gold and silver yarns may be pure gold or silver, the usual product is made by cutting thin strips of the metal and wrapping them around a central core of a strong, flexible material such as silk filament or copper wire. Because of the cost of gold and silver, manufacturers have selected aluminum as a replacement.

Modern aluminum yarns are made by one of two basic procedures. First, aluminum may be encased in a plastic coating of either a polyester or cellulose acetate butyrate. The latter product is cheaper, but the polyester is more desirable. Color is applied either to the plastic coating or directly to the aluminum by an adhesive. This process is called the "sandwich" method, as the aluminum is placed between two layers of plastic. The second technique for manufacturing involves mixing finely ground aluminum, color, and polyester together and then laminating this product to clear polyester. Both types of metallic yarns can be obtained in a variety of colors; gold and silver hues are the most frequently used. The yarns are bright and colorful and do not tarnish. The plastic coating prevents damage from salt water, chlorine, and alkaline detergents.

Metallic yarns are not especially strong, but they are quite adequate for normal decorative purposes. Polyester-coated yarns are stronger than the acetate-butyrate-coated yarns and have been used in fabrics for a variety of end uses including evening wear, theatrical costumes, and various types of home furnishings and domestics. The yarns are colorfast to light and to mild laundering.

The chemical and biological resistance of the yarns depends on the coating material. Cellulose-acetate-butyrate coatings react like acetate fibers, whereas polyester coatings react like polyester fibers. The fibers resist temperatures depending on the coating. Temperatures above 80°C (175°F) should be avoided for acetate-butyrate-coated yarns; polyester-coated yarns can withstand temperatures to 140°C (285°F).

The care given fabrics of metallic yarns or those in which metallic yarns have been used for accent and/or decoration depends upon several factors. Perhaps the most important is the type of coating used for the metallic fiber; but the way in which they have been made, the type of core in wrapped yarns, and the presence of other fibers in the fabric will all influence ultimate care practices. In general, laundering is the recommended procedure; dry cleaning is not suggested unless labels clearly indicate that it is satisfactory. Drying fabric at high temperatures should be avoided, as the plastic coating may soften and be destroyed. Ironing, when needed, should be done at low temperatures, again because the plastic coatings can be destroyed when exposed to high temperatures.

The popularity of metallic yarns is affected tremendously by the dictates of current fashion. A wide variety of home furnishing fabrics, including drapery and curtain fabric, upholstery, bedspreads, towels, and tablecloths contain metallic yarns for accent (Fig. 16.5). Metallics are used to enhance evening gowns, and accessories often use bits of metallic yarn. The luxury of gold and silver, once available only to royalty or the very rich, may be enjoyed today by everyone.

Another metallic fiber available on the market is stainless steel. This fiber may be used as a monofilament fiber, or it may be combined with other fibers in yarn manufacture. Stainless steel in fabrics contributes strength, tear resistance, abrasion resistance, and thermal conductivity. It is finding widespread use in floor coverings as a means of reducing the buildup of static charges. Because it is usually combined with other fibers and is present in small amounts, the care involved depends on the other fibers persent.

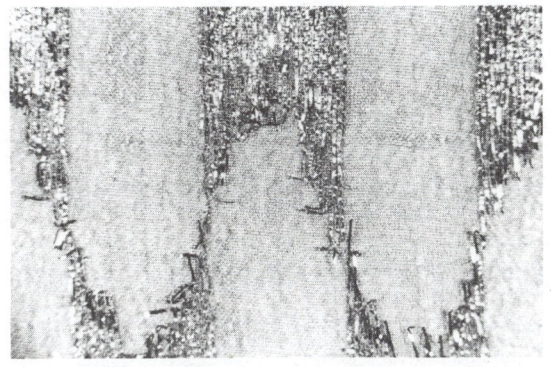

16.5 Fabric using metallic yarns.

Alumina Fibers

A fiber made from aluminum oxide, called alumina, is available for specialized uses as a fiber to embed in metal. The combination forms a metal matrix composite. The alumina fiber has a tenacity of 3.9 grams per denier and a modulus 5½ times that of glass; the fiber is compatible with metals to 1000°C (1832°F). The fibers are 20 microns in diameter. They are made by a combination of textile spinning and ceramic processing; they are spun from a slurry in the form of continuous multifilament yarns; these filaments are shaped into form and inserted into a metal mold, the binder is burned off, metal is added, and the metal solidifes around the filaments. The metals used include aluminum, magnesium, and lead. The fiber-to-metal ratio varies up to 70/30. When alumina fibers are used with aluminum as the metal, a small amount of lithium is added. The major uses for this product are in automotive and jet engines, aerospace structures, and lead-acid batteries.

Other Mineral Fibers

Several other mineral fibers have achieved importance. Strong, stiff, and lightweight fibers are needed for aerospace use particularly, and several mineral fibers have been found to be of value in these applications. Ceramic fibers such as aluminum silicate, silicon oxide, potassium titanate, and aluminum oxide (as described in the section on alumina fibers) are highly successful and of great importance in high-tech industrial uses. These fibers must be able to resist high temperatures and function satisfactorily as part of a composite with other metals or plastic substances. Names associated with these products include Nextel, Fiber FP, Fiberfrax, Alphaquartz, and Capoflex.

Carbon Fibers

Carbon or graphite fibers have been developed for use in various types of industrial textiles and in some types of consumer goods. These fibers are made by converting a precursor filament into 95 to 99 percent carbon. *Graphite* is the term reserved for 99 percent carbon fibers.

Precursor filaments such as acrylic or cellulose (mainly rayon) are carbonized at high temperature.

Graphite fibers are formed under treatment at temperatures above 2500°C (4532°F), which converts the precursor filament to 99 percent carbon. Fibers treated at temperatures up to 1500°C (2732°F), which are converted to 95 percent carbon, are those identified as carbon fibers. Interestingly, the term *carbon* may be used for both types of fibers. Carbon fibers have an extremely high modulus and a low elongation; thus, they are highly suited for uses where high strength and little or no stretch are desired. In addition, they are highly resistant to heat.

The tenacity of the fibers varies from about 3 to more than 19 grams per denier; elongation is less than 1 percent. Tensile strength of fabrics is higher than for any other commerically available fiber except for sapphire whiskers and graphite in whisker form. Modulus of the fibers, the amount of give under initial stress, is rated as higher than for any other fiber by a great amount; the rating is given as an average resistance of 6 million pounds per square inch (420,000 kg/cm^2). Fiber density is approximately 1.5 grams per cubic centimeter. A few carbon fibers may have a density as high as 2, but these are usually designated for very special uses. The fibers are black and have a silky sheen. Carbon fiber is said to be the largest growing fiber in the 1980s.

Carbon fibers have a diversity of applications. They are used to reinforce resins and metals to provide structural materials with high strength and stiffness and light weight. The resulting composites are used in rotor blades for helicopters, compressor blades in jet engines, golf club shafts, crossbows for archery, bicycle parts, skis, keels for canoes, and machinery parts. The carbon filaments are also used to make fabrics that are flameproof and can be used for a variety of protective apparel; they provide for the military where nuclear, biological, and chemical resistance is important; and they are being promoted as an alternative to asbestos. Carbon fibers are used for a variety of electrical applications such as electrostatic precipitation and as resistance units for electrical heating devices.

Predictions are that use of carbon fibers during the 1980s will be divided as follows: 45 to 50 percent for aerospace applications, 24 to 25 percent for textiles, 7 to 8 percent for general engineering uses, 7 to 8 percent for thermoresistant uses, 5 to 6 percent for sports and recreational equipment, and 5 to 6 percent for automotive parts. Currently the United States uses 60 percent of the world's production of carbon fibers.

Boron and Boron Nitride Fibers

Fibers of boron and boron nitride are soft, white in color, strong, and flexible. They are used where heat resistance and flame resistance are important. Boron nitride is the more common of the two fibers. It is used in fabrics for aerospace applications, for certain types of protective apparel, and for heat or thermal-resistant shields. The fiber is considered an industrial high-performance fiber.

STUDY QUESTIONS

1. What are the typical uses for asbestos, and why has its use decreased over the past few years?
2. Describe the properties of glass fibers. What are the important uses for glass fibers? How are glass fibers made?
3. Identify the basic methods used in manufacturing metallic fibers. Cite several uses for metallic fibers and indicate why they are good for those end uses.

Activities

1. Find current references on industrial textiles and geotextiles. Describe fibers involved in such uses. What fibers are of importance in this end use and why?
2. Identify uses for carbon fibers. Describe carbon fibers and state what the basic precursors for carbon fibers may be.

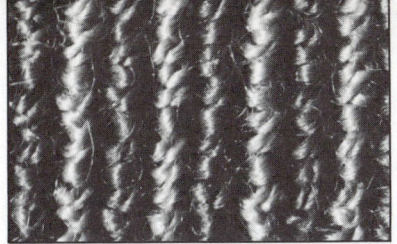

PART III

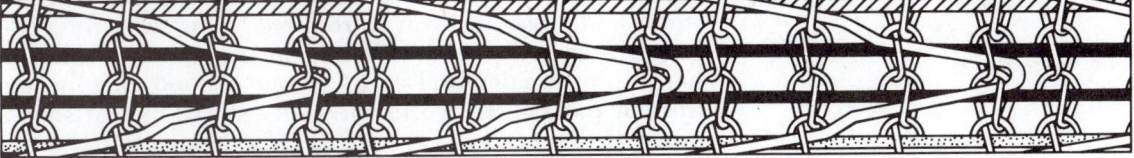

Yarns

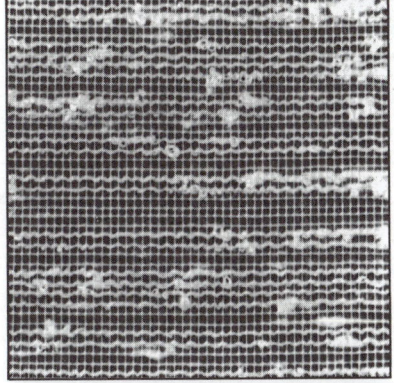

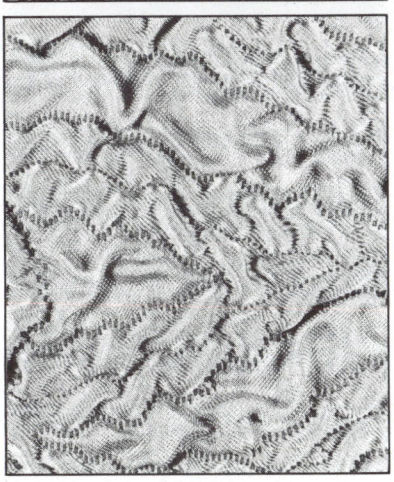

To weave or knit a fabric it is necessary to have yarns. Thus, the making of yarn is nearly as old as the manufacture of fabric and definitely predates recorded history. In prehistoric times, fibers were twisted together in simple ways to form yarns. It is very likely that these early yarn-making techniques involved merely rolling fibers together between the palms of the hand, between the fingers, or between a hand and another part of the body, such as the thigh. As a matter of fact, such techniques are used today by craftsmen and artist-weavers to make special yarns for hand-crafted fabrics.

The next development was the invention of the *spindle*. Various types of spindles have emerged from archeological digs, but the most common device seems to have employed a distaff, spindle, and whorl. Loose fibers were tied to a distaff. The spindle was a short stick notched at one end and pointed at the other. The spinning whorl or weight was secured near the pointed end. The spinner held the distaff under the arm to free both hands for the actual spinning. Fibers were attached to the spindle notch, and the whorl pulled the fibers and the spindle downward in a twirling motion. As the spindle dropped, the spinner drew out the fibers and formed them into yarn with the fibers while the whirling spindle twisted them into a tight strand. When the spindle neared the ground, the spinner took it up, wound the finished yarn around it, and caught the new yarn in the notch. This was repeated until sufficient yarn was made.

Yarns were spun by hand methods until late in the fourteenth century, when a crude spinning wheel, the *high wheel*, was developed. In this device a large drive wheel turned by one hand rotates a spinning head that gives twist to the yarn pulled away from it by the other hand; the yarn must be wound onto the bobbin in a separate operation. The *flyer spinning wheel*, a familiar sight in antique shops and museums, was introduced in the sixteenth century. This wheel, which is in many ways the most efficient hand-spinning device, is still the only method of spinning in some parts of the world and is often used by craftsmen. Since the device is operated by a foot treadle, both hands are free for compressing, extending, and partially twisting the fibers into yarn. The right hand, at the same time, feeds the yarn gradually into the flyer assembly, rotated by the wheel, which gives the final twist to the yarn and winds it evenly onto the bobbin.

During the eighteenth century multiple spinning frames were developed, and the basic machine-spinning techniques used today follow the principles of the early spinning frames. A number of individuals played major roles in the perfection of spinning processes and equipment. Lewis Paul and John Wyatt developed the roller method of spinning in 1737; James Hargreaves invented the spinning jenny in 1764; Richard Arkwright introduced the water power spinning frame in the early 1770s; and Samuel Crompton created the spinning mule in 1779.

The following chapters are concerned with the processes by which yarns are manufactured and with the yarn variations available. The type of yarn used may produce variations in fabric appearance, durability, maintenance, and comfort. It is important to note also that fiber properties have considerable influence on yarn properties.

Yarn Construction

KEY TERMS

air vortex spinning	friction spinning	twist direction
break spinning	open-end spinning	twistless spinning
carded yarns	ring spinning	woolen yarns
carding	rotor spinning	worsted yarns
combed yarns	roving	yarn
combing	self-twist yarns	yarn balance
core-spun yarns	spinning	yarn number
Coverspun yarns	staple yarn	yarn twist
drawing	tape yarns	
filament yarn	thread	

Basic Principles

Yarns are composed of textile fibers. The different ways in which fibers can be joined together aid in providing the variety of structures that, in turn, create a wide variety of fabrics.

The term *yarn* is defined in several ways by various texts and dictionaries, but the definition by ASTM is representative and widely accepted:[1]

a generic term for a continuous strand of textile fibers, filaments, or material in a form suitable for knitting, weaving, or otherwise intertwining to form a textile fabric. Yarn occurs in the following forms:

a. a number of fibers twisted together
b. a number of filaments laid together without twist
c. a number of filaments laid together with more or less twist
d. a single filament . . . monofilament

e. one or more strips made by a lengthwise division of a sheet of material such as a natural or synthetic polymer, a paper, or a metal foil, used with or without twist in a textile construction

The varieties possible include single, plied, cabled, cord, thread, and fancy yarn. Insertion of the phrase "or strands" following "continuous strand" in the first part of the definition above will serve to broaden and clarify the use of the word *yarn* as it is interpreted in this text.

Yarns can be made from short, staple-length fibers or from long filament fibers (Fig. 17.1); some may be made from a combination of both. If filament fibers are used, the yarns may be either *multifilament,* composed of several filaments, or *monofilament,* composed of a single filament. The staple fibers may derive from those natural fibers that are available only in short lengths, or they may be composed of man-made fibers or silk fibers that have been cut into short lengths. In any case, yarns made of short fibers require considerable processing. If both staple and filament fibers are used, they are usually combined by one of a group of new tech-

---

[1]ASTM, *Annual Book of ASTM Standards,* 1983, vol. 07.01, p. 76

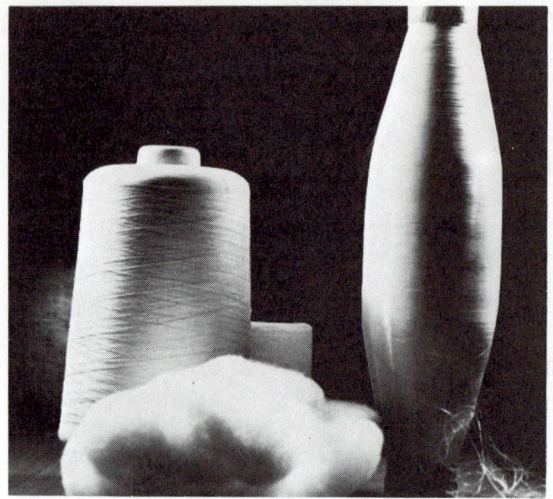

17.1 Staple and filament fibers.

17.2 Spinning filament yarns. As filaments are formed, they are combined, formed into yarns, and wound onto bobbins at the base of the machine. Completed bobbins are placed at the top, then collected for transport to other areas. Empty bobbins are left to be exchanged with a full bobbin. (Celanese Corporation)

techniques developed to produce modern yarns, or they are ply or cord yarns with special characteristics.

YARN PROCESSING

Yarns composed of short, staple fibers may be called either *spun yarns* or *staple-fiber yarns* or simply *staple yarns*. These terms will be used interchangeably. Yarns made from filament fibers may be identified as *filament yarns* or *thrown yarns*. Yarns composed of both staple- and filament-length fibers may be identified by various terms depending on the process used in their manufacture.

Traditional systems used to convert staple fibers into yarns, whether natural or man-made, are the cotton system and the woolen or worsted system. These are grouped together under one general heading of *ring spinning*. Today, much yarn is made by new or nontraditional methods such as *open-end spinning* or *break spinning* and its various subcategories.

Filament Yarns

The manufacture of yarns from filament fibers—whether natural or man-made—is a simple and direct process. Silk is the only natural filament fiber, and the size of silk yarns depends on the number of cocoons reeled off at one time. (See Chap. 6.)

17.3 Spiked lattice that carries fibers from the first opening step through the first blending. (Springs Industries, Inc.)

17.4 Rolls of cotton ready for carding, picker laps. (Cotton, Inc.)

Filament yarns of man-made fibers are made by either the continuous or the discontinuous process. In the continuous process the number of filaments in the final yarn and the number of openings in the spinnerette are the same. The filaments are extruded; drawn to develop strength, molecular orientation, and fineness; and then combined with the desired amount of twist and wound around take-up bobbins (Fig. 17.2). The discontinuous process differs in that filaments, without twist—and, for some types, without drawing—are wrapped onto packages, cakes, or cones. When needed, these filaments are rewound from the package, twist is added, and they are drawn if necessary. The yarn is then rewrapped onto bobbins and beams ready for use in making fabrics.

Filament yarns are smooth and even unless they have been deliberately made irregular for novelty effects. Simple yarns of filament fibers are lustrous and somewhat silky in appearance. The luster can be reduced considerably by the addition of delusterants, but even delustered filaments tend to have more sheen than staple yarns. They can, however, be made to look very much like delustered staple-fiber yarns through texturizing processes discussed in Chapter 19.

Filament yarns have no protruding fiber ends, so they do not pill unless the filaments are broken, and lint is not formed. Round filaments tend to shed soil, whereas multilobal filaments tend to hide or camouflage soil.

The strength of filament yarns is determined by a combination of factors: fiber tenacity, number of filaments combined, denier of the actual yarn, and denier of each of the filaments comprising the yarn. Because the fibers are long, they receive equal pull, and fiber strength is maximized in the yarn structure.

The amount of twist in filament yarns is usually relatively low, but high-twist crepe yarns are made successfully from filament fibers.

Staple-Fiber Yarns

Ring Spinning: Cotton System

OPENING, CLEANING, AND BLENDING Staple fibers arrive at the yarn-processing plant in large bales. To make yarns, fibers must be of similar length and relatively uniform so that the spun yarn can be of uniform quality. To accomplish this, fibers from a variety of production lots, fields, or animals must be blended together.

Several bales or cartons of fibers are placed in the opening, cleaning, and blending area. Some fiber from each bale or carton is fed into the opener and blender. It is important to separate or "open" the fiber mass to a single fiber state, or as close to that as possible. The opening and blending machines separate the fibers and blend fibers from the different bales or cartons. The technique used differs according to the type of opening or blending machine used.

In the intermittent system the fibers are separated from the bales and fed onto a spiked apron or lattice that carries the fibers from the feed area to the cleaning and opening area (Fig. 17.3). The opening operation separates the fibers into a loose, fluffy mass. These loose fibers are fed into a hopper, where a measured amount is laid on a conveyor belt and delivered to the picking unit, where additional blending occurs. The picker further opens, cleans, and blends fibers through a system of rollers and forced air. The blend of fibers is blown onto a collecting cylinder to form a layer from ½ to ¾ inch (1.3–1.9 cm) in thickness. As the cylinder rotates, the layer of fibers is rolled off to form the picker lap (Fig. 17.4). This is then taken to the card unit.

During this operation most of the dirt and impurities that might be present are removed by either gravity or centrifugal force. Cotton fibers receive more opening and blending than man-made fibers, since they have more impurities and greater varia-

17.5 Karousel picker. Automatic unit for delivery of fibers from bales to following processes. (American Textile Manufacturer's Institute)

17.6 Close-up of metal ''fingers'' that pull small tufts of fibers from bales, loosen them, and free them for processing. (Springs Industries, Inc.)

17.7 Card frame. At the back (right of photo) is the picker lap; at the front (left) is the ropelike card sliver as it is doffed or delivered. (Springs Industries, Inc.)

17.8 Card frame with automatic fiber feed shown at rear; the card sliver is doffed in front. (Springs Industries, Inc.)

17.9 Card clothing and brushes on a card. (Westpoint Pepperell, Inc.)

17.10 Layer of fibers from carding frame is gathered into card sliver. (National Cotton Council of America)

tion than do man-made fibers. A picker lap resembles a roll of absorbent cotton, except that it is about 45 inches (1 m) wide and 15 to 18 inches (0.38–0.46 m) in diameter.

The continuous system for making ring-spun yarns takes fibers directly from the bale and processes them automatically through to at least the card sliver state. Further steps may be connected to the card so that the card sliver moves on through additional processes automatically. The various steps in making ring-spun yarns are described in the following paragraphs.

Bales of fiber are placed into some type of automatic fiber feed unit (Fig. 17.5). Metal fingers (Fig. 17.6) pull tufts of fiber from the bale. These fibers are fed to the opening, cleaning, and blending area; they are then conveyed to a hopper for direct feed to the carding frame. Slivers from the card go directly to the drawing frames and may actually be fed continuously through to the roving process.

Yarns made on automatic equipment tend to be more uniform and may be stronger than discontinuous-process yarn. Production speed is considerably faster for continuous processes, labor costs are reduced, and plants stay cleaner.

No matter which system is used, the quality of the final yarn is dependent largely on the selection of fibers and on the thoroughness of the opening, cleaning, blending, and picking operations.

CARDING In the intermittent or discontinuous systems the picker lap is placed at the rear of the card frame to supply fibers (Fig. 17.7). In the automatic system the fibers are held in a hopper and fed in a loose form directly to the card (Fig. 17.8). Carding continues the cleaning of the fibers; it removes fibers too short for use in yarns. The process partially aligns the fibers so that their longitudinal axes are somewhat parallel. Carding is accomplished by wire cards or granular cards. Wire cards contain two layers of *card clothing* consisting of wire flats (rectangular shapes) in which fine wire pins are anchored. The flats are attached to a steel cylinder and to an endless belt that rotates over the top portion of the cylinder (Fig. 17.9). The two sets of pins move in the same direction, but at different speeds, to tease the fibers into a filmy layer, so that a thin web of fibers is formed on the cylinder (Fig. 17.10). This thin web is gathered into a soft mass and pulled into a ropelike strand of fibers about ¾ to 1 inch in diameter (1.9–2.5 cm), called a *sliver*. The sliver is pulled through a cone-shaped outlet and doffed or delivered to cans or to a conveyor belt. Granular cards are similar to wire cards except that the ''card clothing'' is made of a rough granular surface somewhat similar to rough sandpaper.

The card sliver is not completely uniform in diameter, and the fibers are somewhat random in arrangement. Some fabrics are made of yarns that

17.11 Breaker-drawing unit. The front is open to show fiber slivers being smoothed, drawn, and re-formed into one new sliver. (Springs Industries, Inc.)

17.12 Combing frame. From the lap rolls, at the top, layers of fibers are fed to the combing area, where the comb sliver is formed. Waste fibers are discharged at the base. (National Cotton Council of America)

have received only this carding operation prior to drawing and roving formation. However, some fabrics require yarns of finer quality, particularly fine-quality cotton fabrics, and these require combed yarns rather than carded. When cotton and man-made fibers are combined, it is common for the cotton fibers to receive the combing step before the two types of fibers are combined. For yarns that require the additional step, the card sliver goes through the breaker-drawing step and then to the combing operation.

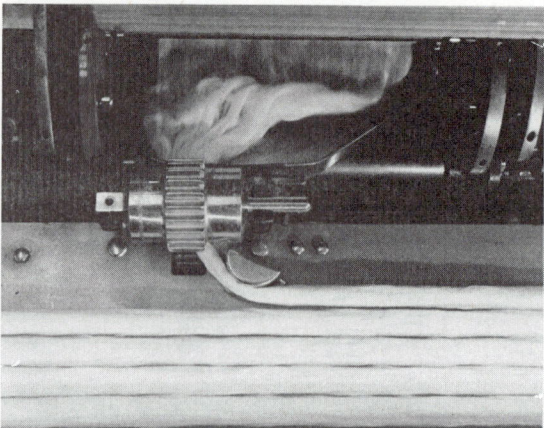

17.13 Close-up of comb sliver as it is formed and laid with other slivers for delivery to drawing frame. (National Cotton Council of America)

COMBING For high-quality cotton yarns of superior evenness, smoothness, fineness, and strength, fibers are combed as well as carded. Card slivers are fed to the breaker-drawing frame, where several card slivers are combined (Fig. 17.11). The breaker-drawing unit smooths out the card slivers, pulls out the fibers into a thin layer, and re-forms a new sliver. The drawing is accomplished by controlling the speed of a series of rollers, each set of which operates faster than the one behind it. The layer of slivers is pulled through the rollers at increasing speeds; as the layer leaves the unit, the fibers are pulled into a new sliver and delivered to cans ready for the combing frame.

Forty-eight slivers from the breaker-drawing unit are combined to form the lap for the comber. These slivers are fed through a lapper that smooths them to a thin layer of fibers which is wound onto a roll. These rolls, each weighing about 30 pounds (13.6 kg), are taken to the combing frame. The layer of fibers is fed into the combing area, where fine metal wires clean out remaining short fibers and impurities and further parallelize the fiber in the comber lap (Figs. 17.12 and 17.13).

During the combing operation as much as 20 percent of the fibers may be removed. This waste is sold to manufacturers of nonwoven products and to others who have use for short fibers. The fibers remaining form a thin web or layer; this web of fibers is pulled together, fed through a cone and under a geared wheel that helps to hold the fibers together, and delivered as a comb sliver.

17.14 Drawing frame. (Zinser Textilemaschinen GmbH)

17.15 The open front of the drawing frame that shows slivers as they are formed and move into receiving cans. (Springs Industries, Inc.)

17.16 Roving frame. Close-up of roller area to show reduction in diameter of the drawn sliver as it moves between rollers and emerges in foreground as roving. (Springs Industries, Inc.)

FINISHER DRAWING Slivers from either the carding unit or the combing unit, depending on the ulitmate yarn desired, are processed through the finisher-drawing or drafting frame (Fig. 17.14). This is the process by which fibers of different types can be blended together to form blended yarns. Eight slivers are drawn together to produce the drawn sliver. If a 50/50 polyester/cotton blend is to be made, there will be four slivers of polyester fiber and four of cotton; if a 65/35 blend is ordered, there will be five polyester slivers and three cotton. As with breaker drawing, rollers moving at different speeds smooth and combine the slivers and pull them into a thin layer and then into the drawn sliver (Fig. 17.15).

The finisher-drawing operation is usually repeated. The second time, however, eight slivers from the first finisher-drawing step are subjected to the same operation. The drawn sliver is about the same size as, or perhaps slightly smaller than, the card or comb slivers. As yet no twist has been imparted into the fiber assemblage, although the delivery of the sliver to the cans tends to twist the sliver slightly.

ROVING Slivers from the finisher drawing are taken to the roving frame, where each sliver will be attenuated until it measures approximately one-eighth of its original diameter. The drawn sliver is fed between sets of rollers (Fig. 17.16). Each set of rollers rotates faster than the set behind it, the front rollers rotate about ten times faster than the back set of rollers. This pulls the fibers out, reduces the diameter of the strand, and further parallelizes the fibers. A slight amount of twist is imparted to give

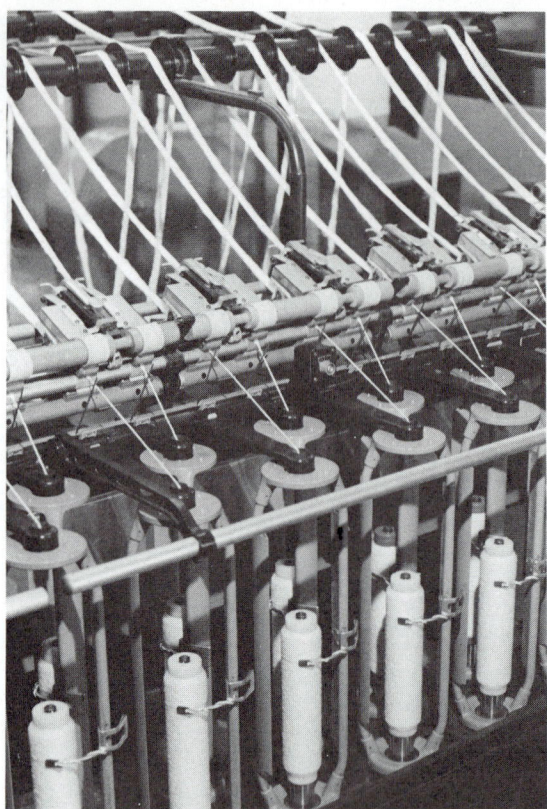

17.17 Roving frame showing slivers entering machine, emerging as roving and wound onto bobbins at base of machine. (National Cotton Council of America)

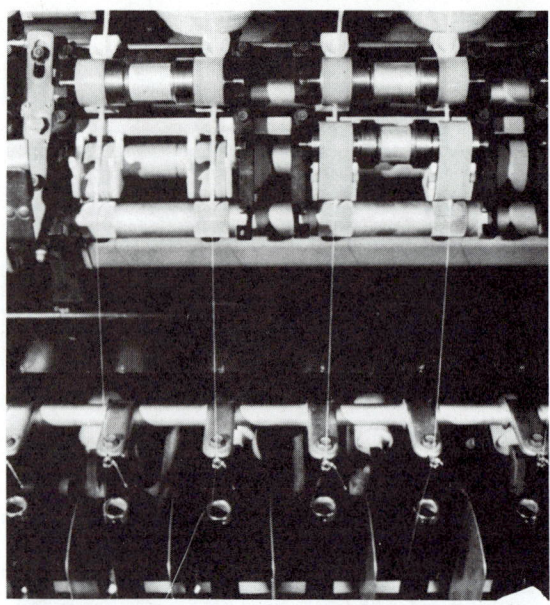

17.19 Close-up of spinning zone to show how roving is extended or drawn out into fine-spun yarn. (Springs Industries, Inc.)

17.18 Spinning frame. (National Cotton Council of America)

17.20 Close-up of traveler, the metal loop that guides the yarn around the spindle and lays it onto the yarn package. (Springs Industries, Inc.)

17.21 Spinning frame with automatic doffing of spun yarn and replacement with blank tubes. (Zinser Textilemaschinen GmbH)

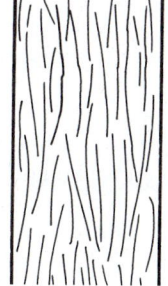

17.22 Woolen yarn *(left)* usually shows fibers lying in a random arrangement. Worsted yarn *(right)* shows highly oriented fiber arrangement.

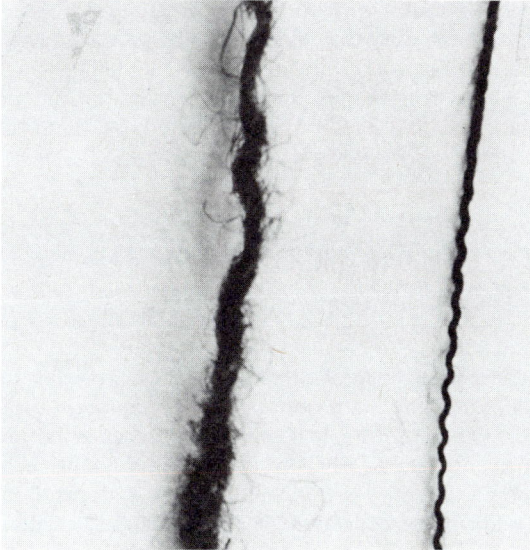

17.23 Woolen and worsted yarns.

strength. The new strand, called roving, is laid onto a bobbin (Fig. 17.17). Roving is wound onto the bobbin package at approximately 30 yards (27 m) per minute. The full bobbins are doffed (removed) from the frame and delivered to the spinning frame.

SPINNING The final process in ring spinning of single yarn is the spinning operation. During spinning the roving is attenuated to the desired diameter, called the *final draft,* and the desired amount of twist is inserted (Fig. 17.18). The roving is fed down into the spinning area, where it feeds between sets of rollers (Fig. 17.19). Just as in the roving step, the front set of rollers rotates faster than the back set. In spinning, the front set rotates about 30 times faster than the back set. This difference in speed attenuates the yarn and makes it even, smooth, and uniform. The attenuated yarn is fed down, guided through a U-shaped guide, called a traveler, which moves around the take-up package or bobbin on a ring, hence the name "ring spinning" (Fig. 17.20). The movement of the traveler and the turning of the spindle on which the bobbin is held combine to introduce twist into the yarn. The spindle turns at about 13,000 revolutions per minute; the traveler is slightly slower. Approximately 12 yards (11 m) of yarn is wound onto the bobbin per minute. The size of yarn and the amount of twist, cited as turns per inch, can be controlled. The yarn manufacturing steps discussed to this point produce a *single* or *singles* yarn (see page 187).

Many new developments have occurred during the late 1970s and early 1980s to make ring spinning competitive with newer methods of yarn manufacture. The combined use of automated doffing systems (removal of spindles of yarn) and automatic winding systems has decreased labor costs, increased productivity, and helped maintain quality (Fig. 17.21).

Ring Spinning: Woolen and Worsted Systems

Wool and man-made fibers cut the length of wool can be spun into yarns by either the woolen or the worsted systems. Woolen yarns are carded and spun; worsted yarns are carded, combed, drawn, and spun (Figs. 17.22 and 17.23).

SORTING Spinning wool fibers into yarns requires some special procedures. The fibers must first be sorted. Each fleece is carefully opened, and an expert grader pulls the fleece apart and sorts the fibers according to fineness, or width, and length, and sometimes according to strength. The grade of fiber determines the type of product for which it will be used. Fine fibers that are relatively long are reserved for sheer wool fabrics and worsteds; medium fibers of short length are suitable for woolens; coarse fibers, both long and short, are made into rough fabrics and carpets.

SCOURING   After sorting, the wool is scoured. This involves washing in warm, soapy water several times, followed by thorough rinsing and drying. Scouring is essential, for it removes the natural grease in the fiber, the suint (dried body excretions of the sheep), dirt, and dust. After the scouring, the fibers are lubricated for ease of processing.

WOOLEN YARNS   To make woolen yarns the fibers are fed to the carding machine, where the fiber assemblage is opened or separated, tangles are removed, fibers are straightened to some degree, impurities are removed, fibers from various supply stocks are mixed, and the fibers are finally pulled from the card in a form called roving or roping. The carding machines are somewhat similar in appearance to those used in carding cotton fibers, but the carding wires are somewhat longer. The carding operation may use several sets of carding cylinders instead of the one used in making cotton system yarns.

The roving or roping goes directly to the spinning frame, where the roving is drawn out to the desired size, twist is inserted, and the woolen yarn is put onto packages for use in weaving or knitting. Several types of spinning systems have been used in making woolen yarns: mule spinning, stand spinning, and ring-frame spinning. Today, most woolen yarn is made on the ring frame, which is similar in action to the ring frame used for cotton yarns.

Because of the absence of drawing in making wool yarns, the yarns have less fiber orientation than carded cotton yarns. They are characterized by nonuniformity, bulk, resilience, good insulation properties, and a rough, hairy surface.

WORSTED YARNS   Following scouring and lubrication, wool fibers are carded. This straightens the fibers, removes impurities, and blends fibers from different batches to provide for uniformity in length and quality. Fibers are arranged in a relatively parallel manner. The card frames are similar to cards used in other processes, but many systems use two cylinders and several feed rolls. The card sliver is drawn and then combed. These steps are

similar to processes used in spinning combed-cotton-system yarns. The wool at this point is often referred to as *top*.

After combing, the comb sliver is drafted or drawn to form a roving, which is delivered to a spinning frame, where the final worsted yarn is made. Worsted yarns can be spun using several methods, but modern worsted yarns are made primarily on ring-spinning frames.

Worsted yarns are characterized by a relatively smooth and even surface, a highly parallel fiber arrangement, a compact structure, resiliency, and good strength. Yarns can be made in various sizes from relatively fine to heavy, and with different amounts of twist.

Processing Staple-Length Man-Made Fibers

Man-made fibers cut into short lengths can be processed on ring-spinning equipment using either cotton systems or wool systems. The choice depends on the staple fiber length. Fibers cut to match the length of cotton are processed on cotton-spinning frames, while fibers cut the length of wool are spun on woolen or worsted equipment.

Man-made staple fibers may be blended with natural fibers at the finisher-drawing stage as described for cotton or at the carding stage for woolen yarns or the carding or combing or drawing stages for worsted yarns. One important step required for using man-made fibers of staple length is to impart crimp or some system that will build in cohesiveness or spinning quality. This contributes a waviness to the fiber that enables it to be processed with natural fibers or with other man-made fibers (Fig. 17.24). Crimp is introduced by texturizing systems (described in Chapter 19) or by building a chemical crimp through polymer formulations.

NEWER METHODS OF YARN PRODUCTION

The past two decades (1965–1984) have seen the development of a series of new techniques for making yarns from staple fibers. These processes are important because they represent considerable economic advantages, including increased speed of production, reduced labor costs, reduced overhead due to reduction in space needs, and reduced energy consumption.

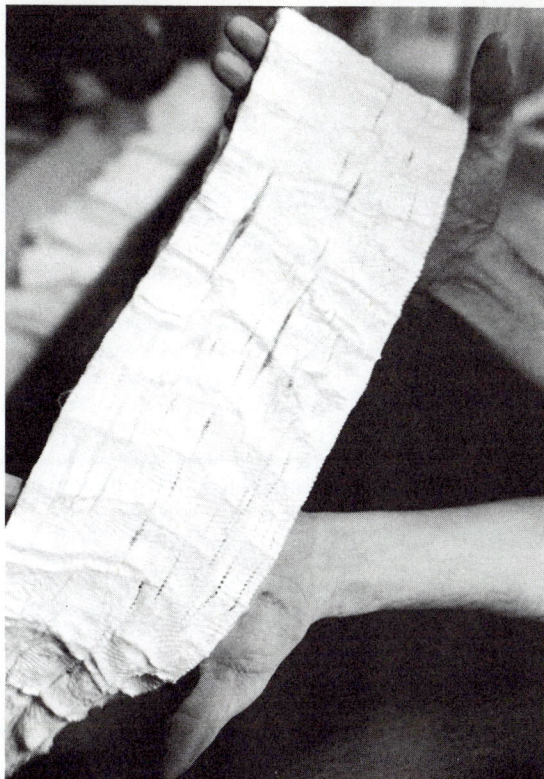

17.24 Crimped tow ready for cutting to make staple fibers for use in making spun yarns. (Celanese Corporation)

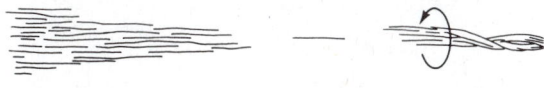

fiber supply   break fiber break   yarn

17.25 Diagram showing the basic principle of open-end or break spinning.

Open-End Spinning

The term "open-end spinning" has frequently been used as a synonym for all new methods of making yarn. This is incorrect, and "open-end" should be applied only to systems where a break occurs in the fiber system. Break spinning and open-end spinning are synonymous (Fig. 17.25).

The essential steps in open-end spinning include the following. A coarse sliver of fibers is fed to an opening system, which opens the sliver to the point where the fibers are individual entities; the individual fibers are fed forward; they are collected together on a small surface and pulled from the sur-

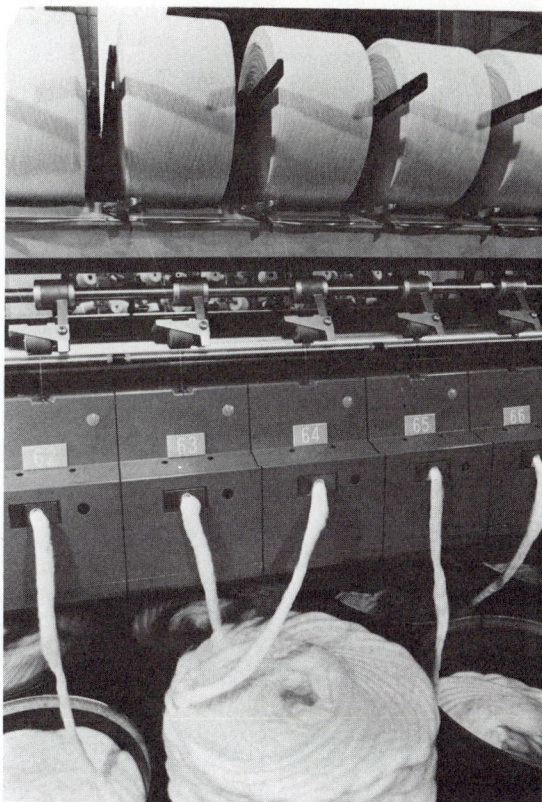

17.26 Open-end spinning frame. Slivers move from below, enter spinning area, and emerge at the top as yarn. (National Cotton Council of America)

face as a thin layer constantly adding to the open end or tail of the forming yarn. The thin layer is attenuated, twist is inserted, and the resulting yarn is wound onto bobbins. Two methods of open-end or break spinning are in use; aeromechanical or rotor spinning and fluid or air or water vortex (jet) systems.

ROTOR SPINNING   Rotor spinning involves the contact of fibers in or on rotating devices such as funnels, cones, baskets, sieves, or needled surfaces (Fig. 17.26). A sliver of fibers is fed into the unit, a current of air forces the fibers into a loose form, and they are collected on the rotating device. As they collect, they are pulled off the rotor by mechanical means to form the yarn, and the new yarn is wound onto packages (Fig. 17.27). Twist is inserted as the yarn is removed from the rotor.

Rotor spinning is a popular process and has replaced some ring-spinning units. There are some differences in quality and characteristics between ring-

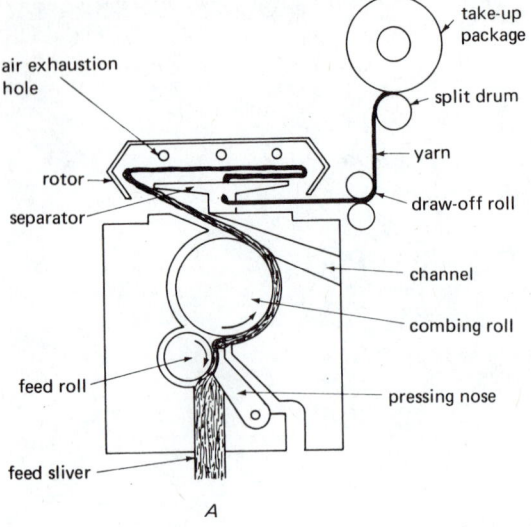

take-up
package

air exhaustion
hole

split drum

rotor

yarn

separator

draw-off roll

channel

combing roll

feed roll

pressing nose

feed sliver

A

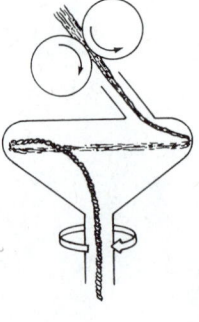

B

17.27 Diagrams of two types of units used in open-end or break spinning. A: Sliver of fibers enters from below and is fed into the rotor, where centrifugal force converts fibers into completed yarn. The take-up package holds yarn ready for further processing into fabric. B: Sliver of fibers enters from above and is fed into the rotating funnel, where centrifugal force converts fibers into completed yarn. Yarn is removed from the base of the funnel.

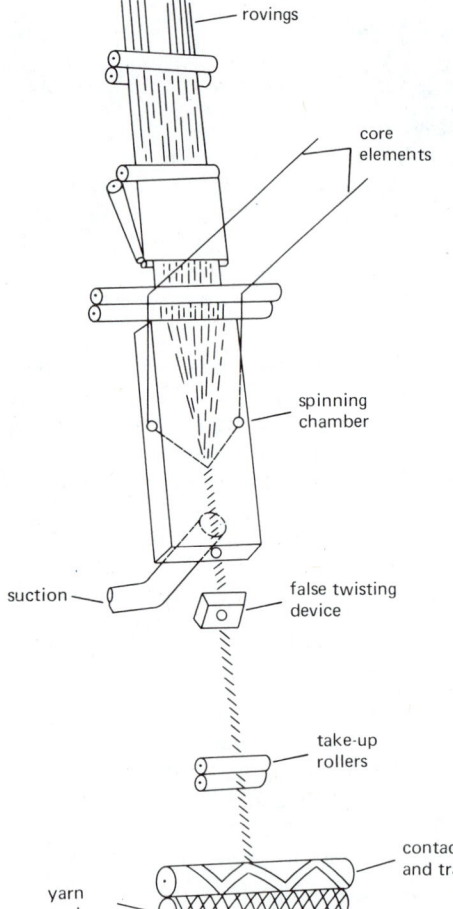

rovings

core
elements

spinning
chamber

suction

false twisting
device

take-up
rollers

contact drive
and traverse

yarn
package

17.28 Diagram of vortex system of spinning.

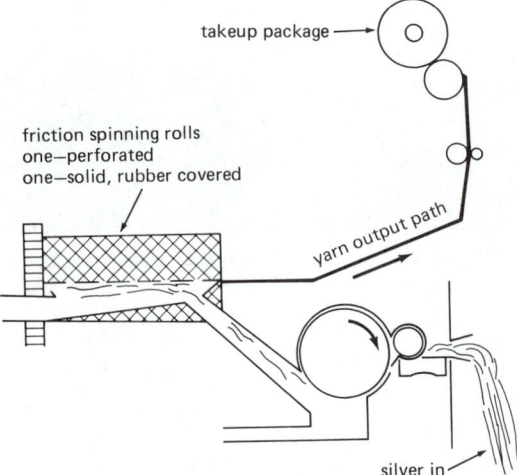

takeup package

friction spinning rolls
one—perforated
one—solid, rubber covered

yarn output path

silver in

17.29 Diagram of one type of friction spinning.

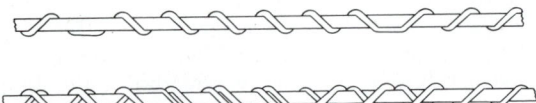

17.30 Diagram showing example of self-twist yarn.

and rotor-spun yarns, but both have some advantages. Many of the disadvantages associated with early rotor-spun yarns are disappearing as the process is improved and perfected. Important aspects of rotor-spun yarn include the facts that they require considerably less plant space, energy requirements and labor needs are reduced, operation is cleaner, and production of yarn is considerably faster than for ring spinning. The same amount and size of yarn spun on the rotor machine in 0.02 hour would take 0.30 hour on a ring-spinning frame.

Some rotor systems, such as the Autocoro® process, take the carded sliver through to the type of package needed for warping or knitting. This process has a built-in unit that pieces slivers to increase uniformity in yarn.

Early rotor-spun yarns tended to be coarse, but modern rotor-spinning machines produce fine yarns as well as medium to heavy or coarse yarns. Furthermore, yarns are even and defects are reduced. Fiber defects may cause problems, but newer systems can eliminate such fibers and discharge them as waste prior to yarn formation.

Properties of rotor-spun yarns compare favorably with those of ring-spun. Fiber distribution is more uniform in rotor-spun than ring-spun, and fiber migration is less in rotor-spun than in ring-spun yarns. Because of the way fibers arrange themselves in rotor-spun yarns, dyeing behavior may differ from that of ring-spun yarns. It has been stated that deeper colors and differential dye techniques are possible with rotor-spun yarns.

End uses for rotor-spun yarns include apparel, home furnishings, and industrial fabrics. In fact, with the current state of the art of spinning, open-end spun yarns, particularly rotor-spun, compete with ring-spun in nearly every possible end use.

AIR VORTEX Spinning of yarns by the air vortex system is similar to the rotor process except that the yarn is formed in moving air rather than on a rotating surface (Fig. 17.28.).

The method is increasing rapidly in use as new equipment has been developed. Air-jet-spun yarns are clean, have good uniformity and even quality, are less irregular than ring-spun yarns, are stronger than much rotor-spun yarns, and have good wash-and-wear characteristics. Air-spun yarns do tend to pill more quickly than other types.

Friction Spinning (Modifications of the DREF Process)

A modification of existing open-end techniques has been introduced that combines mechanical and air current operations. The original system was called DREF after the developer, Dr. Fueher. Several modifications have been made in this technique, and it is now generally referred to as friction spinning.

In this process the sliver enters the system and the fibers are separated and spread onto a combing or carding roll; they are doffed from this roll and transported by air to the friction zone. Two cylinders rotating in the same direction pull the fibers together to form the yarn. The angle of the feed into the friction rolls affects fiber alignment; the smaller the angle, the better the fiber alignment and the more parallel the fibers will be.

Another modification of friction spinning drafts the sliver into a center core of fibers, which is then wrapped by other fibers. It is possible to add filament fibers to the center core.

Friction-spun yarns are uniform, quite free of impurities, fuller with more body than ring-spun yarns, but they tend to have less strength. These yarns can be used successfully for apparel fabrics, home furnishing fabrics, and industrial fabrics of certain types. The process is diagramed in Figure 17.29.

Self-Twist Yarns

Self-twist yarns are essentially two-strand or two-ply (or more) yarns. They may involve one ply or strand of staple fibers and one of filament, two strands of staple fibers, or two of filaments, or multiple combinations of these. A common type is the Selfil yarn, which is composed of one strand of staple fibers with some twist and a filament strand wrapped around the staple strand. The filament strand alternates S and Z twist. A number of combinations of these strands have been made (Fig. 17.30).

Self-spinning produces yarns more cheaply than ring spinning and considerably faster with less labor. Selfil yarns are slightly more even than ring-spun and are much stronger because of the filament wrapping. Furthermore, in knitted structures, Selfil yarns snag and pull less than ring-spun yarns.

Twistless Yarns

Fibers are held together with adhesive to form yarn in the twistless process. A roving is made and then drawn to a fine strand; during the drawing an adhesive is applied by rollers. A common adhesive is starch. The drawn yarn, coated with adhesive, is wound onto packages; the package is steamed, and the adhesive bonds the fibers together.

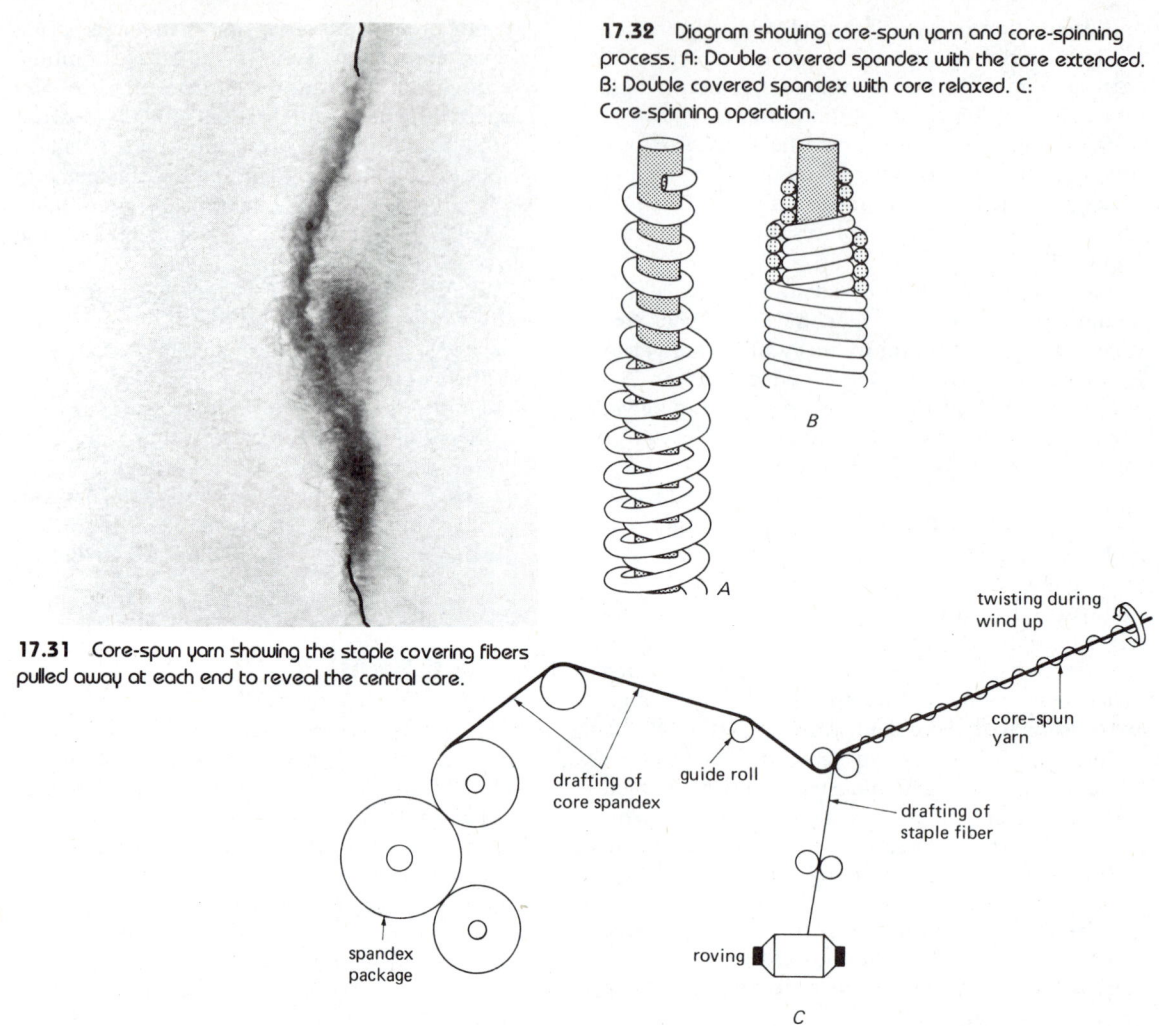

17.32 Diagram showing core-spun yarn and core-spinning process. A: Double covered spandex with the core extended. B: Double covered spandex with core relaxed. C: Core-spinning operation.

B

A

twisting during wind up

core-spun yarn

drafting of core spandex

guide roll

drafting of staple fiber

spandex package

roving

C

17.31 Core-spun yarn showing the staple covering fibers pulled away at each end to reveal the central core.

Characteristics of twistless yarns as compared with ring-spun yarns include the following. Twistless yarn is stiffer than ring-spun and has greater luster, less elongation, and better covering power owing to its ribbonlike character. Also, it is more uniform and somewhat weaker than ring-spun yarn.

Core-Spun Yarns

Core-spun yarns have a central core with a second layer or sheath of fibers wrapped around it. Both core and wrapping may be of the same fiber type, or two different fiber types (or more) may be used. Further, one part may be of filament fibers while the other is of staple fibers; or both parts may be of either filament or staple-length fibers. The outer sheath may completely cover the core. When the outer sheath does not hide the center completely, the two components create interesting appearance effects.

One of the most common types of core-spun yarns is that involving a core of a stretch filament such as spandex with a covering of staple fibers (Fig. 17.31). This process is diagramed in Figure 17.32. It may also be used for a variety of other fiber types and end uses.

A relatively new process for making a special type of yarn is called *Coverspun®*. It can use any type of staple fibers, but it is especially desirable for

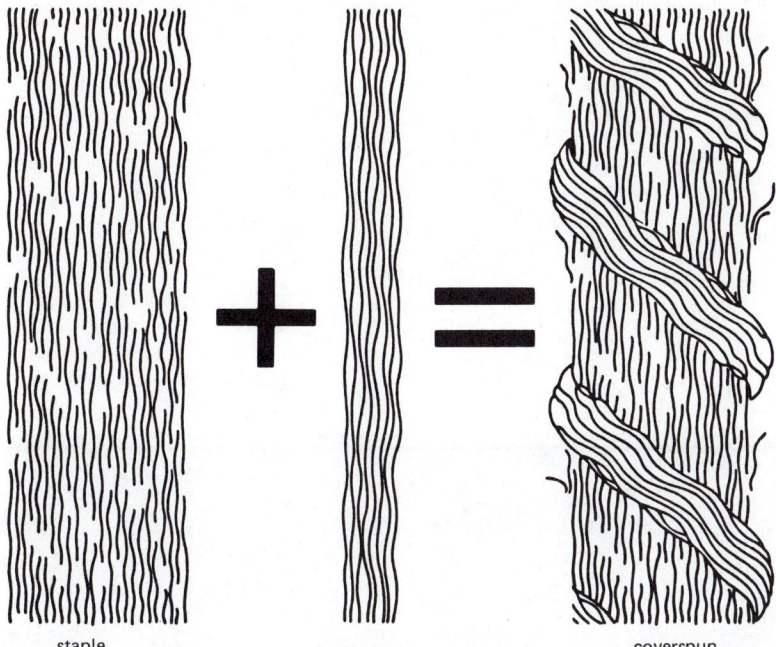

staple
(no twist)

filament

coverspun
yarn

17.33 Steps in making a Coverspun yarn.

wool, and it uses any type of filament fibers. Coverspun is described as a bicomponent yarn made of a center or core of staple fibers that are wrapped with filament fibers that serve as the binder (Fig. 17.33). The process uses a conventional roving as the supply source for the staple fiber core.

A modification of the process involves three components, a center core of filament fibers encircled by staple fibers, then wrapped by filament fibers.

An important factor of this process is that the staple fibers are not twisted, but rather are bundled together. This means yarns can be made rapidly. Coverspun yarns have the following properties:

They are generally stronger than ring-spun yarns. This is due to the filament wrapping and to a high interfiber friction.
They are more even than ring-spun yarns.
They have an elongation equal to ring-spun yarns.
They can be used equally well in knitted or woven fabrics.
Fabrics made of these yarns do not look as if filaments have been used.
Covering power of the yarns is good.
Pilling of yarns in fabrics is reduced.

Fabrics are soft and supple and can be light in weight and thin with little bulk.
Yarns have an attractive appearance.

Stretch and core-spun yarns can be made using the Coverspun system. These can be made economically and exhibit uniformity, reduced torque, good aesthetic appearance, excellent strength, and good dyeing and heat-setting performance.

Tape Yarns

Tape or split film yarns are produced from thin sheets or films of polymer that are cut into narrow strips or ribbons. The major steps in production are extrusion, cooling, slitting, drawing, and winding (Fig. 17.34). Any man-made polymer normally found in fibers has the potential for tape yarns, but in actual practice the majority are polyethylene or polypropylene olefin fibers.

The polymer is extruded through a slot to form a thin layer that resembles plastic wrap, through narrow slots, which eliminate slitting, or through a circular die to form a tube that is then slit. The film is cooled under controlled conditions, and the sheet or tube is then slit into narrow tapes. The tapes are heated before drawing.

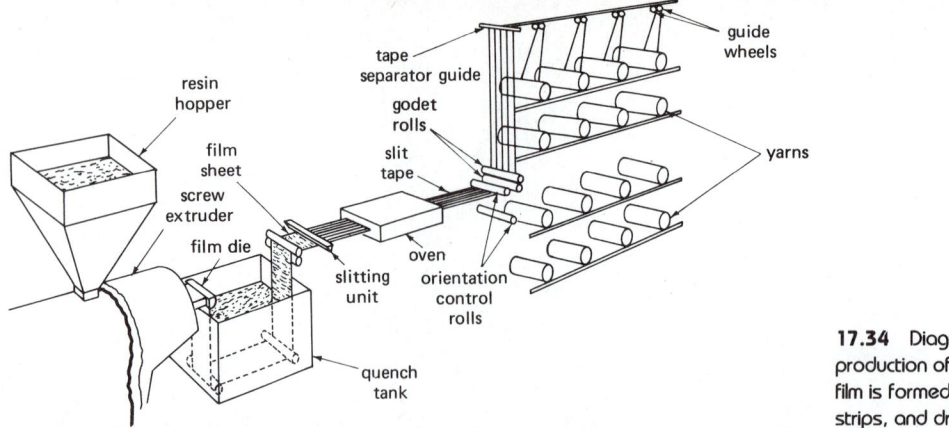

17.34 Diagram showing the production of tape yarns. The film is formed, split into narrow strips, and drawn into yarns.

17.35 An assortment of sewing threads. (Coats and Clark, Inc.)

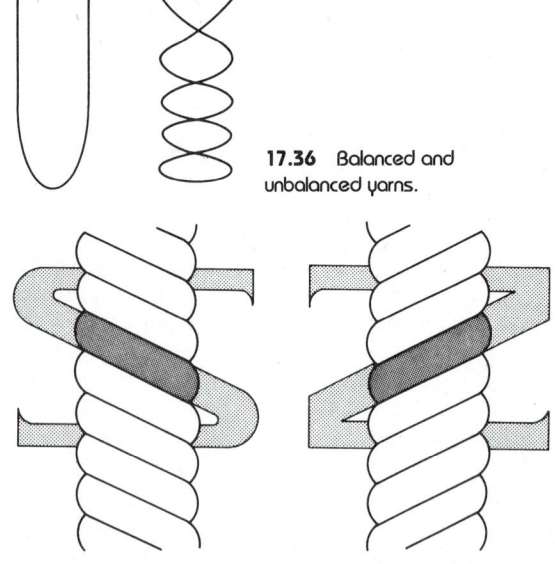

17.36 Balanced and unbalanced yarns.

17.37 Diagram of S and Z twist in yarns.

The drawing operation extends the tape linearly and decreases its width. Molecular orientation occurs, and longitudinal strength is developed. The drawing operation is like that used to draw regular yarns; the tape moves through rollers rotating at different speeds. In general, the greater the degree of stretching during the drawing, the better the fibrillation will be. Fibrillation means that the tape tends to break apart on the longitudinal axis, forming many fibrils, and begins to resemble a coarse filament yarn. The completed yarns are wound onto packages for use on various types of fabric-making machines.

Tape yarns have good strength, good abrasion resistance, and good stability. They are used for carpet backing for tufted carpets, for making sacks and bags, for tarpaulins, for webbings, and for such miscellaneous uses as awnings, blinds, travel goods, swimming pool covers, and some types of rope.

YARN PROPERTIES

Thread and Yarn

Thread and yarn are basically similar. *Yarn* is the term usually applied when the assemblage of fibers is employed in the manufacture of a fabric, whereas *thread* indicates a product used to join pieces of fabric together to create a textile product (Fig. 17.35). Thread is frequently of plied construction. It is fine, even, and strong.

Thread must be constructed so that it can be adapted to either hand or machine sewing as well as embroidery or lacemaking. A satisfactory thread must have high strength and adequate elasticity, a smooth surface, dimensional stability, resistance to snarling, resistance to damage by friction, and an attractive appearance. Several types of thread are available: simple ply threads, cord threads, elastic threads, monofilament threads of man-made fibers, and multifilament threads.

For many decades most types of threads were made of silk or cotton or linen. Today the most common threads are of either polyester or cotton or a blend of the two. In general, polyester and polyester/cotton blends have a higher strength and abrasion resistance, lower shrinkage, and greater sensitivity to high temperatures than cotton.

Most threads are either of a ply construction or core-spun. These have superior strength and durability.

Yarn Twist

Previous paragraphs have described how fibers are formed into yarns with a certain amount of twist in the final yarn. The amount of twist is sometimes identified broadly as low, medium, or high. However, it is more accurate to indicate the actual number of turns, or twists, per inch. The turns per inch (TPI) needed to form the best possible yarns varies with the yarn diameter. As the yarn becomes finer, it requires more twist; heavier yarns can have very low twist and be durable. The strength of yarns is due, in part, to the amount of twist that has been imparted. Strong yarns require considerable twist. However, beyond an optimum point additional twist will cause yarns to kink and finally to lose strength.

Balanced yarns are those in which the twist is such that the yarn will hang in a loop without kinking, doubling, or twisting upon itself. *Unbalanced* yarns have sufficient twist to set up a torque effect, and the yarn will untwist and retwist in the opposite direction (Fig. 17.36). Smooth fabrics require balanced yarns, but for crepe and textured effects, unbalanced yarns are desirable. Crepe yarns are also produced by balanced yarns with sufficient twist to produce the kinking, but this is less common.

The direction of twist is also important. Yarns can be twisted with either a right-hand twist (S twist) or a left-hand twist (Z twist). The direction of the twist conforms to the center bar of the letter S or Z (Fig. 17.37).

Various effects can be obtained by combining yarns of different twist direction, and durability may be increased by efficient plying of S and Z twist single yarns.

Yarn Number

Yarn number is a measure of linear density. *Direct yarn number* is the mass per unit length of yarn; *indirect yarn number* is the length per unit mass of yarn. Yarn number is frequently called *yarn count* in the indirect system. To some extent the yarn number is an indication of diameter when yarns of the same fiber content are compared.

Over the years various methods of determining yarn number have been developed. Cotton yarns are numbered by measuring the weight in pounds of one 840-yard hank; the count is then reported as the number of 840-yard hanks required to weigh 1 pound. For example, if 840 yards, or one hank, of cotton weighs 1 pound, the yarn number is 1s; if it requires 30 hanks to weigh 1 pound, the yarn is a 30s. A heavy yarn would be 1s, a medium yarn a 30s, and a very fine yarn a 160s.

Woolen yarn is measured by the number of 300-yard hanks per pound, whereas worsted yarn is measured by the number of 560-yard hanks to the pound. Silk and man-made fibers are usually measured using the denier system A denier is equal to the weight in grams of 9000 meters of yarn. In this system the lower the number, the finer the yarn. Another direct yarn numbering system is the *tex* system. Tex determines the yarn number by determining the weight in grams of 1 kilometer (1000 meters) of yarn. The result is the tex yarn number. In comparing the various systems used in arriving at yarn number, the following may be helpful. A yarn identified as a cotton 50s would have approximately 41,500 yards per pound; the same yarn, if identified by denier, would be identified as 105-denier yarn; by tex, 12; by the worsted system 75; by the woolen system, 26.

The change to the metric system of measurement should increase the general use of the tex system in all segments of the industry. ASTM has identified the tex yarn number as the recommended standard.

STUDY QUESTIONS

1. Describe the ring-spinning process for making yarns.
2. Describe the various new yarn manufacturing systems.
3. Compare yarns made by the different processes in terms of strength, uniformity, appearance, and other important properties.
4. Compare carded and combed yarns. How do they differ? How are they alike?
5. What are the similarities of and differences between woolen and worsted yarns.
6. Why does thread require more strength than many yarns used in making woven or knitted fabrics?
7. What should consumers look for in yarn construction as it influences recommended care procedures for a textile item?
8. In this day of concern for energy, which yarn construction method or methods would you select for use and why?
9. There has been considerable concern about the manufacture and sale of textile products in the United States because of the high amount of imported goods. As one way to try to help reduce these imports, which one of the yarn construction processes would you use and why?

Activities

1. Remove yarns from several different pieces of fabric and determine if they are single, ply, or cord. (See also Chap. 18.)
2. If a laboratory is available, select yarn samples from various fabrics and measure to determine the yarn number, turns or twists, per inch, and balance or imbalance of the yarns.
3. Look for articles in current journals concerning yarn manufacture and particularly concerning the introduction of robots into the industry. Describe how and where such machines are being used.

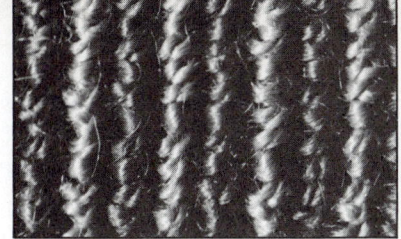

Simple and Complex Yarns

OBJECTIVES

◊ **To introduce terminology related to various types of simple yarns**

◊ **To identify various types of complex or fancy (or novelty) yarns and indicate how they can be described and classified**

◊ **To describe typical end uses for complex yarns**

KEY TERMS

bouclé yarn	grandelle yarn	seed and splash yarns
chenille yarn	loop yarn	simple single yarn
complex yarn	novelty yarn	slub yarn
cord yarn	nub or knot yarn	spiral or corkscrew yarn
fancy yarn	ply yarn	
flock or flake yarn	ratiné and gimp yarns	

Simple Yarns

Yarns that are even in size, have an equal number of turns or twists per inch throughout, and are relatively smooth are called simple yarns. A *simple single yarn* is the most basic assemblage of fibers suitable for operations such as weaving and knitting. These yarns can be made from any of the fibers and by any of the basic systems described in the preceding chapter.

A *simple ply yarn* is composed of two or more simple single yarns plied or twisted together. In naming a ply yarn, the number of singles included usually precedes the word *ply*. For example, if two singles are used, the yarn is called a 2-ply; if three are used, a 3-ply (Figs. 18.1 and 18.2). When more than three singles are used, the term *multi-ply* or *multiple ply* may be used.

Simple cord or *cable yarns* are composed of 2 (or more) ply yarns twisted together (Figs. 18.3 and 18.4). In identifying a cord, it is necessary to indicate the number of plies and singles in the cord. Thus a 3,5-ply cord indicates that each ply has five singles and that three of these 5-ply yarns are combined in making the cord.

Crepe yarns are a variation of simple yarns. However, a crepe yarn possesses a high degree of twist, so the yarn tends to kink or coil. This kinkiness results in the rough texture characteristic of crepe fabrics (Fig. 18.5). As these yarns are evenly twisted and uniform in size, they are identified as simple yarns rather than complex or novelty yarns.

Except for the textured effect achieved by crepe yarns, simple yarns in themselves do not create variation in fabric appearance. Generally speaking, a simple yarn produces smooth fabrics. However, a combination of simple yarns of different size, different amounts of twist, and/or different fiber content can produce many interesting effects. The arrangement of yarns in groups, as in a dimity fabric, can also yield visual variety. Other changes in appearance depend on the number of warp and filling yarns per inch and the type and amount of twist.

Simple yarns are usually considered to be durable, although the durability is affected by such factors as yarn number, amount of twist, and whether the yarn is a single, ply, or cord. However, the uniformity of the yarn helps prevent snagging and tearing. The arrangement of the yarns, the ply or cord construction, and the degree of yarn balance will

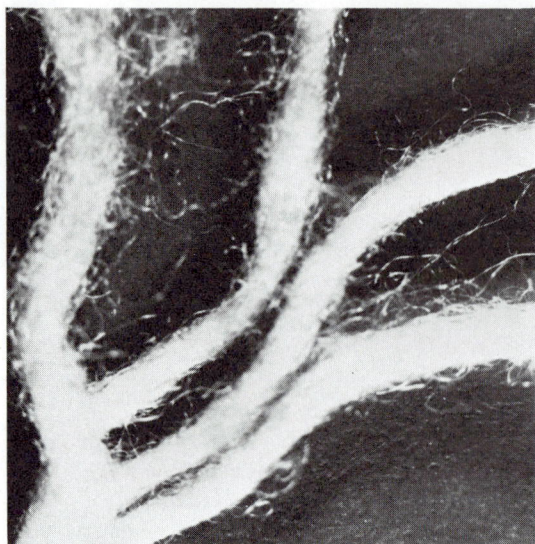

18.1 Simple yarn, magnified. A 4-ply yarn with four singles. The yarn has been separated to show singles and fibers in one of the singles.

18.2 Combining two singles to form a ply yarn. The two yarns are twisted together as they are wound around the bobbin. (Celanese Corporation)

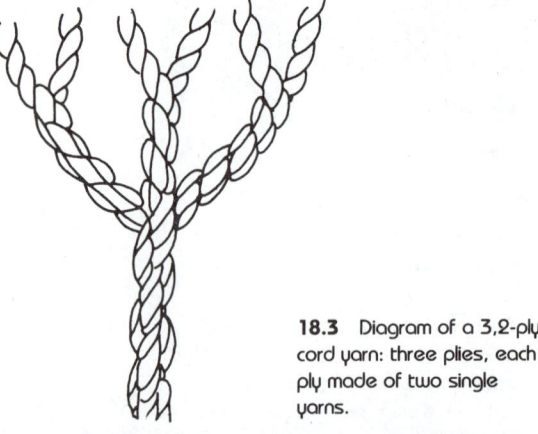

18.3 Diagram of a 3,2-ply cord yarn: three plies, each ply made of two single yarns.

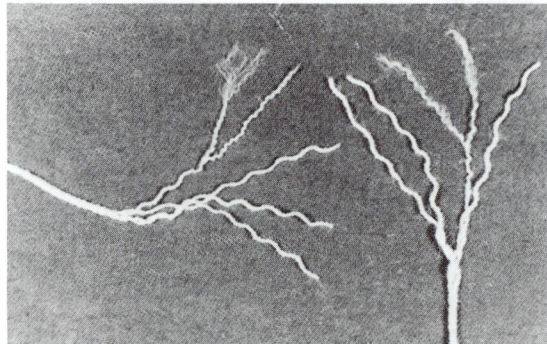

18.4 A 4, 2-ply cord yarn: four plies, each ply made of two singles.

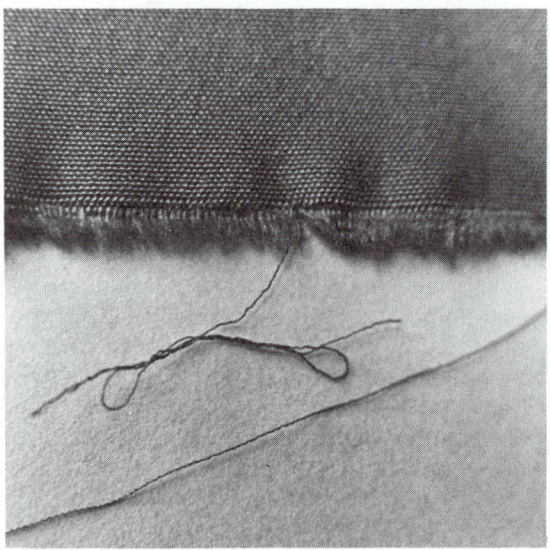

18.5 Crepe yarn and fabric. The high twist in the yarn produces the characteristic crinkled crepe surface.

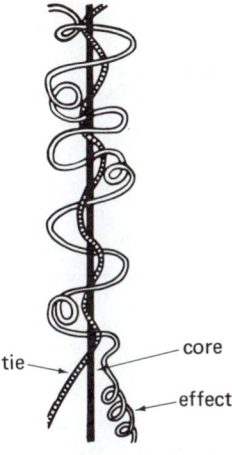

tie → core

→ effect

18.6 Diagram of the basic parts of a 3-ply complex yarn.

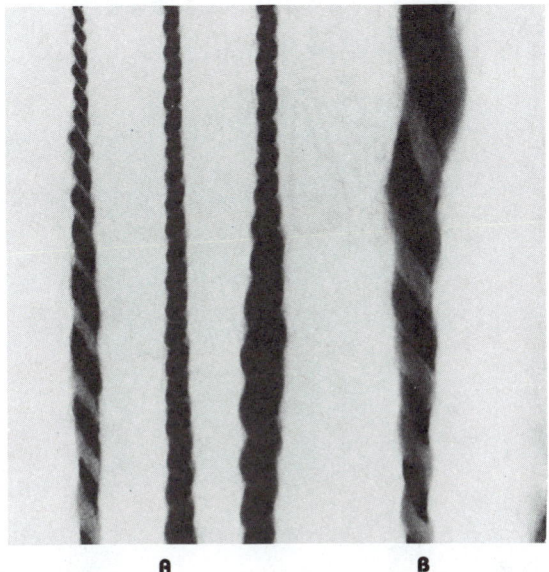

A   B

18.7 Complex slub yarns. A: Single slub. B: Ply slub.

dictate maintenance procedures to some degree. Except for the highly twisted crepe yarns, which tend to shrink during care, simple yarns are most often the easiest to maintain.

The statements made concerning simple yarns are generalizations only and may be incalculably affected by differences in fibers, fabric structures, coloring methods, and finishing processes. It is therefore essential that the student of textiles be aware of the influence of the many fabric dimensions on the durability, maintenance, appearance, and comfort of any fabric.

Complex Yarns

Complex, fancy, or novelty yarns (the three terms are synonymous) are usually uneven in size, varied in color, or modified in appearance by the presence of irregularities deliberately produced during their manufacture. *Single novelty yarns* are produced by the inclusion of slubs or knots. In *plied complex yarns* the irregularities are the result of variable delivery of the component parts and irregularities in size of each of the component single yarns.

Complex yarns are made for their appearance value, and they may be single, ply, cord, or modified cord construction. Complex ply yarns are usually composed of the following: a base or core, an effect, and a tie or binder (Fig. 18.6). The base yarn controls the length and stability of the final yarn. The effect yarn forms the design by the way in which it is applied to the base yarn. The tie or binder yarn is used to attach the effect yarn so that it will remain in position during use and care.

The strength of complex yarns frequently is variable, as the irregularities built in to create the novelty effect may produce uneven distributions of stress; this may result in yarns that are considerably weaker in some areas than in others, causing breakage to occur easily at the weak points.

Several systems are used in naming and classifying complex or novelty yarns. Although these terms are used interchangeably in the literature, ASTM has used the term *fancy yarn* to identify these types of yarns.[1]

Complex Single Yarns

SLUB YARNS A slub yarn may be either a single yarn or a 2 ply. However, the majority are single yarns. These yarns are made by uneven twisting. At intervals, which may be irregularly or regularly spaced, the yarn is left either untwisted or slackly twisted to produce soft, bulky areas (Fig. 18.7). When a 2-ply slub is made, the soft and fluffy portion is held in place by a tightly twisted single. The slubs may alternate between the two singles in a ply slub, or they may all be in one of the singles only. A majority of slub yarns are of single construction and are frequently combined with a simple yarn in order to provide adequate fabric strength. Slub yarns are typical of such fabrics as shantung,

[1]ASTM, *Annual Book of ASTM Standards,* 1983, vol. 07.01, p. 77.

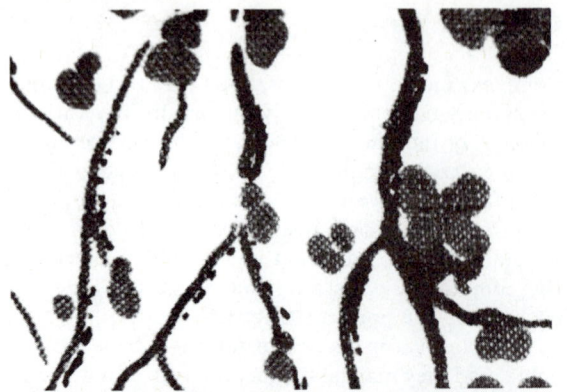

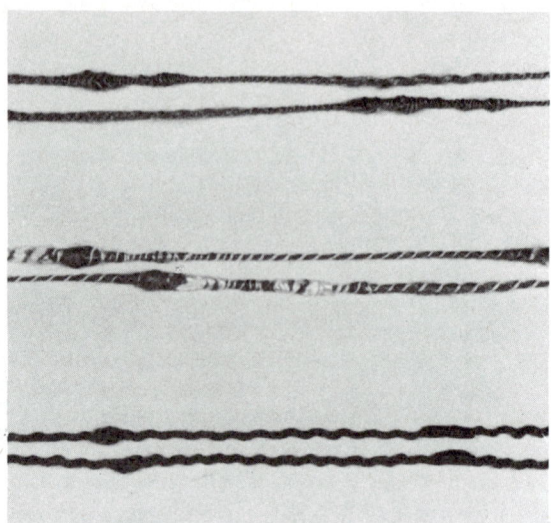

18.10   Nub or knot complex ply yarns.

18.8   Thick-and-thin complex yarn.

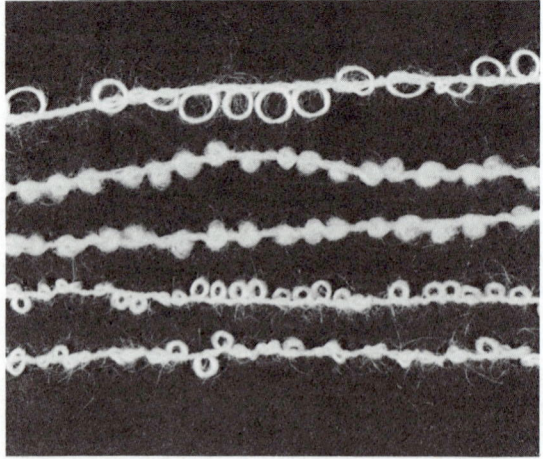

18.9   Loop type complex ply yarns.

18.11   Chenille-type complex yarns.

butcher rayon (frequently made of polyester in to-day's fabrics), and some linen fabrics.

THICK-AND-THIN YARNS Thick-and-thin yarns are similar in appearance to slub yarns. However, the manufacturing process differs, as does the length of the fiber used. Slub yarns are made from staple-length fibers, whereas thick-and-thin yarns are composed of filament length fibers. As filaments are extruded, the pressure forcing the spinning solution through the spinnerette is varied; this causes different amounts of solution to be extruded, and some areas become thicker than others. The resulting yarn has uneven diameter, with some areas thin and others thick (Fig. 18.8).

FLOCK YARNS Flock yarns, frequently called *flake yarns,* are usually single yarns in which small tufts of fiber are inserted at irregular intervals and held in place by the twist of the single yarn. These tufts may be round or elongated and frequently differ in color from the base yarn. Flock yarn is often used to create the tweed effect found in suiting fabrics. One drawback to these yarns is that the flock or tufts of fiber can be pulled loose relatively easily.

Complex Ply or Cord Yarns

BOUCLÉ YARNS Bouclé yarns are characterized by tight loops projecting from the body of the yarn at fairly regular intervals. These yarns are of 3-ply construction. The effect yarn that forms the loops is wrapped around a base yarn, and then a binder or tie yarn holds the loops in position. Bouclé yarns are soft and have a somewhat rough surface and a pronounced fancy or novelty effect. Bouclé yarns can be used in either woven or knitted constructions and are available for hand-knitting or home weaving as well as for commercially made fabrics.

RATINÉ AND GIMP YARNS Ratiné and gimp yarns are similar to each other and, to some degree, are similar to both bouclé and loop yarns. The major difference is that the loops are close together in ratiné and gimp, whereas in bouclé they are more widely spaced, and in loop yarns the loops are much more predominant. A 3-ply structure is usually used. The manufacture requires two distinct twisting operations: after the yarn is made, it is twisted a second time in the opposite direction.

The term *gimp* is frequently used as a synonym for *ratiné.* However, a difference may be evident in some yarns. A gimp yarn may have the loops formed using a soft and slackly twisted single, whereas the ratiné always uses a soft but securely or tightly twisted single to form the loops.

LOOP YARNS A loop yarn is of at least 3-ply construction and may involve more plies; further, it may be a modified cord construction. The base yarn in a loop yarn is rather coarse and heavy. The effect yarn, which makes the loops, is made of either a single or a ply and may be soft, fluffy, or tightly twisted. The loops are held in place with either one or two binder or tie yarns, which may be of either single or ply construction (Fig. 18.9).

Loop yarns are used frequently in coating and suiting fabrics, for interior furnishings, and for specialty fabrics either knitted or woven. Loop yarns are often used in making wool or mohair suiting fabrics, and because of this the term *mohair* has been incorrectly applied to fabrics made of loop yarn when the fiber content was not mohair.

NUB (OR SPOT) AND KNOT (OR KNOP) YARNS The terms *nub, knot, knop,* and *spot* are often used interchangeably; however, there are minor differences. These differences are difficult to identify, so the terms tend to be used synonymously. The minor differences occur in construction. A *nub* yarn is made on a special machine that holds the base yarn almost stationary while the effect yarn is wrapped around the base several times to build up a nub or enlarged segment. Sometimes the effect yarn may be held in place by a tie yarn, but this is not usually necessary, as the twisting operation makes a secure nub. The knot yarn is produced in much the same way, except the knot may be made of different-colored fibers (Fig. 18.10).

GRANDELLE YARNS Grandelle yarns are fancy yarns made by twisting two single yarns of contrasting colors together. They are used to add color effects and are found in suiting, coating, shirting, and home furnishing fabrics.

SPIRAL OR CORKSCREW YARNS The spiral yarn is composed of two yarns of different size; one is fine with a hard twist, the other bulky with a slack or loose twist. The heavy yarn is wound spirally around the fine yarn. A corkscrew yarn can be made by twisting together two yarns of different size or by twisting a fine yarn loosely around a heavy yarn so that it gives the appearance of a corkscrew. Spiral and corkscrew yarns may have greater elongation than other types of yarns. The elongation of the corkscrew is governed by the amount of elongation of the central core.

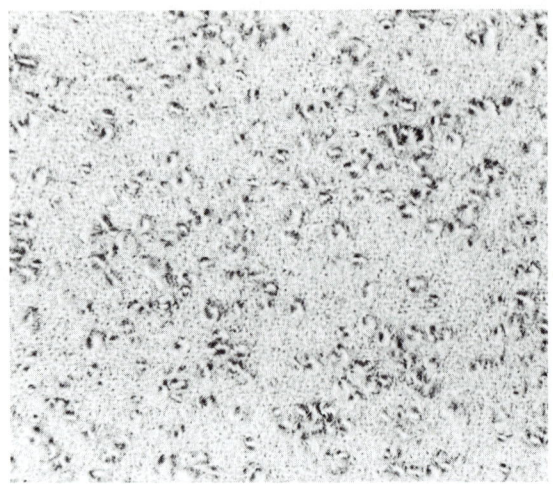

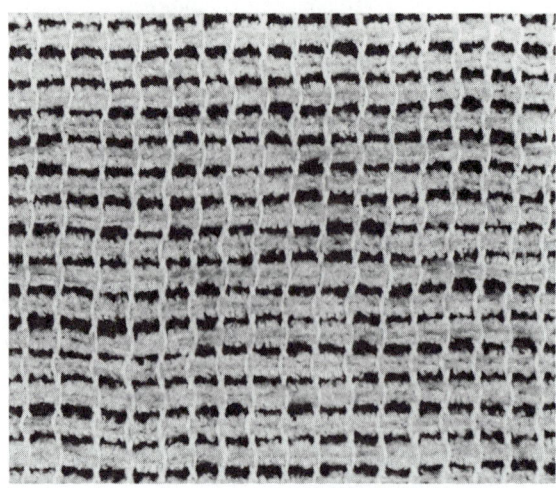

18.13 Fabric made using chenille yarns in filling direction.

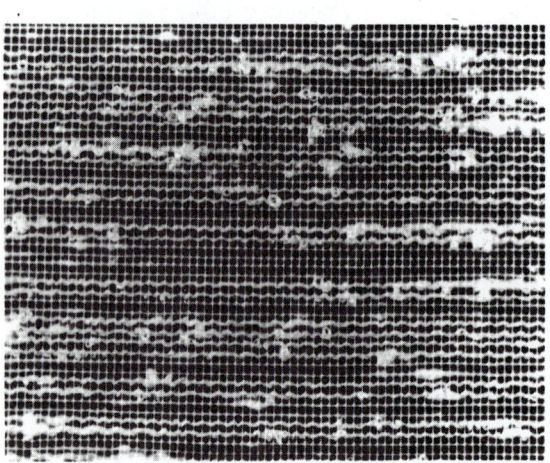

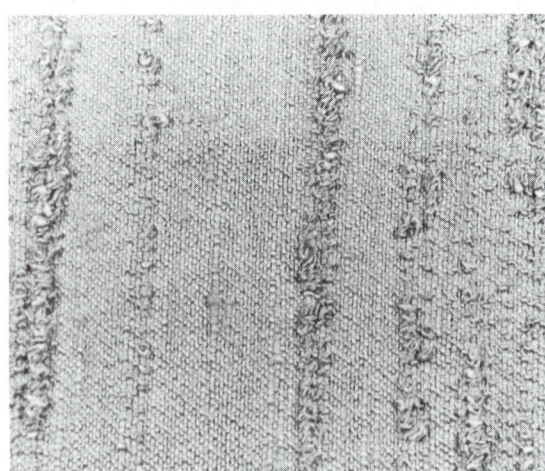

18.12 Fabrics using complex yarns, loop types.

CHENILLE YARNS Chenille yarns are used for special effects in fabrics and in the manufacture of true chenille rugs. The yarn resembles a hairy caterpillar (*chenille* is French for caterpillar). A special doup weave fabric, a leno type of structure, is made and then slit into narrow warpwise strips that serve as yarn. As the special fabric is slit, the loose end of the crosswise yarns, which are soft and loosely twisted, form a pilelike surface. These strips become the filling yarns in weaving, or they can be used in knitting structures. In weaving it is possible to lay the yarns so that all the loose fiber ends are on a single side of the fabric, or they may be placed so that some appear on both the face and back of the fabric (Fig. 18.11).

SEED AND SPLASH YARNS Several authorities classify seed and splash yarns as nub or knot yarns. However, there are some differences. While a nub yarn has an enlarged segment, the splash yarn has an elongated segment that is somewhat longer and thinner than that of the nub yarn; a seed yarn has a much smaller enlarged area than either a nub or splash yarn.

Use of Complex Yarns

Fancy or complex yarns are valued primarily for their appearance. They add texture and design to fabrics (Figs. 18.12 and 18.13). Some complex yarns may be soft and pleasant to the touch, while others may feel harsh and rough. These latter fabrics may be quite uncomfortable for apparel but highly desirable for various types of home furnishings. Loop yarns are considered very comfortable and are used in soft fabrics for a variety of apparel items as well as in upholstery and drapery fabrics.

The rough surface that results from the use of fancy or novelty yarns may cause problems in both use and care. Some types of complex yarns snag easily, causing damage to the fabric; yarns with uneven surfaces are subject to abrasion damage from rubbing, which can result in fabric damage. It is important to identify expected wear for fabrics made of these yarns and determine whether the appearance factors are more important than potential durability.

STUDY QUESTIONS

1. Describe the various types of simple and complex yarns.
2. What types of end uses would typically involve complex yarns?

3. Distinguish between simple and complex yarns. How do they differ? How are they alike?
4. What problems can you expect to encounter in the care of fabrics made from complex yarns?
5. If you wanted to construct a fabric with durability as a primary characteristic, would you select simple or complex yarns? Why?
6. If you wanted to construct a fabric with appearance as a major characteristic, why might you select complex yarns? Is it necessary to select complex yarns for appearance factors? Why or why not?

Activities

1. Locate fabrics on the market or in end-use applications that are made, in part at least, of complex yarns. What type of items do you find? Are they appropriate for these fancy yarns?
2. Can you find fabrics made of cord yarns? If so, what typical end-use products are involved?

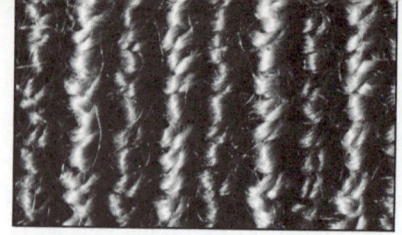

Textured Yarns

KEY TERMS

bulky yarns
draw texturizing
false twist
fluid or air-jet texturizing

gear crimping
knife-edge texturizing
knit-deknit texturizing
sinusoidal curve

stuffer-box texturizing
textured yarn

The term *textured yarn* was for many years just one of several expressions used in describing complex or fancy yarns. Within the past few decades, however, the term has been confined to a select group of yarns, or filaments, that have received specific treatment during manufacture (Fig. 19.1). Textured yarns are composed primarily of filament fibers. The final yarn may be either simple or complex in structure. However, these yarns do possess several special characteristics that make them adaptable to a variety of fabric structures; thus, they are discussed as a separate topic.

ASTM defines *textured yarn* under the general heading of *bulk yarn:*

Bulk yarn: A yarn that has been prepared in such a way as to have greater covering power, or apparent volume, than that of conventional yarn of equal linear density and of the same basic material with normal twist. Varieties include bulky yarn, textured yarn, and stretch yarn.

Bulky yarn: A generic term for yarns formed from inherently bulky fibers such as man-made fibers that are hollow along part or all of their fiber length, or for yarns formed from fibers that cannot be closely packed because of their cross-sectional shapes, fiber alignment, stiffness, resilience, or natural crimp.

Textured yarn: A generic term for filament or spun yarns that have been given notably greater apparent volume than conventional yarn of similar fiber (filament) count and linear density. The yarns have a relatively low elastic stretch. They are sufficiently stable to withstand normal yarn and fabric processing . . . and conditions of use by the ultimate consumer. The apparent increased volume is achieved through physical, chemical, or heat treatments or a combination of these.[1]

Some authorities have used the term *textured yarn* to include all three types identified as bulk yarn by ASTM. However, stretch yarns do have different characteristics as well as different uses; they are discussed, therefore, in the next chapter.

A large proportion of textured yarns are manufactured from thermoplastic fibers. These fibers can be heat-set—influenced in character by the application of heat—which is a necessary property for the production of these types of textured yarn. Others can be texturized through the use of mechanical procedures.

Several processes are used in making textured yarns. These include false-twist texturizing, draw texturizing, air-jet or fluid texturizing, stuffer-box crimping, gear crimping, knit-deknit crimping, and edge crimping.

[1]ASTM, *Annual Book of ASTM Standards,* 1983, vol. 07.01, p. 18.

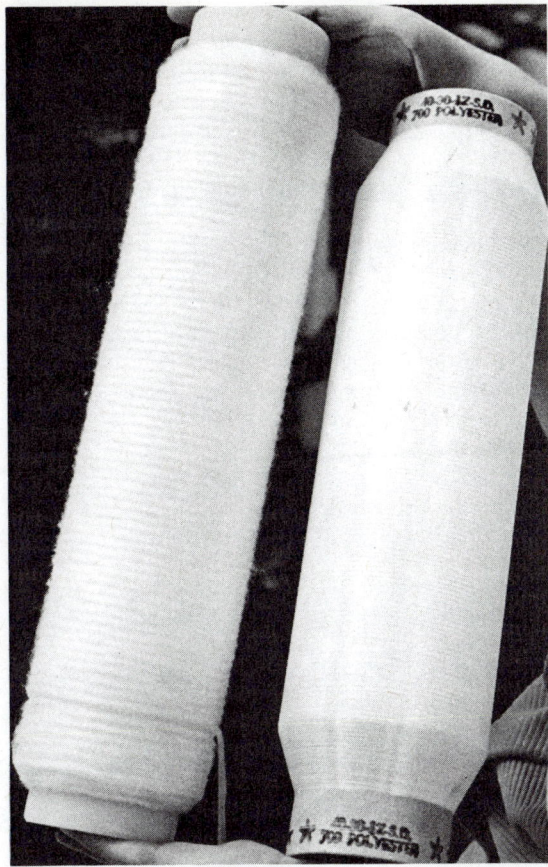

19.1 Textured and nontextured yarns compared. The yarn on the left is textured. (Celanese Corporation)

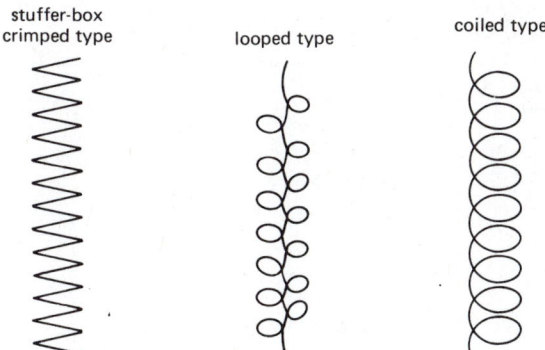

19.2 Diagram of types of textured yarns.

Textured filaments can be cut into staple length for conversion into staple fiber yarns; however, the majority of textured yarns are made of filament fibers. These filament yarns are characterized by little

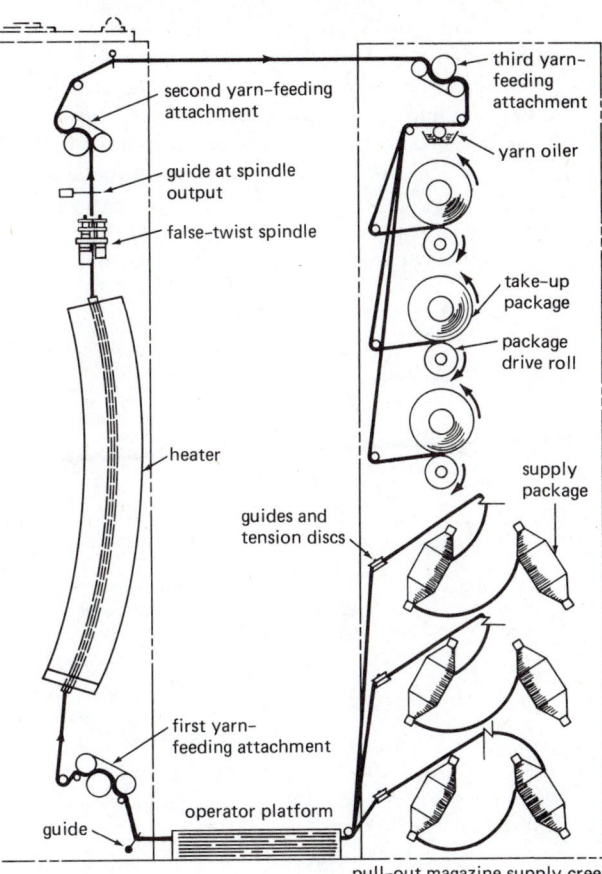

19.3 Diagram of false twist texturizing. (National Spinning Company)

or no pilling, good bulk, exceptional spinning quality, pleasing softness, low or soft luster, and an appearance similar to staple fiber yarns. Figure 19.2 shows some of the shapes built into fiber in the various texturizing processes.

Texturizing Processes

False-Twist Methods

False-twist methods develop texture in filament fibers through the use of controlled heat. The yarn is twisted; exposed to heat, which sets the twist in place; cooled; and untwisted. As the twist is removed, the filaments kink or crimp sinusoidally because of the distortion resulting from the presence of the heat-set twist (Fig. 19.3). A *sinusoidal curve* is defined as a wavy line that has identical amplitude on each side of a central axis (Fig. 19.4). Simple yarns made from these filaments are characterized by either a left- or right-hand torque, so that they tend to be unbalanced and subject to distortion. To prevent the distortion, a right-hand and left-hand twisted single are combined to form a balanced yarn.

The twist method of manufacturing textured yarns produces some stretch in the final product, but this can be controlled by the amount of twist or turns per inch set into the yarn. Yarns are available in a wide range of stretch, from those that can be elongated up to 400 percent and still return to the original size to those with a small amount of stretch but with high bulk. It is possible to stabilize these yarns so that the bulk remains but no noticeable stretch occurs.

To make stretch yarns by the false-twist method, the yarn is fed from the supply package to the heater, where twist is set into the filaments; following the heat setting, the yarns are untwisted and taken up on packages. To produce bulk yarns with little or no stretch, the yarns are heated a second time after being untwisted (Fig. 19.5).

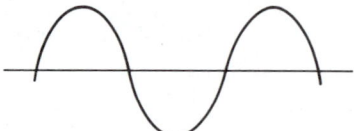

19.4 Sinusoidal curve.

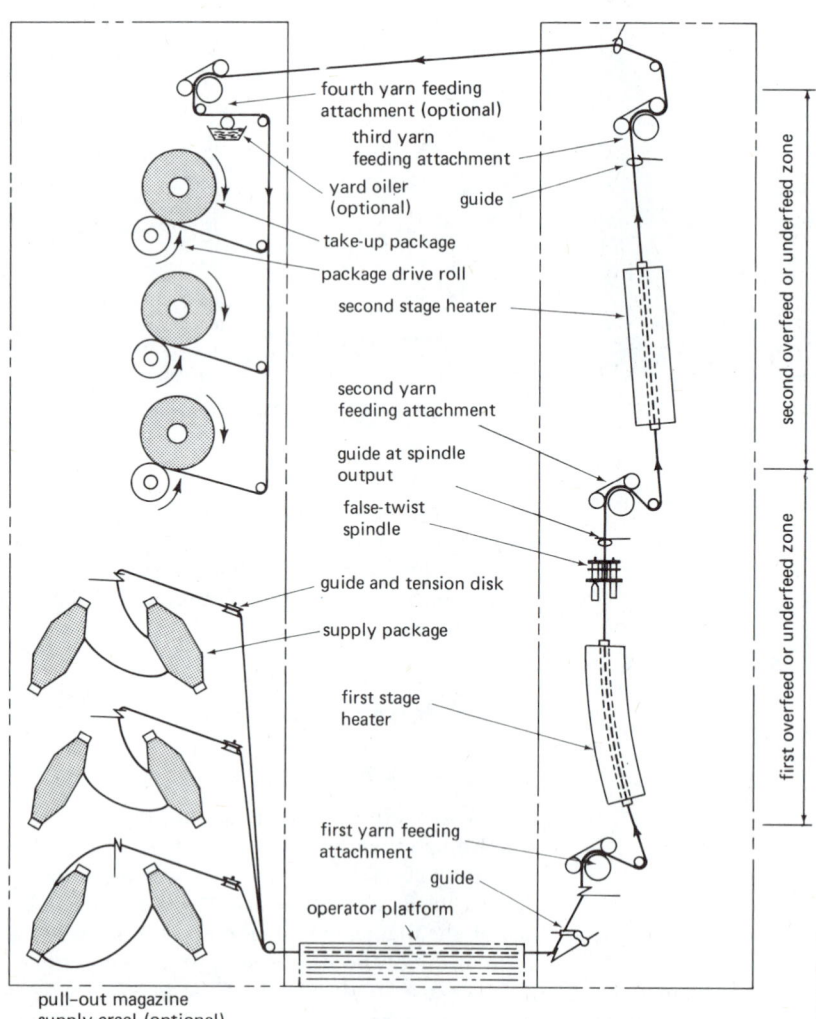

fourth yarn feeding attachment (optional)

third yarn feeding attachment

yard oiler (optional)

guide

take-up package

package drive roll

second stage heater

second overfeed or underfeed zone

second yarn feeding attachment

guide at spindle output

false-twist spindle

guide and tension disk

supply package

first stage heater

first overfeed or underfeed zone

first yarn feeding attachment

guide

operator platform

pull-out magazine supply creel (optional)

19.5 Diagram of false twist texturizing using two heaters.
(National Knitwear and Sportswear Association)

19.6 *Draw-texturizing machine.* (American Barmag Corporation)

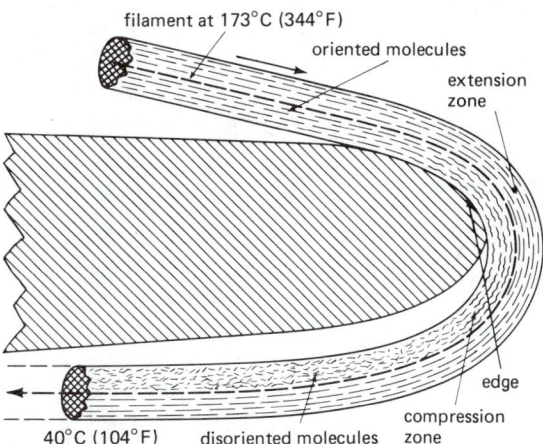

filament at 173°C (344°F)

oriented molecules

extension zone

edge

compression zone

40°C (104°F)   disoriented molecules

19.7 *Knife-edge crimping; molecules are oriented on the side of the filament away from knife edge and disoriented on the side in contact with the knife.* (National Knitwear and Sportswear Association)

Modifications of the basic technique are popular and include, but are not limited to, the following.

1. One type of false twist yarn is made on machines that combine the twist-set-untwist process into a continuous operation. The yarn is highly twisted in one direction by a false-twist spindle on the supply side of the machine. Between the two steps, electrically heated elements set the amount of twist desired. The yarn is then untwisted.

2. Many false-twist machines are designed to process two yarns side by side, imparting S twist to one and Z twist to the other. These yarns are then plied together to produce balanced yarns, which possess many of the same properties as spun yarns made from staple fibers on standard yarn-spinning equipment.

Yarns made by the false-twist systems are often softer and more uniform than those made on other types of texturizing machines. They may have high bulk, little or no stretch to very high stretch, and softness.

Draw Texturizing

Draw texturizing has become extremely popular over the past decade. It combines the final drawing of filaments to align and orient the molecules and establish desired strength and texture. It is particularly effective in handling POY polyester (see page 121). Machinery used in draw texturizing is the same type as that used for false-twist texturizing; the only difference is that the draw-texturizing unit has rollers that extend, or draw, the filaments to orient the molecules and impart the necessary fiber properties (Fig. 19.6). Draw-textured yarns are said to have a crisper hand, better durability and appearance, and superior dyeability when compared with false-twist yarns.

The Knife-Edge Method

Textured yarns made by the knife-edge method possess a spiral-like curl or coil. The yarns are passed over a heated knife edge or are heated and then passed over a cold knife edge while the fibers are still hot. It is easy to visualize this method if one compares it with drawing paper ribbon over a knife blade to get it to curl into attractive spirals and bows for wrapping gifts.

The best-known yarn of this kind is Agilon®, a nontorque yarn frequently used in women's hosiery. The technique consists in drawing a thermoplastic yarn, often nylon, over a hot, sharp knife blade (Fig. 19.7). The edge of the yarn in contact with the heat and blade is changed so that the resulting yarn has a bicomponent quality somewhat similar to wool. Agilon yarns have a high degree of elasticity but retain their sheerness; both properties are highly desirable in women's hosiery.

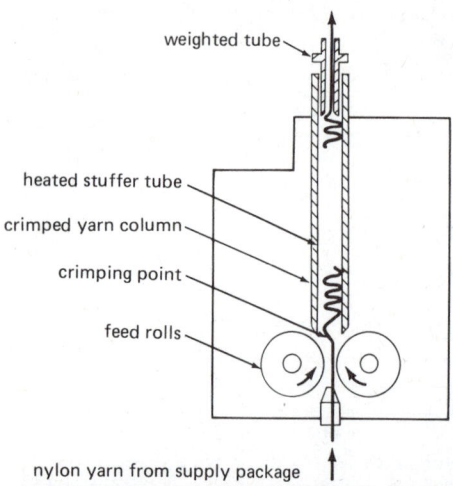

weighted tube

heated stuffer tube

crimped yarn column

crimping point

feed rolls

nylon yarn from supply package

19.8 *Stuffer box crimping.* (National Spinning Company)

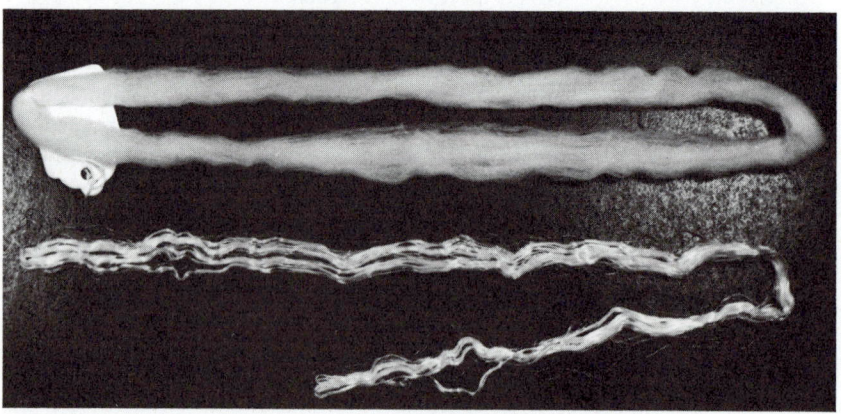

19.9 *Stuffer box textured yarns (above) and filaments before texturing (below).*

The Stuffer-Box Method

In the stuffer-box method, filament fibers are forced into a stuffing box or tube that causes them to develop a sawtoothed crimp. The crimp is heat-set, so when the filaments are removed from the tube, the crimp remains (Fig. 19.8 and 19.9). The greatest amount of bulk and a controlled amount of stretch can be created by this method. Yarns are torque-free and therefore produce satisfactory textured single or plied yarns. The best-known stuffer-box yarn is Ban-Lon®. This process can be applied to any heat-sensitive or thermoplastic fiber. Nylon and polyester are both commonly found in Ban-Lon products. Although most stuffer-box yarns are made from filament fibers, it is possible to texture or crimp yarns of staple-fiber length or to texture filaments following extrusion and then cut these textured filaments into staple length and process into yarn. Filament

fibers are preferred, as they do not pill as badly as staple-fiber yarns.

Stuffer-box crimped yarns are soft, strong, and easy to care for, have a lively hand, have good to outstanding moisture regain and absorption, can be given controlled amounts of stretch, exhibit good dimensional stability, provide adequate air circulation, and produce minimum pilling when filament-length fibers are used. These yarns are sometimes referred to as "textralized" when nylon fibers have been used.

Another product made using the stuffer-box process is Spunize®. To make Spunize, the technique is modified so that multiple ends of yarn can be handled at the same time. While Ban-Lon is typically used in various apparel items, Spunize yarns tend to appear in home furnishings such as carpets and upholstery fabrics and in some industrial fabrics.

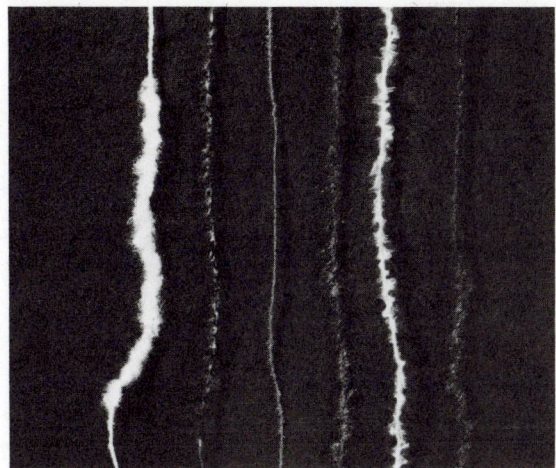

19.10 Taslan textured yarns made to simulate complex yarns. (DuPont Company)

Fluid Texturizing: Air and Steam

Yarns may be textured by means of a jet of air or steam hitting the filaments when they are in a relaxed state. The air or steam forms loops or curls in the filaments. Several manufacturers make equipment for air or steam texturizing, and several different kinds of yarns are available. Taslan® is one of the better-known and oldest examples of air-jet-textured yarn (Fig. 19.10). The process takes the yarn through a zone where it is exposed to turbulent streams of air or steam. Filament fibers are preferred, but staple fiber yarns may be used. The air or steam blows the filaments apart and forms loops in the individual fibers. These tangle with one another and form a yarn that has a high level of bulk but no stretch. Since heat is not required, fibers that are not thermoplastic or heat-sensitive may be bulked using this method. It has proved to be highly successful in making bulky yarns of glass for home furnishing fabrics as well as other uses.

The use of steam is preferred when texturing filament yarns for floor coverings. The resulting yarn, called bulked continuous filament (BCF) yarns, have a three-dimensional crimp, which is considered a highly desirable property for pile yarns typical of those used in carpeting. Fluid texturizing is becoming one of the dominant methods for producing textured yarns for carpet pile of nylon and polypropylene fibers.

Yarns that are bulked by fluid or air-jet methods have the following properties: a permanent change in the physical structure of the yarn; a unique ap-

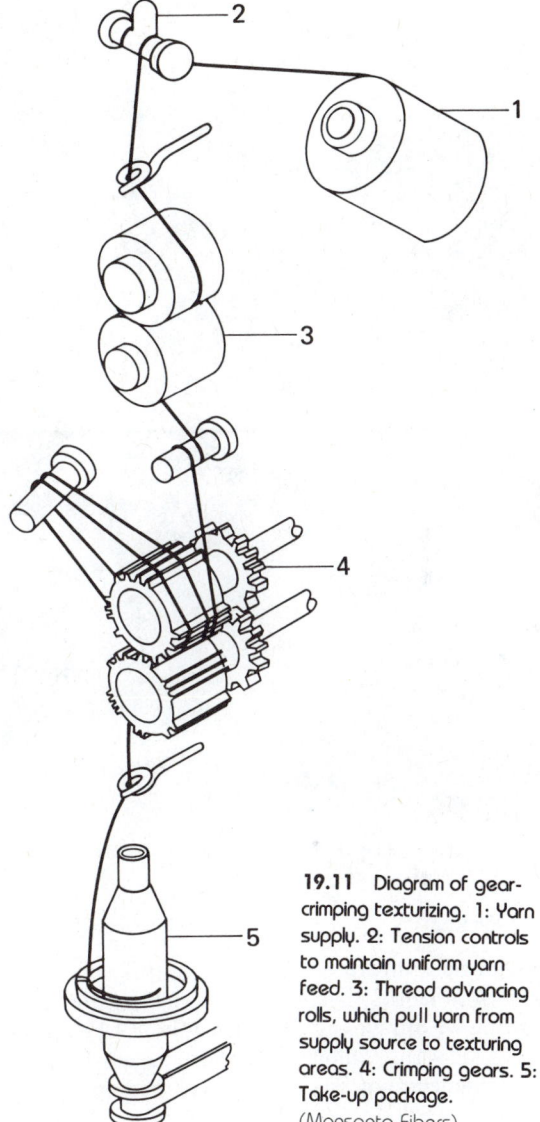

19.11 Diagram of gear-crimping texturizing. 1: Yarn supply. 2: Tension controls to maintain uniform yarn feed. 3: Thread advancing rolls, which pull yarn from supply source to texturing areas. 4: Crimping gears. 5: Take-up package. (Monsanto Fibers)

pearance, hand, and texture; increased covering power; subdued luster; lower yarn strength and elongation; and superior resistance to crushing.

Gear Crimping

In gear crimping, yarns under controlled tension and temperature are carried between rotating intermeshing gears, which give a sawtooth configuration to the filaments (Fig. 19.11). Novelty textured yarns can be formed by positioning the gear rolls out of mesh or by an intermittent crimping.

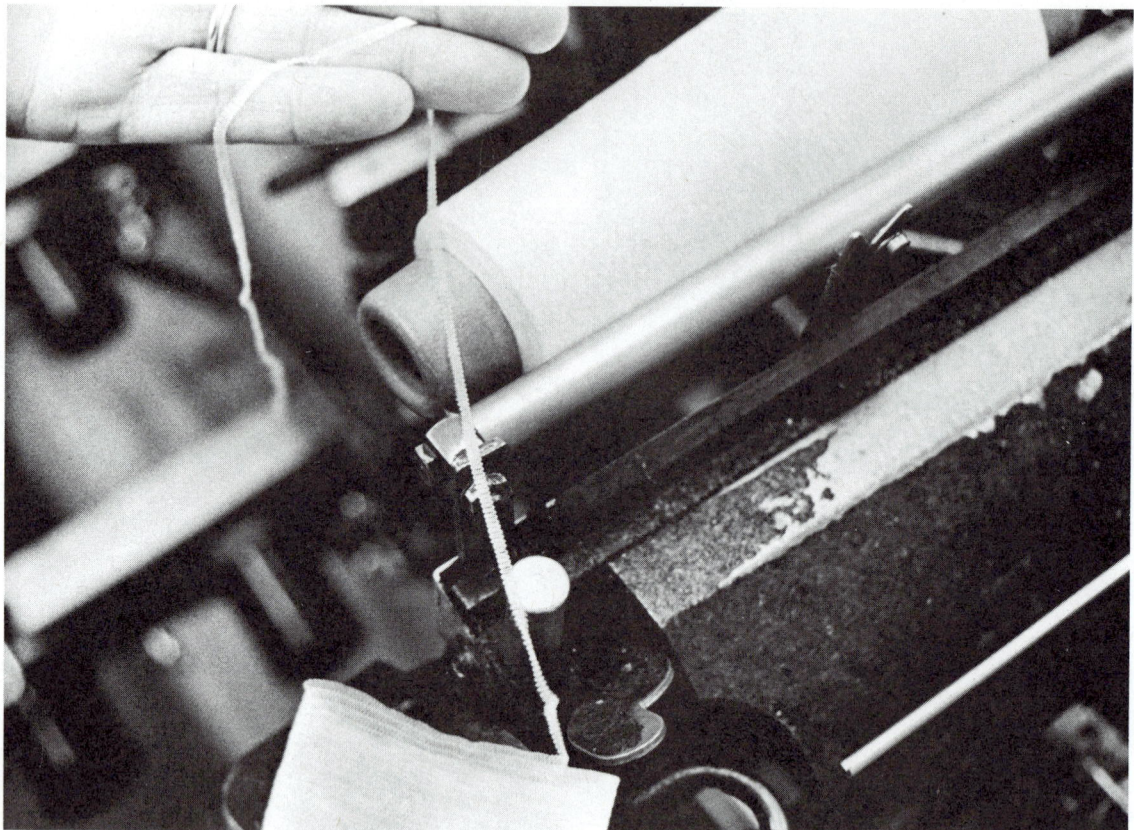

19.12 Knitted tubing that has been heat-set is deknitted to form one type of textured yarn. (Celanese Corporation)

Knit-Deknit

The knit-deknit process involves knitting filament yarns into fabrics, heat-setting the fabric, then deknitting or unraveling the yarn (Fig. 19.12). The unraveled yarns exhibit crimp and are ready for fabric manufacture by any of the usual methods.

Multicomponent Texturing

The formation of bicomponent or multicomponent filaments at the point of fiber spinning can be used to produce textured yarns. Modified formulas of the same generic fiber extruded simultaneously, usually a side-by-side configuration, are used in the production of several textured yarns, including Cantrece® nylon, Sayelle® acrylic, and Wintuk® acrylic.

The filament may be designed so that each component has different shrinkage potential, which results in the kinking or coiling of the filaments as one component shrinks more than the other. Fila-

ments may be designed so that a crimp develops as the fibers are processed in the fabrics; this is called latent crimp and produces fabrics of interesting appearance and texture.

Spinnerette Modifications

A less common method of texturizing may occur with modified spinnerette openings. By altering the shape of the orifice in the spinnerette, it is possible to introduce some bulk into fibers. Other changes that can alter filament texture are by changing the level of air flow at the spinnerette opening or by vibrating the spinnerette.

Use of Textured Yarns

A majority of man-made fiber fabrics are textured through some process. The resulting fabrics have highly desirable properties and are more acceptable to consumers. Textured fabrics tend to be more comfortable, have a more desirable appearance, and be more versatile than nontextured items.

Man-made filament fibers that have not been textured often result in uncomfortable apparel fabrics, because the filaments pack tightly together and prevent the movement of moisture or air through the fabric. Texturizing corrects these problems and produces fabrics that have bulk and space between the filaments so the yarn itself will absorb moisture and provide a desirable level of comfort as well as appearance. Texturizing also helps to create fabrics that have good warmth and can serve as insulators.

Maintenance of fabrics made from textured yarns is similar to the care given the same fiber in other forms. The added moisture retention increases the drying time required for these fabrics, but washing procedures remain unchanged. Care must be taken to avoid snagging, for the crimp, coil, curl, or loops created in the texturizing operation create a rough or raised surface that snags easily. Durability is similar to that of other fabrics made from the same fiber. However, the problem of snagging may lead to broken filaments, which are then subject to pilling, which could shorten the expected life of the product.

The tremendous acceptance of textured yarns has contributed to the continued development of processes that will produce high bulk and/or stretch without any decrease in durability or performance. The manufacturers of equipment have also concentrated on techniques that will produce desirable textured yarns with substantial reduction in costs and increase in speed of production.

STUDY QUESTIONS

1. Describe the methods by which texturization can be accomplished.
2. What limits are placed on texturizing by fibers that are not heat-sensitive?
3. Why are so many of the man-made fiber yarns texturized?

Activities

1. Visit stores and determine what types of products you can identify as having been made of textured yarns. Is this information easy to obtain?
2. Compare fabrics made of textured filament yarns with those that have not been textured. How do they differ? How are they alike?

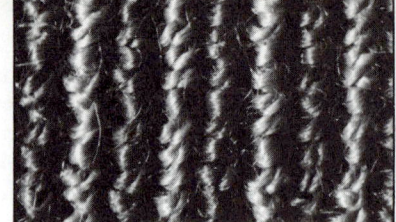

20

Stretch Yarns and Fabrics

KEY TERMS

action or power stretch	piece-goods stretch
comfort stretch	slack mercerization
growth	stretch
mechanical stretch	unrecovered stretch

The concept of stretch dates back to 1589 when the first knit fabric was introduced. Knit fabric constructions can take relatively firm yarns with little or no extensibility and form them into fabrics that do have good elongation or stretch. Since the development of knits, the element of give or stretch in yarns and fabrics for selected end uses has been of utmost interest to consumers. A variety of items provide consumers with satisfaction when stretch is present: selected items of apparel, selected fabrics for home furnishings, and selected fabrics for transportation vehicles. Interest in stretch provided the impetus to develop stretch or elastomeric fibers, stretch yarns, and fabrics with more stretch than knitting would provide.

The word *stretch* has acquired a specific meaning in modern textile terminology. A true stretch fabric has the ability to extend or stretch under tension *plus* the equally important capacity to return to its original size after release of strain. The degree of potential stretch, sometimes referred to as *elongation,* varies from as little as 5 percent to as much as 500+ percent.

Suggested standards for stretch fabrics have been developed; these remain as guidelines for stretch yarns and fabrics. Testing of stretch is done by weighting a 2-inch-wide strip of fabric with a load of 4 pounds to determine the actual percentage of stretch in the fabric (Fig. 20.1). The ASTM indicates that fabrics should stretch at least 20 percent to be identified as a stretch fabric.

There are two categories of stretch fabrics: comfort stretch and action or power stretch. *Comfort stretch* is used to identify fabrics that are used for apparel and home furnishings in which stretch need not be greater than 30 percent. Frequently it will be closer to 20 percent, occasionally less. *Power* or *action stretch* refers to fabrics in which stretch is greater than 30 percent and which have quick recovery when the strain is released. Power-stretch fabrics may have a very high percentage of stretch, but 35 to 50 percent is generally considered sufficient for most uses. These fabrics are used in sportswear for active sports such as skiing, swimming, and running and in such special apparel as foundation garments.

As with many classification systems, there is a somewhat nebulous area between comfort and action stretch. Comfort-stretch fabrics may exceed the 30-percent stretch range, while action stretch may be as low as 30 percent. An important criterion for stretch fabrics is that they meet the end-use requirements and that the fabric recover quickly from the elongation as soon as the stress is eliminated.

20.1 Samples of fabric in static tension tester. Right sample has weight attached to measure amount of stretch.

Stretch can be introduced into fabrics through several procedures. For ease of discussion, the material has been divided into four sections:

1. Fiber stretch—elastomeric fibers and fiber modification
2. Yarn stretch—texturizing and heat-setting processes
3. Fabric stretch—knitting and similar processes
4. Finishing methods—the application of special

finishes to impart stretch after the fabric has been constructed

Fiber Stretch

Stretch has been produced through the use of elastomeric fibers, specifically rubber, since the early 1920s. Fine filaments of rubber were covered with cotton, rayon, or silk, and then woven, knitted, or braided into fabrics. Usually these were combined with other yarns. Narrow elastic fabric is a typical example of early stretch fabrics using fiber stretch. Rubber core yarns were early examples of stretch made through the use of elastomeric fibers. Since the introduction of synthetic elastomeric fibers, rubber has been replaced by spandex in a large percentage of fabric constructions.

Spandex, discussed in Chapter 14, owes its stretchability to its chemical molecular configuration, not to a mechanically imparted property. Spandex fibers can be used in several ways in stretch fabrics. Uncovered or bare spandex filaments are combined with other fibers into yarns that are then constructed into fabrics for such end uses as foundation garments, swimsuits, and surgical supplies such as special types of hosiery and bandages. Bare spandex may be used in comfort stretch, but this is less common than for uses where a high amount of stretch is required or desired. Spandex fibers may be used in core-spun yarns, where the spandex provides the central core, and these yarns may be used in a wide variety of fabrics, especially where comfort stretch is desired. Core spinning is described in Chapter 17. In core spinning the tension under which the elastomeric filament is held is carefully controlled. The resulting yarn has variable degrees of stretch, depending on the controls used. Core-spun yarns have two significant advantages: only 3 to 10 percent spandex is required to produce a high-quality stretch yarn, and the yarn has the appearance of the covering fiber and, depending on what covering fiber is used, may have good moisture absorbency. Core spinning makes it possible to control the amount of stretch that is to be built in—from as low as 10 percent to as much as 200 percent. The majority of core-spun stretch yarns are used in comfort-stretch products and do not exceed 30 percent stretch at standard stress loads. The care of core-spun yarns is basically the same as that required for the covering fibers.

Spandex fibers may be used also in *intimate blend* spinning. This procedure involves the cutting of spandex filaments into staple lengths to match the length of the fibers with which it is to be blended. These are then spun to produce a true blended fiber yarn. The amount of stretch for such yarn depends upon the amount of spandex fiber used.

Yarn Stretch

Yarn stretch can be introduced by texturizing processes. Such yarns are heat-set in such a manner that extensibility is built in. The first yarn of this type was developed by the Swiss firm of Heberlein and Company, A.G. The original goal was to impart crimp to man-made fibers so that they would resemble wool. After initial work on viscose fibers, Heberlein adapted the process to nylon and developed the first stretch nylon yarns. These were introduced in 1947 as Helanca®. This stretch yarn is still employed in a variety of end-use products such as hosiery, leotards, and other figure-conforming apparel.

The current methods used for producing stretch yarns through texturizing include the false-twist methods and the knife-edge method. It is possible to produce stretch yarns using the stuffer-box method, but this is not a common procedure. Texturization as a means of producing stretch is primarily confined to filament fiber yarns; however, it is possible to build yarn stretch into staple-fiber yarns.

In the late 1960s, attempts were made to create stretch yarns from such fibers as cotton using processes called *back twisting* and *crimping*. Although these have not experienced widespread acceptance, they are mentioned here as background knowledge. In the back-twisting method, cotton yarn is treated with a cellulose cross-linking resin such as DMEU (see page 309), which is used in making durable-press or minimum-care fabrics. The yarn is twisted, the twist is cured into the yarn, and the yarn is then untwisted and retwisted in the opposite direction. The resulting yarns are kinky and springy and have good stretch properties.

The crimping process involves treating the cotton with some chemical that reacts with the cellulose to form a cellulose ester or ether that is thermoplastic. The modified cotton is then processed by one of the texturizing methods used for thermoplastic fibers.

Fabric Stretch

The most common method for introducing stretch in the fabric construction stage is knitting. Knits are discussed in detail in Chapter 23. Other fabric construction processes that may provide some type of stretch include braiding and knotting.

Finishing Stretch

The process of imparting stretch to a fabric after it has been constructed is called by such names as *piece-goods stretch, mechanical stretch,* and *chemical stretch.* The first of these is probably the most logical. The actual finishing procedure involves the use of chemicals and results in some chemical change, so, theoretically, the term *chemical* is appropriate. For some procedures a physical or mechanical change takes place. Because both chemical and mechanical changes may occur, it appears to be reasonable to select the term *piece-goods stretch,* which indicates when the stretch is imparted and does not try to identify one specific method.

As the phrase indicates, stretch is introduced into the fabric after it has been constructed (weaving is the most common structure adapted to this process). Cotton, cotton blends, and wool fabrics have been treated in this manner. The procedure used on cotton and cotton blends is called *slack mercerization.* For wool, special processes have been developed but are not widely used.

Slack mercerization utilizes the same principle as those applied in standard yarn or fabric mercerization, except that the fabric is not held under tension, hence the term *slack mercerization.* For horizontal or filling stretch, the fabric is held under lengthwise tension, or if no tension is used at this step, the fabric is restretched and set for length at a later time. If both horizontal and lengthwise stretch is desired, the fabric is treated without tension for the entire process.

The amount of stretch is determined by the concentration of sodium hydroxide used in the solution and by the density of the original fabric. Production of filling stretch by this method has proved successful, but warp stretch has not been widely accepted. The most important reason is that warp stretch tends to be lost during washing and the fabric tends to stretch out to its original length. The use of slack mercerization as a method of producing stretch in fabrics has declined considerably over the past five years.

Use of Stretch Fabrics

Stretch can be produced in the horizontal or filling direction, in the vertical or warp direction, or in both directions (two-way stretch). The last is used primarily for action stretch, whereas comfort-stretch fabrics are usually made with either filling or warp stretch but not both.

Most stretch fabrics do not completely return to their original measurements after elongation. The difference between the original size and the measure after elongation is referred to as *growth* or *unrecovered stretch.* This growth is frequently eliminated in laundering, but it can lead to temporary, or in some cases permanent, deformation. A growth or increase in size of 2 to 3 percent would result in an unattractive product, especially when apparel items are involved. A maximum growth of 2 percent is considered standard.

Several research studies have examined stretch and identified the amount of stretch needed for various end uses. Studies related to apparel have been based on determining the amount the body stretches in various positions. Data from these studies have been summarized and provide the following widely accepted recommendations:

> tailored clothing, 15 to 20 percent stretch
> spectator sportswear, 20 to 35 percent stretch
> active sportswear, 35 to 50 percent stretch
> stretch pants, 40 to 60 percent stretch

The problem of where and how stretch should be used has received considerable attention over the past 15 years. Power stretch is involved for foundation garments, swimwear, active sportswear, and other items where considerable holding power is required or where considerable action is involved. These apparel items require figure shaping as well as providing for considerable body movement. While the amount of stretch should be relatively high, stretch should occur only when considerable force is exerted, in order to prevent a loss of appearance through normal movement.

While considerable attention has been given to the potential for using comfort stretch in the manufacture of garments that are sized so that "one size fits all," this policy is not generally acceptable. Comfort-stretch apparel items should be sized using the same standards as those used for fabrics without stretch. Only in this way can comfort really be a part of each item for each individual.

Consumers must decide whether comfort stretch is needed and, if so, whether it is worth the cost.

Each consumer must evaluate the value of stretch and buy garments that meet his or her individual needs. Consumers must also read labels and make sure to care for the products properly.

Manufacturers must select desirable products in which to use stretch. They must be well informed so as to avoid such mistakes, made in the early years of stretch, as lining stretch apparel items with "rigid" fabrics and constructing seams with threads that prevented any give at the seamlines.

Stretch fabrics have been used in a variety of applications other than apparel. They are used in items for home furnishings, particularly for upholstery and slipcover fabrics and fitted sheets. Stretch fabrics in such end uses provide a textile item that fits well, lies smoothly, and gives a neat appearance. Stretch should be avoided, however, in such home furnishings as curtains or draperies, since the weight of the hanging fabric could stretch the product out of shape. Stretch fabrics are also used in therapeutic products such as bandages and support hose.

Stretch has never quite reached the potential expressed during the early 1970s. However, it is used in a wide variety of items where it can provide the following characteristics: comfort, good fit, shape retention, design flexibility, psychological appeal, wrinkle resistance, appearance appeal, longer wear, and reduced seam puckering.

STUDY QUESTIONS

1. What are the major processes by which stretch is imparted to fabrics?
2. Which methods are most commonly used for modern stretch fabrics?
3. How much stretch is recommended for various activities?
4. What types of end-use products profit from having stretch?

Activities

1. Visit various stores and determine how much apparel is made with stretch as a characteristic. What price levels are involved?
2. What other types of textile products can you find in the marketplace that have stretch built in?
3. Find references concerning stretch fabrics and the determination of how much stretch is required for different purposes. Summarize your findings in terms of how much the body moves and stretches and how this influences the stretch to be built into the product.

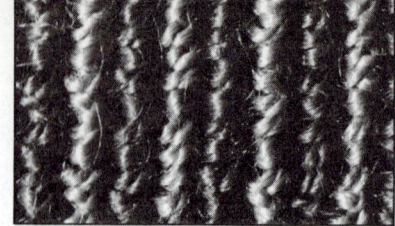

21

Blends and Combination Yarns and Fabrics

OBJECTIVES

◇ To identify the principal methods used in combining different fiber types into fabric structures
◇ To differentiate between a blend yarn and a combination yarn
◇ To identify some of the properties that blends or combination yarns impart to fabrics and how they influence selection, use, and care

KEY TERMS

blend fabric   combination fabric
blend yarn   combination yarn

Blend and combination yarns and fabrics are those in which two or more generic types of fibers are used. These different types of fibers can be combined in the following ways:

1. Two or more different types of fibers can be blended into a single yarn.
2. Single yarns, where each single is of a different fiber type, can be plied together to form a combination ply yarn.
3. Single or ply yarns of one fiber type can be used with single or ply yarns of another fiber type and woven or knitted into a fabric.

As many different fiber types as desired can be used, but each single yarn would be of the same fiber content.

The accepted definition of a blend as cited by ASTM is "a single yarn spun from a blend or a mixture of different fiber species."[1] According to this accepted definition, only the first type of blend or combination cited above qualifies as a *blend yarn*. Further, only a fabric made from such yarns qualifies as a *blend fabric*. Unfortunately, many con-

sumers have come to associate the term *blend* with any fabric containing fibers of two or more different generic types regardless of how they have been used in making a fabric. As a rule, woven fabrics designated as blends by fabric producers employ blended yarns throughout their construction. An exception would be a woven fabric in which yarns of one fiber type are used in the warp while a different fiber type is used in the filling. Other possible combinations might occur when a blended yarn is used in one direction of the fabric and a yarn composed of only one fiber type is used in the other direction. The latter yarn may be of one of the same fibers used in the blend or a totally different fiber type. Fabrics in which blended yarns are used throughout the construction are more likely to give desired performance characteristics during use and care than fabrics made with single fiber component yarns but a different fiber in different yarns.

Knit fabrics may be a true blend; they may be made of a combination of yarns of different fiber types; or they may be made of ply yarns with single components of different fiber types. Nonwoven fabrics are blends when two or more species of fiber are used in constructing the fiber mat.

Blends may be composed of differing amounts of

[1]ASTM, *Annual Book of ASTM Standards,* 1983, vol. 07.01, p. 76.

each fiber involved. A typical fiber blend is cotton and polyester. The amount of each fiber used may be similar, giving a 50/50 blend; the polyester can exceed the cotton, as in a 65/35 polyester/cotton blend or a 80/20 polyester/cotton blend; or the cotton can exceed the polyester as in fabrics with 65 to 80 percent cotton. In a true blend, each yarn has the same proportion of each different fiber type involved as every other yarn.

For a majority of blends on the market, optimum percentages have been established for fibers involved. For example, textile scientists generally agree that in blends of polyester and cotton, the percentage of cotton should range between 35 and 50 percent if the fabric is to combine the properties of easy care, durability, and comfort. If easy care and durability are most important, the polyester component can go as high as 80 percent; if comfort is most important, the cotton content may be as high as 80 percent.

A blend of 55 percent acrylic with 45 percent wool, or a blend of 50 to 65 percent polyester and 35 to 50 percent wool, results in fabrics that provide comfort and can be washed instead of dry-cleaned. A fabric in which as little as 12 to 15 percent nylon is blended with 85 to 88 percent wool and given proper finishing is considered to be a washable wool fabric. In addition, the nylon increases the resistance of the fabric to abrasion damage and helps prevent a high loss in strength that might occur because of the finishing effect on the wool fiber.

In the manufacture of a blend yarn, the fibers may be intimately mixed before yarn manufacturing starts or during the finisher-drawing operation (see page 175). For nonwovens the fibers must be blended before the fiber mat is formed. Unless a thorough blending occurs, the end product will not be uniform.

A factor of importance in building blend yarns is that the different fibers must be cut to the length required by the particular yarnmaking machinery to be used; if natural fibers are involved, any manmade fiber used with them must be cut to the average length of the natural fiber. If different natural fibers are used, it is important to try and use fibers of the same general length. For the most part, manmade fibers are cut to the length of cotton fibers, as most yarns are made on equipment designed for the staple length of cotton fiber.

Blends can be developed to provide consumers with special-performance characteristics and/or to meet predetermined end-use requirements. They may be designed specifically for appearance; to combine appearance and performance; to emphasize easy care; to attract consumers who want to buy luxury fibers for prestige; for reducing cost; or for providing durable-press and easy-care properties. Some typical examples of blend fabrics and the reasons often posed for their development include polyester and cotton to provide easy care, durability and comfort; rayon and acetate to provide appearance and draping qualities; silk, vicuña, and cashmere to add prestige; linen to provide stiffness and appearance.

Blends or combination fiber fabrics are the result of considerable research, development, and testing. Instead of developing new fibers, manufacturers, during the past decade, have concentrated on mixing different fibers to produce yarns and fabrics with desirable properties. A blend that has been properly engineered exhibits properties that represent the best of each fiber involved.

Combination fabrics and yarns may produce outstanding results if the combining process creates yarns with properties that work well together. In the case of a combination yarn, two or more singles, each of different fiber types, are combined into a ply. Such yarns may give outstanding use and be easy to care for. When made into fabric, they should proably give good wear and performance. The major problem with combination fabrics occurs when the yarns in one direction are of one type of fiber while the yarns in the perpendicular direction are of a different fiber type. Such combinations can produce fabrics that do not perform adequately; they may wrinkle badly in one direction or both, they may shrink in one direction, and they may require complex care procedures.

Strength is introduced into combination fiber fabrics by using yarns of high breaking load in the direction that requires extra resistance to force or by spacing strong yarns among yarns of low-tenacity fibers; the strong fibers increase the resistance to breaking. Nylon yarns in the warp direction with some low-tenacity fiber in the filling would produce such a fabric.

Blends and combination fiber fabrics are usually produced for special end uses in which the fabric can be designed to bring out the very best of each of the fiber's properties. However, it is possible to manufacture some fabrics that are not suitable for chosen end uses; in such cases consumers are seldom satisfied with their purchases.

It is particularly important for the fiber content

to be clearly identified. Although fiber content must appear on a label, the law does not require that the arrangement of the fibers be identified. Thus, consumers seldom know if they are buying a blend or a combination fabric. Such information would be helpful, since performance of fabrics is influenced by the method of combining or blending fibers. An example of a product that would not give as good service in a combination as in a blend is a fabric of rayon and polyester. If the combination involved rayon yarns in the warp direction and polyester in the filling, it is quite conceivable that the rayon would wrinkle badly during use and care. However, if rayon and polyester are blended in single yarns, the resulting fabric should provide acceptable performance and be an easy-care fabric.

Consumers should report back to retailers and/or manufacturers when merchandise does not perform as desired. Such reporting helps to inform manufacturers regarding what does or does not work in a combination or a blended fiber fabric.

STUDY QUESTIONS

1. Define a blend yarn and a combination yarn.

2. Define a blend fabric and a combination fiber fabric.
3. How might a combination yarn and a combination fabric differ?
4. What are the reasons for combining fibers of different types?

Activities

1. Look in stores and identify different fabrics in which two or more different types of fibers have been used. What type of information is given the consumer? How many different types of fabrics or end-use items do you find in which there are two or more different generic types of fibers?
2. Locate several samples of fabrics in which two or more different types of fibers have been used. Test them in a laboratory, if available, and compare with fabrics made of only one of the fibers used in the blend or combination.
3. If equipment is available, test fabrics in which two or more different fibers have been used, and try to determine whether they are blends or combinations.

PART IV

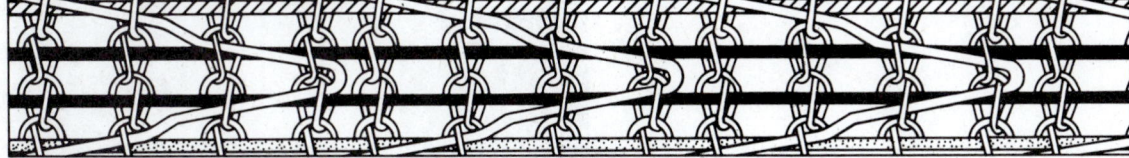

Fabrics

Fibers, yarns, and single fabrics are combined in many ways to produce the multitude of fabrics available to the modern consumer. Part Four outlines techniques used in the manufacture of fabrics. Chapter 22 provides information on woven fabrics, both basic and decorative or novelty weaves. Knitted fabrics are described in Chapter 23. The production of fabrics directly from fibers is described in Chapter 24, and Chapter 25 is devoted to other methods used in fabric construction.

Figures IV.1 and IV.2 illustrate a number of time-honored methods of fabric construction. Fabrics can be knitted, knotted, and coiled from a single yarn; plaiting, tapestry, and weaving employ two or more sets of yarns. Many of these techniques are still in use today, but the repertoire of the fabric manufacturer has been enormously expanded by modern technology, as will be seen in the following chapters.

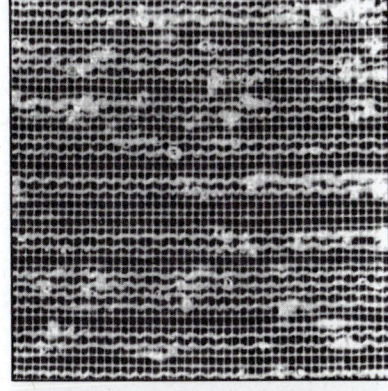

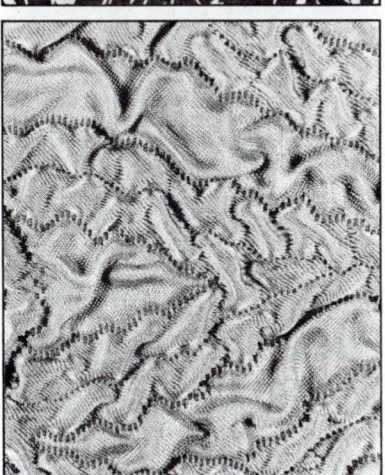

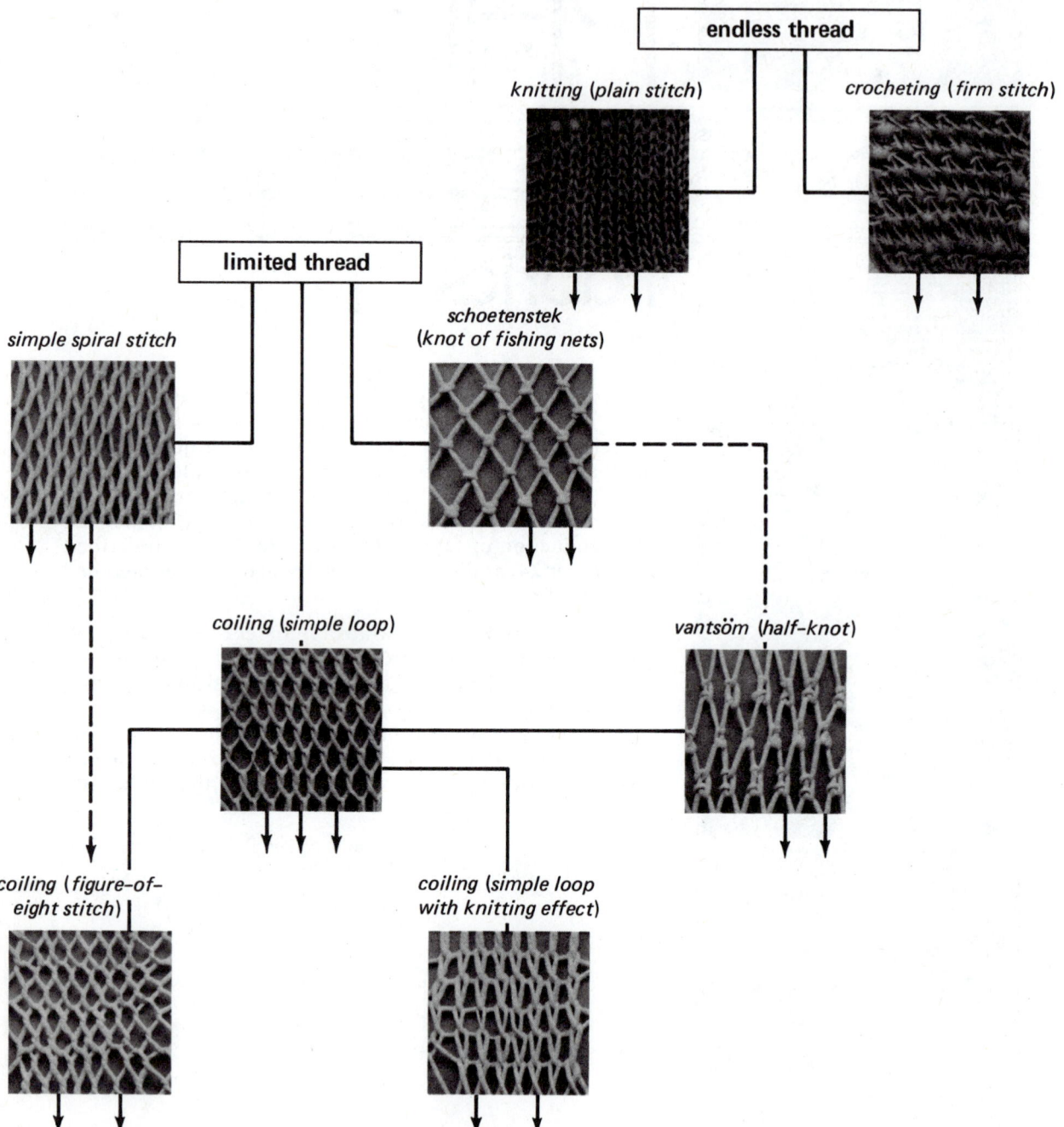

endless thread

knitting (plain stitch)

crocheting (firm stitch)

limited thread

simple spiral stitch

*schoetenstek
(knot of fishing nets)*

coiling (simple loop)

vantsöm (half-knot)

*coiling (figure-of-
eight stitch)*

*coiling (simple loop
with knitting effect)*

IV.1 Examples of early fabrics made from one continuous yarn such as knitted and knotted fabrics.
(Ciba Review)

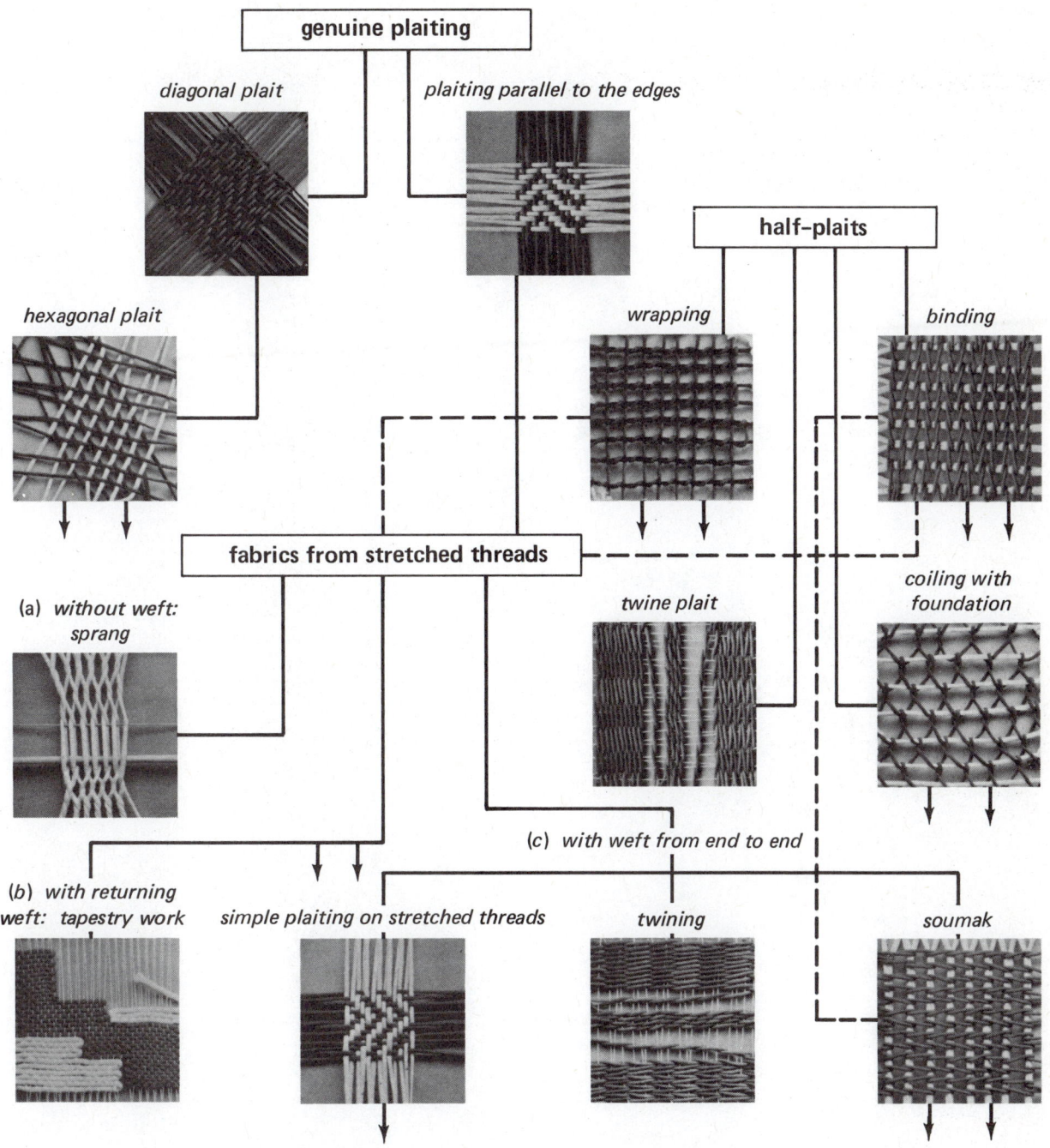

IV.2 Examples of early fabrics made from several yarns, including plaited and braided fabrics. (Ciba Review)

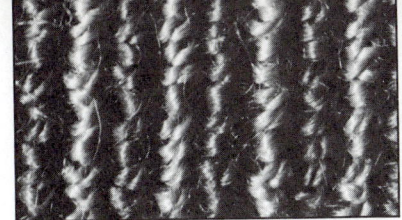

22

Woven Fabrics

KEY TERMS

air-jet weaving	letting off	spot weave
battening	loom	stuffer yarns
biaxial	multiphase weaving	swivel weave
cloth beam	novelty or figure weave	taking up
clipped spot	orthogonal	thread count
dents	picking	triaxial
dobby weaves	picks	twill weave
double cloth	pile weave	uncut spot
ends	plain weave	warp
fabric count	projectile weaving	warp beam
filling	rapier weaving	warp pile
filling pile	reed or beater bar	water-jet weaving
harness	satin weave	weave
heddles	shed	weft
Jacquard weaves	shedding	woof
lappet weave	shuttle	
leno weave	shuttleless	

Weaving is one of the oldest arts known. Although no looms from early civilizations are extant, fabrics of fine quality have been found in the tombs of ancient Egypt, and designs on very old pottery provide indisputable evidence of early skill in weaving. Paintings on pottery also provide some idea of the actual looms used in ancient civilizations.

Woven fabric consists of sets of yarns interlaced at right angles in some established sequence or pattern. The yarns that run parallel to the selvage or the longer diameter of a bolt of fabric are called *warp yarns* or *ends;* those that run crosswise of the fabric are called *filling yarns, weft* yarns, *woof* yarns, or *picks.* The terms *warp* and *filling* are commonly used by retailers and consumers, whereas manufacturers and converters usually use the terms *ends* and *picks.*

Early looms were very crude compared with modern mechanical weaving machines. Nonetheless, all looms or weaving machines, old and new, have basic operating principles that are alike. There is always some system to hold the long warp yarns under tension; there is a way to spread warp yarns apart in some arrangement so that the crosswise yarn can be laid through the opening or *shed* formed; and there is a device to pack the crosswise yarns into position.

Until the early nineteenth century, weaving was done primarily by hand. In the late 1700s and early 1800s scientists, inventors, and engineers, such as Joseph Marie Jacquard and Edmund Cartwright, developed weaving looms that were partially machine-powered. Gradually, looms that were completely mechanical took over, and tremendous changes have since occurred in loom design and operation and in how the pick yarn is laid. Because of

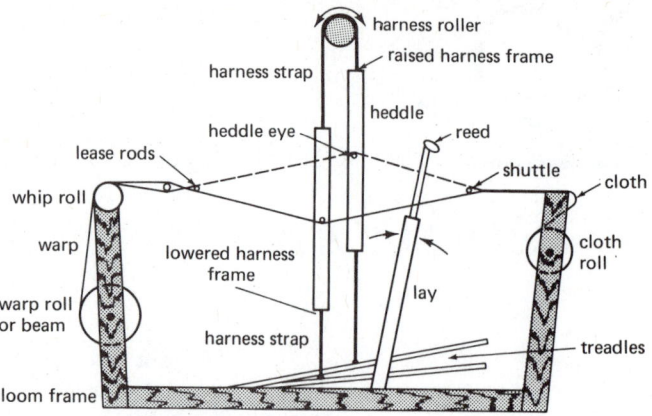

22.1 Diagram of a simple loom.

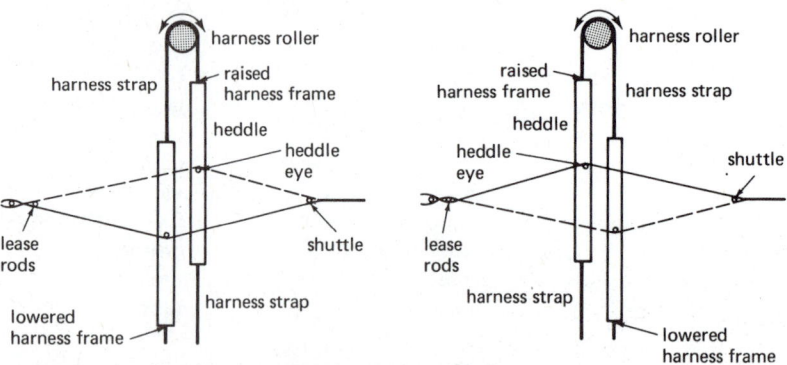

22.2 Diagram showing movement of harnesses and warp yarns to form a shed for the pick in the plain weave.

22.3 Typical shuttle loom. Close-up showing the shuttle about to lay filling yarn through the shed. (Springs Industries, Inc.)

hostility of textile workers to powered looms of any type in the early nineteenth century (workers thought these machines would replace human labor and eliminate their jobs), the development of modern power looms was delayed. Consequently, mechanical or power looms that are extremely rapid in laying pick yarns are a product of the twentieth century. However, the basic principle involved in weaving remains the same; the difference is in how it is achieved and not the basic process itself.

The parts of the basic loom are shown in the diagram in Figure 22.1. The *warp beam* holds the lengthwise yarns. It is located at the back of the loom and is controlled so that it releases yarn to the weaving area of the loom as needed. The *heddles* are wire or metal strips with an eye located in the center through which a warp end is threaded. The *harness* is the frame that holds a group of heddles in position. Each loom has at least two harnesses, and most have more—from four to as many as 32, depending on the type of fabric to be woven. Harnesses can be raised or lowered in order to produce the shed through which the filling (or weft) yarn is passed to provide the crosswise yarn. The order involved in raising and lowering harnesses is responsible for the weave pattern developed. The *shuttle*, or a modern pick layer of some type, carries the yarn across the shed and places the crosswise yarn into preliminary position. The *reed* is parallel to the harness and is responsible for packing the pick or filling yarn into position against the previous placed pick yarn. The *cloth beam* or *cloth roll*, located at the front of the loom, holds the completed fabric.

The basic weaving operation consists of four steps regardless of the kind of loom, its technological state, or the pattern to be woven:

1. *Shedding* is the raising and lowering of the warp ends by means of the heddles and harnesses to form the shed, the opening between warp yarns through which the filling yarn can be passed (Fig. 22.2).
2. *Picking* is the actual procedure of placing the filling or pick yarn into the shed.
3. *Battening*, sometimes called *beating, beating in,* or *beating up* consists in evenly packing the filling yarns into position against the yarns previously placed.
4. *Taking up* and *letting off* involves taking up the newly formed fabric onto the cloth beam and letting off or releasing yarn from the warp beam. The operation maintains uniform distance from harnesses to shed to cloth.

Many fabrics are woven on looms with few harnesses; elaborate fabrics, however, require looms with many harnesses, special attachments, or attachments that control each individual warp yarn and create sheds using methods similar to computer controls. To make a simple plain weave fabric, only two harnesses are required; for twill weaves, three or more harnesses are used; and for satin or sateen weaves, five or more harnesses are needed. Dobby patterns involve as many as 32 harnesses; the Jacquard attachment provides individual control for each warp yarn.

LOOMS: THE STATE OF THE ART OF WEAVING

Shuttle Looms

For centuries the basic loom operated with a shuttle to lay the filling or pick yarn (Fig. 22.3). By the mid-

dle of the twentieth century, shuttle looms were developed to a high level of efficiency and made fabric rapidly with minimum flaws. Speed of weaving had reached an all-time high with optimum results.

Shuttle looms depend upon a shuttle, which encloses a quill or spindle of yarn to lay the pick. As the shuttle moves across the shed, the yarn is laid. The shuttle stops at the opposite side of the fabric, the pick is battened in place, a new shed is formed, and the shuttle returns across the loom to lay a second pick. This is repeated until the fabric is completed. Shuttle looms are extremely noisy, as the hammer or bar that knocks the shuttle across the shed makes considerable noise each time it hits the shuttle. One reason for the wide acceptance of shuttleless looms has been the reduction of noise in weaving rooms.

The textile industry has been concerned about the cost of woven fabrics, particularly those being imported from foreign countries where labor costs are low. Thus, the industry began to look for alternative methods of weaving fabric. Interestingly enough, the newer looms have been developed and manufactured for the most part in foreign countries. Nonetheless, it became apparent that the textile industry in the United States would profit from adopting some type of shuttleless loom.

Shuttleless Looms

Shuttleless looms have replaced a large percentage of shuttle looms in textile mills in the United States and in foreign countries. The major types of these looms include projectile weaving machines, rapier weaving machines, jet weaving machines using either air or water to lay the pick, and multiphase weaving machines.

PROJECTILE WEAVING The projectile machine uses a small metal unit that grips the yarn at the supply package (the package holding the yarn) and carries it across the shed. Only sufficient yarn for the width of the fabric is carried across. There are two types of projectile looms: those with only one projectile and those with many. The latter type is more common today. There are some differences between the two. The single projectile picks up yarn on the supply side, carries it across the shed, and waits for the beating-in action; then either it picks up yarn from a second supply source on that side and returns across the shed to place the next pick,

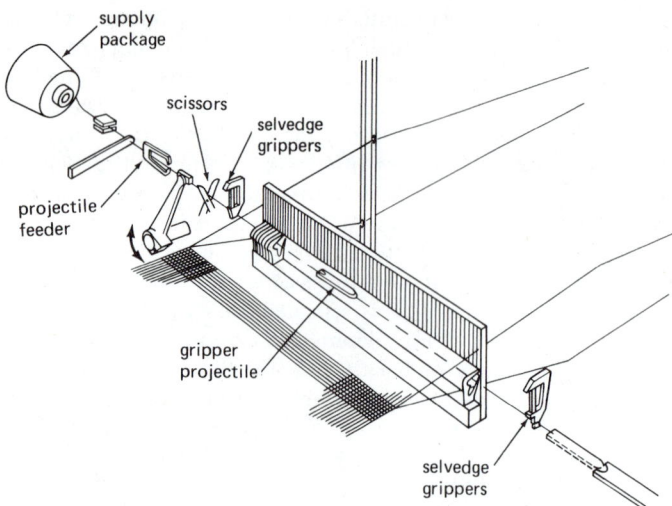

22.4 Diagram of projectile-loom operating principle. (Sulzer-Ruti)

22.5 Shuttleless loom using projectile to lay filling. (Springs Industries, Inc.)

or it may pick up sufficient yarn at the first supply source for two picks so that the first trip across lays half of the yarn picked up and the return trip lays the remainder. In the multiple projectile machines, the projectiles or grippers pick up yarn from the supply source, move across the shed to place that length of yarn, then fall into a conveyor system that returns the projectile to the starting side to pick up new yarn.

Figure 22.4 is a diagram of the projectile weaving system. The projectile (1) picks up thread from the supply package (2) at the projectile feeder (3). It is held by the selvage grippers (4) and cut by scissors (5) before it is released from the projectile. The sel-

22.6 Two-phase rapier weaving machine. (Saurer Textile Machinery)

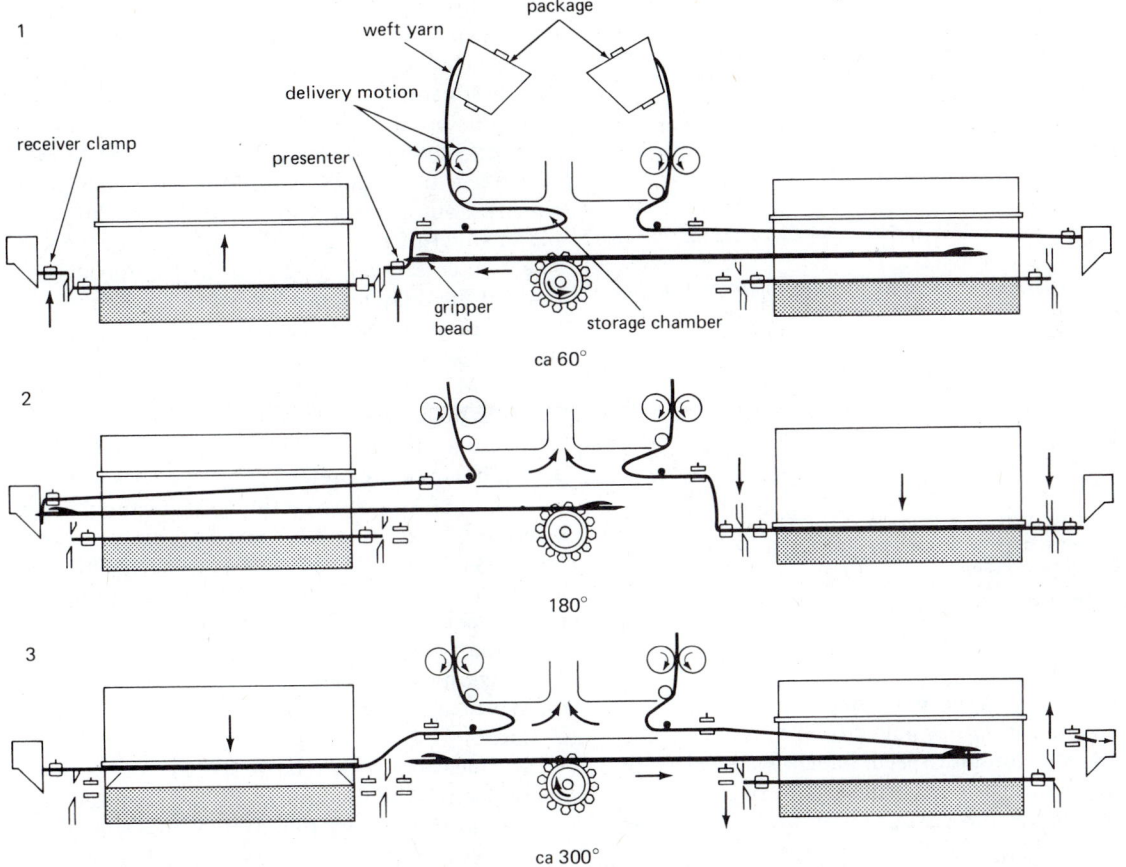

22.7 Diagram showing operation of two-phase rapier weaving machine. A: Supply packages. B: Yarn. C: Delivery wheels. D: Yarn storage. E: Clamps. F: Gripper or rapier head. G: Receiver clamp. (Saurer Textile Machinery)

vage edges are tucked in, and the operation is repeated. The projectile is ejected from the receiving unit and sent by a conveyor system back to the picking position. Figure 22.5 illustrates a modern projectile weaving machine. Projectile weaving machines may be wide or narrow; they are available in weaving widths up to approximately 200 inches. They can accommodate different colors for weft or filling yarns.

RAPIER WEAVING The rapier system operates on the principle of having metal arms, either rigid or flexible, carry yarn to the center of the weaving area, where it is transferred from one arm to the other and carried across the remainder of the fabric width. Newer rapier machines are built with two distinct weaving areas for two distinct fabrics (Fig. 22.6). In these machines, one rapier arm picks up the yarn from the center between the two fabrics

and carries it across one weaving area; as it finishes laying that pick, the opposite end of the rapier picks up another yarn from the center, and the rapier moves back across the surface and lays a pick on the other half of the machine (Fig. 22.7). Figure 22.8 diagrams the action on a single width of fabric for a single rigid rapier system, a double rigid rapier system, and a double flexible rapier system.

Rapier machines weave more rapidly than most shuttle machines but more slowly than most projectile looms. An important advantage of rapier looms is the flexibility that permits the laying of picks of different colors (Fig. 22.9). Rapier looms adapt to any type of fiber and work effectively in weaving fabrics up to 110 inches in width without any modification.

JET WEAVING Jet looms involve the laying of pick yarns by either a jet of air or a jet of water. The

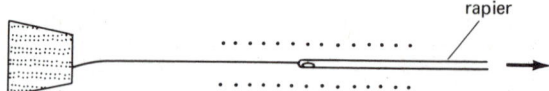

Single rigid rapier. The rapier (a long thin rod) enters the warp from the left and carries one weft thread across the warp on its return journey.

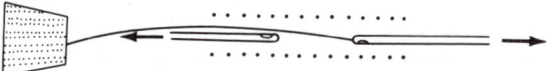

Double rigid rapiers. The two rapiers enter the warp simultaneously and meet in the center. The left-hand rapier carries the weft thread to the center of the warp and then hands it over to the right-hand rapier.

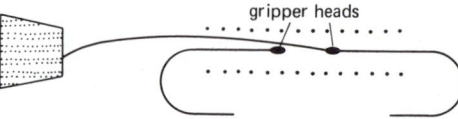

Double flexible rapiers. Same principle as with rigid rapiers but the rigid rods are replaced by flexible steel or plastic tapes which follow a curved path.

22.8 Diagram of other rapier systems for laying picks.

most popular are air-jet weaving machines. Figure 22.10 illustrates the basic steps in weaving using jets of air. The yarn is pulled from the supply package (1) at a constant speed, which is controlled by the rollers at position 3; the length of the yarn is determined by the measuring disk (2) and is based on the width of the fabric being woven. With the clamp closed, the yarn is held ready for insertion in the storage area (6) in the form of a hairpin (5) by the air stream from an auxiliary nozzle (4). Immediately before the clamp (7) opens, the main nozzle (8) starts blowing air so that the yarn is set in motion when the clamp opens. The hairpin shape is stretched out, and the yarn is blown into the guiding channel of the reed (10) with the shed open. The yarn is carried through the shed by the air currents of the relay nozzles (9) along the channel. At the end of each insertion cycle the clamp closes, and the yarn is beaten in and cut (11) after the shed is closed. Maximum width for air-jet weaving machines is about 140 inches (Fig. 22.11).

Water-jet looms are less commonly used than air-jet, but they are preferred for some types of fabrics. Figure 22.12 shows a filling yarn being laid in position by a jet of water. Both air- and water-jet looms weave rapidly, provide for laying different colors in the filling direction, and produce uniform-quality fabrics. They are less noisy and require less space than most other types and do minimal damage to warp yarns during the weaving operation, as there is no abrasion on warp yarns by the jets of air or water.

As a measure of the relative speeds of these shuttleless looms, the amount of filling yarn laid per minute provides interesting data. A projectile loom

22.9 Rapier loom designed to lay picks of different colors. Design is controlled by a dobby attachment operated by electronic controls. (Saurer Textile Machinery)

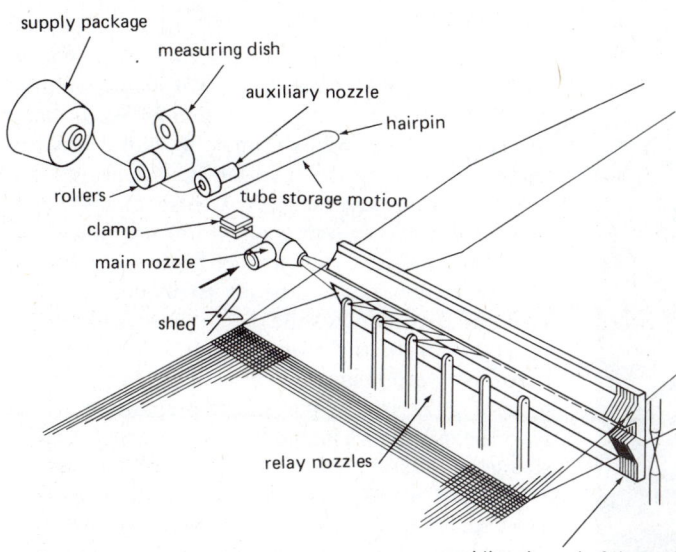

supply package

measuring dish

auxiliary nozzle

hairpin

rollers

tube storage motion

clamp

main nozzle

shed

relay nozzles

guiding channel of the reed

22.10 Diagram of operation of air-jet loom. (Sulzer-Ruti)

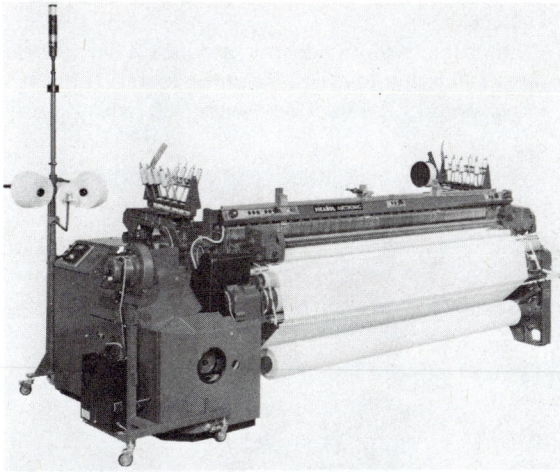

22.11 Air-jet weaving machine. (Picanol, Belgium)

22.12 Laying the filling yarn with a jet of water. The jet of water is fast and efficient and will lay 420 picks per minute. (Springs Industries, Inc.)

can lay between 1000 and 1350 yarns per minute; the rapier loom lays about 750 to 900 yards per minute; the air-jet machine lays about 1800 yards per minute.

MULTIPHASE WEAVING Multiphase weaving is characterized by the near simultaneous insertion of several picks across the width of the fabric. This also requires different shedding motions for each pick that is to be laid. These looms weave at a phenomenal rate of speed. The process transforms weaving into a continuous process rather than a cycle of shedding, picking, and battening. The operation is based on a series of wavelike motions across the weaving surface. In general, fabrics woven on these looms do not have a true 90° angle relationship between warp and filling; therefore, the filling yarns are in a slightly slanted position. Multiphase weaving is limited to special types of fabrics, but it can be expected to gain acceptance in the years ahead.

Fabrics of different widths can be woven on almost any type of weaving machine. The widths cited, in general, are maximum. The actual width of the fabric depends on the number of warp yarns placed on the warp beam and the width between each warp yarn in the final fabric. Preparing warp beams involves several steps. Yarns from packages taken from the spinning operation are placed on creels and fed first to a warper beam (Fig. 22.13). Several warper beams are placed in position in a machine that prepares the actual warp beam; here, the yarns from the warper beams are combined onto one warp beam, which will be placed on the loom (Fig. 22.14). As part of the preparation of the warp beam, the yarns are usually finished with a sizing compound, called slashing (see Chap. 26).

Modern weaving rooms are well lighted; constant removal of lint from the weaving operation maintains a clean and healthful environment. Figure 22.15 provides a good example of a modern weaving area.

Shuttleless looms do not produce a selvage on fabrics like that made with shuttle looms. If the selvages on shuttleless looms were left without any

22.13 Winding a warper beam from the creels in the background. (Celanese Corporation)

22.14 Winding a warp beam from the warper beams in background. (Celanese Corporation)

22.15 Typical large weaving room. (Springs Industries, Inc.)

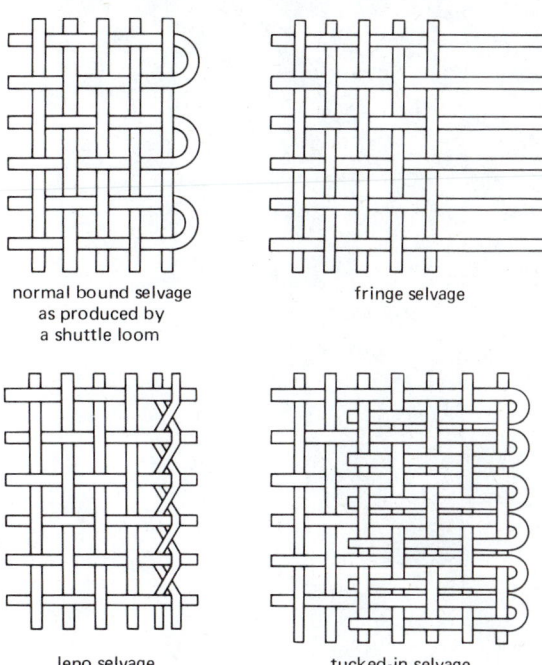

normal bound selvage
as produced by
a shuttle loom

fringe selvage

leno selvage
(note twist)

tucked-in selvage

22.16 Diagram comparing selvages produced by shuttleless looms with the traditional selvage of a shuttle loom.

modification, the fabric edge would resemble a raveled piece of fabric, with loose yarn ends extending from it. To achieve fabric edges similar to those made by shuttle looms, various methods have been adopted that provide unconventional selvages that look very much like those from a shuttle loom. Most shuttleless looms are equipped with an attachment that produces a selvage like one of those illustrated in Figure 22.16. The most common edge is the tucked-in selvage. Fabrics of thermoplastic fibers may use the leno selvage and apply heat to provide a heat-sealed edge. Some machines lay a narrow line of adhesive or resin along the edge to seal the yarns and prevent raveling. The use of nontraditional selvages is increasing rapidly as the use of shuttleless looms increases.

BASIC WEAVES

Plain Weaves

The plain weave is the simplest form of yarn interlacing and consists of the alternate shedding of warp yarns to provide a fabric in which each filling

22.17 Plain-weave fabric

22.18 Point diagram of plain weave.

22.19 Plain-weave fabric using yarn-dyed yarns.

22.20 Rib-weave variation of the plain weave.

22.21 A 2 × 2 basket weave.

22.22 A 4 × 4 basket weave.

yarn passes over one warp and under the adjacent warp. An adjacent filling yarn reverses the interlacing so that it passes over the warp that was on top of the preceding filling yarn and under the warp that lay on top of the preceding filling yarn. Figure 22.17 is an illustration of the plain weave. Figure 22.18 is referred to as a point diagram. Each black square indicates that the warp yarn is on the surface. The squares paralleling the vertical diagram (and the page) should be visualized as the warp direction of the fabric, and the horizontal rows represent the filling yarns.

Many woven fabrics are constructed using the plain weave. Figure 22.19 is an example of a plain-weave fabric in which variety has been provided through the use of different-colored yarns. Unless colors have been printed onto the surface, plain-weave fabrics are generally considered to be reversible. In making plain-weave fabrics, yarns can be packed loosely or tightly together, and the number of warp yarns may equal the number of filling yarns in each inch or may vary considerably. Yarns can vary in diameter and type to produce interesting fabrics. When the number of warp yarns per inch is approximately the same as the number of filling yarns per inch, the *thread count*, sometimes called *fabric count*, is considered balanced; when the number of yarns per inch differs considerably between warp and filling, the fabric count is unbalanced.

The plain weave is comparatively inexpensive to produce. A variety of designs can be made using various coloring and finishing processes on the finished fabric. In addition, some of the most durable fabrics are manufactured by the plain-weave technique. Examples of plain-weave fabric include muslin, percale, cheesecloth, chambray, gingham, batiste, organdy, chiffon, shantung, and homespun.[1]

Rib Variation of the Plain Weave

Interesting and attractive fabrics can be obtained by utilizing the rib variation of the plain weave (Fig. 22.20). The rib effect is produced by using heavy yarns in the filling or warp direction (usually the filling direction), by grouping yarns in specific areas of the warp or filling, or by having more warp than filling yarns per inch.

Many rib fabrics have heavy yarns inserted as picks. Examples of this construction include poplin,

[1]Definitions and descriptions of fabrics cited are provided in the Glossary.

faille, bengaline, and ottoman. Dimity derives from alternation of fine and heavy yarns at planned intervals in the warp direction. Cross-bar dimity uses fine and heavy yarns at planned intervals in both the warp and filling directions. Broadcloth results from using many more warp yarns per inch than filling yarns. As these yarns pack together in the warp, they produce the fine rib characteristic of a broadcloth.

Comparative size of the ribs in some of the more commonly encountered rib fabrics is one method of fabric identification. The following is a selection of rib fabrics listed in order from fine to heavy rib: broadcloth, poplin, faille, grosgrain, bengaline, ottoman.

Basket Variation of the Plain Weave

The basket weave is generally defined as having two or more warp ends interlaced as an unit with one or more filling yarns treated as a unit. This construction is not as firm as regular plain weaves and frequently has lower strength. However, basket weaves are attractive and have interesting surface effects. A basket variation in which two warps pass over and under one filling is called a 2 × 1 weave. Other fabrics of the basket-weave type can be found in 2 × 2 (Fig. 22.21), 2 × 4, 3 × 2, and 4 × 4 arrangements (Fig. 22.22).

Oxford cloth, a 2 × 1 basket weave, is a popular fabric for shirtings and sports blouses. The two warp yarns equal in size the single filling yarn. The fabric is soft and comfortable. Some authors have listed oxford cloth as a separate modification of the plain weave, but the majority still cite it as a basket variation.

Monk's cloth is one of the best-known examples of basket-weave construction. It is available in a variety of modifications, 2 × 2, 4 × 4, 8 × 8, and occasionally in uneven arrangements such as 4 × 3 and 2 × 3. Rather coarse yarns are used. Yarn slippage may occur because of the loose structure. Basket-weave fabrics are often used for draperies and in coating and suiting fabrics. Examples, in addition to oxford and monk's cloth, include hopsacking and flat duck.

Other Plain-Weave Variations

In addition to the variations produced in plain-weave fabrics by modification of the weaving pattern, other design effects can be introduced without structural modifications. The use of complex or novelty yarns, at either regular or irregular intervals, may create interesting surface textures. The amount of twist in the yarns is another basis for diverse appearance and textures.

Yarns of different fiber content, for example metallic yarns and cotton yarns, or of different colors can be combined to develop interesting fabrics. Chambray and gingham are classic examples of plain-weave fabrics created by using yarns of two (or more) different colors. Spacing the yarns in various arrangements also produces variety. Fabrics can be loose, with yarns spaced widely apart, or compact, with yarns packed closely together.

Twill Weave

The second basic weave pattern used in manufacturing fabrics is the twill weave. This technique is characterized by a diagonal line on the face, and often on the back, of the fabric. The face diagonal can vary from a low 14° angle *(reclining twill)* to a 75° angle *(steep twill)*. An angle of 45° is considered to be a medium diagonal or a *regular twill*. The regular twill is the most common. The angle of the diagonal is determined by the closeness of the warp ends, the number of yarns used per inch, the diameter of the yarns used, and the actual progression forming the repeat.

Twill-weave fabrics have a distinctive and attractive appearance. In general, fabrics made by the twill-weave interlacing are strong and durable. Twills differ from plain weave in the number of filling picks and warp ends needed to complete a repeat pattern. The simplest twill uses three picks and three warp ends to form the repeat. At least three harnesses are required on looms if a twill weave is to be made.

The warp yarn goes over, or *floats* over, two filling yarns and under one in the ⅔ twill. In a regular twill each succeeding float begins one pick higher or lower than the adjacent float. In more complicated twills the progression may vary, but the diagonal effect will remain visible. The number of pick yarns required to complete the twill pattern determines the number of harnesses required for weaving. Some twill patterns may require as many as fifteen harnesses.

Twill fabrics have either a right-hand or left-hand diagonal (Figs. 22.23 and 22.24). If the diagonal moves from the lower left to the upper right of

22.23 A right-hand, ½ twill.

22.24 A left-hand, ¾ twill.

22.25 A herringbone twill.

22.26 A satin-weave fabric.

22.27 A sateen-weave fabric.

the fabric, it is referred to as a *right-hand twill;* if it moves from upper left to lower right, it is a *left-hand twill.* In even twill fabrics the filling yarns pass over and under the same number of warp yarns, whereas in uneven twills the pick goes over either more or fewer warps than it goes under. Uneven twill fabrics have a right and a wrong side and therefore are not considered reversible. *Filling-faced* twills are those in which the picks predominate on the face of the fabric; *warp-faced* twills have a more evident warp on the surface. Even twills have the same number of warp and filling yarns on both the face and back and can be considered reversible. Of course, finishes and coloring methods may make one side the face and prevent reversing the fabric.

Yarns used in making twill-weave fabrics frequently are tightly twisted and exhibit good strength. The twill weave permits the packing of yarns closer together because of fewer interlacings. This close packing combined with strong yarns can produce a strong, durable fabric. However, if the yarns are packed too tightly, the fabric will have reduced tearing strength, abrasion resistance, and wrinkle recovery.

In addition to appearance and good strength, twills tend to show soil less quickly than plain-weave fabrics. However, twills are more expensive to produce than plain-weave fabrics because of the more complicated weaving techniques and looms required.

A frequent variation of the twill weave is the herringbone. In this design the twill direction is reversed at predetermined intervals to form a series of inverted Vs (Fig. 22.25).

Examples of fabrics made by the twill weave include denim, jean, gabardine, surah, wool sharkskin, some flannel fabrics, and some tweeds.

Satin Weave

Satin fabrics are characterized by long floats on the face of the fabric (Fig. 22.26). These floats are caught under cross yarns at intersections as far apart as possible for the particular construction. At no time do adjacent parallel yarns come in contact with one another at a point of interlacing. This reduces the possibility of a diagonal effect occurring on the face of the fabric. However, some satins do have a faint diagonal effect owing to the low number of yarns used to form the repeat.

In a satin fabric it is the warp ends that float on the surface. A variation of the satin weave in which the filling picks float on the surface is referred to as *sateen* (Fig. 22.27). Filament fiber yarns are generally used in making satin fabrics, while staple-fiber yarns, often of cotton, are more common in sateen fabrics. There are, however, exceptions; cotton satins as well as filament yarn sateens have been made.

The long floats of the satin weave create a shiny surface and tend to reflect light easily. This is accentuated if bright filament fiber yarns with a low twist of ½ to 1 turn per inch (about 0.2–0.4 turns/cm) are used for the floating yarns. Floats in satin and sateen fabrics tend to snag and abrade easily; thus, such fabrics are not as durable as plain- or twill-weave fabrics.

The length of the floats in satin structures is governed by three factors: the number of harnesses, which is determined by the number of filling yarns involved in forming the repeat; the number of yarns per inch, or fabric count; and the yarn size. Of these, the most important are fabric count and yarn size. A satin fabric may have as few as five harnesses to form the repeat (in which case it is called a 5-shaft satin), or it may have many more. The number of yarns per inch influences the length of the float along with the number of harnesses. Among fabrics with the same number of yarns required for the repeat, a fabric with a high fabric count will have shorter floats than one with a low yarn count. When fabric count and yarn size are held constant, the length of a float over four yarns will obviously be shorter than a float over seven yarns.

Satin-weave fabrics are lustrous and are selected primarily for appearance and smoothness. Satins are frequently used as lining fabrics in coats and suit jackets, as they make it easy to slip the apparel item on and off over other materials. Satins and sateens

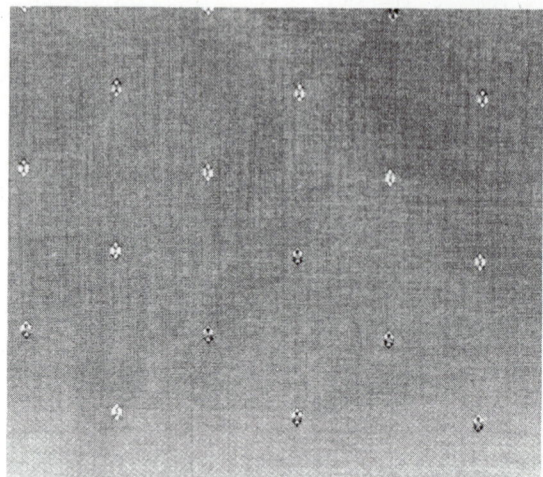

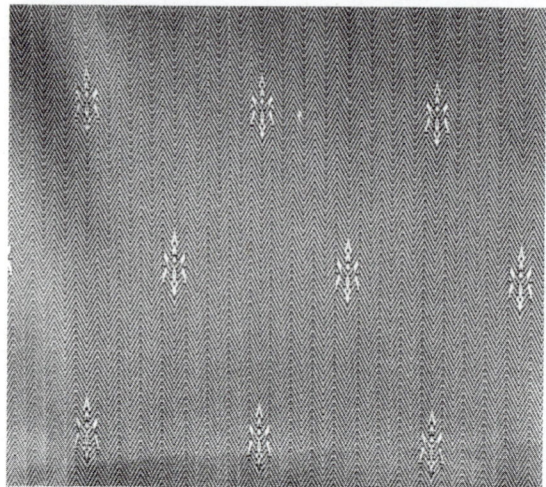

22.29 Close-up of the pattern roll in one type of dobby loom. The pattern roll works somewhat like a player piano. For each shed, one horizontal row of perforations determines which harnesses are raised and which are lowered. (Springs Industries, Inc.)

have a definite face and back. Variations in satin fabrics can be produced by using highly twisted yarns in the filling to create a *crepe-back satin;* when the crepe side is intended to be used as the right or face side of the fabric, it is called a *satin-back crepe.*

Examples of satin-weave fabrics include antique satin, slipper satin, crepe-back satin, faille satin, bridal satin, and moleskin.

FIGURE WEAVES

Figure weaves, also identified as *fancy* weaves, *decorative* weaves, or *complex* weaves, are formed by predetermined changes in the interlacing of the warp and filling yarns. At least two different types of basic weaves will be found in most figure-weave fabrics. Figure weaving can be accomplished by using various attachments above or on the loom to increase the control of warp yarns and provide for a variety of changes in the shedding process. Weav-

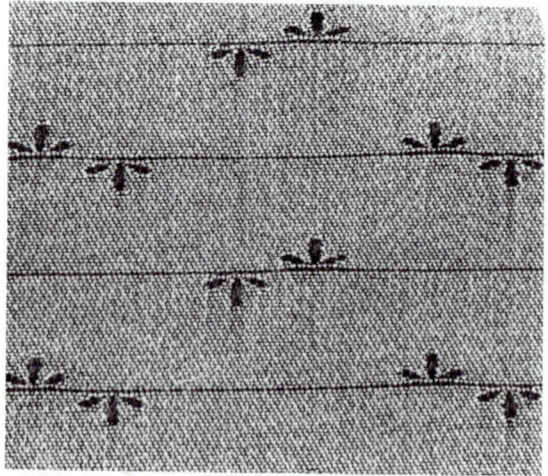

22.28 Dobby-weave fabrics.

22.30 Dobby loom using electronic controls (computer) to determine pattern. (Picanol, Belgium)

ing processes discussed in this group include dobby, Jacquard, leno, pile, and double-cloth weaves, as well as the use of extra warp or filling yarns in the formation of special spot types of designs.

Dobby Weaves

Dobby designs are characterized by small figures such as dots, geometric designs, and small floral patterns that have been woven into the fabric (Fig. 22.28). These designs are produced by the combination of two or more basic weaves, and the loom may have up to 32 harnesses to control the shedding operation. The design is produced by a dobby pattern chain, which may be made of wool with metal pins or perforated metal, paper, or plastic rolls. The pattern chain controls the harnesses and determines which are to be raised or lowered in order to produce the desired pattern. Figure 22.29 illustrates one type of control system used in the weaving of dobby designs. Each crossbar or row of holes in the roll controls a row of the pattern and mechanically determines which warp yarns (harnesses) will be raised and which lowered. Older dobby controls limited the potential design possibilities, but modern developments in dobby controls, such as double-cylinder controls and electronic controls, have increased the number of designs that can be made by this method (Fig. 22.30).

Examples of fabrics produced by dobby weaving are piqué, waffle cloth, shirting madras, and huck

toweling. Piqué may utilize heavy yarns, called *stuffer yarns,* to produce an accentuated pattern.

Jacquard Designs

Fabrics with extremely complicated woven designs are manufactured using Jacquard loom attachments. The major advantage of the Jacquard attachment is its ability to control each individual warp yarn instead of a series as in regular harness looms. This separate yarn control provides great freedom for the fabric designer because large, intricate motifs can be transferred to fabric. The present state of the art makes it possible to produce extremely elaborate patterns depicting narrative scenes taken from paintings or photographs as well as the typical elaborate designs usually associated with Jacquard patterns.

Jacquard weaves are among the older types of weaving, and the use of the Jacquard attachment, developed by Joseph-Marie Jacquard, dates back to the early 1800s. Until recently all Jacquard designs were created using a set of pattern cards similar to enlarged IBM cards or a player-piano roll. The pattern desired is transferred to a series of perforated cards or a roll; one card, or one section of a roll, is required for each shedding and placing of a filling pick. The holes in the card permit the lifting of needles on the machine that determine which warp yarns are to be raised in forming the shed. The shed is formed and the pick is placed into position (Fig.

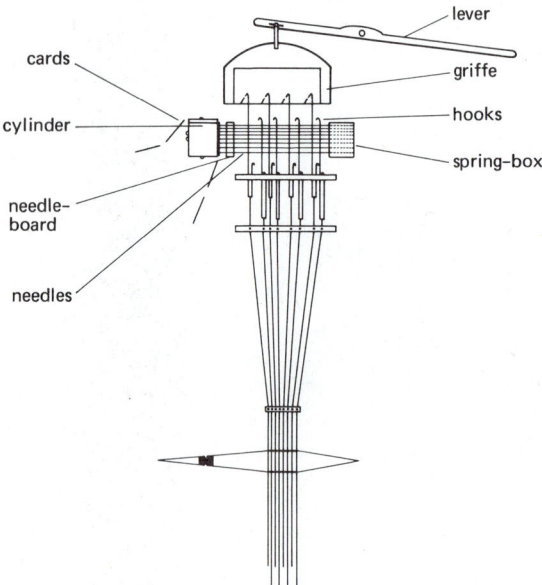

22.31 Diagram of Jacquard mechanism.

cards
cylinder
needle-board
needles
lever
griffe
hooks
spring-box

22.32 Jacquard pattern cards that control warp yarns to produce the pattern in the final woven fabric.

22.31). Figure 22.32 illustrates a set of punched cards in place on a loom that control the shedding required to form a complicated design. Each card stops on the cylinder for its particular pick, the pick is placed, the card moves on, and a new card takes its place. This continues until all cards are used and one repeat of the pattern is formed; the process is then repeated for as long as needed. Many Jacquard attachments in use today are controlled by computer tapes rather than cards. The process is basically the same, but the computer tape identifies which yarns are to be raised to form the desired shed. Complicated patterns can be developed using various kinds of graphics software that permit the drawing of designs directly onto monitors that are then converted into the pattern tape for controlling the shedding of the warp yarns. Figure 22.33 shows a loom with a Jacquard attachment that is controlled by cards, seen at the right side of the photograph. Looms using computer controls appear very similar except that the cards are missing and the controls are housed in the upper-level control box.

Jacquard designs involve at least two of the basic weaves in various arrangements to form the pattern. Jacquard weaves are expensive to produce, as the machinery is complex, complicated to operate, and costly to build. Jacquard fabrics are used for home furnishings, apparel, domestics such as table coverings and napkins, and other elaborate and decorative fabrics.

Examples of fabrics woven by Jacquard techniques include damask, tapestry, brocade, brocatelle, matelassé, and some bedspread fabrics (Fig. 22.34).

Leno Weaves

The leno weave may also be referred to as a *doup* weave or a *gauze* weave. In the most correct use of terms, *doup* is the name for the attachment on the loom that forms the specific interlacing characteristic of the leno weave. The doup attachment controls the warp threads and moves horizontally as well as vertically. Thus, the warp yarns can be interlaced and crossed between the picks.

When a distinction is made between leno and gauze weaves, the term *gauze* is used to identify an open-mesh type of fabric, whereas *leno* applies to fabrics made by the special interlacing-intercrossing process. Another difference that may be encoun-

22.33 A Jacquard loom using cards to control yarn sheds. (Sulzer-Ruti)

22.34 Examples of Jacquard-weave fabrics.

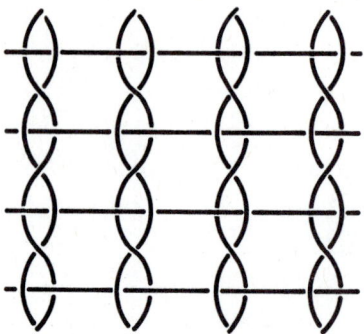

22.35 Diagram of a standard leno weave.

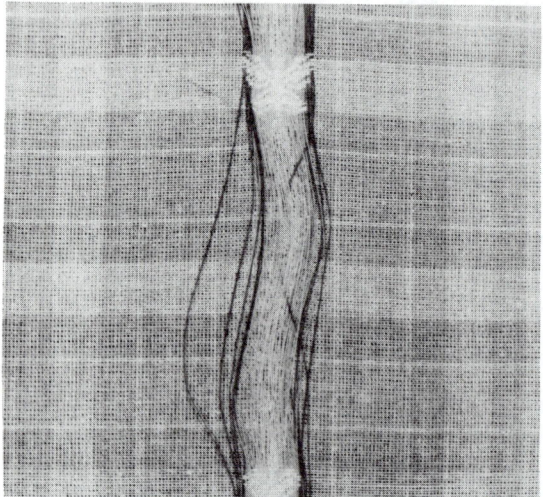

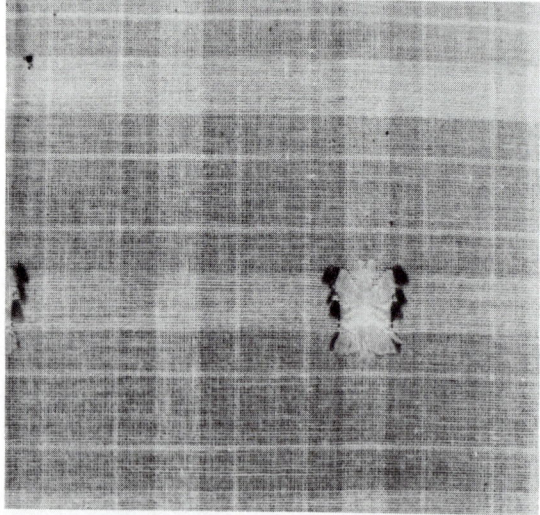

22.36 Clipped spot. *Top:* Back before cutting extra yarns. *Bottom:* After cutting extra yarns.

tered relates to the number of filling yarns inserted between the crossings of the warp yarns. If only one filling is involved in each crossing, the term *gauze* is permitted; if more than one filling is involved, the term *leno* is preferred. It is important to note that fabrics sometimes identified as gauze fabrics may not be constructed by the gauze or leno weave; rather, they may be nothing more than a loosely woven plain-weave fabric.

The leno weave produces open-textured fabric that may be sheer or heavy. The unusual warp interlacing (Fig. 22.35) prevents slippage of the filling yarns, reduces shrinkage, and prevents fabric distortion that could occur in loosely woven plain-weave structures. Further, the construction gives strength to sheer fabrics. In some fabrics, the leno weave is combined with other construction processes.

Examples of fabrics made with the leno weave include marquisettes used for window curtains and similar uses, mosquito nets, household or food bags, interlock embroidery canvas, and special fabrics used in interior design and for special apparel.

Surface-Figure Weaves

Extra warp and filling yarns can be employed to produce many different designs. When extra warp yarns are used, they are wound on an additional warp beam and threaded into separate heddles so that they can be controlled as needed to form the pattern. Depending on the complexity of the pattern, the design may be controlled with dobby attachments or Jacquard mechanisms. When the design is to be made using extra filling yarns, the extra yarns are inserted, usually by means of a special shuttle and either a box loom or a regular shuttle loom. The box loom is preferred, as it produces more satisfactory fabrics and permits considerable flexibility in design. The three main types of fabric construction that involve the use of extra warp and filling yarns are lappet, swivel, and spot or dot.

Lappet Weave

Lappet is a form of weaving in which extra warp yarns are introduced in a manner that creates designs over predetermined portions of the base fabric. Patterns are woven by means of an attachment to the loom that consists of a frame or rack fastened to the loom near the reed. Long needles are carried in the frame, and the yarns to be used in making the design are threaded through the needles. When the rack is lowered, the needles are pressed to the bottom of the shed and held in position while the picks are laid. The rack is then raised, and the pick is beaten into the cloth. Next the rack is shifted sideways to a new location, and the same action is repeated. Each time the frame or rack moves sideways, it carries the yarn in the needle across the surface of the fabric and creates a row of the pattern. If long floats are formed on the back of the fabric, they may be cut away; however, if the floats are short, they are usually left. This presents both an advantage and a disadvantage. If the floats are left, the pattern will be durable, but the floats may be easily snagged, causing damage to the fabric. If the floats are cut, the design area is weakened and may be removed during use and care. The lappet weave is considered strong and durable, but it is comparatively expensive. Currently, no lappet fabrics are being made in the United States. Any that are found have been imported, primarily from European countries.

Swivel Weave

The swivel weave differs from the lappet in that swivel designs are produced by extra filling yarns. The yarns to be used in each pattern are wound on quills and placed in small shuttles. These shuttles are strategically located at each point where the design is to occur. The pattern mechanism causes a shed to be made, and the shuttle carries the yarn through the shed the distance of the pattern only. This may mean that it passes over very few warp yarns to form the design. This process is repeated for each row of the design pattern. Between repeats of the pattern, the extra filling yarn floats on the back of the fabric and is cut away after the weaving is completed.

The swivel process permits the weaving of different colors in the same row because each figure has its own shuttle; however, each column would consist of repeats of the same color. In fabrics with small designs the swivel will save material and give figures a prominent, raised appearance. This method fastens the yarn securely as each figure is completed, and it cannot pull out without severely damaging the fabric. Swivel weaves can be recognized by the fact that the yarn used to form the pattern creates the same effect on both the face and the back of the fabric. There is little or no swivel-weave fabric currently made in the United States, and only limited amounts are being imported.

Spot Weave

Spot or dot designs can be fabricated with either extra warp or extra filling yarns. The yarns are inserted the entire length or width of the fabric in predetermined areas, and the pattern is formed using either dobby controls or Jacquard attachments for the area where the designs are located. When small, widely spaced designs are made, the floating yarns on the reverse or back side of the fabric are cut away; this leaves dots that can be pulled out of the fabric with a small amount of effort. The simplest designs use extra warp yarns that may be different in weight, color, or type from those used in the base fabric. Designs in which the floats are clipped away are called *clipped-spot* (or cut-spot) patterns (Figs. 22.36 and 22.37).

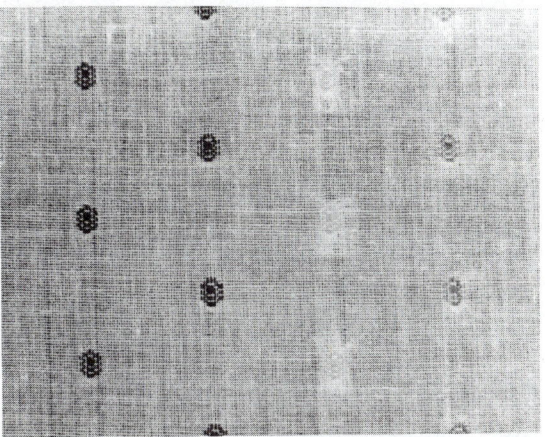

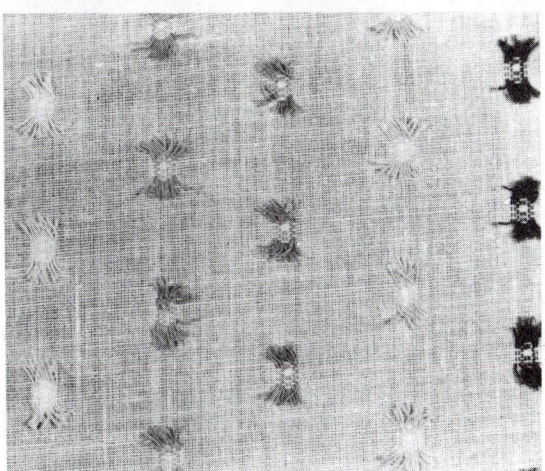

22.37 Face and back of a clipped-spot fabric.

22.38 Dotted swiss. Inset at right is cut side.

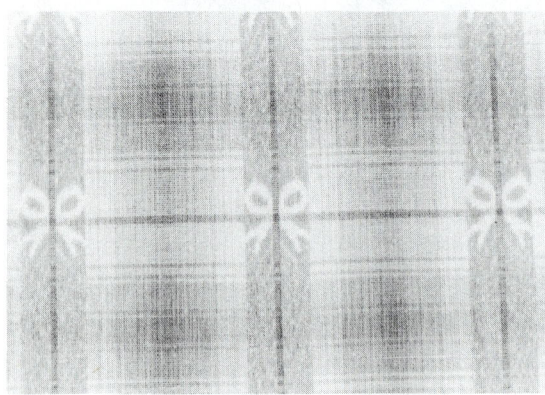

22.39 Uncut spot. Above: Face. Below: Back.

Filling floats are relatively easy to cut, but warp floats are rather difficult to cut and require special apparatus. The durability of a spot design depends on the compactness of the background yarns that hold the design yarns in place and the smoothness or roughness of the yarns used for either the foundation fabric or the design, or both. Spots in compact weaves are quite stable; in loose weaves they can be pulled out of the fabric rather easily, thus destroying the intended pattern. Standard *dotted swiss* fabric, made using a true spot weave, is a clipped-spot fabric (Fig. 22.38). Considerable dotted swiss fabric is being made using a flocking finish instead of the spot weave (see Chap. 27). Such flocked fabrics are not clipped-spot designs and may not have the same level of durability that a true clipped-spot pattern would. There are many different types of clipped-spot patterns; for example, fabrics with long fringed effects on the surface may also be produced by the clipped-spot technique.

Spot designs in which the floating yarns are not cut are referred to as *uncut-spot patterns* (Fig. 22.39). The amount of yarn that is left to float may involve very short spans, or the floats may be long. Frequently, uncut-spot patterns are used for border designs, and these usually have very short spaces between the design repeats. Such fabrics, in fact, may be made to be reversible so that the pattern on the face side is complete and the pattern on the back side is the reverse of the design. Uncut-spot patterns may be made using either dobby or Jacquard attachments, depending on the complexity of the design. In both clipped-spot and uncut-spot patterns, it is possible to remove the yarns forming the design without disintegrating the base fabrics. However, removing such yarns results in a less compact fabric and may reduce durability considerably. Obviously, removing pattern yarns would be undesirable.

Pile Weaving

Woven-pile fabrics are those in which an extra set of warp or filling yarns is interlaced with the ground warp and filling in such a manner that loops or cut ends extend from the base fabric. The base fabric may be constructed using either a plain or a twill weave.

Filling Pile

Filling-pile fabrics are produced with two sets of filling yarns and one set of warp. Although the ground

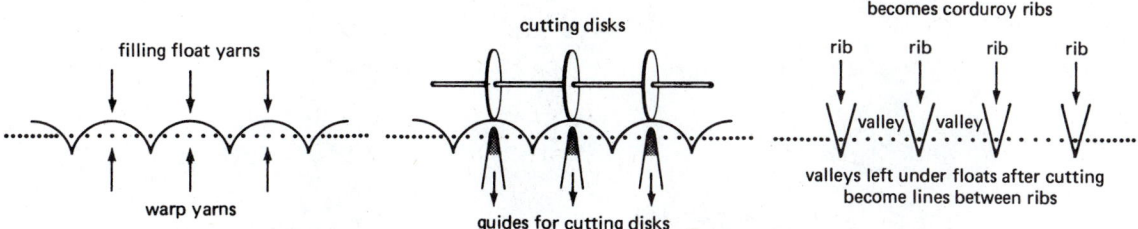

22.40 Diagram showing the formation of corduroy.

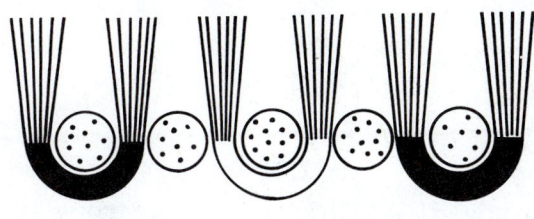

22.41 V and W interlacings for pile fabrics: after cutting.

may be of either twill or plain weave, a twill base is preferred for its durability. The extra set of filling yarns floats over three or more warp yarns; frequently the floats are over five or seven yarns. After weaving is completed, the floats are cut and brushed up to form the pile surface. Velveteen and corduroy are both manufactured by this method. Corduroy differs from velveteen in that the floats are interlaced in such a manner that rows of floats are formed with sufficient space between them so that when they are cut and brushed the face of the fabric has a ribbed effect. Velveteen, however, has the floats of such a length and closeness that when cut and brushed they produce an all-over effect rather than a ribbed effect. Figure 22.40 diagrams the procedures involved in making corduroy.

Corduroy and velveteen are prepared for cutting in the same manner. The floats are treated to give them cutting surface, and the fabric is stiffened so that it will remain smooth and firm. The pile may be cut by hand with a thin steel blade, but as this is tedious, time-consuming, and costly (except in countries where labor is cheap), machine cutting is generally used. The fabric is held under tension and moves under sharp knife blades. The blades cut the floats without damage to the base fabric. After the pile yarns have been cut, the fabric surface is brushed to bring the pile yarns into a position perpendicular to the fabric surface. Novel surface effects can be achieved by having different-length floats or shearing the floats to different lengths to produce patterns. Cutting some floats and leaving others uncut can also be used to create interesting fabric surfaces.

The floats for filling pile fabrics are interlaced using either a V or W interlacing (Fig. 22.41). The depth of the pile is controlled by the length of the floats, which is determined by a combination of the number of warp yarns over which the filling yarn is to float and the compactness of the base fabric. The W form of interlacing is more durable than the V, as the pile yarns are held down by two ground yarns instead of one.

Warp Pile

Warp-pile fabrics are those in which the pile is formed by extra warp yarns. Velvet, velour, rug velvet, and Wilton and Axminster rugs are made using extra warp yarns to form the pile. One set of the warp yarns interlaces with the set of filling yarns to form the base fabric, while the extra set of warp yarns is used to create the pile. Three general methods are used to make warp-pile fabrics: the wire-cut pile method, the looped-pile or terry cloth method, and the double-weave or double-cloth process.

The wire method involves the following steps. When a row of pile is to be formed, the warp yarns forming the pile are raised and a shed is formed with the ground yarns. A wire is inserted through the shed; the size of the wire is determined by the height the pile is to be. When the warp-pile yarns are lowered into place, they lie smoothly over the wire. The next filling for the ground is laid into position to hold the pile yarns in place. The wire is

22.42 Terry weaving machine with Jacquard attachment. (Picanol, Belgium)

22.43 Four-color rapier terry weaving machine. (Saurer Textile Machinery)

22.44 Double cloth using five sets of yarns.

then withdrawn. If a cut pile is to be produced, a very sharp knife is attached to the end of the wire and as it is pulled out it cuts the warp-pile yarns. If an uncut pile is made, the wire does not have a knife at the end and as it is withdrawn, it leaves the loops intact. If cut-pile fabrics do not have a uniform pile surface, the fabric may be sheared (see Chap. 27).

The wire method is frequently used in constructing fabric for floor coverings, and different-colored yarns may often be involved in producing the desired pattern. In some instances, several different-colored pile yarns may be carried along with ground yarns; this produces a very thick foundation or ground and increases the durability of the carpet.

The terry or looped-pile construction process depends on tension to form the loops. This construction is used to make terry cloth and may be used in making velour if the pile loops are sheared (cut) to form a cut-pile surface. The loops formed in this process are the result of control of tension on the yarns used in forming the pile. When the loops are to be formed, the extra warp yarns have the tension released so that they will be loose. When the reed packs the filling yarns into place, the warp yarns without tension form loops between the pick or filling yarns. Usually loops are formed on both sides of the fabric. The warp yarns forming the ground fabric are held under tension so that those yarns and the filling yarns produce a firm base or ground fabric. Warp yarns used for the pile in terry cloth are soft, fluffy, and highly absorbent, and have a low twist. This type of uncut-pile fabric is found in terry towels, robe fabric, some upholstery fabrics, and other home furnishing items. Patterned terry cloth, or any loop-pile construction using warp yarns for the pile, may be made into fabrics with complex de-

signs by having dobby or Jacquard attachments on the loom (Fig. 22.42). The loom for terry cloth requires two warp beams. One beam is at the rear of the loom, while the second beam is placed at the back but above the weaving surface (Fig. 22.43). This particular loom uses a rapier to place the filling yarns. The ground warp yarns are white; the yarns forming the loops provide the color. Filling yarns vary in color depending on the pattern. Shuttle looms and other types of shuttleless looms may be used in making pile fabrics just as they may be used for all types of woven fabric.

Double Weaves

Double-weave fabrics are made using two sets of warp yarns, two sets of filling yarns, and, if a true double weave, a fifth set of yarns that serve as the tie or binder holding the two layers of fabric together. Some double cloth does not use the fifth set of yarns.

Pile fabrics may be made using the double-weave construction as noted above. These fabrics are cut apart after the weaving to produce two distinct pile fabrics. Warp-pile fabrics, especially velvets, are frequently constructed using this process. In forming these fabrics, the yarns that become the pile are interlaced with one set of warp and one set of filling, forming one ground or base fabric. They then are passed to the other set of warp and filling, forming the second layer of fabric. When the fabrics have been woven, they are cut apart with a sharp knife. The pile yarns are severed and leave a cut-pile surface on each of the fabric layers. The fabric pile may be sheared (see Chap. 26) to even the pile height.

Other double fabrics are constructed with the tie or binder yarns held close to the surface of the two base fabrics so that they remain as a unit. A person may be able to separate such fabrics at selected locations; the ease of separation depends on the frequency of the tie or binder yarns, the strength of the yarn, the closeness with which they hold the two fabric layers together, and the interlacing pattern. Fiber type may also determine how well such fabrics hold together. Yarns of such fibers as wool tend to hold double fabrics together because of the surface characteristics of the wool fibers (Fig. 22.44).

Double fabrics are also made using two sets of warp and two of filling yarns without the tie or binder set. In these constructions, the interlacing process is controlled so that one set of warp and one

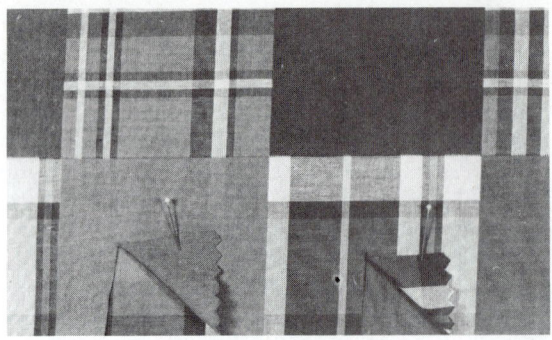

22.45 Double cloth using four sets of yarns.

set of filling yarns form one fabric layer and the other set forms the second layer; these may move from one fabric layer to the other in such a way that the fabrics interlock but in some locations remain distinct. One layer of the fabric cannot be destroyed without destroying the total fabric (Fig. 22.45).

A third type of double cloth, more accurately called a *backed fabric,* uses two sets of warp yarns and one set of filling yarns *or* two sets of filling yarns and one set of warp yarns. These are frequently interlaced so that each side of the finished fabric is of a different color. Blankets are frequently constructed using this method. Fabrics with two sets of warp yarns are called *warp-faced,* while those with two sets of filling are called *filling-faced.*

The double-weave construction is used in making a variety of fabrics. Heavy fabrics with complicated designs that are reversible are frequently double fabrics; such fabrics are often made with different-colored yarns so that the design exhibits different colors on each side of the fabric. For example, a coat fabric of double cloth might have a plaid face and a plain color back; or one side may have a plaid effect and the other stripes. Some double fabrics are not reversible. The second layer of fabric may be designed to provide stability only. Such fabrics are frequently designed for use in home furnishings, especially upholstery.

Matelassé and brocatelle fabrics are examples of double cloth in which extra sets of yarns are inter-

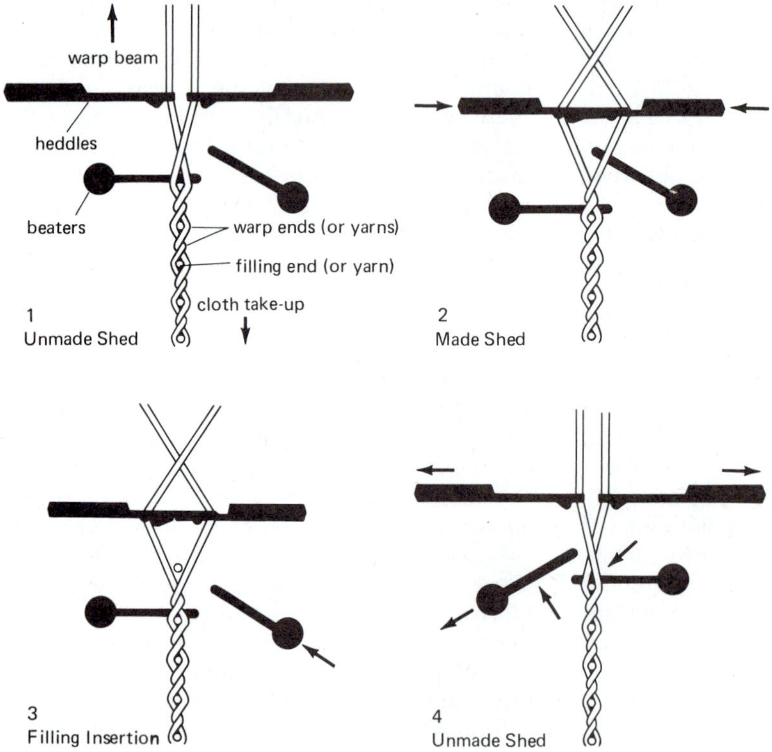

warp beam

heddles

beaters

warp ends (or yarns)

filling end (or yarn)

cloth take-up

1
Unmade Shed

2
Made Shed

3
Filling Insertion

4
Unmade Shed

(a) Shed formation

22.46 Diagram of triaxial weaving: shed formation.

(b)

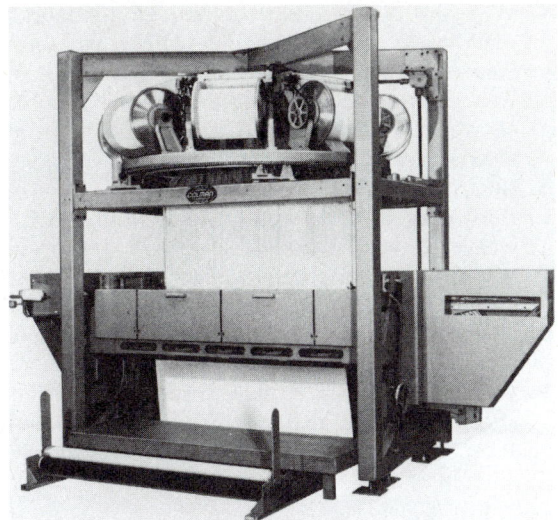

22.47 Triaxial weaving machine. (Barber-Coleman Company)

woven so as to create puffed effects on the face of the fabric. These fabrics may be lightweight and suitable for apparel or heavy enough for use in upholstery and draperies. By combining yarns of different colors, size, and types using dobby or Jacquard attachments, a wide variety of double-woven fabrics can be obtained.

Triaxial Weaving

Woven fabrics discussed to this point are *biaxial* or *orthogonal* structures. They are produced by interlacing warp and filling at 90° angles. Triaxial weaving uses three sets of yarn, which are interlaced at 60°

angles (Fig. 22.46). The warp is mounted on beams located above the weaving area; these beams rotate and release warp yarns as the weaving progresses. The warp yarns move vertically downward to the weaving zone, where the yarns change from a parallel path to a plane in opposing 60° angles. Filling is inserted using a rigid rapier system (Fig. 22.47). The fabric does not have a standard selvage since the warp yarns form the selvage as they cross back into the weaving plane. The warp yarns form a diagonal path from one side of the fabric to the other, then reverse and return to the opposite side. This is repeated for all warp yarns during the weaving process. The filling yarns are inserted and packed into position using open beater fingers rather than a standard reed in the battening or beater frame. One set of fingers maintains the previous filling end in position while the next filling is being inserted and then packed into place.

Triaxial fabrics have exceptionally high burst resistance, which makes them highly desirable for end uses where great pressure is focused on the fabric. Because of the three-way construction, they have outstanding tear resistance. Further properties include uniform strength in all directions, no distinct bias weakness or extra stretch, ravel resistance, and good resistance to shear forces.

Another advantage of triaxial weaving is that it can produce strong fabrics that are lighter in weight than biaxial fabrics of the same strength. Less raw material is required because of the greater strength of the fabric. Products tend to have a longer wear life than biaxial weaves; there is high seam efficiency or strength with little slippage; and fabrics can be designed for special end uses.

22.48 Triaxial weave constructions. Left: Basic weave. Center: Basic basket weave. Right: Bi-plain weave. (Barber-Coleman Company)

Triaxial fabrics are finding widespread use in technical applications, and there have been some general-purpose applications. Three basic types of triaxial weaves are currently produced: the basic triaxial weave, a basic basket weave, and a bi-plain weave (Fig. 22.48). A major use of the process has been in the production of carbon fabrics to be used in composite fabrics for aerospace and industrial applications. Other uses for triaxial fabrics include gas-fired balloons, sailcloth, truck covers, and apparel, particularly uniforms and outerwear where light weight, wrinkle resistance, and a good hand are desired. Uses under consideration include upholstery fabric for home furnishings, airplane seats, bus and other automotive seats, foundation garments, swimsuits, athletic uniforms, and canvas shoes. Triaxial fabrics are successful as the base for coated fabric; they work well in geotextile applications. It is anticipated that triaxial weaving will become increasingly popular during the coming decade.

STUDY QUESTIONS

1. How do the plain weave, twill weave, and satin weave differ? How are they alike? List various modifications for each of the basic weaves.
2. What developments in weaving fabric have occurred during the past two decades? What effect has the increased use of shuttleless looms had on the cost of woven fabrics? What other factors have been influenced by these new weaving machines?
3. What are figure weaves? How do they differ from basic weaves?
4. What are typical care requirements for fabrics made using the plain weave, twill weave, satin weave, dobby weave, Jacquard weaves, spot weaves (both cut and uncut), leno weave, double weave, pile weaves (both cut and uncut), and triaxial weaves?
5. Describe the basic steps in weaving.
6. How does a satin weave differ from a twill weave? How are they alike?
7. Which of the basic weaves is generally the most durable? Why?
8. How can plain-weave fabrics be given a variety of appearances?
9. What differences are there in the care, appearance, and durability of dobby-weave fabrics and Jacquard-weave fabrics? What accounts for the differences?

Activities

1. Using cardboard and yarn, prepare samples of fabrics made from the plain weave, basket weave, twill weave, and satin weave.
2. Select samples of a variety of woven fabrics currently on the market and analyze them to determine the type of weave used.
3. If a laboratory is available, perform various physical tests on woven fabrics such as the determination of strength, abrasion resistance, tearing strength, shrinkage, crease resistance, and strength of seams made in the fabrics. Then compare results among the different fabrics.
4. Visit fabric departments in stores and identify the particular type or types of weaves that are currently popular.

23

Knitted Fabrics

KEY TERMS

circular knitting machines
course
crochet knits
double knit
filling knit
flatbed knitting
 machine
gauge
interlock

jersey or flat stitch
knit loop
milanese knits
miss stitch
purl or reverse
 loop
raschel knits
rib knit
simplex knits

single knit
stockinette stitch
tricot knits
tuck-loop
wale
warp knit
warp-knitting
 machines
weft insertion

Knitted fabrics date back to at least A.D. 256. Other examples support the premise that knitting was used as a method for forming fabric structures in very early civilizations. The use of knitted structures made by machines dates from 1589, when an Englishman, William Lee, developed the first mechanical knitting frame. This machine was a flatbed unit and used spring-beard needles. It remained substantially the same for over 200 years. J. Strut developed a ribbing device during the late eighteenth century, and M. Brunel invented the circular knitting machine in 1816. M. Townshend patented the latch needle in 1849. Although major improvements have been made in knitting machines during the twentieth century, the basic principle of interlooping of yarns remains much the same.

Production and consumption of knitted fabrics increased dramatically between 1866 and the mid-1950s. Even greater advances, particularly in controls and computerization of knitting machines, have occurred during the 1970s and early 1980s. Knitted fabrics continue to be used in a wide variety of end uses, and during the latter half of the twentieth century, these types of fabric structures have

found widespread use in many areas thought to be the sole province of woven structures. In the early 1960s, knitted fabrics represented 24 percent of all apparel fabrics; by the mid-1970s this had risen to approximately 50 percent. Since that time knitted fabrics have maintained a relatively constant level of popularity, although the early 1980s saw a return to woven fabrics, particularly for outer wearing apparel.

There are several reasons for consumer acceptance of knitted fabrics. Knits can be made rapidly, so yarn-to-fabric expenses are much lower and quality fabrics can be produced at comparatively low cost. The increase in travel, especially by air, resulted in the need for lightweight and comfortable clothes that require little care and maintain their neat appearance after sitting or packing. Knitted fabrics fit these needs. The tendency for knits to resist wrinkling has been an important factor in their acceptance and continued use.

Knitting is commonly defined as forming a fabric by means of interlooping yarns. In machine knitting, loops of yarn are formed with the aid of thin pointed needles or shafts. As new loops are formed, they are drawn through the previously shaped loops. This interlooping and the continued formation of new loops produces a knit fabric. Two general methods are used in making knit fabrics: *weft knitting* (or *filling knitting*) and *warp knitting*.

In the construction and analysis of knit fabrics, two terms are used frequently: *wale* and *course* (Fig. 23.1). *Wale* refers to a column of loops that are parallel to the loop axis. The wales also run parallel to the longer measurement of a knit fabric. A *course* is a series of successive loops lying crosswise of the knit fabric, that is, at right angles to a line passing from the open throat to the closed end of the loops.

WEFT OR FILLING KNITTING

Weft or filling knitting is a construction process in which the fabric is made by a yarn forming loops across the width of the fabric or around a circle. Each yarn is fed at more or less a right angle to the direction in which the fabric is built. The term *weft*

is taken from weaving terminology. In weaving, the term is used synonymously with filling or pick to refer to the crosswise yarns that are laid during the weaving operation. Weft-knit fabrics can be made by machines; weft knitting is also the technique usually used in hand-knitting. A considerable amount of filling-knit fabric is made on a circular knitting machine, in which a series of needles is arranged around the circumference of a circle. Fabric

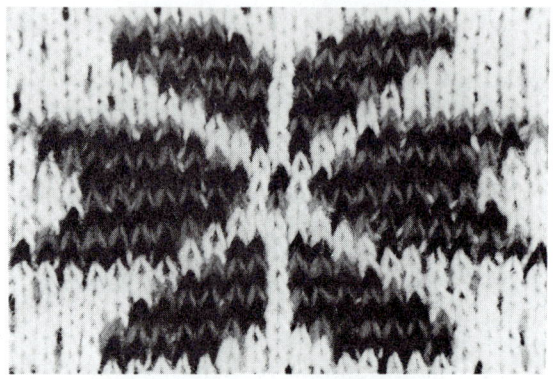

23.1 *Knit fabric showing wales and courses.*

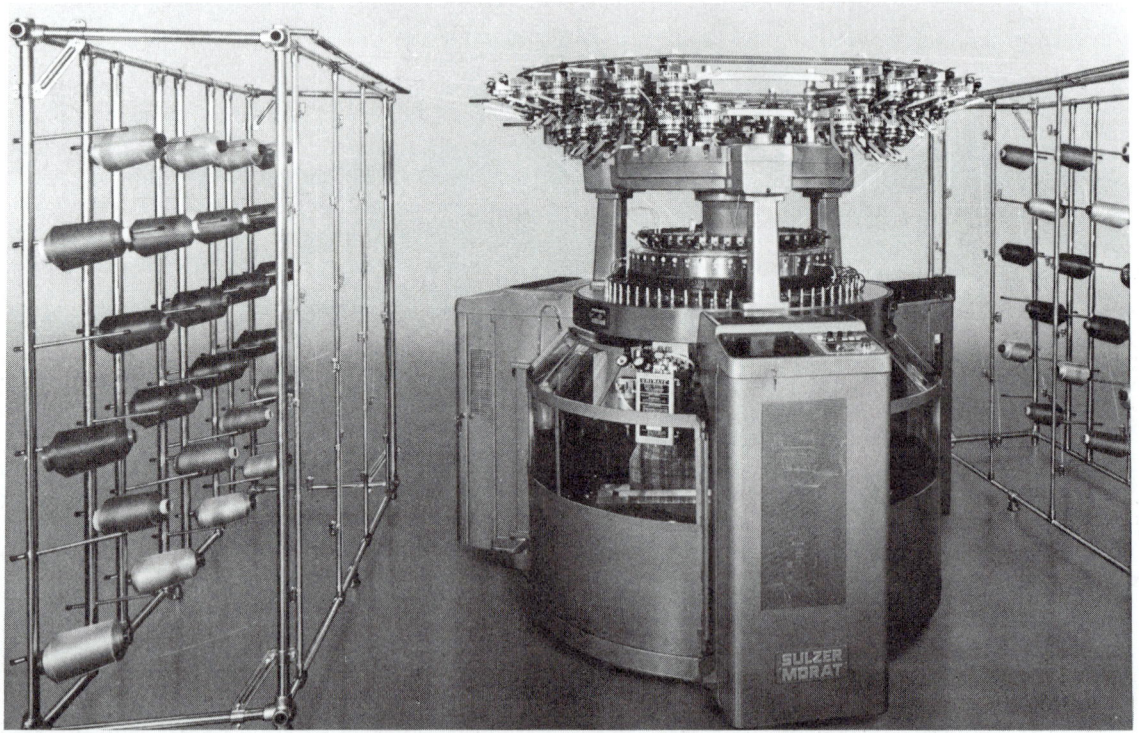

23.2 *Circular knitting machine for weft knitting.* (Sulzer-Morat)

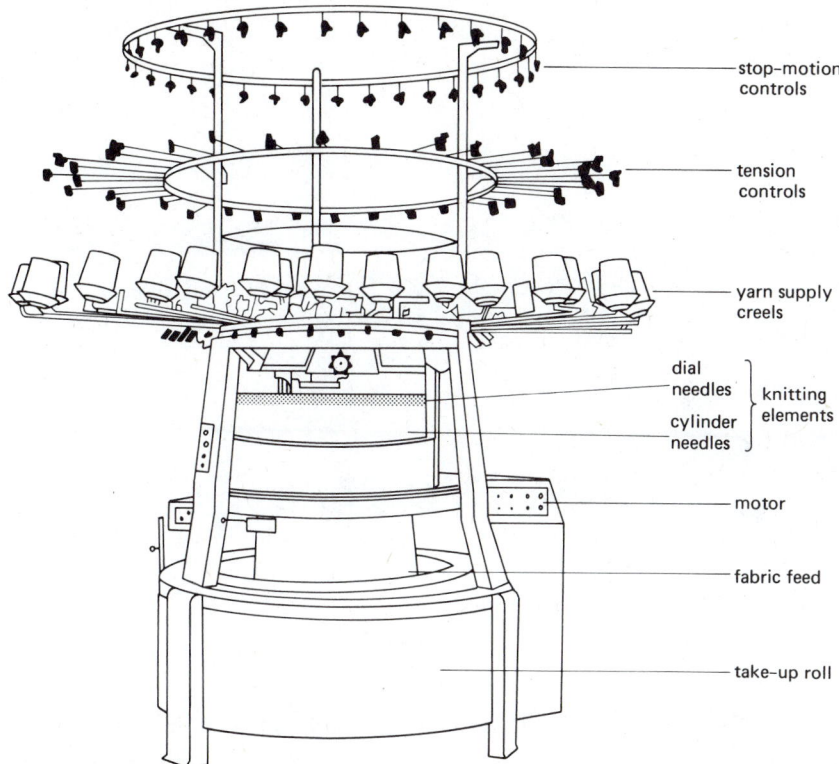

stop-motion controls

tension controls

yarn supply creels

dial needles } knitting elements
cylinder needles }

motor

fabric feed

take-up roll

23.3 Diagram of a circular knitting machine. This is a double-knit unit. Yarns feed from the supply packages to the top and then down through various controls to the knitting area.

may be made in the shape of a tube; if a flat fabric is desired, the tube can be cut open. Many fabrics, in fact, are made with a specific location for slitting the fabric open. Such knits could not be used in tube form. Other circular knits are designed so that they may be used in the cylinder or tube form in which they are made; adjustments are made for shaping to a figure or form for end use. Figure 23.2 is an example of a modern circular knitting machine with large creels for the yarn packages from which yarn is fed directly to the knitting positions. Figure 23.3 is a diagram of a circular knitting machine in which the yarn packages are located on the upper portion of the machine.

Knitting machines used for weft knitting may also be of the flatbed type. In these the needles are arranged parallel to each other in a flat plane (Fig. 23.4). Flatbed machines that are used to make ribbed knit fabrics have two sets of needles arranged to form a V shape with the open end of the V parallel to the base of the machine (Fig. 23.5).

Knitting requires four basic components: a yarn

supply source; knitting elements or needles, which form the loops and build the fabric; fabric take-down; and fabric collections. The yarn supply for weft knitting may be located above the knitting area or on large creels at the side. If at the side, the yarns are carried to the top of the knitting machine and are fed down to the knitting area. The knitting process includes the needles that permit the loops to be formed, held on the needle until a new loop is made, and then "knocked off" to gradually build the knit structure. After the knitting, the fabric is carried to a roll at the base of the machine.

The actual knitting elements include the needles, sinkers, the needle bed or frame that holds the needles, and the yarn carriers that lay the yarn in knitting position. There are two basic types of needles, latch and beard (Fig. 23.6). Although either may be used for weft knitting, the latch needle is more common. The action of the needles is controlled by cams of various types, which determine the appearance of the knit fabric. Considerable weft knitting is done on circular machines. Flatbed ma-

23.4 *Flatbed knitting machine.* (Universal Maschinenfabrik.)

23.5 *Close-up of **V** bed knitting machine.* (Universal Maschinenfabrik.)

chines are desired for knitting specific shapes and for producing "full-fashioned" knit pieces. Both circular and flatbed machines can produce highly patterned fabrics through the use of various types of controls such as computer controls. Attachments similar to those used for Jacquard weaves may be used to create elaborate knit patterns, which may be called Jacquard knits.

There are two general types of weft-knitting machines: single knitting frames and double knitting frames or machines. Single knitting machines can be either of the flatbed type or circular (Fig. 23.7). Double knits are usually produced on circular knitting machines.

Four types of loops or stitches can be formed in regular knitting. This process is controlled by the cams, which in turn control the needle action. The loops are identified as the *knit* or *plain loop,* the *tuck loop,* the *purl* or *reverse loop,* and the *miss stitch* (Fig. 23.8). The knit or plain loop is the basic stitch and occurs as a result of the steps cited for both single and double knits.

The knit stitch shows the neck of the loop on the face of the fabric and the head of the loop on the back. These stitches produce a fine fabric with a smooth face; there is a definite face and back or reverse side.

The purl or reverse knit stitch forms a fabric that resembles the reverse side of the knit or plain stitch

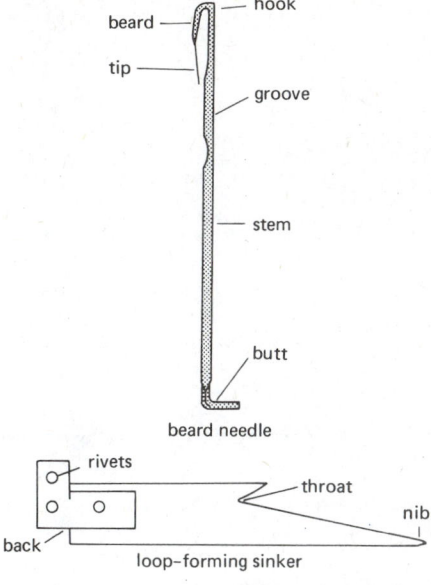

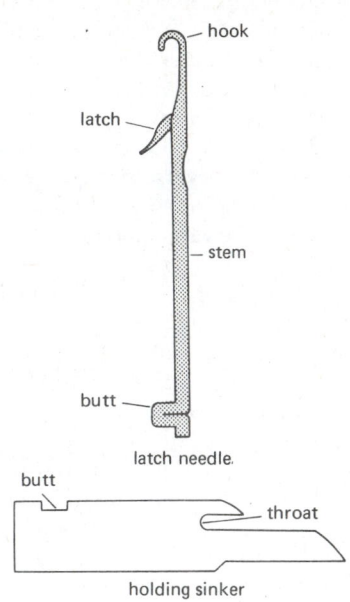

beard
hook
tip
groove
stem
butt
beard needle

rivets
throat
back
nib
loop-forming sinker

hook
latch
stem
butt
latch needle

butt
throat
holding sinker

23.6 Diagram of latch and beard knitting needles.

23.7 Single knit circular machine. (Mayer and Cie)

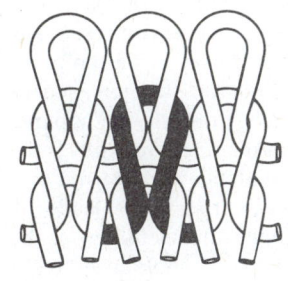

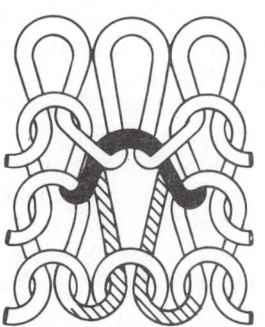

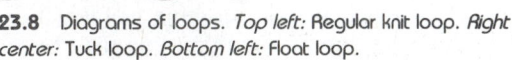

23.8 Diagrams of loops. *Top left:* Regular knit loop. *Right center:* Tuck loop. *Bottom left:* Float loop.

Knitted fabrics **243**

on both face and back. The purl stitch produces a fabric that is fuller and puffier than that made by the plain stitch. The fabric is reversible, as it does appear the same on face and reverse side.

The miss stitch or loop is characterized by yarns floating unlooped on the reverse side of the fabric. The needle in a miss loop or stitch does not move into position to accept the yarn, and no actual stitch or loop is formed.

The tuck stitch or loop is formed when the needle raises only partially and retains the previous stitch as well as picking up yarn to form a second stitch in the same needle. Tuck stitches may hold more than two stitches for some designs. The tuck stitch tends to create open spaces and is used to form lace effects, mesh designs, open-work patterns, blister effects, and bumpy textures in knit fabrics.

Plain knit fabrics have distinct but flat vertical lines on the face and dominant horizontal lines on the reverse side (Fig. 23.9). Hand-knitters recognize this effect as the *stockinette* pattern, which is used more frequently than any other because the process is rapid and inexpensive. Furthermore, flat stitch knitting can be varied to produce run-resist and fancy patterned knit fabrics. Jersey or flat knits are used in making hosiery, lingerie, sweaters, sportswear, and a variety of fabrics, primarily for apparel.

A major disadvantage of regular plain knits is the ease with which they drop stitches if the yarn is broken. This results in vertical "runs" or "ladders," which destroy the appearance and usefulness of the fabric. Some plain knits, such as wool jersey, resist running because of the tendency for the wool fibers to cling together. A variety of variations in the plain stitch have been developed as one measure to reduce runs in knit fabrics. One variation is diagramed in Figure 23.10.

The purl stitch (Fig. 23.11) produces fabrics that are similar to the reverse side of the jersey stitch. These are identified as purl knits. The purl stitch is frequently used in the manufacture of bulky knits such as sweaters and a variety of other apparel fabrics. Recently this stitch has been popular in fashion articles. As the purl stitch produces fabric with the same appearance on both sides, there is no problem in cutting and preparing it for the construction of end-use items, especially when no design has been applied to one side. Knitters consider the production of this stitch to be a slow process and thus more costly; some believe that machine maintenance is required more often for purl knitting than for reg-

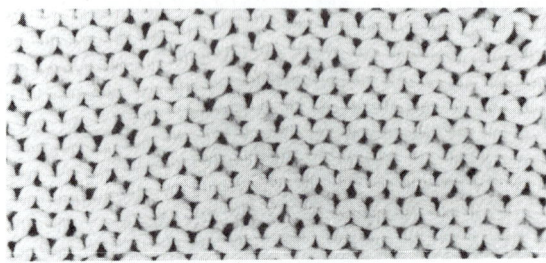

23.9 Flat or jersey knit, face and back.

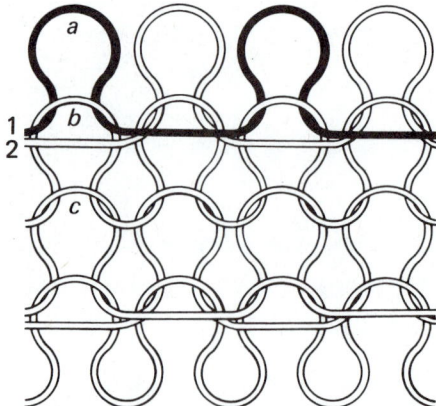

23.10 Diagram of a run-resist flat-knit stitch used for some hosiery and similar fabrics. Numbers indicate horizontal yarns; letters identify loops.

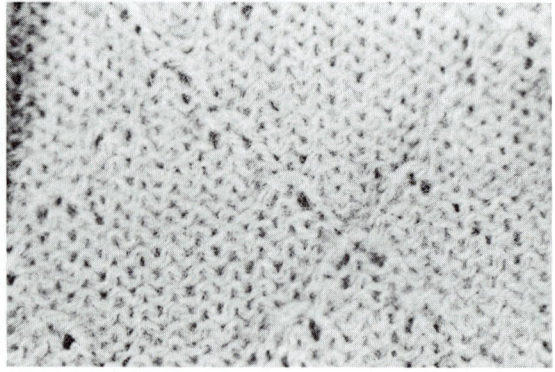

23.11 Purl stitch.

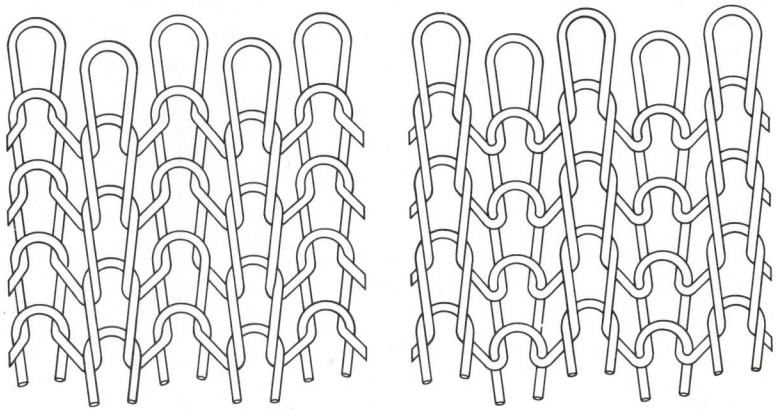

(a)

(b)

23.12 Diagram of rib knits. A: 1 × 1 rib face. B: 1 × 1 rib knit, back.

23.13 Rib-knit fabric.

23.14 Diagram of interlock fabric.

ular plain jersey or stockinette knitting. However, there is some evidence that new knitting machines do not present these problems. The purl stitch creates fabrics with considerable stretch in both directions and with more bulk than other knit stitches.

The rib knit (Fig. 23.12) is usually made on a V-flatbed machine where two sets of needles face each other and form a V. The stitches intermesh in opposite directions on a walewise basis, and the frequency of intermeshing determines the type of rib. If intermeshing occurs at every other wale, it is a 1 × 1 rib; if it occurs every two wales, the result is a 2 × 2 rib (Fig. 23.13). Uneven ribs can be produced by interlooping in one direction for a certain number of wales and a different number in the other direction. Rib fabrics can be knitted on circular knitting machines equipped with both cylinder and dial needles.

The rib pattern is used whenever stretch is desired, and the resulting fabric has an excellent degree of elasticity. Rib knits also tend to be warm. The primary disadvantage of rib knits is high cost due to the increase in fabric weight and the use of more yarns per area. Production of fabric using the rib pattern tends to be lower than for jersey or purl stitches. Rib-knit fabrics are found at lower edges of sweaters and sleeves, at necklines, and wherever considerable stretch but close fit is desired.

The interlock knit (Fig. 23.14) is a variation of the rib knit. In construction it resembles two separate 1 × 1 rib fabrics that are interknitted. Interlock fabrics are thicker and heavier than regular rib fabrics of the same gage. *Gage* or *gauge* refers to fineness of a knit fabric and is identified by the number of needles per unit of width, per inch or per 1½ inches. Most recent literature uses the number of needles per inch as the gage.

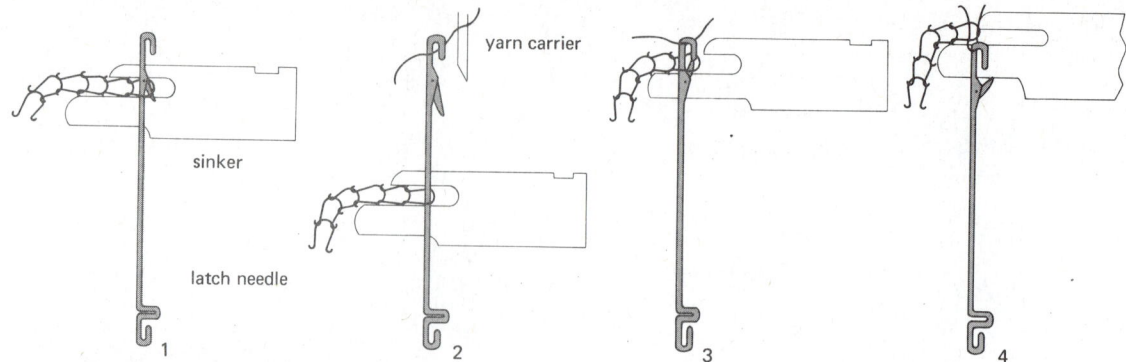

23.15 Diagram of stitch formation in single knitting.

23.16 Double-knit fabric

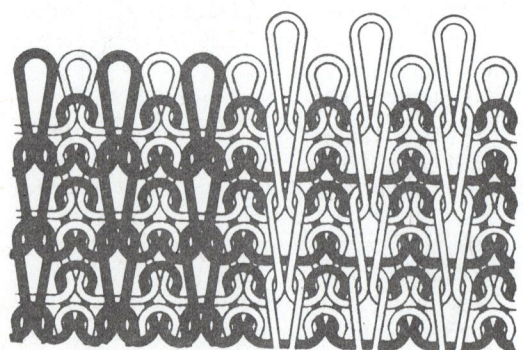

23.17 Diagram of an example of a Jacquard knit.

Interlock fabrics are constructed so that they appear identical on both face and back or reverse side. This characteristic can be modified through surface design or through the use of different-colored yarns in selected locations. Interlock knits have a soft hand, good moisture absorbency, and high dimensional stability. They can be cut easily for construction, do not curl at the edges, and sew easily. Yarns of most any weight may be used; fabrics are firm and have good durability.

Interlock knits may be constructed using the same type of machines as those used for plain, purl, or rib knit. However, the majority of interlock knits made since the late 1970s are constructed on circular double-knit machines.

Single Knits

Single-knit fabric may be plain, ribbed, highly patterned, or a combination of these. The knitting elements are latch needles, holding sinkers, and the yarn carrier. The basic steps in stitch formation, as shown in Figure 23.15, are as follows:

1. The needle is in the running or rest position. The last-formed loop is on the latch of the needle, and the sinker is ahead holding the fabric.
2. The needle is pushed up by the cam to the uppermost or clearing position. The previous loop has slipped off the latch and lies on the stem of the needle. The sinker is still forward, holding down the formed loops. The yarn carrier feeds the yarn to the hook.
3. After the yarn is in the hook, the needle begins to lower. The holding sinker retracts to permit the needle to drop low enough so that the yarn in the hook is pulled through the previously

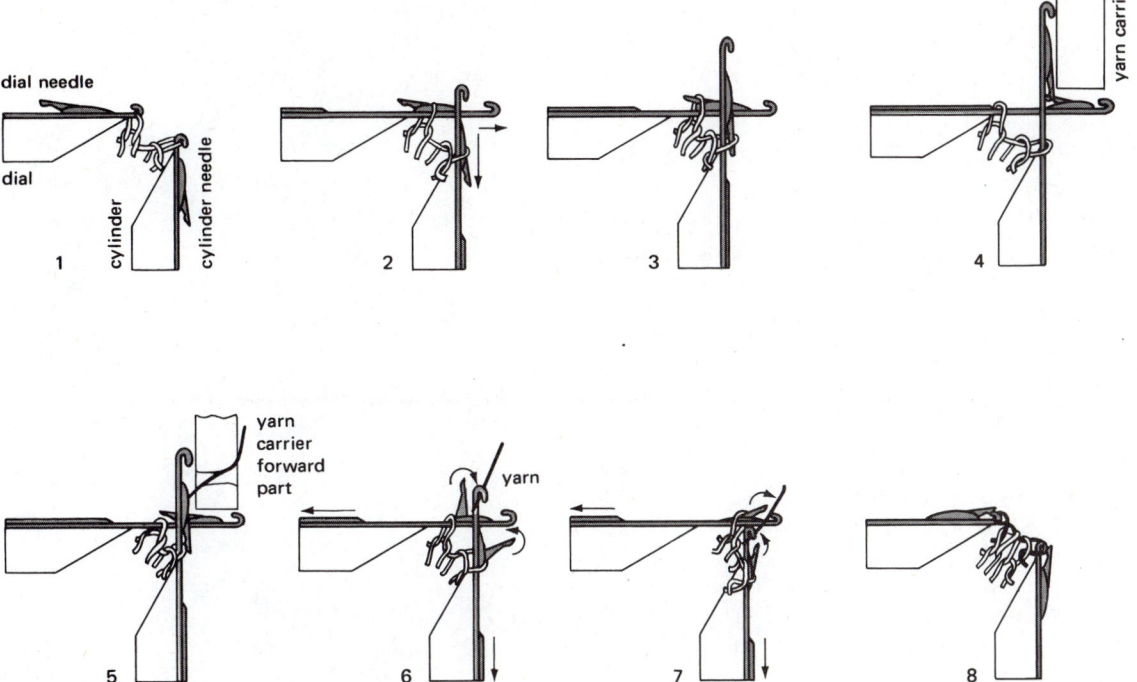

23.18 Diagram of stitch formation in double knitting.

formed loop. The old loop closes the latch, and thus the yarn is held securely in place, ready for a new loop.

4. The needle drops to its lowest position, forming the new loop. The sinker begins to move forward to push the old loop ahead and hold the fabric. The process is then repeated until the fabric is ready to be removed from the machine.

Double Knits

Double knits are produced using the interlock stitch (Fig. 23.16) and by variations of that process. Both surfaces of the fabric appear somewhat riblike. Decorative effects can be achieved using special Jacquard attachments for individual control of yarns. Most of these attachments in use today are controlled by some type of computerized program or electronic controls. The flexibility provided by the individual control of the needles makes it possible to produce a wide variety of fabric designs.

Double knits can be made also by knitting two distinct filling- or weft-knit fabrics that are periodi-

cally bound together by an additional set of yarns. Figure 23.17 is a diagram of a double knit in which two different-colored yarns have been used in developing a pattern.

The manufacture of double knits requires special circular machines with two sets of needles (see Fig. 23.3). The dial needles lie parallel to the floor around the circumference of the central knitting area; the cylinder needles are perpendicular to the floor and lie against the cylinder on which the dial needles are placed. Steps in forming the stitches for double knits are as follows (Fig. 23.18):

1. The needles are in the nonknit or running position, with the previously formed loops in the hooks of both dial and cylinder needles.
2. The dial needle starts its forward motion and the cylinder needle starts upward. As the dial needle moves, the cylinder needle holds the previously formed loop in place.
3. The needles continue their motion; while the cylinder needle holds the stitch on the dial needle, the dial needle simultaneously holds the stitch on the cylinder needle.
4. The two needles reach their forward and upward

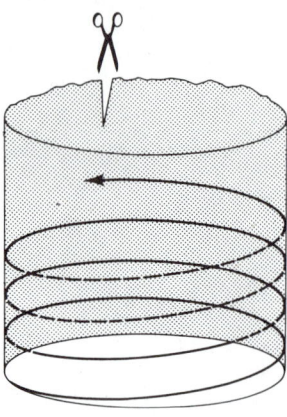

23.19 Diagram of a circular knit showing the spiral yarn path that results from feeding many yarns nearly simultaneously.

motions, and the yarn carrier moves into position to make certain the latches on the needles stay open. Note that the previously formed loops are on the needle stems behind the latches.

5. The yarn carrier continues its movement and lays new yarn in the hooks. The needles are moving back and down, and the old loops are beginning to lift the latches.

6. The needles continue their reverse motion; the old loops are moving up and partially closing the latches.

7. The yarn is in the dial hook and the cylinder hook. The latches are almost closed, and the old loops are almost ready to slide over the ends of the needles.

8. The needles are in the back or down position. The latches are closed, and the new loops have been pulled through the old loops. The last step is frequently called knocking off or knocking down the stiches.

The action occurs simultaneously for each end of yarn being fed. For most double knits, about 48 ends of yarn feed to the knitting area, and there are about 1800 needles in the cylinder and 1800 in the dial. The fabric builds up in a spiral form rather than at a true 90° angle, as occurs in the interlacing of warp and filling in weaving (Fig. 23.19). Single knits made on circular machines are also constructed using this spiral configuration.

Double knits are usually constructed on circular knitting frames; the interlock stitch, used in making some double-knit fabrics, can be done on flatbed machines that have two sets of needles set into the V position. All double knits require two sets of needles, whereas single knits require only one set.

23.21 Double-knit fabric: face and back of Jacquard design.

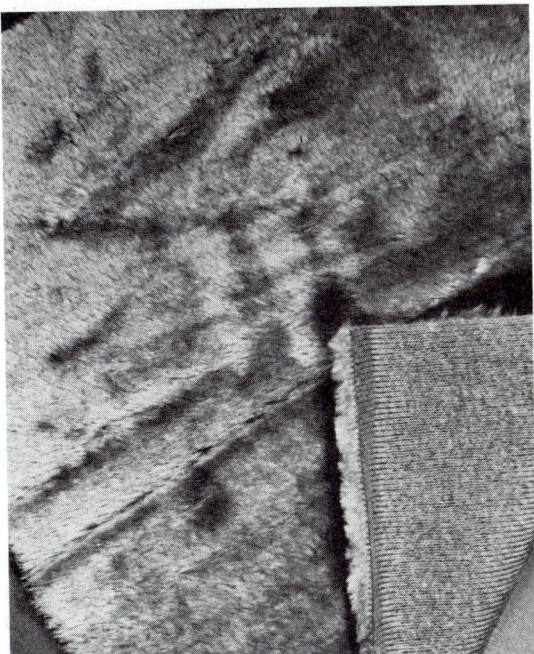

23.22 Pile fabric with weft-knit base.

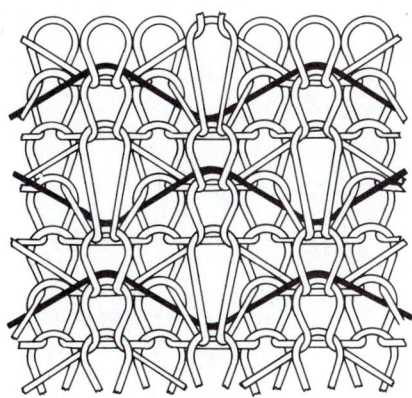

23.23 Diagram of laying extra yarns in weft insertion.

During the past few years the production of patterned or Jacquard knits has become highly sophisticated. Most double-knit machines have design capabilities that are controlled electronically. These computer-assisted-design controls make possible complex design changes in a matter of minutes. Even for older knitting machines, the time required to change patterns is considerably shorter than that needed in changing patterns for the weaving process. The use of electronic controls makes it possible to reproduce complicated designs and to copy art in a matter of minutes instead of months as required a few decades ago (Figs. 23.20 and 23.21).

Double knits have better stability than most single knits and resist the formation of runs. Double knits are easier to sew than single knits and do not tend to curl at the edges as many single knits do. Double knits are firmer, heavier, less stretchable, and more resilient than single-knit fabrics. Single knits can be made considerably finer and sheerer than double knits.

Knitted-Pile Fabrics

Knitted-pile fabrics are usually made by the weft- or filling-knit process, using procedures that closely re-

semble double knitting. To produce the pile, an extra set of yarns is drawn out in long loops and then cut or left uncut depending on the desired effect. The base fabric is generally a plain stockinette stitch. Many pile fabrics made to resemble fur are actually made using a knit-pile construction (Fig. 23.22). Many knit-pile fabrics now are constructed using a soft yarn sliver for the pile rather than regular yarns. The sliver is fluffy and soft and creates a rich, luxurious fabric.

Yarn Insertion

Yarn insertion or *laying-in* techniques involve the addition of extra yarns as the fabric is being knitted. The process permits the use of a variety of novelty yarns that might not have the strength to be processed by the regular knitting operation. Furthermore, yarns with considerable surface interest can be used for laying-in even though these yarns might not be acceptable to the action of feeding through needles. Such fabrics tend to have a high surface interest. Laying-in is also used as a method of inserting heavy-duty yarns that will be held to the back of the fabric and provide strength, stability, and warmth rather than having visual or even tactile value. Yarn insertion techniques for weft knitting can be used in making either single- or double-knit fabrics with special designs. A typical example of insertion, in this case a double knit, is shown in Figure 23.23.

Loosely twisted yarns, which adapt well to brushing or raising techniques, can be used in making fabrics with inserted or laid-in yarns. Following construction, the surface of the fabric is brushed or

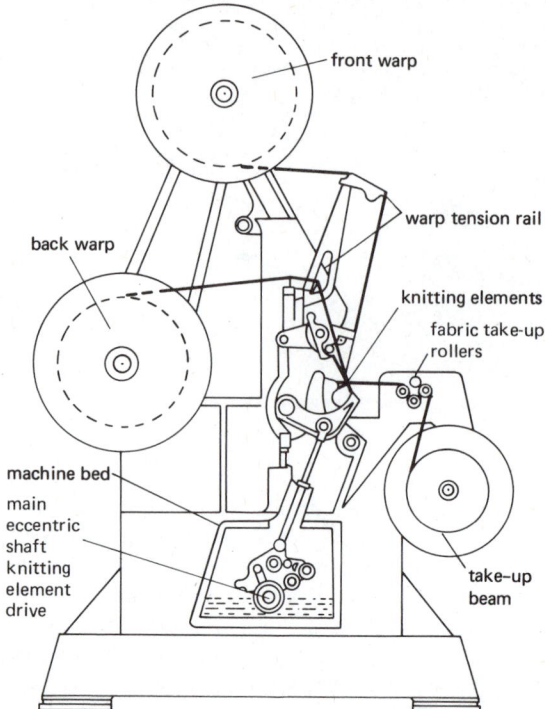

23.24 Diagram of tricot knitting machine.

cation of the yarn supply, and the interlooping of parallel yarns, the machines used are sometimes called *knitting looms* (Fig. 23.24).

Essentially, warp knitting is a system for producing fabric that is flat, has straight side edges, and is manufactured rapidly and in large quantities. Warp knits are classified according to the type of equipment used and to special characteristics of the resulting fabrics. The types are tricot, raschel, milanese, and simplex. The most common types are tricot and raschel.

Warp-knit fabrics have some elongation or stretchability, although it may be less than for filling knits. The amount of extension is influenced by the type of construction (such as single bar tricot, double-bar tricot, raschel); the tightness of the knitting (the tighter the knit, the lower the amount of stretch); finishing techniques, which can impart good dimensional stability; gage (number of needles per unit of width); and type of yarn (for example, core-spun stretch yarns, complex yarns with little or no stretch, single or ply yarns of high dimensional stability).

The strength of warp-knit fabrics may be increased by using yarns of strong fibers, yarns of balanced construction, and a high gage with strong, fine yarns. A combination of yarns of different fibers, or of different types of yarns (simple, ply, complex), and space between loops affects the strength of the fabric.

napped to give a soft, attractive appearance and hand. If done correctly, these processes do not reduce fabric strength.

WARP KNITTING

The term *warp knitting* is also adapted from weaving technology. Warp knitting differs from weft or filling knitting in that the loops are formed in a vertical or warpwise direction and yarns lying side by side are interlooped. Machines used for warp knitting tend to look somewhat like weaving machines. All of the yarns are placed on beams and are located behind and above the actual knitting area. All yarns feed into the knitting area at the same time. Each yarn is manipulated by one specific needle as the interlooping proceeds; however, guide bars control the placement of the yarn, and the particular needle forming the loop may vary from one interlooping action to the next. Jacquard attachments can be used to provide for special needle controls and the making of highly patterned warp knits. Because of the knitting process used in warp knitting, the lo-

Tricot Knits

Tricot knits originated in England during the latter part of the eighteenth century. Plain or decorative tricot fabrics can be made on the same machine; the difference is determined by the patterns used in the interlooping operation. This means that a variety of knit fabrics can be manufactured at the same general price level and at the same speed. The interlooping of the adjacent yarns can be controlled so that yarns lying next to each other are interlooped or yarns lying a few yarns away from each other can be interlooped. This flexibility helps to provide the different types of tricot knits and the resulting variety in fabric appearance and character.

Tricot fabrics, like weft knits, can be made using either latch or beard needles. However, beard needles are the most common for tricot knitting. Therefore, the steps for making a tricot are diagramed (Fig. 23.25A) showing beard needles.

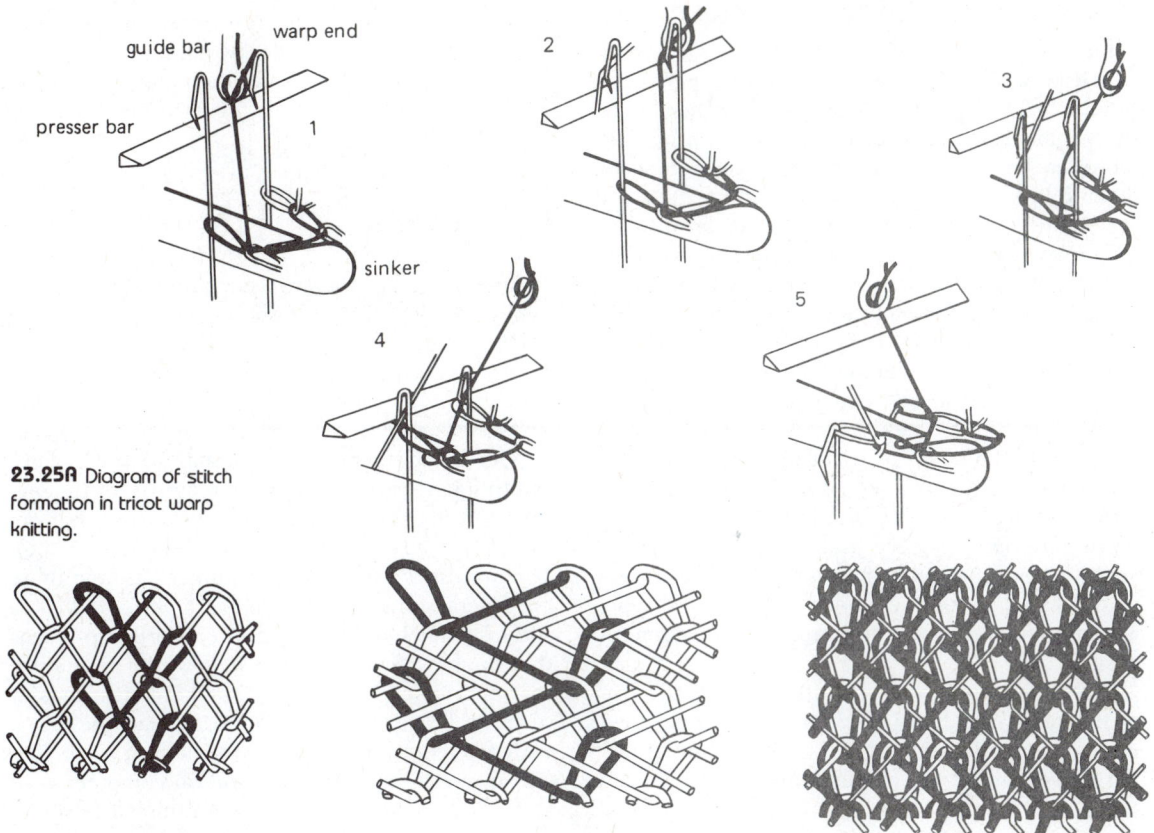

23.25A Diagram of stitch formation in tricot warp knitting.

23.25B *Left:* Single-guide-bar diagram. *Center:* Single guide bar with 2-stitch underlap. *Right:* Two-guide-bar diagram.

1. Step 1 shows the various parts that make tricot knitting possible. Note the warp end, which would be coming from the beam of yarn on the knitting machine, the guide bar that controls the placement of each yarn, the presser bar that helps control the closing of the needle, the sinker that helps to control the movement of formed loops and fabric. The beard needles have a spring type of hook without any latch (see Fig. 23.6). In step 1 the needles are in their highest position, the previous loops are on the stems of the needles, and the sinker is holding down the formed fabric.

2. The guide bar carrying the yarn that formed the last loop on the left needle moves to the right to place the yarn in the needle to the right. A yarn from the far left is being placed in the left needle.

3. The yarn is against the needle stem, and the needles are starting their descent. As the needles move down, the yarn is trapped in the hooks. The presser bar moves toward the needles, and the sinker moves away.

4. The yarn is in the hook. The presser bar moves in and forces the tips of the needles against the stems to hold the yarn in place and to permit the needles to pull the yarn through the previously formed loops.

5. The needles have moved to their lowest position, the new loops are formed, and the old loops have been knocked off. The sinker moves back in to hold the fabric. The needles will return to the upper position, and the steps will be repeated. The guide bar carries the yarn to either the right or left in order to form the vertical interlooping of stitches.

Tricot knits are identified as single-guide-bar, two-guide-bar, or more, depending on the number of yarns and guide bars used for each needle in making the interlooping pattern. The simplest tricot is the single bar with movement between adjacent needles only (Fig. 23.25B, left). A single-bar tricot in which the guide bar moves over two needles is shown in Figure 23.25B, center. In forming this fabric, each guide bar carries the yarn over one needle and lays the yarn into the second needle from the one in which the previous loop was formed.

A two-guide-bar tricot in which two different colors of yarn have been used is shown in Figure 23.25B, right. With two or more guide bars, a variety of designs can be made using different types and colors of yarns in each guide bar. Most modern tricot machines have between two and four guide bars.

The characteristics of tricot knits include good air and water permeability, softness, crease resistance, good drapability, nonfray or nonraveling properties, run resistance, and elasticity. Tricot fabrics can be given special finishes that control dimensional stability, and the choice of fiber, yarn type, and closeness of yarn help provide the strength desired.

The thickness of tricot is influenced by the size of the yarns used, by the tightness or compactness of the stitches (the gage), the length of the guide-bar movement as well as the number of guide bars used, and finishing techniques such as calendering (see Chap. 26). Fabrics with a sheer and filmy appearance, such as those used for fine lingerie and nightwear, are made from fine yarns, usually of strong fibers such as nylon. Firm, relatively opaque fabrics are made from medium-size yarns closely spaced. A special finishing procedure using calendering may be applied to tricot knits to decrease thickness of the fabric and at the same time increase the opacity.

Prices for tricot-knit fabric have been generally higher than for weft knits; however, they are usually less costly than woven fabrics. Price is influenced by the cost of machinery and operation, as well as the cost of preparing the beams of yarn. Even though these fabrics may be made more rapidly than weft knits, other factors combine to influence the actual cost.

Tricot-knit fabrics appear in a variety of end uses. Typical applications include lingerie fabrics, nightwear, blouses, dresses, and other apparel items. Tricot may be used for some home furnishings, but because of the extensibility of such fabrics, this use is considerably less common. Tricot is frequently used as the backing fabric in multicompo-

nent structures (see Chap. 25), where it may serve as a built-in lining. Because tricot knits can be lightweight and are less expensive than most woven fabrics, they have been used as a lining for some quilted bedspreads.

Raschel Knits

Raschel knitting is a warp-knitting technique that offers the manufacturer tremendous flexibility in fabric design. It is one of the most versatile methods for producing fabric and is particularly important in making highly patterned knit fabrics and crochet knits.

The equipment used is similar to tricot warp knitting in that all of the yarns required for the regular knitting portion are placed on beams that are in turn placed on the raschel machine (Fig. 23.26). The machines usually use beard needles, and there are several guide bars for the warp yarns as well as special guide bars to control the insertion of yarns that can be "laid in" during the knitting to produce special design effects. Not all raschel knits use laid-in yarns, however. Raschel knitting machines use a variety of controls to develop the pattern in the fabric; most new machines depend on computer controls. The computer can be programmed to direct

23.26 Raschel knitting machine with electronic controls for pattern design. Fabric would be rolled on other side of machine. (Cidega Manufacturing Company)

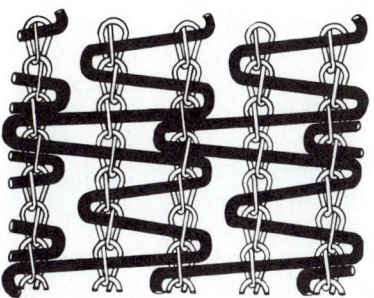

23.27 Diagram of a simple raschel crochet knit. (National Knitwear and Sportswear Association)

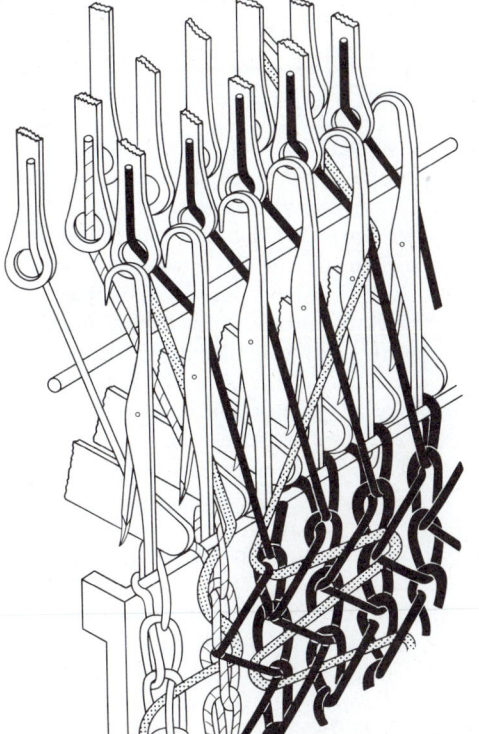

23.28 Diagram showing laying in yarn to form design.

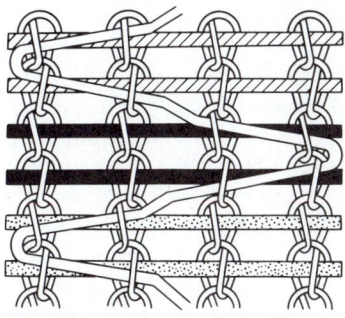

23.29 Diagram of warp-knit fabric with laid-in yarns.

the machine to knit a wide variety of fabric designs, and changes in design can be made quickly and accurately. Any type of yarn, including bulky yarns and novelty yarns of all types, can be used in producing raschel knit fabrics. These machines are especially adaptable to using heavy novelty yarns for the laid-in yarns. A range of fabrics, from very sheer and lacy to heavy, coarse, and thick, can be made on raschel equipment.

The needle action may resemble that used in making a single knit except that the yarns are interlooped in a vertical direction, with weft yarns laid into position when desired. Figure 23.27 illustrates the interlacing of a simple raschel knit; Figure 23.28 indicates the guide bars and the laying in of yarns as a part of the knitting operation. Figure 23.29 shows the interlooping of the warp yarns with placement of laid-in yarns in the filling or weft positions. These diagrams provide some idea of the complex types of fabrics that can be knitted using raschel frames.

Raschel machines may have as many as 65 guide bars, which provides for the tremendous choice of fabric designs possible on such machines. As raschel fabric is knitted, the fabric is pulled down from the knitting area at an angle of about 150° and then wound on cloth rolls.

A considerable amount of net-type fabric is made today on knitting machines. These fabrics may be constructed on either tricot or raschel machines, but the majority are made on raschel units. Knitted nets result when, at planned intervals, there is no connection between two adjacent wales. The fabric spreads at those points, leaving the opening characteristic of nets (Fig. 23.30).

Because of the wide flexibility in design and the capacity to use almost any type of yarn, raschel knits have a wide variety of end uses. There are dressy apparel fabrics, upholstery fabrics, power nets, and elastic fabrics for decoration. Raschel knits can be made with excellent dimensional stability or fabrics can have considerable stretch or extension; fabrics may have outstanding strength depending on the type of fibers and yarns used; and the design flexibility is nearly unlimited.

Milanese Knits

Milanese is a method of warp knitting that is similar to the tricot process. The milanese fabrics also resemble warp knits; however, the interlooping process produces a visible angle (Fig. 23.31).

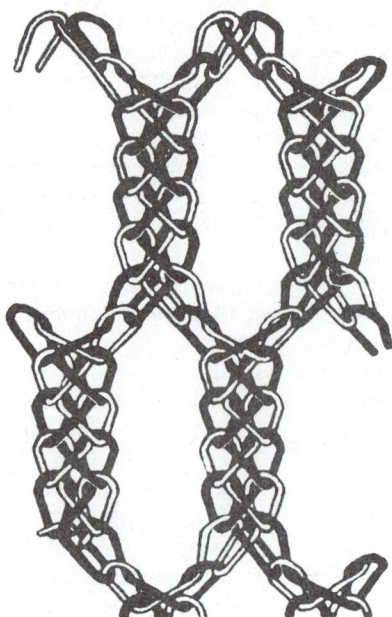

23.30 Diagram of a knitted net.

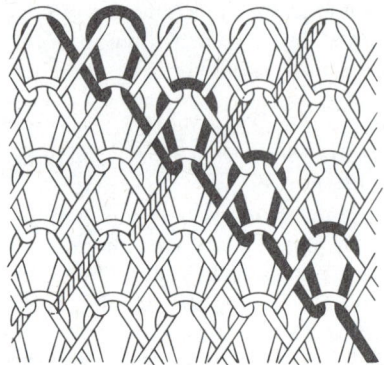

23.31 Diagram of a typical milanese knit.

Milanese knits are smoother, more regular in structure, have greater elongation, and are higher in tear strength than tricot knits. These fabrics are produced in limited quantities only because they do not have the flexibility in design capability that other knits do.

Simplex Knits

Simplex knits were popular in the early years of the twentieth century, then disappeared almost completely for a time. Now they are reappearing on the market for use in apparel, upholstery, accessories such as gloves, and moldable items where the knit provides the fabric base. Forecasts have indicated that these knits will become increasingly popular, but as yet, use is limited.

Properties of simplex knits include the following: there is no running, splitting, or raveling; they have substantial bulk and compactness; they exhibit excellent snag and abrasion resistance; they possess good elastic recovery; they have a smooth, fine surface; they do not tend to curl at the edges; and they tailor well. It will be interesting to observe what happens to this group of fabrics over the next few years.

USE OF KNITTED FABRICS

A wide selection of knitted fabrics is available to the consumer. They offer the user several important and desirable properties. The most important, probably, are excellent elongation or stretch combined with good elastic recovery, and outstanding resistance to wrinkling and crushing. These properties make knit fabrics a good choice for travel, as wrinkles hang out quickly. Knit fabrics pack in a limited space, and they are comfortable to wear.

The care of knit fabrics depends on several factors. The fiber content should give some guidance as to whether the fiber can be laundered or dry-cleaned. The type of knit construction needs to be considered. Is it loosely or tightly knit? What type of yarns have been used? Will they snag during care? What finishes are present? Instructions on care labels should be closely followed.

End-use items of knit fabrics should be chosen carefully. Knit apparel items have many outstanding characteristics, but if the item is not properly constructed it may stretch or shrink out of shape during use and care. Knit fabrics used for upholstery should be firm enough so that they do not stretch unattractively. However, that very stretch property makes knits a good choice for furniture throws, as it can be shaped around the furniture piece.

Knitted structures are porous and permit good air circulation; this increases fabric comfort. Knits allow for freedom of movement while reducing fabric deformation. Care is relatively easy, as many knits require laundering only; no ironing is needed. Because of the many desirable properties of knits, it is expected that they will continue to be popular fabrics (Fig. 23.32).

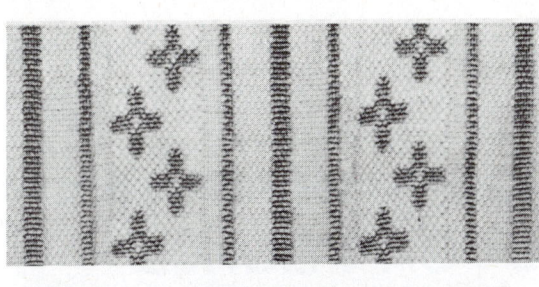
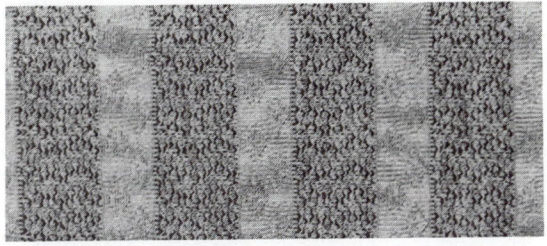

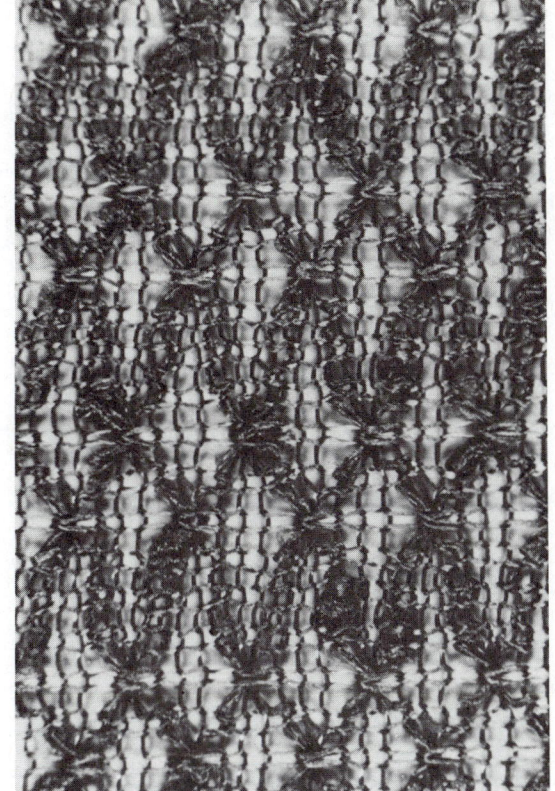

23.32 Example of knit fabrics.

STUDY QUESTIONS

1. Distinguish between the construction of warp knits and that of filling knits.
2. What is the difference between knit and woven fabrics?
3. What are the four basic types of stitches or loops used in knitting? Describe each.
4. Describe the differences between single and double knits. How could these differences influence use and care?
5. What types of knit constructions tend to run badly and why?

Activities

1. Using yarn and a pair of knitting needles, construct pieces of fabric that represent the stockinette or jersey stitch, the purl stitch, and the rib stitch.
2. Locate a variety of knit fabrics available on the market, and identify whether they are filling or warp knits, what type of filling or warp knit they are, and what care procedures are recommended.
3. Select several different types of knit fabrics, and prepare care labels for each.

24

OBJECTIVES

◇ **To identify methods of constructing nonwoven fabrics**

◇ **To provide information concerning the use and care of different types of nonwoven fabrics**

◇ **To provide information about differences among nonwoven, woven, and knitted fabrics**

◇ **To describe new technology used in the production of nonwoven fabrics**

Nonwoven Fabrics

KEY TERMS

air-lay process	dry process	nonwoven
binder	felt	spunbonded process
bonded-fiber fabric	film-extrusion process	spunlaced process
carded webs	needle-punched felt	wet process

Nonwoven fabrics include both the oldest and the newest methods of making cloth. The term *non-woven* has become widely accepted to include traditional felts, needle-punched felts, adhesive-bonded fabrics of various types, and various special structures that do not use yarn. The definition of nonwoven fabric as stated by ASTM limits nonwoven structures to those made of textile fibers: "A textile structure produced by bonding or interlocking of fibers, or both, accomplished by mechanical, chemical, thermal, or solvent means and combinations thereof."[1]

According to this definition the starting raw material for any nonwoven is a mass of textile fibers. These fibers may be natural, man-made, or combinations thereof, or fibrous forms obtained by various processing of films.

From the starting material a web is formed. This may be done by air to form a random fiber arrangement; by the carding process (see Chap. 17), coupled with arrangement units that either (a) place layers of fibers so that the fibers in each layer are parallel to the layers above and below or (b) place the fibers in a cross lay where the fibers in one layer are at right angles or perpendicular to the layer above or below; by forming a web through the wet-lay technique used in making paper; or by disintegration of a film.

Following the formation of the web of fibers, the next step is to bond them together. The fiber itself can serve as a bonding material; adhesives or solvents may be added; the fiber web may be needled; the web of fibers may be interlocked by mechanical action; or the web may be formed by thermal action.

FELTS

Human ingenuity in forming flexible covering materials first expressed itself in the making of felt. The manufacture of felt is dependent on the physical and, to some extent, chemical properties of wool, hair, or fur fibers. Wool, the fiber usually associated with felt, has been used for centuries in this type of fabric construction. Fur fibers are used in felt for special end uses such as hat bodies, and these fibers may be blended with wool for special fabrics requiring certain textural and aesthetic properties. Man-made fibers such as rayon are frequently blended with wool in making felt today.

ASTM defines felt as follows:[2]

---

[1]ASTM, *Annual Book of ASTM Standards,* 1983, vol. 07.01, p. 31.

[2]ASTM, *Annual Book of ASTM Standards,* 1983, vol. 07.01, p. 32.

Felt, wool: a textile composed wholly of any one or combinations of new, reprocessed, reused wool fibers physically interlocked by the inherent felting properties of wool and produced by a suitable combination of mechanical work, chemical action, moisture, and heat, but without weaving, knitting, stitching, thermal bonding, or adhesives.

Felt, part wool: a textile composed of wool fibers in combination with any one or any combination of natural or man-made fibers.

Further clarification of felt fabric includes the following from ASTM: "Felt is a textile characterized by the densely matted condition of most or all of the fiber of which it is composed."

The ability of wool fiber to coil upon itself, interlock, and shrink when subjected to heat, moisture, and pressure (including friction and agitation) is responsible for the felting action. Long before recorded history, people found that they could take wool fibers, apply heat and water, and then pound the fibers with rocks to create a cloth that would hold together. These fabrics could be used on floors or wrapped around the human body to provide warmth and comfort.

Today the manufacture of felt is highly mechanized and scientifically controlled. Wool fibers, alone or in combination with other fibers, are cleaned, blended, and carded. The card is formed into a wide web of fibers rather than into a card sliver as done in preparation for making yarns. Two or more layers of card web are arranged at right angles to one another. The number of layers depends on the planned ultimate thickness of the felt; but every layer alternates in fiber direction to the one directly below or above. The final thickness of the felt fabric depends on the thickness of the arrangement of fiber webs. Felt fabrics may vary from a thin 1/64 inch to over 3 inches (0.4–76 mm). Apparel felts are usually 1/32 to 1/16 inch thick; while felts for use in home furnishings or as carpet padding may approximate 1/2 inch in thickness.

The layers of carded fibers are passed through machines where they are trimmed and rolled. The rolls of fiber are put through the felting machine where moisture and heat are applied; the batts or layers of fibers move between heavy plates. The top plate vibrates, producing friction, agitation, and pressure, which cause the fibers to become entangled and pressed tightly together. The machinery is controlled auotmatically, so it stops when the desired thickness, hardness, and degree of felting is at-

tained. Following the felting action, the cloth is fulled. *Fulling* consists in shrinking the felt into a compact mass by the application of soap or sulfuric acid and then pounding with wooden hammers. Finally, the felt is neutralized, scoured, rinsed, dried, and then stretched to the desired width.

Although wool, hair, and fur fibers can all be used in making felt, wool from sheep is the most frequently employed fiber, as it possesses the best felting properties. Animal fibers of any kind can be combined with a wide variety of nonfelting fibers in the production of felt fabrics. The majority of felts made today do include fibers other than the animal hair fibers. The fibers commonly found in felts along with wool include rayon (the most common), waste fibers of various types, and some cottons.

Felt fabrics have many industrial and domestic or consumer applications. Felts have good to excellent resilience; are good shock absorbers; are easy to shape; will not ravel, so edges need no finish; absorb sound; have good insulating properties, with resultant warmth; will not tear, though fibers may pull apart; and can be finished to be mothproof, water-repellent, fire-resistant, and fungi resistant.

The breaking load of felts is low when compared with many woven or knitted fabrics. However, with intelligent selection of type and thickness, the consumer can obtain a felt that will be satisfactory for a variety of end uses. Felts for apparel pose some problems, as they do not have the give and flexibility that most apparel fabrics require. They must be constructed into relatively loose apparel items; they tend to retain the shape acquired as a result of deformation rather than return to the original shape and form.

Felts are used primarily for home furnishing items, crafts and decorative accents, and industrial purposes (Fig. 24.1). The method of construction enables the manufacturer to produce both flexible fabrics and comparatively stiff products. Flexible felts are used for apparel, such as skirts and jackets, and for home furnishing items such as floor matting, underliners for upholstered furniture, table pads, pillow backing, and similar items. Thick and firm felt fabrics are frequently used for insulation and for rug pads.

Care procedures for felt fabrics depends partially on the fiber content, but the most important factor is the construction method and the thickness of the felt. Because of the absence of yarn formation, the soft, thin felts have comparatively low tensile strength; therefore, they require careful handling.

24.1 Felt fabrics used in making stuffed animals.

Thick, firm felts may be handled with somewhat greater ease; however, because of the size of many felt objects and because of the low flexibility, it is recommended that dry cleaning be used.

NEEDLE-PUNCHED FELTS

Needle-punched felts resemble felt in appearance, but they are made primarily from fibers other than wool. These fabrics have high density but retain some bulk; they are available in different weights and thicknesses. Weight may vary from 1.7 to 10 ounces per square yard, and thickness may range from 15 to 160 mils.

Construction involves the following basic steps. The fiber web or matt, prepared using either carding, garnetting, or air-laying techniques, is fed into a machine equipped with groups of specially designed needles. The fabric moves between a metal bed plate and a stripper plate; the needles punch through the plates and the fiber web, and reorient the fibers so that mechanical interlocking or bonding occurs among the individual fibers (Figs. 24.2 and 24.3). The matt or web of fibers may be fed into the punching area on a substrate of filaments, a scrim, or some other substrate; the substrate also may be placed in the middle of the fiber web. This improves the strength and structural integrity of the finished needle-punched fabric.

The strength of needle-punched fabrics depends also on the fiber arrangement within the webs. If fibers are placed parallel to each other, the finished fabric will have good strength in that direction but will tend to be weak in the opposite direction. If the fibers are in a random arrangement, strength is equal in all directions. The machines may employ a two-step process: first the web is tacked with 30 to 60 punches per square inch (4.7–9.3/cm^2); this is followed by the regular punching, in which 800 to more than 2500 punches per square inch (125–390/cm^2) complete the final punching, and the fabric is ready for any final processing or finishing. The higher number of punches is used for fabrics that will receive considerable handling during use and care, such as blankets, while the lower number is used for fabrics destined primarily for padding.

The properties of needle-punched fabrics depend on the length and characteristics of the fiber or fibers used; the thickness, evenness, and weight of the fiber web; the arrangement of fibers in the web (parallel, crisscross, or random); the density and pattern arrangement of needles in the needle board; the number of punches per second and the total number per unit area; the speed of movement of the web through the machine; and the size of the needles and the number and arrangement of the barbs on the needles.

Most needled fabrics lack any structural pattern because the needles punch and intermingle the fibers in such a way that the fabric surface is uniform in appearance. Needle-punched fabrics can be made, however, that resemble loop-pile, velour, and

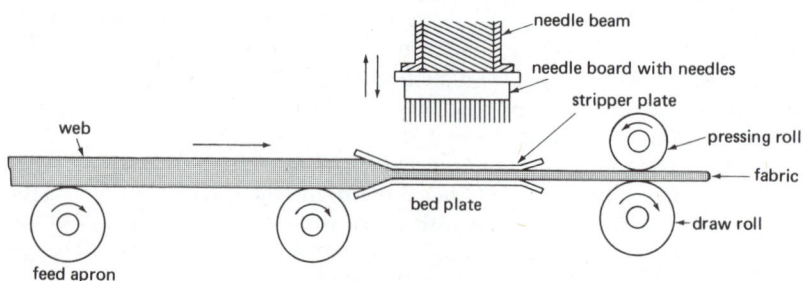

24.2 Diagram showing the basic principle of needle punching.

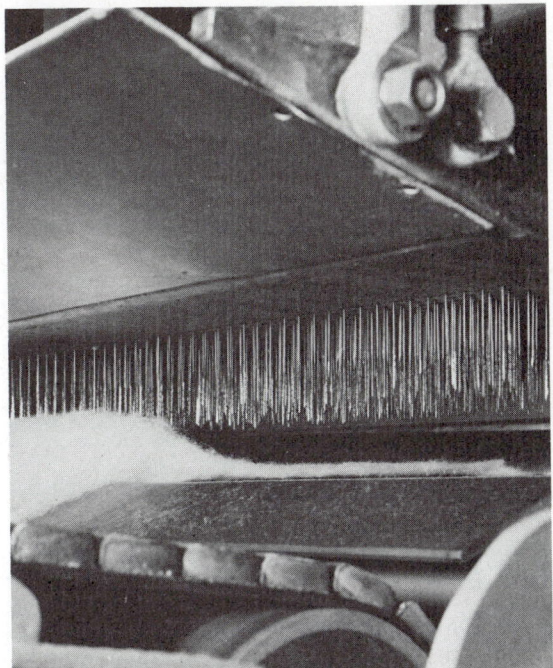

24.3 Needle board used in punching fiber webs to form needle felts. (Monsanto Fibers)

velveteen structures. Such fabrics require special needles that punch beyond the surface to form loops on one side. These loops may be left uncut, or they can be cut and brushed to give the appearance of velveteen, velour, or other similar pile-woven fabrics. Both the needle bed and the type of needles used must be modified for this type of needle punching.

Needle-punched fabrics are frequently found in carpeting and other floor coverings, wall coverings, blankets, padding material, insulation materials, industrial fabrics, and fabrics for various types of vehicles.

BONDED-FIBER FABRICS

Bonded-fiber fabric dates back to the early 1930s. At that time a few textile companies began experimenting with bonded materials as one way of utilizing cotton waste. During the late 1940s, a few more companies became interested in nonwovens, and the industry has grown to its present important status. The use of nonwovens in 1983 was estimated as worth $1.3 billion. Each year this section of the textile industry increases in importance.

The basic sequence of steps in manufacturing bonded-fiber fabrics is as follows: preparation of the fiber; web formation; web bonding; and drying, curing, and finishing.

Fibers are selected on the basis of their properties and what performance can be expected in end uses. Natural or man-made fibers can be used; in nonwoven technology at present, the preference is for first-quality fibers that have not been used for some other process. The length of fibers used may vary from ½ to 2 inches (1.3–5.1 cm). Filament fibers may be used in making some types of bonded-fiber fabrics. Since no spinning is involved, it is possible to mix or blend together fibers of different lengths as well as fibers of different generic categories. The selection of fibers to be used depends on the product to be made, the care typically given to it, and the expected or desired durability. The cost of the fibers used is important, as it in turn influences the cost of the final product. After fibers have been selected, they are given a cleaning and bleaching if necessary, thoroughly mixed, and prepared for web formation.

Web Formation

Dry Process

Dry carded webs may serve as the base for nonwoven fabrics. These webs are formed by mechanical means. The fibers are metered and uniformly distributed on a moving belt. All the fibers in the web may be parallel to each other (a parallel-fiber arrangement); they may be placed at right angles to one another by building layers of fibers in which each layer is at right angles to the layer beneath it (a crosswise arrangement); or the web may have a random arrangement in which the fibers have no specific pattern. Fiber bonding is achieved either through the use of a binder or adhesive or by the inclusion in the blend of heat-sensitive fibers, which help seal the final fabric as a result of their ability to soften and fuse with other fibers.

Air-Lay Process

In the air-lay process, the fibers are suspended in an airstream and then blown or forced onto a continuously moving belt where the web is formed. The arrangement of these fibers is primarily random, and the webs exhibit relatively uniform characteristics.

After the air-laid web is formed, the fibers are bonded together either through the application of an adhesive binder, the softening of some fibers within the fiber mix, or the use of solvents, which soften some of the fibers so that they will bind the fiber mat together. The mat is stable after the solvent has been removed.

Wet Process

The web of fibers may be formed from a suspension of the fibers in water. This technique is used in making paper and has been adapted to forming fiber webs. The process permits manufacturers to use very short fibers, even those less than ½ inch long; dry-laid webs require fibers at least ½ inch in length. Wet-laid webs are less costly than dry-laid, they can be formed more rapidly than dry-laid, and they can use waste fiber if that is desired.

The fibers are suspended in water, then deposited from that suspension onto a special type of support where the water is removed and the web is formed. The web is then dried. The bonding agent may be incorporated in the suspension either through the use of thermosensitive fibers or as an adhesive of some type. As the web is dried, the adhesive or heat-sensitive fibers bind the web together. Alternatively, the web can be sprayed with a binder following formation, and as the web dries, the binder seals the fiber together.

Adhesives and Binders

Binders and adhesives used in making bonded-fiber fabrics include acrylic latices, polyvinyl acetate copolymers, SRL latex, polyvinyl chloride copolymers, nitriles, ethylene vinyl chloride, vinyl acetate-ethylene. These have different properties and are used in making different types of bonded-fiber fabrics. However, regardless of which one is chosen, the following properties must be considered when selecting the binder: cost, bond strength, adhesion properties, recovery and bounce, resistance to chlorine, aging properties, and color retention. The properties to consider in relation to the fabric itself include tear strength, tensile strength, hand and drapability, washfastness and dry-cleanability, and absence of free formaldehyde. The binder selected as well as the amount used will influence these properties. For example, high percentages of binder usually increase fabric strength but also increase stiffness and thus decrease hand and drapability.

Acrylic latices produce fabrics with softness and resilience, high wet abrasion resistance, easy launderability and dry-cleanability, and good hand. The polyvinyl acetate copolymers are used primarily on fabrics that are designed to disintegrate rapidly, such as disposable diapers and sanitary products. SRL latex results in fabrics with a soft hand and high tensile strength and that are formaldehyde-free so there is a minimum or no odor. These fabrics are generally used for interlinings, carpets, and carpet underpadding. Polyvinyl chloride copolymers are chosen for synthetic leathers and coatings for fabrics to be used in automotive door panels and upholstery. This adhesive is flame-resistant. Nitriles have excellent tolerance to low temperatures and retain flexibility. They are frequently used for luggage, footwear, simulated leather, and artificial chamois. Ethylene vinyl chloride is being used in medical-surgical products. Vinyl acetate-ethylene is used mostly in wet wipes, towels, and other products designed for one-time use.

Solvents of various types may be used as binders for bonded fiber fabrics. The web is coated with a material that normally has no effect on the fibers but can be activated by heat. The web is heated, and the substance attacks the fibers and forms a spot-weld effect at points of contact. The solvents selected evaporate at higher temperatures and leave a structure of fibers only, sealed together at the weld point. Because no extraneous material is left on the fabric, these products are softer and more drapable than those sealed with adhesives.

Spunbonded Process

Spunbonding is a process by which fabrics are produced directly from the polymers. One or several polymers, such as polyester, nylon, polypropylene, or polyethylene, are fed into an extruder. The polymers are converted to a liquid state, usually by melting, and extruded through a spinnerette, cooled slightly in the air, and laid on a moving conveyor belt to form a continuous web. As the web cools completely, the fibers seal together.

The pattern of the fabric and arrangement of the fibers is determined by several factors. The spinnerette may be rotated to deliver filaments in different patterns and arrangements; a jet of air can be introduced to tangle the filaments; and the conveyor can be moved at different speeds to collect different amounts of filaments at different locations. The fabric achieves bonding through heat or chemical treatments, which affect the fiber polymers used to form the filaments. Fabrics made by this process include Mirafi 140 of nylon and polypropylene, Celestra of polypropylene, Reemay® of polyester, Tyvek® of polyethylene, Typar® of polypropylene, Bondtex® of polyester, Cerex of nylon, and Bidim of polyester.

Spunlaced Process

In the spunlaced process a fibrous web is subjected to high-velocity water jets that entangle the fibers and form a fabric by mechanical bonding (Fig. 24.4). The process results in fabrics that are lightweight, soft, and drapable. The products that best identify this group are the Nexus® fabrics made by Burlington, which are available in several patterns and can be dyed or printed. They are either washable or dry-cleanable. Fabrics range in weight from 0.7 to 2.2 ounces per square yard and in thickness from 3.5 to 25 mils.

Typical end uses include quilt backing fabrics, mattress pad ticking, substrates for coated fabrics of various types, interlinings, curtains, table coverings, and selected items of apparel. Typical trade

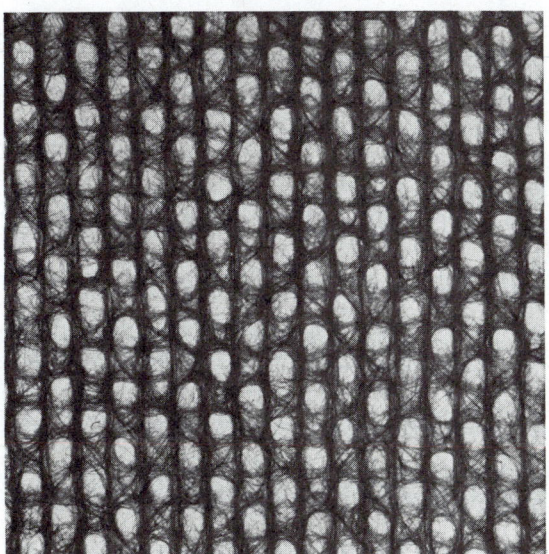

24.4 Spunlaced Nexus® fabric of 100% polyester. Magnified 5×. (Burlington Industries)

names for these products include Nexus®, Sontara®, and Polyspun®, all made of polyester. Although the majority of spunlaced fabrics on the market are made of polyester, it is possible to use other fibers.

Melt-Blown Process

In the melt-blown process the molten polymer is forced through the spinnerette, and as it emerges a high-velocity air stream hits the filaments as they form. This breaks the filaments into short lengths; the short fibers are collected in a web form on a moving belt. The force of the air stream entangles the fibers. Thermal bonding is used to secure the web. These fabrics are comparatively new. It is expected that their uses will be similar to spunbonded and spunlaced constructions. All of these find use in industrial fabrics as well as the uses identified.

Ultrasuede® and Other Artificial Leathers

A product resembling suede, Ultrasuede, was introduced in the late 1960s and met with immediate success. It appeared in high-fashion apparel and upholstery fabrics. It has been used since that time for a wide variety of apparel, home furnishing fabrics, luggage, accessories, and special items for which "fabric" covers are popular. The product is made in Japan, and information on its construction is limited to patent literature.

It would appear that the manufacture involves the following steps:

1. A special matrix fiber of polyester and nylon is spun in such a manner that the polyester forms very fine fibrils in a matrix of nylon.
2. The special fibers are cut into 2-inch (5-cm) staple length and blended with regular polyester fibers of the same length.
3. A web of fibers is formed by one of the dry-laid techniques.
4. The web is needle-punched to interlock the fibers.
5. The web is impregnated with polyurethane and cured.
6. The fabric is treated with acid to dissolve the nylon matrix in the special fibers and leave the tiny polyester fibrils.

7. The fabric is dried and then brushed to give the suede texture. The final composition is polyester and polyurethane.

Ultrasuede is easily washed and dried in automatic laundry equipment and retains its appearance for long periods. It is strong and durable, has the comfort of woven or knitted textiles, and has the appearance and feel of a top-quality suede leather. It is available in a variety of colors but only in one thickness at the present time. It drapes well but performs more like suede leather than other types of fabrics. Ultrasuede is still sold only in high-cost items; yardage is available in a limited amount at high cost.

A variety of other artificial leathers and suedes are also available on the market. Some are made of bonded-fiber fabric with a coating that resembles leather or suede. Some involve the use of knitted or woven fabrics with a surface coating or finish. Only those artificial leathers and suedes that use a bonded-fiber base are considered nonwoven products.

Finishing, Uses, and Care of Nonwovens

The final stage in the manufacture of nonwovens involves drying, curing, and finishing. This stage is important, as it provides for the removal, by evaporation, of solvents used in the application of the adhesives. The drying action can be done in hot-air ovens, under infrared lights, by rolling over heated cans, or by high-frequency electrical equipment. The choice is based on the fibers used, the binder or adhesives used, and the thickness of the product. Bonded-fiber fabrics that do not use any solvents may need various finishing operations to prepare the fabric for its final appearance and end use. Many of these finishes are similar to those used for standard woven or knitted fabrics (see Chaps. 26 and 27).

The use of nonwoven products is expanding each year. These fabrics are no longer relegated to situations in which they are hidden from view. While such uses as interlinings, substrates for coated fabrics, the base for tufted carpeting, insulation, and disposable products all continue to be important, nonwovens are finding widespread use in home furnishings, commercial and industrial uses, apparel, and geotextile applications.

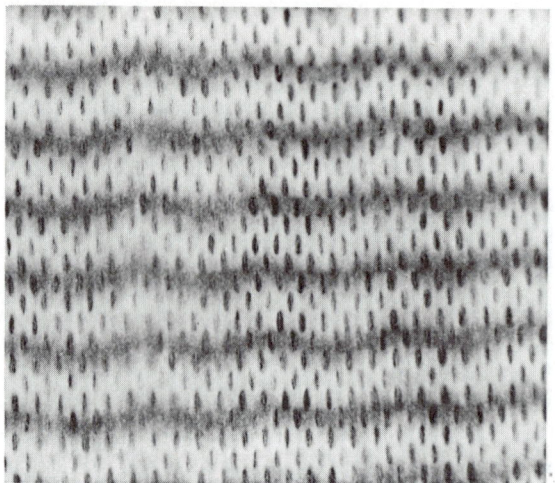

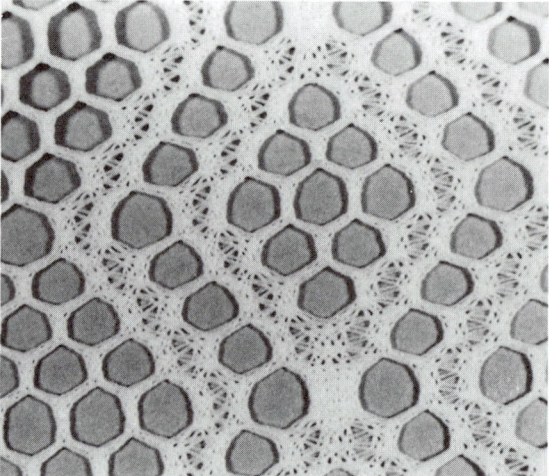

24.5 Examples of nonwoven fabrics.

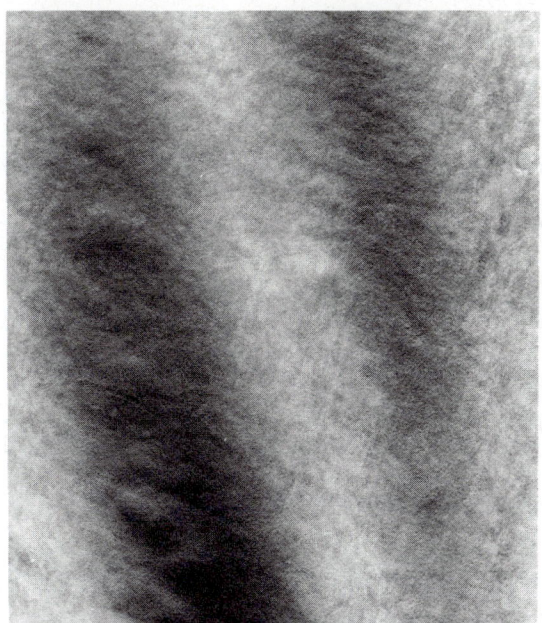

24.6 Ultrasuede® nonwoven fabric.

the lack of yarn structure, thin nonwoven fabrics should have wrinkling or twisting kept to a minimum. Figure 24.5 shows a few examples of nonwoven fabrics. These are intended for limited use. A nonwoven fabric for long-term use (Ultrasuede) is illustrated in Figure 24.6.

STUDY QUESTIONS

1. Define a nonwoven, a felt, and a needle-punched felt.
2. Describe how felts are made, how needle felts are made, and how bonded-fiber fabrics are constructed.
3. What properties must an adhesive be able to contribute in making a bonded-fiber fabric?
4. What factors influence the end use of the various types of nonwoven fabrics?

Activities

1. Locate several different nonwoven fabrics and determine how they respond to laundering procedures, to pull-stress, and to folding.
2. Describe typical end uses for each of the following and collect samples: a wool felt, an acrylic needle-punched fabric, a sheer nonwoven, and a spunlaced nonwoven.

Care of nonwovens depends on several factors: fiber used, web formation in terms of thickness and direction of fiber lay, adhesives used, and finishes and colors applied. If a care label is present, it should provide the directions for care. Because of

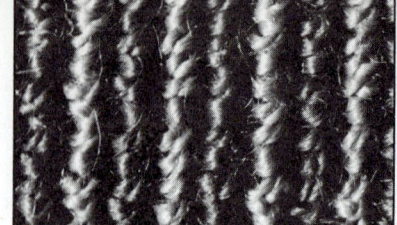

25

Other Fabric Construction Processes

OBJECTIVES

◇ To identify and describe methods of fabric construction other than weaving, knitting, and nonwoven processes
◇ To indicate where and why these additional processes are used
◇ To describe recommended methods of care for these types of fabrics
◇ To note typical end uses for these fabrics
◇ To describe their importance to the textile industry

KEY TERMS

bonded fabric
braid
chemstitched
foam-backed fabric
lace
laminated fabric
Malifol
Malimo

Malipol
Malivlies
Maliwatt
multicomponent fabric
narrow fabric
net
Pinsonic bonding
quilted fabric

Schusspol
stitch-bonding
stitch-knitting machines
tufted
ultrasonic energy
Voltex

Fabric construction processes discussed in this chapter include those other than weaving, knitting, felting, or fiber bonding. Methods that are used only for very specialized types of fabrics are included as well as those that are gaining in popularity. In most cases, the construction methods described herein require the use of yarns; some types require the use of thread (sewing) as well as yarn; and some require the use of more than one layer of fabric that has already been constructed by one of the common methods.

STITCH-BONDED FABRICS

Stitch-bonded fabrics may be described as fabrics in which fibers, yarns, fibers and yarns, or fibers and a base of substrate fabric are held together by stitching with some type of thread or yarn. There are sev-

eral methods of making these types of fabrics, but only two companies manufacture the *stitch-knitting machines* used in their construction. Only one has been used to any extent in the United States, and that is the group of machines generally identified by the name Mali.

These machines can be grouped into three distinct types: The first type stitch-bonds fabrics using yarns that are then joined by sewing with thread. The second stitch-bonds fibers together without the use of yarn or thread. The third stitch-bonds using a prefabricated fabric substrate and stitching loops into the surface with threads, yarns, or slivers.

Fabrics Made with Yarns and Threads

There are four types of fabric in this group. They are typically identified by the names Malimo, Schusspol, Maliwatt, and Malifol.

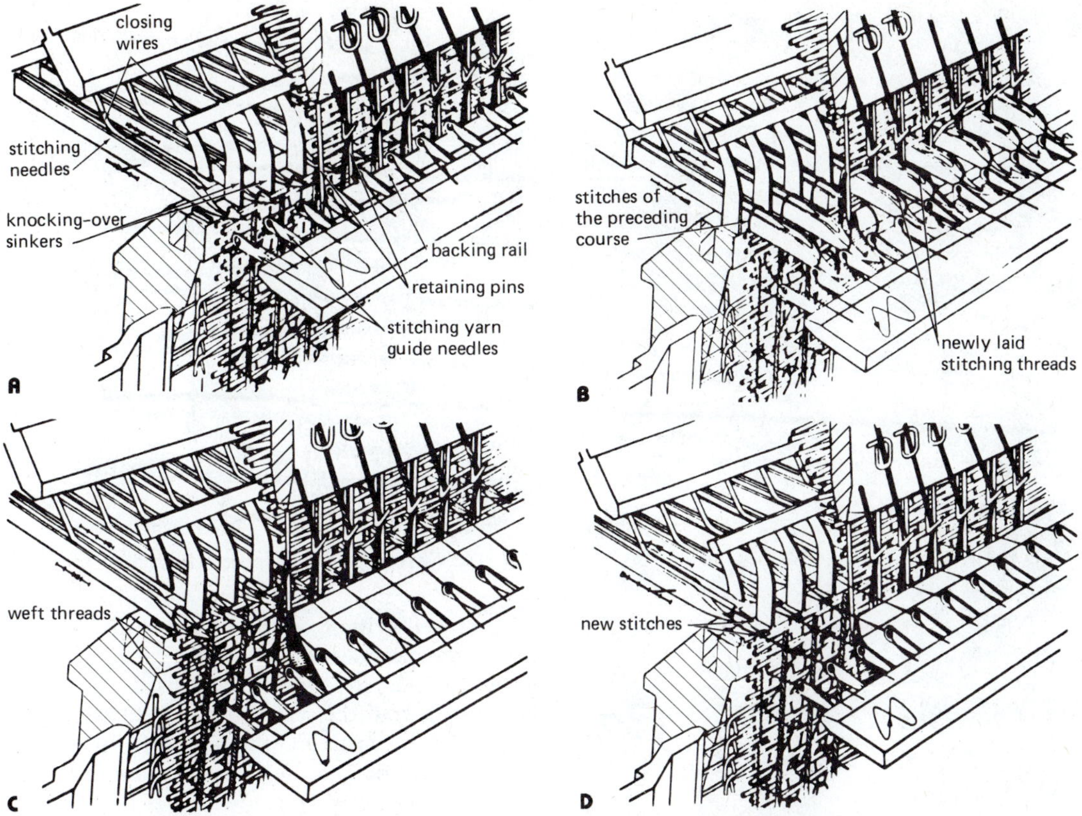

25.1 Steps in making a Malimo fabric. The process involves four steps: A: The stitching needles pierce through the sheets of weft threads. The previously formed stitches hang in the hooks of the stitching needles. B: The previously formed stitches slide over to the stitching needle shafts and closing wires. In order to form new stitches, the stitching threads are laid into the hooks of the stitching needles. C: The hooks of the stitching needles together with the newly inserted stitching threads are covered by the closing wires so that the previous stitches may slide over them. D: Knocking over of the previous stitches and formation of the new course of stitches.

MALIMO The Malimo process uses two sheets or layers of yarns, one lying in the lengthwise or warp direction and one in the weft or filling direction. These are joined together with threads, which are stitched over the yarns to hold the layers of yarn in position. The stitching process resembles a chain stitch and looks somewhat like tricot knitting. A modification of this process uses only weft yarns; the stitching yarns then form the warp direction. New machines of this type have been made that use two guide bars, which permits greater design capabilities. Figure 25.1 diagrams the basic steps in the manufacture of Malimo fabrics, and Figure 25.2 is a diagram of a typical Malimo stitch-bond fabric.

The characteristics of the fabric depend on the weight and diameter of the yarns used in the base

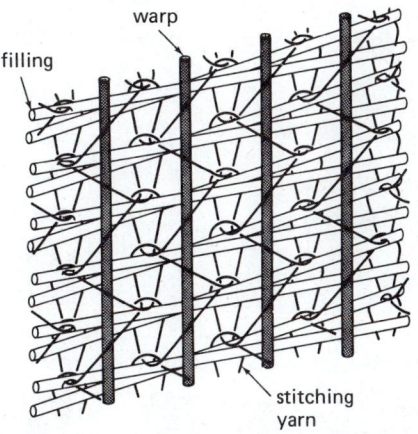

25.2 Diagram of a typical Malimo stitch-bond construction.

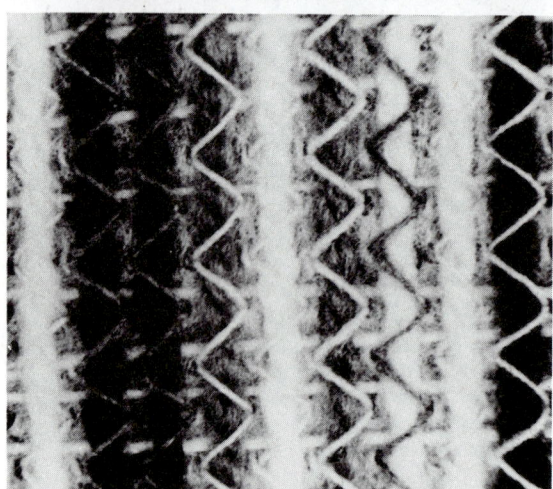

25.3 Three examples of Malimo-type stitch-bond fabrics.

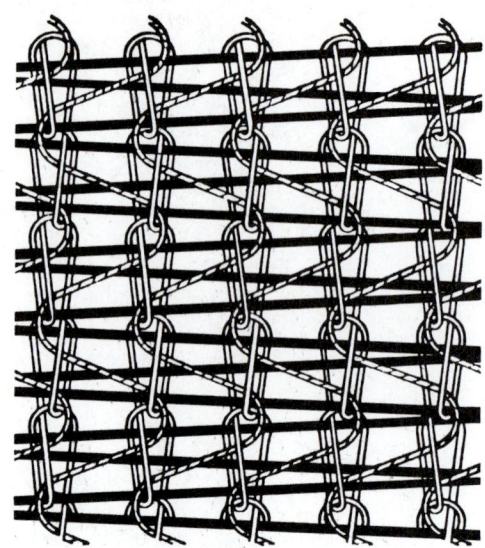

25.4 Diagram of a Schusspol fabric. (Textima)

layers as well as the type and weight of the stitching thread, the closeness of the yarn arrangement and of the stitching, the type of yarns used, the type of fiber used, and the elasticity or extension and strength of the yarns and threads. When the stitching thread is fine and the base yarns are thick, the fabric resembles a woven structure, as the stitching threads tend to disappear into the surface; when the stitching thread is dominant, the fabric surface tends to resemble a knit structure.

Malimo fabrics are used for decorative textiles such as upholstery, wall coverings, and pillow covers; for apparel such as suitings, beachwear and other sportswear, blouses, dresses, and shirting materials; and for technical fabrics such as conveyor belts, packing materials, base fabrics for coatings, and layers in laminated structures (Fig. 25.3).

SCHUSSPOL Schusspol fabrics require the use of a sheet of weft yarns, yarns or thread used for stitching, and a set of yarns that form a pile. The process is diagramed in Figure 25.4. While the stitching threads combine with the weft layer of yarns to secure the fabric, the pile yarns form a pile on one side of the fabric only. The stitching threads hold the pile yarns in place. The major uses for this type of stitch-bond is floor coverings, upholstery, and wall coverings.

MALIWATT Maliwatt fabrics are made by stitch-bonding a layer or web of fibers with yarns or threads. A cross-laid or random fiber web forms the

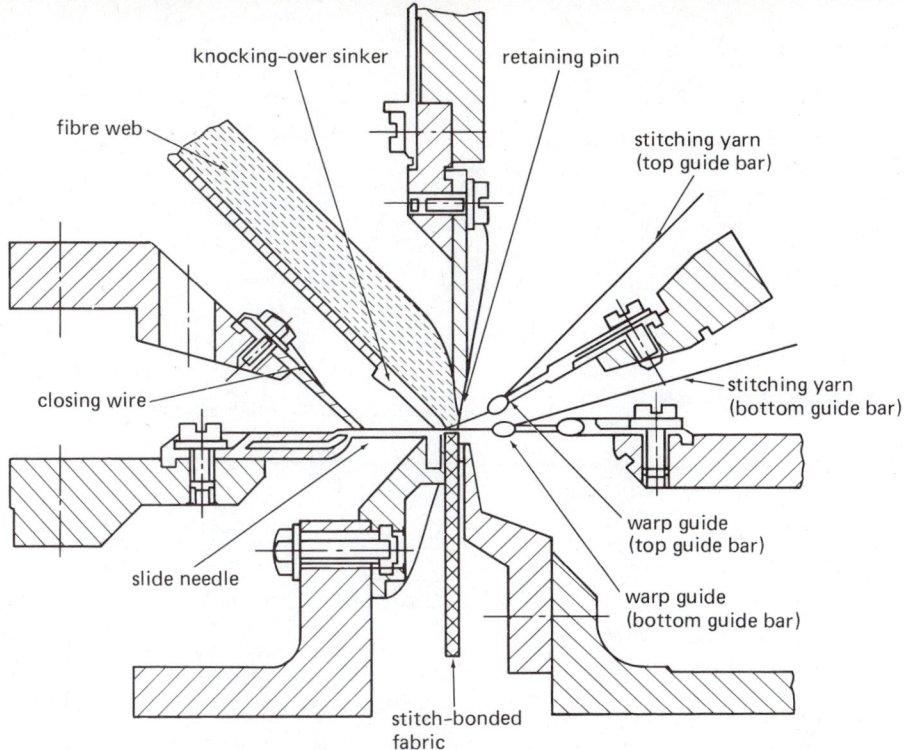

25.5 Diagram of a Maliwatt stitch bond. (Textima)

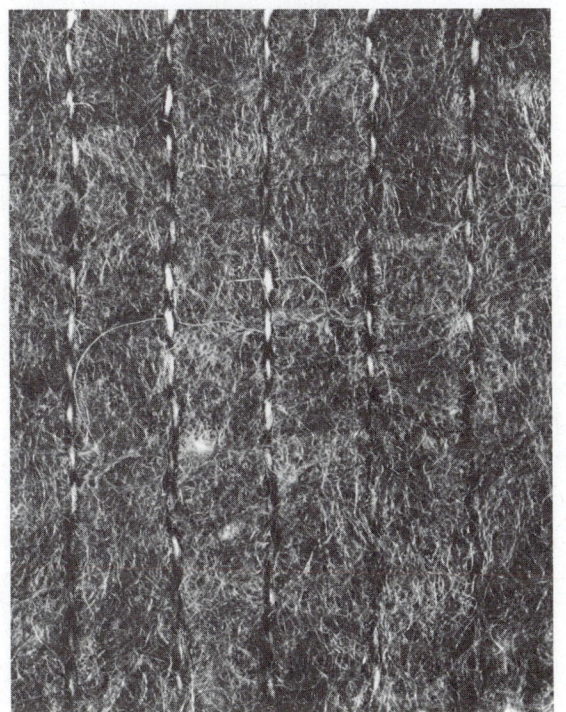

25.6 Examples of Maliwatt-type stitch-bond fabrics.

base and is held together by rows of stitching. Figure 25.5 diagrams the basic principles of the Maliwatt process.

Maliwatt fabrics can range from quite thin to relatively heavy and thick. They are recommended for use in such products as interlinings for apparel, decorative fabrics, wall coverings, cleaning rags, backing fabrics for surface coatings, insulating and temperature control linings, and padding for floor coverings. Depending on the size of the thread used in stitching, these may resemble needle-punched fabrics (Fig. 25.6).

MALIFOL The Malifol type is relatively new, and little has been published concerning its construction and use. However, it is known that the base for this is a layer of strips of polyester film that are joined together with stitching thread.

Fabric Made with Fiber Mats

The fabric type identified in the fiber-mat group is *Malivlies.* This fabric is made using a mat of fibers that is "stitched" without thread in the needles. Obviously, this would tend to be very similar to the needle-punching operation described as a non-woven construction. Fabrics do resemble needle-punched constructions; however, the process by which the needles intermesh the fibers is such that the resulting fabric tends to have the look of actual thread stitches on the surface. These fabrics can be made in very wide widths and in varying weights. They are recommended for use in packing materials, as decorative felts, and for insulating materials.

Fabrics with a Preconstructed Base

MALIPOL The Malipol construction uses a prefabricated fabric as the base; to this, yarns are fed to form a pile surface. Figure 25.7 diagrams the Malipol construction. The pile stitches can be short or long, made with fine to heavy yarn or thread, left uncut or cut and sheared. Fabrics can be made to resemble terry cloth, blankets, plush fabrics such as velours, and imitation furs. Malipol fabrics can be used for the same applications as regular terry cloth: beachwear and casual wear, upholstery, imitation furs, and floor coverings. These fabrics are durable and have good pile density, and the pile loops are securely anchored into the base fabrics (Fig. 25.8).

VOLTEX A second type of fabric using a preconstructed base is the Voltex type. In this construction a web of fibers is stitched into a preconstructed fabric base. The fiber web may be of staple length or filament fibers. The stitching process produces a fabric with a pilelike surface and what appear to be stitches on the back. The surface of these fabrics may be left as constructed, in which case the surface may have uncut loops, particularly if filament fibers were used; or the surface may be sheared to produce a uniform pile effect. Figure 25.9 is a diagram of the Voltex process. Fabrics made by this method are used for such products as imitation furs, lining materials for footwear and clothing, overcoating fabrics, upholstery fabrics, plush fabrics for toys, and blankets.

Use and Care of Stitch-Bonded Fabrics

Stitch-bonded fabric care is based on the type of fiber or fibers used, the type of yarn construction involved, the closeness of the stitches, the type of base, and the looseness or compactness of the structure. If a care label is included, the directions pro-

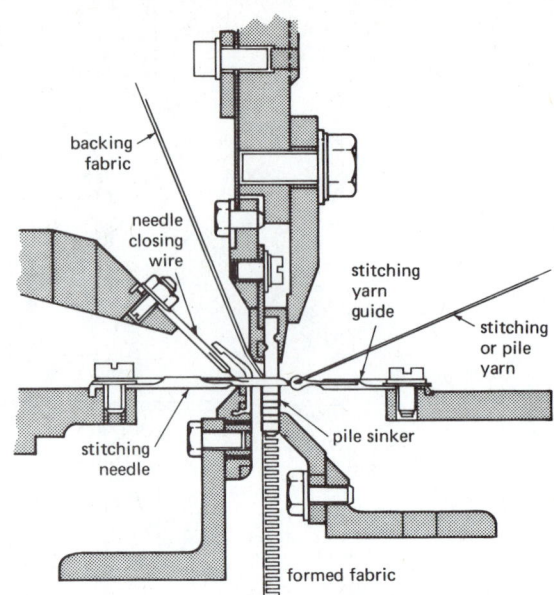

25.7 Diagram of Malipol-pile stitch-bond process. 1: Backing fabric. 2: Needle closing wire. 3: Stitching needle. 4: Stitching yarn guide. 5: Stitching or pile yarn. 6: Pile sinker. 7: Formed fabric. (Textima)

vided should be followed. As these fabrics tend to resemble structures previously discussed (weaving, knitting, felting, and fiber bonding), the care is similar to that recommended for the common types of structures with which most people are familiar.

Stitch-bonded fabrics are relatively new and have not become as popular in the United States as they are in some other countries. However, they do offer several advantages: they are usually less expensive to produce, equipment requires less space, and the design potential is outstanding. As yet the production of these fabrics is limited, but there is an increase yearly. Much of this type of fabric is being used for interiors as decorator fabrics.

THE METAP SYSTEM

The METAP system was developed in Czechoslovakia. The machine forms fabrics using a combination of knitting and weaving. It is reported to involve between 75 and 85 percent weaving and 15 to 25 percent knitting. The fabric is characterized by a series of woven stripes separated by tiny wales of knitting (Fig. 25.10). The machine uses a warp yarn arrangement much like any weaving loom with a

25.8 Two examples of Malipol-pile stitch-bond fabrics.

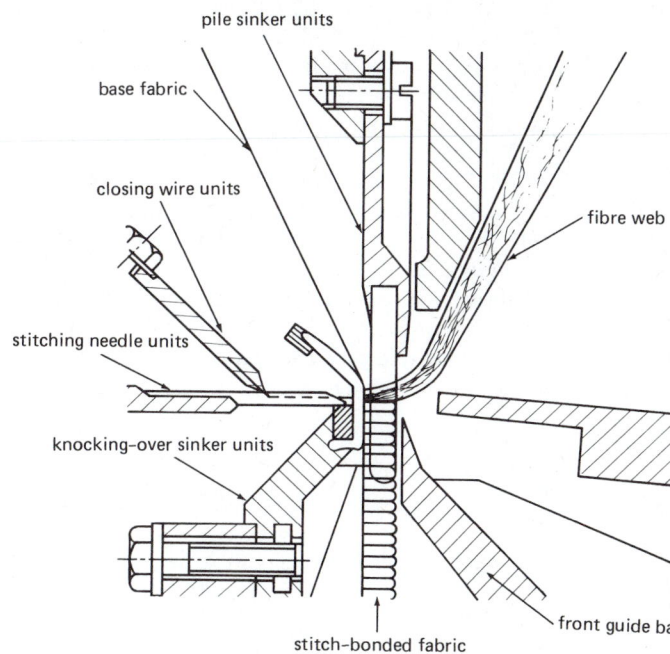

pile sinker units

base fabric

closing wire units

stitching needle units

knocking-over sinker units

fibre web

stitch-bonded fabric

front guide bar

25.9 Diagram of Voltex stitch-bond fabric. (Textima)

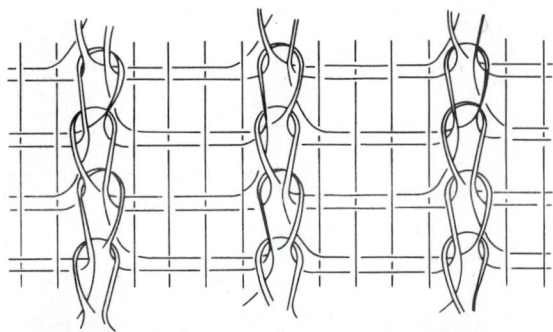

25.10 Diagram of the METAP construction process

25.11 Braided fabric used for trimming.

25.12 Net fabric.

shedding operation similar to standard weaving. However, interspersed is a series of yarns that are interlooped using a warp-knitting system. The fabric is described as having greater extensibility and greater comfort than woven fabrics; it has good crease resistance, it drapes well, and it is porous, so air permeability is good.

Fabrics made by this process are recommended for apparel and home furnishings. There are good design possibilities for these fabrics. Care would be similar to either woven or knitted fabrics of the same general weight and sheerness. The construction process is faster than weaving.

BRAIDED FABRICS

Braided fabrics are characterized by a diagonal surface effect. They are made by plaiting three or more yarns that originate from a single location and lie parallel before the interlacing occurs (Fig. 25.11). The yarns intercross from one side to the other, resulting in a column of horizontal Vs. Narrow braids can be joined together to form wide fabrics for large items such as rugs. Braids are made either in flat or in circular form.

Circular braids appear in such everyday items as shoelaces and insulation for electric wires. Flat braids are used for trimming. Braids may be stretched in one direction, but as they are stretched they tend to compact in the other direction. This characteristic is used frequently in manipulating braids in various end uses; it is particularly helpful when using braids as edge trimming, for it permits the curving of braid around corners in such a way that it continues to lay flat. Some uses of braids include cord for use on window blinds, special trims, and netlike fabrics.

Fabrics may be braided using forms other than yarns. Cut strips of fabric, strips of leather, straw, and other flexible products can be braided to create attractive and unusual fabrics.

NETS

Nets are open-mesh fabrics with large geometric interstices between the yarns (Fig. 25.12). Early nets were made by knotting the yarns at each point of intersection, and this is still done when true knotted

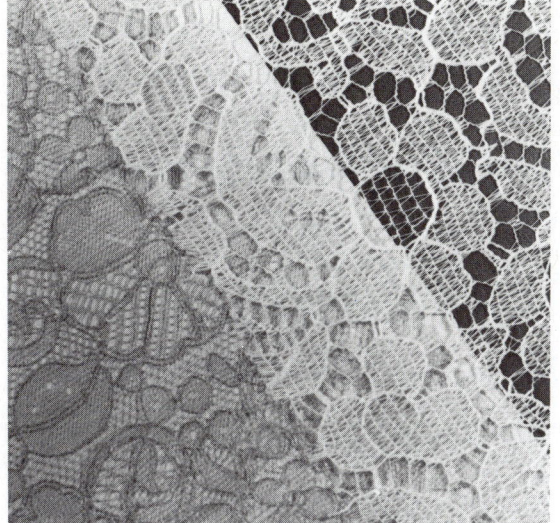

25.13 Lace fabric.

nets are constructed. These nets have a comparatively large mesh and will not slip, spread, or become distorted in use. Before 1809 nets were made by hand, but in that year a machine was developed that produced knotted nets that were so close to hand-knotted fabrics that few people could tell them apart. In recent years most nets have been constructed on either tricot or raschel knitting machines, where the yarns are only interlooped and not knotted. The knitted nets are not as durable as those made by the knotting technique. Because of the knotting, true nets are strong; this factor, combined with the open area or interstices, makes nets that are very effective where high strength with an openwork structure is required. They are used in fishing to permit easy drainage of water but retain the fish without damage. Nets are used for hammocks and screens because of the air circulation and strength. Knotted nets were widely used for evening apparel and for hats; however, this use has been taken over to a great extent by knitted nets.

Nets require careful handling because they can be snagged easily. However, if strong fibers and strong yarns are used, the fabric exhibits good performance and durability. If washable fibers have been used, the fabrics are easily washed, provided other items that might get caught in the open interstices are not placed in the laundry bath with the nets. It is important that the laundry equipment not have rough spots that could catch the net and result in damage.

LACES

Lace has been defined in many ways, and authorities differ about what really constitutes lace. However, it is safe to state that lace is an openwork fabric consisting of a network of yarns formed into intricate designs (Fig. 25.13).

It is not known when lace was first made, but specimens in museums have been dated as early as 2500 B.C. No other material is as difficult to make, requires such artistry in manufacture or such complicated machinery, and is as delicate.

The development of lacemaking equipment involves some interesting history. In 1808 John Heathcote completed a machine that successfully made knotted net, and this set the stage for the development, by John Leavers, of the Leavers machine, in 1813, that would interknot yarns into complex designs. By 1837, Leavers and his coworkers had incorporated the principle of the Jacquard attachment and was able to produce a wide variety of lace designs.

The Leavers machine is considered the most complex of all textile equipment and requires more floor space than most other machines. There are about 40,000 parts, each built to a tolerance measured in thousandths of an inch. A single machine weighs over 30,000 pounds (13,600 kg) and requires 500 square feet (46 square meters) of floor space. This giant is capable of producing the delicate fabrics known as lace.

In the Leavers machine the yarns are placed on small bobbins, spaced approximately 19 to the inch (7.5/cm). The machine controls the bobbins in creating the knotted structure.

Yarns used in making lace must be strong and firmly twisted in order to withstand the construction process. The adoption of man-made fibers such as nylon for making laces has added durability to many lace fabrics. Some laces are still made by hand, which requires many hours of labor, and thus are very costly. Other laces today are frequently made on raschel knitting machines. These are knitted fabrics and not true laces. However, it is very difficult for most people to distinguish between the two. Furthermore, the durability of knotted and of knitted laces is so similar that it is nearly impossible to say that one is better than the other.

Laces may be manufactured in various widths. Edges may be even or in some form of design such as curves or points. Several well-known laces are characterized by specific features; the reader should review special references on laces for details concerning these fabrics. A few of the common laces available include Alençon lace, antique lace, Chantilly lace, galloon lace, insertion lace, rose-point lace, tatting lace, Valenciennes lace, and Venice lace.

True lace is expensive, so knitted lace is the commonly found lace on the market. Lace requires some care in handling to prevent snagging and damage during laundering or dry cleaning. Depending on the fiber, care should be gentle with as little handling as possible. Nylon laces, which are popular on the market, give good service and performance and can be handled with minimum difficulty.

FILM FABRICS

Films are not true textiles since they are not made from fibers; however, they are made from the same generic polymers used for many man-made fibers. Furthermore, when such films are used in applications where woven, knitted, or other types of textile constructions are used, they are generally referred to as textiles.

Films may be clear and transparent, colored and transparent, translucent, or opaque (Fig. 25.14). Such fabrics are used for such items as shower curtains, rainwear, and protective apparel. To manufacture films, the polymer is extruded in a sheet form rather than in filament-fiber form. The films vary in thickness from very fine to relatively heavy layers destined for use in upholstery. Films may be supported with a woven, knitted, or nonwoven backing. These supported films have greater strength and tear resistance than nonsupported. Technically, however, this type of structure becomes a multicomponent fabric.

Nonsupported films vary in durability and performance depending somewhat on thickness and somewhat on type of polymer used. Care of such fabrics usually involves the simple act of wiping the surface with a damp cloth or with soap and water. They may crack and break when dry-cleaned, or they may become so weakened that they break during the agitation of laundering. If a care label is attached to the item, the recommended care should be observed.

NARROW FABRICS

It is difficult to place a discussion of narrow fabrics, as they may be made by nearly every method discussed so far. Thus mention here will be brief and confined to the production of narrow woven fabrics.

To weave narrow fabrics, a different type of loom is required than that used for standard broadwidth fabrics. It is designed to have several positions where the shuttles can be located and yarn can be fed into the filling direction. As most narrow fabrics require a selvage of some type, there must be some method of forming a firm selvage edge. Thus, most narrow fabrics are made on modified shuttle looms.

Narrow fabrics are used for a variety of products: safety belts and harnesses, ribbons, elastic tapes, labels, bindings, belting, webbings, and a variety of industrial products. Care of such a fabric depends on the other fabrics with which it has been combined. If it is used alone, care depends on the type of fiber as well as the construction. Heavy duty narrow fabrics respond well to any type of care procedure. Some narrow fabrics can be wiped with a damp cloth, some require laundering, and some may be considered for short-term use and not require care. Narrow fabrics may be highly patterned and made using dobby or Jacquard attachments; others may be simple basic weave structures. The main property that distinguishes these fabrics from other woven fabrics is that they are narrow, they have finished edges, and several are made on the same "loom" at the same time. Each width has its own shuttle and its own set of warp yarns.

25.14 Film fabric with design painted on surface.

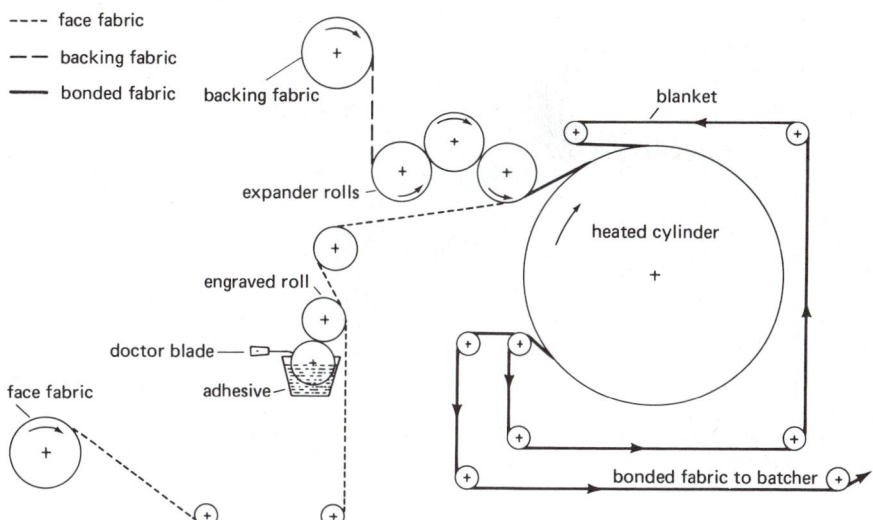

- - - - face fabric
- - backing fabric
—— bonded fabric

backing fabric

blanket

expander rolls

heated cylinder

engraved roll

doctor blade

adhesive

face fabric

bonded fabric to batcher

25.15 Diagram of fabric-to-fabric bonding process.

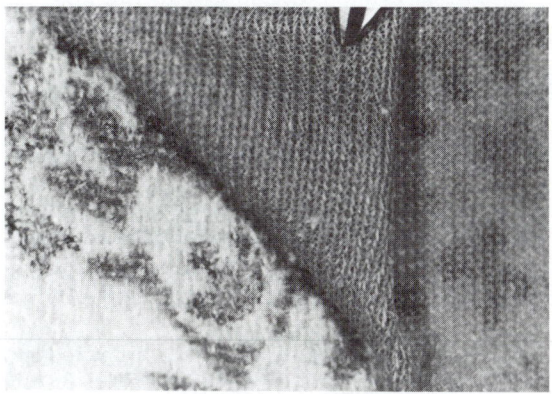

25.16 Bonded fabric-to-fabric construction.

MULTICOMPONENT FABRICS

Multicomponent fabrics include *bonded fabrics, laminated fabrics, foam-backed fabrics,* and *quilted fabrics.* A multicomponent fabric is one in which at least two layers of material or fabric have been sealed together. Adhesives may be used such as thermosetting resins, thermoplastic substances, or heat-treated polyurethane foam, or thread may be used to stitch the layers together.

One of the most common multicomponent fabrics is made of two layers of fabric securely bonded together with an adhesive (Figs. 25.15 and 25.16).

These structures may involve two fabrics, either of which can serve as the face fabric; or they may involve the use of a tricot knit as the backing, which provides a self-lining and helps to stabilize the fabric. Bonded fabrics have resistance to stretch and deformation and a low incidence of raveling.

Another multicomponent fabric is composed of a layer of fabric bonded to a layer of foam. The foam adds stability and warmth (Fig. 25.17). A modification of this type is the sandwich structure in which two layers of fabric are sealed together using a layer of foam in the center. The foam may serve as the adhesive agent. Figure 25.18 illustrates the fabric-to-foam-to-fabric bonding process.

Bonding Using Ultrasonic Energy

Fabric may be sealed together using ultrasonic energy. This process, frequently identified as Pinsonic® bonding, can be used to seal two or more layers of fabric or two layers of fabric with a fiber mat between. The product typically appears similar to a quilted fabric, which is made by machine-stitching (or hand-stitching) layers of fabric together.

Ultrasonic energy is mechanical vibratory energy that operates at frequencies beyond the level of audible sound, usually 20–40 kHz. Pressure and vibration are applied to the area to be bonded, which results in intermolecular mechanical stress and causes melting to occur at the points of contact.

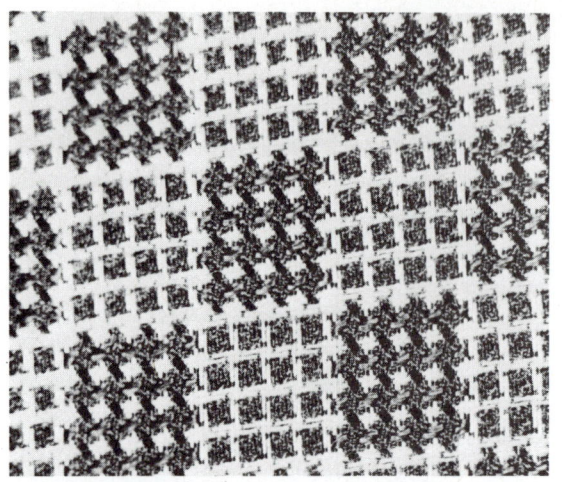

These points of contact can be made to resemble stitches found in standard sewing (Fig. 25.19 and 25.20). The process is fast and is less damaging to fibers than thermal bonding. It has been reported that approximately half of all mattress pads and bedspreads are "quilted" using ultrasonic energy.

Other applications for ultrasonic bonding include the production of fabrics for home furnishings and industrial uses. Staple-fiber webs may be bonded into a nonwoven fabric using this technique.

Other Multicomponent Fabrics

Other types of multicomponent fabrics include the following:

1. A layer of film laminated to a fabric (Fig. 25.21). A variety of design effects can be created depending upon the type of film used, the thickness of the film, and the design effects added to the layer of film through various finishing and coloring methods.
2. Film can be laminated to foam. These fabrics are frequently built for use where insulation is desirable; the fabrics are durable unless the film layer is so thin that it can be damaged easily.
3. Two fabrics with or without a filling between can be sealed together by heat and/or adhesives. Fabrics with various types of designs can be developed owing to the method used in sealing, the type of adhesive used, and the type of fibers and yarns used in making the fabric. *Chemstitching* may be used for this. Chemstitching produces fabrics with a crinkled or rippled effect on the

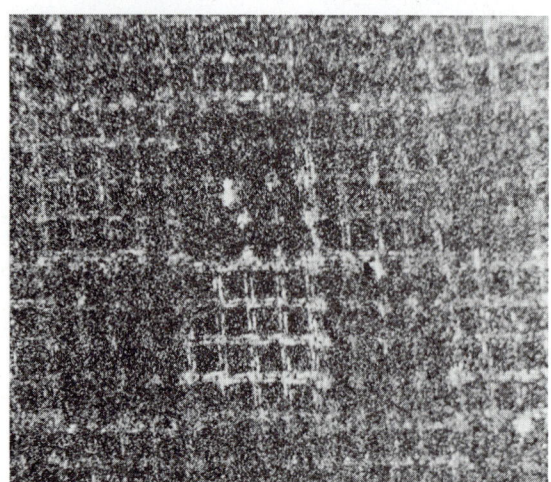

25.17 Bonded fabric-to-foam construction.

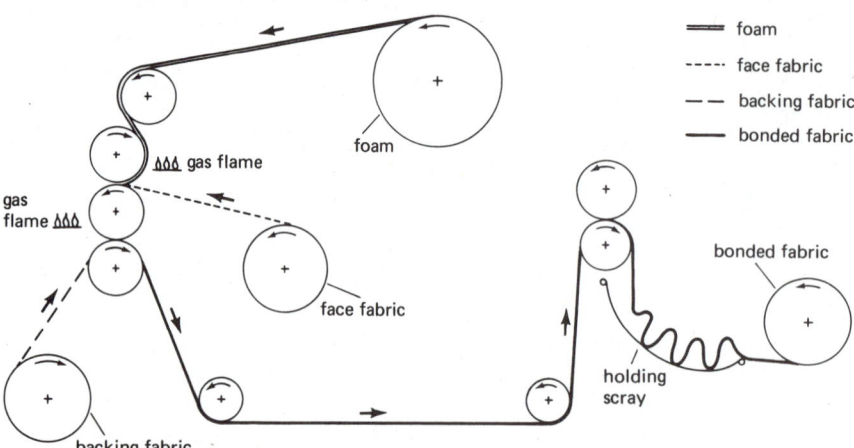

25.18 Diagram of fabric-to-foam-to-fabric bonding process.

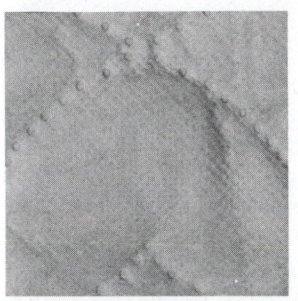

25.19 Pinsonic® process used to form multicomponent fabrics.

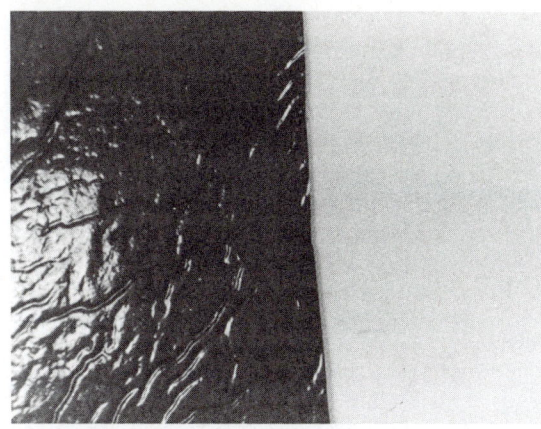

25.21 Vinyl surface laminated to a background fabric.

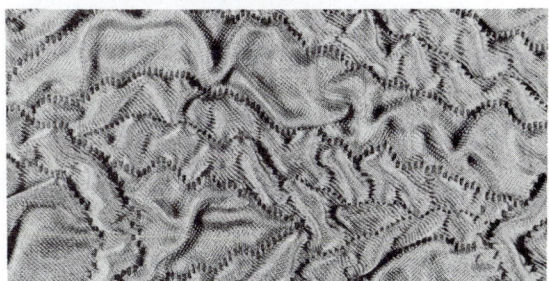

25.22 Chemstitched fabric.

25.20 The Pinsonic® unit as it seals fabrics together (Branson Sonic Power)

25.23 Down-filled jacket quilted to hold face, lining, and down in position (L. L. Bean)

face (Fig. 25.22). These fabrics are made by sealing one fabric that will shrink when heated to another fabric that will not. As they seal, the fabric that does not shrink tends to crinkle or wrinkle to produce the appearance.

4. A layer of fabric bonded to a layer of fibers is another form of multicomponent fabric. These structures are used for special purposes where warmth, insulation, and bulk are required.

5. Two fabrics with or without a layer of fibers between may be joined by stitching. This creates fabrics identified as *quilted* structures. The stitching may be done by hand or machine. The designs used for the stitching may be relatively simple or highly complex patterns (Fig. 25.23). Currently, the production of quilted fabrics has increased tremendously. Both commercially and handcrafted quilted structures are found in a wide variety of uses. Quilted fabrics are no longer relegated to use as bedspreads and robes.

Selection of Multicomponent Fabrics

When purchasing multicomponent fabrics, the consumer should consider the following:

The layers should have been sealed together securely and firmly, so that it requires considerable pull to separate them.

When both fabrics are woven, the grain lines in each should be parallel to those of the other fabric, and filling yarns in one fabric should be perpendicular to the warp yarns in the same layer as well as to those in the second layer.

Adequate care labels should be securely attached. It is hard to prescribe generalized care for multicomponent fabrics, as there are many different combinations for the face and back fabric; thus, care labels are essential.

There should be no odor, and the fabrics should not be stiff or brittle.

An adhesive, if used, should not be visible.

If foam is used, it should retain its light color unless it was dyed to blend better with the surface fabrics and their color.

For quilted fabrics, the stitching should be small, stitches should be even in size, and there should be no breaks in the threads used for the stitching.

TUFTED FABRICS

Handmade tufted fabrics originated in the early American colonial period. At that time hand-tufting was practiced as an art and was limited to making fabrics for special uses. About 1900 the craft was revived, and machines were developed to produce tufted fabrics at rapid speed.

Tufting is a process of manufacturing pile fabrics by inserting loops into a base fabric. The base or ground fabric may be of any type and may be composed of any type of fiber, but the majority of tufted fabrics available today use cotton, polyester, polypropylene, nylon, or rayon fiber for the base fabric. The tuft yarns may be of almost any type of fiber. Those commonly used include cotton, rayon, wool, acrylic, nylon, polyester, and acetate.

The pile loops are inserted with needles and held in place either by a special adhesive coating or by untwisting the tufting yarn and shrinking the base fabric so that it becomes more compact and will hold the fibers forming the pile.

One of the major uses of tufted fabrics is for floor coverings. Tufted carpets and rugs first made their appearance in the early 1950s. The success of these fabrics for floor coverings has been phenomenal; currently (1986) approximately 90 percent of all carpets and rugs sold in the United States are made by the tufting process. Such fabrics are less costly to produce than similar types of fabrics made by weaving or knitting; durable fabrics can be made; and these floor coverings retain their shape.

The size of the loop in such fabrics is determined by the distance the needles carrying the pile yarns protrude beyond the surface of the base cloth. The tuft loops may be cut or uncut. Special design units determine the distance the various needles will pass into the fabric, and this in turn can result in fabric surfaces with loops of different heights.

Many tufted fabrics, particlarly those for floor coverings, have been sealed to a backing fabric. This makes it difficult to determine precisely what type of construction has been used. However, it may be possible to pull back a segment of the backing fabric and determine whether the surface is a tufted fabric (Fig. 25.24).

Coloring of tufted fabrics can be achieved in the same manner as for other fabrics. The fabric may be piece-dyed; yarns of different colors may be tufted into the base following an electronic design control

25.24 Tufted fabric. Top: Face. Bottom: Back.

system that determines which color a needle puts through the fabric at any specific location; or different fiber variants may be used that accept different types of dyes (see Chap. 28). Some tufted fabric is made in light weights for use as apparel fabric and home furnishings such as bedspreads, upholstery, and pillow covers.

Care of tufted fabrics that can be safely and conveniently cleaned at home would depend on the fiber type used, the closeness or looseness of the pile or tufts, the type of yarn structure (simple or complex), and the size of the article. Most tufted fabrics found in household articles or apparel that are of a size that would fit into home laundry equipment are probably washable. However, if care labels are provided, it is essential to follow all care directions carefully.

STUDY QUESTIONS

1. Describe each of the following and indicate special considerations involved in the care of each: (a) stitch-bond fabrics of the Malimo, Maliwatt, Malipol, and Schusspol types; (b) braids; (c) nets; (d) multicomponent fabrics; (e) tufted fabrics; (f) lace.
2. What are typical uses for film fabrics? What care would they require?

Activities

1. Locate fabrics made using the various constructions described in this chapter that are available on the consumer market. What is the typical cost? How much of the type of fabric is available? In what types of items? Why?
2. Locate some multicomponent fabrics, and determine whether the fabric layers can be separated and, if so, how easily.
3. For tufted fabrics, see how easy it would be to pull out the yarns that form the loops. If you find a difference among such fabrics, explain why the difference might have occurred.

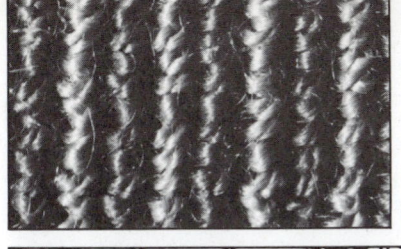

PART V

Finish and Color Application

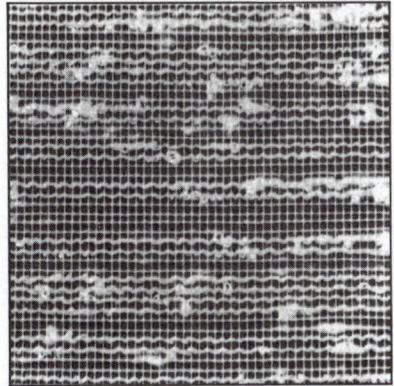

Finishes are an essential ingredient in the making of any textile fabric. Without finishes, we would not have modern fabrics as we usually know them.

The amount of finishing depends on the type of fabric and the purpose for which it is intended. Most fabrics that reach the consumer market have received one or more finishing treatments. Moreover, except for white fabrics, color in some form has been applied. The textile industry considers the application of dyestuffs as part of the finishing or wet processing of fabric. However, for convenience in discussion, dyestuffs and methods of applying color are discussed in separate chapters in this text.

The history of finishes, excluding color, is sketchy. Smoothing fabrics on flat stone surfaces was the forerunner of calendering; application of white clay was a rudimentary sizing. The first recorded information describing special finishes refers to mercerization. John Mercer, in 1853, discovered the effect of caustic soda on cotton; the process was perfected by H. A. Lowe in 1889. Shrinkage control, durable press, water repellency, and most other finishes are products of the mid-twentieth century. Wash-and-wear finishes were developed and used during the second quarter of the twentieth century, whereas durable press was not introduced until 1964.

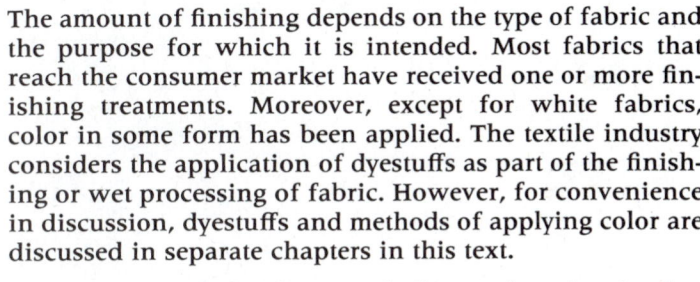

This text divides the discussion of finishes into two chapters. Chapter 26 discusses the various forms by which finishes are applied, including traditional finishing, foam technology, and solvent finishing. That chapter also includes information regarding finishes that are considered preparatory to additional processes. These may also be

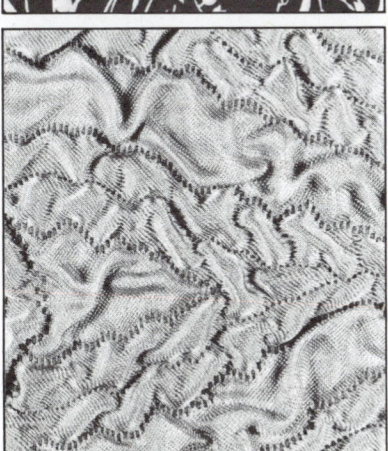

called routine finishes, and they are usually a part of the preparation of all fabrics. Chapter 27 discusses finishes that have been developed to alter appearance, function, and/or performance or to modify characteristics resulting from construction, fiber content, and yarn type.

Chapter 28 discusses the various types of dyestuffs and methods by which dyes and pigments are applied to textiles. Chapter 29 is concerned with the application of surface design through the use of color.

OBJECTIVES

◇ **To describe the processes by which finishes are applied to textile fabrics**

◇ **To describe the various routine, general, and/or preparatory finishes used on textile fabrics**

◇ **To identify how finishes effect fabric performance, maintenance, durability, and appearance**

26

Finishes: Part I

KEY TERMS

bleaching
brushing
calendering
carbonizing
crabbing
decating
desizing
foam finishing technology
fulling

heat setting
inspection
liquid ammonia
  treatments
mercerizing
pressing
scouring
shearing
singeing

sizing
skew
slashing
solvent finishing
stoving
tentering
water-bath finishing
weighting

The application of finishes is the province of the converting industry. Converters devote their research and development to improving, discovering, or otherwise modifying existing finishing operations in an effort to produce the most desirable textile product. Fabrics are said to be in the *greige* (or gray) before finishing. This term does not indicate a specific color, for the unfinished fabric may be tan, gray, white, or already colored through yarn or fiber dyeing techniques.

Finishes can be classified by several different systems. They can be mechanical or chemical, permanent or temporary, durable or renewable, and preparatory, functional, and/or appearance-enhancing.

Mechanical finishes are applied to fabric by equipment such as copper plates, cylinders, or tentering frames. Chemical finishes are those that use some type of chemical substances such as acids, alkalies, bleaches, resins, or other substances and that result in some chemical change in the fabric.

Finishes are said to be durable if they withstand

a "normal" amount of wear and care. "Normal" is obviously a relative term, and one person's interpretation may differ greatly from another's. The industry measures the durability or performance of a finish by its ability to withstand tests designed to simulate average use and care. Renewable finishes are those that rub off or are removed easily by washing or dry cleaning. They can be replaced, in some cases, during the care period.

Finishing is a basic procedural step in preparing fabrics for use. The order in which finishes are applied will vary depending on fabric types, fiber type, and ultimate fabric appearance. A typical sequence of procedures for a cotton or a cotton/polyester blend fabric would be singeing, desizing, scouring, bleaching, mercerizing, tentering, calendering, and inspection. Further finishing might involve the application of durable-press finishes and other types of functional finishes or the application of finishes designed to modify appearance. For a wool fabric the preparatory finishes include scouring, fulling, carbonizing, crabbing, decating, and inspection.

FINISHING PROCESSES

Finishes may be applied to textile fabrics or substrates by one, two, or three techniques or by combinations of them. Various finishes may be applied by all three, or only one may be practical. These processes are the use of a water bath or liquid with a water base, the use of foam technology, and the use of solvents.

Water-Bath Finishing

For years the use of water in finishing has been the typical process. As long as water was plentiful, no one was concerned about environmental pollution, and while energy was plentiful, the use of water baths was considered logical. Water-bath finishing requires saturation of the fabric in a liquid bath with water as the base for the solution. Throughout the finishing process, whenever the fabric needs wetting out, water has been the chemical used.

The various finishing processes described in this and the next chapter have used water until recently, when converters became concerned with energy conservation, pollution, and water preservation. Then these manufacturers turned to alternative finishing processes whenever they were appropriate or could be adapted without damage to fabric or the people involved.

Solvent Finishing

Solvent finishing, as well as foam technology, was developed to reduce water pollution and to reduce energy costs through reduced energy consumption. Further, solvent processing was considered an effective method of removing fabric impurities. It was thought to be a good method for finishing yarn- or fiber-dyed fabrics without affecting the color, and it was seen as a process in which desizing and scouring could be accomplished simultaneously.

The solvent process utilizes chemicals other than water as the basis for application of finishing materials, for cleaning or scouring fabric, and for removing impurities from fabric. A desired solvent process includes the recovery and purification of the solvent so that it can be reused. Solvent finishing is used for processing considerable wool fabric as well as some man-made fiber fabrics.

Foam Finishing

Foam finishing was also developed, in part at least, as a means of reducing energy consumption, water pollution, water consumption, and, to some extent, labor costs. Foam finishing is a process for treating textile substrates with foamed chemicals at a very low wet pickup or low add-on of liquid. It involves the use of a rapidly breaking medium for finishing chemicals, precise metering and flow control for the delivery of the foam to the substrate, pressure-driven impregnation of the foam into the substrate, and an applicator system designed to allow uniform high-speed application and collapse of the foam in a single step. A semistable foam is necessary to get spontaneous foam collapse and spread through the substrate; this method is in contrast to the system where stable foams are used. Stable foams are specified as part of various foam-coating processes normally requiring a separate step to break and distribute the foam through the textile material. Both systems are used in finishing operations. Manipulation and precise control make possible the application of a wide variety of chemical agents to substrates ranging from lofty and thick fabrics such as rugs and carpets to thin, sheer fabrics. Use of a dual head–dual feed applicator makes it possible to apply, sequentially, different chemicals such as resins and softeners without intervening drying steps.

Methods of foam finishing include the application of stable foams that can be broken upon application to the fabric. These require the use of presser rolls, which break the foam down and force it into the fabric. This method tries to ensure that application is uniform but with low wet add-on. Only the finishing chemicals readily penetrate the substrate textile. Of concern in the application of finishes by foam technology is the stability of the foam; it must remain in foam form until it can be applied to the fabric surface and pressed into the fabric substrate.

Foams used in textile finishing are primarily of the dispersion type. These are made by introducing and mixing gas from an external source into a liquid. Mechanically generated foams include those used in fire fighting and in making whipped cream as well as foams for textile finishing.

There are many different ways to apply foams to textiles. Foams can be printed onto the fabric substrate with printing rollers; they can be laid on the fabric and spread with a knife blade; they can be applied on one side of the fabric only or to both sides of the fabric at the same time; and they can be

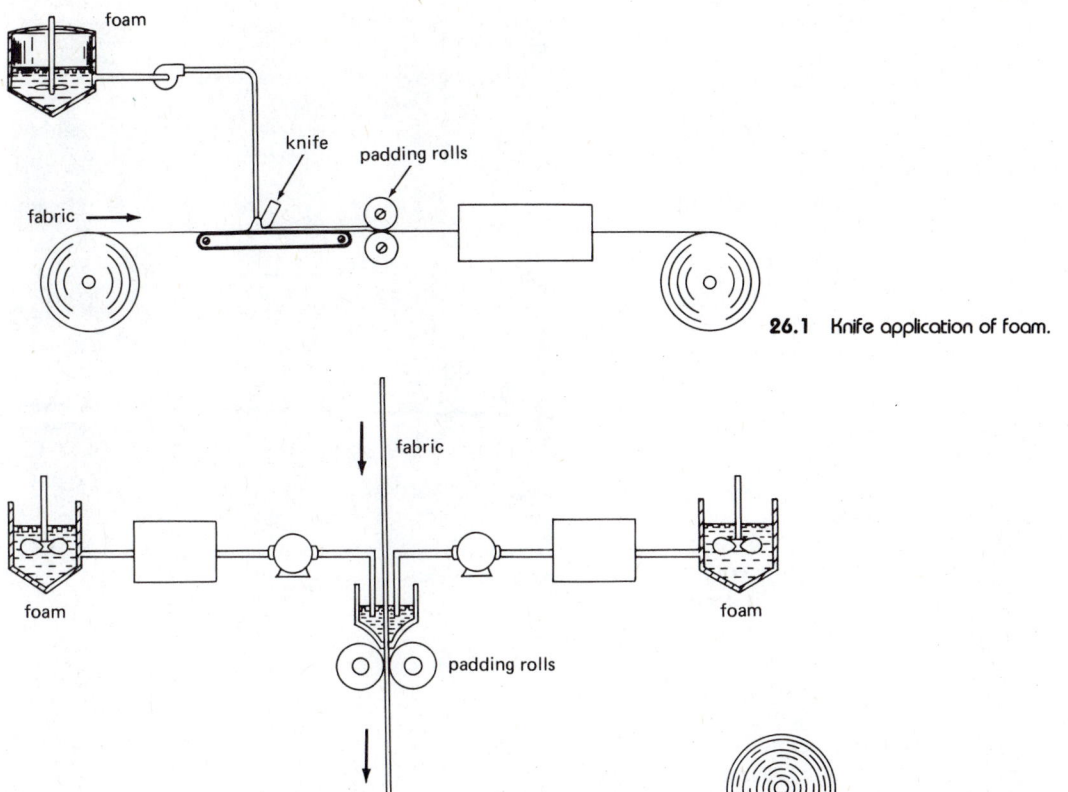

26.1 Knife application of foam.

26.2 Horizontal padder application of foam.

applied in a semistable form based on the foam finishing technology (FFT) process (Figs. 26.1–26.3).

Finishes that have been applied successfully by foam methods include durable press, water repellency, soil release, softeners, mercerization, and fabric stabilizers. Dyeing and printing may be done using foam.

It has been found that foam finishing for durable press on a polyester/cotton blend can be achieved with only half the wet pickup used in normal wet-processing techniques. In some cases, the amount of durable-press chemicals required were reduced when foam finishing was used.

The reduced amount of liquid and resulting reduced wet pickup (the amount of liquid picked up by the fabric) result in a considerable reduction in the energy needed for drying fabrics and may make it possible to omit drying between some finishing processes.

Finishes discussed in this chapter include those that are considered essential in the preparation of a

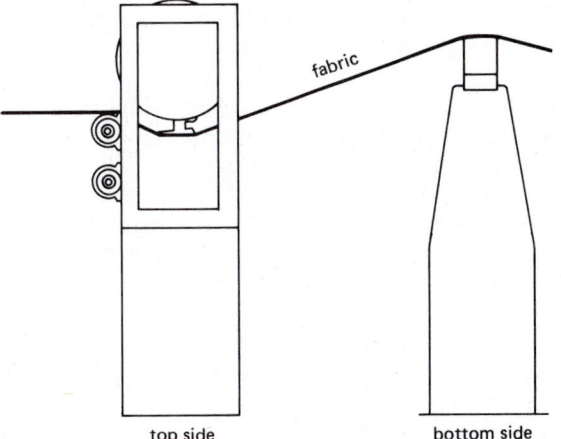

26.3 FFT application of foam to both sides of fabric simultaneously.

majority of fabrics. The processes are described as they would occur in a typical application system. Further, the finishing processes are described as they are applied to staple-fiber fabrics such as cotton, cotton/polyester blends, rayon, rayon blends, and wool. The procedures may be used on some filament-fiber fabrics, but there are several that would be omitted when processing filament-fiber fabrics.

The descriptions of the processes are primarily those used when water-bath finishing is involved. However, the same general procedures are required with foam finishing and to some extent with solvent finishing. The difference lies in the medium used, the time involved, and the equipment involved.

BASIC ROUTINE FINISHES

Singeing and Desizing

Singeing and desizing are frequently combined operations. Singeing removes protruding ends of fibers in order to produce a clear, smooth, uniform surface. Desizing removes chemicals applied before fabric construction, especially during weaving. Desizing immediately follows singeing in most instances, as it prevents possible latent damage to fabric that might occur from singeing flames or heated plates.

A typical singeing and desizing operation includes the following steps:

1. Fabric is opened to full width and fed onto storage scrays to allow ample fabric to be fed to the singers at the speed necessary to prevent fabric damage.
2. Fabric surfaces may be brushed lightly to raise unwanted fiber ends before singeing so that fabrics will be singed quickly and uniformly.
3. Fabric enters the singeing area, where it is held at full width and kept flat to minimize wrinkles or creases and to prevent selvage edges from curling. Singeing may be done with heated plates or open flames (Fig. 26.4).
4. Fabric leaves the singeing area and immediately enters the desizing bath. The desizing bath stops any singeing afterglow that might damage the cloth. The desize enzymes saturate the fabric, which moves into additional baths containing more enzymes and detergents that loosen the sizing present and prepare the fabric for the next step in processing. Fabric moves through the singeing and desizing processes between 230 and 270 yards (210–247 m) per minute.

26.4 Open flame singeing. (Springs Industries, Inc.)

Singeing is basically a chemical finish, since the reaction is one of oxidation. However, no chemical change occurs in the fabric itself. The first desizing bath contains water and enzymes that "digest" the sizing chemicals. This process loosens the sizing and makes it easy to remove during the washing operation that follows.

Desizing involves chemical action on the sizing substances applied during the stages of fabric construction; however, no chemical change occurs in the fabric. As the fabric leaves the desize bath, it is either rolled onto large beams in full width or pulled into a rope form for storage prior to scouring and bleaching.

Bleaching and Scouring

Fabric, yarn, or fibers can be bleached to prepare them for dyeing or printing or to make them white. Bleaching is a chemical finish; scouring is much like any washing process. Scouring and bleaching procedures vary depending on the fiber or fibers involved. Some fabrics are sold as they come from the loom or other fabric construction machines; others are scoured to remove foreign matter that may be present; some may require scouring for both reasons. The foreign matter that may be involved includes natural waxes, dirt, processing oils, and the sizing chemicals that might not have been removed during the desizing process. Fugitive colors that may have been introduced during fabric construction as aids in fiber or yarn identification are removed during the bleaching and scouring steps.

Soaps or synthetic detergents with alkaline builders are common scouring agents for fabrics in which cellulose is a component. For protein fibers a neutral or slightly acidic synthetic detergent is used. Despite the use of chemicals, no molecular change occurs in the fabric. Scouring removes the chemicals used in bleaching as well as any residual substances remaining after desizing.

The consumer seldom considers the effect of bleaching during manufacture on colored fabrics. However, if a fiber or fabric has not been properly bleached during preparatory finishing, it may return to its natural color, which would cause a change in the color applied to the fabric. The particular chemical used for bleaching depends on the textile fibers involved. Cellulosic fibers are bleached with chlorine compounds (sodium hypochlorite is one of the most commonly used) and/or hydrogen peroxide; many bleaching operations use a combination of both chemicals. Perborate bleaches are available for home use, but they are seldom applied commercially since hydrogen peroxide reacts in much the same way and is more effective.

Chlorine compounds used on protein fibers would result in severe strength loss and eventual destruction; thus, hydrogen peroxide is preferred for silk and wool. Sulfur dioxide may also be used for protein fibers; in water it forms sulfurous acid, which acts as a reduction bleach. Hydrogen peroxide and chlorine compounds are oxidation-type bleaches. Bleaching of protein fibers, particularly wool, using sulfur dioxide is called *stoving* rather than bleaching; it is less durable than other types of

bleaching, as the wool may reoxidize in air and return to its original color.

Man-made fibers may require some bleaching; the choice of compounds used depends on the type of fiber and, if blended with natural fibers, the type of fibers in the blend. Much fabric made of 100 percent man-made fiber will require little or no bleaching unless it has been stained during manufacture.

Fabrics may be bleached in rope or open-width form. In rope bleaching the fabric is pulled together to form a somewhat circular mass of cloth that is open enough to permit penetration of the finishing solutions but is not under any tension. In open-width finishing, the fabric is held flat and under tension.

Rope Bleaching

Typical steps in rope bleaching and scouring of fabrics that contain cellulose are as follows: fabric is fed in sequence to a prewasher, caustic saturator, J-box, washers, peroxide saturator, J-box, washers, and finally to storage bins (Figs. 26.5 and 26.6).

1. The rope of fabric is fed into the prewasher where desizing may occur if it was not done previously. If no additional desizing is required, the prewasher saturates the fabric with water and wetting agents.
2. Fabric goes from the prewasher to the caustic saturator. The caustic bath is made of a 2 to 4 percent sodium hydroxide (NaOH) solution with additional wetting agents and emulsifiers as needed to remove any remaining waxes, foreign matter, and discoloration.
3. Saturated fabric is fed into a J-box, where time, heat, and chemical action scour and clean. Movement of the fabric through the J-box is

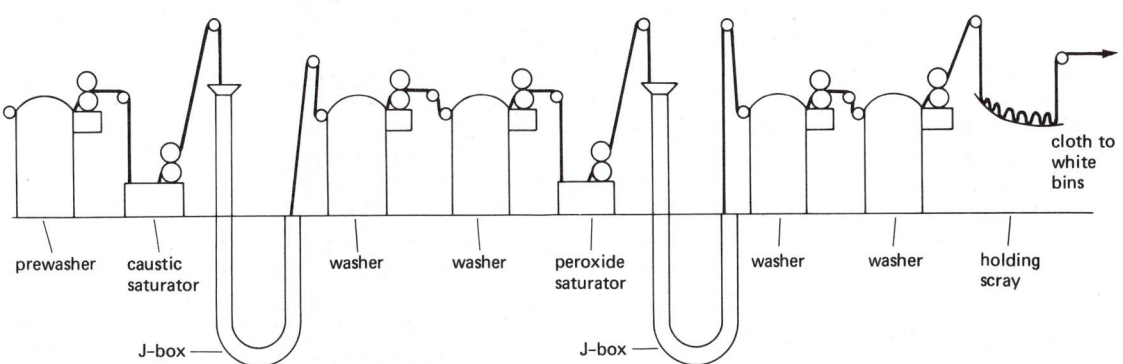

26.5 Diagram showing basic steps in rope bleaching and scouring.

26.6 *Rope bleaching range.* (Gaston County)

controlled to ensure that each yard of fabric will remain inside the box from 75 to 90 minutes. This provides the necessary time for the solution to act on the fabric to remove impurities.

4. The fabric leaves the J-box and goes to washers that remove the caustic NaOH solution and prepares the fabric for a peroxide bath.

5. Fabric enters the peroxide bath, where it is saturated with a solution of hydrogen peroxide, a silicate, and NaOH.

6. The saturated fabric is fed into a second J-box for final bleaching. Again, it remains in the J-box for the required amount of time. Time may vary depending on fiber and fabric construction.

7. From the saturator J-box the fabric goes to the final washers, where all chemicals are removed and the fabric is ready for further processing and/or drying.

Fabric moves through the rope-bleaching range at 100 to 200 yards (91–183 m) per minute. Considering that each yard must remain in a J-box for a relatively long time, one can get some idea of the total amount of yardage involved in scouring and bleaching at any one time.

Open-Width Bleaching

Open-width bleaching differs from the rope method in minor ways. The fabric is handled in open flat width under tension to prevent the formation of undesirable wrinkles and crease marks. Instead of passing through J-boxes, the fabric passes through steamers on a series of rollers, where it is kept flat and under tension (Figs. 26.7 and 26.8). Fabric moves through the open-width unit at 80 to 120 yards (73–110 m) per minute.

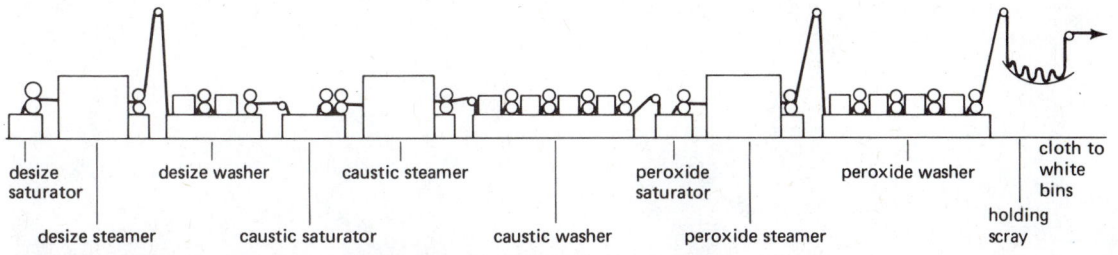

26.7 Diagram showing basic steps in open-width bleaching and scouring.

26.8 Overall view of open-width finishing frame for bleaching and scouring. (Springs Industries, Inc.)

Scouring may be done using solvents rather than water-based solutions. This procedure is increasing in use, particularly in scouring fabrics of wool and blends of man-made fibers such as polyester and wool.

Tentering

Tentering is a mechanical straightening of fabrics. It is a part of many finishing operations such as mercerizing, resin finishing, drying, and shrinkage control. A clip or pin tenter (or stenter) frame may be used (Fig. 26.9). The fabric is held horizontally by each selvage between clips or on pins. The chains holding the fabric gradually move apart to the desired width for the cloth before they enter drying units or other processes requiring tentered cloth. The tenter chains carry the fabric through the process and release the cloth to be rolled onto take-up rolls.

By feeding the cloth to the pins or clips at a speed slightly greater than the speed at which the chains are moving, some lengthwise shrinkage can be pro-

26.9 Tentering of fabric. (Westpoint Pepperell)

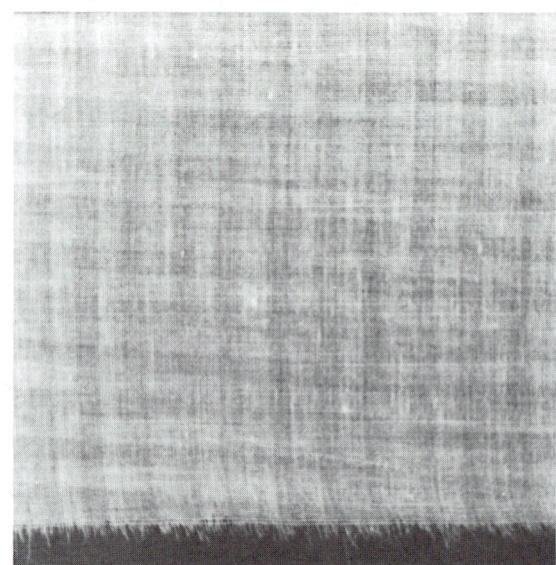

26.10 Fabric that has been printed off-grain. Note lines of pattern that are not parallel with torn edge of fabric.

duced during drying, which helps to reduce shrinkage occurring later.

If the fabric is picked up by the tenter chains in such a way that the filling yarns are not absolutely perpendicular to the warp yarns, the fabric is finished off-grain and exhibits *skew.* This produces problems in use as the fabric will not hang correctly and patterns may become distorted (Fig. 26.10). When resin finishes have been applied, or if fabrics are thermoplastic (heat-sensitive) and have been heat-set, the grain cannot be corrected. If patterns are printed off-grain, as in the illustration, it is not possible to have the straight grain and the print design in their proper relationship, and the fabric will not give consumer satisfaction.

There are a number of devices that help to set the fabric on a true grain. A tenter wtih a variable chain drive enables the operator to slow down one chain and keep the filling threads in their proper location. The same variable mechanism can be controlled by electronic controls that adjust the speed of the chains and bring the filling and warp into proper relationships automatically, or else the sensors can stop the unit so that operators can adjust the chains and make certain that warp and filling yarns are at right angles to each other.

The marks of the clips or pins used to hold fabric on the tenter chains are often visible in the fabric selvage. Many fabrics have selvages that are heavier than the rest of the fabric in order to minimize damage from tenter clips or pins.

Heat setting of man-made fiber fabrics is frequently combined with tentering. If the feed rolls operate more rapidly than the fabric take-up rolls, slack occurs in the width and permits the fabric to shrink to new dimensions. If previously heat-set fabrics are stretched during tentering, shrinkage may occur in laundering, tumble drying, or ironing at temperatures considerably less than those used for actual heat setting.

Mercerizing

Mercerization is a chemical finish applied to cellulose fibers, especially cotton. It adds luster to fabric, improves dyeing characteristics, and increases strength. Steps in mercerizing are the following: wetting out the fabric with water, saturating with caustic solution, timing to permit mercerizing action to occur, tentering to set fabric dimensions, washing, neutralizing, washing, and drying (Figs. 26.11 and 26.12).

1. Fabric is thoroughly wet out in a water bath and fed between rolls to remove excess water.
2. Fabric enters the mercerizing caustic bath, which contains between 16 and 27 percent so-

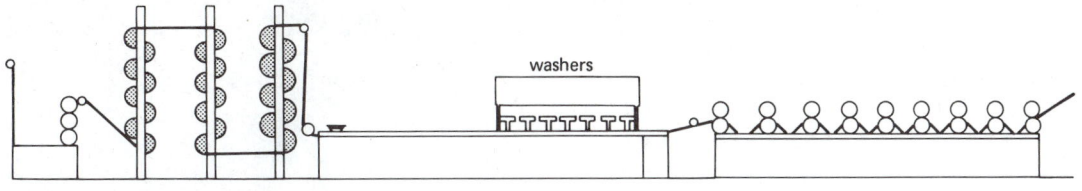

washers

caustic bath   timing cans   tenter frame   8-compartment washer

26.11 Diagram showing basic steps in mercerizing. (Springs Industries, Inc.)

26.12 Mercerizing machine. (Springs Industries, Inc.)

dium hydroxide (the typical concentration is 20–23 percent NaOH).

3. Saturated fabric is fed between further sets of rollers to ensure uniform penetration of the solution and to remove any excess.

4. Fabric is fed around a series of timing cans— large metal rolls that keep the fabric flat and smooth and of uniform width—for a specified time to control saturation and effect of the solution on the fabric.

5. Fabric is fed onto the tenter frame, which holds the fabric under tension and maintains specified dimensions.

6. Fabric on the tenter chain passes under a series of washers that force water through the fabric to start removal of the caustic. As the fabric moves under the washers, the temperature is gradually reduced to 160° to 180° F (71°–82° C).

7. Fabric is taken from the tenter chains, held open and flat, and fed into a washer; neutralizing chemicals are applied to prevent any latent damage to the fabric by the caustic chemicals.

8. Washed fabric is thoroughly rinsed and fed to the dryer, which consists of a series of heated cans, metal rolls similar to the timing cans.

9. Smooth, mercerized, dry fabric is wound onto large rolls and is ready for any additional processing required.

Fabric moves through the mercerizing unit at 80 to 120 yards (73–119 m) per minute, depending on fabric weight and compactness and on the concentration of the NaOH used.

Recent developments in finishing have included the use of foam processes for mercerization. The caustic is applied in the form of foam, which reduces the amount of liquid required and the amount of time needed for drying.

Mercerization finish swells cellulose fibers, giving them a round cross section that reflects light to create a gloss or sheen. The natural twist of cotton fiber is largly removed during mercerization; fibers have increased strength; and fibers have an increased affinity for dyestuffs.

Although chemicals are used in the mercerization process, the change in the fiber is actually physical. The cellulose fibers experience some molecular rearrangement, and the fiber is swollen. The crystallinity is decreased, and the arrangement of the molecules is such that they share stresses more equally than before giving the fiber increased tenacity.

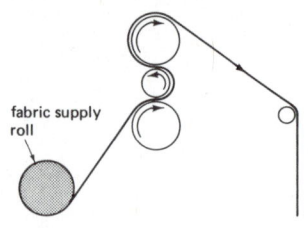

26.13 Diagram of calender rolls showing path of fabric between and around rolls.

26.14 Calender machine. (Westpoint Pepperell)

26.15 Perches used for inspection of fabric. (Springs Industries, Inc.)

Calendering or Pressing

Calendering is applied to cotton, linen, silk, rayon, and other man-made fiber fabrics. *Pressing* is the term used for wool fabrics. Basic calendering and pressing are mechanical processes. The finish is similar to ironing but is done with much greater pressure (Figs. 26.13 and 26.14). The process produces fabrics with smooth surfaces.

Pressing is usually done by flat presses. The fabric feeds between flat, heated platens or metal plates. Fabric can be held between pieces of card clothing, or needle boards, which are similar to the card clothing used in carding of fibers in yarn manufacture. These needle boards help retain a napped or pile finish or other raised textured surfaces and preserve the surface appearance while removing wrinkles from fabric and giving it a smooth surface. When flat, smooth surfaces are desired for wool fabrics and other fiber fabrics similar to wool, pressing may be done with a press cloth between the fabric and the pressing unit.

Fabric going through a standard calender unit moves continuously, but fabric to be pressed moves intermittently. In regular calendering the fabric moves at a speed similar to that of other operations that might be in tandem with the calendering. In pressing, a length of fabric moves into position, is pressed, then moves on, and a new length moves into position.

There are several calendering processes that impart design features to fabric. These include moiréing, embossing, and schreinering, which are described in some detail as a part of decorative finishes in Chapter 27.

Inspection

Fabric inspection has traditionally involved three steps: perching, burling, and mending. For many years only wool fabrics received detailed inspection; today all fabrics are given some inspection at least once during their manufacture. Some fabrics may be inspected several times depending on the processing involved.

Perching

Perching is a visual inspection. The name is derived from the inspection frame used, called a perch. This frame consists of frosted glass panels with lights behind and above. The fabric passes over the perch and is inspected visually (Fig. 26.15). Flaws, stains or spots, yarn knots, and any other imperfections are marked. The type of marking used depends on the stage in manufacture and the severity of the flaw. Some marks may be placed at the point of the flaw, while others may be marked in the selvage edge. Whether or not the flaw is corrected depends on the severity of the flaw, the location, the type, and the fabric quality.

Much inspection done today involves the use of electronically controlled devices or laser beams. The latter are becoming increasingly important. Laser inspection is rapid and highly accurate. It reduces manufacture time while increasing accuracy in identification of flaws.

Burling

Burling is the removal of yarn knots or other imperfections that can be repaired without producing inferior fabrics. The decision to repair is based on quality and price level of the fabric as well as the fiber content.

Mending

Mending is the actual repair of imperfections. It may leave marks in the fabric, which reduces the quality level, or it may be done so that the repair is not visible to the consumer.

SPECIAL FINISHES FOR WOOL FABRICS

Wool fabrics are subjected to a series of finishing operations that are specific to that fiber or to blends including wool. These processes include carbonizing, fulling, crabbing, and decating.

Carbonizing

Carbonizing is a chemical finish. Wool yarns and fabrics frequently contain vegetable matter that was not removed during carding. To eliminate this contaminate, wool fabric is immersed in a solution of sulfuric acid, then subjected to high temperatures for a brief time. The acid and heat react to convert the vegetable matter to carbon, which is easily removed by a final scouring and, if necessary, by brushing. The process must be carefully controlled to prevent damage to the wool fiber.

Crabbing

A mechanical finish applied to wool fabrics, crabbing permanently sets the construction. The fabric is immersed in hot and then cold water, and then it is passed between rollers. If it is properly fed into the rollers, the warp and filling yarns in a woven fabric are set at a true 90° angle to each other. For other constructions, the crabbing process is designed to stabilize the construction. Improper crabbing may produce "off-grain" fabrics, which never look or handle satisfactorily.

Decating

Decating is a mechanical finish used on wool and sometimes on silk, rayon, and blends of silk or rayon with wool. It can be done wet or dry. The finish helps to set the luster. For fabrics with wool content, decating develops a permanent sheen. On fabrics of other fiber content, the process softens the fabric hand.

The decating process involves pressure and moisture. In dry decating, steam and then cold air are forced through the fabric; in wet decating, hot and then cold water are forced through. For both types the final step is pressing.

Fulling

Fulling is a mechanical finish applied to wool and to some wool blends to produce a compact, closely constructed fabric. It is used primarily on woven fabrics. When a wool fabric is removed from the loom, it bears little resemblance to the fabric the consumer will see. It is loose or open in weave and hard and stiff in texture. The fulling process helps to pull yarns together and to soften them at the same time. Moisture, heat, and friction are used. The same action occurs in felting, and if wool fabrics are handled too roughly during fulling, they may become more like a felt than the intended fabric.

SELECTED OTHER FINISHES

The following finishes are important in preparing fabrics for the ultimate consumer, and they impart characteristics frequently associated with specific fabrics. Some may replace traditional processes used prior to the 1970s.

Heat Setting

Thermoplastic (heat-sensitive) fibers are generally given a heat-setting finish to produce a special shape or to ensure a stable fabric. Both filament- and staple-fiber fabrics composed of heat-sensitive fiber types are heat-set. The process is physical, and it alters the physical characteristics of the fiber.

Heat-sensitive fibers have both a melting temperature and a glass transition temperature (T_g). The glass transition temperature is the point at which the amorphous regions of the fiber develop flow or ''melt.'' At this temperature fibers can be shaped. Only the interior of the fiber need reach the T_g temperature. In addition to the flow in the amorphous regions, there are some changes in the crystalline areas of the polymer. Small crystallites may disappear and large crystallites may grow larger and assume the configuration in which the fiber is held—smooth, bent, folded, uneven, or wrinkled.

The rules for heat setting are that (1) fiber temperature must reach or exceed the glass transition temperature before the fiber is allowed to cool, and (2) any subsequent resetting or reshaping must be done at a temperature greater than that used in the first heat-setting operation.

A major reason for heat setting is to introduce dimensional stability; the degree of dimensional stability is determined by the temperature, the pe-

riod of exposure, and the amount of force used to hold the fabric in the desired shape and size during heat setting. Other characteristics that may be built into fabric by heat setting include resiliency, which contributes to wrinkle resistance; elastic recovery, which aids in size control; and design details. Fabrics can be heat-set in whatever shape desired. The fabric may be flat, pleated, or with various design details, including a smooth surface.

Both the temperature used and the time for which the fabric is exposed to that temperature are important considerations in heat setting. If a heat-set fabric is exposed to temperatures higher than those used in the heat setting, or if it is subjected to heat over an extended period of time—longer than that used in the original heat setting—the fabric will tend to assume the new shape. For example, if the fabric is wrinkled or folded where it should not be, these undesirable conditions may be permanently set into the cloth. To prevent this, laundering, drying, and smoothing temperatures below the glass transition temperature and at a point below that used for heat setting must be maintained during any type of use and care.

Brushing

Brushing is a mechanical finish that removes short, loose fibers from the surface of fabrics. Cylinders covered with fine bristles rotate over the fabric, pick up loose fibers, and remove them by either gravity or vacuum pull. The finish is usually applied to fabrics of staple-fiber content; filament-fiber yarns normally do not have loose fiber ends.

Brushing may also be a preliminary step to shearing, particularly when shearing is done to even off surface nap or pile. In this procedure the brushing operation raises fiber ends so that the fabric surface is uniform. Improper brushing may raise fiber ends unevenly and result in poor-quality fabrics. When a smooth pile surface is desired, brushing is important in raising all fiber and yarn ends to ensure that subsequent processes result in acceptable fabrics.

Liquid Ammonia Treatments

The use of liquid ammonia has been adopted as an alternative to several preparatory finishes or processes involved in finishing fabrics. It is an impor-

26.16 Shearing blades that smooth fabric surface. (Springs Industries, Inc.)

Shearing

Shearing is a mechanical finish applied to fabric of most natural fibers and to a relatively large proportion of fabrics from staple-length man-made fibers. Shearing involves cutting off undesirable surface fiber ends to even the nap or pile of the fabric surface.

After preliminary singeing and subsequent processing, fiber ends or loose fibers may protrude from the fabric surface. Shearing removes these ends and permits a clear view of the weave or knit construction. For pile or highly napped surfaces, shearing evens the surface to provide a uniform appearance. Special controls used on the shearing machine make it possible to produce a variety of designs in which there are both cut and uncut pile sections.

The shearing machine has a wide, spiral cylinder to which cutting blades are attached. It resembles a lawn mower in action. The fabric passes over brushes that raise the fiber ends or the fiber nap and then moves under the cutting blades where the shearing occurs (Fig. 26.16).

Sizing and Slashing

Sizing is the application of stiffening materials to yarns or fabrics. Sizing or size is composed of starches or resins. It is applied to warp yarns to prevent damage during the weaving operation (Fig. 26.17); in this case, the process is called slashing. When size is added to fabrics, it produces a firm, stiff fabric. The process is chemical in the sense that substances are added to the fabric. When resins are used instead of substances that are easily removed during subsequent processing, chemical change may occur in the fiber molecule as a result of cross-linking of the fiber molecules and the resins.

Starch and dextrin sizes are applied to cellulosics, particularly cotton, to create a luster and to improve the body of the fabric. These substances add weight and can make an inferior fabric look attractive. Since such finishes tend to be removed by laundering, the consumer must replace the size during care in order to maintain satisfaction with the item. The application of starch, whether by the manufacturer or by the consumer, prevents fabrics from soiling as quickly. However, their use is limited to fabrics that are to have a firm hand. Acrylic copolymers are frequently used for sizing, especially when preparing warp yarns for weaving. These substances give the

tant alternative in mercerization and in processes leading to the application of functional finishes (see Chap. 27). It is used primarily on cotton, cotton blends, and other cellulosic fiber fabrics.

The ammonia swells the cotton fiber in much the same way as caustic soda, used in the old traditional processes. Ammonia-treated fabrics have good luster and good dyeability, but caustic mercerization produces somewhat better depth of color. However, the ammonia treatment appears to result in better crease recovery, less damage from abrasion, and less loss of strength following easy-care finishing, such as durable press, than caustic treatments.

Ammonia treatments have been successful in stabilizing the size of cotton fabrics. Fabrics treated with ammonia are not as stiff or as harsh as fabrics mercerized by the caustic treatment.

Because of the improved resilience of the ammonia-treated cotton and the low internal frictional forces, the amount of cross-linking resin required for easy-care finishes is less than that needed following caustic treatments. This is responsible for the good strength and abrasion resistance of easy-care fabrics finished using liquid ammonia rather than caustic soda.

26.17 Application of sizing to yarns before weaving: slashing. (Springs Industries, Inc.)

26.18 Application of starch sizing to a fabric. (Springs Industries, Inc.)

yarns high strength and good abrasion resistance; they have good adhesion, stick to the yarns well, and are easily removed.

One procedure for sizing involves passing the fabric through the starch or sizing solution and then between rollers that pad the starch into the fabric and remove excess solution (Fig. 26.18). Starch is generally considered to be a temporary finish; res-

ins used for stiffening are generally considered durable.

Weighting

Weighting is a special sizing technique applied to silk fabrics. After complete degumming, silk fibers are very soft. To make heavy, firm, or stiff fabrics, manufacturers resort to weighting the fibers by some method. The usual process is to add metallic salts, such as stannous chloride, to the silk. The absorbency of silk protein makes this a feasible procedure; however, weighting, if overdone, causes silk fabrics to crack and split. To protect consumers, the Federal Trade Commission established rules related to weighting of silk (see Chap. 32). The sericin part of the silk as well as metallic salts may be reapplied to silk to add firmness.

Weighting either by salts or by sericin poses problems in the care of silk fabrics. Sericin works satisfactorily as long as products are dry-cleaned. Laundering removes the sericin gradually, and its presence increases the possibility of water spotting. Metallic salts do not create problems during laundering or dry cleaning, but over a period of time they tend to cause the fibers to split, which results in cracks and slits in the silk fabric.

Weighted silk has body and density, but the fabrics are not as durable as silk fabrics without any weighting. Weighted silk fabrics are more sensitive to sunlight, air, and perspiration damage than silk with no weighting.

FINISHING KNITTED FABRICS

Many of the finishing processes described in this chapter are applicable to both woven and knitted fabrics. Differences occur in the methods of handling the fabric during the operation. For example, knit fabrics are tentered carefully so that the fabric can be adjusted to the desired density—compactness of stitches and thickness of fabric—as well as the maintenance of uniform width and relation between wales and courses. Heat setting is extremely important in the finishing of knit fabrics made of heat-sensitive fibers in order to adequately stabilize these fabrics.

Machinery used in finishing knits differs somewhat from that used with woven fabrics; however, the general procedures are the same. Knit fabrics are singed, scoured, bleached, heat-set if made of heat-sensitive fibers, stabilized, brushed, sheared when appropriate, calendered or pressed, and inspected. Because of the difference in construction procedures, knit fabrics that are flat may have an adhesive added to the edges to reduce edge damage.

STUDY QUESTIONS

1. What is the difference between rope and open-width finishing procedures? When is it important to use the open-width process?
2. What is foam finishing? Why has it become popular?
3. What is solvent finishing? When is it used?
4. Why are routine finishes important to consumers?
5. Why are yarns "slashed" prior to weaving?
6. What is calendering and how does it differ from pressing?

Activities

1. Select several fabric samples. Take a sample and rub it and handle it to determine whether any finishing compounds are easily removed by this handling. If so, what type of finish (or finishes) was (were) involved? Take a second sample from the same fabric and wash it. Has the hand or appearance been changed as a result of laundering? If so, how and why?
2. Describe the basic finishing processes that are considered a routine part of the manufacture of fabrics, and collect fabric samples that illustrate these different processes.

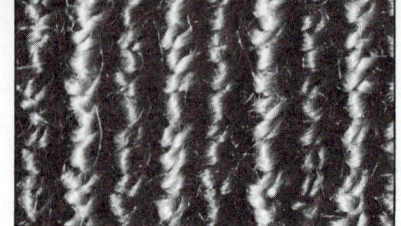

27

Finishes: Part II

OBJECTIVES
◇ **To provide information regarding methods used in wet-processing fabrics for appearance and performance**
◇ **To provide information regarding the application of finishes that modify or alter appearance and/or hand of fabric**
◇ **To provide information concerning application processes used to affect the function or performance of a fabric**
◇ **To identify typical chemicals used in wet processing**
◇ **To describe finishes used for serviceability**

KEY TERMS

abrasion resistance
absorbent finishes
antislip finishes
antistatic finishes
appearance and/or hand
  modifiers
bacteriostats
beetling
burned-out designs
ciré
delusterants
durable press
embossed finishes
flame resistance

flame retardants
flocking
fume fading
functional finishes
gigging
glazed finishes
minimum care
moiré
mothproofing
napping
optical brighteners
plastic coatings
plissé
schreinering

shrink-resistant
softeners
soil release
stabilization
stain and soil
  resistants
stiffeners
sueding
wash and wear
waterproof
water-repellent
wet processing

Finishes may be added to fabrics to alter appearance, hand, or performance. Some of the processes are an integral part of creating specific fabrics. Others are added to create aesthetic interest, and some are designed to modify the performance or function of a fabric in end use.

This chapter is divided into two main divisions. The first section describes finishes that change or modify the appearance and/or hand of a fabric. The second section is devoted to functional finishes, those that modify, change, and usually improve the performance characteristics of the fabric.

An important part of any finishing procedure is drying the fabric after the finish is applied. This is especially important when any type of liquid, including water or foam, is involved in the process. As a result of concern for the conservation of energy and cost reduction, several procedures are available for drying fabric after finishing. Fabrics

may be dried by means of heated cans or metal rolls, radiant heat chambers, radio frequency, and microwaves.

The use of dry cans is still considered the most cost-effective and efficient. Cans (heated rolls or drums) can handle any type of fabric except that which needs to be tension-free during drying. Dryers that use radiant heat include those in which the fabric is fed through the hot-air chamber on flat conveyor-type belts with large interstices in them. This process is commonly used when processing carpeting. Another type of dryer feeds the fabric through in a series of loops. This is effective for fabric that does not require tension control.

In dryers using high-frequency waves, the textile is passed between two electrodes; this process is effective at temperatures below 100°C (212°F). Dense fabrics are dried rapidly, and fabric in a variety of packages can be dried without overdrying, yellowing, or color migration. Microwave drying is similar except that the wavelengths used differ. Drying may occur with fabric on tenter chains; these are particularly helpful in hot-air drying in enclosed chambers or ovens.

Drying may be accelerated by removing moisture just before the drying operation. A method of interest involves the passing of high-pressure steam through a narrow slot. Fabric passes over the slot, where the high-velocity steam flow creates a pressure differential across the fabric and the water is literally blown out of the fabric. The use of foam finishing, discussed in Chapter 26, reduces the time and energy required for drying, as the fabric has considerably less moisture to remove.

In the discussion that follows, no attempt is made to establish any relative significance of finishes. The order in which they are cited should not be construed as indicative of importance. Rather, finishes are selected for specific purposes and to provide fabrics with various desired characteristics.

FINISHES THAT ALTER APPEARANCE AND HAND

Special Calendering

The preparation of some fabrics involves special calendering—smoothing under pressure—which imparts design to the fabric surface. The process is usually mechanical; permanence or durability depends on several factors. If the fibers used are thermoplastic, the calendering can actually soften them and impart a permanent design; if a resin is applied to the fabric, a durable calender design can be produced; if pressure alone is used on nonthermoplastic fibers, the design will generally be lost during the first laundering. Temperatures used for calender rolls vary from low or cold to 500°F (260°C); pressure ranges from 200 pounds per linear inch to 2500 pounds per inch.

Schreinering

Schreinering is produced using a special schreiner calender (Fig. 27.1). The metal roll has a series of fine lines, from 250 to 350 per inch (100–140/cm), engraved so that they form an angle of roughly 26° to the construction of the cloth. The angle is usually such that the lines are parallel to the twist in the

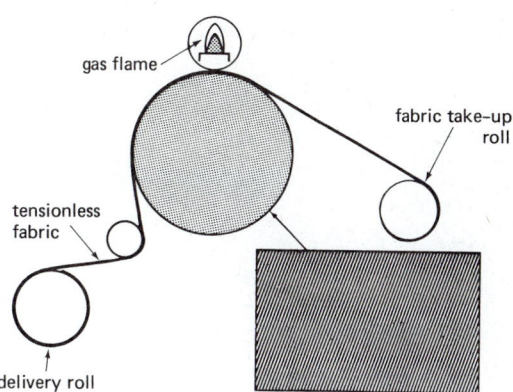

27.1 Diagram of a schreiner calender. Insert shows lines on face of roll.

yarns. The fabric is fed between the large roll with the engraved lines and a smaller roll that is heated. The finish produces a soft, silklike luster and is frequently used on cellulosic fibers such as cotton and linen. The rolls flatten the yarns and create a smooth and compact fabric. The process is also used in tricot knits to produce lingerie fabrics that are soft and opaque.

Moiré

In the days before man-made fibers, moiré fabrics were also identified as "watered" fabrics and the process was used primarily on silk. With the development of man-made fibers, a moiré finish can be applied to a variety of fibers, and the term "watered silk" has nearly disappeared from use.

The process is relatively simple. Two layers of identical fabric are placed face to face and then subjected to heat and pressure. Although flat presses may be used, large calender rolls are more economical. Two rolls are needed: a large roll covered with a surface, usually cloth, that has a slight give and a small roll that has design lines etched into the surface. As the two layers of fabric pass between the rolls, a pattern of parallel lines formed by the weft threads of one fabric is impressed upon the weft threads of the second layer of fabric and vice versa. When thermoplastic fibers are used the finish is durable; if a resin has been used as part of the finishing operation, the finish is usually considered durable. For some moiré fabrics both rolls are clear— no design lines are required—and the weft yarns in the fabric create their own design.

Rib-weave fabrics work best in creating moirés;

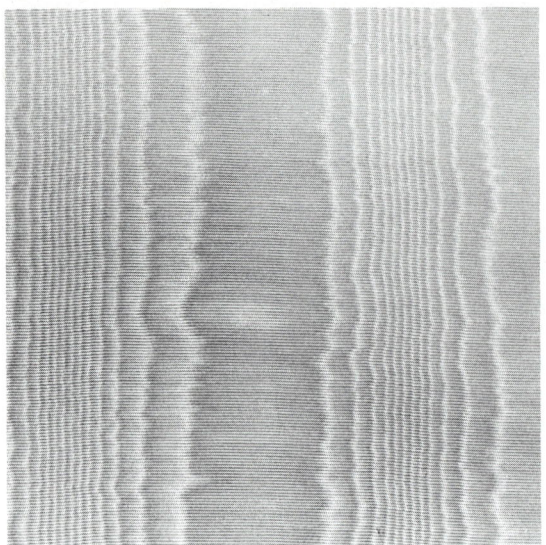

27.2 Moiré fabric.

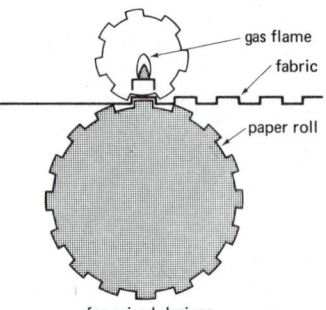

27.3 Diagram of embossing rolls.

gas flame
fabric
paper roll

for raised designs

27.4 Embossed fabric.

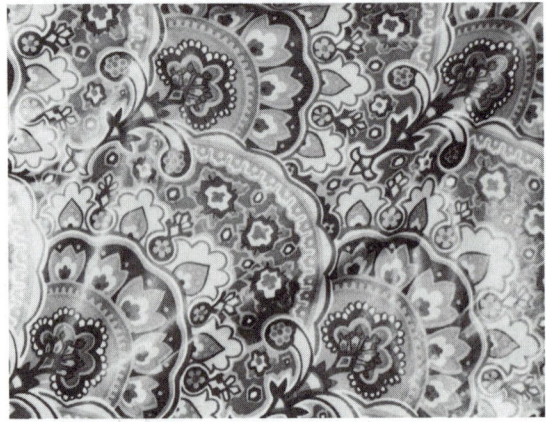

27.5 Glazed fabric.

failles and taffetas are particularly common for this use. Both layers of fabric must be identical, and a prominent rib-weave effect is recommended. Recently some knit fabrics have been given a moiré finish.

A moiré finish is characterized by a soft luster and an optical effect caused by the reflection of light. The specific reflection results from interference between light rays reflected from sets of reasonably parallel lines (Fig. 27.2).

Embossed Surfaces

Embossed fabrics are characterized by three-dimensional designs. Before the introduction of resin finishes, embossing lacked durability, but now resins aid in making these patterns relatively permanent. Thermoplastic fibers also produce fabrics that will hold embossed designs.

The calenders used for embossing consist of either two or three rolls per set. In the two roll method, one roll is of cotton or paper, and the other is made of metal and carries the engraved design (Fig. 27.3). The metal roll is heated and is half the diameter of the cotton or paper roll. In the three-roll process, two of the rolls are of cotton or paper and the third is the engraved metal roll.

The design is engraved onto the steel roll, the large roll is dampened, then the machine is run without fabric passing through until the pattern on the steel roll is deeply impressed into the soft roll. When the impression is sufficiently deep, the machine is run until the soft roll is dry. Now the fabric may be fed through the calender, and the design is embossed into the fabric. Any type of design can be adapted to embossing that can be engraved into the steel roll. Repeat size depends on the diameter of the metal roll (Fig. 27.4).

Polished Surfaces

Friction calenders along with special chemicals are used to produce fabrics with a high level of surface polish or shine. The two most common processes produce glazed surfaces or ciré finishes.

Glazed Surfaces

Glazed chintz or polished cottons are typical of fabrics that involve a polished surface (Fig. 27.5). Three rolls are required. The center roll is of cotton or paper and the other two are metal. The metal rolls operate at a very high speed, while the other roll turns at a slower speed. The polish is developed by the friction created by the speed of the metal rolls.

To make a polished surface durable, the fabric may be impregnated with a resin before calendering. Nonpermanent glazed surfaces are easily destroyed by care procedures such as laundering. Glazed or polished surfaces may be accented by the use of wax, starch, and/or shellac.

Ciré

Ciré is a high-polish finish accomplished by impregnating the fabric with wax or a thermoplastic substance of some type and then passing it through a friction calender. The durability of the finish will depend on the type of substance used on the surface, the fiber content of the cloth, and the care methods used. To make a ciré-finished fabric, the base cloth must be made of yarns that are exceedingly smooth and uniform in diameter and the fabric construction must be even and compact.

Raised Surfaces

Surfaces of cloth may be raised by several different methods. Gigging, napping, and sueding are those most frequently used. Flocking produces a surface somewhat similar in some instances, but the method used differs considerably and is discussed separately. Fabrics that are to be gigged or napped must be made of staple-fiber yarns. The filling yarns are usually of a low twist, and the yarns are lubricated to ease the extraction of the fiber ends from the cloth. The raising action is mechanical and is considered durable. The raised surface or nap hides the individual yarn shape and the base fabric struc-

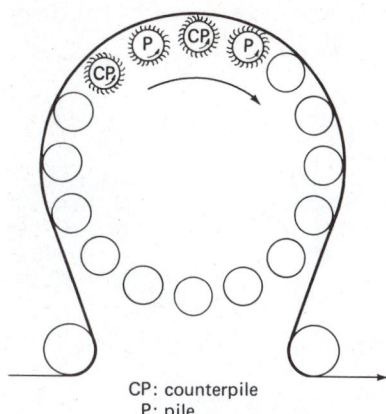

CP: counterpile
P: pile

27.6 Diagram of the napping process. Fabric moves from left to right, passing over napping rolls with alternating curved wires.

ture. The surface is soft, somewhat hairy, and textured. The base cloth may be made by various methods of construction, but weaving is the most common.

Gigging

Gigging is a napping or raising process used on wool, rayon, and other fibers when a short lustrous nap is desired. Teasels obtained from a special variety of thistle plant are attached to a cylinder. The fabric is then fed into the machine, and the teasels gently tease or pull the fiber ends to the surface to produce the nap. The process is gentle, does little damage to the fabric, and produces a soft surface. Gigging is not used as frequently now as in the past because in many cases napping and sueding methods can duplicate the nap surface obtained by gigging at less cost.

Napping

Napping is applied to cotton, rayon, wool, and other staple-fiber yarns when a deep nap or raised surface is desired. This process utilizes cylinders on which there are fine metal wires with small hooks (Fig. 27.6). Napping units have between 24 and 30 raising rolls evenly spaced around a large cylinder. Each raising or working roll is covered at 1 1/16-inch intervals with 1/2-inch-long wires set at a 45° angle to the surface to be raised. The wires on each roll are set at opposite angles to the rolls on either side. These are called pile (P) and counterpile (CP) rolls. The wires pull fiber ends to the surface of the fabric.

27.7 Napped fabric. The napping hides the actual fabric base construction. (Collins and Aikman)

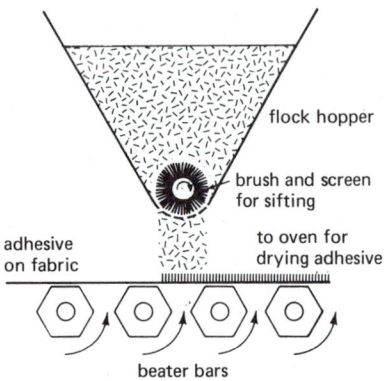

27.8 Diagram of mechanical flocking.

Labels in figure 27.8: flock hopper; brush and screen for sifting; adhesive on fabric; to oven for drying adhesive; beater bars

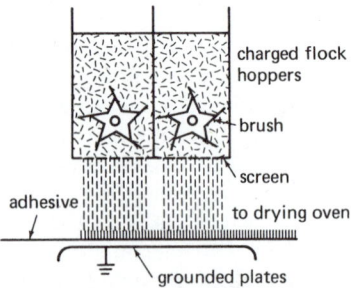

27.9 Diagram of electrostatic flocking.

Labels in figure 27.9: charged flock hoppers; brush; screen; adhesive; to drying oven; grounded plates

27.10 Fabric with flocked design.

27.11 Organdy with design areas not made transparent.

The pile rolls create long nap fibers on the fabric surface, while the counterpile rolls create short nap. In order to produce a specific degree of napping, the cloth is held under tension during the operation, and the fabric may be passed through the napper as many as 30 times to obtain the desired depth and compactness of nap. Napping can be done on one or both sides of the fabric (Fig. 27.7). The final napped surface may be evened by shearing. Napping can produce different surface effects. Raised loop napping pulls fibers away from the surface without breaking them, thus uncut loops are formed on the fabric surface. Regular napping raises the fibers and breaks them. A third type is designed so that fibers are raised and then tucked back into the fabric, creating a felted effect.

Fabrics used for napping should contain soft-spun yarns with low twist and comparatively loose fibers. Plain- or twill-weave fabrics with soft filling yarns are usually preferred. In these fabrics the warp yarns are strong and provide strength to the fabric. The loose filling yarns are easily napped. Knitted fabrics need to be made with yarns of low twist for napping. For some knits, yarns of low twist are alternated with yarns of high twist in order to give the finished fabric adequate strength. Fabrics of other construction processes are seldom used for napping, with the possible exception of needle-punched fabrics.

Fabrics with napped surfaces include flannels, flannelettes, blankets, and some coating and suiting materials. Duvetyns are made by napping the fabric and then shearing to produce a uniform surface. Napped fabrics should not be confused with pile surfaces produced by fabric construction methods (see page 232).

Sueding

Sueding occurs when the fabric is rubbed with a revolving sandpaper-covered roll. The sandpaper cuts the fibers that are on the face of the fabric and produces a fuzzy surface. One sueding process uses a support roll for the fabric. These machines rotate from 400 to 1200 revolutions per minute, and the cloth feed varies from 10 to 50 yards (9–45 m) per minute. The sandpaper varies from a very fine to a rough grit. A second process holds the fabric stretched taut between two sets of rollers. The sandpaper-covered roll drops onto the surface of the fabric between the rollers. The amount of suede effect depends on the tension of the cloth and the amount the sueding roller is dropped—that is, the amount of contact between roller and fabric.

Brushing

Brushing (see page 292) can be used to produce a raised surface similar to that obtained by sueding or napping.

Flocking

Flocking consists in attaching very short fibers to the surface of the fabric by means of an adhesive. The result is a textured appearance. Frequently, some areas of a fabric are flocked while others are left smooth to produce a pattern. The flock is usually made of rayon fibers because they are inexpensive. The best fibers for flocking are those that can be cut so that they are square on the ends.

The adhesive is printed onto the fabric in the desired pattern; then the flock is applied by one of two methods. The vibration or mechanical method is used to apply flock to one or both sides of the fabric.

The flock is circulated in a container under which the fabric passes (Fig. 27.8). As the fabric moves, it vibrates and builds up static that attracts the flock. The flock adheres to the areas where adhesive has been applied. The fabric then moves into a drying chamber, where the adhesive dries with the flock firmly embedded. Finally it is brushed to remove flock in areas where there is no adhesive as well as flock that did not adhere to the adhesive.

The second method, the electrostatic or electrocoating technique, depends on electric charge of fibers and the presence of an electric field above and below the fabric (Fig. 27.9). The fabric, printed with the adhesive, passes over an electric field, which establishes an atmosphere that forces the loose fibers in the area away from one of the electric fields and toward the second. With the fabric moving, the loose fibers strike the adhesive, and the electrical field orients the fibers and pulls them into the adhesive. The fabric moves into a drying area, where the adhesive is dried to hold the fibers in place.

Flocking is comparatively permanent to laundering as long as high temperatures are avoided. Dry cleaning, however, may cause damage by softening or dissolving the adhesive.

Recently, flocking has been applied to a wide variety of fabric types for use in both apparel and home furnishings. Interesting designs can be produced on the base fabric (Fig. 27.10). Solid flocked surfaces that resemble napped or pile materials are available. Among the fabric types duplicated by flocking are imitation suede, velour, and cut-pile carpeting.

Acid Finishes

Transparent or parchmentlike fabrics of cellulose are produced by treatment with sulfuric acid. The cotton fabric is immersed in the acid bath under controlled conditions for a brief time and then quickly neutralized. The type of finish can be applied to the entire fabric to produce a clear organdy. By printing an acid-resistant substance on the fabric before treatment, designs can be developed with both opaque and transparent areas (Fig. 27.11). The finish is most effective on mercerized cotton, but it can be used on any natural cellulosic fiber. The durability of organdy depends on the quality of the finish. A well-applied finish will be lasting and will not weaken the cloth. Organdy fabrics wrinkle during maintenance and require considerable ironing.

27.12 Fabric with burned-out design.

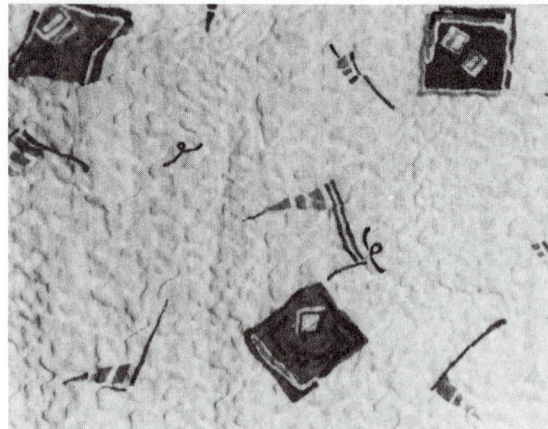

27.13 Plissé fabric. The crinkled effect is obtained by finishing with caustic soda.

A second acid finish produces *burned-out designs* (Fig. 27.12). It employs a fabric composed of two properly selected fibers—one that is easily destroyed by acid, such as cellulose, and another that is acid-resistant, such as polyester or acrylic fiber. The fabric is exposed to an acid, usually sulfuric, which burns away the sensitive fiber to leave sheer areas in the fabric. The nonaffected fiber remains to provide integrity to the fabric. The acid can be printed onto a fabric, in a paste form, to produce interesting and intricate designs. Careful planning of the fiber content and arrangement of the fibers in yarns and in the fabric construction is essential for satisfactory results.

Basic Finishes

The application of chemical bases or alkalies—frequently called caustics because of their corrosive action—produces interesting fabrics. *Plissé* crepe, a crinkled or crepelike cotton fabric, results from the action of sodium hydroxide on cotton fabric in selected areas. Caustic soda in a paste form is printed onto the fabric in predetermined areas. This causes the coated areas to shrink and the untreated areas

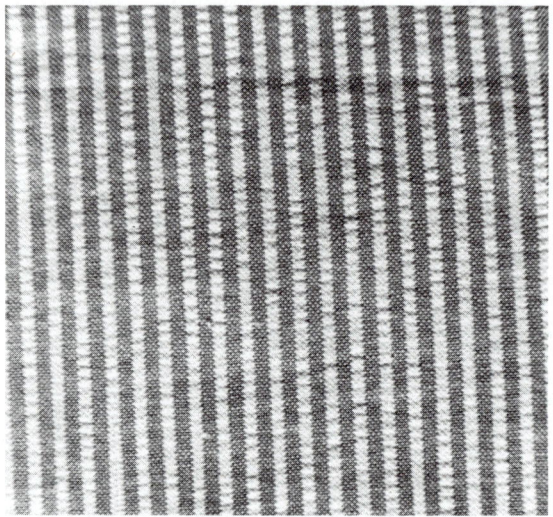

27.14 Seersucker fabric. The crinkled effect is obtained by control of warp yarns during weaving.

to pucker because of fiber shrinkage around the puckered area (Fig. 27.13). After the caustic is removed, the crinkled effect is comparatively durable. However, heavy or prolonged ironing will stretch out the fabric and result in dimensional change, so ironing is not recommended.

Crinkled, embossed, or plissé effects in various types of designs on nylon fabrics can be obtained by using phenol. The organic base accomplishes the same result on nylon as caustic soda does on cotton fabrics. The operation must be carefully controlled to prevent fiber damage.

Polyester, nylon, and other synthetic-fiber fabrics that resemble seersucker (Fig. 27.14), which is made by weaving as opposed to finishing, can be made through the use of different types of fibers. Combining a nylon or polyester, for example, that has one shrinkage potential with another fiber of the same generic type or one of some other generic type that has a different shrinkage level produces a fabric similar in appearance to seersucker or plissé. Such fabrics develop their appearance during the finishing operation when the one type of fiber shrinks a set amount and the remaining fiber shrinks a different amount. The one with the least shrinkage will pucker as the fibers around it shrink.

Depending on the fiber used in the fabric construction, various patterns can be achieved by burning out one type of fiber while leaving the other fibers unaffected. This method may be used for special designs in which acetate is one of the component fibers. Acetone removes the acetate at planned locations, leaving a fabric with sheer sections.

Stiffening Finishes

Sizings, discussed in Chapter 26, contribute a temporary stiffness to fabrics. However, a comparatively durable stiffness can be built into fabric through the use of thermosetting resins or plastic compounds of various types. They may be used to keep sheer fabrics crisp and prevent sagging and slipping of yarns. Stiffeners reduce the formation of lint and help maintain a surface that is resistant to snags and abrasion.

Softening Finishes

Softening finishes improve the hand and drape of fabric. They may add body to fabric, facilitate application of other finishes, subdue the coarseness imparted during other processing, and increase the life and utility of fabric. Batiste is an example of a common fabric treated with a softener.

Softeners are more common than many other finishes. They include a variety of products, such as oils, fats, wax emulsions, soaps and synthetic detergents, substituted ammonium compounds, and silicone compounds. The silicone compounds produce relatively durable softening.

Softening finishes are of great importance as a part of durable-press finishing. Durable press (see page 307) stiffens fabrics considerably, so softeners are included in the finishing process in order to maintain a pleasant hand.

A wide selection of softeners is available to the consumer for home care. These products, usually quaternary ammonium salts, maintain or restore fabric softness following care and reduce static cling. However, consumers should be aware that the use of fabric softeners may mask or destroy other fabric characteristics. Continued use of softeners tends to decrease absorbency, which can be very undesirable in the case of such items as towels. Softeners also inhibit flame resistance. Consumers should read care labels and follow directions for the use of softeners to avoid dissatisfaction with the end-use product. If no directions for the use of softeners are given, it may be helpful to remember the primary use of the product and then decide if softeners are useful or not.

Optical Finishes

Delusterants

Man-made fibers such as rayon, acetate, nylon, and polyester often have a high degree of luster because their relative transparency or their shape reflects considerable light. A few long light rays reflected from a surface give more luster than many short rays, because the short rays are diffused as they cross and blend. Luster may be controlled by selection of fibers or yarn construction techniques. However, when this is not feasible, supplementary substances can be added to the fiber during manufacture. A common system is to introduce pigments into the spinning solution. Titanium dioxide, a white pigment, reduces luster by the breakup of light reflection, thus creating an opaque and dull fiber. The amount of delustering can be controlled by the amount of titanium dioxide used.

External delusterants may be applied to the surface of fibers or yarns. Barium salts, such as barium sulfate, are the most common. They are applied in a two-bath procedure that results in the formation of an insoluble deposit on and in the fiber. Other external delusterants are applied in a single bath and deposited on the fiber surface. These include china clay, aluminum oxide, zinc oxide, and methylene urea.

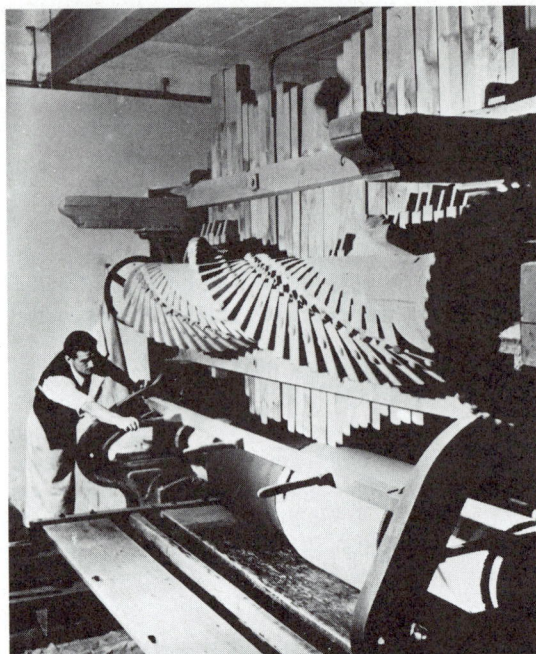

27.15 *Beetling machine.* (International Linen Promotion Commission)

Optical Brighteners

Many fabrics lose their brightness, whiteness, and clearness during processing and maintenance. In an attempt to prevent this and to maintain white and bright fabrics, optical brighteners are used by fabric converters in finishing, and they are added to many home laundering agents so the consumer can restore brightness each time a product is laundered. The substances attach themselves to the fabric and create an appearance of whiteness and/or brightness by the way in which they reflect light. These substances absorb invisible ultraviolet light and reflect it as visible blue light. Many products used in the care of textile products include some type of optical brightener in their composition. These substances are sometimes called fabric brighteners.

Beetling

Beetling is a mechanical finish applied to cotton, linen, and some rayon fabrics to increase the luster of the fabric and to produce a fabric that tends to lie flat. Beetling involves the use of a machine with many large hammers that rise and fall on the surface of the fabric (Fig. 27.15). The continued pounding flattens the yarns, closes the weave, and in-

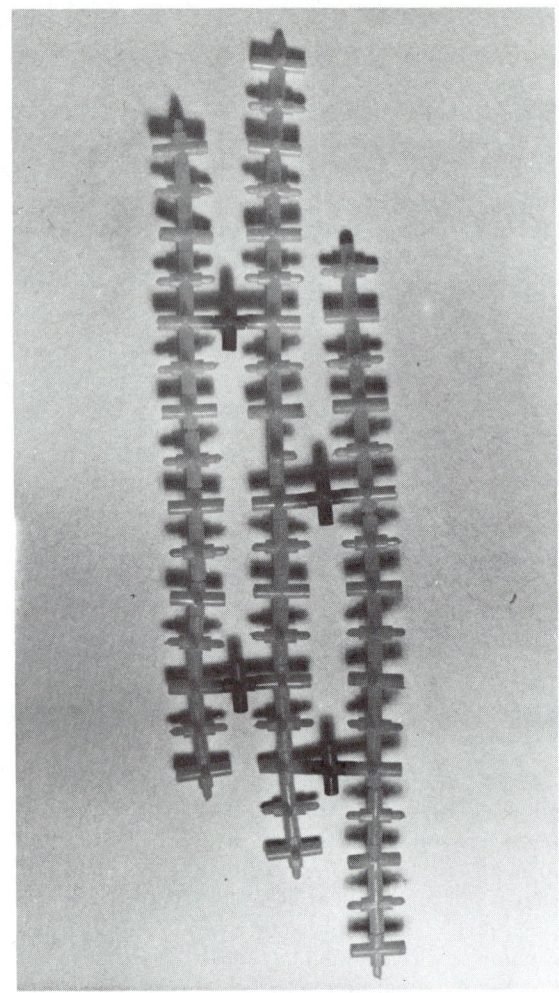

27.16 *Model simulating cross-linking of molecular chains, which introduces stability and adds such features as durable press.*

creases the light reflectance—hence the sheen—of the fabric. Beetled fabrics will withstand wear and maintenance if the fabric is laundered carefully and ironed with adequate pressure.

Other Finishes That Affect Appearance and Hand

Several finishes discussed in Chapter 26 produce changes in the appearance of the textile. These include regular calendering, mercerizing, fulling, and singeing. Finishes such as sizing, fulling, and heat setting influence the hand and drape of fabrics.

FUNCTIONAL FINISHES

Functional finishes are of two basic types: external finishes and internal finishes or chemical modifiers. External finishes are those applied to the surface of fibers, yarns, and/or fabrics that do not combine chemically with the fiber. They include softening agents; film-forming agents such as starches; selected thermosetting and thermoplastic resins; surface deposits, such as delusterants and hygroscopic agents; and some of the various corrective finishes used as water repellents, flame resistants, moth repellents, and/or bacteriostats. External finishes may alter the appearance and hand of fabrics as well as the performance.

Internal finishes are deposited within the fiber. They may combine chemically with the fiber molecule, or the finish may be mixed with the fiber molecules but not actually chemically attached to them. Some internal finishes produce a cross-linking of the fiber molecule, as shown in the simulation in Figure 27.16.

Internal finishes are applied to fibers with porous surfaces. They include thermosetting resins used for dimensional stability and durable press, and chemical modifiers that alter the fiber chemistry. Internal finishes do not alter the appearance of the fabric, but they may modify the hand to some degree.

Resin finishing is used to alter a variety of fabric characteristics. Typical steps in resin finishing are wetting the fabric, drying, applying the resin and other chemicals, drying, curing in an oven while on a tenter chain, washing, softening, and finally drying (Fig. 27.17). Several modifications to this sequence are being used at the present time. One is the use of foam finishing, which reduces the amount of moisture absorbed by the fabric and consequently the amount of drying needed. Another modification is to apply the resins without drying between the first wetting step and resin application.

A concern of the industry recently has been the need to reduce the amount of formaldehyde vapor that is released after finishing processes. Research has focused on the selection of the chemicals to be used and the methods of application. Several products have been tested, and a few are being promoted as having extremely low release of formaldehyde. This concern is of most importance in durable-press finishing.

The various functional and performance finishes are discussed without concern for relative importance, as the importance of any functional finish is a matter of consumer needs and wishes. Finishes are discussed in alphabetical order.

Abrasion-Resistant Finishes

Some manufactured fibers, particularly nylon, have inherent resistance to abrasion. However, natural fibers and some man-made fibers may be damaged by rubbing. To reduce this type of fabric damage, manufacturers may do one of two things: (1) blend fibers of high abrasion resistance wtih those of low resistance or (2) apply soft thermoplastic resins, which appear to increase the fabric's resistance to abrasion damage. Acrylic resins may improve abrasion resistance; however, the acrylic resin must be selected with care, as some are too soft to be effective and others are too hard and introduce brittleness to the fabric.

The problem of abrasion is extremely complex,

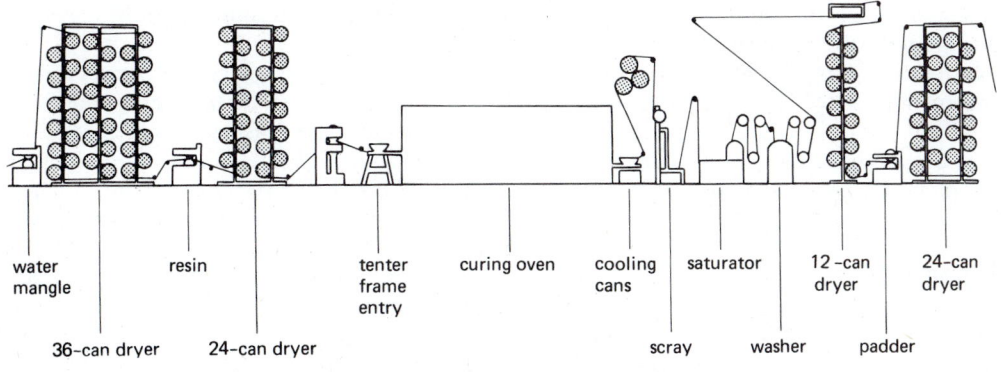

water mangle   resin   tenter frame entry   curing oven   cooling cans   saturator   12-can dryer   24-can dryer

36-can dryer   24-can dryer   scray   washer   padder

27.17 Diagram showing basic steps in resin finishing. (Springs Industries, Inc.)

but it is believed that a substantial part of the resistance produced by resins results from the fact that the resin binds the fibers more firmly into the yarns and thus increases the time and amount of abrasion required to roughen the surface by fiber breakage.

Recent evidence indicates that abrasion-resistant finishes may increase the wet soiling of fabric. These finishes are popular on fabric to be used for trouser pockets, waistband linings, hat bands, and similar uses where abrasion cannot be avoided.

Absorbent Finishes

Absorbent finishes increase the moisture-holding characteristics of the fiber. This helps the cloth absorb more moisture and increases the drying action of such fabrics. At the same time, the time needed to dry the fabric is increased. One type of absorbent finish causes the absorbed moisture to break up into small micelles that evaporate readily. A second type holds the moisture by absorption and disperses it into the yarns.

Absorbent finishes have been applied to towels, underwear, sport shirts, and other items where moisture absorbency is desirable. These finishes may aid in the application of dyestuffs. They are external coatings of yarn and fabric, and they are applied from aqueous baths. Durability of such finishes is only fair.

Antipesticide Protective Finishes

Concern for people involved in the application of pesticides or who work in areas where there are large concentrations of pesticides has gained widespread attention. Antipesticide finishes are designed to prevent penetration of the pesticide through clothing and to permit easy removal of any pesticide on the surface of clothing by laundering. Special fabric constructions may also be used. As yet, little information is available concerning finishes for this purpose, but it is expected that considerable work will be done in this area during the 1980s.

Antislip Finishes

Finishes applied to a fabric to reduce or eliminate yarn slippage are called antislip, slip-resistant, or nonslip finishes. They help keep yarns in their proper position in the fabric and reduce seam fraying.

Three types of products have been used. (1) Rosins, hard waxy substances left after the distillation of volatile turpentine, have been widely applied, but they have poor washfastness unless treated with metallic salts such as zinc acetate. (2) Colloidal dispersions of silica decrease slippage by reducing surface smoothness; these materials are not durable. (3) Urea and melamine formaldehyde resins are effective agents in reducing yarn slippage and are considered durable.

Antistatic Finishes

Static buildup in fabrics has long been recognized as a problem both to the manufacturer and to the ultimate consumer. With the development of man-made fibers such as acetate, nylon, polyester, and acrylic, the problem of static electricity increased in importance. Difficulties in manufacturing and processing fibers, even in humid rooms, were evident, and some type of system to reduce static became essential.

Antistatic finishes work by one or more of three basic methods. (1) The finish may improve the surface conductivity and thereby help the electrons to move either to the ground or to the atmosphere. (2) The finish may attract molecules of water to the surface, which in turn increase the conductance and carry away the static charges. (3) Chemical finishes may develop an electric charge opposite that of the fiber, which neutralizes the electrostatic charges.

The most effective finishes work in all three ways. However, fibers differ in the types of static charges they generate—some are positive and some are negative. Thus, in order for the third method to be effective, there must be different finishing agents for different fibers.

Most antistatic agents are cationic surface-active chemicals based on quaternary ammonium compounds. Many of these finishes are not durable and require replacement during laundering or drying.

Static buildup on fabric is annoying to consumers, is actually dangerous in some situations, and increases the speed of soiling. Thus, finishes to reduce static are highly desirable to consumers. Several special antistatic fibers are available on the market; some are designed for special end uses such as carpeting, while others may be used for a variety of purposes. Trade names of some antistatic fibers currently available include Ultron® nylon, Antron® nylon, Staticgard® nylon, and Anso® nylon.

The consumer may add static resistance to fabrics laundered at home through the addition of fabric softeners. These products coat the fibers with a substance that increases conduction and prevents buildup of electrons along with the softening action. Some softeners are added to the rinse cycle during laundering; others are impregnated into small sheets or strips of nonwoven fabric and used in the clothes dryer. Spray antistatic finishes are available for consumers to spray directly onto fabrics before wearing.

Bacteriostats

Bacteriostats, or antimicrobial finishes, are applied to fabric for three basic reasons. They may control the spread of disease and reduce the danger of infection following injury; they help to inhibit the development of unpleasant odors from perspiration and other soil on cloth; and they reduce damage to fabrics from mildew-producing fungi and rot-producing bacteria.

Evidence indicates that substances to prevent fabric deterioration from microorganisms were known in ancient Egypt and were used to preserve the fabrics used to wrap mummies. The current use of bacteriostats dates from the early 1900s; it was World War II, however, that made people aware of the value of these finishes. The German army treated soldiers' uniforms with quaternary ammonium compounds, and records indicate that men wearing these treated fabrics suffered considerably less infection from wounds. Currently, fabrics for a variety of end uses are treated with bacteriostats. These finishes may be durable or renewable. The renewable ones are external finishes that produce a "climate" unfavorable to the microorganisms. Some durable finishes are surface coatings that have been made insoluble so that they remain on the fabric during use and care; other finishes are internal and are insolubilized within the fiber structure. The preferred type is the durable finish.

Some of the successful compounds used as antimicrobial or bacteriostatic finishes include the following:

1. Methylol melamine or similar durable-press chemicals in combination with zinc nitrate, ammonium chloride, and zinc chloride.
2. Organofunctional silanes. One successful compound is 3-trimethoxysilylpropyldimethyloctadecyl ammonium chloride. It has been found to be highly successful on carpeting and produces a product that is bacteriocidal, fungicidal, and algicidal.
3. Zinc acetate with hydrogen peroxide and acetic acid. This system has been evaluated as excellent on cotton and durable to a minimum of 50 launderings.
4. Copper zirconia compounds; rated good to excellent.
5. Dodecyldimethyl benzyl ammonium naphthenate; rated very good.
6. Alkyl ammonium naphthenate, rated good.
7. Triethanolamine plus acetic acid plus a metal salt, rated good.
8. Antibiotics such as neomycin and bacitracin; ratings vary depending on the fiber substrate.

Although some of these finishes will withstand 50 launderings, or more, others may be removed after as few as 15. It is recommended that fabrics with bacteriostats or antimicrobial finishes be laundered carefully. Bleach should be avoided if possible, as it tends to remove many of these finishes.

Finishes to prevent the growth of microorganisms appear on fabrics for a wide variety of applications: apparel, home furnishings, fabrics for hospitals, and other medical sites, various types of commercial fabrics, and industrial fabrics where exposure to microorganisms can cause problems. Specific end-use items that are frequently finished with some type of antimicrobial agent include socks, shoe linings, sportswear, babies' clothing, sheets, pillowcases, mattress padding and coverings, carpeting and carpet underpadding, blankets, towels, tentage, tarpaulins, auto convertible tops, and various geotextiles.

A number of research projects have supported the value of bacteriostatic finishes. A lower incidence of reinfection from athlete's foot was noted when shoe linings were treated. Homemakers have remarked on the absence of musty odors that accompany mildew in hot, humid climates when floor coverings were protected with these finishes.

Durable Press

Durable press is the term used to refer to the ability of a fabric to retain its original surface appearance and/or shape following laundering, with little or no ironing required. *Wrinkle recovery* is a term used in technical literature to indicate the ability of a fabric to recover from folding deformation while it is dry. *Crush resistance* is used to describe the ability of a fabric to recover from crushing; frequently this term is applied to pile fabrics. These properties can be imparted to fabrics either through fiber choice or by finishing. This discussion is limited to the application of finishes and is aimed primarily at durable-press finishing.

A recognized defect of cellulose fibers is their tendency to wrinkle badly during wear and care. Unattractive products result that require considerable ironing to restore their original appearance. Before the 1920s the only method known to minimize wrinkling of cellulose-fiber fabrics was to apply starch, and that was a temporary solution only. The first measurements of fabric creasing were made in 1919 and set the groundwork for the development of finishes designed to reduce wrinkling and creasing. Finishes developed during the 1920s and 1930s had one characteristic in common: they caused considerable loss of strength and fabric deterioration. Fabrics made of linen had considerable inherent strength owing to the fiber; thus, these could be treated with the early finishes and still provide the consumer with adequate wear. The finish on these fabrics made the item so much more attractive that consumers asked for similar treatments on other cellulosic-fiber fabrics. Cotton, however, did not stand up well to these finishes, and as recently as the end of the 1940s, less than 1 percent of cotton fabric was treated with minimum-care finishes.

Consumers were impressed with the few examples they saw and did not seem to realize, or maybe they did not care, that such fabrics were considerably less durable. One of the best-kept secrets of the textile industry was the fact that easy-care finishes caused a considerable loss in fabric strength and in abrasion resistance.

The introduction of man-made thermoplastic fibers that could be heat-set to build in optimum appearance made easy care an attainable goal of the textile industry. The introduction of durable press (or permanent press, as it may be called) occurred in 1964. Since that time, most fabrics with any cellulose-fiber content are receiving some type of durable-press finish. To reduce the damage caused by the loss of strength and abrasion resistance of the cellulosic fibers, most durable-press fabrics now include a strong man-made fiber such as polyester or nylon. Polyester is the most common fiber to be combined with cellulose, especially with cotton, in fabrics made since the early 1970s.

There have been two major theories about why the finishing process improves wrinkle resistance and reduces the care required. It is quite probable that most durable-press fabrics combine these two theories. One theory states that the finishing resins build a memory into the fiber so that it returns to the size and shape it had during the finishing operation. The second theory holds that the finishing agents react chemically with cellulose and bring about a cross-linking of the cellulose molecules. This causes the molecules to experience strain whenever they are moved into a new position; then, when the strain is removed, they return to the original arrangement and the fabric is once again flat. If the finish is cured on a creased or pleated fabric, the fabric will return to its creased or pleated state after deformation.

In simplified terms, the durable-press operation consists in padding liquid into the fabric, drying on a frame to desired dimensions, curing at an elevated temperature, scouring to remove residual chemicals, and final drying. Durable-press finishes can be cured at either of two points in the process. Precured durable press is given the final cure at the plant, followed by the final drying. Delayed cure or deferred cure involves additional steps or a different order of processing. The fabric may be partially cured in the flat fabric state, making certain that part of the resin is unpolymerized. The fabric is then dried and made into the end-use item. Following construction of the item, the resin is given a final cure, at which time the remaining finish is polymerized within the fiber. Some fabrics may have finishes applied, be dried, then be made up into end-use items with no curing at all until after the fabric has been constructed into the end-use product.

Various types of chemicals are used for durable-press finishing. The major chemical used for deferred-cure methods is dimethylol-dihydroxy-ethylene urea (DMDHEU). The precured process uses a variety of resins including DMDHEU, dimethylol-ethylene urea (DMEU), dimethylolpropylene urea (DMPU), and methylated hexamethylolmelamine. For precured white fabrics, carbamates and DMPU are effective. Melamine, triazones, and imidazolidones are used for some durable-press finishing.

Each of the chemicals used can bring about a cross-linking between cellulose molecules. This occurs as the finishing chemical releases an OH group and becomes attached to the cellulose molecule, which releases a hydrogen atom. The finishes and fibers cross-link and give off molecules of water. The action with DMDHEU is diagrammed as follows:

DMDHEU   +   cellulose ⟶

cross-linked cellulose + water

Formulas for some of the other chemicals used are diagrammed. Note that in each case there is either an $-OH$, $-H$, or $-NH_2$ group that can react with the cellulose to cross-link the molecules.

1. Dimethylolethylene urea (DMEU):

2. Methylol carbamates (a specific example is hydroxyethyl methyl carbamate):

3. Dimethylolpropylene urea (DMPU):

4. Melamine (used to give good fabric hand and drape):

5. Imidazolidone (note that the R, R', and R″ will vary, but some of these will be groups such as $-CH_2OH$, $-H$, $-CH_3$, $-NH$, $-NH_2$, $-OH$):

6. Triazone (used much less frequently than in the past):

Durable-press finishing utilizes a cross-linking resin, catalysts to initiate the cross-linking action, a softening agent to help maintain the quality of the fabric, and a wetting agent to increase the speed of the penetration of the finish into the fabric. Durable-press fabrics do have reduced tear strength and abrasion resistance, but there is a difference in degree. According to Weaver:[1]

> There is a direct, positive correlation between wrinkle recovery or durable-press appearance and the amount of resin applied—and there is also a direct (negative) correlation between the wrinkle recovery or durable-press behavior and the tear strength. Some systems give a little better strength than others, but they all lower the strength by 40 to 50 percent in order to give durable-press properties to fabrics.

If fabrics are not thoroughly rinsed after the final cure, it is possible for some of the catalyst and free formaldehyde to be left in the fabric. These chemicals can set up a reverse action and break the cross-links formed. Another problem arises when these resins gradually wash away, resulting in decreased self-smoothing characteristics.

Perhaps a more serious problem has been the release of formaldehyde vapor into the air. There is evidence that free formaldehyde is a carcinogen; thus it is extremely important to limit the amount of this vapor delivered into the air. Efforts to control this release have included the use of finishing resins

[1]J. W. Weaver, personal communication.

that have a very low formaldehyde content or none at all. One successful method appears to be the use of methylated DMDHEU with magnesium chloride and citric acid as the catalysts; another is the use of DMDHEU with carbohydrazide with the subsequent removal of formaldehyde-carbohydrazide as insoluble solids. Still another process uses methylated DMDHEU and washes the cured fabric thoroughly to reduce any free formaldehyde to trace levels. A further process has replaced 35 percent of the DMDHEU with alkyl nitro-alcohol. Since nitrate and magnesium chloride were used as buffers, up to 60 percent less released formaldehyde occurred with durable-press performance compared with other processes.

It is desirable to achieve durable press with as little strength loss as possible—zero loss is the goal—and there should be no change in soiling or comfort characteristics from nonfinished fabric. The finishing process should use as little energy as possible, should have rapid curing, and, as noted, should allow as low a level of free formaldehyde released as possible.

Although the majority of durable-press fabrics include some polyester fiber in a blend with cotton, currently (1984) some 100 percent cotton durable-press fabrics are available.

A concern to consumers in the use of durable-press fabrics has been the tendency for such fabrics to discolor when bleached with chlorine bleaches. Some cyclic reactants give good durable-press properties and are not visibly damaged by chlorine. However, fabric may be weakened and wear is reduced. Triazones may show less damage than other substances because they are highly basic, and the basicity nullifies the action of any acid formed. However, if not adequately rinsed after curing, the triazones may develop a fishy odor that makes them undesirable. Carbamates are used on white fabrics because they do not yellow during the curing operation. They provide good self-smoothing characteristics and resist damage from chlorine bleaches.

Finishes can be cured by either a wet fixation, which involves the use of a high-temperature wet bath, or a vapor phase (steam) process; or they can be fixed by gamma radiation or low-energy beta radiation treatments.

Durable-press finishes work only on cellulosic fibers. When cellulose is blended with polyester, for example, the polyester does not accept the finish. However, the polyester and other man-made fibers that might be used are not damaged by the finishing process or the chemicals used. The use of blends in durable-press fabrics is popular because the thermoplastic fiber adds strength to the fabric and makes it possible to produce good durable-press fabrics that are light in weight, comparatively sheer, and serviceable.

Despite the popularity of durable-press fabrics, they do pose problems to consumers. Deferred-cure fabrics are almost impossible to alter or change after construction into end-use items. Precured fabrics are difficult to shape into end-use items. Nonetheless, durable-press and other easy-care fabrics are sought by consumers because of the reduced care involved and the retained appearance during use and care.

Durable press appears in a wide variety of end-use items. Apparel, home furnishings, and fabrics for various commercial and industrial applications are usually given some type of durable-press finish if the fiber content involves cotton or other cellulosic fiber. It is probable that consumers will continue to select items with durable-press or easy-care finishes in order to reduce or eliminate time spent in care of these textile items.

Flame Resistance

Most textile fibers will burn if the environmental conditions are right. Some fibers are self-extinguishing if nothing around them supports a flame; others require special treatment to reduce danger from fire.

Finishes that reduce the flaming, charring, or afterglow of fibers and fabrics are important for safety. Most finishes in this group produce fabrics that will burn in the direct path of flame but that self-extinguish when the source of flame is removed. Finishes cannot provide a completely safe product. They can, however, reduce the danger and provide a margin of safety that may prevent serious harm to people and property.

Flame resistance is defined as that property of a material whereby flaming combustion is prevented, terminated, or inhibited following application of a flaming or nonflaming source of ignition, with or without subsequent removal of the ignition source. Flame resistance can be an inherent property of the basic material, or it may be imparted by specific treatment (finishing, for example). *Flame-retardant treatment* is a process for incorporating or adding flame retardants to a material or a product. A *fire-*

proof substance is one that is totally unaffected by fire. Very few substances are fireproof. The only possible textile fiber that can be described as fireproof is asbestos. Although glass does not burn, it will melt and thus its form is destroyed.

Flame-retardant treatments are not new. The history of these finishes can be traced back at least 300 years. In 1821 J. L. Gay-Lussac produced some flame retardants for Louis XVIII of France. Versmann and Oppenheim did comparative studies of flame retardants in 1859 and found ammonium phosphate and tungsten salts to be effective. These are still used in some renewable finishes. In 1922 Kling and Florentin studied the use of borax and boric acid and arrived at a recommended mixture of these substances. These were further tested by Ramsbottom and Snoad in 1947. Home methods for flame resistance still use borax and boric acid.

Various government rules and regulations pertain to flame resistance of textile items. These are discussed on page 373. To satisfy these various rules and regulations, flame-resistant finishes should be durable through normal care for a normal use life. This has been defined in the legislation as 50 launderings.

The finish should be bound to the fibers in such a way that it will release flame-retardant chemicals at the time flaming temperatures are reached but not at any other time. Improperly applied finishes can result in fabric degradation. Finishes should not change the hand or appearance of the fabric. However, it is recognized that some flame-retardant treatments do affect certain dyes and may increase the harshness of the fabric. It should be obvious that such finishes do not produce fabrics that will survive a fire with no damage; their purpose is to provide an element of safety so that damage is reduced and danger to life is reduced or eliminated.

Flame-resistant finishes are classified in one of the following groups:

1. Water-soluble compounds that might be reapplied after exposure to moisture. These include borax, boric acid, ammonium phosphate, ammonium sulfate, and various mixtures of these chemicals.
2. Salts dissolved in a suitable solvent, which is applied to the fabric and either evaporated or made to react with a second compound to render the salts insoluble. These salts include metal oxides such as ferric oxide, stannous oxide, and manganese dioxide.
3. Oils, waxes, or resins that incorporate chlorinated substances, bromine compounds, phosphorus compounds, antimony compounds, or other similar flame-retardant material.
4. Substances that react with the fiber to produce molecular change. These are usually confined to cellulose fibers and produce cellulosic ethers or esters with flame-resistant properties.
5. Substances combined with man-made fiber polymers in the solution or melt form and extruded as an inherent part of the fiber.

Not all types of finishes are suitable for all fabrics. The selection of finish for the particular fiber and fabric is determined by such factors as anticipated use, appearance, desired hand, and chemical reactions of the fiber molecules.

Some of the chemicals and/or finish trade names used for flame-retardant treatments include the following:

1. Provatex CP, an organic fiber-reactive phosphorus compound, used primarily on cellulose fibers.
2. THPC, tetrakis hydroxymethyl phosphonium chloride, one of the important chemicals used for cellulose and cellulose blends.
3. THPOH-NH$_3$, tetrakis hydroxymethyl phosphonium hydroxide plus ammonia, trademarked by Cotton Incorporated as Firestop®. It is used for cellulose and cellulose blends.
4. Fyrol 76, a reactive vinyl phosphorus ester, is used with N-methyl acrylamide and colloidal antimony/halogen systems. It produces good flame resistance and can be used with durable press effectively. Zinc nitrate is used as a catalyst.
5. TM-DABT, tetramethyl 2,4 diamino 6(3,3,3 tribromo-1 propyl)1,3,5 triazine, effective on 100 percent cotton. In combination with colloidal antimony oxide, the finish is effective on polyester/cotton blends.
6. Proban, an ammonia-cured finish that produces a cross-linked phosphorus/nitrogen polymer within cellulose fibers.
7. Astro® pyropruf, used on nonwoven fabrics.
8. Spartan®
9. Flamegard®
10. Glotard®
11. Fireway®
12. Caliban®
13. Protogard®

A desirable method of providing flame resistance is to use fibers that are inherently flame-resistant. Such fibers include aramids, modacrylics, Cordelan polychal, novoloid, vinyon, asbestos, and glass. In addition, flame-resistant modifications of rayon, polyester, and nylon fibers are available. Trade names for fibers that are considered flame-resistant include: HEIM polyester, Extra FR polyester, Orlon® FLR modacrylic, SEF® modacrylic, Teviron vinyon, Valren vinyon, Leacril vinyon, Cordelan® polychal, Nomex® aramid, Kevlar® aramid, Kynol® novoloid, and fiberglass fibers.

Flame-retardant treatments act in various ways:

1. They release gases or foams that provide a flame-smothering atmosphere.
2. They make the products of pyrolysis less flammable by causing a change in the type of pyrolysis products formed. These give rise to materials that are less flammable than those from the non-flame-resistant substrate. In cellulose this includes the formation of Lewis acids (acceptors of electrons) at flaming temperatures; these acids catalyze the dehydration of cellulose to carbon and water.
3. Substances may be released that accelerate the degradation of cellulose with the release of volatile products that inhibit flaming.
4. Products that interfere with the burning reaction may be formed. These change the mechanisms of the chemical reactions during burning to prevent continued propagation of the flame.
5. Substances may reduce the transfer of combustion heat back into the substrate.
6. Substances may reduce the diffusion rate of pyrolysis products to the flame.

It is possible that several of these actions may occur at the same time.

Consumers and textile students should be aware of the problems related to flame resistance. If fiber blends are involved, flame resistance may be extremely difficult to attain. For example, cotton can be made flame-resistant relatively easily, as can polyester; however, if the two fibers are combined, the problem becomes difficult, and as yet there is no really good treatment for these blends.

Flame-retardant treatments may influence the hand of fabrics and result in fabric that is stiff and rough in texture. This can be a problem particularly with fabrics for sleepwear. Dimensional stability of fabric may be improved by such finishes.

Flame-resistant finishes delay the speed of fire spread in fabrics and make it possible to extinguish the flame before major damage occurs. Nonetheless, such fabrics can give a false sense of security. These fabrics do burn, and they may give off toxic fumes that can be hazardous. Some finishes may increase the amount of smoke produced. Further, flame-resistant fabrics tend to cost more than similar fabrics without such finishes. However, it is important that they be available to consumers who want them, as they do provide a safety factor. Whether they should be mandated for all fabrics for selected end uses is a philosophical question that cannot be easily answered.

The care of flame-resistant fabrics requires attention. Soaps mask the effectiveness of the finish and render it inactive within three launderings. Bleaches destroy the finish, and fabric softeners destroy the effect and increase the ease of burning. Calcium in hard water reduces the effectiveness of flame resistants, and nonphosphate detergents may stop the flame-resistant action. It is important to remember that the property of a fiber in relation to its behavior in flame may be changed by the presence of normal processing substances such as dyestuffs. The presence of soil may increase flammability.

The most satisfactory method of care for flame-resistant fabrics is to launder with phosphate detergents. Avoid fabric softeners and chlorine bleaches. When bleaching is needed, use perborate bleaches, and if phosphate detergents cannot be used in the geographical area, try citrate detergents or nonionic commercial detergents.

Fume-Fading-Resistant Finishes

Certain dyestuffs on certain fibers are subject to color loss or change as a result of exposure to atmospheric fumes that include oxides of nitrogen and various sulfur compounds.

Dyes applied to acetate fibers are particularly susceptible to fume fading, and the same type of dyestuff may cause problems when used on nylon or polyester fibers. A major step in efforts to reduce fume fading was taken when pigments were introduced into the fiber polymer solution before extrusion. However, not all fabrics subject to fume fading can be dyed economically by pigment coloration.

For items requiring coloration after yarns and fabrics have been constructed, finishes can be added to reduce fume fading. Simple alkaline substances such as borax are sometimes used, but these are not permanent and require replacement after laundering. Comparatively durable finishes are produced by various tertiary amines.

Metallic and Plastic Coatings

In an effort to produce fabrics that reflect heat, fabric converters developed finishes in which an aluminum coating was applied to the back of fabrics. This coating modified the warmth or coolness of the fabric. A current use for metallic and plastic coatings is for drapery linings. The fabric helps maintain constant room temperatures; the aluminum coating will reflect sunlight in summer and retain heat in winter; plastic coatings close the interstices of the fabric and delay the passage of heat through the fabric.

Aluminum finishes with adhesives that resist solvents will dry-clean fairly well; some, however, are lost when dry-cleaned. Fabrics with closely packed yarns and with smooth surfaces serve as good substrates for such finishes. Plastic coatings help reduce the amount of soil that will penetrate and attach itself to fabric.

A different use of plastic coatings on fabrics is to create designs. Plastic coatings can be treated so they resemble leather. Depending on the end use of the fabric, coatings can be applied either to the face or the back of the fabric. For drapery linings and similar uses, the coating is attached to the back or wrong side of the cloth; when the coating is to provide appearance value, such as a leather effect, it will be applied to the face of the cloth.

A problem with either metallic or plastic coatings is that they may crack and peel off the substrate fabric. This is especially true of plastic coatings that are mistreated or cleaned incorrectly. It is important to read and follow any care instructions attached to the fabric.

Mothproofing

Fiber containing protein, such as keratin in wool, are susceptible to damage by moths and carpet beetles. The cystine amino acid residues in keratin are believed to be what the moths prefer, and this explains why they eat hair fibers containing keratin and not the fibroin of silk. Carpet beetles, on the other hand, will eat keratin, fibroin, and some other protein substances.

Fibers other than protein may be damaged by insects trying to escape confinement and reach desirable food. The same situation exists when protein fibers are blended with other types of fibers. Wool is the most susceptible protein fiber and is the one most frequently damaged.

There are several different types of moths and carpet beetles that will eat protein fibers. It is the larvae stage of the insect that does the eating; during the eating period the larvae increase in weight approximately 300 times.

Chemicals used for mothproofing include the following:

1. Pyrethroids of the type 2-substituted 3,3-dimethyl 1-cyclo-propane-1-carboxylates. These are considered highly effective against the clothes moth and the black carpet beetle. A typical example is 1,3-dimethyl-5-phenyl carbamoyl-2,4,6-trioxo-hexahydropyrimidine derivatives.
2. Alpha-substituted phenyl acetates. These are also effective against the moth and the carpet beetle but not as good as the first product. A typical example is 1,3-disubstituted 5-phenyl-carbamoyl-2,4,6-trioxo-hexahydropyrimidine derivatives.
3. Compounds such as 1,3-dimethyl-5-phenyl carbamoyl-2,4-6 trioxo-hexahydropyrimidine derivatives have been effective against the furniture carpet beetle or moth. A typical example is 1,3-disubstituted 5-phenyl carbamoyl-4,6-dioxo-2-thione-hexahydropyrimidine derivatives.

A look at each of these examples will provide evidence of the similarity among these chemicals.

Other products based on pyrethroids and pyrimidines are among the other successful substances to be used in mothproofing.

Good practices in the care of wool or wool-blend fabrics should be observed. Soiled wool should never be stored, for it is a prime candidate for damage. Closets should be kept clean; spraying of closets periodically is an added precaution. Carpets of wool should also be kept clean.

It is common to apply moth-resistant finishes along with other finishes when processing wool. A common combination includes mothproofing chemicals and soil-resistant substances.

Soil-Release Finishes

The increased use of durable press and synthetic fibers in general has brought some problems to the consumer. There is increased difficulty in removing soil from such fabrics. To alleviate the problem, manufacturers are incorporating soil-release finishes into these fabrics. When durable press is involved, the soil-release finish is usually a part of the general finishing process.

Soil-release finishes operate on one of two principles. They provide hydrophilic surfaces that attracts the water and permits it to lift off soil, or they coat the fibers so that the soil does not penetrate.

Soil-release finishes are similar to soil-resistant finishes (see page 317). They often provide several side benefits such as preventing soil redeposition, introducing antistatic properties, and improving the softness and hand of fabrics.

Chemicals used for soil release include the following. (1) Acrylic soil-release agents include copolymers of acrylic monomers and carboxylic groups. Acrylic, methacrylic, itaconic, and maleic acid are common monomers. (2) Fluorochemical soil release agents are generally copolymers of polyoxyethylene and acrylate polymers combined with fluoroaliphatic groups. Hydrophilic compounds of polyoxyethylene and polyethylene terephthalate units have been successful on fabrics with polyester fiber content.

The acrylic soil-release agents give excellent oily soil release. The only negative aspect is that they may increase the stiffness of some fabrics. Special fluorochemical finishes provide some oil repellency as well as soil release. This finish can be used on a wide range of fabrics, as it does not affect durable-press properties or the hand of fabric. Soil-release finishes involving polyethylene terephthalate are used only on 100 percent polyester fabrics. They provide soil release and impart a soft, silky hand.

Another process for obtaining soil release on durable-press fabrics involves the copolymerization of cotton with polyacrylonitrile (PAN). This process decreases the susceptibility of cotton to oily soil and to waterborne soil. However, there is considerable evidence that if oily soil is in the fabric, the presence of polyacrylonitrile agents increases the difficulty of removing it.

Research on soil release is continuing. The problem has not been solved to the satisfaction of textile experts or consumers. A true soil-release finish should make it possible for the consumer to remove all types of soil by home laundering with common detergents. This includes the removing of common stains, both oil- and water-based. Further, the finish should not result in any color change in the fabric, and it should be durable.

Stabilization Finishes

One of the most frequently asked questions about a textile item is whether the fabric will shrink. The problem of fabric shrinkage is as old as fabrics. Some solutions to the problem were developed by the consumers themselves—they simply washed the cloth before converting it into an end-use item. During the 1930s, manufacturers became aware that stabilization of fabric was extremely important to consumers, apparel manufacturers, and makers of fabrics for home furnishings.

Fabric converters and processors recognize two distinct types of strinkage: relaxation or residual shrinkage and felting shrinkage. *Residual* or *relaxation shrinkage* is that shrinkage remaining in a fabric when it is purchased; the actual shrinkage occurs when some factor causes a release of stress imposed during the fabric manufacturing and finishing operations. *Felting shrinkage* is caused by certain fiber characteristics and may occur over a long period of time. The term *shrinkage* indicates a change in dimensions of a fabric in either the length or the width measurement, or both. The term *dimensional change* refers to either a loss or reduction in measurements or a growth or enlargement of measurements.

Relaxation shrinkage is rather complex. It is the most common type and occurs when some operation such as laundering releases the tensions imposed during fabric manufacture, so that the yarns return to their original length. This type of shrinkage is sometimes progressive in that all of the potential shrinkage may not take place during the first laundering. The delay may be caused by the presence of various finishing agents, and as they are gradually removed, the additional relaxation shrinkage occurs. Dry cleaning can also cause relaxation shrinkage, especially if a wet cleaning process is used.

A second problem with relaxation shrinkage is that although shrinkage occurs during laundering, ironing will often restretch or strain the fabric. This may continue for the life of the garment, so that the size will vary with each care period.

Some fabrics shrink or stretch with changes in humidity. This is a fiber property, but it is reflected in the fabrics. It occurs when a fiber is more easily stretched or elongated when humidity is high and the fabric's weight causes fibers and yarns to extend or elongate. As humidity decreases, the fiber returns to position. This type of shrinkage is visible in some drapery fabrics, when an actual variation in length can be noticed on damp and dry days. Chain weighting in draperies increases the effect. This property is sometimes called the "elevator effect."

If a fabric has been held under tension on the lengthwise yarns during drying, it may shrink in that direction upon release of stress and stretch in the perpendicular direction. Nearly all fabrics composed of natural fibers and many of man-made fibers exhibit relaxation shrinkage; the amount will vary, but if left uncontrolled it will result in an unsatisfactory product. Such shrinkage is seldom the result of fiber characteristics. Rather, the stress put on fibers when making yarns as well as the stress applied in making fabrics causes relaxation shrinkage when such stresses are released.

Felting shrinkage is primarily a characteristic of hair fibers. It occurs when fibers entangle as a result of heat, moisture, pressure, and/or agitation. Wool fabrics are particularly susceptible to felting shrinkage. This characteristic is used to advantage in routine finishing of wool, where it is called *fulling*. However, if not controlled in some way, it is a distressing characteristic to the ultimate consumer.

Techniques used to control shrinkage vary with different fiber types. In recent years fabric stabilization has become a part of other finishing operations, particularly durable press.

Shrinkage Control

CELLULOSIC FIBER FABRICS The primary method for eliminating shrinkage in cellulose-fiber fabrics is mechanical. A simple method, frequently employed by the consumer, is to wet the fabric thoroughly, dry it in a tensionless state (slack drying), then smooth it out by calendering or ironing. Another method involves feeding the cloth into the tenter frame in a slack condition and applying stretch to the filling. The method that is probably most commonly used and most successful is called *compressive shrinkage*. This process produces fabrics that will have between 0 and 2 percent shrinkage. The normal shrinkage for fabrics of this type is about 1 percent.

27.18 *Compressive shrinkage machine.* (Springs Industries, Inc.)

In compressive shrinkage the fabric is fed in open width to the shrinkage area (Fig. 27.18). Fabric, slightly damp, and a thick rubber blanket are fed over a roller and then against a heated cylinder (Fig. 27.19). As the fabric and blanket pass over the roller, the outer surface of the blanket is extended, and the shoe plate above ensures that the fabric tightly adheres to the blanket surface. As the blanket and fabric leave the guide roll, the blanket retracts and the fabric is forced to comply. Thus, the fabric is compressed or physically shortened. Fabrics carrying the trade names of Sanforized® and Rigmel® are examples of compressive shrinkage.

Other chemical treatments to control shrinkage include resin impregnation. This process controls shrinkage as long as the resin remains on the fabric. Weaver states that there is a continuous relationship among shrinkage control and durable press.[2] Any good cross-linking resin will control shrinkage

[2]J. W. Weaver, personal communication.

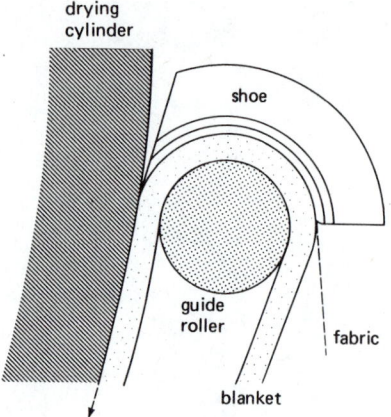

27.19 Diagram illustrating the principle of compressive shrinkage.

at as little as 2 to 3 percent add-on (that is, 2 to 3 percent increase in weight); durable-press properties require considerably greater amounts. The disadvantage of resin treatment for shrinkage control alone is that fabric character may be altered. There is a tendency for treatment with resins to result in harsh and stiff fabrics. Further, as the resins are gradually removed during use and care, shrinkage can occur late in the life of the textile product.

NYLON AND POLYESTER Man-made fibers, particularly nylon and polyester, can be controlled for shrinkage by heat setting. This process stabilizes the fabrics, and unless care procedures are incorrect, the fabrics will retain their size during use and care. For a discussion of heat setting see page 292.

WOOL FABRICS Wool has always posed many problems in relation to shrinkage. In addition to relaxation shrinkage, wool has a high degree of felting shrinkage. Felting shrinkage is a result of the behavior of wool fiber. Sponging or steaming of wool fabric will eliminate much of the relaxation shrinkage that can occur, but felting shrinkage calls for much more drastic treatment. Some of these processes have been identified and discussed in the chapter on protein fiber (see pages 51–52).

Other finishing processes can impart some control against felting shrinkage of wool. Silicone finishes that provide water repellency tend to increase fabric stability. A process to produce a wool that is both flame-resistant and shrink-resistant is available. It involves the use of isocyanate and a halogen-ated acid anhydride. The process is effective and requires less energy, less time, and less money than many other processes used in shrinkage control.

The use of acrylic copolymers effectively establishes cross-links with the wool fiber and controls shrinkage. Successful substances used for this include acrylic acid, 2-sulfoethyl methacrylate, and glycidyl methacrylate. Vapor-phase ozone treatment is another method for stablizing wool. This process produces a wool fabric with uniform shrinkage control; costs are generally lower than for other methods.

Shrink-Resistant Treatments for Knit Fabrics

Because of the fabric structure, knit fabrics must be processed somewhat differently than woven structures. Knits of thermoplastic fibers can be heat-set for stabilization. Although knits of natural fibers or blends use the same type of chemicals as woven fabrics, the mechanical process of compacting is used for knits. This method mechanically pushes knit stitches closer together in the lengthwise direction. The fabric is steamed with pressure to provide durability. It is important to provide support to knit fabric during such processing, as it would stretch when wet unless there is support. Rolls or conveyor belts can be used. There is some similarity in the concept of compacting knit stitches and compressive shrinkage for woven fabrics—they both push yarns closer together.

Use and Care of Shrink-Resistant Finishes

The advantages of shrink-resistant finishes are obvious. A fabric that shrinks or stretches and changes size results in a product that no longer fits, whether it is apparel or a home furnishing item.

According to the Federal Trade Commission, textile products that are labeled with respect to shrinkage should give the percentage of maximum shrinkage that may occur. However, there are no regulations that *require* information concerning shrinkage. It might be a wise precaution in buying yardage to test a sample of fabric before using it. This is even more important when fabrics are to be tumble-dried. For example, the Sanforized shrinkage statements are based on flat drying. Tumble drying, a much more common method today, causes more shrinkage than flat drying. Greater shrinkage than is indicated on a label is apt to occur.

Many fabrics of man-made fibers are considered highly dimensionally stable. However, it is generally advisable to preshrink yardage before cutting, particularly for polyester knit fabrics, which tend to shrink considerably if not heat-set adequately.

Consumers should be aware of problems that shrink-resistant finishes may cause. For example, if wool is labeled as shrink-resistant, a consumer may encounter problems in constructing that fabric into an apparel item. Tailoring of wool has depended in the past on the ability to shrink wool into various shapes during the tailoring. When wool has been treated to be shrink-resistant, it is impossible to shrink out fullness during construction. If the weave is loose and yarns can be packed more tightly together, problems may be eliminated, but this does not occur when using closely woven fabrics.

Stain and Soil-Resistant Finishes

Removal of stains from fabrics has been a constant problem for consumers. Finishes that reduce staining and soiling are therefore welcome. Soiling or staining of fabrics occurs in three different ways: redeposition of soil during laundering or dry cleaning; deposit of dry soil from the air or by contact; and spot soiling or staining by contact with foreign matter.

Soil is redeposited when fabrics are laundered incorrectly. Inadequate rinsing is a common error. Materials such as carboxy methyl cellulose (CMC) aid in preventing redeposition and are frequently included in detergents. Substances used to produce fabrics with resistance to waterborne stains are similar, in some cases identical, to chemicals used for water repellency. Silicone chemicals and fluorochemical finishes are effective for both water repellency and soil resistance to waterborne stain or soil. This does not hold for oily stains. Fluorochemicals can be used to produce fabrics that are resistant to oily stains, but the amounts and types usually differ from those used for water repellency.

Soil-resistant finishes reduce the rate of soil redeposition on a fabric either by creating an electric charge that repels the soil or by producing a smooth surface to which soil will not adhere. Fabrics treated with soil-resistant finishes are therefore easily cleaned. Finishes used to reduce soiling act as direct barriers, as the finish occupies places on the fiber that would otherwise be filled by the soil. A smooth surface is created and the soil falls off.

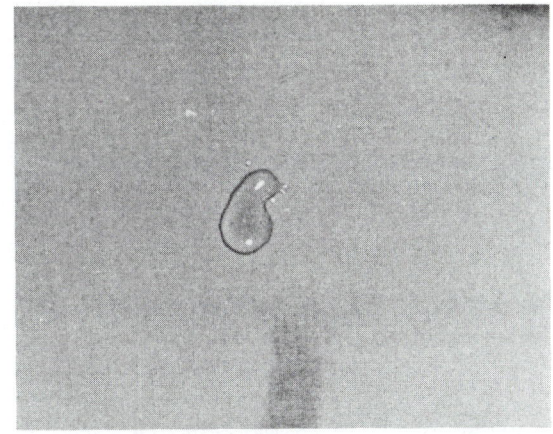

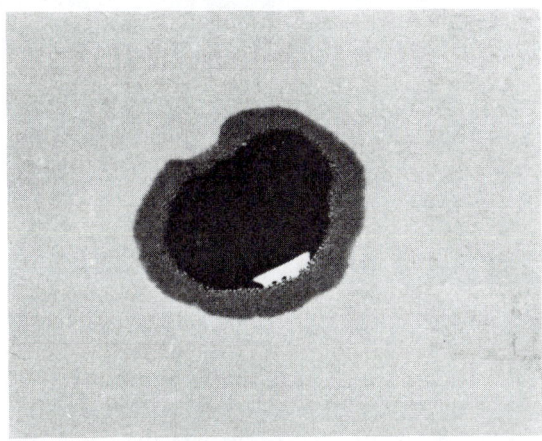

27.20 Fabric with fluorochemical finish *(top)* and same fabric without finish *(bottom)*. Oil does not penetrate the treated sample but it soaks in and spreads rapidly into the untreated fabric.

Spot staining causes the most problems in the care of fabrics, so finishes that prevent stains are a real aid to the consumer. Stain-repellent finishes are made from such compounds as silicones, fluorochemicals, waxlike derivatives, triazine compounds, and pyridinium compounds. The presence of the finish prevents stains from penetrating the fabric by developing a high degree of surface tension on the fabric; by producing a substrate on the fabric so that oil and water actually float; or by presenting a surface with a very low free-energy factor, which prevents reactions between the stain and the surface. Fluorochemicals are among the best in this group (Fig. 27.20). They create a surface with a low free-energy factor and are considered extremely successful.

One problem has become apparent with the increased use of stain-repellent finishes. If dry soil becomes embedded in the fabric, it is nearly impossible to remove. Frequent cleaning will help, but if the soil is in the fabric, it tends to stay there. Liquid stains are relatively easy to remove, but any stain should be cleaned as soon as possible if optimum use of the finish is to be achieved.

Water-Repellent and Waterproof Finishes

Waterproof finishes are those that coat or seal a fabric so that water does not pass through it. Such fabrics are nonpermeable to air and thus are not comfortable in wearing apparel. Water-repellent finishes result in a fabric that resists wetting and is relatively porous.

Early methods used to produce waterproof fabrics coated the fabric with rubber, oxidized oil, or varnish. Although they prevented water from passing through, some were heavy and bulky, and all were uncomfortable as apparel. Oiled silks were light in weight, but they were not as durable as rubber- or varnish-coated fabrics. Although these early methods are still used for some fabrics, most modern waterproof fabrics are produced by coating a substrate with a synthetic polymer of some type.

Water-resistant and water-repellent finishes are popular in consumer goods because the fabric lets air through; thus, they are comfortable, they retain their original appearance, and fabric hand is modified only slightly. Water repellency is determined by both fabric construction and finish. The fabric should be made so that the largest interstices between yarns or fibers are smaller than raindrops. The yarns should be soft and the yarn count high. The fabric still has adequate air permeability.

Early water-repellent coatings were easily removed in dry cleaning or laundering. The first "durable" water repellent was introduced in the United States in 1942. It was used by the armed forces for protective apparel and was based on the use of quaternary ammonium compounds. At present, durable, semidurable, and renewable water-repellent finishes are available on various types of consumer goods. Durable finishes are based on silicone compounds, pyridinium compounds, fluorochemicals, methylol stearamide, and ammonium compounds. Semidurable finishes are based on zirconium compounds or salts of the rare earth elements. These are combined with a special type of soap during application to the fabric. Renewable water repellents are generally composed of aluminum compounds or wax emulsion. As the term implies, renewable finishes must be reapplied after cleaning. The fluorochemical finish Scotchgard® is available in aerosol spray cans and can be applied to fabrics in the home. This product tends to be nondurable, but it does serve a purpose for limited use.

It is important to note any care instructions with fabrics treated with water repellents. Some may be removed by dry cleaning but not damaged by laundering; others may be removed by any method of care. Most dry-cleaning establishments can reapply a water-repellent finish to fabrics.

Multiple Finishing

A trend in processing modern fabrics is to apply several different finishes to fabrics so as to provide a variety of characteristics. Durable press, soil release, and softeners are frequently applied together to produce a fabric that is easy to maintain, is comfortable, and has a pleasing hand. The durable-press finish may provide dimensional stability as a part of the easy-care processing.

Flame-resistant finishes are often applied in conjunction with other finishes, such as water repellency, crease resistance, and soil resistance. The durability of such combinations tends to vary widely. Consumers should seek labels to determine any information regarding care and/or guarantees concerning such products.

The finishing industry conducts research on a continuous basis. It is important to identify new finishes that may make fabrics more adaptable for specific end uses, satisfying in today's world, compatible with scarcities of raw materials and energy, and appealing to consumers. It is safe to say that research in finishing will continue to demand attention and financing.

STUDY QUESTIONS

1. List and describe the main types of finishes that provide special appearance characteristics.
2. Identify finishes that modify or alter the hand of fabric.
3. List the most important functional finishes, de-

scribe what they do, the care required, what chemicals are usually used, and how they are applied to fabric.

4. What is the difference between a durable finish and a renewable one?
5. What is a permanent finish?
6. One of the more important finishes is that providing durable press. What methods are available to produce durable-press characteristics, and what are the advantages and disadvantages of each?
7. What is the difference between a flameproof and a flame-resistant fabric?
8. What is the difference between a waterpoof and a water-repellent finish?
9. Identify some of the chemicals used in finishing, and note particular finishes for which they work the best.

Activities

1. Locate samples of a variety of different fabrics. Determine whether any labels accompany these fabrics. If laboratory equipment to test the fabrics is available, test for the performance of various finishes.
2. Visit various stores and locate different kinds of fabrics. See what information may be provided about the presence of finishes and care procedures. How much information concerning finishes is available on fabrics or textile end-use products?

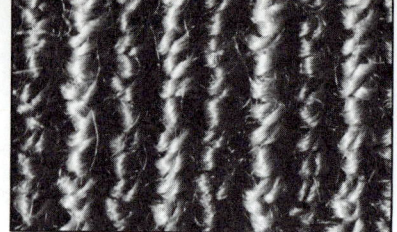

28

Dyestuffs and Their Application

OBJECTIVES
◇ **To provide information concerning the different types of dyestuffs and their composition**
◇ **To provide information about methods used in applying dyes to fabric substrates**
◇ **To provide information about how people see color**
◇ **To indicate processes used in applying dyestuffs and how they influence colorfastness**

KEY TERMS

acid dyes	dye	piece dyeing
auxochromes	dyestuff	pigment colors
azoic dyes	fiber dyes	product dyeing
cationic dyes	indigo	reactive dyes
chromophores	leveling	solution dyeing
cochineal	mass pigmentation	substantive
continuous dyeing	metallized dyes	sulfur dyes
direct dyes	mordant dyes	vat dyes
disperse dyes	naphthol dyes	yarn dyeing

The appeal of color is universal; it repeatedly serves as a common language. Consumers are usually more concerned with color than with any other characteristic of a textile product.

The textile industry is aware of the consumer's desire for appealing colors. Manufacturers and retailers know that the consumer who selected an item because of its color will be extremely annoyed if the color is not maintained for the anticipated life of the product. Consequently, research by dyestuff manufacturers has resulted in coloring agents that satisfy the aesthetic demands of consumers and provide lasting pleasure if the color is properly applied and the fabric carefully maintained. However, it is important to note that there are some dyestuffs that do not produce durable colors when applied to some type of fibers. The dyer must be an expert in dye technology to know what dyes work with what type of fibers and how durable they will be in end use.

Historical Review

Dyestuffs and dyeing are as old as textiles themselves, predating written history. Fabrics dating from 3500 B.C. have been found in Thebes that still possess the remains of blue indigo dye. Fabrics discovered in ancient tombs in Egypt were colored yellow with dye obtained from the safflower plant. Beautifully colored fabrics dating back several thousand years have been unearthed in China, Asia Minor, and some sections of Europe. Until 1856 all dyestuffs were made from natural materials, mainly animal and vegetable matter with a few minerals for special colors.

One of the animal sources was a tiny insect native to Mexico, from which a bright red dye was extracted. This insect was used by the Aztecs to color their fabrics, and when the Spaniards invaded Mexico in 1518, they called the insect and the dyestuff *cochineal.* Cochineal is an anthraquinoid type of dye and has the following formula:

COCHINEAL (Carminic Acid)
Natural Red 4, CI #75470

A tiny mollusk, *Murex brandaris* and *Murex trunculus,* found on the Phoenician coast near the city of Tyre, produces a beautiful purple.

TYRIAN PURPLE
Natural Vat dye #75800

By 1500 B.C. Tyre had become the center for the trading and manufacture of this purple dye. It was extremely costly to produce, because approximately 12,000 tiny animals were needed to obtain just 1 gram of dyestuff. The expressions ''royal purple'' and ''born to the purple'' came into being as a result of the fact that only the wealthy could afford the dye.

Logwood, extracted from the pulp of the logwood tree, produced excellent dark colors, particularly blacks and browns, and is still employed to some extent in coloring fabrics for special purposes.

LOGWOOD (Haematin)
Natural Black 1, CI #75290

Another extremely old color that is still used today is indigo. This blue color has become popular in making special types of designs for modern fabrics. This formula for blue indigo (indigofera) is

INDIGO CI #75780

Early efforts at coloring fabrics posed serious problems because few of the natural dyes formed a colorfast combination with fibers. Eventually, scientists found that this defect could be partially overcome by the use of *mordants*—mineral compounds that render colors insoluble.

As long as people depended on animals and vegetables for dyestuffs and on minerals for mordanting, progress was limited by the operator's skill in mixing the natural dyes and in perfecting the techniques of application. As with many of nature's products, the quality of materials varied considerably, and so the results were somewhat unpredictable.

The year 1856 marked a turning point in the history of dyes. Sir William H. Perkin, while trying to make artificial quinine from coal tar, accidently produced the first synthetic dyestuff, a purple color called mauve, a basic dye. This discovery launched the modern dyestuff industry. Today, nearly all dyes are synthetically compounded, and in most cases they are superior in every way to natural dyes.

The development of artificial dyes has been rapid, and the available dyes number in the thousands. However, research in the development of dyes continues. New fibers and fiber modifications frequently require a new type of dyestuff; various finishes applied influence the dye selected and create a need for something better; the desire for new and different colors creates a need; the continued search for colors that will withstand all possible environmental conditions encourages the researcher to continue to seek new types of dyestuffs; and the emphasis on discontinuing the use of chemicals suspected of being potential carcinogens has made it essential to try to find new dyes to replace those identified as hazardous to health.

Seeing Color

Color is a visual sensation. It results from the reflectance of certain visible light rays that strike the retina of the eye and stimulate cells in the nerves of the eye. The nerves send a message to the brain, which in turn produces the sensation of a specific hue. Thus, we ''see'' color. When all the visible light rays are reflected, an object appears white; if none of the rays is reflected, it appears black. When one or more rays are reflected, the viewer senses the color produced by the specific reflected ray or combination of rays.

The purpose of a dye is to absorb light rays on a selective basis, causing the substrate fabric to reflect the rays that are not absorbed. In other words, if all the rays except those producing blue are absorbed, the viewer sees blue. The ability of an organic compound to create this desired color derives from the presence of chemical groups called *chromophores.* Substances that include chromophores in various arrangements produce the sensation of different color hues.

Chromophores are made up of such organic molecular arrangements as the azo group, the thio group, the nitroso group, the nitro group, the azoxy group, the anthraquinoid group, the quinoid nucleus, the pyrazine ring, the quinophthalone structure, the lactone ring, the carbonyl group, and the tetrabenzoprophyrazine nucleus.

$$-N{=}N-$$
azo group

$$={=}C{=}S \quad \text{thio group} \qquad -NO_2 \quad \text{nitro group}$$
$$-N{=}O \quad \text{nitroso group} \qquad -N{=}N \quad \text{azoxy group}$$
$$\underset{O-}{\overset{|}{}}$$

anthraquinoid group

$$-N{=}\!\!\!\bigcirc\!\!\!{=}N-$$

quinoid nucleus

pyrazine ring   oxazine ring

thiazine ring   quinoid structure A

thiazole ring   quinoid structure B

quinophthalone group

lactone ring   carbonyl group

All chromophores contain an extended conjugated system of alternate double and single carbon-to-carbon bonds. To produce color visible to the human eye, the dyestuff must have a least two chromophore groups. To obtain deep and intense colors, the number of chromophores is increased and weak chromophore systems are replaced by strong.

Although chromophores confer color on a substance, the intensity or brightness of the color depends on the presence of one or more substances called *auxochromes.* Furthermore, the auxochromes may give water solubility to a dye and provide the groups that form associative bonds with a fiber. These include $-SO_3H$, $-N(CH_2)_2$, $-NHCH_3$, $-NH_2$, $-NaO_3S$, $-NC_2H_5$, $-OH$, and $-OCH_3$. Dyestuffs themselves or combinations of other chemicals with dyes in the dye bath contribute both chromophores and auxochromes for the actual dyeing process.

The technical definition of a *dye* is a compound that can be fixed on a substance in a more or less permanent state and that evokes the visual sensation of a specific color or hue. *Dyestuff* is a synonym for dye in this technical sense.

TYPES OF DYES

Dyes can be classified in several ways: according to hue produced, according to chemical class, and according to the method of application and types of fibers to which they are successfully applied. The approach used in this text is based on the method of application; however, the identification of chemical class becomes an important part of this system.

The important groups of dyestuffs discussed here include substantive or direct dyes, azoic or naphthol dyes, acid dyes and mordant or metallized dyes, cationic or basic dyes, disperse dyes, vat dyes, sulfur dyes, reactive dyes, and pigment colors. Although pigment colors are somewhat different from dyes, they are included in this discussion since they are used in coloring fibers and fabrics.

The development of each type of man-made fiber has necessitated, in most instances, the creation of a special group of dyestuffs for each specific fiber type. The majority of dye manufacturers develop these dyes as the fibers are being perfected so that colored textiles can be available to consumers with the introduction of a new fiber. Fiber chemists must also consider what existing dyestuffs will work on a new fiber or fiber variant introduced to the public.

Some dyestuffs attach themselves to the surface of a fiber, some are absorbed into the fiber with no actual chemical reaction between fiber and dye, and some react chemically with the fiber molecule to form a strong bond.

Colorfastness of all dyestuffs will vary to some degree. It is desirable, when purchasing a textile item, to seek any label information that provides clues to the colorfastness of the dyes and recommended care. Although care information is required (see Chap. 32), information about colorfastness is not required; however in some cases it is provided voluntarily by the manufacturer as a help to consumers.

Substantive or Direct Dyes

Substantive or direct dyes comprise the largest and most commercially significant group of dyestuffs. Direct dyes are water-soluble; they are applied primarily to cellulose fibers and occasionally to protein fibers and polyamides. Most direct dyes belong to one of two main groups:

1. Azo dyes: these may be monazo, diazo, triazo, or polyazo. Examples are given below.

   These dyes have either two or more azo groups as chromophores or one azo group and other chromophores such as the carbonyl group.

2. Direct dyes derived from benzidine, triphenyl methane, or phthalocyanine. It should be noted that dyes based on benzidine have been removed from the American market, as there is some evidence that they may be carcinogens. However, they may still be available from foreign dye manufacturers. Auxochromes found in the various types of direct dyes include $-NaO_3S$, $-NH_2$, $-OH$, and $-OCH_3$. An example of a dye derived from triphenyl methane is Direct Blue 41 and one derived from phthalocyanine is Direct Blue 86.

Direct Red 64, CI #17875; monazo dye; red

CI Direct Red 2, CI #23500; a diazo dye, bright red

Direct Blue 11, CI #30350; triazo, dull blue

Direct Blue 86, CI #74180; phthalocyanine
type, tetrabenzoporphyrazine nucleus

Direct Blue 41, CI #42700; triphenylmethane type;
greenish blue

To apply direct dyes, the dyestuff is dissolved in a water bath, and a salt is added to control the absorption rate of the dye by the fiber. The fabric is then immersed in the dye bath. The amount of dye stuff absorbed depends on two main factors: the size of the dye molecule and the size of the pore opening in the outer surface of the fiber. Direct colors are easy to apply and are considered the most inexpensive dyes on the market. They require no special equipment.

Direct dyestuffs exhibit relatively good colorfastness to sunlight, and some are considered to have excellent lightfastness. However, the colorfastness to washing may be poor. Because they are soluble in water, the laundry process tends to dissolve some of the dye and remove it from the fabric. In cases where a fabric requires good lightfastness but is not laundered frequently, direct dyes are adequate. For example, they prove to be highly successful on fabrics for draperies but of little or no value on apparel that is laundered frequently. The problem of poor washfastness can be solved to some degree by the application of selected finishing compounds such as those substances used to provide easy care. Formal-

dehyde aftertreatment of direct dyes has been quite successful in making direct dyes relatively resistant to the effect of laundering.

There is no chemical *reaction* between direct dyestuffs and the textile fibers to which they are applied, but there is a chemical *attraction*. Nevertheless, at no time can it be assumed that the colors are completely fast to outside environmental influences.

Developed Direct Dyes

Developed direct dyes are processed after application to develop the color on the textile substrate and make it more durable to care procedures and environmental factors. The developers are usually naphtholic compounds, and the end product is similar to the azoic dyes discussed in the next section. To develop a direct dye, the dye molecule must have a radical, usually an amino group, that will react with the naphtholic developer. The resultant dye is insoluble, possesses a molecule of such size that it will not pass through the fiber surface pores, and has improved attraction to the fiber or actually forms a chemical bond with fiber molecules. Developing direct dyes frequently changes the hue of the dyestuff.

Developed direct dyes have superior washfastness compared with nondeveloped direct dyestuffs; however, many of them also have decreased lightfastness. Both direct and developed direct dyes are used for bright shades and for coloring fabrics to be sold at medium to low prices.

Azoic or Naphthol Dyes

Azoic dyes are used on cellulose fibers and to a limited extent on man-made fibers, notably polyester. Azoic dyes produce color as a result of a chemical action in the fiber between a diazotized amine and a coupling agent. The diazo compound is often applied to the fabric first, but for certain procedures the two may be applied simultaneously. The starting compounds are colorless; it is the coupling of the two that produces the color. Typical coupling agents include the following:

Coupling Component 5, CI #37610; 4,4'-bi-*o*-acetoacetotoluidine

CI Coupling Component 2, CI #37505;
3-hydroxy-2-naphthanilide

Azoic Coupling Component 36, CI #37585;
3-hydroxy-2-(o-anthrotoluidine)

Azoic Coupling Component 25, CI #37590;
2-hydroxy-2'-methyl-11H-benzo(a)carbazole-
3-carboxy-p-anisidine

The component CI #37610 is used primarily in the formation of azoic yellow colors. Chromophores for azoic dyes are present in the azo compounds, and the number increases as a result of the reaction between the azo component and the coupling agent.

The dyestuff used with the coupling agent is often an azo compound of some type, frequently a diazo dye similar to that diagramed for direct colors. Azoic dyes are sometimes referred to as "ice" colors because they are applied from a low-temperature water bath. After the dye application, however, the fabric is treated in hot detergent solution to attain or develop the desired color.

Azoic dyestuffs produce brilliant shades, particularly reds, violets, and burgundy. They offer good fastness to washing, light, chlorine, and peroxide bleaches, but they have poor resistance to rubbing or crocking. They are low in cost and can be applied in the same amount of time as that required for direct and vat dyes.

Acid Dyes

The name *acid dye* is derived from the fact that these dyes are applied in the presence of an inorganic or organic acid such as sulfuric or formic acid. The term identifies a large group of anionic dyes with relatively low molecular weight that carry from one to three sulfonic acid groups ($-SO_3H$) or nitro groups ($-NO_2$) in the dye molecule. Acid dyes be-

long to subclasses such as nitro, nitroso, monoazo, diazo, triphenyl methane, zanthene, azine, quinoline, ketone-imine, and anthraquinone. Typical formulas follow.

Acid Yellow 4, CI #18695; a monoazo dye

Acid Yellow 1, CI #10316; a nitro dyestuff

Acid Orange 25, CI #20160; a diazo dye

Acid Yellow 2, CI #47010; a quinoline dye

The chromophores in these dyes include the azo group ($-N=N-$), the carbonyl group ($=C=O$), and variations of the quinoid structure. Auxochromes are formed, in some instances, as a result of reactions between the dyestuff and the acid bath.

Acid dyes have no affinity for cellulosic fibers; rather, they are used on protein fibers such as wool and silk, on polyamide fibers, and on certain modified acrylic and polyester fibers. They function particularly well on fiber containing nitrogenous basic radicals that attract the acid dye molecule, so that associative bonds or forces are established between the dye and the fiber. These dyes cannot be used on fibers that are sensitive to acids, as the acid bath would prove destructive.

Acid dyes exhibit varying degrees of colorfastness. The selection of an acid dye, therefore, should be based on the fiber content, the planned use of the fabric, the anticipated method of maintenance or care, and the type of colorfastness properties desired.

Mordant or Metallized Dyes

Mordant or chrome dyes, often called metallized dyes, have many properties in common with acid dyes. They are effective on the same types of fibers, and the actual dye is an acid type of dyestuff. The major difference is that a metal is added to the dye molecule. This metal may be added during the dyeing process or just before the application of dye to the textile. The metal reacts with the dye to form relatively insoluble dyestuffs with improved wet colorfastness and lightfastness. The metal most often used is chromium, which produces the so-called chrome dyes. Other metals that may be used include cobalt, aluminum, and nickel. Copper serves as the metal mordant in some acid dyeing of acrylic fibers. Metallized dyes usually have good colorfastness to dry cleaning, which is of considerable importance to wool and silk fabrics that are more frequently dry-cleaned than laundered.

Cationic or Basic Dyes

Cationic dyes, frequently referred to as basic dyes, are salts of colored organic bases. This group includes the oldest synthetic dyestuff, mauveine, discovered by Perkin, as well as some of the natural dyes. The important factor in cationic dyes is that the colored portion of the dye molecule (the cation) is positively charged. Basic or cationic dyes fall into the following major categories:

1. Triphenyl methane derivatives. An example is

Basic Red 9, CI #42500

2. Azines, including oxazines and thiazines. Examples include the following:

Basic Red 2, CI #50240, an azine dye

Basic Blue 24, CI #52030, a thiazine dye

3. Zanthene dyes. An example:

Basic Red 8, CI #45150

4. Mauveine, the oldest synthetic dye:

Basic Dye, Mauve; CI #50245

Chromophores for cationic dyes include the thiazine ring, quinoid groups, and oxazine rings. Auxochromes include $-NH_2$, $-NHCH_3$, and $-NHCH_2CH_3$.

Cationic dyes are excellent for coloring acrylic fibers. There appears to be a chemical reaction between a cationic dye and the radicals at each end of the polyacrylic molecules. The dyes therefore produce relatively colorfast products. Cationic dyes are successful on special nylon and polyester fibers that have been modified to accept basic or cationic dyes.

Basic dyes were formerly used on cellulosic and protein fibers, but because they produce fugitive colors (those that fade quickly), their popularity for these fibers has decreased. Basic or cationic dyes occasionally serve as "topping" colors to increase the brilliance or brightness of a fabric.

Disperse Dyes

Disperse dyes, formerly called *acetate* dyes, were originally developed for acetate fibers. They can be applied to acetate, acrylic, aramid, modacrylic, nylon, olefin, polyester, saran, and triacetate fibers.

For acetate, polyester, and triacetate fibers they are the only practical means of coloration. Disperse dyes belong, in most instances, to one of the following two types:

1. Azo, mainly monoazo with some diazo dyes. Examples include:

Disperse Blue 11, CI #11260; a monoazo type

Disperse Orange 15, CI #26080; a diazo type

A wide variety of colors is available from dyestuffs in this group.

2. Anthraquinone dyes. Examples include:

Disperse Blue 1, CI #64500

Disperse Orange 11, CI #60700

Colors found in this type are primarily in the orange, red, and blue hues.

Chromophores include the azo group, the anthroquinone group, and the nitro groups. Auxochromes include the $-NH_2$, $-OH$, and the $-OCH_3$ groups.

Disperse dyes require special fabric preparation for uniform dye application. Nonionic surfactants and alkali are used in an initial scour at a temperature range from $140°$ to $210°F$ ($60°-99°C$). This accomplishes three objectives: dirt removal, removal of size or oil, and fabric shrinkage. This is followed by a second scour, which may include a solvent to remove excess oil and residuals left during the first scour.

Disperse dyes are only slightly soluble in water, but they are easily dispersed throughout a solution. The colored particles attach themselves to the fiber surface and then dissolve into the fiber. This reaction occurs between disperse dyes and thermoplastic fibers such as acetate and polyesters. These dyes are subject to fume fading and may lose color when exposed to nitrogen oxides in the atmosphere.

Colorfastness to light, laundering, and dry cleaning is good. The reaction with nitrogenous oxides does not occur as quickly or as seriously when the dyes are used on polyester fibers as when used on acetates. If disperse dyes are applied to polyesters at low temperatures, carriers are required to bring about penetration of the dye molecules into the fiber. The combination of high temperatures and high pressure eliminates the need for carriers. The *thermosol* process also eliminates the need for carriers, but high temperature is involved. The thermosol process entails padding the dye into the fabric and passing the fabric into a heat zone where the dye is fixed in the fibers. Thermosoling can be achieved by heated dry air, by contact with hot surfaces, or by exposure to infrared heating zones. The time of exposure to heat varies from 10 seconds for the infrared technique to 30 to 60 seconds for heated dry air. The most common is the heated dry air method, and many dyes are fixed at approximately $205°C$ ($400°F$) in 30 to 60 seconds.

Disperse dyes do not dissolve in the dye bath; rather they are dispersed through the bath. They are absorbed by the fiber, then tend to dissolve or diffuse into the fiber. Because of their lack of solubility in a water bath, they tend to be extremely colorfast to laundering.

Vat Dyes

The dyestuffs frequently publicized as having the best colorfastness are the vat dyes. In general, vat dyes do exhibit outstanding colorfastness properties, although their lightfastness may be somewhat inferior. Furthermore, the dyes in this category exhibit some variation in colorfastness because of differences in chemical structure.

Vat dyes were originally developed in Europe about 1910 and derived their name from the equipment used in applying the dye, which included a large vessel or vat. Today these dyes can be applied in vats or by continuous feed methods. Vat dyes fall into one of two main categories, indigoid and anthraquinoid. An example of the indigoid type is one of the synthetic indigo dyes:

INDIGO, Vat Blue 1, CI #73000

This dye is based on the classical indigo formula. Modifications of this basic formula produce variations of blue such as

Vat Blue 5B, CI #73070

Another example of an indigoid dye is

Vat Red 41, CI #73300

Many vat dyes are of the anthraquinone type. Examples include the following:

Vat Red 10, CI #67000

Vat Yellow 4, CI #59100

Vat Orange 9, CI #59700

Vat Blue 6, CI #69825

Chromophores for vat dyes include the anthraquinoid group and indiquinoid structures. Auxochromes include the $-NH_2$ group and others formed as the dye is reacted with various alkaline substances in the dyeing operation.

Vat dyes are insoluble in water and have no affinity for fibers until they are converted to a product that is soluble in an alkaline solution. The solution of dye and alkaline substance is called a *leuco* bath. All vat dyes are characterized by the presence of a $=C=O$ group, which may be reduced to a

$$\overset{\backslash}{\underset{//}{C}}-O-H$$

group that is soluble in sodium hydroxide. In the NaOH it changes form to a

$$\overset{\backslash}{\underset{//}{C}}-O-Na$$

group that is substantive to selected fibers. After application in the leuco state, the dye is reoxidized to its original form, at which time the final color develops. The reoxidized color is insoluble and thus is highly resistant to water and many other environmental factors, which gives it outstanding colorfastness properties.

Vat dyes are used primarily on cellulosic fibers such as cotton and rayon. They may be used to dye some nylons, and they are used in the dyeing of cotton/polyester blends. In this latter use they may stain the polyester as well as dye the cotton, but they do not color the polyester sufficiently, so other dyes such as disperse dyes are used for such combinations. These two types are commonly applied to cotton/polyester blends and usually involve the thermosol process for the disperse dyes used for the polyester.

A wide choice of colors is available in vat dyes, and they have good to excellent colorfastness. It is because of their superior behavior and colorfastness that the term *vat dye* has become almost synonymous with *colorfast dyes*.

Sulfur Dyes

Sulfur dyes are compounds containing either sulfur or a mixture of the color component and sulfur in a form that will create a soluble product. Most sulfur dyes are of unknown composition. Examples of three sulfur dyes with known formulas are

Sulfur Violet 2, CI #53760;
8-amino-10-phenyl-2(10H)-phenazinone

Sulfur Blue 6, CI #53460;
N-[p-(p-acetamido anilino)phenyl]-
p-quinoneimine

Sulfur Black 3, CI #53180; p-aminophenol

Sulfur dyes are used primarily on cellulosic fibers, particularly cottons and rayons, and they produce good to excellent colorfast hues. They are widely selected for dark shades such as browns, blacks, and navy blues. Some newer sulfur dyes are available in bright colors.

When sulfur dyes are applied correctly, they give good performance. If the application procedure does not follow specific directions, the colors may cause fabric breakdown through tendering and weakening of the textile fiber. Eventual disintegration can occur. Most sulfur dyes are relatively low in cost and can be used on a variety of cellulosic fabrics intended for low-cost products.

The application of sulfur dyes is similar to that of vat dyes, as they must be made soluble before being absorbed by the fibers. The dye is reduced in an alkaline solution, the textile is fed into the bath, where it absorbs the color. The fabric is then washed; the color remains on the fiber but is converted into an insoluble form by the washing. Sulfur dyes do not have good colorfastness to bleaches.

Reactive Dyes

The first practical reactive dyes were introduced in 1956, one hundred years after the discovery of the first synthetic dye. Originally, reactive dyes were used primarily on cotton. This is still somewhat true, although a few reactive dyes are now finding use on wool and man-made cellulosic fibers. An important use of reactive dyes is their application, along with disperse dyes, on blends of cotton or other cellulosic fibers and polyester.

Reactive dyes are combined with the fiber molecule through a complex system utilizing a reactive molecule on both the dye and the fiber. The connection may be diagramed as follows:

fiber molecule — reactive coupling agent — dye

The reactive dye unites with the fiber molecule by addition or substitution. When the coupling agent is separate from the dye molecule, the dye combines with the coupling agent, which then reacts with the fiber molecule.

The three major types of coupling agents include mono-, di-, or trichlorotriazinyl compounds, pyrimidine derivatives, and vinyl sulfone. The major chromophore systems include the azo group, the anthraquinone structure, and the phthalocyanine or tetrabenzoporphyrazine nucleus.

Examples of reactive dyes include the following:

Reactive Brown 1, CI #26440; diazo type monochlorotriazinyl reactive system

Reactive Red 17, CI #18155, a monoazo and amine chromophore, trichloropyrimidinyl reactive system

Reactive Red 22, CI # 14824; monazo chromophore, vinyl sulphone reactive system

Reactive Blue 4, CI #61205; anthraquinone chromophore, dichlorotriazinyl reactive system

Reactive Blue 7, CI #74460; phthalocyanine (CUP) chromophore, monochlorotriazinyl reactive system

Bright colors with excellent colorfastness, particularly good washfastness, are available with reac-tive dyes. Although these were costly when first introduced, the cost has dropped and their use has continued to increase. They are desirable for fabric for a wide variety of end-use products in which cellulosic fibers comprise part or all of the fiber content. Colorfastness to light is excellent for most reactive dyes.

One of the few major problems with reactive dyes is that some of them have a high susceptibility to damage from chlorine bleaches. Colorfastness to crocking or abrasion, to perspiration, to dry cleaning, and to fume fading varies from very good to excellent depending on the particular dyestuff.

Pigment Colors

Technically, pigments are not dyes; but they are used to color some textiles, so it is essential that they be included in a discussion of coloration of fabric. Pigments are not considered dyes because they are completely insoluble in water or in the solvents typically used in dyeing. They must be applied by some other mechanism.

Pigment colors are made from both organic and inorganic compounds. A typical example of inorganic pigment would be cobaltous aluminate. Depending on the formula, either a blue or a green color can be obtained. For blue the formula is $CoO \cdot Al_2O_3$; for green the formula is $4CoO \cdot Al_2O_3$.

Other inorganic compounds used include cadmium sulfide (CdS), a red pigment; arsenic trisulfate (As_2S_3), a yellow pigment; cobalt ammonium phosphate ($CoNH_4PO_4 \cdot H_2O$), a violet pigment; and copper arsenite ($3CuAs_2O_3$), a green pigment.

Pigment colors obtained from organic compounds include the following four basic types.

1. Azo compounds, which are available primarily in yellows, oranges, and reds. Chromophores for this type include the azo groups and the nitro groups. The —OH group is the major auxochrome.

Pigment Orange 2, CI #12060; monoazo pigment

2. Anthraquinones, mainly in red, blues, and violets. Pigment Violet 5 is usually obtained using the aluminum salt of the compound. The chromophore is the anthraquinone group, and the auxochromes are the —OH group and the —SO₃H group.

Pigment Violet 5, CI #58055:1;
anthraquinone type

3. Phthalocyanines, used primarily for blues, blue-greens, and greens. In Pigment Blue 15, the tetrabenzoporphyrazine nucleus is the chromophore.

Pigment Blue 15, CI #74160,
phthalocyanine type copper complex

4. Most purple pigments are either dioxazines or triaryl methanes. In Pigment Violet 23, the oxazine ring is the chromophore; —NC₂H₅ is the

Pigment Violet 23, CI #51319; dioxazine type

In addition to being insoluble in water, pigments have no affinity for fibers. To fix them on fabrics, some type of adhesive, resin, or bonding agent must be employed. The colors thus produced are relatively permanent, except that as the resin or bonding agent wears away, the color will also disappear. Even mild abrasion may erode some of the color.

It is possible to mix pigments thoroughly with the fiber solution so that the fiber is colored as it is formed. When pigment colors are added to the fiber solution or molten polymer, the term *dope dye, mass pigmentation,* or *solution dye* is used. Fibers colored in this manner exhibit good colorfastness to laundering, dry cleaning, light, perspiration, and crocking or abrasion.

Pigment colors are used in solution dyeing of acetate, rayon, nylon, polypropylene, polyester, glass, and other man-made fibers that will accept color during the solution state. The process is extremely popular for fibers that are difficult to color with dyestuffs. This is especially true of the olefin fibers, both polypropylene and polyethylene, so these are frequently colored with pigments. Pigments can be attached to textile surfaces as part of a printing process if they are securely affixed by means of some type of bonding agent. Glass fiber fabrics are frequently printed with pigments that are bonded to the fabric using an adhesive.

APPLICATION OF COLOR

Dyes can be applied to textile products at various stages in their manufacture. Natural fibers can be colored as separate fibers, a process called loosestock dyeing; in sliver form, called top dyeing; in the yarn form; or as completed fabric, frequently called piece dyeing. They may be colored after the final end-use product has been made.

Man-made fibers can be colored in all of the same stages listed for natural fibers. In addition, they can be colored in the solution state (mass pigmentation or solution dyeing) and in the gel state when fibers have begun to form but before they have set. Another stage for dyeing man-made fibers is in the tow form—the mass of filaments after formation but before cutting into staple lengths.

When dyes are applied to a fabric substrate they do not always color the fabric evenly. To eliminate this problem, *leveling* agents are used in the dye bath. These agents help to maintain an even appli-

28.1 Fiber stock and dye kiers (vats). (Morton Machine Works, Inc.)

28.2 Fiber-dyed fabric.

28.3 Yarn dyeing in skein form. (Service Yarn Dyeing Corporation)

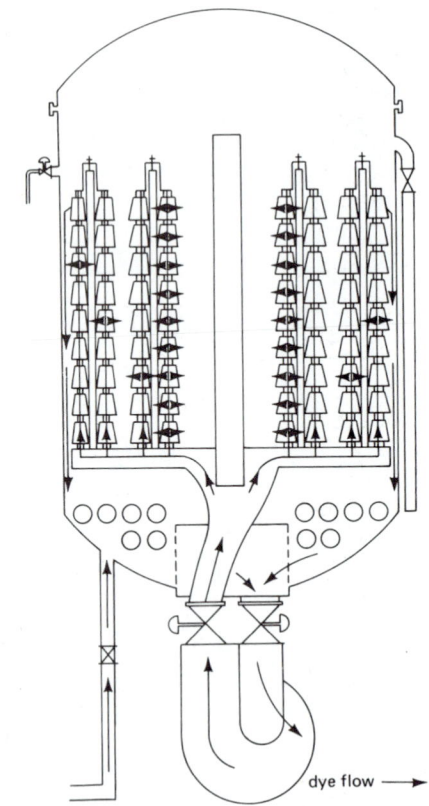

28.4 Diagram illustrating the principle of package dyeing. Packages of yarn are mounted on posts in a dye beck. Dye solution moves up the posts and out through port openings, and it is forced through packages from center to outside. (Springs Industries, Inc.)

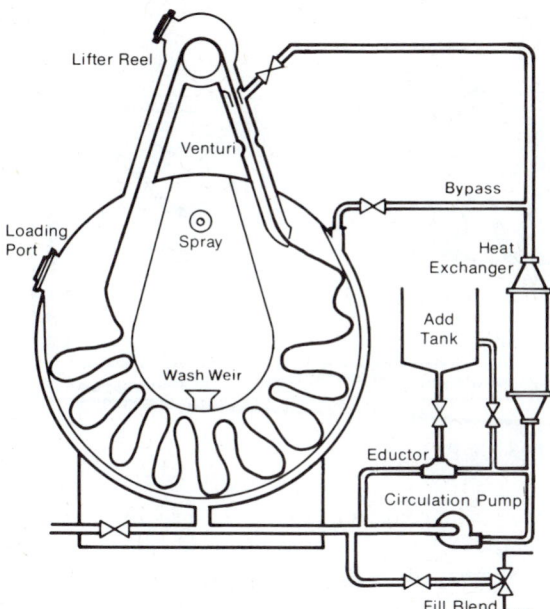

28.5 Diagram and illustration of Aqualuft machine used for piece dyeing. (Gaston County)

cation of dyes. The chemicals used in leveling differ depending on both the dyestuff used and the fiber content of the textile substrate.

Solution Dyeing or Mass Pigmentation

In the manufacture of man-made fibers, color can be added to the chemical solution before it is forced through the spinnerettes. If the pigment is good, this method ensures not only even dyeing but colors that are an integral part of the fiber and therefore fast to most outside influences. This method is preferred for fibers that are difficult to dye by other methods. This process is of particular importance to acetate and olefin fibers, especially polypropylene.

Gel dyeing incorporates color into the fiber while it is still in a soft or gel form before the solution hardens. It is similar to mass pigmentation, and similar dyeing agents are used.

Fiber Dyeing

Tow, top, and fiber dyeing involve adding color to filaments or staple fibers before they are processed into yarns and/or fabrics. The type of dyestuff selected depends on the fiber involved. This method provides for a deep penetration of the dye into the fiber and gives uniform coloration with good to excellent colorfastness properties—provided, of course, that good dyestuffs were selected for use. Figure 28.1 illustrates the dyeing of loose fiber, while Figure 28.2 is an example of a fabric for which the fibers were dyed before the yarns were formed.

Yarn Dyeing

One of the oldest systems of dyeing textiles is to color the yarns. This process is still widely used, in three main variations. (1) Yarns are dyed in skein form (Fig. 28.3). (2) Yarns are rolled on tubes and then dyed; this system is called *package dyeing* (Fig. 28.4). (3) Yarns are rolled onto warp beams and then dyed; this system is called *beam dyeing.* Yarn dyeing provides good color absorption and adequate penetration. It permits the use of various colored yarns in one fabric, thus giving the fabric designer wide scope in designing plaids, checks, stripes, muted color arrangements, and iridescent effects.

Yarn or package dyeing has several advantages. It requires less labor than fiber dyeing; the packages dry rapidly; high temperatures can be used. When yarn is packed into cones or packages, reeling of yarn into hanks and then into packages or creels for further processing is eliminated.

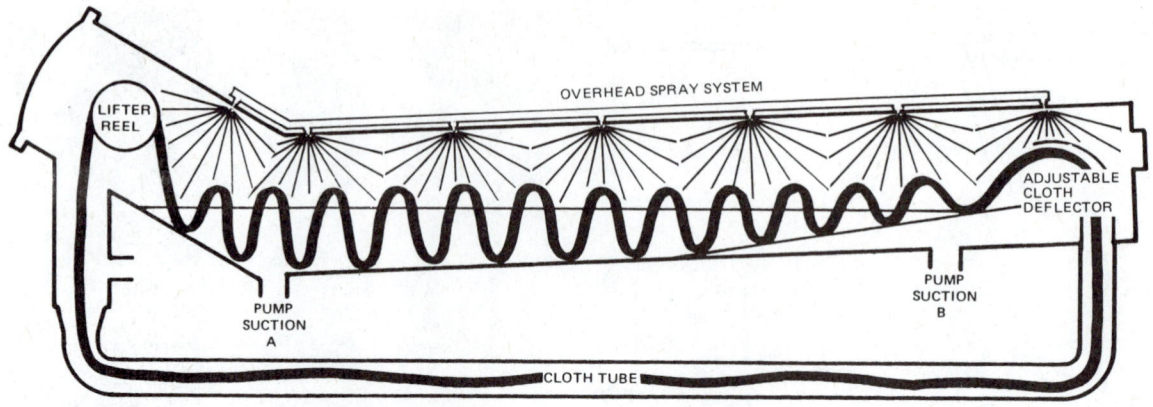

OVERHEAD SPRAY SYSTEM

LIFTER REEL

ADJUSTABLE CLOTH DEFLECTOR

PUMP SUCTION A

PUMP SUCTION B

CLOTH TUBE

28.6 Futura piece-dyeing machine for fragile and pressure-sensitive fabrics. (Gaston County)

Piece Dyeing

Most solid-color fabrics are dyed after the fabric has been constructed. This is piece dyeing, the easiest and cheapest method of adding color (Figs. 28.5, 28.6, and 28.7). Manufacturers can color fabrics as ordered and need not maintain a large stock of dyed fabrics that might become obsolete if fashions change. Piece dyeing does not always provide a thorough penetration of dyestuff into the fabric, but for many uses it is quite satisfactory. Normally, piece-dyed fabrics are a single color, but when a fabric contains more than one fiber, a pattern can result from the different absorption rates of the fiber and different levels of attraction or reaction between dyes and fibers. Further, different types of dyestuffs may be used so that one fiber is colored by one type of dye and another fiber is colored by a

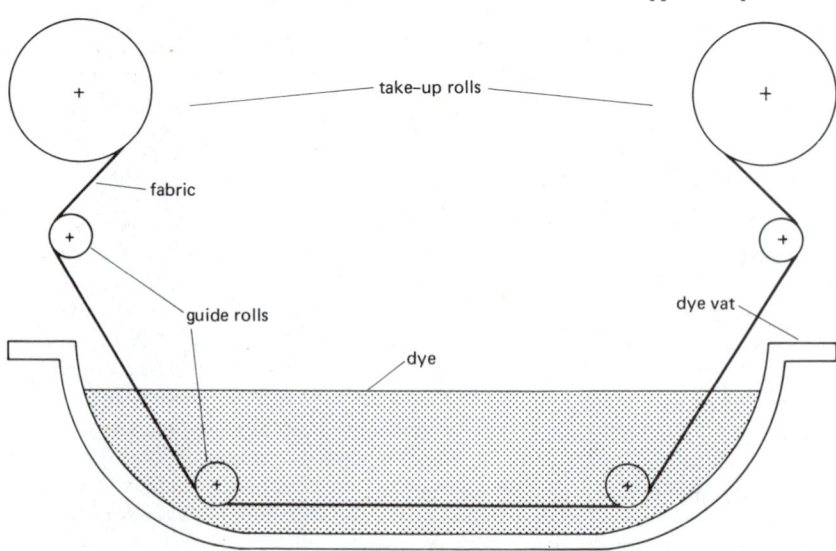

take-up rolls

fabric

guide rolls

dye vat

dye

28.7 Diagram illustrating the principle of jig dyeing. Fabric moves from one take-up roll to the other through the dye and then reverses, moving back to the first roll. (Springs Industries, Inc.)

different dye. There are two important processes used when fabrics are made of two or more different fiber types or fiber variants. These are union dyeing and cross dyeing.

Union Dyeing

In union dyeing a fabric containing two or more different generic fiber types or fiber variants of one generic type is dyed a single uniform color. Various dyestuffs are applicable only to certain fiber types, so when a fabric contains two or more types of fibers and is to be colored a solid color, the dyes must be carefully selected and properly applied in order to ensure color uniformity. If possible, dyes should be chosen that can be applied simultaneously to the fabric. However, in some cases dyers have found it

preferable to introduce the dyes individually, each by its recommended procedure. These two methods are often called *one-bath* and *two-bath* processes.

Cross Dyeing

In cross dyeing a fabric containing two or more fiber types or fiber variants is dyed so that each fiber type or variant accepts a different type of dyestuff and becomes a different color. In some cases, the dye bath is planned so that certain fibers will accept no color at all and instead will remain white. The end product depends upon the fiber arrangement within the fabric. It may be a check, a plaid, a tweed, a stripe, a muted color, a heather effect, or some other design.

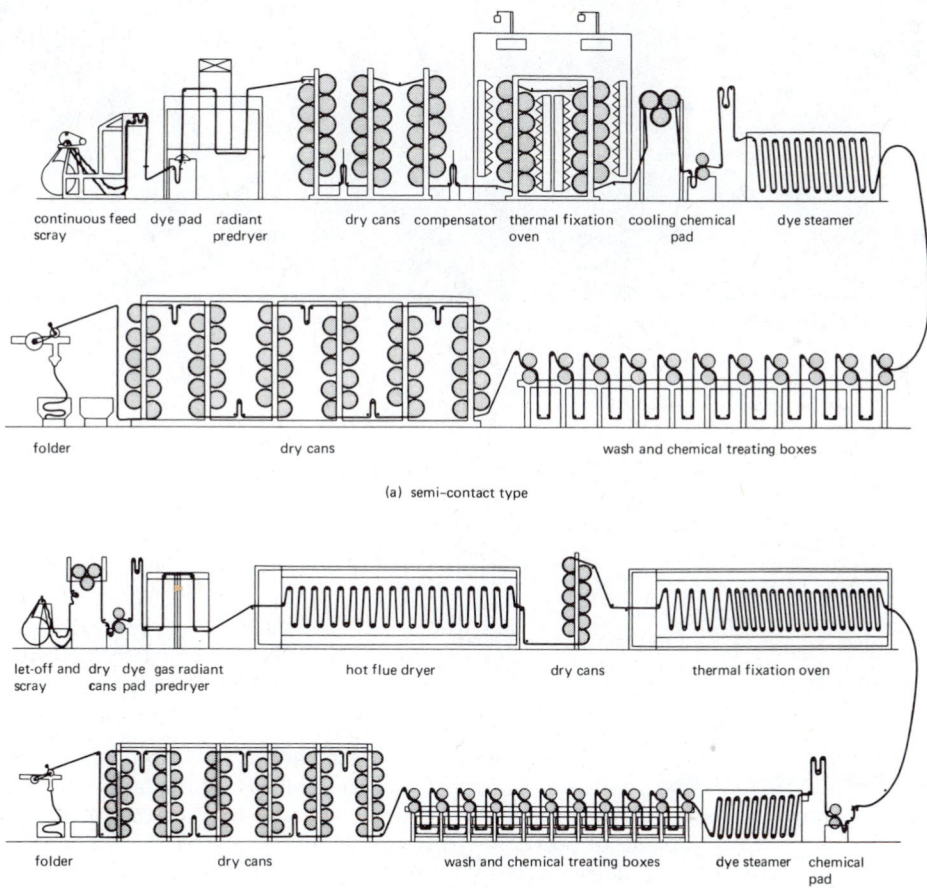

28.8 Typical thermal fixation dyeing ranges. A: Semi-contact type (Aztec Corporation). B: Hot flue type (Courtesy of Proctor and Schwartz, Inc.).

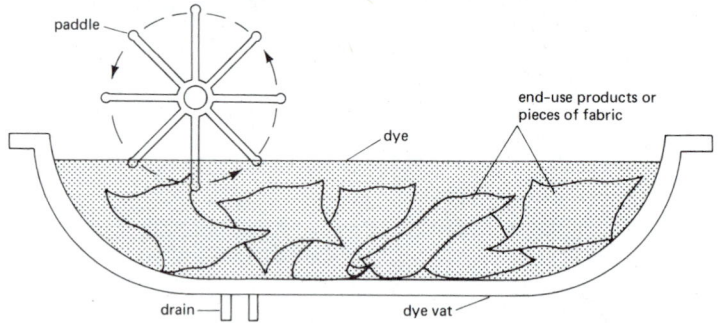

28.9 Kusters continuous dyeing range. (Zima Corporation)

paddle

end-use products or
pieces of fabric

dye

drain

dye vat

28.10 Diagram showing paddle dyeing.
The paddle keeps both fabrics and dye
solution in motion. (Springs Industries, Inc.)

Continuous Dyeing Process

One of the more common types of fabrics available
to consumers is composed of a blend of polyester
and cellulose (usually cotton). The dyeing procedure for this blend requires two types of dyes, and
a continuous dyeing system is commonly used. Figure 28.8 diagrams the steps involved in this process.

If disperse and vat dyes are used, the dyes are combined and padded into the fabric; this is followed by
a predry and then by a thermosol, or thermofix, step
where the disperse dyes are firmly attached by the
application of high temperatures for a brief period.
This step colors the polyester.

The fabric then moves into a chemical bath to
activate the vat dyestuff. It moves to a steamer for a

brief time and then into a cold wash where the vat dye is oxidized. A last wash is given to remove loose dye and any chemicals that may remain in the fabric; this is followed by a final rinse and drying. When reactive dyes are used on the cellulose instead of vat dyes, the cold wash and oxidation steps are omitted. Continuous dyeing units are widely used in dyeing single-fiber fabrics as well as blends (Fig. 28.9). In such instances only one dyeing method would be involved.

Product Dyeing

It is possible to make a complete end-use textile product and then dye it. In such cases, the dyeing technique commonly used is *paddle dyeing* (Fig. 28.10). This method is not considered practical for general use by apparel manufacturers, but it is used for some specialty items like couture apparel, and it is frequently used for home furnishings such as towels, bedspreads, and similar items.

Other Methods

Other methods of dyeing include batik and tie-and-dye. These are discussed as part of applied design in Chapter 29.

COLORFASTNESS OF DYES

Dyestuffs are evaluated in terms of their colorfastness to a variety of environmental situations. Further, fabrics may be colorfast to one or two situations but not to all of those to which the product might be exposed. Some of the situations to which color is exposed are laundering with water, detergent, and/or bleach; dry cleaning, both wet and dry; sunlight; crocking, rubbing, or abrasion; perspiration; environmental gas fumes (ozone and smog); and pressing, both wet and dry. Tests for determining whether the textile is resistant to the various factors can be found in several resources, such as the yearly *Technical Manual* published by the American Association of Textile Chemists and Colorists (AATCC).

When dyes are lost after exposure to certain types of situations, they are identified as not colorfast or with varying degrees of colorfastness. A few dyes are made for the sole purpose of providing temporary markings during various processing steps. Such dyes are called fugitive tints and are removed easily during a wash cycle.

If colors are lost into a water bath or cleaning bath, the color is said to *bleed*. Bleeding can be observed when color is lost from the textile and seen in a water bath as part of laundering or in cleaning solvents during dry cleaning. *Migration* of dyes occurs when colors spread in adjacent areas of fabrics and stain those areas. Migration and bleeding frequently occur together.

Colorfastness of dyes is important to the consumer. Unfortunately, there are no legal rules or regulations that require that information about colorfastness be provided the consumer. Care labels must identify methods of care, but that does not mean that colors will necessarily be retained at their original level during care, even when recommended care procedures are used. Information concerning colorfastness properties of a textile would be of interest and help to most consumers.

STUDY QUESTIONS

1. When was the first synthetic dyestuff discovered? How? By whom?
2. What was used for dyeing before the discovery of synthetic dyes?
3. Identify the various types of dyestuffs, cite examples, and indicate what fiber types are usually dyed with each specific dye type.
4. How do pigments differ from dyes, and how are they applied?
5. When can dyes be applied to textile products? How do the processes differ in relation to colorfastness and dye penetration?
6. What is meant by colorfastness, and why is it difficult to evaluate?
7. What is a mordant and why is it used?
8. Define *chromophore* and *auxochrome*.

Activities

1. Study textile items available on the market, and determine what, if any, information is given identifying the colorfastness of the dyestuff used.
2. Select various samples of fabrics of different fiber types, wash the samples, and determine what, if anything, happens to the color.
3. Select several samples of dyed fabrics, and determine how each was colored: fiber, yarn, piece, or product?

Applied Designs

OBJECTIVES
◇ **To provide information that will make it possible to identify different techniques used in applying surface designs to fabric**
◇ **To identify various methods of applying surface designs and to describe each process**
◇ **To indicate factors to use in evaluating performance of fabrics with surface designs**
◇ **To identify special processes used in applying surface designs to fabrics**
◇ **To provide a look at the historical background of printing and surface decoration of fabrics**

KEY TERMS

batik	ikat	roller printing
block printing	jet printing	rotary screen printing
direct printing	kasuri	screen printing
discharge printing	photographic printing	stencil printing
duplex printing	polychromatic printing	tie-dye
embroidery	printing	tjanting
flatbed screen printing	resist printing	transfer printing

PRINTING

Printed fabrics are defined as fabrics that have been decorated by a motif, pattern, or design applied to the surface of the fabric after it has already been constructed. The art of printing fabrics is thousands of years old. It is not known exactly when the first fabrics were given surface decoration, as these early fabrics were colored with "dyes" of temporary value and color did not last. Pictures found on the walls of the tomb of Beni Hassan (c. 2100 B.C.) in Egypt show figures costumed in fabrics with small conventional print motifs. Remains of printed fabrics have been found in both India and China that have been identified as belonging to the period around 500 B.C.

The oldest textile prints found in Europe have been dated at about A.D. 600. In the Americas, examples of printed fabrics have been discovered in pre-Inca remains in southern Peru, dated between A.D. 300 and 500. However, it was not until the sixteenth century that textile printing attained general acceptance, and even then it did not achieve the distinction that it reached in the eighteenth century when Christophe Phillippe Oberkampf opened his textile printing factory at Jouy, France, and began to produce the famous "Toiles de Jouy." These are considered by many art historians to be the finest patterned textile fabrics in the world (Fig. 29.1).

Resist Printing

Some historians consider resist printing to be one of the oldest methods, if not the oldest, of applying design to cloth. Early Javanese batiks and Japanese stencil prints are examples of resist printing, as is plangi tie-dye, which was developed in Asia, probably in China or India. The basic principle of resist printing is to protect areas of the fabric that are not to be colored so that dye cannot penetrate at those protected locations. The basis of protection may be paper or metal coverings, chemicals painted onto the fabric, or wax coatings painted onto the fabric.

29.1 Toile de Jouy. Copper-plate print on linen (detail). **Jouy, France.** (Los Angeles County Museum of Art, Gift of Mr. and Mrs. John Jewett Garland)

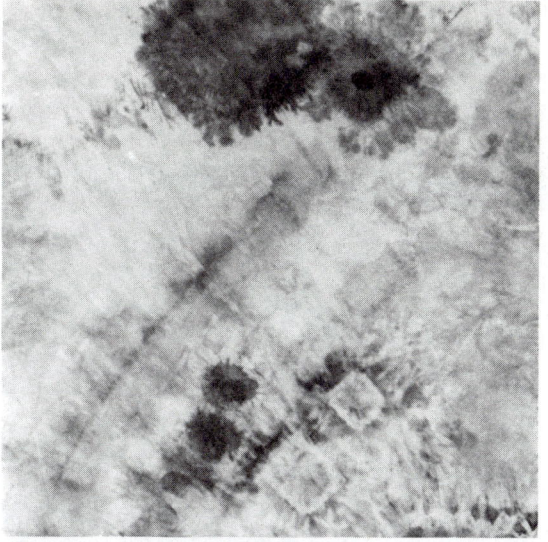

29.2 Modern example of tie-dyed fabric.

Plangi Tie-Dye

Plangi resist methods were used by ancient peoples in the Far East, and early designs were extremely delicate. In this technique tiny puffs of fabric were pulled over a pointed object, and waxed thread was tied tightly below the small puff. Wherever the fabric was to resist the color, it was tied securely with the waxed thread. After tying, the fabric was dipped into a dye bath. If two, three, or more colors were to be used, the thread was removed after each application of a color, and the fabric was retied to protect it at new locations.

A method called *tritik* involves hand or machine stitching. The stitching is put in according to special designs, and the thread is pulled to draw the fabric together. The fabric resists the dye penetrating in the specific tied areas.

Modern Tie-Dye

Modern tie-dye designs are usually characterized by large blotchy areas of color (Fig. 29.2). The principle is the same, but the thread used for tying is not necessarily waxed. Further, other methods may be used to tie off portions of the fabric. Materials such as yarn, thread, cloth, or metal strips may be used to protect the fabric at selected points and provide the resist needed to create interesting designs.

Today, tie-dyed fabrics are made primarily as craft items. Designs that resemble tie-dye available in commercial quantities may have been done using other printing methods such as screen printing or direct roller printing. Good examples of tie-dye may be art forms intended for wall hangings or other display items.

Batik

A resist method perfected by the Javanese, batik has recently been revived (Fig. 29.3). In batik prints wax serves as the resist substance. Using a *tjanting*—a copper cup attached to a reed handle—the batik printer applies wax to the fabric where it is to resist the dye (Fig. 29.4).

An important part of producing batik prints is the preparation of the fabric. It must be thoroughly washed to remove any slashing or sizing and treated with oil or some other material to facilitate dye penetration. The fabric is washed to remove any impurities acquired during the oiling, and then it is stiffened with a special starch made from tapioca to produce a smooth surface on which the design can be drawn. The starch prevents the spread of the wax beyond areas where it is planned.

A batik design is produced following these steps:

1. Melted wax is applied with the tjanting to all

29.3 Batik from Malaysia.

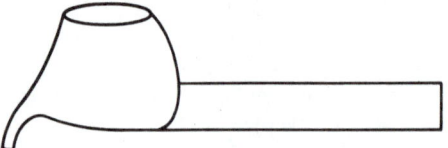

29.4 Tjanting used to apply wax resist in the batik process.

areas that are to remain unaffected or clear of the specific color to be applied. For some designs, the wax may be applied using special blocks with wires forming the design that is to remain clear of the specific color. Further, for some large designs the wax may be painted on with a brush.

2. The cloth is dipped in dye. All waxed areas repel the dyestuffs, so only the untreated areas absorb the color. It is important to note that some batik prints are made by painting the dye onto the fabric with a brush instead of dipping the fabric into a dye bath. This latter method makes it possible to hold the fabric taut and prevents cracking of the wax.

3. The wax is removed in a boiling water bath. As the water cools, the wax solidifies, floats to the surface of the water, and can be recovered for reuse. For some designs, the wax may be cracked first, and large segments of the wax may be removed by hand before dipping the cloth in the water bath.

4. The process is repeated for each color required. Wax covers areas already dyed except where combinations of colors are needed to produce the desired design color.

For some designs the wax is cracked before dipping or applying in order to create fine background lines. These are often identified as specific characteristics of batik fabrics; however, some of the new batik fabrics made in Indonesia and Malaysia have designs without the thin lines.

The block that may be used in applying wax is called the *tjap*. It is dipped in melted wax and then placed on the cloth. The wax coats the fabric in the design that has been created on the block.

Using the tjanting, Javanese or Malaysian women require from 30 to 50 days to complete a 4-meter length of fabric. The tjap shortens the time considerably, and a 4-meter length can be made in less than 10 days. The tjap did not replace the tjanting; rather it has simply added to the ease of creating various designs. Fine designs are still made with the tjanting.

Ikat (Kasuri)

Ikat, also called kasuri, is a resist method in which only the warp yarns are printed. The areas not to receive color are tied. The yarns are dipped in the dye bath; the tied areas remain white, the untied areas become colored. If more than one color is to be used, then several tyings will be necessary. After coloring, the yarns are placed on the loom ready for weaving.

Today, kasuri and any fabric identified as a warp print are made by modern printing processes. The warp yarns are put through a printing operation just a fabric would be, using either resist or direct printing methods (Fig. 29.5). Ikat and kasuri made according to the old process are still produced in several Asian countries.

Stencil Printing

Stencil printing was first developed in Japan and was the precursor of modern screen printing processes. In stencil printing, design areas are cut from thin metal sheets or from sheets of special paper coated with wax or some similar substance such as varnish. A separate stencil is cut for each color. Each stencil must be cut so as to register with every other stencil so that the final design is accurately matched to produce a perfect print. A difficulty with stencil prints is that the design areas must be connected in some way to other areas so as to prevent the loss of any part of the design. The Japanese developed a system of using extremely fine silk filaments or human hair to tie the design pieces together. When printed, these filaments were so fine that there appeared to be no connection between the design parts. Most modern stencil prints use rather bold patterns with obvious connections among the pieces. Color may be applied by hand-painting the open areas of the stencil as was done for early stencil printing, or by applying dye with an airbrush or spray gun of some type. Stencil printing is used for limited yardage, one-of-a-kind scarves, and similar products. For the most part, it has been replaced by screen printing.

Screen Printing

Many textile technologists consider screen printing to be the newest technique for decorating fabric surfaces, even though it was probably developed from stencil printing and other resist methods used many decades ago.

A screen is made by covering a frame with a cloth of silk, metal, nylon, or polyester filaments. The fabric is then covered with a film of some type, and the design areas are cut out of the film, leaving

29.5 Silk kasuri, warp-printed fabric.

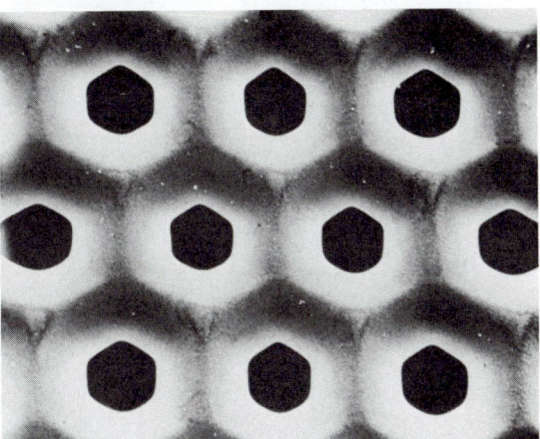

29.6 Screen material magnified 600×, 125 mesh (openings per inch). (Stork Screens America, Inc.)

the fine-mesh fabric open for the dyestuff to pass through and coat the fabric (Fig. 29.6). In modern screen printing mills, screens are prepared by photochemical processes, chemical-resist reactions, or engraving techniques. The completed screen is attached to whatever type of frame is required for the printing—either a flatbed frame or a rotary frame.

In *flatbed screen printing,* the frame is laid on the

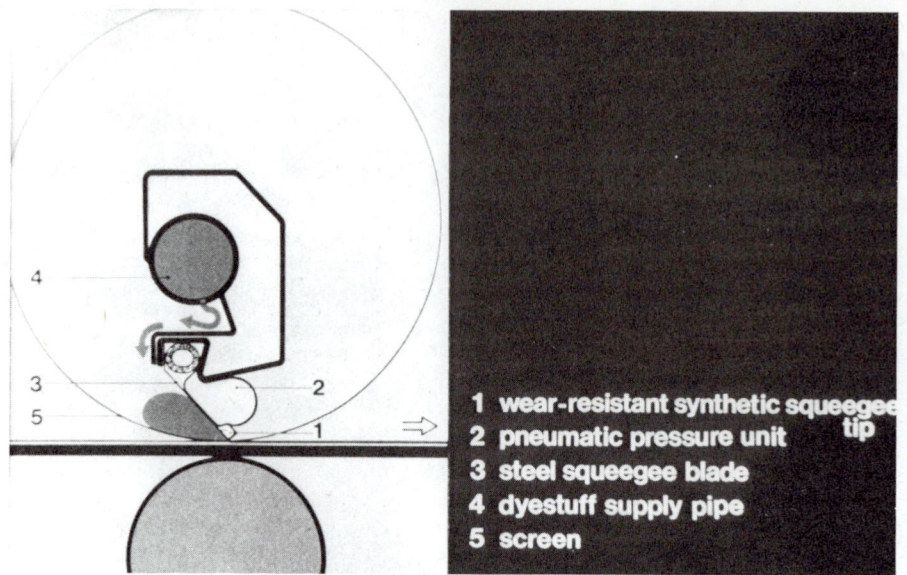

1 **wear-resistant synthetic squeegee tip**
2 **pneumatic pressure unit**
3 **steel squeegee blade**
4 **dyestuff supply pipe**
5 **screen**

29.7 Inside schematic of print roll for rotary screen printing. (Stork Screens America, Inc.)

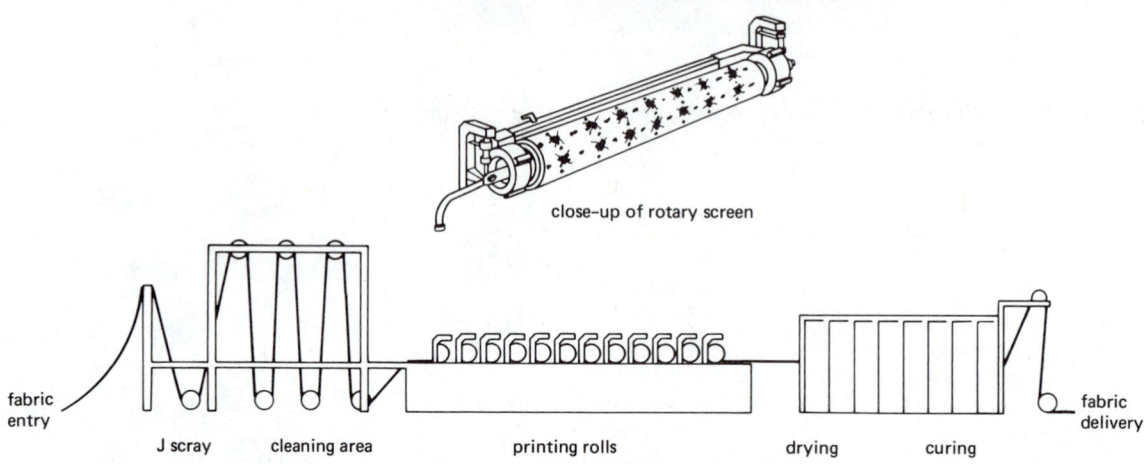

close-up of rotary screen

fabric entry | J scray | cleaning area | printing rolls | drying | curing | fabric delivery

29.8 Diagram showing basic steps in rotary screen printing. (Springs Industries, Inc.)

surface of the fabric to be printed, the dye is placed at one edge of the frame or screen, and a rubber knife or squeegee moves the dye across the screen and forces the color through the open areas and onto the fabric. One screen is prepared for each color, and the size is made to correspond to the planned repeat size of the pattern. All screens used for a specific design are arranged so that they register, or fit together, to form a clean, neat, perfect print pattern. Modern flatbed machines are equipped with a variety of electronic controls to ensure that screens are carefully matched.

Rotary screen printing uses rolls on which the screens have been securely fastened. The dye is fed into the center of each roll, and a squeegee blade forces the dye through the open areas of the screen and onto the fabric as it passes beneath the design rolls (Fig. 29.7).

Flatbed screen printing has been automated to some degree, but it remains a relatively slow process. The printing rate is about 7 yards (6.5 m) per minute. This is considerably faster than hand methods, however. Rotary screen printing is considerably faster than other screen printing methods; ro-

29.9 Placing rolls into position in rotary screen printing machine. (Stork Screens America, Inc.)

29.10 Rotary screen printing.

tary units can print from 60 to 100 yards (55–91 m) per minute. The amount of dye forced through the screens can be controlled so that the layer of color can be very thin or somewhat thick. Figures 29.8, 29.9, and 29.10 illustrate rotary screen printing processes.

The size of the roll determines the size of the repeat unit that may be produced. As screen diameters can vary, it is possible to vary design size as long as it does not exceed the circumference of the roll used. Artists may develop designs that seem to be much larger than they actually are; however, close

inspection will indicate that the repeat is indeed no larger than the circumference of the roll. Flatbed screens may be of any size; thus, it is possible to develop patterns that fill large sections of fabric (Fig. 29.11).

Before automatic screen printing was introduced, the amount of yardage that could be printed at one time was limited by the length of the printing table, the speed of the operators, and the number of colors to be used. The fabric was spread flat on a padded table and fastened securely to the table. The operator(s) laid the screens in place, one at a time,

29.11 Screen-printed fabric.

29.12 Example of discharge-printed fabric.

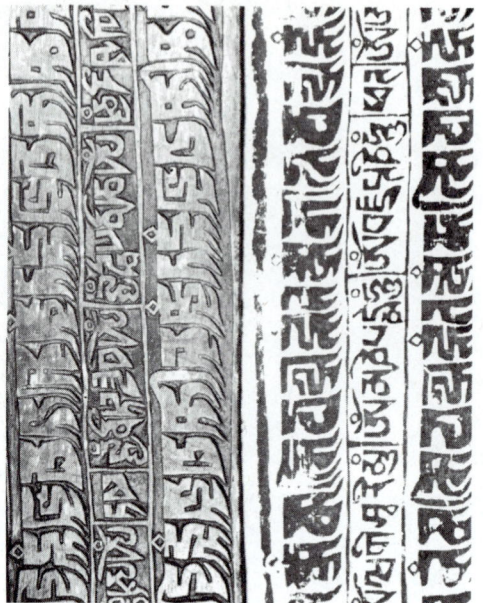

29.13 A wood block *(left)* and the fabric *(right)* printed using the block.

and forced the dye through the openings in the screen with a squeegee. This was repeated as many times as there were screens and colors for the particular design. When the fabric was completed, it was moved to racks over the printing table to dry.

Today, rotary screen printing is competing with direct roller printing. It can print as fast as direct printing and in some cases much faster; it is possible to make screens much more rapidly and more economically than the engraved copper rolls used in direct roller printing; it is practical for producing short runs of special designs in limited yardage; and it is easy to change design, colors, or add screens.

An important aspect of both rotary screen printing and flatbed screen printing is that the fabric is carried through the printing process on a flat surface and securely attached to a backing blanket to prevent distortion of the fabric. This process is especially good for printing knitted fabrics. Fabrics up to 200 inches (5 m) in width can be successfully printed with screen printing machines.

It is believed that as direct roller printing units become inoperative or obsolete, they will be replaced with rotary screen units. It should be noted that although most rotary screen printers have the rolls in a horizontal arrangement to keep the fabric flat, some new rotary screen printers have the screens arranged vertically or even around a central cylinder similar to that used for direct roller printing.

Screen printing is used for large designs on fabrics for apparel and home furnishings. It is useful for both yardage and completed end-use products. It has proved to be highly useful for printing such products as terry cloth towels, bedspreads, sheets, and draperies.

Discharge Prints

Discharge printing involves the removal of dye from a fabric in such a manner that a pattern is formed. The area where the dye has been removed may be left white, or another color may be placed in the pattern area. Discharge printing is applied to fabrics that have been previously dyed a solid color and is particularly useful when print fabrics with dark color backgrounds are to be made. To remove the dye, a design roller is coated with a bleach that removes the base dye and leaves the white pattern on a dark background (Fig. 29.12). The process may involve reprinting the white area with some other color. This is done by having a second roll apply the desired color to the area where the original background color has been discharged or bleached out. Any number of colors can be applied in the discharged areas depending on the desired pattern.

Some discharge processes entail combining the discharge of the base color and the application of a new color in a single bath. When this is done, the solution used to discharge the base color must not have any effect on the replacement color, and the bleach and dye are mixed in a single solution.

Discharge printing may cause weakening or tendering of the fabric at the points where the chemical was applied to remove the foundation dye. It is important that the dyer use the proper chemicals and that any chemical used to remove color be thoroughly rinsed away as part of the operation.

Direct Printing

Direct printing remains one of the most important methods for imparting pattern to cloth. Direct roller printing accounts for a large proportion of printed fabric, although its use is decreasing as other methods, namely screen printing and transfer printing, gain in use and acceptance. Block printing, a direct method, is used for special designs and for limited yardage. It is used to some extent as a crafts process. Direct methods may be involved in duplex and photographic printing.

Block Printing

Ancient samples of fabric stamped with block prints have been discovered by archeologists and dated as early as 1600 B.C. Wall paintings indicate a possible application of a pattern by block stamping as early as 2100 B.C. These fabrics appear to have been printed with small blocks no larger than 1 to 2 inches (2.5–5 cm) in diameter. By the fifteenth century blocks were between 12 and 18 inches (30–46 cm) in diameter and 2½ to 3½ inches (6.4–8.9 cm) thick. Block printing is still practiced today, primarily as a handicraft. Each block prints only one color, so if a design of several colors is desired, a block must be made for each color. In preparing a block, one carves away the background while leaving the design areas raised.

The making of a block print begins with the fabric laid flat on a table that has been covered with a protective padding. The fabric is securely attached to the table to prevent movement during printing. Either the block is dipped in printing paste (dye) so that only the raised portions pick up the color, or a roller is coated with the paste and then rolled over the block, depositing a coating of color on the raised areas. The block is then pressed onto the fabric surface with sufficient pressure to force the color into the fabric (Fig. 29.13). The fabric is then left to dry.

Roller Printing

Direct roller printing had its origin in the use of flat plates or blocks on a flat printing press. This was a natural development from block printing. The flatbed direct printing press was used by Oberkampf at Jouy in producing his famous printed fabrics. Thomas Bell of Scotland invented the roller print machine in 1783. His process combined metal engraving with color printing. Improvements have been made over the years, but the basic idea developed by Bell is still the foundation for direct roller printing operations.

Direct roller printing has been the most popular and involves the most yardage since its development. However, at present it is being challenged by both screen printing and transfer printing, and direct printing is decreasing in use.

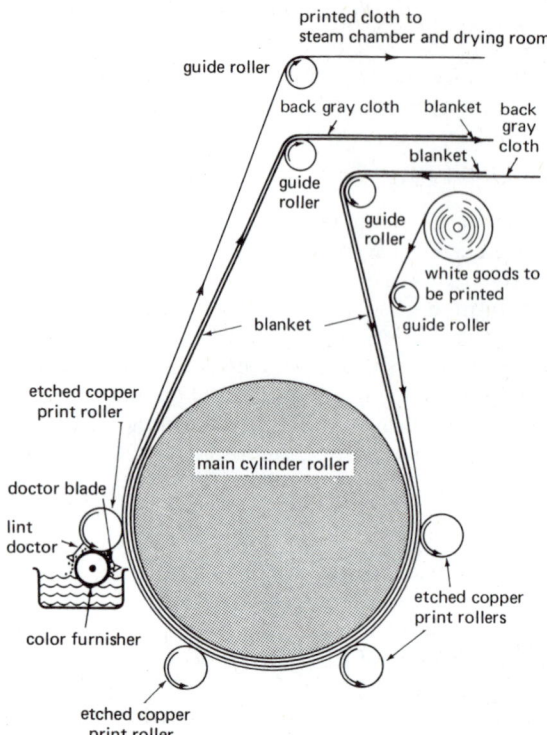

29.14 Diagram of a direct roller printing machine.

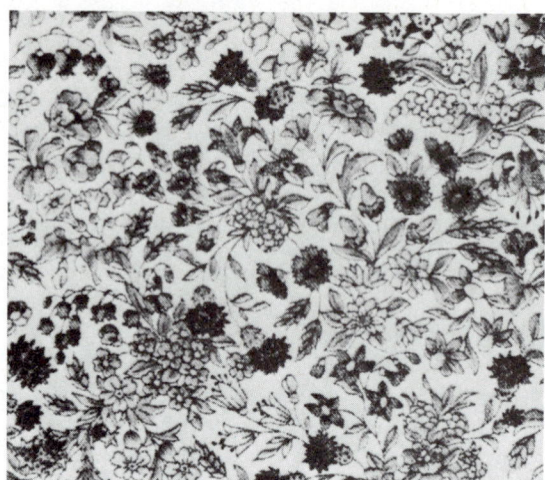

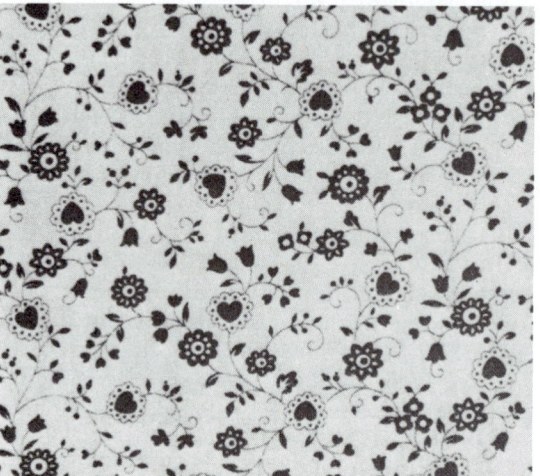

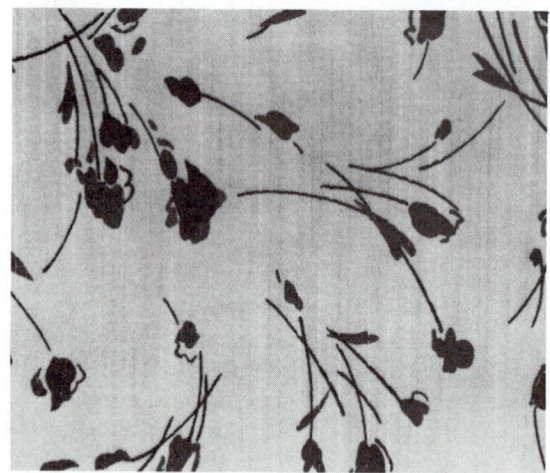

29.15 Direct roller printed fabrics.

In roller printing the design repeat cannot exceed the circumference of the rolls used. The design is developed so that it can be engraved on copper rolls and each color will have its own engraved roll. Figure 29.14 diagrams a typical direct roller printing machine. However, it must be noted that actual machines have provision for many more color rolls than shown in this diagram.

After the design is made and the colors have been clearly identified and separated, the portion of the design for a specific color is transferred to a roll by means of a pantograph or other mechanism. Some transfer units today depend on computer graphics for transferring the design to the copper roll. The pantograph controls an instrument that outlines the design on the roll. The area of the roll that is to print the specific color remains clear, while the other areas of the roll are coated with a chemical-resistant paint. The roll is dipped in acid, which etches or burns away the surface layer of metal wherever there is no chemical-resist coating. After etching, the resist coating is removed and the roll is polished. A direct roll has the design area de-

29.16 Photographic print fabric.

feeds around the padded roll, and a "back gray" cloth is often used on top of the printing blanket. The cloth to be printed is on the outer surface. The layers move together from the supply rolls around the cylinder, under the etched copper rolls where the printing takes place. As it reaches the end of the printing area, the cloth leaves the cylinder and is fed into drying ovens, which set the color. The base fabrics return to the supply rolls for reuse.

Roller printing machines can print at a speed of approximately 40 to 50 yards (37–45 m) per minute. The end result depends on the accuracy of roll preparation and efficient machine operation and control. Colored backgrounds can be printed onto fabrics from etched rollers at the same time that the designs are applied, and predyed fabrics can be printed if colors to be added can be seen on the colored base without distorting color schemes. A wide variety of direct roller printed fabrics can be made. The type of design is limited only by the size of the repeat, which is limited by the size of the engraved rolls. Most direct roller printing machines do not print fabric much wider than 48 to 54 inches; for wider fabric, screen printers are usually used. Examples of fabrics printed by a direct roller printing process are shown in Figure 29.15.

Duplex Prints

Most duplex prints are prepared on direct roller printing machines that have been modified to print both sides of a fabric at the same time. However, some duplex printing is now being done using screen printers with the print rolls arranged vertically, with two sets of rolls placed so that fabric passes between them. For either system, the rolls are placed in parallel vertical arrangements and the fabric passes between the two sets; thus, both the face and the back of the fabric are printed simultaneously.

Duplex-printed fabric may have the same design on both sides of the fabric; the same design with two different color arrangements may be printed; or two distinctly different designs can be used so that they resemble yarn-dyed or fiber-dyed patterns. In some cases duplex prints may resemble decorative or novelty weaves. Duplex prints are usually more expensive than single-side prints; however, the design possibilities are worth the cost to many consumers.

pressed to hold the dye rather than spreading the color onto raised areas as in block printing.

The engraved rollers are arranged around the main cylinder and locked into place on the printing machine. As many as sixteen rolls may be used. Each roll has a trough for its particular dye and a doctor blade, which scrapes the dye away from the smooth raised surface, leaving that portion of the roll without any color while dye remains in the depressed or etched sections. Modern equipment uses electronic controls to ensure that all the rolls are in perfect register with each other in order to produce a clear, even, and well-matched pattern.

The large cylinder in direct printing is covered with a padding blanket. A moving printing blanket

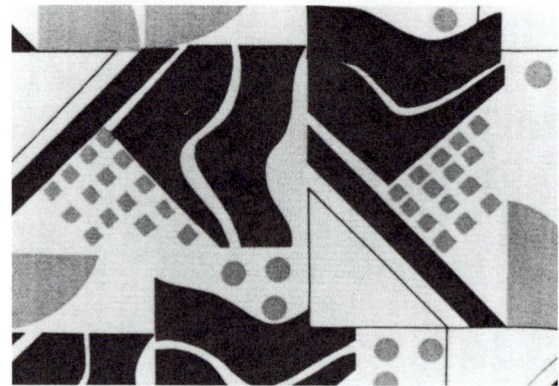

29.17 Transfer prints. Left: Paper before printing along right edge and after printing in center.
Right: Fabric after printing.

Photographic Prints

Photographic prints on fabric are made in a manner very similar to that used in making photographs. Designs may be in black and white, or multicolored patterns can be reproduced (Fig. 29.16). The fabric is treated with a light reactive chemical, a negative is placed on the fabric, light is transmitted to it, then the color is developed. After stabilization, the fabric is thoroughly washed, and the print becomes as permanent as any good photograph.

Transfer Printing

In comparison with most printing methods, transfer printing of fabric is a relatively new technique. The process involves the transfer of color from one surface, usually paper, to a second surface, the textile fabric (Fig. 29.17). There are three basic methods used: vapor-phase transfer; wet transfer, sometimes called migration printing; and melt transfer. The most common is the vapor-phase method; this is sometimes referred to as sublimatic or sublistatic transfer printing.

Although the history of transfer printing dates back to the mid-nineteenth century, the major work on this process did not occur until the early 1930s, and the majority of the development dates from 1968. The process is a competitor to both direct roller and rotary screen printing. However, its use has not grown as predicted, and there appears to be no attempt to replace either direct roller or rotary screen methods with transfer methods except for specialized uses.

The basic principles of the process are as follows:

1. The vapor-phase method uses disperse dyes or other dyes capable of sublimation. These dyes are printed on paper to form the desired pattern. The dyes are transferred from the paper to the textile substrate at temperatures between 180° and 220°F (82°–104°C). Contact time between paper and fabric is approximately 30 seconds. In the vapor-phase method the dye sublimates or changes to a vapor. As the dyestuffs have little or no affinity for the paper and a great affinity for the fabric, they move from the paper to the textile fabric in the vapor form. The vapor condenses on the fabric, and then heat and pressure are used to set the pattern in the fabric.
2. Wet-transfer printing involves moisture in the contact of paper and textile. The dyes on the paper are dissolved briefly in water and printed onto the fabric under heat and pressure or through the use of radio-frequency treatment.
3. The melt-transfer system entails printing the dyes or pigments together with a thermoplastic binder onto paper and then transferring the color and the binder onto the textile under heat and pressure.

During the late 1960s and early 1970s the vapor-phase method was used to print polyester fabrics with disperse dyestuffs. It was particularly successful for printing knitted fabrics. Gradually the process was expanded to print woven fabrics; then development of the wet and melt methods made it possible to print fabric of other fibers than polyester. The method is used successfully on polyester, polyester/cotton blends, polyester/wool blends, nylon, acrylic, 100 percent cotton, and 100 percent wool fabrics. The average speed for transfer printing is about 15 yards (13.7 m) per minute.

Transfer printing has become an important process for knit fabrics because it does not distort the fabric during the printing operation. Further, transfer printing can be used on fabric of almost any width; the only limit is the way the transfer paper has been prepared and the width of the transfer printer carriage. It is also possible to transfer patterns onto completed garments such as T-shirts. This latter art has resulted in a distinctive merchandising program in which garments are given a print of the customer's choice at the time of purchase.

Transfer printing should continue to grow in popularity for these reasons:

1. The process is highly efficient, and the amount of second-quality print fabric can be reduced, as the paper carrier can be checked before printing and any inferior-quality sections can be eliminated before the fabric is printed.
2. A wide variety of interesting patterns can be prepared on transfer paper.
3. Unskilled labor can be used for the transfer operation. All that is needed is someone able to operate the transfer press.
4. An important advantage is that there is less pollution of water and considerably less water is required.
5. Fabrics can be printed as needed, reducing storage costs as well as losses due to unsold printed yardage that became outdated because of fashion changes.
6. Considerably less space is required at the textile printing site. This reduces overhead costs and limits the need for large amounts of energy.

One of the major advantages of transfer printing lies in the flexibility of designs. It is possible to transfer large scenic photographic prints, pictorial prints such as found in tapestries, and imitation figure-weave effects. In addition to savings in space, water, and energy, transfer printing reduces or eliminates the need for auxiliary chemicals at the transfer site.

However, one must not forget that the transfer paper must be prepared. This is usually done using a rotary screen printing operation. Consequently, cost is involved in the preparation of the designs and the dyes used in preparing the transfer medium.

Jet Printing

Jet printing is achieved by controlling continuous dye streams. The dye streams are deflected by air or mechanical devices in such a way as to be directed onto or away from the fabric, depending on the pattern desired. There are several methods of jet printing. Only a few will be highlighted here.

THE TAK METHOD The TAK method applies two or more colors in a random shower, and rotating wire-chain bands break the dye streams into tiny droplets, which fall onto the fabric surface. Variations are further achieved by modifying the viscosity or consistency of the dye liquor. Sharp and distinct or large and diffused color spots can be obtained. Design effects depend upon control of the wire chain, comb devices, and doctor blades. The TAK system is widely used to print carpeting.

THE POLYCHROMATIC PROCESS The polychromatic process produces patterns that may be similar to screen printing designs; they may also tend to resemble some tie-dye patterns. There are two basic techniques involved: the dye-weave method and the flow-form process (Fig. 29.18).

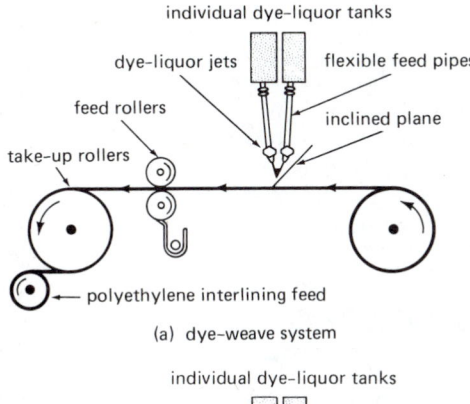

(a) dye-weave system

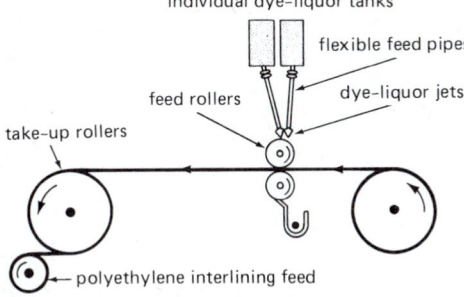

(b) flow-form transfer system

29.18 Polychromatic dyeing. A: Dye-weave system. B: Flow-form system.

In the *dye-weave* method, the dye is forced through jets onto a metal plate at a 45° angle to the fabric. The dye runs down the plate and onto the fabric. The design is influenced by the distance the dye must flow on the plate before it hits the fabric. A short flow area gives sharp, clean patterns; longer flow produces more indistinct and blurred designs. In the *flow-form* process, the dye is fed onto a roller, which in turn rolls the color onto the fabric. This method tends to give a marbelized effect to the design.

For either method, the jets can be placed into a rail and moved sideways to increase pattern complexity. The speed of movement of the cloth, the amount of color extruded at any one time, the arrangement and number of the color jets or applications, and the movement of the jets all combine to determine the pattern that will be formed on the fabric. There may be little or no evidence of any repeat in the design.

The dyes for polychromatic printing are selected on the basis of appropriateness to the fiber involved. They are fixed onto the fabric by the method most suited to the type of dye and the fiber.

The polychromatic method is used for fabrics for both apparel and home furnishings, although it is used more often for carpeting and other home furnishings than for apparel. The process is particularly good for tufted carpeting, either cut or uncut pile, because the dye will penetrate the pile very satisfactorily.

THE MILLITRON PROCESS The millitron process is similar to screen printing. The fabric is carried on an inclined plane under a series of jet bars, one for each color. There are ten jets per inch across the bar. The pattern is controlled by computer systems that generate electronic signals to control jets of air blown at right angles to the dye jets. When dye from a jet is to hit or print the fabric, the air jet is off. If no print is to occur, the air deflects the dye from the jet into a trough, and it is recycled. The computer controls make it possible to change patterns quickly and frequently.

THE CHROMOTRONIC PROCESS The chromotronic process may be compared to a flatbed screen printer. The fabric is moved intermittently, and printing is achieved as a print unit moves from side to side while the fabric is held stationary. During the move across the fabric, needle valve jets in the print head are opened at the appropriate moment to feed a drop of dye to the fabric. The pattern is developed by computer controls. Each color has its own print head.

The greatest use of jet printing methods is for carpeting. The amount of dye can be controlled, yet sufficient color can be fed into the pile carpet construction so that adequate color saturation is achieved. The processes may be used for other textile end-use items; however, the major use of these techniques remains carpeting. The methods do provide for a wide variety in pattern design within the same product, easily changed designs without major cleaning and change of rolls and dye supplies, and the possibility of controlling the actual printing by computer.

Bubble Printing

A relatively new method of printing involves the use of foam technology whereby the dye is dispensed onto the fabric in the form of bubbles. The majority of designs using bubbles involve geometric shapes similar to hexagons or modified geometric figures. The dye is dispensed in the foam according to the planned pattern; the bubbles move into the fabric substrate; the dye is permanently set. Patterns can involve the use of a single color or multiple colors. Since the process is relatively new, few examples of fabric are available. As this process involves foam technology, it is probable that it will receive increased use. It would be a system that reduces energy costs because of the reduced drying time required, and probable reductions in application time can occur.

EMBROIDERY

The application of yarn, thread, or floss is a very old method of decorating fabric (Fig. 29.19). Exquisite embroideries were made in Europe during the fourteenth, fifteenth, and sixteenth centuries, and some of these are now treasured museum pieces. Although this chapter has concentrated on surface design using dyestuffs, embroidery is included here as it does involve applied surface design.

Today, most embroidered fabrics are produced by machines, somewhat like those used in creating laces (Fig. 29.20). Embroidery can be applied to fabric of almost any weight. In fact, some embroidery is done so that the final fabric resembles a lace

29.19 Embroidered fabrics.

rather than an embroidered product. This is accomplished by embroidering onto a special shear fabric made of easily dissolved fibers. When the embroidery is complete, the base fabric is dissolved away, leaving only the embroidery pattern. Using cotton embroidery on a silk base would provide such a fabric if the silk were dissolved away following embroidery by the use of caustic soda, which would not harm the cotton. Another system might use a soluble vinal fabric for the base, which could be removed by standard washing procedures. However, most embroidered fabrics use a durable base fabric that remains as part of the fabric. Embroidery can be done with a variety of fiber yarns or thread, but probably the majority of embroidered products use cotton, silk, polyester, or wool.

MISCELLANEOUS METHODS OF FABRIC DECORATION

In addition to the methods described, fabrics can be decorated by appliquéing cut-out pieces of fabric onto the surface of a base fabric. Quilting can be used to make surface patterns on fabric. Some fabrics can be the result of a combination of several processes. The important thing is that surface de-

29.20 Automatic embroidery machine. (Saurer Textile Machinery)

sign depends on a base fabric structure upon which the surface design is added. The base fabric can be made by any fabric construction process. The majority of surface designs are applied to fabrics with simple yarn structures in order to minimize distortion of design as a result of uneven fabric surfaces.

In addition to the various processes described here, surface designs can be created through the use of selected finishing processes. These include plissé, moiré, embossing, flocking, glazing, and burned-out patterns, which have been discussed in previous chapters.

STUDY QUESTIONS

1. Briefly indicate the early history of printing designs onto fabric surfaces.
2. Describe the different types of printing procedures.
3. What are the major differences among resist, direct, and discharge printing?

4. Why has rotary screen printing become so popular?
5. What typical end-use product may be printed by means of jet or polychromatic printing processes?
6. Why has transfer printing become widely used for knit fabrics? Why is its use increasing for all fabrics?

Activities

1. Locate a variety of printed fabrics on the market. Try to determine what process or technique was used to print each one. Can you give reasons why the different processes were probably used?
2. Select several printed fabrics, and, if equipment is available, test for colorfastness to such conditions as rubbing or abrasion, washing, perspiration, dry cleaning, and pressing.
3. Locate several printed fabrics, and try to determine how many different color dyes were required to prepare the print design. Have some colors been printed over others to create a color?

PART VI

Fabric End Use

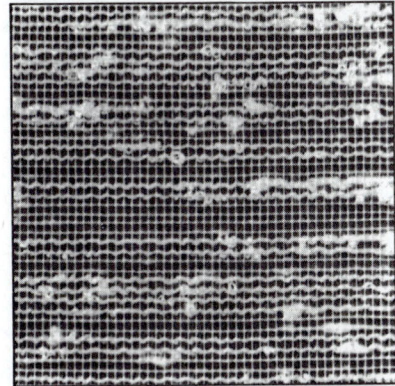

Fibers, yarns, fabrics, finishes, dyes—all are directed toward one goal: the end use of a product. With a few exceptions, textiles are meant to be worn, sat on, walked on, or enjoyed in some other form. They protect us as well as enhance our appearance and our near environment.

The concluding chapters in this text attempt to pull together the study of textiles. Discussion includes a review of textile performance and methods of testing; factors that need to be considered in selecting a fabric for a designated end use; legislation that affects the textile industry and textile consumers; and voluntary performance standards and test methods available for manufacturers that desire them. The final chapter considers fabrics in very highly specialized uses including geotextiles, high-performance textiles, and textiles in medicine.

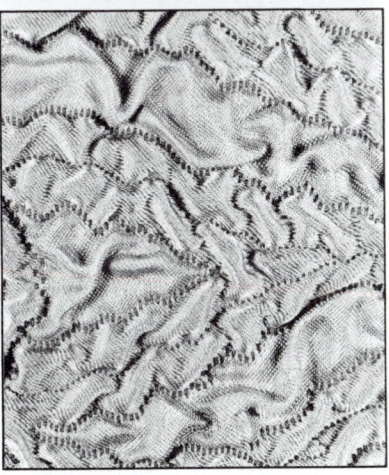

30
Fabric Geometry

KEY TERMS

abrasion resistance	moisture relationships
air permeability	soiling
clo	tear strength
dimensional stability	tensile strength
hand and drape	thermal-ohm
heat transmission	tog
maintenance	

The properties of any textile product are governed by a variety of factors. One determining factor is the geometrical relationships that exist among the component parts of a textile: fiber, yarn structure or fiber arrangement, fabric structure, finish, and color. How these components are assembled influences the properties of the textile fabric, especially the geometrical arrangement of fibers into yarns and fabrics.

Consider the component parts and how each one can vary; then consider how such variations influence the final fabric. Fiber properties are determined by the inherent characteristics of the base polymer and such geometric features as fiber length, cross-section shape and area, amount of crimp or texturization, stiffness or softness, and surface contour. Yarn properties are influenced by fiber characteristics and such geometric features as amount of yarn twist, shape and diameter, compactness of fibers within the yarn, and the basic yarn structure—simple, complex, single, ply, cord. Fabric properties are the result of fiber and yarn characteristics or the method of arranging the fibers in making the fabric plus the special geometry of the fabric structure itself. This includes the type of fabric structure (weave, knit, nonwoven), the size of

yarns used, the number of yarns per inch in wovens, the number of loops per inch in knits, the fiber arrangement in nonwovens, the tension on the yarn or fiber components, and the presence of dyes and finishes that influence the behavior of the fiber, yarn, and fabric.

Fabric geometry can be defined as the relationship, or interrelationships, of fibers and yarns to their ultimate shape and arrangement in the finished fabric (Fig. 30.1). Geometric factors influence the following properties important to consumers:

Tensile and tearing strength of the fabric.

Transmission of heat or cold through fabric, or its prevention and/or control.

Transmission of moisture and moisture absorbency, except that caused by inherent fiber properties. An example would relate to water repellency of a fabric.

Dimensional stability—the amount of shrinkage or stretch that can be expected for a fabric.

Abrasion resistance—the ability of a fabric to resist damage from rubbing.

Fabric soiling and cleaning problems—the influence of fiber, yarn, and fabric features in relation to soil resistance and soil release.

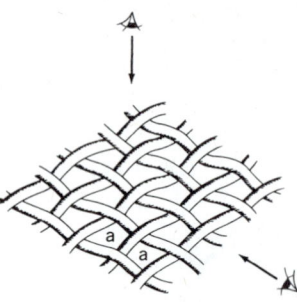

30.1 Diagram showing the interlacing of yarns that contribute to fabric geometry. Closeness and size of yarns influence the bend in the yarns and the resulting properties of the fabric. *A* identifies the interstices or openings between yarns.

Finishes must be considered here as they may influence geometric features to some degree.

The hand and drape of a fabric—the influence of geometric features on product appearance, product manipulativeness, and product texture.

Knowledge of geometric features and their interrelationships provides clues to possible fabric behavior and can be used by the informed consumer as a basis for fabric selection, use, and care. It is important to emphasize that many finishing techniques in current use will alter fabric properties despite known inherent features and geometric factors. On the other hand, some finishes may optimize inherent properties and improve the effectiveness of a fabric in use and care because of their interrelation with geometric features.

Tensile and Tearing Strength

Any fabric should possess adequate resistance to tearing and stress. Fabrics that are made from inherently strong fibers will tend to have adequate strength for the selected use and care. However, other factors may influence the properties, and the fabric may be subject to quick wear because of low resistance to tear and pulling stress (tensile strength).

Combined geometric features that produce a highly durable fabric that resists both tearing and pulling stress are found in fibers such as nylon, which has inherently high tensile strength; filament fibers, which tend to possess better resistance to tear and tensile stress; yarns of ply construction;

and a plain-weave fabric structure with sufficient yarns to provide good strength but not so many as to make the fabric stiff. Changing one factor can reduce the combined geometric properties and reduce the resistance to tearing or pulling forces.

Tearing strength can be increased by using strong fibers in strong yarn constructions in both warp and filling directions of a woven fabric and by general use of knitted structures. However, tearing strength is also affected by yarn mobility within the structure. High tearing strength can be achieved when yarns that have relatively low strength are combined into a fabric using a loose open structure. Low tearing strength can result when strong yarns are combined into a compact structure. As yarn mobility is decreased, tearing strength may be decreased.

Tensile strength can be improved by using strong fibers and yarns in both directions of a woven fabric and in all yarns for a knitted fabric; however, if the yarns in one direction of a woven fabric, or alternate yarns of reduced strength in a knit, are used, the resulting fabric may be relatively weak in the one direction and be subject to damage from a small amount of pull or stress in that particular situation or direction. A fabric that has been constructed with 80 yarns per inch in both the warp and filling will be stronger than a fabric made of 80 yarns in the warp and only 60 in the filling—provided the yarn size is consistent between both fabrics. Conversely, a fabric made of 80 yarns per inch in both warp and filling may be considerably weaker than another fabric made of the same number of yarns but composed of fibers that are inherently stronger. Further, a fabric with 80 yarns per inch in each direction but of yarns that are smaller in diameter and with low levels of twist would be considerably weaker than a fabric with 80 yarns per inch but of a heavier diameter or denier and with medium to high twist.

Tensile and tearing strength can also be influenced by the type of yarn used. A single- or simple-ply yarn in which the fibers and twist are uniformly distributed will probably give better resistance to stress than novelty or complex yarns where there may be areas of reduced strength owing to uneven twist, uneven distribution of fiber, and uneven yarn diameter.

Balanced woven fabric constructions will tend to resist tearing or pulling stress more successfully than fabric of unbalanced construction, as the yarn distribution is equalized in the balanced fabric and thus strength is equalized. Knit fabrics that are made of yarns of the same size but with a different number of loops per inch will differ in their resistance to pulling force. Obviously, the more yarns, the higher the strength—up to an optimum point.

Nonwoven fabrics will resist tear or pulling stress best when the fiber arrangement is spread over all directions and when the method of sealing the fibers together resists pull or tearing stress.

The presence of finishes will influence tear and tensile strength of fabrics despite the strength created by the choice of fibers, yarns, and construction processes. Regardless of the geometric factors at work, certain finishes do reduce resistance to tearing and pulling. The use of easy-care or durable-press finishes reduces the resistance of a fabric to tearing stress; consequently, in making good durable-press fabrics it is important to select the most optimum geometric factors in order to provide a fabric with adequate resistance to damage from tearing—the most seriously affected property by the presence of such finishes.

If consumers keep in mind fibers that provide the most inherent strength, types of yarn or fiber arrangement that contribute good resistance to stress, and a fabric construction that is well balanced and uniform, they may be able to choose a fabric that exhibits outstanding resistance to damage from either tearing or pulling forces.

Thermal Properties

Fabric for use in selected items of wearing apparel and home furnishings must have properties that make it adaptable for various climatic conditions. Thermal properties for apparel are of concern to most everyone, and that aspect will be emphasized in this discussion; however, much of what is said can be applied to fabrics used for draperies and similar furnishings.

The end use of a fabric may require that the fabric hold heat against the body, prevent heat from penetrating to the body, or conduct heat away from or toward the body.

For clarity in understanding the relationship of thermal properties and fabric geometry, a brief discussion on the mechanisms involved in heat loss is included. Heat can be lost from the body by conduction, convection, radiation, and evaporation of perspiration.

Heat loss by *conduction* occurs when materials known to be good conductors are placed next to the body. The conductor carries the body heat to the surrounding atmosphere, where it is dissipated into the air, cooling the body.

Heat loss by *convection* occurs when air currents move over and around the body and carry the heat away. This chill factor is one reason why a person feels colder on a windy day than on a day when no wind is apparent, even when air temperatures are identical.

Heat loss by *radiation* means that heat is given off from the body in the form of rays. This occurs when the air temperature is below body temperature.

Heat loss by *evaporation of perspiration* results from a physiological mechanism to control body temperature. When the body becomes too warm, noticeable amounts of fluid are given off through the skin. This fluid, perspiration, evaporates and the body is cooled. The cooling takes place because the water requires heat of vaporization to evaporate, and this heat comes from the body.

Fabrics used in cold environments should entrap and hold body heat. They should prevent heat loss by conduction, convection, or radiation. To reduce heat loss by conduction, fibers should be combined into yarns and fabrics in such a manner that air spaces are left to serve as insulating areas.

To prevent heat loss by convection and, to some degree, by radiation, the following features would be desirable: (1) a fabric with smooth yarns that are packed densely and (2) a high thread or fabric count with very tiny interstices between yarns to reduce air permeability.

There are measurements that help to identify thermal properties of fabric. The *clo* identifies a unit of thermal resistance defined as the insulation required to keep a resting person comfortable in an environment at 20°C, air movement of 0.1 meter per second, or roughly the insulation value of typical indoor clothing. The thermal resistance of a fabric is identified as the R value. These values may be determined scientifically and provide some indication of the thermal properties of fabrics or assemblies of fabric. It has been suggested that the total apparel for wear on a hot day should not exceed 0.5 clo, but on a cold winter day in cold climates a person may need 4.0 to 5.0 clo to be warm. Clo values depend on the ability of a fabric or layers of fabric to control the movement of air through them.

Another measure used for thermal comfort of fabrics is the *tog*. This is equal to 0.645 clo and is considered to be approximately the insulation of light summer clothing. Still another measure of thermal comfort is the *thermal ohm.* This equals 6.45 clo or ten times a tog unit.

Some items of clothing for cold climates are made of two layers or more of fabric. The inner layer is often a napped or pile fabric made of fibers that are poor conductors, whereas the outer layer is a tightly woven fabric such as taffeta, poplin, or broadcloth. In addition to preventing the loss of heat by convection, the outer fabric reduces heat loss from radiation because it will stop the heat and may in some cases actually reflect heat back to the body.

In warm areas clothing should accelerate or at least aid in heat loss. Where a minimum of insulation is desired, fabrics of loose weaves, smooth yarns, fine diameter yarns, and large interstices will be wise selections. These fabrics contribute to heat loss by convection, for air currents can circulate freely; by radiation, since the open spaces permit the rays to move to the surrounding air; and by evaporation, because the moisture vapor can move easily into the air. If the fibers are good conductors and if the fabrics have few or no spaces to entrap air, heat loss by conduction is aided.

In regions where air temperatures exceed 98°F (37°C), particularly desert and tropical regions, fabrics are sometimes chosen that prevent passage of heat toward the body. These fabrics are similar to those recommended for cold climates, and the purpose is to hold the high temperature out instead of letting it pass through the fabric to the body.

Air Permeability

The air permeability of a fabric is closely related to thermal properties and is frequently a major factor in body comfort and in protection against moisture buildup as well as heat retention or release. Fabrics with good air permeability encourage heat loss by air movement. As air freely moves through a fabric, heat can be dissipated to the outside; conversely, heat can pass through the fabric to the body.

The air permeability of a fabric is influenced by several factors: the type of fabric structure, the design of a woven or knit structure, lacy structures versus compact weaves or knits, the number of warp and filling yarns per inch (or centimeter), the number of loops per inch in knit fabrics, the amount of twist in yarns, the size of the yarns, the type of yarn structure, and the size of the interstices in the fabric. Fabric with low thread counts

and fine yarns usually have good air permeability, whereas compact fabrics with high thread counts or gage and very tiny interstices between yarn interlacings or interloopings will naturally limit the passage of air. In addition to influencing heat loss by convection, air permeability may be related to the movement of moisture or water vapor adsorption, absorption, and/or wicking properties. To make comfortable hot-weather apparel from hydrophobic fibers, fabrics should be of a porous construction so that they permit air permeability, moisture diffusion, and wicking.

Moisture Relationships

The movement of moisture into fibers or along the surface of fibers, yarns, and fabrics is the result of wicking, moisture absorption, and moisture regain properties. Hydrophilic fibers will absorb moisture and allow it to pass through geometric openings in the fabric if those openings are of sufficient size. Hydrophobic fibers do not absorb moisture; however, these fabrics provide for moisture transmission by geometric openings, by adsorption onto the surface or between fibers, and by wicking. Both hydrophilic and hydrophobic fabrics allow moisture transmission if the fibers have a tendency to wick.

The movement of liquid moisture and vapor through fabric is dependent on the compactness or looseness of the weave or fabric structure, the yarn structure or fiber arrangement, and the wicking and adsorption characteristics. When fabrics are composed of hydrophilic fibers, vapor will move through both the fibers and the fabric interstices. Hydrophobic fibers permit the passage of moisture vapor through the interstices, between fibers within yarns, and along fibers and yarns.

The transmission of liquid moisture may be enhanced by loose fabric structures; however, liquid moisture moves comparatively well through a porous structure even though that structure may be compact, provided the fibers do have wicking properties. Wearer comfort and discomfort appear to be closely allied to the ability of a fabric to pick up water by means of wicking, adsorption (adherence of moisture to the surface of the fiber), or absorption (moisture actually entering the fiber). In addition, the fabric should provide for some water vapor transmission. Fabrics constructed of hydrophobic fibers may be uncomfortable if the fabric's geometric features are not properly planned and if wicking is not present or is hindered in some way.

Blends that include cellulosic fibers are especially good in water transmission because cotton fibers have a high degree of wickability as well as absorption. Other cellulosic fibers also improve moisture passage. They are extremely efficient in picking up water from the skin surface and carrying it into the fibers within the yarns and fabrics.

The type of fiber, filament or staple, is an important aspect of comfort. Studies indicate that filament-yarn fabrics tend to plaster themselves to the skin when liquid moisture is present, whereas spun- or staple-fiber yarns are held away by the minute fiber ends extending from the surface.

Water repellency is determined to some degree by the geometry involved in relation to moisture characteristics. Fabrics with large interstices will permit rapid transfer of water, but fabrics constructed with very tiny interstices tend to repel water. This behavior can be enhanced by using fibers that are hydrophobic, nonwicking, and nonabsorbent and have a high surface tension.

Fabrics made of soft cotton yarns can provide good water repellency by virtue of their ability to absorb considerable moisture and swell. As the fibers swell, so do the yarns, the interstices are closed, and transmission of moisture is reduced.

Sometimes a high degree of water absorption is desired in a fabric. The geometric features for such fabrics are altered to provide a maximum surface of soft yarns with good absorptive properties. For example, terry cloth is frequently selected for its absorbency. The geometry of this fabric includes relatively dense construction with yarns that are soft and loosely twisted. Furthermore, the loops of yarn tend to hold moisture within the pile until it moves into the yarns and base fabric structure.

Wrinkle Recovery

Fabric geometry is important in relation to wrinkle recovery. The following points indicate some of the interrelationships between wrinkle recovery and geometric features.

1. Very short fibers tend to be displaced easily when yarns are folded and will therefore retain permanent deformation including wrinkles and creases. Medium-length staple fibers in relatively firm and stable yarn structures, long staple fibers in medium-firm yarns, and filament-fiber yarns produce good wrinkle recovery if properly combined into yarns and fabrics.

2. Actual fiber diameter and shape influence wrinkle recovery. Fibers that are round in cross section tend to resist bending and folding. Fibers that resist bending and folding usually recover rather quickly from light to medium folding stress. However, if sharp, heavy wrinkles are formed in round fibers, they recover slowly because the factor of strain tends to hold the creases in place.

3. The amount of yarn twist contributes to wrinkle recovery. Yarns of medium twist provide little or no opportunity for fiber displacement, so these yarns tend to return to their original position. Yarns with very low twist permit fiber displacement when bent or folded, and, upon release from strain or stress, the fibers do not return to their original position. High-twist yarns do not recover as well as medium-twist yarns because the high twist tends to hold folds or creases as a result of strain or stress on the fiber and/or the yarn.

4. Coarse yarns composed of fine staple fibers or filaments resist wrinkling and, if wrinkled, recover more effectively than yarns made of coarse fibers, filaments, or monofilaments.

5. Woven fabrics of basket, twill, or satin-weave constructions recover more easily from wrinkling than plain-weave fabrics if the fabrics are of equal compactness and yarn size. The basket, twill, and satin weaves have higher yarn mobility than the plain weave because they have fewer yarn interlacings. In general, the lower the number of yarns per inch (or centimeter), the better the wrinkle recovery.

A compact twill weave fabric with a relatively high thread count made of fine yarns will probably have a lower wrinkle recovery than a coarse plain weave made from larger yarns. However, in general, any type of fabric, regardless of the weight or tightness of construction, would give better easy-care performance if constructed from weaves with fewer interlacings than the plain weave.

It must be noted, however, that the wrinkle recovery of many fabrics is the product of a combination of factors including geometry and chemical finish. Fabrics with durable-press finishes, for example, will behave quite differently than a similar fabric without such a finish. Even fabrics that would normally not be wrinkle-resistant can be made wrinkle-resistant through the use of chemical finishes.

6. Thick fabrics that result from coarse yarns usually exhibit good wrinkle recovery.

7. Rough surfaces are less likely to show wrinkles than smooth fabrics. This is due, in part, to visual effects. When fabric surfaces have fibers napped or inserted at right angles to the base, such as pile constructions, they tend to obscure any wrinkles that are formed.

Dimensional Stability

The dimensional stability of fabric is its ability to resist shrinking or stretching. Although fiber content has some influence on this property, geometric factors are extremely important. One of the most significant elements in dimensional stability is the degree of tension under which yarns are held during fabric construction. Warp yarns are held taut during weaving; after removal from the loom they relax. This relaxation is accelerated when the fabric is first subjected to moisture. As the yarns relax, they return to their original length, which means they become shorter and shrinkage occurs. Extremely compact fabrics with firm yarns and a high fabric or thread count or gauge are less subject to size change than those with loose, soft yarns and low thread count. Firm yarns spaced to give a low thread count may shrink as much as soft yarns.

Although it is well known that wool fibers shrink because of their inherent physical properties, they are also subject to relaxation shrinkage following the release of any tension used during fabric construction. Heat-sensitive fibers shrink when exposed to temperatures above that at which the fabric, yarn, or fiber was heat-set. Many of these fibers show very little relaxation shrinkage if properly heat-set, and the fabrics have good dimensional stability. Relaxation shrinkage can occur on such fabrics if the heat-setting process was improperly done.

Abrasion

Fabrics can be damaged by flat abrasion or rubbing, by flex abrasion, or by edge abrasion. Damage from abrasion is the result of certain inherent fiber properties and selected geometric factors. Smooth fabrics constructed of firm yarns with optimum yarn interlacing and relatively compact yarn arrange-

ment are less subject to damage by flat abrasion than fabric with irregular surfaces, low yarn count, and minimal yarn interlacing. The latter are easily roughened and snagged by rubbing. Loop yarns and other complex yarns, as well as pile fabrics, are subject to abrasion damage. Knit structures tend to be abraded more quickly than woven fabrics because of the interlooping, which tends to give a textured surface.

The size of yarns also influences abrasion resistance. Thick yarns resist damage from abradants, whereas fine yarns may abrade easily. Yarn uniformity is important, for irregular yarns may show wear very quickly in selected locations. The surface of satins and sateens can be abraded because of the floating yarns on the surface.

Despite the abrasion resistance of firm fabrics, the consumer should be aware of at least one disadvantage of extremely compact fabrics. With use, these fabrics tend to lose some of their flexibility, and if they become too rigid, abradants can do considerable damage.

Flex abrasion damage occurs when fabric is flexed or folded upon itself or other fabrics. Edge abrasion is effected by the same factors applicable to flex damage and rubbing of the surface.

Soiling and Care

Geometric factors play an important role in soiling, soil resistance, and maintenance of fabrics. Fibers with a smooth surface and a comparatively large diameter, made into smooth yarns and relatively firm fabrics, tend to resist soiling because they do not provide as many places for soil to be lodged in the fabric structure. Normal cleaning procedures remove dry surface or occluded soil rather easily. However, oily or waterborne soil or stains are not always easy to remove.

Fabrics of a rather loose structure tend to permit penetration of soil into the interstices. This may hinder cleaning. Fibers with irregular cross sections retain soil more easily than round fibers; however, the fabrics do not show the soil as quickly when made of fibers with irregular cross sections because such fibers tend to hide the soil. They do not appear dirty. This is partly due to the way light is reflected by the irregular or lobal cross sections.

Loosely twisted yarns that are somewhat coarse are readily penetrated by soil, as are yarns composed of short staple fibers. The latter may be somewhat difficult to clean, for the soil may be lodged tightly in the yarns and resist efforts at removal.

Hand and Drape

Geometric factors are important to the hand and drape of a fabric. The hand of fabrics is influenced by flexibility (pliable to stiff), compressibility (soft to hard), extensibility (stretchy to nonstretchy), resilience (springy to limp), density (compact to open), surface contour (rough to smooth), surface friction (harsh to slippery), and thermal character (cool to warm). Several of these characteristics can be measured objectively by standard test procedures. However, in describing the overall property of hand, consumers depend primarily on subjective evaluation. They may describe a fabric as soft or firm, smooth or rough, springy or limp, stretchy or rigid, compact or loose, pliable or stiff; but they will seldom describe it using technical terms and instrumental measurements.

The geometric factors involved in the development of a subjective description for a fabric and its hand and drape include fiber contour, cross-sectional shape, and length; arrangement of the fibers in yarns or various other forms for conversion to fabric; and the arrangement of yarns or fibers in the actual fabric construction.

The way a fabric will hang and drape depends on the same general factors that influence hand. In one study consumers were unable to make an adequate distinction between the terms *hand* and *drape*. The two expressions are probably almost synonymous to the average person. They are descriptive and must be explained subjectively. To do this, consumers must actually fold, bend, and handle the fabric to understand and express their impression of the draping characteristics.

Summary

The purpose of this chapter has been to alert the student and the consumer to the fact that fabric is characterized by geometric factors as well as by inherent fiber properties. Knowledge of the geometric factors, coupled with personal observation and an understanding of fiber, yarn, and fabric properties, should help optimize consumer judgment in the selection of fabric for desired end uses.

STUDY QUESTIONS

1. Describe fabric geometry and what it means to consumers.
2. What factors are most involved with fabric geometry?
3. Why are geometric factors important in the area of wearing apparel?
4. Can geometric factors be of importance in fabrics for home furnishings? If so, state what some of the factors are and what impact they would have on fabric for interior design such as drapery fabric, domestic applications such as sheets and towels, and upholstery fabric.

Activities

1. Select a group of fabrics of the same fiber content but with different geometrical characteristics, and observe their differences in behavior when water is placed on the surface, when the fabrics are creased or folded, and when the fabric is handled in relation to drape and design.
2. Identify several different end used for a fabric; then describe what characteristics of the geometric factors should be most desirable.

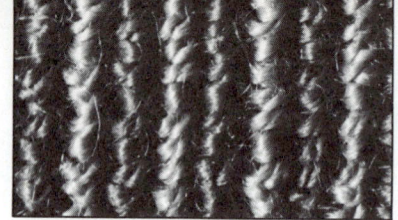

31

Selection and Care of Fabrics

OBJECTIVES
◇ **To identify factors that influence the appearance of a textile**
◇ **To identify factors related to fabric durability**
◇ **To identify factors related to the comfort of textiles**
◇ **To identify factors that influence the maintenance (care) of textile fabrics and end-use items**

KEY TERMS

appearance   durability
comfort   maintenance

The components of a textile fabric—fiber type, yarn structure or fiber arrangement, fabric structure, finish, and color—must all be considered in the selection, use, and care of a textile product. The relative importance of each of the factors is closely related to the appearance, durability, maintenance, and comfort of the product. The relative importance of each depends upon the planned end use of the textile. For best results, it is important that the consumers' choice be similar to that identified by the manufacturer. Selecting a product for a drapery that the manufacturer intended for use in evening apparel could result in a very dissatisfied customer. To avoid problems of this type, the consumer should become familiar with the different factors involved in choosing textile products and make a selection based on known facts and on those that can be determined through the individual's knowledge of how to evaluate textiles.

Appearance

The appearance of a fabric can be described as the visual effect on consumers, who, in addition, make use of the sense of touch to further comprehend what they see. Thus, both the visual and tactile senses are involved in appearance.

Fiber luster and texture influence the appearance of fabric. Shiny, lustrous fibers make it possi-

ble to make shiny, lustrous fabrics. Dull fibers may be made into fabrics with a dull appearance; however, it is possible to add finishes to dull fibers to enhance their luster. The yarn structure or fiber arrangement of a fabric influences appearance. Complex yarns produce a fabric with appearance characteristics that differ markedly from the surface obtained with uniform simple yarns. Yarns or fiber arrangement can be responsible for varying character through the special shapes and forms that characterize such yarns and fiber groupings. Fabric structure is important in appearance. Woven fabrics differ from knitted fabrics; both differ from nonwovens; lace and braid are still different. One can easily recognize different methods of constructing fabric, and each method creates special appearance qualities. Color is an obvious part of appearance and is one of the most important factors in the selection, use, and care of the product. Finish may alter or enhance appearance. Specific attention given the various sections of this text will enable the reader to discern how the components fit together in developing the appearance of fabric.

Depending on the interaction of the various factors, fabrics may appear to be soft or stiff, rough or smooth, delicate or coarse, lustrous or dull, bulky or sheer, bright or dull, light or dark. A continuum can be established for each of these comparisons, and any one fabric can be ranked or rated at some position along the scale used.

The importance of appearance as well as the characteristics of the desired appearance for selected end uses will depend on the consumer. Further, after one has determined the type of appearance desired, one considers the significance of that appearance, and then it becomes equally important to determine methods of care that will preserve the appearance as long as the consumer wishes. Thus, it is necessary to identify care procedures that are applicable to the fiber or fibers involved, the type of yarn or fiber arrangement, the type of fabric structure, the finishes involved, and the dyestuff used.

Durability

Durability is defined as the ability to last or endure, the power to last or continue in any given state without deterioration or destruction. Consumers, in general, do not wish to have fabrics last a lifetime. Thus, for purposes of this discussion, fabric durability is considered to be the ability to retain properties and characteristics for a reasonable period of time.

Factors involved in durability are also important to appearance, as retained appearance depends on the durability of the textile. The following generalizations concerning durability are based on the component parts of any textile fabric.

Fiber content influences durability. Some fibers, such as acetate, are valued for their beauty of hand and drape rather than for their wearing qualities, whereas, nylon is frequently selected because of its strength, abrasion resistance, and other properties that contribute to durability. It is important to study each fiber group and identify the properties that contribute to durability, such as relative tenacity (strength) and flexibility. Strong fibers are more durable than weak fibers if other factors are held constant; fibers with good flexibility are more durable in apparel than stiff fibers because of the bending that is required, but a stiffer fiber may be better for some home furnishings where it could resist crushing and retain its shape. It is, once again, important to identify the end use of the product and select the fiber or fibers that will give good durable service in that specific end use.

Yarn structure or fiber arrangement determines the durability of a textile to a degree. In general, fabrics made with yarns tend to have greater durability than nonwovens that have been made with fiber arrangements. This is particularly true for fabrics designed for apparel. However, fabrics made using

fiber arrangements, rather than yarns, may be a very durable product in some home furnishings and for some commercial and industrial uses.

Complex yarns, for example, made with loops or similar surfaces are easily snagged, producing damage and reducing fabric usefulness or durability. Simple yarns with medium twist will give good wear, and yarns with even twist throughout their length are less likely to show wear than those with irregularities found in complex yarn structures. Slub yarns with areas of low twist may be pulled apart in some situations and cause fabric breakdown.

Fabric structure is an important factor in durability. Plain- and twill-weave fabrics are more durable than satin weaves; the floating yarns in a satin weave are subject to snagging, breaking, and damage from abrasion. Decorative weaves that include long floats are easily damaged by rough or sharp objects, which may snag the floating yarns. Decorative or novelty weaves with short floats, high thread counts, and strong yarns and fibers may give more satisfaction than inferior plain-weave fabrics. Filling- or weft-knit fabrics of plain design are subject to runs when the yarn is broken. A run spreads more rapidly when fibers and yarns are smooth. Yarns of rough fibers, such as wool, tend to adhere to each other, and damage from runs is reduced. Warp-knit fabrics, such as tricot, are comparatively run-resistant. They also have sufficient fabric give to resist damage from bending or extending.

Felt fabrics usually have good durability unless they are subjected to considerable pulling force or abrasion. Nonwovens may be durable or disposable, depending on the planned end use. Nonwoven interfacings should be able to withstand various methods of maintenance to give satisfactory life in the final product.

In general, basic weave constructions and plain knit fabrics are more durable than complicated fabric constructions, which could show signs of wear as a result of surface distortion or damage. Fabrics with medium to high yarn count are usually considered more durable than fabrics with low count; however, this is greatly influenced by the type of yarn structure and the fiber involved.

Color selection and method of application influence durability. Choosing the proper dyestuff for each fiber type is essential if the fabric color is to give good service. The consumer, however, should be aware of scientific, economic, and fashion affects on color. It is impossible to find all colors in all classes of dyestuffs, and this may mean selection of a second-choice dye in order to obtain a currently popular or fashionable color. Moreover, not all dyes within any one class are equally good, and it is difficult to find dyes in all colors that prove to be colorfast to all degrading environmental conditions. Dyestuffs differ in cost and in expense of application; thus, it is necessary to choose dye that will be consistent with a reasonable price. Furthermore, dye selection should be based on the planned end use of the fabric. This, too, may mean a compromise.

The consumer should be willing to accept advice and select fabric for the end uses for which it was planned. The use of a dress fabric for draperies, for example, may lead to trouble. It is very unlikely that the dress fabric color was tested to determine resistance to sunlight, while the drapery fabric was probably checked for resistance to sunlight but not to laundry. Loss of color during maintenance as well as during use will result in consumer dissatisfaction and premature discard of the textile item.

Finishes, whether applied for appearance or to alter certain behavioral properties, often affect fabric durability. Surface finishes such as glazing can be removed by improper care, so that the useful life of the product is reduced. Most wrinkle-recovery, minimum-care, or permanent-press finishes reduce fabric tear strength, breaking load, elongation, and abrasion resistance. However, minimum-care finishes, despite reduced durability, are frequently more attractive than comparable fabrics that do not have such finishes. This may compensate many consumers who are willing to accept a shorter use life for such products. Of equal importance is the fact that easy-care finishes reduce the time spent in maintenance, which provides many consumers with a high level of satisfaction.

Durability is determined by several factors. Consumers should determine the relative importance of durability in terms of product end use and make their selection accordingly.

Comfort

The importance of comfort, like that of appearance, will vary according to the predetermined end use of the product and the preferences of the consumer. Such considerations as air permeability, thermal retention, texture and tactile characteristics, moisture absorbency, wicking properties, weight per unit area, and rigidity versus stretch appear to be related to comfort.

Comfort is affected by various psychological considerations, which are not easily discerned. For example, loss of color would hardly influence physical comfort, but it might help create a psychological atmosphere leading to an illusion of physical discomfort. Since no two people are identical, fabric comfort is related to individual differences and requires careful decision making on the part of each consumer. However, it is safe to say that comfort depends on the following factors: surface smoothness or roughness of the fabric, moisture absorbency, wicking, type of yarns used, type of fiber or fibers used, air permeability, and potential allergenic reactions.

Maintenance

The care given a textile product is dependent on the fiber or fibers used, yarn structure or fiber arrangement, fabric construction, method of imparting color, type of dyestuff used, finishes and methods of application, and geometric factors.

Inherent and geometric fiber properties influence care. Thought should be given to the reactions various fibers exhibit when laundered, dry-cleaned, spot-cleaned, or otherwise maintained. Yarn structure or fiber arrangement may affect maintenance. Such characteristics as the number of turns per inch and the type of construction of yarns—simple, complex, single, ply, cord—all play a part. For example, a yarn with a very high number of turns per inch (or centimeter), such as crepe yarns, may shrink when subjected to moisture and undergo excessive shrinkage. A complex yarn can be damaged by abrasion from equipment or other fabrics and trims during the maintenance process.

Blended yarns should receive the type of care recommended for the more easily damaged fiber. However, proper blending may result in easier care for both fibers. For example, a blend of a thermoplastic fiber with cotton produces a fabric that is easily laundered, dries quickly, and requires lower ironing temperature than pure cotton. A blend of wool and acrylic can be home-laundered, whereas dry cleaning is recommended for pure wool.

Fabric construction is related to maintenance in several ways:

1. Fabrics with long floating yarns, such as satins, can be damaged during cleaning. This results in

unattractive surfaces, destruction of appearance, and weakening of the fabric. These fabrics should be laundered or dry-cleaned with gentle handling. Sharp instruments or rough edges may damage such fabric surfaces.

2. Knitted fabrics may need only a minimum of ironing, but some require reblocking and reshaping to retain size and appearance after maintenance procedures.

3. Sheer fabrics of leno-weave construction might require careful handling, but they are easier to maintain than sheer fabrics of plain weave. The interlocking of the warp yarns reduces yarn slippage. However, other factors, such as fiber content, may alter the care of sheer fabrics.

4. Nonwoven fabrics demand careful consideration concerning the maintenance method to select. Incorrect care may result in loss of adhesive and concomitant fiber separation.

5. Fragile fabrics, such as lace, may require special handling; this is influenced by fiber content. Fragile, sheer fabrics of strong, tough fibers are easier to maintain than firm fabrics of weak fibers.

6. Pile fabrics may require brushing to remove lint from the surface. Those that can be laundered look better if tumble-dried, because the dryer action tends to raise the pile and fluff the fabric.

7. Tufted fabrics can generally be laundered. It is important to tumble-dry such products in order to maintain the appearance of the tufts on the surface.

Proper laundering techniques should be observed for all washable fabrics. Instructions on care labels contribute specific knowledge and should be followed if durability is to be achieved. Consumers should recognize that many factors influence laundry results, including type of detergent used; laundry additives used; length of the wash cycle (in most cases this should not be more than 10 to 12 minutes); type of bleaches selected in relation to the fiber content, dyestuffs, and finishes involved; water softeners selected; and fabric softeners.

Color is an important aspect of care. Whether fabrics are dyed or printed, color may be lost during laundering or dry cleaning. Tests for evaluation of color are described in Chapter 33. When convenient, it is a good idea to determine colorfastness of dyestuffs before using a specific care procedure. As this is extremely difficult, if not impossible in many cases, most consumers are left with the care instructions on the label as the only guide. Finishes applied to fabrics may make maintenance or care easier, but they may also cause new problems. Some finishes respond well to dry cleaning but are destroyed by laundering; others respond to laundering but are destroyed by dry cleanings. Again, information on the care label should be studied carefully. Further, information concerning special finishes may be a source of valuable information concerning fabric care.

The selection, use, and care of fabrics depend on many factors. Appearance, durability, comfort, and maintenance vary in relative importance. It is the responsibility of each consumer to evaluate the qualities of a fabric in view of its ultimate end use and then make the best decision concerning proper methods of care and best possible end uses for the fabric, as well as best possible fabric for the specific end use.

STUDY QUESTIONS

1. What factors are important in determining the appearance of a fabric? the comfort of a fabric? the maintenance of a fabric? the durability of a fabric?

2. How do appearance, comfort, maintenance, and durability combine to give some idea of the performance and serviceability of a fabric?

3. How do the various components of a textile fabric fit together to create fabrics that meet the consumers' desires for a specific end use product? What must be considered?

Activities

1. Identify a variety of end uses for textile fabrics. Indicate various kinds of textile fabrics that would be satisfactory or appropriate for each end use. Note the type of fiber or fibers desired, yarn structure or fiber arrangements, fabric structure, finish, and color.

2. Select samples of textile fabrics and indicate for what end uses they would be most appropriate. Describe how you arrived at your decision.

32

Textile Legislation: Rules and Regulations

OBJECTIVES

◊ **To provide current information on the status of legal rules and legislation relating to textile materials:**

> The Wool Products Labeling Act
> Pure Dye Silk Labeling (weighted silk)
> Fur Products Labeling Act
> Textile Fiber Products Identification Act (TFPIA)
> Care Labeling
> Wheeler Lee Act of 1938
> Flammable Fabrics Act

◊ **To identify information that must be provided to consumers by law**

◊ **To indicate consumer responsibilities in relation to textile products and label information**

KEY TERMS

dry-cleanable
flame-resistant
flameproof
labeling

launderable
new wool
recycled wool

To help provide consumers with important information at the point of sale, and to provide protection to some degree, the U.S. government has enacted various rules and regulations that pertain to textile fabrics and products. These rules and regulations are designed to provide protection and sufficient information concerning various aspects of textiles so that consumers have the necessary data to provide long-term care, to make knowledgeable selections, and/or to feel somewhat safe and secure regarding the purchase of the item. It is these various rules and regulations that are identified and described in this chapter.

Wool Products Labeling Act

The Wool Products Labeling Act (WPL) was passed in 1939. It is a measure to protect producers, manufacturers, distributors, and consumers from the unrevealed presence of substitutes and mixtures in spun, woven, knitted, felted, or otherwise manufactured wool products.

The act requires that any textile product of wool or part wool must be labeled to indicate the quantity and type of wool present. Several terms are defined by the act and its amendments. Since the enactment of the legislation there have been several amendments, the last made in 1980. Current definitions used in labeling wool products include the following.

Wool means the fiber from the fleece of the sheep or lamb or hair of the Angora or Cashmere goat (and may include the so-called specialty fibers from the hair of the camel, alpaca, llama, and vicuna) that has never been reclaimed from any woven or felted wool product.

Recycled wool means (1) the resulting fiber when wool has been woven or felted into a wool product which, without ever having been utilized in any way by the ultimate consumer, subsequently has been made into a fibrous state, or (2) the resulting fiber when wool or reprocessed wool has been spun, woven, knitted, or felted into a wool product which, after having been used in any way by the ultimate consumer, subsequently has been converted back into a fibrous state.

Wool product means any product, or any portion of a product, which contains, purports to contain, or in any way is represented as containing wool, reprocessed wool, or reused wool.

Reprocessed wool fits definition 1 for recycled wool, while *reused wool* fits definition 2 for recycled wool. The term *recycled wool* supersedes the use of *reprocessed wool* and *reused wool* as of the amendment of 1980. However, the terms *reprocessed* and *reused* still appear in some cross references concerning the WPL and the labeling of wool products.

Fibers from animals other than the sheep may be identified by the name of the animal as long as it is clear that it is a type of animal hair fiber. However, the use of special animal names is not required; thus, any fiber, such as Cashmere, may be identified and labeled as wool without any other terminology.

The Federal Trade Commission is responsible for the enforcement of the WPL and provides both manufacturers and consumers with helpful information concerning this act.

Other terms that may be used in identifying wool include the following. *Virgin* or *new* may be used with the term *wool* only when the fiber is new and has never been reclaimed from any type of woolen product. The term *fur fiber* may be used to identify fibers taken from animals normally used for fur. The term may not be used with wool or specialty fibers. The use of the name of one of the specialty animals, such as the Cashmere goat, Angora goat (mohair), vicuna, and others may be applied only when fiber from those animals is actually involved. The term *lamb's wool* is not defined in the rule as it now stands. However, the term is used to represent wool taken from animals under eight months of age.

In general the quality of recycled wool is usually lower than that of new fibers. During the garnetting process that separates the fibers back into a fibrous mass from yarns or fabrics, some damage may occur to the fibers. However, the warmth factor is not affected, and recycled wool is satisfactory in such products as interlinings, padding for carpeting, inexpensive blankets, and similar products.

As a help to consumers, the manufacturers of wool products may use the trademark for pure 100 percent wool products, called the Woolmark; the Woolblend mark may be used for products that include wool but are not 100 percent wool.

Pure Dye Silk

The Pure Dye Silk regulation concerns the labeling of silk that has or has not been weighted. The regulation has been on the government books for many years. Although the regulation receives little recognition at the present time, it is still a requirement in the identification and labeling of silk products. Any silk item, other than black fabrics, must be labeled as "weighted silk" if the fiber has more than 10 percent weighting (see Chap. 26). If the fabric has 10 percent weighting or less, it may be labeled as "pure dye silk." Black silk fabrics may be labeled as "pure dye silk" with up to 15 percent weighting. As weighting of silk tends to reduce the wear life of the fabric, it is considered important that such labeling be clearly included for any silk fabric or product.

Fur Products Labeling Act

The Fur Products Labeling Act was passed in 1952; it has been amended slightly but the basic act has not been changed. It was passed to protect consumers and others against misbranding, false advertising, and false invoicing of fur products and furs.

The act requires that labels identify the true English name of the animal from which the fur is taken, the country of origin, and information about whether the fur product is composed of used, damaged, or scrap fur, or fur that has been dyed or bleached. One amendment provided a set of names for identification of animals, and a further amendment added the provision that furs that have been pointed, dyed, bleached, or artificially colored must be labeled as such.

Important terms that relate to the identification of fur and fur products include the following.

Fur means any animal skin or part thereof with hair, fleece, or fur fibers attached thereto, either in its raw or processed state, but shall not include such skins as are to be converted into leather or which in processing shall have the hair, fleece, or fur fiber completely removed. *Used fur* means fur in any form which has been worn or used by the ultimate consumer. *Fur product* means any article of wearing apparel made in whole or in part of fur or used fur, except that such terms shall not include such articles as the Federal Trade Commission (FTC) shall exempt by reason of the relatively small quantity or value of the fur or used fur contained therein. *Waste fur* means the ears, throats, or scrap pieces which have been severed from the animal pelt and shall include mats or plates made therefrom.

Textile Fiber Products Identification Act (TFPIA)

The TFPIA was passed in 1958 to be effective in 1960 and has been amended several times. The most important amendments have been the addition of generic terms to be used in labeling textile fibers. The act requires that textile products be labeled to identify fiber content by percentage (except for fibers present in amounts less than 5 percent, which may be identified as "other"). The act further established generic terms for manufactured fibers. These have been clearly identified in chapters concerning fibers and are defined in the Glossary as well. The original act identified 17 generic terms; amendments have increased the number to 21.

The act further indicates that natural fibers, other than wool, which is included under the Wool Products Labeling Act, must be identified by name. All fibers must be identified by percentage, with the fiber of highest percentage given first, followed by the next percentage component and so forth, ending with the fiber with the lowest percentage. The act exempts some textile products such as certain coated fabrics, industrial fabrics of some types, and upholstery that is already installed on furniture. Both the textile product itself and any advertising of such products must identify the fiber content.

The TFPIA identified generic terms that must be used for all manufactured fibers. If trade names or trademarks are to be used, they must be accompanied by the generic term for the fiber. The trade name or trademark shall be capitalized; the generic term is not, except where both words are completely written in capital letters.

The act requires that correct fiber content be transmitted by fiber producers to product manufacturers, who, in turn, must provide adequate and accurate information concerning fiber content to the retailer. The retailer is responsible for labeling the product at the consumer level.

When fabrics are composed of two or more fibers, the label must identify the actual percentage of each fiber in descending order as noted above. If less than 5 percent of a fiber is present, this low percentage may be indicated as "other fibers"; however, if the fiber serves a clearly established purpose or function, such as an elastomeric fiber, it may be identified by percentage, generic name, and significant property imparted.

Clear and concise guidelines concerning the TFPIA have been prepared by the FTC, and both retailers and consumers may obtain copies from the FTC free of charge. The FTC is responsible for the enforcement of the act. However, the real responsibility for enforcement may, in fact, rest with the consumer. Unless consumers are willing to report evidence of noncompliance with the act, the actual value of the legislation may be reduced owing to lack of enforcement funds.

Retailers are frequently lax in maintaining properly labeled textile merchandise, especially when customers seem uninterested. This situation emphasizes the need for consumer education, the need for consumers to demand proper label information, and, most important, the need to provide information about how fiber content data can be used to advantage. It is the responsibility of every consumer to report the absence of fiber content labeling or mislabeling to the Federal Trade Commission office.

In addition to fiber content, the label must also identify the manufacturer, either by name or by identification number. If the product has been imported, the name of the country where the product was made or processed must be included.

It is important to note one component of the act. If a textile product is advertised, the fiber content may or may not be given. If no reference is made in the advertisement to fiber content, then no content need be identified in the ad. However, if any reference is made to fiber content, then the advertisement must carry all the information, including percentages of the component fiber or fibers. Regardless of information in advertisements, the actual product must be accurately labeled with fiber content.

For quick reference, the generic terms identified by the TFPIA which are defined in the Glossary and the fiber chapters include the following: acetate, acrylic, anidex, aramid, azlon, glass, lastrile, metallic, modacrylic, novoloid, nylon, nytril, olefin, polyester, rayon, rubber, saran, spandex, triacetate, vinal, vinyon.

Care Labeling

Care labeling is required under a trade regulation rule. This rule was enacted first in 1972; it was amended in late 1983 to be effective in 1984. This rule requires manufacturers and importers of textile wearing apparel and certain piece goods to provide regular care instructions through the use of care labels or other methods described in the rule at the time such products are sold to purchasers or consumers.

Before labeling products for care, the manufacturer must evaluate (or test) the product using the care instructions designated to determine their accuracy. Results of all such testing must be retained by the manufacturer and made available to consumers or others if requested. This will undoubtedly increase product cost.

Definitions of importance concerning this rule include the following.

Care label means a permanent label or tag, containing regular care information and instructions, that is attached or affixed in such a manner that it will not become separated from the product and will remain legible during the useful life of the product.

Certain piece goods means textile products sold by the piece from bolts or rolls for the purpose of making home-sewn textile wearing apparel. This includes remnants, the fiber content of which is known, that are cut by a retailer, but does not include manufacturer's remnants up to 10 yards long that are clearly and conspicuously marked "pound goods" or "fabrics of undetermined origin."

Dry cleaning means a commercial process by which soil is removed from products or specimens in a machine which uses common organic solvents. The process may also include adding moisture to the solvent, up to 75 percent relative humidity, hot tumble drying up to 160°F (71°C) and restoration by steam press or steam-air finishing.

Machine wash means a process by which soil is removed from products in a specially designed machine using water, detergent or soap, and agitation. When no temperatures are given (e.g., warm or cold), hot water up to 150°F (66°C) can be regularly used.

Regular care means customary and routine care, not spot care.

The current Care Labeling Rule provides specific information concerning the labeling of wearing apparel. These include the following:

(a) Manufacturers and importers must attach care labels so that they can be seen and easily found when the product is offered for sale to consumers. If the product is packaged, displayed, or folded so that consumers cannot see or easily find the care label, care information must also appear on the outside of the package or on a hangtag fastened to the product.

(b) Care labels must state what regular care is needed for the ordinary use of the product. In general, labels for textile wearing apparel must have either a washing instruction or a drycleaning instruction. If a washing instruction is indicated, it must comply with the requirements set forth in paragraph (1) of this section [cited below]. If a drycleaning instruction is included, it must comply with the requirements set forth in paragraph (2) below. If either washing or drycleaning can be used on the product, the label need have only one of these instructions. If the product cannot be cleaned by any available cleaning method without being harmed, the label must so state.

(1) Washing, drying, ironing, bleaching, and warning instructions must follow these requirements:

i. Washing: The label must state whether the product should be washed by hand or machine. The label must also state a water temperature that may be used. However, if the regular use of hot water will not harm the product, the label need not mention any water temperature.

ii. Drying: The label must state whether the product should be dried by machine or by some other method. If machine drying is called for, the label must also state a drying temperature that may be used. However, if the regular use of a high temperature will not harm the product, the label need not mention any drying temperature. (For example, "tumble-dry" means that a high, medium, or low temperature setting may be used. "Tumble-dry at medium temperature" means that the product can be tumble-dried, but the temperature used should never exceed the medium temperature setting.)

iii. Ironing: Ironing must be mentioned on a label only if it will be needed on a regular basis to preserve the appearance of the product, or if it is required under section v. Warning: if ironing is mentioned, the label must also state an ironing temperature that may be used. However, if the regular use of a hot iron will not harm the product, the label need not mention any ironing temperature.

iv. Bleaching: (A) If all commercially available bleaches can safely be used on a regular basis, the label need not mention bleaching. (B) If all commercially available bleaches would harm the product when used on a regular basis, the label must say "No bleach" or "Do not bleach." (C) If regular use of chlorine bleach would harm the product, but regular use of a nonchlorine bleach would not, the label must say "Only nonchlorine bleach, when needed."

v. Warnings: (A) If there is any part of the prescribed washing procedure which consumers can reasonably be expected to use that would harm the product or others being washed with it in one or more washings, the label must contain a warning to this effect. For example, if a shirt is not colorfast, its label should state "Wash with like colors" or "Wash separately." (B) Warnings are not necessary for any procedure that is an alternative to the procedure prescribed on the label. For example, if an instruction states, "Dry flat," it is not necessary to give the warning "Do not tumble-dry."

(2) Drycleaning:

i. General: If a drycleaning instruction is included on the label, it must also state at least one type of solvent that may be used. However, if all commercially available types of solvents can be used, the label need not mention any type of solvent. The terms "Drycleanable" or "Commercially dryclean" may not be used in an instruction.

ii. Warning: If there is any part of the drycleaning procedure that consumers or drycleaners can reasonably be expected to use that would harm the product or others being cleaned with it, the label must contain a warning to this effect. For example, if steam will harm the product, the label should state "Professionally dryclean, no steam." A warning is not necessary for any procedure which is an alternative to the procedure prescribed on the label. For example, if a label reads "Professionally dryclean, fluorocarbon," it is not necessary to add the warning "Do not use perchloroethylene."

Care labels must also be provided for piece goods (yardage) except for certain exemptions. The label must provide information concerning regular care and must be available to give to customers at the time of purchase.

If a product carries no label, it is to be assumed that any method of care can be applied without damage to the item—hot water, hot drying, hot ironing, bleaching with all types of bleaches, and dry cleaning by any method. Such products, however, must have some indication at the point of purchase that any care procedure can be used safely. Examples of care labels are illustrated in Figure 32.1.

The "Glossary of Standard Care Terms" as established in the amended care rule is given here for reference.

1. Washing, Machine Methods

a. *Machine wash*—a process by which soil may be removed from products or specimens through the use of water, detergent or soap, agitation, and a machine designed for this purpose. When no temperature is given, e.g., *warm* or *cold*, hot water up to 150°F (66°C) can be regularly used.

b. *Warm*—initial water temperature setting 90° to 110°F (32° to 43°C) (hand comfortable).

c. *Cold*—initial water temperature setting same as cold-water tap up to 85°F (29°C).

d. *Do not have commercially laundered*—do not employ a laundry which uses special formulations, sour rinses, extremely large loads or extremely high temperatures or which otherwise is employed for commercial, industrial, or institutional use. Employ laundering methods designed for residential use or use in a self-service establishment.

e. *Small load*—smaller than normal washing load.

f. *Delicate cycle or gentle cycle*—slow agitation and reduced time.

g. *Durable press cycle or permanent press cycle*—cool down rinse or cold rinse before reduced spinning.

h. *Separately*—alone.

i. *With like colors*—with colors of similar hue and intensity.

j. *Wash inside out*—turn product inside out to protect face of fabric.

k. *Warm rinse*—initial water temperature setting 90° to 110°F (32° to 43°C).

l. *Cold rinse*—initial water temperature setting same as cold water tap up to 85°F (29°C).

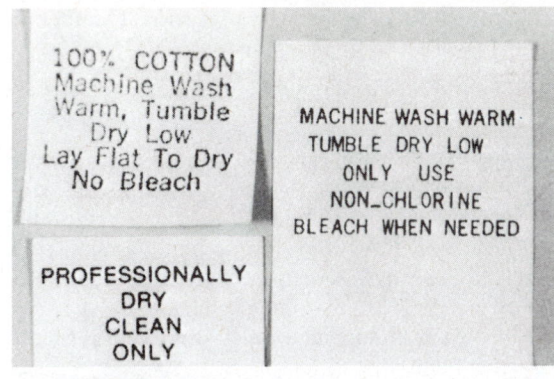

32.1 *Examples of care labels in use, 1984.*

m. *Rinse thoroughly*—rinse several times to remove detergent, soap, and bleach.

n. *No spin* or *Do not spin*—remove material start of final spin cycle.

o. *No wring* or *Do not wring*—do not use roller wringer, nor wring by hand.

2. Washing, Hand Methods

a. *Hand wash*—a process by which soil may be manually removed from products or specimens through the use of water, detergent or soap, and gentle squeezing action. When no temperature is given, e.g., *warm* or *cold,* hot water up to 150°F (66°C) can be regularly used.

b. *Warm*—initial water temperature 90° to 110°F (32° to 43°C) (hand comfortable).

c. *Cold*—initial water temperature same as cold water tap up to 85°F (29°C).

d. *Separately*—alone.

e. *With like colors*—with colors of similar hue and intensity.

f. *No wring or twist*—handle to avoid wrinkles and distortion.

g. *Rinse thoroughly*—rinse several times to remove detergent, soap, and bleach.

h. *Damp wipe only*—surface clean with damp cloth or sponge.

3. Drying, All Methods

a. *Tumble-dry*—use machine dryer. When no temperature setting is given, machine drying at a hot setting may be regularly used.

b. *Medium*—set dryer at medium heat.

c. *Low*—set dryer at low heat.

d. *Durable press or permanent press*—set dryer at permanent-press setting.

e. *No heat*—set dryer to operate without heat.

f. *Remove promptly*—when items are dry, remove immediately to prevent wrinkling.

g. *Drip dry*—hang dripping wet with or without hand shaping and smoothing.

h. *Line dry*—hang damp from line or bar in or out of doors.

i. *Line dry in shade*—dry away from sun.

j. *Line dry away from heat*—dry away from heat.

k. *Dry flat*—lay out horizontally for drying.

l. *Block to dry*—reshape to original dimensions while drying.

m. *Smooth by hand*—by hand, while wet, remove wrinkles, straighten seams and facings.

4. Ironing and Pressing

a. *Iron*—ironing is needed. When no temperature is given, iron at the highest temperature setting may be regularly used.

b. *Warm iron*—medium temperature setting.

c. *Cool iron*—lowest temperature setting.

d. *Do not iron*—item not to be smoothed or finished with an iron.

e. *Iron wrong side only*—article turned inside out for ironing or pressing.

f. *No steam* or *Do not steam*—steam in any form not to be used.

g. *Steam only*—steaming without contact pressure.

h. *Steam press* or *Steam iron*—use iron at steam setting.

i. *Iron damp*—articles to be ironed should feel moist.

j. *Use press cloth*—use a dry or a damp cloth between iron and fabric.

5. Bleaching

a. *Bleach when needed*—all bleaches may be used when necessary.

b. *No bleach* or *Do not bleach*—no bleaches may be used.

c. *Only nonchlorine bleach, when needed*—only the bleach specified may be used when necessary. Chlorine bleach may not be used.

6. Washing or Drycleaning

a. *Wash or dryclean, any normal method*—can be machine washed in hot water, can be machine dried at a high setting, can be ironed at a hot setting, can be bleached with all commercially available bleaches, and can be drycleaned with all commercially available solvents.

7. Drycleaning, All Procedures

a. *Dryclean*—a process by which soil may be removed from products or specimens in a machine which uses any common organic solvent (for example, petroleum, perchloroethylene, fluorocarbon) located in any commercial establishment. The process may include moisture addition to solvent up to 75% relative humidity, hot tumble-drying up to 160°F (71°C), and restoration by steam press or steam-air finishing.

b. *Professionally dryclean*—use the drycleaning process but modified to ensure optimum results either by a drycleaning attendant or through the use of a drycleaning machine which permits such modifications or both. Such modifications or special warnings must be included in the care instruction.

c. *Petroleum, Fluorocarbon,* or *Perchloroethylene*—employ solvent(s) specified to dryclean the item.

d. *Short cycle*—reduced or minimum cleaning time, depending upon solvent used.

e. *Minimum extraction*—least possible extraction time.

f. *Reduced moisture* or *Low moisture*—decreased relative humidity.

g. *No tumble* or *Do not tumble*—do not tumble-dry.

h. *Tumble warm*—tumble-dry up to 120°F (49°C).

i. *Tumble cool*—tumble-dry at room temperature.

j. *Cabinet dry warm*—cabinet-dry up to 120°F (49°C).

k. *Cabinet dry cool*—cabinet-dry at room temperature.

l. *Steam only*—employ no contact pressure when steaming.

m. *No steam* or *Do not steam*—do not use steam in pressing, finishing, steam cabinets, or wands.

8. Leather and Suede Cleaning

a. *Leather clean*—have cleaned only by a professional cleaner who uses special leather or suede care methods.

It is important to remember when reading a care instruction that

1. Only the washing or dry-cleaning process listed in the instruction has been checked for safe use.
2. If no temperature is mentioned, it is safe to use any temperature or setting—hot, warm, or cold.
3. If no ironing instruction is given, it should not be necessary to iron the product.
4. If bleach is not mentioned, any type of bleach may be used.
5. If no warnings are given, you do not need to make adjustments to the care processes listed in the instructions.

If a care label says, "Wash or dry-clean, any normal method," it means that a garment or fabric can be machine-washed in any temperature water; tumble-dried at any temperature setting; ironed at a hot setting, if ironing is necessary; bleached with any type of bleach; and dry-cleaned in all common solvents. If specific care methods are given, instructions must include information on washing, drying, ironing, bleaching, and/or dry cleaning.

The National Retail Merchants Association developed a series of symbols that might be used as a part of care instructions. These are illustrated in Figure 32.2. Such symbols can provide the following advantages: a quick glance could interpret the information given; symbols can be universal in their use and application; symbols require little space but provide valuable information; and symbols can be easily learned by all segments of the public.

Readers who want detailed information on care of textile products, including information on spot and stain removal will find the references listed under "Care" in the Bibliography helpful. Particular attention is directed to the publications by Maytag and by Sears, Roebuck and Co.

Wheeler Lee Act of 1938

In addition to the acts and regulations discussed to this point, the Wheeler Lee Act provides controls related to advertising. This act is directed against false or misleading advertisements. The law prohibits advertisements that are misleading not only because of what they do say but also because of what they do not say. The regulations written into the act are particularly valuable in preventing statements in

The code basically consists of the following symbols, each of which is variable.

 The washing Process A number and a temperature in the wash tub symbol indicates that the article can be washed safely either by machine or hand. The figure which appears above the waterline in the tub represents the full washing process and the figure below the waterline represents the water temperature. The symbol may, be accompanied by a box containing a written description of the process. There are nine numbered processes in the international code but only seven are likely to be used in the UK. These can be seen in detail on most washing product packets.

A hand in the wash tub indicates that the articles must not be washed by machine. The appropriate hand wash instructions may be added in a box alongside the symbol.

The wash tub crossed out indicates tha the article must not be washed.

 Chlorine Bleaching A triangle containing the letters CL △ indicates that the article may be treated with chlorine bleach. If it is crossed out ⧄ this means that chlorine bleach must not be used. The symbol refers to chlorine bleach only and does not apply to other types of bleach.

Ironing There are four variations of the ironing symbol. The temperatures shown in brackets are the maximum sole plate temperature indicated by the dots in the symbol.

| HOT | WARM | COOL | |
| (210°C) | (160°C) | (120°C) | DO NOT IRON |

Dry Cleaning Letters placed in a circle indicate that the article may be dry cleaned and which type of solvent may be used. Only the letters A, P and F are recognized. In some circumstances the circle containing P or F may be underlined. This indicates that special procedures are required as these goods are sensitive to dry cleaning.

 = Normal goods dry cleanable in all solvents.

 = Normal goods dry cleanable in perchloroethylene, white spirit, Solvent 113 and Solvent 11.

 = May be dry cleaned professionally. Do not 'coin-op' clean.

 = Normal goods dry cleanable in white spirit or Solvent 113.

 = Do not dry clean.

Drying The vast majority of textile articles can safely be tumble dried. Care labels may be used to indicate either that tumble drying is the optimum drying method for a particular article, or that tumble drying should not be used if the article is likely to be harmed by this treatment.

 = Tumble drying beneficial.

 = Do not tumble dry.

In cases where the tumble drying prohibition symbol is used, any special positive instructions, such as "dry flat" for heavier weight knitwear, should be given in words.

32.2 Suggested international "Sure-Care" symbols.

advertising that imply that fabrics will respond in a certain manner when, in actuality, they will not. The act also forbids unfair or deceptive practices in commerce.

Despite this, there are always examples to be found of misleading advertising, deceptive methods of selling, and unfair competition. The cause is a combination of lack of adequate controls for enforcing the laws and ignorance on the part of the retailer or seller, the advertising media, or the consumer. It should be noted, however, that regulations concerning advertisements in various media require that the advertisement must conform to what is true and that evidence to support statements must be available to any interested consumer.

Flammable Fabrics Act

The initial Flammable Fabrics Act was passed in 1953 to regulate the manufacture for sale in interstate commerce of all highly flammable wearing apparel fabrics. It was specifically designed to prohibit the sale of exceedingly hazardous or "torch"-type fabrics. At that time it was under the control of the Secretary of Commerce; the Secretary of Health, Education, and Welfare; and the Federal Trade Commission. Since then the jurisdiction for responsibility and enforcement has been given to the Consumer Products Safety Commission.

The original act was modified in 1967 to cover a wide range of clothing, and interior furnishings were added. Since that time various standards have been added to provide for control of specific items such as carpets and rugs, mattresses and mattress pads, children's sleepwear sizes 0–6X and 7–14, and some upholstery fabrics.

The amendments provide for strict controls on the items identified in the amendments.

It is important to define key terms used in relation to flammability. These definitions are those accepted by ASTM in 1984.[1]

Flame resistance (noun): The property of a material whereby flaming combustion is prevented, terminated, or inhibited following application of a flaming or nonflaming source of ignition with or without subsequent removal of the ignition source.

[1]ASTM, *Annual Book of ASTM Standards*, 1984, vol. 07.02, pp. 30–31.

Flame-resistant (adjective): Having flame resistance.

Flame-retardant (adjective): Undefined. This term should not be used except in the terms "flame retardant treated" and "flame retardant treatment."

Flame retardant (noun): A chemical used to impart flame resistance.

Flame retardant treatment (noun): A process for incorporating or adding flame retardants to a material or product.

The current standards and requirements include the following.

Flammability of Clothing Textiles, Title 16, CFR 1610. This covers articles of wearing apparel, but excludes interlining fabrics and certain hats, gloves, and footwear. The standard requires that a piece of fabric, placed in a holder at a 45° angle and exposed to a 5/8-inch flame for one second, should not ignite and spread flame up the length of the sample in less than 3.5 seconds for smooth fabrics or 4.0 seconds for napped fabrics. This standard has been effective since July 1, 1954.

Flammability of Vinyl Plastic Film, Title 16, CFR 1611. This became effective in 1954 and requires that vinyl plastic film for wearing apparel, placed in a holder at a 45° angle, should not burn at a rate exceeding 1.2 inches per second.

Large Carpets and Rugs, Title 16, CFR 1630, FF1-70. This standard became effective in April 1971 and includes carpets which have one dimension greater than 6 feet and a surface area greater than 24 square feet. Linoleum, vinyl tile, and asphalt tile are excluded. The test for this standard requires that a 9 by 9-inch (23 by 23-cm) specimen that is exposed to a burning tablet placed on the center of each specimen not char more than 3 inches in any direction; the burning tablet is intended to simulate small ignition sources such as a match or cigarette dropped on the carpet.

Small Carpets and Rugs, Title 16, CFR 1631, FF2-70. This standard became effective in December of 1971 and covers carpets with no dimension greater than 6 feet and a surface area not greater than 24 square feet. Again, it excludes linoleum, vinyl tile, and asphalt tile. The same test is used as for large carpets. If the product does not meet the standard, it may be labeled to indicate that the item failed to meet the standard.

Mattresses and Mattress Pads, Title 16, CFR 1632, FF4-72. This standard became effective in June 1973 and covers ticking filled with a resilient material intended or promoted for sleeping upon, including mattress pads. Excluded are pillows, box springs, sleeping bags, and upholstered furniture. The test requires that a minimum of nine cigarettes be allowed to burn on the smooth tape edge and quilted or tufted locations of a bare mattress. The char length on the mattress surface must not be more than 2 inches in any direction from any cigarette. Tests are also conducted with nine cigarettes placed between two sheets on the mattress surfaces. Items that do not meet the standard must be labeled as not complying with the standard and may be subject to ignition. Mattresses that do meet the standard do not need to be labeled, but many manufacturers do label to indicate that the product meets the standard for flame resistance.

Children's Sleepwear, Sizes 0–6X, Title 16, CFR 1615, FF3-71. This standard, effective in July 1972, includes any product of wearing apparel up to and including size 6X such as nightgowns, pajamas, or similar or related iems such as robes intended to be worn primarily for sleeping or activities related to sleeping. Diapers and underwear are excluded. Fabrics sold by the yard intended or promoted for use in children's sleepwear must also meet the standard. The test process requires that five samples, each 3.5 by 10 inches (8.9 by 25.4 cm), be tested. The specimens are suspended vertically in a holder in a cabinet and exposed to a 1½-inch gas flame along its bottom edge for 3 seconds. The specimens may not have an average char length of more than 7 inches, and no single specimen may have a char length of 10 inches. This test must be passed when the product is new and following 50 washings and dryings. Any item intended for children's sleepwear manufactured since July 1973 must meet the standard. Although a label does not have to be provided indicating that the product meets the standard, many manufacturers do provide such information as a service to consumers.

Children's Sleepwear, Sizes 7–14, Title 16, CFR 1616, FF5-74. This standard became effective May 1975 and covers any product of wearing apparel, sizes 7 to 14, such as nightgowns, pajamas, or similar items intended to be worn primarily for sleeping or activities related to sleeping. Fabrics intended for such use must also meet the standard. Basically, this standard extends that established for sizes 0 to 6X, and testing procedures are the same.

In 1983 both of the standards relating to children's sleepwear were revised, but no major changes were made in the provisions of the act. It is important to emphasize that all children's sleepwear, sizes 0–14, and fabric intended for such use shall meet the standard of the act. Further, it is important to note that the term *flame-resistant* does not mean "flameproof." Flame-resistant fabrics will burn, but they resist flames better than other fabrics do. Typically, flame-resistant sleepwear would be self-extinguishing or incapable of supporting combustion when the ignition source is removed. Informative booklets describing the flammability act are available from the Consumer Products Safety Commission of the United States government.

Compliance with flame-resistant legislation has presented many difficulties. Technology concerning effective and safe finishing substances has encountered many problems, including the banning of one of the most popular finishing compounds, tris, because of its carcinogenic properties. Detergents other than the phosphate type do not work well with flame-retardant finishes, and in some locations phosphate detergents are banned because of environmental pollution problems. Soap should not be used in the care of flame-resistant products, as it masks the finish and renders the product quite flammable. Fabric softeners increase the flammability of fabrics; bleaches may destroy the finish. Fibers that have been made inherently flame-resistant cause the least problems in care, but the use of softeners to reduce static charge can reduce the flame resistance of these products. It is important to look for care instructions on any flame-resistant product and make certain that care instructions are followed exactly. (See also page 369.)

Whether the law has been of value in reducing deaths and serious injury from fire or whether the increased public awareness of the potential hazards from burning fabrics has made individuals more cautious has not been determined. In any case, since the passage of the Flammable Fabrics Act amendments and the development of standards for children's sleepwear, mattresses, and floor coverings, there has been a noticeable decrease in deaths and injury due to fire associated with textiles. A concern expressed by some consumers, however, is that the act has reduced their freedom of choice in the marketplace at an added cost.

Toxic Substances Control Act

The Toxic Substances Control Act is important in relation to the textile industry and consumers of textiles. This act requires that new chemical substances must be proven safe to humans and the environment before they can be used. It is due to this act

that formaldehyde, widely used in finishing fabrics, has been identified as a carcinogen, and the amount released into the air is to be controlled. This act will prevent the use of any new product until it has been identified as safe and will result in the modification or elimination of products in current use that have been identified as potentially toxic.

Cotton Dust Standard and OSHA

Concern for workers in the processing of cotton, particularly those who developed byssinosis, or "brown lung" disease, resulted in the development of standards that would control the amount of dust or lint in the work area. There has been considerable disagreement over the cause of byssinosis; some medical authorities say it is not due to cotton dust and lint. However, changes in the work environment that resulted in decreased levels of dust and cotton lint have also resulted in a decrease in pulmonary infections associated with byssinosis. Evidence also indicates that the improved working conditions have been obtained without increases in the cost of production. The enforcement of such standards as this are a part of the federal Office of Safety and Health Administration (OSHA).

Consumer Responsibility

The provision of information about the fiber content, care, and flame resistance of selected textile items is mandated by legislation. The success of such legislation is determined, to a great extent, by the consumer. If information required by law is not provided, the consumer has a responsibility to identify that lack and request such information from the seller. Consumers tend to ignore their responsibilities, and this reduces the enforcement of such rules and regulations. Each time label information is missing, the consumer should express concern to the merchandiser or the manufacturer of the unmarked or mismarked merchandise in order to make certain that those attempting to sell such products are aware that the product does not conform to legislative requirements.

Manufacturers and retailers are in business to make money. Many apparel manufacturers and retailers as well as some fiber and fabric producers are marginal concerns and sell whatever they can at whatever price they can get for it as long as they can get away with it. If merchandise is exceptionally poor, these companies go out of business quickly; if consumers refuse to buy unmarked and inferior merchandise, the company goes under even more quickly. Some manufacturers do not even use a trade or company name. Such companies are difficult to trace to assign responsibility for poor products. It is best to buy items that are labeled to clearly identify the manufacturer and to carry all the necessary information. To reduce problems, a consumer has the responsibility to return inferior or unmarked (or incorrectly labeled) merchandise that does not perform satisfactorily to the retail establishment and, whenever possible, notify the manufacturer of the item of its failure to perform properly.

The development of guides or standards for the production and sale of quality merchandise at fair prices is the responsibility of manufacturers, retailers, and consumers. Legislation can never replace intelligent buying. Various service groups and agencies associated with manufacturers and retailers such as the Better Business Bureau, the National Retail Merchants Association, the Man-Made Fiber Producers Association, the Wool Bureau, the National Cotton Council, the Amercian Society for Testing and Materials (ASTM), and the American National Standards Institute are only a few of the organizations that promote quality products and adequate information for manufacturers, retailers, and consumers.

In addition to various legislative rules and regulations that place various controls on textile products, there are a variety of voluntary standards for performance of textile items. ASTM has accepted and published 46 voluntary performance standards that are used frequently as the basis for contracts for buying and selling among fiber, fabric, and textile product producers. They are also used by manufacturers, wholesalers, and retailers who wish to have merchandise with established specifications. Some retailers have established their own standards, which they use in negotiating contracts with suppliers. These performance standards help the consumer in that they encourage the marketing of quality products.

It is important that students and consumers recognize the impact of textile legislation on the textile and end-use product industries. Because of rules and regulations, consumers can expect, within limits, products that are relatively safe, that have reliable information on care, and that identify fiber content. Manufacturers that adhere to various voluntary standards for performance add another advantage for consumers. However, consumers must recognize that conforming to various rules, regulations, and voluntary standards can cause problems in the ultimate use and care of an item and add to the cost of the product.

Decisions a consumer makes when buying should be the result of a storehouse of textile knowledge used with the label information provided. Fiber content will give clues about basic principles of fabric care. Some technical knowledge of fabric structure, color, finish, and geometric factors will aid in the decision-making process.

Information gained from textbooks, lectures, periodical articles, and practical experience helps the consumer make choices in the marketplace and to estimate performance or behavior of an item. To determine the criteria to be used in making a textile purchase, the consumer should consider such factors as the length of time the product is expected to last, maintenance procedures that would be used, the relative importance of durability or long life, the relative importance of comfort, and the relative importance of appearance.

The behavior of a textile product in relation to appearance, comfort, durability, and maintenance is usually specific to each item, and the importance of each is specific to each consumer. An informed consumer will make the best use of the available information and apply it in decisions related to the selection, use, and care of textile products.

STUDY QUESTIONS

1. What are the current rules and regulations under the supervision of the Federal Trade Commission? How do they help consumers?
2. What regulation is under the supervision and control of the Consumer Products Safety Commission that relates to textile products? Of what importance to consumers is this legislation?
3. What is the consumer's responsibility in relation to enforcement of legal rules and regulations concerning textile products?
4. How can manufacturers and retailers profit by adherence to rules and regulations concerning textile products?

Activity

Contact the nearest Federal Trade Commission office and the Consumer Products Safety Commission office, and determine what changes have occurred in rules and regulations relating to textile products since 1984.

33

Fabric Performance and Testing

KEY TERMS

air permeability	colorfastness	specifications
bleeding (of color)	fabric description	standards
breaking strength	fabric thickness	testing
color migration	performance	yarn slippage

Textile fabrics can be subjected to a variety of standard test procedures as well as ''home'' tests to gain some knowledge of their performance in end use. This chapter identifies some of the standard test methods, some home tests, and performance standards that have been developed to help evaluate textile fabrics and products in relation to use and care.

Scientific studies of textiles yield quantities of information concerning performance of a product; expected performance; and basic physical, chemical, biological, and microscopic properties of textile fibers and fabric. However, they may increase the number of questions that consumers may ask, and frequently they make it impossible to give a yes or no response concerning the item. Further, consumers differ, and what would make a product adequate for one consumer's end use might make it very unsatisfactory for another's. Nevertheless, performance standards and testing methods can provide information of value to every student of textiles and can serve as a valuable foundation in the classroom or the laboratory.

Test methods identified in this text have been taken from the 1984 *Technical Manual* of the American Association of Textile Chemists and Colorists and the *Annual Book of ASTM Standards*, volumes 07.01 (1983) and 07.02 (1984), published by the American Society for Testing and Materials.

Performance Standards

Some years ago the American National Standards Institute published a set of performance requirements for textile fabrics in various end uses. This set of requirements, called L-22, set the stage for the development of performance standards of various types. During the 1970s, the ANSI group relinquished the performance standards, and the American Society for Testing and Materials (ASTM) assumed the responsibility for developing performance standards. Currently ASTM has accepted and published performance standards for 46 different end uses of textile fabrics. Most of these have been accepted by ASTM since 1980, so they represent the current state of the art in relation to fabric performance in end use.

An example of these standards is D4038-81: Performance Specifications for Women's and Girls' Woven Dress and Blouse Fabrics. This performance specification covers woven fabrics intended for use in women's and girls' dresses and blouses that are composed of any textile fiber or mixture of textile fibers. The standard identifies the various test methods to be used in determining whether the fabrics meet the specifications. Reference is made to test procedures developed by both ASTM and the American Association of Textile Chemists and Colorists

(AATCC). This particular specification includes minimum performance for both sheer and nonsheer fabrics. Included are specifications for breaking strength; resistance to yarn slippage; tongue tear strength; dimensional change when new, after five launderings, and after three dry cleanings; colorfastness to laundering and dry cleaning; resistance to gas fume fading; colorfastness to crocking, both dry and wet; colorfastness to perspiration; colorfastness to light; fabric appearance following laundering or dry cleaning (durable-press performance if indicated); and flammability performance.

These performance standards may be used as a part of sales agreements between manufacturer and retailer. They may be used in advertising, and they may be provided on attached labels as information to consumers. At the present time, performance specifications, for the most part, are voluntary standards and are used only when there is some interest on the part of both manufacturer and retailer. They may be required when the government is involved in the purchasing of such items.

Some of the other performance specifications apply to men's and boys' woven dress shirt fabrics; bedspread fabrics, woven, knitted or flocked; career apparel fabrics; coat fabrics, knitted and woven; curtain and drapery fabrics; fabrics for swimwear; and upholstery fabrics. In addition to the 46 performance specifications already adopted by ASTM, others are in the development stage and will be appearing in the near future. Readers should obtain the most current edition of both the *Annual Book of ASTM Standards* and the AATCC *Technical Manual* to determine the current test methods approved by these two groups. The ASTM *Annual Book,* volumes 07.01 and 07.02, would be the best source of performance specifications currently approved. As stated, performance standards, for the most part, are strictly voluntary. However, consumers who are interested may wish to express such interest to retailers and to manufacturers to encourage them to provide information on some type of hang tag that would accompany the textile item involved.

Although data on test results and performance standards are helpful to consumers and provide valuable information to guide decision making related to the selection, use, and care of textile fabrics, it must be remembered that other factors can play a large part in fabric performance. Accidental damage is an obvious variable; human differences in handling may be less obvious but are nonetheless important.

In order to test for performance, there must be accepted or standardized test methods. Both ASTM and AATCC have published standardized test methods for use in evaluating textile fibers, yarns, fabrics, dyes, and finishes. Only a few will be discussed here, but they are basic to understanding and testing textile products.

Tests for Fabric Characteristics

Fabric Description

Fabric description involves ASTM test methods D3773-79 for length of woven fabric; D3774-79 for width of woven fabric; D3775-79 for fabric count of woven fabric (the number of ends and picks per inch); D3776-79 for width per unit area of woven fabric; D3882-80 for bow and skewness in woven and knitted fabrics; D3883-80 for fabric crimp of woven fabrics; and D3887-80 for specifications for knitted fabric.

A woven textile fabric is described citing its average width, length, number of yarns per inch in warp and filling, yarn size, and weight in ounces per square or linear yard. This information is important to product manufacturers who are billed for the fabric. If fiber content is known and constant, it provides a basis for price comparison and for determination of suitable end uses.

The width suggests how patterns must be laid for efficient cutting; the length and width indicate how many items can be cut per linear yard. Width is important to the home consumer in determining the amount of yardage to buy.

The number of yarns per inch and the yarn size give some idea of the compactness and density of the fabric. Balanced thread counts—in which the number of yarns per inch in the warp and filling and the yarn size are similar—frequently are considered to offer better wearing qualities than unbalanced counts. However, this is also influenced by yarn size or yarn number (ASTM tests D1059-83 and D1907-80) and by the type of yarn (staple- or filament-fiber). Whether the yarn is a ply or a single is also important. If yarns in one direction have a tiny diameter and yarns in the opposite direction are thicker, the number of threads per inch may vary considerably and still provide a satisfactory fabric. The same may be true if yarn type varies.

Fabric weight determines to a great extent the weight of the end-use product. It is important to fabric hand, appearance, and comfort.

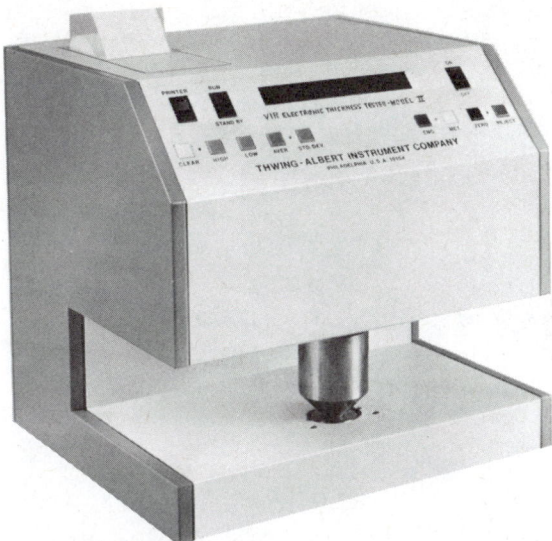

33.1 Fabric thickness tester. (Thwing-Albert Instrument Company)

Knitted fabrics are tested for weight, width, and length using ASTM D231-62 (reapproved 1975). Instead of measuring yarns per inch, for knit the number of wales and courses or loops per inch are counted. This provides information concerning the density of the fabric in relation to the closeness of yarns. The fineness of knitted fabrics is expressed (to some degree) as the gauge (or gage), which identifies the number of needles per unit width. The gauge may sometimes be cited as the number per 1½ inches. In general, for knitted fabrics the number of needles per inch determines the size of yarns that may be used; the greater the number of needles, the finer the yarn.

Fabric Thickness

Fabric thickness (Fig. 33.1) can be determined by using ASTM test method D1777-64 (reaffirmed 1975). The thickness of a fabric is one of its basic characteristics. It is usually expressed in thousandths of an inch or in millimeters. Warmth in textile products can be estimated from the thickness of fabric. Tests that measure change in thickness resulting from rubbing or shrinkage are helpful in evaluating performance.

Air Permeability

Air permeability or air flow is determined using ASTM D737-75 (reapproved 1980). Air flow is expressed as cubic feet of air per square foot of fabric

at a given pressure drop across the fabric; it can be expressed in metric units as cubic centimeters of air per square centimeter of fabric. The ability of a fabric to permit flow of air and water vapor through it is one aspect of comfort. Air permeability may also indicate which fabrics are suitable for protective apparel and coverings.

Thermal Properties

Thermal transmission tests also provide data on fabric comfort. ASTM test D1518-77 cites procedures for the determination of the amount of heat that passes through a fabric and thus the relative insulative value. A low degree of heat transfer would indicate a good fabric for insulation and protection from undesirable temperatures. Weight and thickness of fabric are calculations used in evaluating thermal properties and hence serve as factors in end-use performance. A fabric with good resistance to heat transfer could be a poor choice if too heavy and too thick for comfort.

Abrasion Resistance

The abrasion resistance of any fabric can be measured by a variety of test methods and testing machines. ASTM tests D3886-80, D1775-80, D3884-80, D3885-80, and D4157-82 plus AATCC test 93-1978 are all procedures for determining abrasion resistance of fabrics, and each one depends on a different type of testing machine. Results are influenced by both the type of machine used and the type of abradant used. Further differences are due to the size of the area abraded, the tension on the sample, and the abrading action. Because of the variety of factors involved, the reliability of test results concerning abrasion resistance is limited. However, if the same instrument, the same procedure, and the same abradant are used on a set of fabrics, good comparable results can be obtained. Figure 33.2 shows one example of an abrasion tester.

Resistance to abrasion is affected by such textile factors as the inherent and geometric properties of fibers, yarns, and fabrics and the kind and amount of finishing substances used. The results of abrasion testing must be interpreted carefully.

Pilling and Snagging

The pilling and snagging of fabrics can be determined using ASTM test methods D3511-82 and D3512-82 and AATCC test 65-1979. The way a fab-

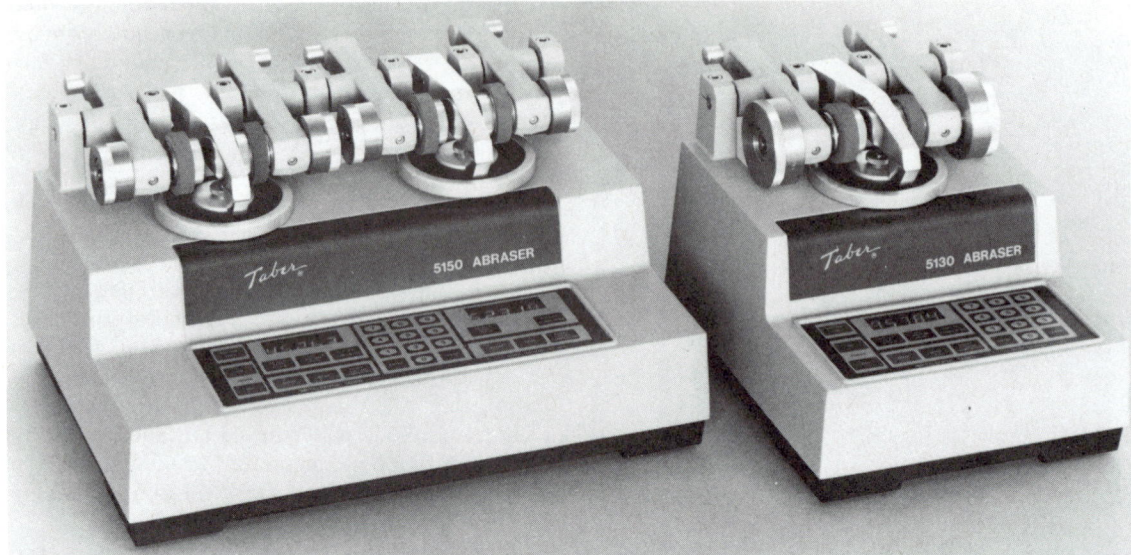

33.2 Taber abrasion tester. Single and dual digital abrasers with LED readout. (Taber Instrument Company)

33.3 Evaluating the amount of pilling on fabric against standards. (Celanese Corporation)

ric pills and the way snags form are important factors in retention of fabric appearance and hence in fabric use and serviceability. Fabrics made of staple fibers tend to pill considerably more than fabrics made of filament fibers. Fabrics of strong fibers and yarns show pilling more quickly and more severely than fabrics of weaker fibers, as the strong fibers tend to ball up into pills and remain on the fabric surface, while the weaker fibers ball up and break away easily. Both pilling and snagging are important to consumers as a factor in appearance. Snagging may occur more readily with filament yarns where rough or sharp surfaces can pull filament yarns away from the fabric plane. Pilling testing is shown in Figure 33.3. Testing for snagging is shown in Figure 33.4

Strength or Breaking Load of Fabrics

ASTM tests D1682-64 (reapproved 1975) for woven fabrics and D3787-80a for knit fabrics provide directions for determining strength of either a woven or a knit fabric structure.

Woven fabric strength is usually expressed as the force in pounds per inch (or kilograms per centimeter) required to break or rupture the fabric sample. Breaking strength for woven fabric is determined by cutting samples to a specific size and subjecting them to a continuously increasing force

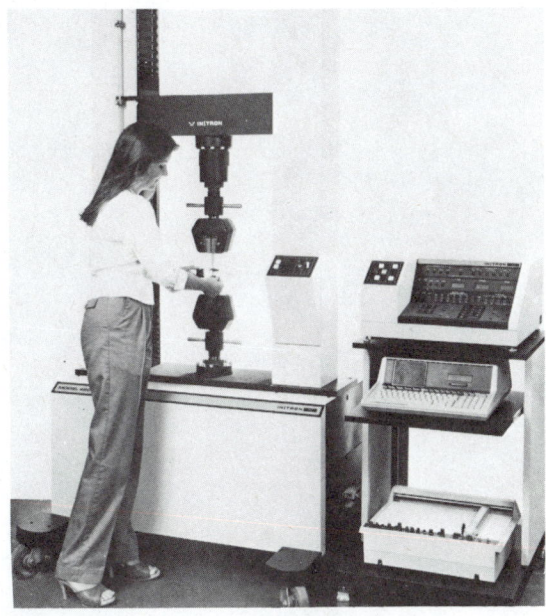

33.4 Testing knitted fabrics to determine resistance to snagging. (Celanese Corporation)

to determine the point of rupture or break. Several different types of testing instruments may be used. Figure 33.5 is an Instron machine used to measure strength of fibers, yarns, or fabrics. Figure 33.6 is a Scott tester, model J, used for determining strength of fabric and with modification can be used for yarn. The Scott machine shown in Figure 33.7 is normally used for testing the strength of fibers or yarns. Figures 33.8 and 33.9 show a strength-testing machine determining the strength of yarn and the strength of fabric. Yarn slippage can frequently be determined by the same test procedures.

Knitted fabric strength is expressed as the force per square inch (or grams per square millimeter) required to rupture the fabric.

When using breaking or bursting strength data, it is important to have the data from the same type of instruments for comparisons; otherwise the results may be misleading and will not truly represent differences or similarities among fabrics.

In addition to measuring strength of fabrics, data and results obtained on strength-testing machines may provide valuable information on yarn slippage.

33.5 Instron tester for measuring strength of fibers, yarns, or fabrics. (Instron Corporation)

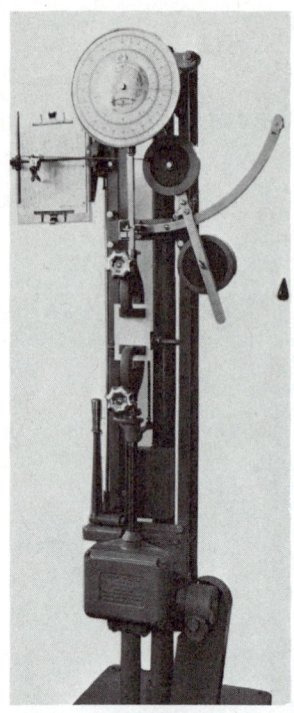

33.6 Scott tester, model J, measures strength and elongation of fabric or yarn.
(Scott Testers, Inc.)

33.7 Scott IP-2 tester for measuring strength and elongation of yarn and fibers.
(Scott Testers, Inc.)

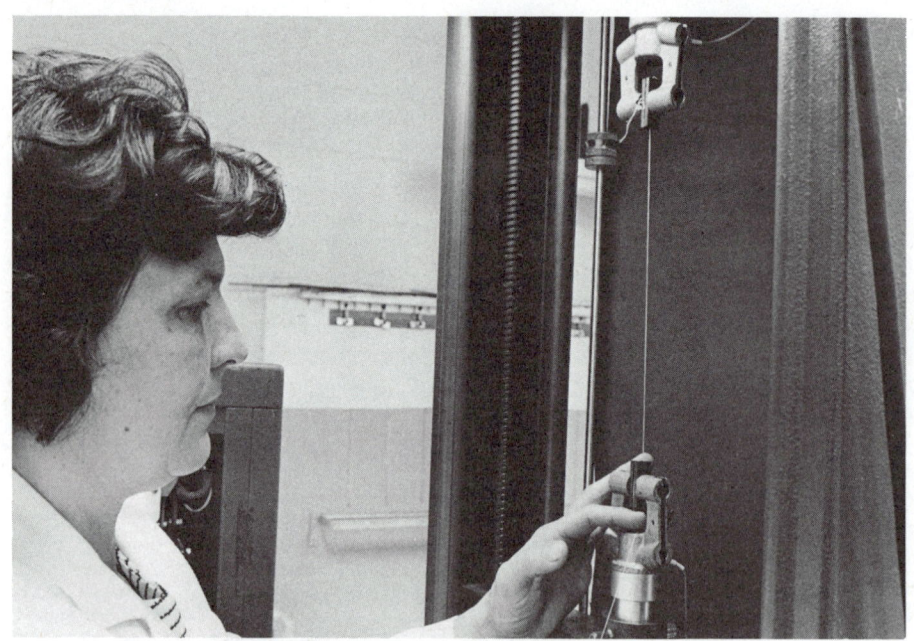

33.8 Preparing yarns to test for strength. (Celanese Corporation)

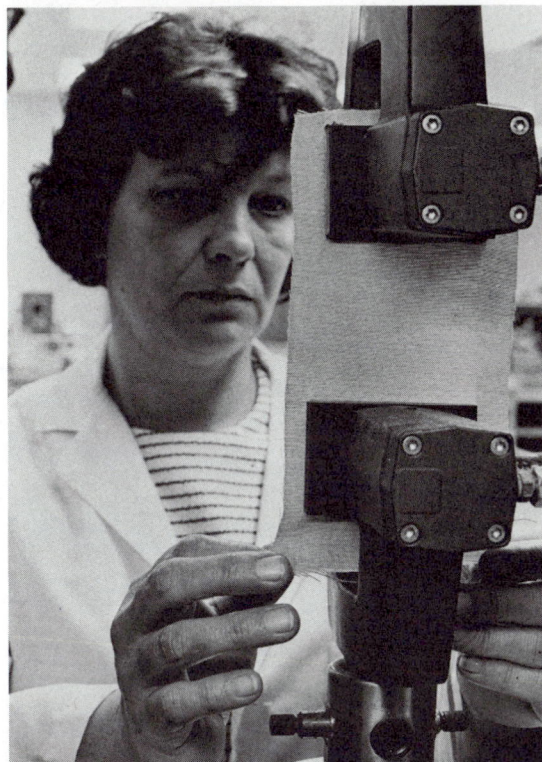
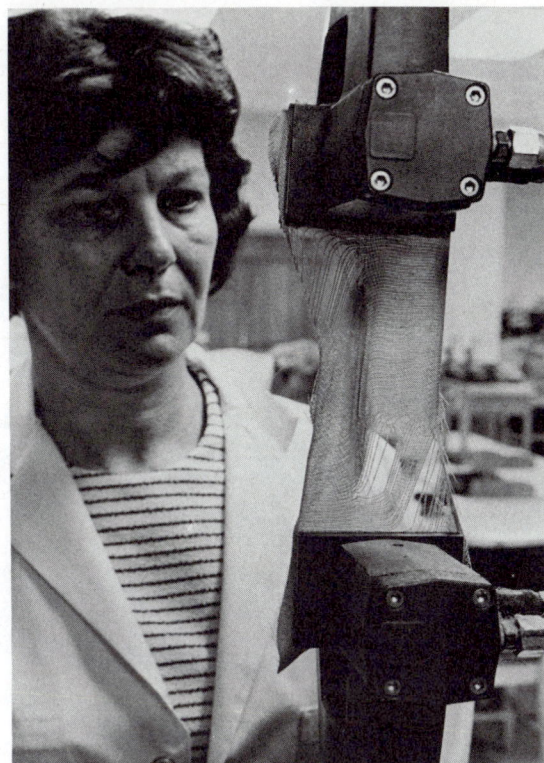

33.9 Left: Placing a specimen in testing unit. Right: Pulling fabric to determine strength and yarn slippage.

33.10 Elmendorf tearing-strength tester. (Thwing-Albert Instrument Company)

As with all tests, different fabrics will have different strengths, the specification for a selected end use may identify a minimum strength for that use; data may also be compared to identify which fabrics provide the most strength. However, the end use should be a major factor in determining what strength level is desired in a fabric.

Tearing Resistance

ASTM test D1424-83 cites the procedure for determining the resistance of a fabric to tearing. This differs from breaking strength, as the fabric is tested in such a manner that the pull required to tear the fabric is determined rather than the force required to rupture or break the fabric. Figure 33.10 shows one of the standard tearing testers.

It should be noted that tearing strength is one of the characteristics that is negatively affected by the addition of durable-press finishes to fabrics. Thus, it is important that fabrics with these finishes be tested for resistance to tearing in order to predict possible durability and serviceability of the fabric.

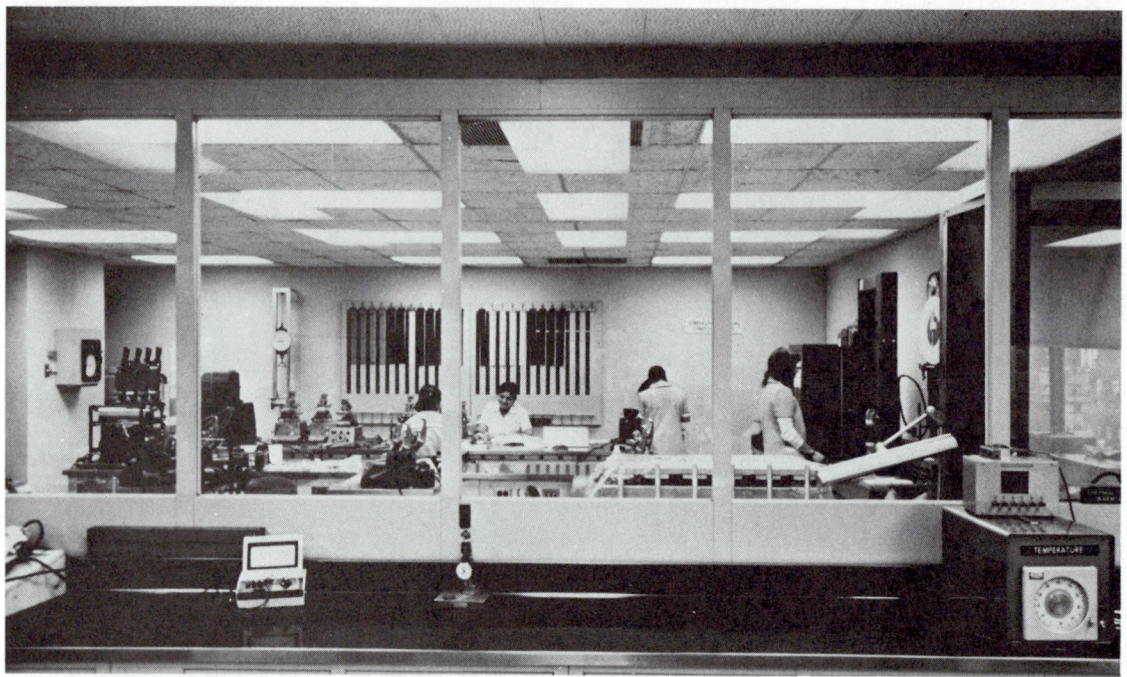

33.11 Conditioning room in the merchandise testing center. (J. C. Penney Company, Inc.)

33.12 Soxhlet apparatus in use to identify types and amounts of finishes on a fabric. (Celanese Corporation)

Yarn Slippage at Seams

ASTM test method D434-75 provides the method for determining how a fabric will resist pulling damage at seamlines. Yarn slippage refers to the way yarns pull closer together on the side of force and further apart on the side away from force—the seamline in this test. As seams are construction procedures that determine, to a great extent, the life of a product, it is important to have an idea of what pull will do to fabrics at these seam lines. Slippage may be followed very quickly by the development of rips or tears in fabric. Slippage occurs more readily on fabrics made from filament yarns, which tend to be somewhat slippery. Resistance to slippage is expressed as the number of pounds per inch, or newtons per meter, of pull across a seam required to produce an elongation of ¼ inch (6.35 mm) in excess of the normal fabric stretch.

Tests for Finish Performance

This section identifies some of the standard tests for qualities that depend on the addition of finishes to fabric as well as fiber, yarn, and fabric properties.

The scope and procedures of these tests are described briefly. Methods included are taken from AATCC and ASTM.

The typical consumer has no access to laboratory equipment; however, several simple tests can be conducted at home or in the classroom that will provide at least an idea of how fabrics will perform. These home tests are described in brief. However, if a laboratory is available. it is imperative that it be used in the determination of standard behavior of fabrics. Figure 33.11 is a typical quality-control laboratory. The analysis of finishes often involves the chemical testing of fabrics (Fig. 33.12).

Both home tests and laboratory tests are identified together by type of property under investigation. Home tests should not be used as a substitute for laboratory testing; they can provide only comparative information on a group of products tested in the same way and under the same environmental conditions. Such tests give limited information about fabric and finish behavior. They do, however, provide insight into care problems so that consumers can develop procedures for fabric maintenance.

Instructors and students can use some of the home tests when there is no regular testing equipment. By conducting a series of tests in an identical manner, comparisons can be made among the fabrics tested, but, as stated above, generalizations about fabrics and/or finishes should be avoided.

Resistance to Loss of Finish in Laundering or Dry Cleaning

AATCC tests 94-1977 and 61-1980 cite procedures for determining quantitatively the amount and kind of finishing substances used on a fabric. By checking fabrics before and after laundering or dry cleaning, the amount of finish lost can be determined as well as the total amount of finish on a new fabric. In addition to this quantitative analysis, a subjective analysis will provide information of interest to the consumer concerning changes in appearance and hand of fabric.

Resistance to Water

RAIN TEST AATCC test 42-1980, rain test, is applicable to any fabric with or without water-repellent finishes. It measures the fabric's resistance to penetration of water by impact and predicts the behavior of the fabric in rain. Equipment used for this test can apply water under different amounts of pressure so that performance of fabric in various conditions can be determined.

SPRAY TEST AATCC test 22-1980, the spray test, is used on fabrics that may or may not have been treated for water resistance or water repellency. It measures the resistance of fabrics to wetting and provides a visual standard to determine fabric ratings. Ratings range from 100 (no sticking or wetting of the upper fabric surface) to 0 (complete penetration of the fabric). This method is recommended for measuring the water repellency of apparel fabrics. It is especially useful in evaluating the effectiveness of water-repellent finishes. Results depend primarily on the water resistance of fibers, yarns, and finishes and not on fabric construction.

WATER REPELLENCY This test may be used to obtain a general idea of the water repellency of a fabric in situations where standard test equipment is not available. With a clothes sprinkler or eye dropper, drop or shake water onto fabric that has been laid on a smooth surface or placed in an embroidery hoop and held at a 45° angle. If the water forms tiny beads and rolls off without penetrating, the fabric may be considered to have some degree of water repellency. As this test does not provide any force behind the water hitting the fabric, other than that provided by gravity, the test provides only an indication of fabric performance.

Resistance to Insect Damage

AATCC tests 24-1980 and 28-1980 are designed to measure the damage to fabrics that might be caused by insects such as moth and carpet beetles. As these insects cause millions of dollars of damage each year, such a test is of value not only to potential consumers but to manufacturers and retailers. Besides the economic factor, a consumer may have to discard a well-liked article, or articles of historical value, because of damage from such insects. The purpose of these tests is to ascertain the susceptibility of a fiber to insects and the efficacy of finishes applied as a means of preventing such damage.

Resistance to Mildew and Rot

Fabrics composed of fibers damaged by mildew or rot, or those that contain substances attacked by mildew or rot, can be treated to resist such destruction. AATCC test 30-1981 determines the suscepti-

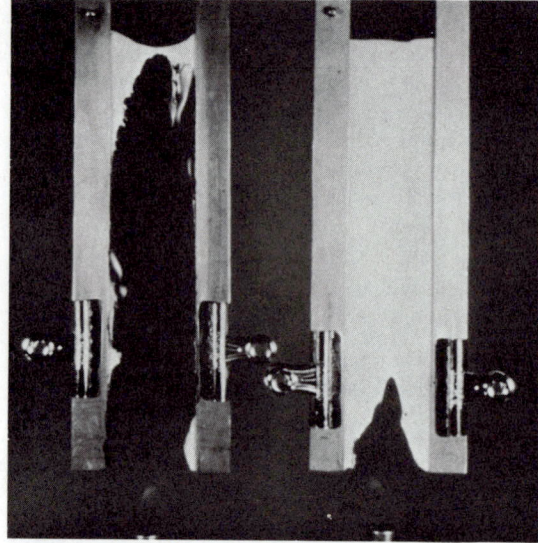

33.13 Sequence showing progressive flame-test results on nontreated fabric *(left)* compared with flame-resistant fabric *(right)*.

bility of a fiber and fabric to mildew damage as well as the effectiveness of mildew preventives. Several methods are given for testing fabrics under varied conditions. Soil contact tests are used for items such as tarpaulins and sleeping bags.

Resistance to Fire: Flammability of Textiles

Tests designed to determine the flame resistance of fabric include AATCC test 33-1962 and ASTM tests D1230-83, D2859-76, D3659-80, D4108-82, and D4151-82. Federal laws regarding flammability of textiles are concerned with reducing the speed of burning and the pattern of burning for a textile fabric; they do not require that burning be eliminated completely. Testing for flame resistance is a complex operation. There are several test procedures in use. Various tests apply to fabrics for various end uses; some are directed to apparel fabrics, others to blankets, others to mattresses, and still others to carpeting. Tests for use in evaluating children's sleepwear have been published as a part of the Flammable Fabrics Act. No single test is applicable to all textiles, and no single test has been identified as best. In fact, there is controversy over test methods used for the determination of flammability; many questions about the reliability and validity of test results are still unanswered.

Testing for flammability identifies fabrics that burn rapidly enough to be dangerous; such tests eliminate from the consumer market any fabric that does not meet the minimum flammability standards. In addition, it determines the effectiveness of flame-retardant treatments. Fabrics are rated according to the speed and manner in which they burn; results include information on the burning rate, ignition rate, char length, residue, afterglow, and smoke generated (Fig. 33.13).

FLAME RESISTANCE The following simple test procedure may be used either in the home or classroom to determine some evidence of the flammability of a textile fabric.

1. Hold a piece of fabric in a pair of tongs.
2. Place a lighted match or candle at the lower edge until the fabric appears to flame or burn.
3. Remove the source of flame and observe the behavior of the fabric. If the flame extinguishes itself, the fabric has some degree of flame resistance. It is essential to observe extreme caution in doing this test to prevent injury to persons as well as possible damage to surrounding furnishings.

The federal test for children's sleepwear requires that five samples, 3.5 by 10 inches (8.9 by 25.4 cm), be oven-dried, cooled, and placed in special vertical holders; these are then placed in a chamber for drying, after which they are inserted into a special test chamber where they are tested individually. A 1½-inch flame is held at the lower edge of each strip for 3 seconds. The flame is removed and the fabric is allowed to burn until flame and afterglow are extinguished. The sample is then measured to deter-

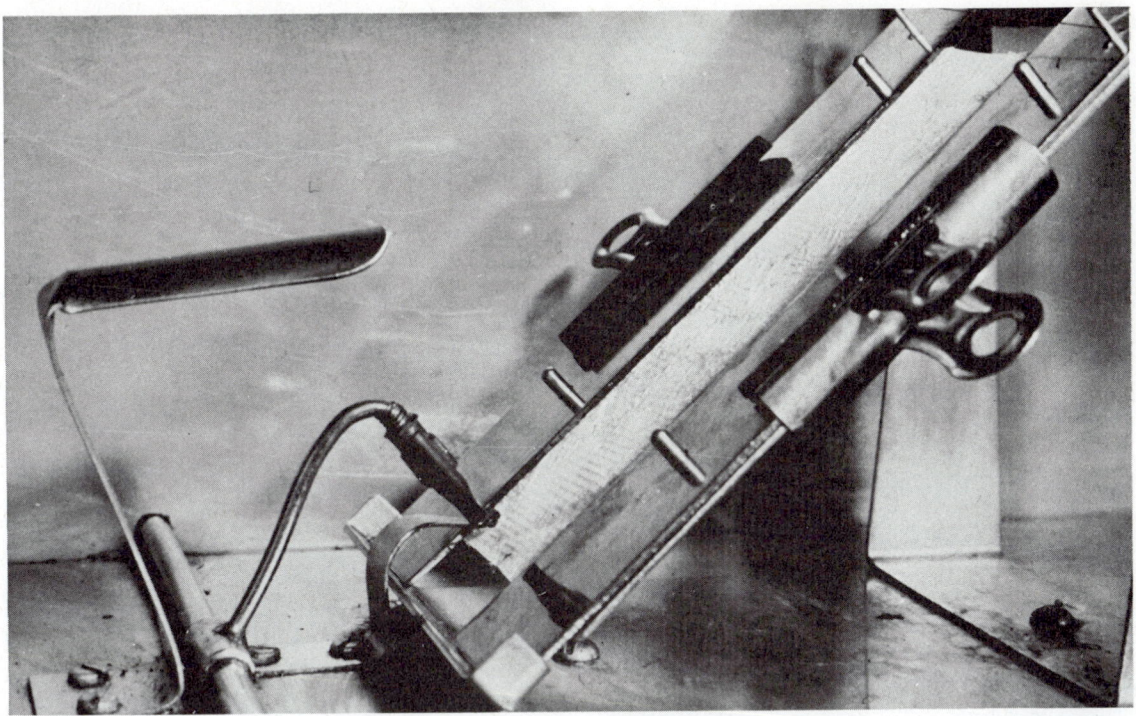

33.14 Testing for flame resistance: the 45° angle method. (Springs Industries, Inc.)

mine the char length; time of burning for any residue that has fallen to the bottom of the test chamber is also recorded. The average char length in any set of five specimen cannot exceed 7 inches (17.8 cm), and if any sample chars the entire 10 inches the fabric is considered to fail the test. All flaming residue must extinguish within 10 seconds or less after removal of the flame. Test methods for children's sleepwear did include a ban on afterglow. However, that portion of the test was eliminated in 1981 as a requirement for approval.

Other tests for measuring flame resistance of fabric include the following:

1. A sample is held at an angle of 45° to the floor and is ignited for a specific amount of time, in seconds; then the behavior of the sample is evaluated in a manner similar to that cited for the vertical test (Fig. 33.14).

2. Samples are held horizontally to the floor, ignited for a set time, and then observed; after burning, the amount of char is measured.

3. For carpets and rugs a burning tablet is placed in the center of a square that has been oven-dried; the distance that the damage extends beyond the tablet is measured and recorded.

4. As in the mattress test described in Chapter 32, burning cigarettes are used to test the flame resistance of upholstered furniture and mattresses.

It should be noted that the standard test procedure for apparel fabrics other than children's sleepwear uses the 45° angle test. Another testing procedure that has been used for some research studies placed fabric upon special mannequins to determine how fabrics burn when on the human body.

Dimensional Change: Effect of Laundering

Tests to determine dimensional change (shrinkage or stretch) include AATCC tests 96-1980, 99-1983, 135-1978, 150-1979, 158-1979, and 160-1980. Perhaps one of the greatest disappointments for the consumer is to have a textile product shrink or stretch out of shape so that it no longer fits, hangs correctly, or looks attractive. The dimensional change of fabric in dry cleaning or laundering can be determined by standard test procedures. Methods used approximate normal laundering or dry-cleaning procedures. The standard laundering test provides for the best laundering method for the specific type of fabric to be tested. Thus, the test identifies

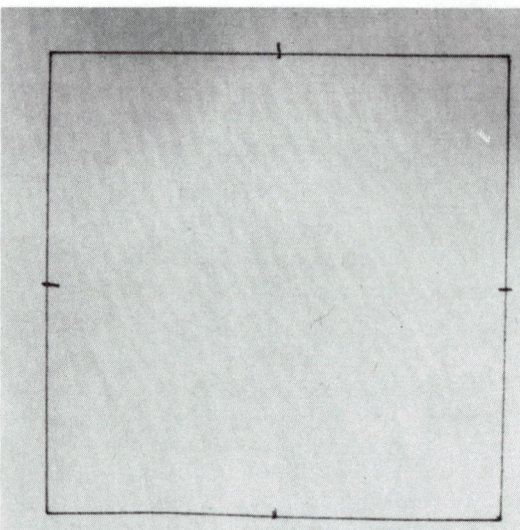

33.15 Fabric with 10-inch (26-cm) square marked for shrinkage testing.

33.16 Small sample to be tested for shrinkage after laundering by comparing sample with marked outline.

different washing temperatures, laundering agents, drying procedures, and restoration procedures for various types of fabrics and end uses.

Label information regarding shrinkage or stretch is desirable. If dimensional change exceeds 2 percent, the fit of the item will be altered noticeably. It is hoped that care labels provide directions that will prevent fabric shrinkage, but this cannot be assumed unless some mention has been made concerning the amount of shrinkage consumers should expect.

The standard test procedure for dimensional change can be easily adapted to home laundering equipment provided there is sufficient yardage of fabric for the test. If a 22-inch (56-cm) square of fabric is available, the procedure that follows will provide results that can be compared with standard results. Mark a 20-inch (52-cm) sample area within the test specimen, launder, restore to normal appearance, then measure to determine dimensional change. It is not often that a 22-inch specimen can be found from purchased articles or even from yardage remaining after construction of an item; however, a 12-inch square may be available. The following process applies to a specimen of that size.

1. Cut a 12-inch square on the grain of the sample, clearly mark a 10-inch (26-cm) square on the sample, and make certain that the warp and filling directions are clearly identified (Fig. 33.15).
2. Launder the sample with a regular wash load using conditions that would normally be used for the particular type of fabric.
3. Dry according to normal procedures for the item.
4. Restore using ironing or smoothing when this would be typical procedure.
5. Measure in three different locations for both the warp and the filling (or wale and course direction for knits). By simple mathematical calculations, the percentage of shrinkage or stretch can be measured:

$$\text{percentage shrinkage or stretch} = \frac{\text{original meas.} - \text{final meas.}}{\text{original meas.}} \times 100$$

Calculate for both warp and filling separately or for wale and course direction in knits. A shrinkage or stretch of more than 3 percent is said to cause a full size change in wearing apparel. A 2 percent change is usually considered maximum for consumer satisfaction.

If the consumer is interested in determining whether drying in a dryer has an effect on dimensional change distinct from the change due to washing procedures, two samples may be prepared. One sample is laundered and air-dried, the other laundered and dryer-dried, and the results are compared.

Another test procedure can be employed when only a small sample is available. This requires a piece of fabric about 4 by 5 inches (10 by 13 cm).

1. Trim the sample so that the cut edges are parallel to warp and filling in woven fabrics and to wales and courses in knitted fabrics. Clearly indicate the warp or wale direction. Try to cut the sample so that the longer dimension is the warp or the wale.
2. Place the test sample on paper, and draw around it so that there is a clear record of the original sample size (Fig. 33.16).
3. Wash the sample by hand, using water temperature and detergent recommended for the specific type of fabric. If water temperature normally used is too hot for hand-washing, select a pint jar that can be tightly sealed and place sample and washing solution in the jar. Shake the jar vigorously to simulate washer action.
4. Rinse the sample thoroughly, dry, press if needed, and compare with the original size.

This method does not provide for change in size caused by raveling, and a fabric in which raveling of yarns does occur will give misleading results. Some idea of change can be determined in such samples by applying a close zigzag stitch to the sample edges before testing. However, such stitching may tend to affect stability to some degree and influence results.

Dimensional Change: Resistance to Dry Cleaning

Shrinkage in dry cleaning is usually caused by water added to the cleaning solvent to remove waterborne soil and stains, by agitation in the presence of water, or by steam pressing. Fabrics that are to be dry-cleaned can be tested to determine shrinkage resulting from moisture and pressure alone by marking a 12-inch square sample as used in the laundering test and thoroughly pressing with steam and pressure. Some idea of the potential shrinkage or stretch of a fabric during dry cleaning can be determined by the following procedure:

1. Prepare a sample like that used in testing for the effect of laundering.
2. Wet the sample in water and remove all excess moisture.
3. Place the sample in cleaning solvent and agitate frequently by stirring, shaking, or rubbing. Continue for 8 to 10 minutes.
4. Remove from the solvent, squeeze out excess fluid, and dry.
5. Measure and calculate the dimensional change using the same formula as given for laundering.

Make certain that all safety precautions are observed when working with cleaning solvents.

The laundering and/or dry-cleaning tests will also provide other information that may be of interest. Observation of the sample can indicate retention of such appearance finishes as glazing, polish, and flocking as well as finishes that influence the hand of fabric, such as sizing.

Recovery from Wrinkling

Consumers want fabrics that will resist the formation of undesirable wrinkles, and if wrinkles do develop, they want them to disappear during care. The purpose of AATCC tests 66-1978 and 128-1980 is to determine the recovery of fabrics from creasing. Any fabric may be tested for crease recovery, but the test is usually applied to woven fabrics and to both the warp and filling directions. Further, it may be an important test for any fabric that has been given a crease-resistant or a durable-press finish.

The following procedure can be used in the home or classroom to provide some indication of how well a fabric recovers from wrinkling.

1. Fold a 2-inch (5-cm) square sample of fabric twice so as to make a 1-inch (2.5-cm) square.
2. Place a 1-pound (0.45-kg) weight on top of the folded sample. Let it remain on the sample for 5 minutes.
3. Remove the weight and unfold the sample, but do not smooth with the hands.
4. Observe to see whether wrinkles spring out quickly and disappear.
5. After 5 minutes, observe the sample a second time to determine what has happened.

Although this is not a scientific test, it does provide information about the recovery of a fabric from wrinkling or creasing.

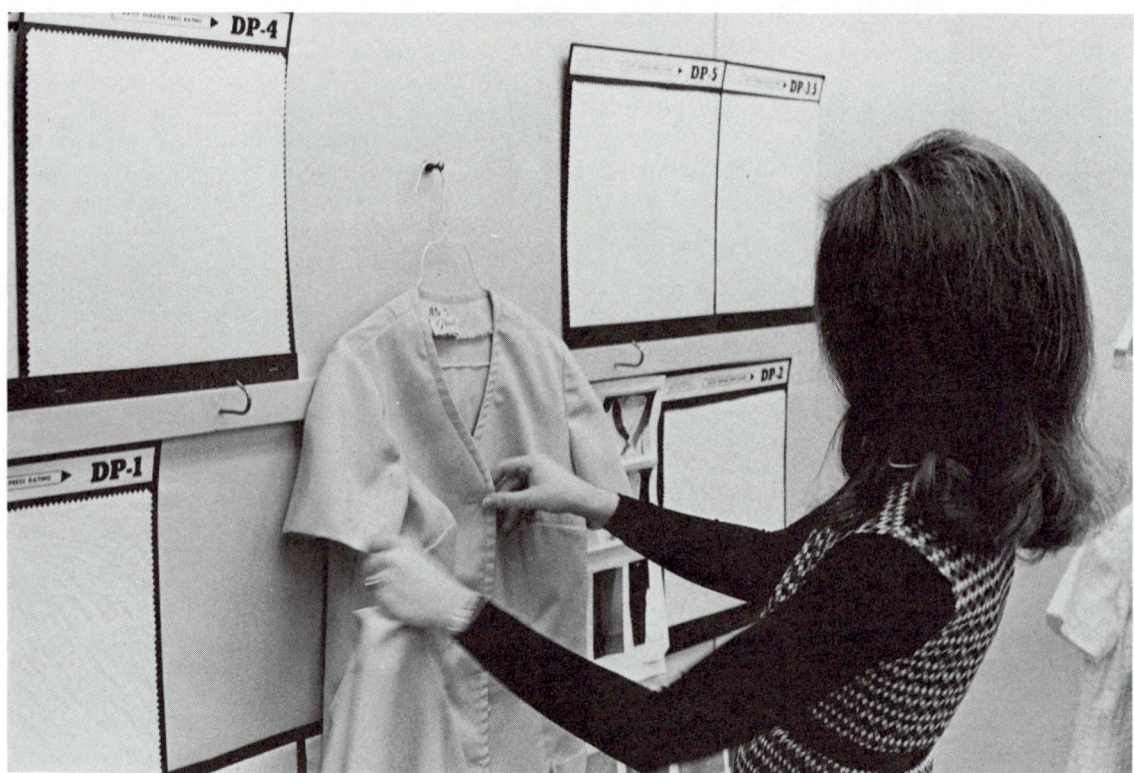

33.17 Evaluating a durable-press finish against rated standard samples. (Celanese Corporation)

Durable-Press Properties of Fabrics

The purposes of AATCC tests 124-1983, 88B-1981, and 88C-1975, developed to determine durable-press properties, are to identify how such fabrics perform during use and care and how well they retain their original appearance. The analysis is somewhat subjective even in professional laboratories. Plastic replicas and photographs of fabrics at various steps of wrinkling are used as standards. The item being tested is compared with the standards and rated according to the replica or photograph it most closely approximates in appearance. The test should be repeated periodically to determine the expected duration of a satisfactory appearance. The test cites specific conditions for amount and type of light to be used and for distance of sample from light and from the observer. Fabric surface, seam construction, and planned pleats or creases are all studied (Fig. 33.17).

To test for durable press in the classroom, in the home, or in laboratories that do not have standards, the following procedure may be used:

1. Prepare a test sample of about 10 to 20 inches square.
2. Launder the sample according to the recommended care procedures.
3. Air- or tumble-dry using recommended procedures.
4. Evaluate by visual inspection, before pressing. Determine the need, if any, for touch-up ironing, and rate on some comparative basis how well the fabric returns to a smooth surface. Note clearly whether ironing is required to accomplish the smooth surface.

Although this method is completely subjective, it does give some indication of the durable-press properties of a fabric.

Soil Release Properties

AATCC test 130-1981 is one procedure to measure the ability of a fabric to release oily soil during laundering. Fabric is stained with oily substances in a specified manner; it is then washed according to standard procedures. The test fabric is compared with stain-release standards and evaluated. Many new finishes and some fibers tend to hold oily stains. This test yields data that will give the consumer as well as the manufacturer some idea of care requirements and appearance retention.

Students or consumers can obtain a general idea of the soil release properties or resistance to oilborne stains by following these steps:

1. Place a drop of salad oil on a piece of fabric.
2. If the drop of oil forms a bead and can be easily removed with a blotter or a piece of absorbent tissue, leaving no stain, the fabric has repellency to oilborne stains and liquids.
3. If the stain does not form a bead, but sinks into the fabric, launder the fabric using standard procedures.
4. After laundering, see whether the stain has been removed. Is so, soil-release properties are considered successful.

Summary: Finish Performance

Some finishes are destroyed by the first laundering or dry cleaning; others last for more than 50 washings or cleanings. When purchasing fabrics with various finishes, the consumer should carefully note labeling information and observe all recommended care procedures. The purchase of any textile fabric or product is a matter of choice, but the intelligent consumer will follow care directions and know how to evaluate a product at the point of sale.

Testing techniques are often impossible to use on ready-made articles. For these, consumers must depend on label information, which is often meager, or they must wait and see what happens after the first laundering (or more), when the results can be traumatic and disappointing.

Again, consumer responsibility requires that merchandise that does not perform according to expectation when handled according to the directions provided should be returned to the place of purchase. A request that the manufacturer be informed is necessary if products of similar performance are to be eliminated. Without complaints about unsatisfactory merchandise, neither the retailer nor the manufacturer is aware that problems exist.

Tests for Colorfastness

Standard tests are available to test for the colorfastness of fabrics to laundering (AATCC 61-1980),

bleaching (AATCC 3-1979 and 101-1979), crocking (AATCC tests 8-1981 and 116-1983), light and weather resistance (AATCC 16-1982, 111A-1978, and 111A-1983), perspiration (AATCC 15-1979), water (AATCC 107-1981), dry cleaning (AATCC 132-1979), and pressing (AATCC 133-1979). Additional tests may be found in the AATCC *Technical Manual* published each year.

The various tests identify procedures used to simulate environmental conditions that may cause fading or color change in a textile item. Results may be compared with standard test fabrics or special charts; they may also be compared with other fabrics.

Dyestuffs may cause problems for consumers despite the tremendous development in dye chemistry over the past century. Dissatisfaction may be the result of improper fabric care—either the consumer ignores the care information on an attached label, or adequate care instructions are not provided. (Although labels are required by law, they may be missing or the amount of information may be incorrect or incomplete.) Problems can result from improper dye selection by the converter or dryer or from the use of inferior-quality dyes in an attempt to produce a product at a cost less than what would be typical when using recommended dyestuffs.

Consumers should be alert to problems that arise as a result of the type of light used in viewing colored textiles. Fabrics may appear to be identical in color under one type of light but quite different under another light source. This matching problem, called metamerism, can cause serious problems during color selection and can result in consumer dissatisfaction.

When label information about care seems inadequate, consumers may wish to perform their own tests to determine the behavior of color in various situations. Several nontechnical tests are included here as guides. Using them may prevent some dissatisfaction and disappointment with a textile item. However, small samples of fabric are required for such tests, and these may not be available for items purchased ready to use.

Home Tests for Colorfastness

DRY CLEANING

Test 1. Sponge a sample of fabric (or the seam allowance at a point where it is hidden) with a dry cleaner or spot remover, using a clean white cloth.

If the color is not fast to cleaning, it will run onto the cloth. Dry-cleaning solvents and spot removers should be used in well-ventilated areas, and some must never be used near flames. It is important to avoid inhaling the vapor of these substances.

Test 2. If a sample of sufficient size, approximately 2 by 4 inches (5 by 10 cm), is available, immerse it in cleaning solvent for 10 to 20 minutes. Observe to determine whether any color has bled into the cleaning solution; then dry and compare the sample with an original piece of fabric to determine whether color change has occurred or if the bleeding represents excess dye only.

LAUNDERING

Test 3. A small fabric sample is required. This can be clipped from the seam allowance or hem if a fabric scrap is not available. When yardage is used, a 2 by 2-inch (5 by 5-cm) swatch is adequate.

1. Use a pint jar and water at the temperature suggested for the fiber content involved.
2. Put one cup of water and one level teaspoon of soap or synthetic detergent into the jar.
3. Add the fabric sample.
4. Shake the jar frequently and allow the fabric to remain in solution for 10 minutes.
5. Observe the color of the wash water.
6. Rinse the sample in warm water at least twice, and observe any loss of color into the rinse water.
7. Dry the sample, and compare it with the original fabric to determine whether any color change has occurred.

Laboratory testing usually involves a testing machine such as the Launder-O-Meter (Fig. 33.18).

LAUNDERING WITH OTHER GARMENTS

Test 4. When dye is evident in the wash water, you may wish to see whether it will discolor other fabrics laundered at the same time.

1. Repeat Test 3 with a new sample of fabric, and include in the jar small samples of white fabrics of cotton, nylon, polyester, rayon, acrylic, and acetate.
2. Observe the white samples to determine whether they have picked up any color from the sample being tested.

Bleeding is the term used to indicate that color has been lost from a sample into a cleaning medium

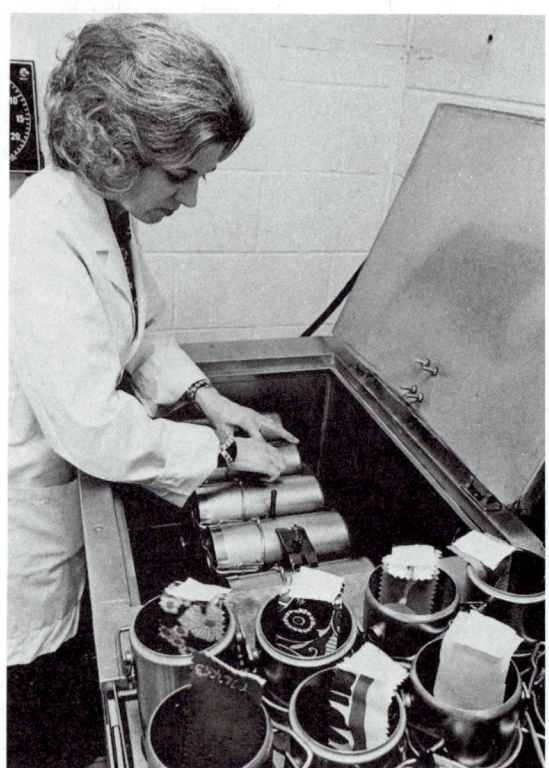

33.18 Preparing a Launder-O-Meter for testing for colorfastness to laundering. (Celanese Corporation)

such as water. *Migration* identifies the movement of color from one location on a fabric to another location on the same fabric *and* movement of color from one fabric to other fabrics in the same wash bath.

Colorfastness to laundering, *washfastness,* is desirable in any textile item that requires frequent cleaning with water and detergents. When color is picked up by other fibers or fabrics, the consumer must launder the item alone or with fabrics that are not affected. Fabrics may lose color, or bleed, without giving visible evidence of color change in the item itself. This occurs when excess dye has remained in the product. In such instances the product requires separate care until all excess dye has been removed; then it may be laundered with other items if migration does not occur.

Label information can be misleading. Although a label may state that a fabric is colorfast, it may not be colorfast to laundering. The term *washfast* is preferred, as it does indicate that the item will not bleed color and migration should not occur. To some extent, care labeling compensates for the absence of such information. Care labels are supposed to be written to assure consumers that the care given the product will not result in changes that cause consumer dissatisfaction.

SUNLIGHT

Test 5. Textile fabrics that will be exposed to sunlight for many hours each day, such as curtains, draperies, and sportswear, should be colorfast to sunlight—referred to as *lightfastness.* While it is difficult to carry out accurate tests at home, it is possible to assess lightfastness to some degree.

1. Expose a sample of fabric to sunlight between 10:00 A.M. and 4:00 P.M. standard time, between May and September.
2. Keep a record of the number of hours of exposure. It is also helpful to maintain a record of rainy, cloudy, and sunny days.
3. Compare the sample with an original piece of the textile that has not been exposed to light. Make this comparison at intervals during the exposure period. Fabric is not considered satisfactory for use at windows or on patios unless it will resist fading for a minimum of 120 to 140 hours. A consumer wishing to pretest a fabric sample before final purchase has the problem of time. Frequently, by the time lightfastness or sunfastness has been checked, the product is no longer available on the market. Thus, for most situations, consumers must depend on label information and past experience. If the word *lightfast* or *sunfast* appears on a label or on tags, the consumer should expect good service and satisfaction.

OTHER ENVIRONMENTAL FACTORS

Other conditions that can affect color include atmospheric fumes and smog. Testing for colorfastness to these conditions is difficult, if not impossible, except in well-equipped laboratories. Fume fading may be observed if a small sample of fabric is suspended in a gas oven with a pilot light functioning. As most new gas ovens depend on electronic ignition, a pilot light is frequently not available. Tests for smog require special chambers into which mixtures of gases and impurities can be fed.

The Weather-O-Meter or Fade-O-Meter shown in Figure 33.19 is used in laboratories to test a fabric for colorfastness to sunlight, humidity, and other weather conditions that might affect color.

IRONING

Test 6. Color may be altered by ironing or pressing with either dry or wet heat. When dry heat is used, the fabric will usually return to its normal color upon cooling. The consumer can check this satisfactorily with an iron on either a sample of fabric or an inside seam allowance.

1. Press the fabric with an iron set at the temperature recommended for the fiber. Observe any color change.
2. If color does change, observe the fabric as it cools to determine whether it returns to its original color.
3. If not, try a lower ironing temperature or hand smoothing. When all else fails, contact the retailer to determine whether the item should be returned.

Pressing with steam or with a damp press cloth may affect some dyes. Fabrics can be checked as for dry heat, using steam or a wet press cloth on the fabric. If colors change with this test and not with the dry heat, or vice versa, the consumer knows which ironing or pressing method should be used. Dyes affected by wet heat may stain the ironing board cover, the press cloth, or, under certain circumstances, other fabrics. Such behavior should be observed and considered in relation to care.

RUBBING OR CROCKING

Test 7. Colors may be removed or affected by rubbing, called crocking. To test for colorfastness to rubbing follow this procedure:

1. Place a small square of white cotton fabric, muslin or percale, over the forefinger.
2. With even pressure rub the white fabric at least ten times over a colored fabric at the same location.
3. Observe whether the color rubs off onto the white fabric.
4. Repeat the process using a piece of white fabric that has been thoroughly wet-out or moistened.

For laboratory testing the Crockmeter (Fig. 33.20) is used.

Summary: Colorfastness

The amount of color change in a fabric is evaluated by comparing samples with standards as well as

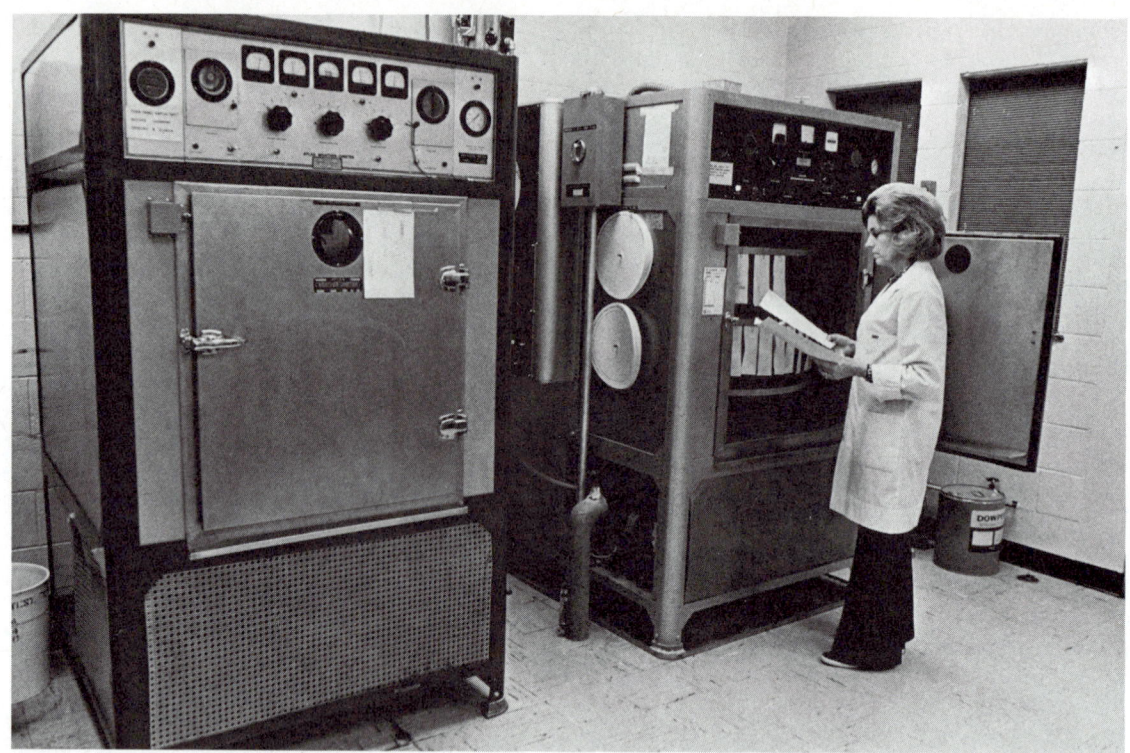

33.19 Fade-O-Meter and Weather-O-Meter used for testing for colorfastness to sunlight, ultraviolet light, and weather. (Celanese Corporation)

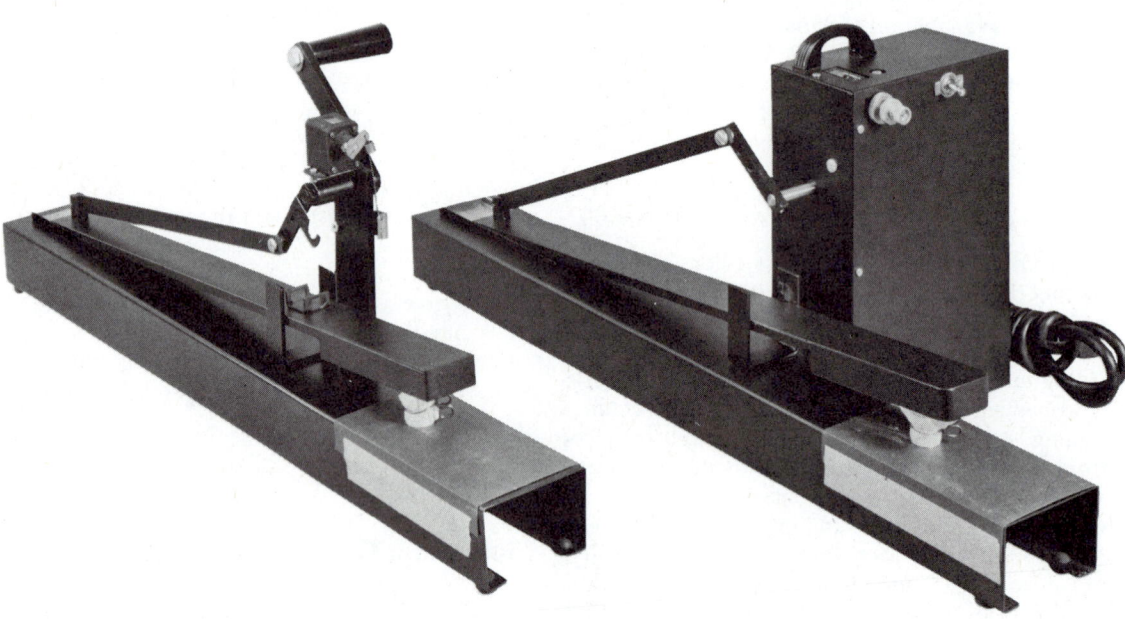

33.20 Crockmeters: test for colorfastness to rubbing or crocking. (Atlas Electric Devices, Inc.)

33.21 Evaluating colorfastness test results. (Celanese Corporation)

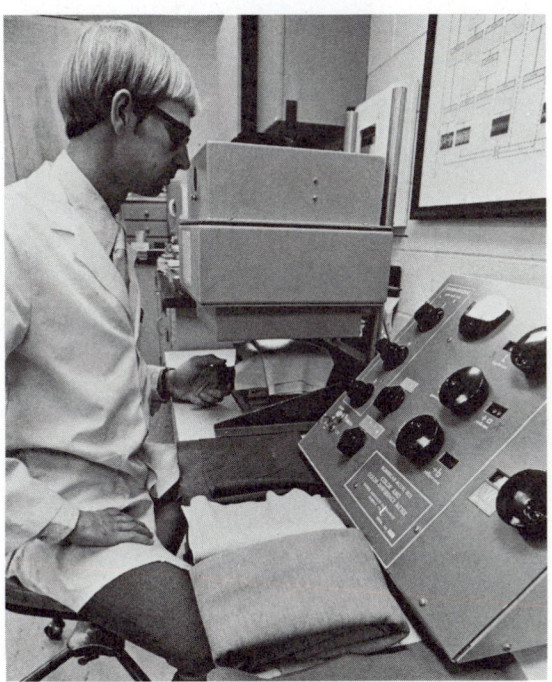

33.22 Evaluating change in color with a Color-Difference Meter. (Celanese Corporation)

with the original fabric. Figure 33.21 indicates some of the various standards available for use in such comparisons. Figure 33.22 illustrates one type of colorimeter that mechanically determines color change. Consumers may see obvious change simply by comparing the tested sample with a piece of the original product.

Test results and label information can provide consumers with valuable data concerning the care a textile item should be given as well as identifying situations that should not be used. It is then the responsibility of consumers to decide how to care for the products they have purchased.

While care information is required for most textile items, it seldom identifies colorfastness properties. The consumer may assume that the care prescribed will retain color during maintenance, but that does not mean that it will withstand various environmental conditions that it encounters during use. Products that do not provide consumer satisfaction should be returned so that retailers and manufacturers are made aware of poor-quality merchandise.

A very important point, however, is that consumers must follow the care directions provided if they wish to have a product retain its appearance and serviceability. Improper care is not the fault of the retailer or the manufacturer; it is the fault of the consumer.

Testing: A Summary Statement

Modern test procedures and equipment provide a means by which fabric performance can be predicted. Such predictions are of help to consumers who are willing to consider these results and who are willing to adhere to care instructions. The knowledgeable consumer has the advantage in obtaining the best textile product for each potential end use.

Ideally, any textile product can have a label affixed that indicates what the fabric will and will not do or endure. No item, however, will give satisfaction to its owner if it shrinks even one size, if colors fade, or if the fabric wrinkles badly. Consumers who use their textile knowledge can make intelligent selection of textile products and should receive long-term satisfaction.

STUDY QUESTIONS

1. What are performance standards? Locate the current ASTM *Annual Book of ASTM Standards* and determine what products have established performance standards.
2. How will performance standards be used, and how can they help a consumer?
3. How can care labeling, described in the previous chapter, help consumers in relation to the selection, use, and care of textile items? What tests help determine the information that care labels must include?

Activities

1. Select a group of fabric samples, and perform various tests to describe the fabrics, determine finish durability and performance, and determine colorfastness.
2. Describe various tests that can be used to determine the reaction a textile product might have to environmental conditions.

34

Textiles for Specialized Uses

KEY TERMS

fiber reinforced   high-performance textiles
geotextiles

Specialized fibers and specialized uses for textile fabrics are achieving widespread importance in today's high-tech world. This chapter describes a few of the more common geotextile uses of fibers and fabrics; identifies a few of the high-performance fibers and fabrics that may be encountered in consumer goods as well as in industrial and commercial uses; identifies textiles used in medicine; and notes some of the typical uses for fibers that may not be easily observed by the average consumer. This discussion provides only a brief look at special high-performance fibers and fabrics. But no book on textiles written in the 1980s can afford to ignore these high-tech fibers and fabrics.

Geotextiles

One of the most rapidly growing uses for textiles is in geotechnical applications. Geotextiles include textiles for ground stabilization, erosion control, drainage, asphalt and moisture proofing, and special "exotic" high-performance uses.

Both woven and nonwoven fabrics are used in geotextile applications. These fabrics are made of such fibers as polypropylene olefin, polyester, nylon, and acrylic. Nonwoven fabrics exceed woven in use. The most important fiber, or most used, is

polypropylene. Polyester would provide the best performance, but it is considered too costly for widespread use; acrylics are also considered too expensive despite the fact that they have superior properties for such uses.

Probably the most common geotechnical use of textiles is in the area of soil stabilization, erosion control, and drainage in ground installations. They serve as a separation layer to form a stable boundary between layers of soil to maintain the integrity, character, and performance properties of each layer. This usage occurs in such situations as constructing an embankment of soil or laying ballast for a road or railroad. These textile materials act as a barrier to the movement of soil particles but permit the flow of water necessary for adequate drainage. Drainage can occur from one soil layer to another through a geotextile layer, or drainage can occur within a single plane or layer where the geotextile serves as the drain vehicle. The geotextile material reinforces a structure and reduces erosion by equalizing stresses over a wide area.

Textiles are used as a support or stabilizer for concrete in the construction of dams, canals, drainage systems, and retaining walls for ponds or lakes. They are used in road construction in various ways. They may be laid over the soil and rock base to help segregate the subsoil and the fill, and they may be laid over the base and directly under the surface asphalt layers. The former use provides for equalization of stress as well as segregation of subsoil and fill; the latter reduces cracking of the road base and asphalt surface and reduces the amount of asphalt required for good stability of the road surface. Both uses tend to improve drainage.

The properties of a geotextile need to include the following. They must be stable to the conditions into which they will be placed; this means they must resist damage from microorganisms and insects. They must be stable to the range of temperatures that will be encountered both in application and in use. They must be stable to chemicals that may be encountered, and they must be resistant to possible damage from light. Whatever the extreme of environmental conditions encountered, the geotextile must be able to withstand those conditions. Geotextiles must be strong and have special stress-strain properties that are required for the specific end use. Various physical properties will be engineered to suit the particular use. Some situations require very thick layers that are highly rigid, strong, and resistant to creep; others require a thin layer with plenty of pores to provide for the passage of fluids through the surface.

Although some woven fabrics are required, the majority of geotextiles are nonwovens made by spun bonding, fuse bonding, or needle punching. Spun bonding involves the melt extrusion of thermoplastic polymers to form a web of intermingled filaments that are fused together at their crossing or intersecting points as the fabric is formed. When the filaments cool, the fabric is securely formed. Typical examples of spun-bonded geotextiles include Typar®, a polypropylene nonwoven, and Mirafi®, a polyester nonwoven.

Fuse-bonded geotextiles are formed from solid fibers or already-formed filament fibers. The fibers are laid into a planned arrangement and then fused by heat to form a cohesive fabric that is rigid and durable. This process has been called ''melding'' in some recent literature. An example of fuse-bonded textiles is Terram®, a geotextile used in layer separation, filtration, and drainage.

Needle punching is accomplished just as it has been described previously (Chap. 24). These fabrics tend to be thicker than the bonded or fused fabrics. Bidim®, a polyester fiber fabric made by Monsanto, is an example of a needle-punched fabric designed for geotextile use.

Combinations of needle-punched layers with bonded fiber layers are used for some specialized installations. These composites are designed to meet a combination of requirements such as high resistance to stress, resistance to sunlight and ultraviolet light, toughness, and high durability.

Other interesting applications of geotextiles include their use in airport runways and in stabilizing ground in areas of high earthquake liability.

Woven fabrics are being used in the construction of special platforms, in building road beds, and in making jacketing material for retaining walls.

In agricultural uses, geotextiles reduce erosion from sprinklers and other irrigation systems, serve as windbreakers, make excellent shades for seedlings and small plants, work effectively in turf protection to prevent damage from weather, and provide a base as protection for seeds.

It will be important for any student of textile science to keep current with developments in geotextiles and have at least a basic understanding of how these textiles are used, what properties they must have, and how they are improving various environmental states.

High-Performance Fibers and Fabrics

Mention has already been made in previous chapters of specialized uses for some of the man-made fibers. These include the use of high-tenacity rayon, nylon, and polyester in tires for general vehicle use as well as for airplanes and other aerospace applications. In addition, glass and steel fibers are used in tire manufacture, among a variety of other uses. Aramid fibers are high-performance fibers that serve in a wide variety of special high-tech uses, including tires for general automobiles and for high-performance use in aerospace, as a protective fiber for bulletproof clothing, and other end uses not typical of uses by the average consumer. This section is included to outline, in brief, a few of the high-performance fibers and information on how they are used for selected situations.

A special type of fabric, called Thinsulate®, is available from the 3-M Company. This special product has unique insulation properties owing to the microfiber construction (Fig. 34.1). This microfiber construction provides more surface area to capture or trap insulating air more efficiently than larger fibers of the typical high-loft polyester. It is stated

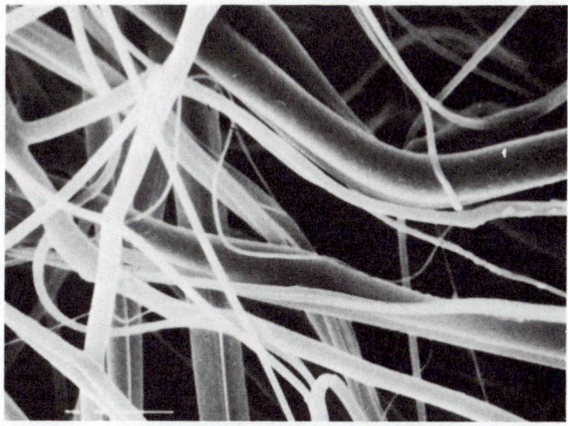
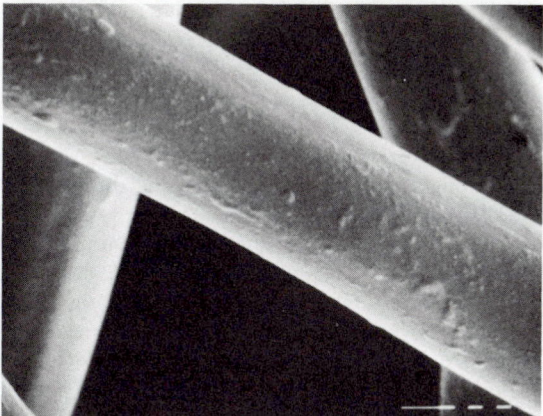

34.1 An example of Thinsulate® fibers compared with a 6-denier hollow fiber. (3M Corporation)

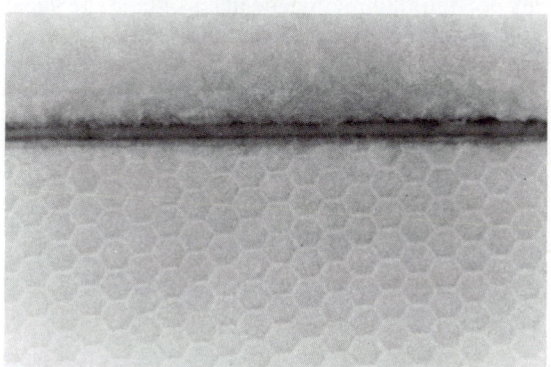

34.2 Examples of fabric composed of Thinsulate®.

34.3 Examples of apparel using Thinsulate®. (3M Corporation)

that Thinsulate provides nearly twice the warmth of down or other high-loft insulations when equal thicknesses are compared. It has been used in a wide variety of sportswear where warmth is a critical property, for example in diving suits and in apparel for mountain climbing. The product is breathable, providing comfort as well as warmth. It retains its insulating properties even when damp. Thinsulate is made primarily of olefin fiber. Selected types of Thinsulate also include polyester fibers (Fig. 34.2). The olefin microfibers contribute superior insulating properties, while the polyester fibers function as bulking fibers providing improved drape and a softer hand. The olefin microfibers are about 2 to 4 microns in diameter, which is about ten times smaller than typical synthetic fiber filaments. Typical garments in which Thinsulate has been used are shown in Figure 34.3.

Teflon, polytetrafluoroethylene fiber, has been described previously. It is considered a high-performance fiber because of the major types of uses. It has been used in blends and alone for high-performance fabrics where there is a need for outstanding soil and stain resistance. The product is also used as a finish on fabrics for the same purpose.

Gore-Tex® is a membrane type of textile made from polytetrafluoroethylene fibers that have been expanded. These expanded microfibers are bonded to a fabric and provide pores of only 0.2 microns. The resulting product is waterproof, yet it permits moisture to evaporate and heat to dissipate. An important use for this product is as a barrier to bacteria, which will not pass through the layer. It is being used in protective clothing for people who will be exposed to such things as dangerous bacteria or insecticides, and it is finding some medical uses. The membrane layer is so fine that 1 square yard of the fabric weighs only ½ ounce.

Fiber-reinforced plastics and metals have been available for some time. The use of fibers as reinforcements increases the resistance of the plastic or metal to rupture stress and increases strength while providing a product light in weight. Some of the fibers typically used as reinforcements are fiberglass, aramid, carbon, graphite, and specialty items such as sapphire whiskers. Some products use a combination of two or more fibers as the reinforcement. The polymer frequently used as the plastic base is polyester, while the metals that may be reinforced are frequently steel or aluminum.

Special fibers for fire-protective clothing have been noted in fiber chapters. These include Kynol novoloid, Nomex® aramid, modacrylic fibers, carbon fibers, Celiox®, the polychal Cordelan®, and selected polyvinyl chloride fibers. Refer to the fiber chapters for details on these. Fire-protective clothing must insulate the body from flame and heat as well as have a very high ignition temperature. It must be made so that seams do not permit ready passage of heat and flame. Such clothing must be lightweight, comfortable, and nonrestrictive of body movement.

Textiles in Medical Applications

Textiles have long been used for such routine applications as uniforms, bedding, hospital furnishings, bandages, and dressings and in such locations as hospitals, clinics, medical centers, and doctors' offices. Recent uses for highly specialized medical applications are worthy of mention.

For bedding in hospitals, cotton is still a favorite fiber for sheets, as they can be easily sterilized to kill bacteria. Cotton, acrylic, and some olefin fibers are being used in blankets, as these can be easily laundered and sterilized when needed. The use of non-woven fabrics is increasing, particularly for areas of highly infectious illnesses, as these fabrics are sterile when first used and are destroyed following their use.

Clothing for use in operating rooms must be antistatic, and cotton is generally used to meet this requirement. To reduce the danger of the transfer of bacteria from the medical team to a patient, the use of Gore-Tex has been successful. The micro-thin layer of Gore-Tex is used in apparel for surgeons and to some extent for other members of the surgical team.

An important use of textiles in medicine is for sutures. Yarns may be made of silk, cotton, linen, polyester, nylon, and polypropylene. Monofilament, multifilament, and spun yarns are used. In some special orthopedic surgery, sutures of stainless steel filaments may be useful.

Fabrics are also used for prosthetic devices, to replace some parts of the body. Some of the typical uses include artificial blood vessels and hearts. Polyester knitted into tubes works well for the blood vessels, especially main arteries. Other prostheses include artificial tendons made of either polyester or carbon fibers; and bone repair involving polytetrafluoroethylene fibers or graphite fibers.

Collections of glass fibers are a means of providing light at locations within the body to help doctors to make diagnoses. These fiber optics instruments represent an important step; they can convey regular light or laser beams.

Forecasts indicate a rapid growth in the use of special fibers for medical applications as well as new medical uses for fibers, yarns, or fabrics.

Summary

Each year new uses for textiles are identified. Many of these are never seen by the average consumer. Many consumers fail to recognize specialized fibers when they do encounter them. For example, how many think about the special properties that fabrics used in airplanes must possess? They must be flame-resistant or flameproof, light in weight, and durable, and for cabin furnishings they must be comfortable and attractive. The same is true when purchasing an automobile. The fabrics used for floor coverings, upholstery, ceiling, and side wall panels must be durable yet attractive and comfortable. Few, however, think about the fact that they should be highly resistant to sunlight and ultraviolet light, particularly if they are to sit in the sun during the day while their owner is in a comfortable air-conditioned building. Vinyl coatings on car tops must also resist damage from the sun and weather.

Students and consumers can profit, in the long run, if they do give thought to how a textile should perform in whatever end use it is found. Only then can textile items provide consumer satisfaction and prevent consumer dissatisfaction.

STUDY QUESTIONS

1. What are typical geotextile applications for textile fibers and fabrics?
2. What is meant by *high-performance fibers* or *fabrics*?

Activities

1. Locate examples of geotextiles, and describe their properties and how they differ from textiles used for home furnishings or apparel.
2. Develop some special situations that might require a textile, and describe what type of textile would be needed and the properties that it should possess.
3. Locate examples of materials in which textile fibers have been used as reinforcement either in plastic or metal. Why do you think they have been used in such situations?

Metric Conversion Tables

When dealing with foreign suppliers or consulting references printed abroad, the textile manufacturer, scientist, or student should be able to convert readily from the U.S. system of weights and measures to the metric system, employed by virtually every country outside the United States. The following tables provide multipliers for converting from metric to U.S. and the reverse; the multipliers have been rounded to the third decimal place and thus yield an approximate equivalent.

METRIC TO U.S.			U.S. TO METRIC		
To Convert from	**To**	**Multiply the Metric Unit by**	**To Convert from**	**To**	**Multiply the U.S. Unit by**
Length					
meters	yards	1.093	yards	meters	.914
meters	feet	3.280	feet	meters	.305
meters	inches	39.370	inches	meters	.025
centimeters	inches	.394	inches	centimeters	2.540
millimeters	inches	.039	inches	millimeters	25.400
Area and Volume					
square meters	square yards	1.196	square yards	square meters	.836
square meters	square feet	10.764	square feet	square meters	.093
square centimeters	square inches	.155	square inches	square centimeters	6.451
cubic centimeters	cubic inches	.061	cubic inches	cubic centimeters	16.387
Liquid Measure					
liters	cubic inches	61.020	cubic inches	liters	.016
liters	cubic feet	.035	cubic feet	liters	28.339
liters	U.S. gallons*	.264	U.S. gallons*	liters	3.785
liters	U.S. quarts*	1.057	U.S. quarts*	liters	.946
Weight and Mass					
kilograms	pounds	2.205	pounds	kilograms	.453
grams	ounces	.035	ounces	grams	28.349
grams	grains	15.430	grains	grams	.065
grams per meter	ounces per yard	.032	ounces per yard	grams per meter	31.250
grams per square meter	ounces per square yard	.030	ounces per square yard	grams per square meter	33.333

*The British imperial gallon equals approximately 1.2 U.S. gallons or 4.54 liters. Similarly, the British imperial quart equals 1.2 U.S. quarts, and so on.

Bibliography

GENERAL INTEREST

Alexander, Patsy R. *Textile Product Selection, Use, and Care.* Boston: Houghton Mifflin, 1977.

Bendure, Z., and G. Pfeiffer. *American Fabrics.* New York: Macmillan, 1947.

Cohen, Allen C. *Beyond Basic Textiles.* New York: Fairchild Publications, 1982.

Collier, A. M. *A Handbook of Textiles,* 3rd ed. New York: State Mutual Book and Periodical Service, 1982.

Considine, Douglas M., ed. *Chemical and Process Technology Encyclopedia.* New York: McGraw-Hill, 1974.

Corbman, Bernard P. *Textiles: Fiber to Fabrics,* 6th ed. New York: McGraw-Hill, 1983.

Creekmore, Anna M., and Ila M. Pokornowski. *Textile History.* Washington, DC: University Press of America, 1982.

D'Harcourt, Raoul. *Textiles of Ancient Peru and Their Techniques.* Seattle: University of Washington Press, 1974.

Encyclopedia of Textiles, 3rd ed. Englewood Cliffs, NJ: Prentice-Hall, 1980.

Farnfield, Carolyn A., ed. *Textile Terms and Definitions,* 7th ed. Manchester, England: The Textile Institute, 1975.

Hall, A. J. *Standard Handbook of Textiles,* 8th ed. New York: Halstead Press, 1975.

Hearle, John W. S.; Percy Grosberg; and Stanley Baker. *Structural Mechanics of Fibers, Yarns and Fabrics,* vol 1. New York: Wiley-Interscience, 1969.

Hollen, Norma; Jane Saddler; and Ann Langford. *Textiles,* 5th ed. New York: Macmillan, and London: Collier Macmillan, 1979.

Joseph, Marjory L., and Audrey Gieseking-Williams. *Illustrated Guide to Textiles,* 4th ed. Canoga Park, CA: Plycon Press, 1985.

Kaswell, E. R. *Textile Fibers, Yarns, and Fabrics.* New York: Reinhold, 1953.

Kvaraceus, Catherine, and Larry Salmon. *From Fiber to Fine Art.* Boston: Museum of Fine Arts, 1980.

Labarthe, Jules. *Elements of Textiles.* New York: Macmillan, 1975.

Linton, George E. *The Modern Textile and Apparel Dictionary,* 4th ed. Plainfield, NJ: Textile Book Service, 1973.

Lyle, Dorothy Siegart. *Modern Textile,* 2nd ed. New York: Wiley, 1982.

Man-Made Fiber and Textile Dictionary. New York: Celanese Corp., 1974.

Mark, H. F., N. G. Gaylord, and N. M. Bikales, eds. *Encyclopedia of Polymer Science and Technology,* 15 vols. New York: Wiley-Interscience, 1964–1971.

Needles, Howard L. *Handbook of Textile Fibers, Dyes and Finishes.* New York: Garland, 1980.

Nettles, John E. *Handbook of Chemical Specialties: Textile Fiber Processing, Preparation and Bleaching.* New York: Wiley, 1983.

Pankowski, Edith, and Dallas Pankowski. *Basic Textiles: A Programmed Manual.* New York: Macmillan, 1972.

Pizzuto, J. J. *Fabric Science,* 4th ed, revised by Arthur Price and Allen C. Cohen. New York: Fairchild Publications, 1980.

Seagroatt, Margaret. *A Basic Textile Book.* New York: Van Nostrand Reinhold, 1975.

Smith, Betty F., and Ira Block. *Textiles in Prospective.* Englewood Cliffs, NJ: Prentice-Hall, 1982.

Taylor, Marjorie A. *Technology of Textile Properties.* London: Forbes Publishers, 1972.

Textile Handbook, 5th ed. Washington, DC: American Home Economics Association, 1975.

Tortora, Phyllis G. *Understanding Textiles,* 2nd ed. New York: Macmillan, 1982.

Volbach, W. Fritz. *Early Decorative Textiles.* London: Paul Hamlyn, 1969.

Wingate, Isabel. *Dictionary of Textiles,* 6th ed. New York: Fairchild Publications, 1979.

Wingate, Isabel, and June Mohler. *Textile Fabrics and Their Selection,* 8th ed. Englewood Cliffs, NJ: Prentice-Hall, 1984.

FIBERS

Alexander, Peter; Robert Hudson; and Christopher Earland. *Wool: Its Chemistry and Physics.* New York: Reinhold, 1963.

Asquith, R. S., ed. *Chemistry of Natural Protein Fibers.* New York: Plenum Press, 1977.

Black, W. Bruce, and J. Preston. *High Modulus Wholly Aromatic Fibers.* New York: Marcel Dekker, 1973.

Brown, H. B., and J. O. Ware. *Cotton.* New York: McGraw-Hill, 1958.

Brown, T. D. *Wool in Double Jersey.* Watford, England: Merrow Publishing Co., 1973.

Carroll-Porcznski, C. Z. *Asbestos.* Manchester, England: The Textile Institute, 1956.

Carroll-Porcznski, C. Z. *Manual of Man-Made Fibers.* New York: Chemical Publishing Co., 1961.

Carroll-Porcznski, C. Z. *Natural Polymer Man-Made Fibers.* New York: Academic Press, 1959.

Carter, Mary E. *Essential Fiber Chemistry.* New York: Marcel Dekker, 1971.

Chapman, C. B. *Fibres.* Plainfield, NJ: Textile Book Service, 1974.

Cook, J. Gordon. *Handbook of Polyolefin Fibres.* London: Merrow Publishing Co., 1967.

Cook, J. Gordon. *Handbook of Textile Fibres,* 2 vols. London: Merrow Publishing Co., 2nd ed., 1985.

Crawford, M. D. C. *The Heritage of Cotton.* New York: Putnam, 1924.

Hamby, Dame S., ed. *The American Cotton Handbook,* 3rd ed., 2 vols. New York: Wiley-Interscience, 1965.

Hearle, J. W. S., and R. H. Peters. *Fiber Structure.* New York: Butterworth and Co., 1963.

Heyn, A. N. J. *Fiber Microscopy.* New York: Interscience Publishers, 1954.

Hochberg, B. *Fibre Facts.* Berkeley, CA: Textile Artist Supplies, 1981.

Identification of Textile Materials, 7th ed. Manchester, England: The Textile Institute, 1975.

Jeffries, R. *Bicomponent Fibres.* Watford, England: Merrow Publishing Co., 1971.

Leggett, W. S. *Story of Linen.* New York: Chemical Publishing Co., 1945.

Leggett, W. F. *Story of Wool.* New York: Chemical Publishing Co., 1947.

Lennox-Kerr, Peter, ed. *Deskbook of World Fibers.* New York: McGraw-Hill, 1981.

McKelvey, John B. *Cotton Modification with Oxiranes.* Watford, England: Merrow Publishing Co., 1971.

Mark, H. F.; S. M. Atlas; and E. Cernia. *Man-Made Fibers,* 3 vols. New York: Interscience Publishers, 1968.

Meredith, R. *Elastromeric Fibres.* Watford, England: Merrow Publishing Co., 1971.

Moncrieff, R. W. *Man-Made Fibers,* 7th ed. Woburn, MA: Butterworth, 1984.

Morton, W. E., and J. W. S. Hearle. *Physical Properties of Textile Fibers.* London: Butterworth & Co., 1975.

Pajgrt, O., et al. *Processing of Polyester Fibers.* New York: Elsevier Science Publishing Co., 1980.

Peters, R. H. *Textile Chemistry,* vol. 1. New York: American Elsevier Publishing Co., 1963.

Peters, R. H. *Textile Chemistry,* vol. 2. New York: American Elsevier Publishing Co., 1967.

Textile Fibers and Their Properties. Greenboro, NC: Burlington Industries, 1972.

U.S. Department of Agriculture, Bureau of Mines. *Asbestos: Materials Survey.* Washington, DC: Government Printing Office, 1959.

Von Bergen, Werner. *Wool Handbook,* vol. 1, 3rd ed. New York: Wiley-Interscience, 1963.

Von Bergen, Werner, *Wool Handbook,* vol. 2, part 2, 3rd ed. New York: Wiley-Interscience, 1969.

Von Bergen, Werner. *Wool Handbook,* vol. 2, part 2, 3rd ed. New York: Wiley-Interscience, 1970.

World Textile Fibers. Cleveland, OH: Predicasts, 1981.

YARNS

Goswami, B. C., J. G. Martindale, and F. L. Scardino. *Textile Yarns: Technology, Structure and Applications.* New York: Wiley, 1977.

Henshaw, D. E. *Self-Twist Yarn.* Watford, England: Merrow Publishing Co., 1971.

Hossack, D. C. *Tape Yarns.* Watford, England: Merrow Publishing Co., 1971.

Lord, P. R. *Spinning in the '70's.* Watford, England: Merrow Publishing Co., 1970.

Selling, H. J. *Twistless Yarns.* Watford, England: Merrow Publishing Co., 1971.

Studies in Modern Yarn Production. Manchester, England: The Textile Institute, 1968.

Wilkinson, G. D., ed. *Draw-Textured Yarn Technology.* Monsanto Textile Co., 1974.

The Yarn Revolution. Manchester, England: The Textile Institute, 1976.

FABRIC CONSTRUCTION

Buresh, Francis M. *Nonwoven Fabrics.* New York: Reinhold, 1962.

Emery, Irene. *The Primary Structures of Fabrics.* Washington, DC: The Textile Museum, 1966.

The Fabric Revolution. New York: State Mutual Book and Periodical Service, 1981.

Gioello, Debbie Ann. *Profiling Fabrics.* New York: Fairchild Publications, 1981.

Gioello, Debbie Ann. *Understanding Fabrics.* New York: Fairchild Publications, 1982.

Greenwood, K. *Weaving: Control of Fabric Structure.* Watford, England: Merrow Publishing Co., 1975.

Krcma, Radko. *Manual of Nonwovens,* 2nd ed. Manchester, England: Textile Trade Press, 1971.

Lancashire, J. B. *Jacquard Design and Knitting.* New York: National Knitted Outerwear Association, 1969.

Lennox-Kerr, Peter, ed. *Needle Felted Fabrics.* Manchester, England: Textile Trade Press, 1972.

Lord, P. R., and M. H. Mohamed. *Weaving: Conversion of Yarn to Fabric,* 2nd ed. Watford, England: Merrow Publishing Co., 1982.

New Ways to Produce Textiles. Manchester, England: The Textile Institute, 1972.

Reichman, Charles. *Double Knit Fabric Manual.* New York: National Knitted Outerwear Association, 1961.

Reichman, Charles. *Knitted Stretch Technology.* New

York: National Knitted Outerwear Association, 1965.

Reichman, Charles, ed. *Handbook of Knitted Yarns and Knitwear Dyeing Processes.* New York: National Knitted Outerwear Association, 1962.

Reichman, Charles, ed. *Knitted Fabric Technology.* New York: National Knitted Outerwear Association, 1974.

Reichman, Charles, ed. *Knitting Dictionary.* New York: National Knitted Outerwear Association, 1966.

Reichman, Charles, ed. *Principles of Knitting Outerwear Fabrics and Garments.* New York: National Knitted Outerwear Association, 1961.

Reichman, Charles, J. B. Lancashire, and K. D. Darlington. *Knitted Fabric Primer.* New York: National Knitted Outerwear Association, 1967.

Reisfeld, A.; C. Rotenstein; D. F. Paling; and J. B. Lancashire. *Fundamentals of Raschel Knitting.* New York: National Knitted Outerwear Association, 1958.

Robinson, A. T. C., and R. Marks. *Woven Cloth Construction.* Manchester, England: The Textile Institute, 1973.

Smirfitt, J. A. *An Introduction to Weft Knitting.* Watford, England: Merrow Publishing Co., 1975.

Studies in Modern Fabrics. Manchester, England: The Textile Institute, 1970.

Thomas, D. G. B. *An Introduction to Warp Knitting.* Watford, England: Merrow Publishing Co., 1971.

Ward, D. T. *Tufting: An Introduction.* London: Textile Business Press, 1969.

Wheatley, B. *Raschel Lace Production.* New York: National Knitted Outerwear Association, 1972.

FINISHING AND COLORING

Adrosko, Rita J. *Natural Dyes and Home Dyeing.* New York: Dover Publications, 1971.

Backer, S.; G. C. Tesoro; T. Y. Toong; and N. A. Moussa. *Textile Fabric Flammability.* Cambridge, MA: MIT Press, 1976.

Beech, W. F. *Fibre Reactive Dyes.* New York: SAF International, 1970.

Bhatnagar, Vijoy Mohan. *Flammability of Apparel,* vol. 7, ''Progress in Fire Retardancy'' Series. Westport, CT: Technomic, 1975.

Billmeyer, Fred W. *Textbook of Polymer Science,* 2nd ed. New York: Wiley-Interscience, 1971.

Bird, C. L., and W. S. Boston, eds. *The Theory of Coloration of Textiles.* West Yorkshire, England: Dyers Company Publications Trust, 1975.

Brunello, Franco. *The Art of Dyeing in the History of Mankind,* trans. Bernard Hickey. Vicenza: Neri Pozza Editore, 1973.

Clarke, W. *An Introduction to Textile Printing,* 4th ed. New York: Wiley, 1974.

Colour Index, 3rd ed., vols. 1–6. Bradford, Yorkshire, England: Society of Dyers and Colourists and Research, and Triangle Park, NC: The American Association of Textile Chemists and Colorists, 1971 (vols. 1–4) and 1975 (vols. 5–6).

Dempsey, E. P., and C. E. Vellins. *Heat Transfer Printing.* Sale, Cheshire, England: Interprint, 1975.

Gentille, Terry A. *Printed Textiles.* Englewood Cliffs, NJ: Prentice-Hall, 1982.

Giles, Charles Hugh. *A Laboratory Course in Dyeing,* 3rd ed. Bradford, Yorkshire, England: The Society of Dyers and Colourists, 1974.

Hall, A. J. *Textile Finishing,* 3rd ed. New York: Chemical Publishing Co., 1966.

Harper, R. J. *Durable Press Cotton Goods.* Watford, England: Merrow Publishing Co., 1971.

Hearle, J. W. S., and L. W. C. Miles. *The Setting of Fibres and Fabrics.* Watford, England: Merrow Publishing Co., 1971.

LeBlanc, R. Bruce, ed. *Proceedings of the Symposiums on Textile Flammability, 1973–1979.* East Greenwich, RI: LeBlanc Research Corp., 1973–1979 (annual).

Lee, R. W. *Printing on Textiles by Direct and Transfer Techniques.* Park Ridge, NJ: Noyes Data Corp., 1981.

Lew, Jennifer F., and Richard M. Proctor. *Surface Design for Fabrics.* Seattle: University of Washington Press, 1983.

Lyons, John W. *The Chemistry and Uses of Fire Retardants.* New York: Wiley-Interscience, 1970.

McPhee, J. R. *The Mothproofing of Wool.* Watford, England: Merrow Publishing Co., 1971.

Manly, Robert H. *Durable Press Treatments of Fabrics.* Park Ridge, NJ: Noyes Data Corp., 1976.

Mark, H. F.; Norman G. Wooding; and Sheldon M. Atlas, eds. *Chemical Aftertreatment of Textiles.* New York: Wiley-Interscience, 1971.

Markinson. *Shrinkproofing of Wool.* New York: Marcel Dekker, 1979.

Marsh, J. T. *Textile Finishing,* 2nd ed. Metuchen, NJ: Textile Book Service, 1966.

Miles, L. W. C. *Textile Printing.* New York: State Mutual Book and Periodical Service, 1983.

Moilliet, J. L., ed. *Waterproofing and Water Repellency.* Amsterdam: Elsevier Publishing Co., 1963.

Montgomery, Florence M. *Printed Textiles.* New York: Viking Press, 1970.

Peters, R. H. *Textile Chemistry,* vol. 3, *The Physical Chemistry of Dyeing.* New York: American Elsevier Publishing Co., 1975.

Pettit, Florence. *America's Printed and Painted Fabrics.* New York: Hastings House, 1970.

Reeves, Wilson A., and George L. Drake, Jr. *Flame Resistant Cotton.* Watford, England: Merrow Publishing Co., 1971.

Reichman, Charles, ed. *Transfer Printing Manual.*

New York: National Knitted Outerwear Association, 1976.

Sadano, Charles S. *Water and Soil Repellents for Fabrics.* Park Ridge, NJ: Noyes Data Corp., 1979.

Storey, Joyce. *Textile Printing.* New York: Van Nostrand Reinhold, 1974.

Szilard, Jules A. *Bleaching Agents and Techniques.* Park Ridge, NJ: Noyes Data Corp., 1973.

Trotman, E. R. *Dyeing and Chemical Technology of Textile Fibres,* 5th ed. London: Griffin & Co., 1976.

Venkataramen, K., ed. *Analytical Chemistry of Synthetic Dyes.* New York: Wiley, 1977.

Venkataramen, K., ed. *Chemistry of Synthetic Dyes,* 8 vols. New York: Academic Press, 1952 (vols. 1–2), 1970–1974 (vols. 3–7), 1978 (vol. 8).

Williams, Alec. *Flame Resistant Fabrics.* Park Ridge, NJ: Noyes Data Corp., 1974.

Williamson, R. *Fluorescent Brighteners.* New York: Elsevier Science Publishing Co., 1980.

PERFORMANCE AND TESTING

AATCC 1984 Technical Manual. Research Triangle Park, NC: American Association of Textile Chemists and Colorists, 1984.

ASTM. *Annual Book of ASTM Standards* (published annually), vols. 07-01 and 07-02. Philadelphia: American Society for Testing and Materials, 1983.

ASTM. *Performance Standards for Textile Fabrics.* Philadelphia: American Society for Testing and Materials, 1983.

Booth, J. E. *Principles of Textile Testing,* 3rd ed. New York: Butterworth, 1969.

Earland, C., and D. J. Raven. *Experiments in Textile and Fibre Chemistry.* London: Butterworth & Co., 1971.

Fourt, Lyman, and Norman R. S. Hollies. *Clothing Comfort and Function.* New York: Marcel Dekker, 1970.

Garner, W. *Textile Laboratory Manual,* 3rd ed., 6 vols. London: National Trade Press, 1967.

Hall, David M. *Chemical Testing of Textiles.* Auburn, AL: Auburn University, 1975.

Hollies, Norman R. S., and Ralph F. Goldman. *Clothing Comfort.* Ann Arbor, MI: Ann Arbor Science Publishers, 1977.

Lyle, Dorothy Siegart. *Performance of Textiles.* New York: Wiley, 1977.

Perenich, Theresa, and Barbara Reagan. *Textile Laboratory Manual.* Athens, GA: Prince Scientific Press, 1980.

Renbourn, E. T. *Physiology and Hygiene of Materials and Clothing.* Watford, England: Merrow Publishing Co., 1971.

Weaver, J. W., ed. *Analytic Methods for a Textile Laboratory,* 2nd ed. Research Triangle Park, NC: American Association of Textile Chemists and Colorists, 1984.

CARE OF TEXTILES

Alexander, Patsy R. *Textile Product Selection, Use and Care.* Boston: Houghton Mifflin, 1977.

Gioello, Debbie Ann. *Understanding Fabrics.* New York: Fairchild Publications, 1982.

Lyle, Dorothy Siegart. *Performance of Textiles.* New York: Wiley, 1977.

Magtag Company. *Encyclopedia of Home Laundering.* New York: Popular Library, 1965.

Mellan, Ibert, and Eleanor Mellan. *Removing Spots and Stains.* New York: Chemical Publishing Co., 1959.

Tortora, Phyllis G. *Understanding Textiles,* 2nd ed. New York: Macmillan, 1982.

Your Guide to Brighter Wash Days. Chicago: Sears Roebuck & Co., n.d.

RECOMMENDED PERIODICALS

American Dyestuff Reporter
American Fabrics and Fashions
America's Textile Reporter
Journal of the Society of Dyers and Colourists
Journal of the Textile Institute
Knitting Times
Modern Textile Business
Textile Chemist and Colorist
Textile Industries
Textile Month
Textile Organon
Textile Research Journal
Textile World
Textiles

Glossary of Textile Terms

absorption The attraction and retention of gases or liquids within the pores of a fiber; also, the retention of moisture between fibers within yarns, and between fibers or yarns within fabrics.

acetate A manufactured fiber in which the fiber-forming substance is cellulose acetate. Where not less than 92 percent of the hydroxyl groups are acetylated, the term *triacetate** may be used as a generic description of the fiber.

acrylic A manufactured fiber in which the fiber-forming substance is any long-chain synthetic *polymer* composed of at least 85 percent by weight of acrylonitrile units

$$\left(\begin{array}{c} -CH_2- \; C - \\ | \\ CN \end{array} \right)$$

addition polymerization Formation of large polymolecules by means of rearrangement of the chemical bonds. The formula for the repeating unit is identical to that of the *monomer* or monomers used.

adsorption The retention of gases, liquids, or solids on the surface areas of fibers, yarns, or fabrics.

alginate A fiber formed from a metallic salt of alginic acid, which is a natural component of seaweed. Alginate fibers are soluble in water.

alpaca Long, fine fibers (hair) from the alpaca, an animal native to South America.

angora Fine, lightweight fiber (hair) from the Angora rabbit. See also *mohair.*

anidex A manufactured fiber in which the fiber-forming substance is any long-chain synthetic *polymer* composed of at least 50 percent by weight of one or more esters of a monohydric alcohol and acrylic acid ($CH_2 = CH—COOH$).

*Italics within a definition denotes a cross-reference within the Glossary.

animal fibers Any fiber taken from animal life, such as *wool, alpaca, mohair, silk.*

antique satin A *satin-weave* fabric made to resemble silk satin of an earlier century. It is used for home furnishing fabrics.

aramid A manufactured fiber in which the fiber-forming substance is a long-chain synthetic *polyamide* in which at least 85 percent of the amide linkages

$$\left(\begin{array}{c} -C- \; NH- \\ || \\ O \end{array} \right)$$

are attached directly to two aromatic rings.

art linen A heavy *plain-weave* fabric used for tablecloths and as the basis for many types of embroidered household items.

asbestos A mineral fiber obtained from rock formations. The fiber is completely nonflammable.

azlon A manufactured fiber in which the fiber-forming substance is composed of any regenerated naturally occurring proteins.

balanced yarns Yarns in which the twist is such that the yarn will hang in a loop without kinking, doubling, or twisting upon itself.

barathea A closely woven *dobby-weave* fabric with a characteristic pebbly surface. It is generally made from silk or rayon, often combined with cotton or worsted. The fabric is used for dresses, neckties, and lightweight suits.

batiste A fabric named for Jean Baptiste, a French linen weaver. (1) In cotton, a sheer, fine *muslin,* woven of combed yarns and given a mercerized finish. It is used for blouses, summer shirts, dresses, lingerie, infants' dresses, bonnets, and handkerchiefs. (2) A rayon, polyester, or cotton-blend fabric with the same characteristics. (3) A smooth, fine wool fabric that is lighter than *challis,* very similar to fine nun's veiling. It is used for dresses and negligees. (4) A sheer silk fabric, either plain or figured, very similar to silk mull. It is often called batiste de soie and is made into summer dresses.

Bedford cord Lengthwise ribbed durable cloth for outergarments or sport clothes. The corded effect is secured by having two successive *warp* yarns woven in plain-weave order. Heavier cords are created with wadding—a heavy, bulky yarn with very little twist—covered by *filling* yarns.

beetling A finish primarily applied to linen whereby the cloth is beaten with large wooden blocks in order to flatten the yarns.

bengaline A ribbed fabric similar to *faille*, but heavier, with a coarser rib in the *filling* direction. It may be silk, wool, acetate, or rayon *warp*, with wool or cotton *filling*. The fabric was first made in Bengal, India. It is used for dresses, coats, trimmings, and draperies.

bicomponent fibers See *composite fibers*.

biconstituent fibers See *composite fibers*.

bilateral fibers A filament composed of two generic fiber types or two variants of the same generic fiber extruded simultaneously in a side-by-side relationship.

blend A yarn obtained when two or more types of *staple fibers* are joined in the textile operation for producing spun yarns. See *combination fabrics*.

blister knit A *knit* fabric with an irregular raised surface that gives the impression of "blisters." The blisters are formed during knitting special yarn on selected cylinder needles only to form the surface-texture fabric. A base yarn is knitted on dial and cylinder needles to form the base fabric.

bouclé A fabric woven with bouclé yarns, which have a looped appearance on the surface. In some bouclés only one side of the fabric is nubby; in others, both are rough. Sometimes the bouclé yarn is used as a *warp* rather than a *filling*. Bouclé yarn is very popular in the knitting trade; there are many varieties and weights.

braid A narrow textile structure formed by plaiting several strands of yarn. Braid is usually used in trimming. Braids may also be made by plaiting several strips of fabric.

breaking load The minimum force required to rupture a fiber, expressed in grams or pounds.

brins The two adjacent silk *filament fibers* extruded by the silkworm.

broadcloth A term used to describe several dissimilar fabrics made with different fibers, weaves, and finishes. (1) Originally, a silk shirting fabric so named because it was woven in widths ex-
ceeding the usual 29 inches (72 cm). (2) A tightly woven, high-count cotton cloth with a fine crosswise rib. Fine broadcloths are woven of *combed* yarns, usually with high thread counts, such as 136 × 60 or 144 × 76. They are usually mercerized, Sanforized, and given a soft, lustrous finish. (3) A closely woven wool cloth with a smooth nap, velvety feel, and lustrous appearance. Wool broadcloth can be made with a two-up-and-two-down *twill weave* or *plain weave*. In setting up a loom to make the fabric, the loom is threaded very wide to allow for great shrinkage during the fulling process. The fabric takes its name from this wide threading. In higher qualities the cloth is fine enough for garments that are to be closely molded to the figure or draped. Its high-luster finish makes it an elegant cloth. Wool broadcloth is 10 to 16 ounces per yard (312 to 499 grams per meter) and is now being made in chiffon weights. (4) A fabric made from silk or man-made *filament fiber* yarns, woven in a plain weave with a fine crosswise rib obtained by using a heavier *filling* than *warp* yarn.

brocade Rich Jacquard-woven fabric with an all-over interwoven design of raised figures or flowers. The name is derived from the French word meaning "to ornament." The brocade pattern is emphasized with contrasting surfaces or colors and often has gold or silver threads running through it. The background may be either satin or twill weave. It is used for dresses, draperies, and uphostery.

brocatelle Supposedly an imitation of Italian tooled leather, in which the background is pressed and the figures are embossed. Both the background and the figures are tightly woven, generally with a *warp* effect in the figure and a *filling* effect in the background. Brocatelle is employed mainly in upholstery and draperies.

buckram A low-count fabric heavily sized to give a stiff and boardy character. It is used for linings where extreme firmness is required, in bookbinding, and in millinery.

bunting A *plain-weave*, loosely woven fabric that is soft, flimsy, and similar to *cheesecloth*. Available in white or bright colors, it is used primarily for flags, draped pennants, and temporary decorations.

burlap A coarse, heavy, *plain-weave* fabric made of *jute*. It is frequently used for bagging, as it tends to be highly resistant to slipping; thus bags can be stacked easily.

cambric A closely woven white cotton fabric finished with a slight gloss on one side.

canton flannel A heavy, warm cotton material with a twilled surface and a long soft nap on the back produced by napping the heavy soft-twist yarn. It is named for Canton, China, where it was first made. The fabric is strong and absorbent; it is used for interlinings and sleeping garments.

carbon fibers Fibers with high strength made by heating precursor filaments, usually *rayon* or *acrylic,* to appropriate temperatures that convert the substance to primarily pure carbon.

card sliver A ropelike strand of fibers about ¾ inch to 1 inch (1.9 to 2.5 cm) in diameter; the form in which fibers emerge from the *carding* machine.

carding A process by which staple fibers are sorted, separated, and partially aligned.

casement cloth A general term for lightweight, sheer fabrics used for curtains and as a backing for some special decorative drapery fabrics.

cashmere The soft fiber (hair) from the cashmere goat.

cavalry twill A sturdy *twill-weave* fabric with a pronounced diagonal cord. It is used for sportswear, uniforms, and riding habits.

cellulose fibers Fibers composed of cellulose either from natural sources or regenerated by man-made operations. Examples include *cotton,* flax, *rayon, jute.*

ceramic fibers Fibers made from such substances as aluminum silicate. These strong fibers are frequently used in reinforcing plastic materials.

challis or challie One of the softest fabrics made, named from the Anglo-Indian term *shalee,* meaning soft. It is a fine, lightweight, *plain-weave* fabric, usually made of *worsted* yarns. Challis was formerly manufactured with a small flower design, but now it is made in darker tones of all-over prints and solid colors, in the finest quality fabrics.

chambray (1) A plain-woven fabric with an almost square count (80 × 76), a colored *warp* and, usually, a white *filling,* which gives a mottled, colored surface. It is used for shirts, children's clothing, and dresses. The fabric is named for Cambrai, France, where it was first made for sunbonnets. (2) A similar but heavier carded-yarn fabric used for work clothes and children's play clothes.

chameleon A fabric with a variable multicolor effect achieved by using *warp yarns* of one color and two *filling yarns* of two different colors in each *shed.*

cheesecloth A very loosely woven *plain-weave* cotton fabric. The yard width is called tobacco cloth. It is used for curtains, costumes, and cleaning cloths.

chiffon A term used to describe many light, gossamer sheer, *plain-weave* fabrics. Chiffon can be made of silk, wool, or man-made fibers. It is an open weave with tightly twisted yarns.

china silk A lightweight, soft, *plain-weave* silk fabric used for lingerie, dress linings, and soft suit linings.

chino A type of army twill made of combed, two-ply, *mercerized* yarns in a vat-dyed khaki color. It is not available in a variety of colors.

chintz A highly lustrous *plain-weave* cotton fabric with a bright, glazed surface, generally made by finishing a print cloth construction.

cloque fabric A fabric with a surface that is characterized by an irregular raised blister effect.

coated fabric A fabric to which a surface layer such as lacquer, plastic, resin, rubber, or varnish has been firmly attached.

cohesiveness The ability of fibers to adhere to one another in yarn-manufacturing processes.

color abrasion Color abrasion, frequently called frosting, refers to color change that occurs in localized areas of a garment or product. It is due to differential wear of different fibers in the fabric, such as differences due to performance of cotton and polyester which have been given permanent-press finishes.

combination fabrics Fabrics that contain two or more different types of fibers. However, these differ from *blends* in that any one single yarn in a combination fabric is composed of only one fiber type.

combination yarn A plied yarn in which each single component is composed of one fiber type but at least two different fiber types occur in the final plied yarn.

combing A process by which staple fibers are sorted and straightened; a more refined treatment than *carding.*

composite fibers Fibers composed of two or more *polymer* types or variants of one type of polymer in a sheath-core or a side-by-side configuration.

condensation polymerization A *polymerizing* process in which the repeating unit in the *poly-*

mer has fewer atoms than in the *monomer* or monomers. Generally, the separation of a simple substance such as water or ethylene glycol is the result of this type of reaction.

copolymer A *polymer* composed of two or more different *monomers.*

corduroy A ribbed, high-luster, cut-pile fabric with extra filling threads that form lengthwise ribs or *wales.* The thread count varies from 46 $\times$ 116 to 70 $\times$ 250.

core yarn A yarn in which the base or foundation yarn is completely wrapped by a second yarn. May be called core-spun.

cotton A natural fiber obtained from the cotton plant.

cotton linters Cotton fibers that are too short for yarn or fabric manufacturing.

course A series of successive loops lying crosswise of a knitted fabric.

covert Generally called covert cloth, a closely woven *warp*-face *twill.* Its characteristic flecked appearance is produced by using a two-ply yarn so that one dark thread alternates with a light thread. Covert is generally made of wool or cotton, but man-made fibers and *blends* can also be used.

crepe A lightweight fabric of silk, rayon, cotton, wool, man-made, or blended fibers, characterized by a crinkled surface that is produced by hard-twist yarns, chemical treatment, weave, or embossing.

crepe-back satin or satin-back crepe A fabric made so that it can be reversible with one face a satin finish and the other a crepe effect. The filling yarns are of a crepe twist; and there are two or three times more ends per inch than there are picks. The satin side of the fabric is smooth and lustrous, the crepe side is dull and crinkly.

cretonne A plain-weave fabric similar to unglazed *chintz,* usually printed with large designs.

crimp The waviness of a fiber, usually visible only under magnification.

crystallinity The degree to which fiber molecules are parallel to each other, though not necessarily to the longitudinal fiber axis.

cuprammonium rayon *Rayon* fibers formed by precipitating cellulose dissolved in a solution of copper oxide and ammonia.

damask A firm-textured fabric with raised patterns, similar to *brocade,* but lighter and reversible. Table damasks are *Jacquard*-woven in lustrous designs.

degree of polymerization The number of *monomer* units occurring in an average polymeric unit.

denier A unit of yarn number equal to the weight in grams of 9000 meters of the yarn. See also *tex.*

denim A twilled fabric made of hard-twist yarns, with the *warp yarns* dyed blue and the *filling yarns* undyed. Sports denim is softer and lighter in weight. It is now available in many colors and in plaids and stripes.

density Mass per unit volume, usually expressed as grams per cubic centimeter. See also *specific gravity.*

dimensional stability The degree to which a fiber, yarn, or fabric retains its shape and size after having been subjected to wear and maintenance.

dimity Literally, double thread; a fine checked or corded cotton sheer made by bunching and weaving two or more threads together.

dobby A term applied to machine or fabric. (1) A dobby control on a loom governs the operation of each harness to permit the weaving of small geometric-type designs. (2) A dobby fabric is one that has been constructed on a loom with the dobby attachment; it is characterized by small geometric-type designs.

dotted swiss A sheer, crisp cotton fabric with either clipped spot or swivel dots.

double-knit fabric A circular-*knit* fabric produced by using a knitting machine equipped with two sets of needles: dial and cylinder needles. The fabric is double in thickness.

double-weave fabric A fabric woven with two complete sets of *warp* and *filling* yarns. Only one set is visible on the face at any one point.

doupion Silk yarns made from two cocoons that have been formed in an interlocked manner. The yarn is uneven, irregular, and larger than regular *filaments.* It is used in making *shantung* and doupioni.

drawing (1) The process by which *card slivers* of staple fibers are pulled out or extended after *carding* or *combing.* (2) The stretching, either hot or cold, of continuous filament yarns to align and arrange the molecular structure within the filament.

drill A strong cotton material similar to *denim,* which has a diagonal 2 $\times$ 1 *twill* running up to the left *selvage.*

duck The term duck covers a wide range of fabrics. These are among the most durable fabrics used in consumer goods. Duck is a closely woven, heavy fabric. The most important fabrics in this group are known by such terms as army duck, flat duck, ounce duck, and number duck. Number and army ducks are always of plain weave with medium- or heavy-ply yarns; army ducks are the lighter of the two. Flat and ounce ducks are similar; they have single warp yarns woven in pairs and single or ply filling yarns.

duvetyn A very high-quality cloth that resembles a compact *velvet*. It has a velvety *hand* resulting from the short nap that covers its surface completely, concealing its *twill weave*. It is used for suits and coats.

elastic recovery The ability of a fiber, yarn, or fabric to return to its original length after the tension that produced *elongation* has been released.

elastique A firm worsted fabric with a distinct double twill line on a rather steep twill; the double line creates a series of narrow and wide wales on the diagonal.

elongation The amount of stretch or extension that a fiber, yarn, or fabric will accept.

end A term used in the textile industry to identify individual *warp yarns*.

faille A soft, slightly glossy silk, rayon, or cotton fabric in a rib weave, with a light, flat, crossgrain rib or cord made by using heavier yarns in the *filling* than in the *warp*.

fasciated yarn A yarn consisting of a core made up of discontinuous fibers with little or no twist and fibers with twist wrapped around the core.

felt A nonwoven fabric in which the fibers develop a tight bond and will not ravel. Felt is used for coats, hats, and many industrial purposes.

fiber A unit, either natural or man-made, which forms the basic element or "building block" of fabrics and other textile structures. Most fibers are characterized by having a length at least 100 times their diameter.

fiber morphology The form and structure of a fiber, including its biological structure, shape, cross section, and microscopic appearance.

fibrils Bundles of fiber cells.

filament fibers Long, continuous fibers that can be measured in meters or yards or, in the case of man-made fibers, in kilometers or miles.

filling yarns Yarns that run perpendicular to the longer dimension or *selvage* of a fabric; also called picks.

finish (1) A substance or combination of substances added to a *textile* to improve its properties. (2) A physical or chemical process applied to textile materials to alter their properties.

flannel A catch-all designation for a great many otherwise unnamed fabrics in the woolen industry. Flannel is woven in various weights of *worsted, wool,* or a mixture of both. It can even be made of man-made fibers. The surface is slightly napped in finish. A wide range of weights is available: an 11-ounce flannel is made for suits, and there are tissue-weight flannels for dresses.

flannelette A soft *plain-* or *twill-weave* cotton fabric lightly napped on one side. The fabric can be dyed solid colors or printed. It is popular for lounging and sleeping garments.

flat duck See *duck.*

flat-knit fabric (1) A fabric constructed on a flatbed knitting machine instead of a circular knitting unit. In the textile trade the term "flat knit" is used to refer only to weft knits made on a flat-bed machine. (2) In the underwear trade the term "flat knit" is used to indicate a fabric with a flat surface as opposed to a ribbed surface.

fleece Wool sheared from a living lamb.

flexibility The property of bending without breaking.

float (1) In woven fabrics, a portion of a *warp* or *filling* yarn that extends over two or more adjacent filling picks or warp ends for the purpose of creating design. (2) In knitted fabrics, a portion of yarn that extends for some length on the fabric surface without being knitted into the structure.

formed fabric An assembly of textile fibers held together by such techniques as the mechanical interlocking of fibers in a web, by fusing of thermoplastic fiber, or by bonding fibers with added adhesive substances.

foulard A ligweight silk, rayon, cotton, or wool fabric characterized by its *twill weave*. Foulard has a high luster on the face and is dull on the reverse side. It is usually printed, the patterns ranging from simple polka dots to elaborate designs. It is also made in plain or solid colors. Foulard has a characteristic *hand* that can be described as light, firm, and supple.

frosting See *color abrasion.*

gabardine A hard-finished, clear-surfaced, *twill-weave* fabric made of either natural or synthetic fibers. The diagonal lines are fine, close, and steep and are more pronounced than in *serge*. The lines cannot be seen on the wrong side of the fabric.

gauze A *plain-weave* fabric with widely spaced yarns, used for such things as bandages. Some weights of gauze can be stiffened for curtains or other decorative or apparel purposes.

gingham A light- to medium-weight *plain-weave* cotton fabric. It is usually yarn-dyed and woven to create stripes, checks, or plaids. The fabric is *mercerized* to produce a soft, lustrous appearance; it is sized and calendered to a firm and lustrous finish. Gingham is used for dresses, shirts, robes, curtains, draperies, and bedspreads. The thread count varies from about 48 × 44 to 106 × 94.

glass A manufactured fiber in which the fiber-forming substance is glass.

greige The state of a fabric before a finish has been applied.

grenadine A tightly twisted *ply yarn* composed of two or three *singles*.

grosgrain A closely woven firm, corded fabric often made with a cotton filling. The cords are heavier than in *poplin,* rounder than in *faille.*

habutai A soft, lightweight silk dress fabric originally woven in the gum on handlooms in Japan. It is sometimes confused with Chinese silk, which is technically lighter in weight.

hackling A *combing* process that separates short bast fibers from long fibers.

hand The "feel" of a fabric; the qualities that can be ascertained by touching it.

handkerchief linen A very fine, sheer, linen fabric used mainly for handkerchiefs and lightweight apparel. Plain weave.

hemp A coarse, durable bast fiber. Hemp is used primarily for industrial and commercial textiles.

herringbone A fabric in which the pattern of weave resembles the skeletal structure of the herring. It is made with a broken *twill weave* that produces a balanced zigzag effect; it is used for sportswear, suits, and coats.

homespun A coarse *plain-weave* fabric, loosely woven with irregular, tightly twisted, and unevenly spun yarns. It has a hand-woven appearance; it is used for coats, suits, sportswear, draperies, and slipcovers.

homopolymer A *polymer* composed of one substance or one type of molecule.

honan Originally, a fabric of the best Chinese silk, sometimes woven with blue edges. It is now made to resemble a heavy *pongee,* with slub yarns in both *warp* and *filling.* Honan is manufactured from silk or from man-made fibers. It is used for women's dresses.

hopsacking An open-basket-weave *ply-yarn* fabric of cotton, linen, or rayon. The weave is similar to the sacking used to gather hops, hence the name. It is used for dresses, jackets, skirts, and blouses.

huck or huckaback A toweling fabric with a honeycombed surface made by using heavy *filling yarns* in a *dobby* weave. It has excellent absorbent qualities. Huck is made in linen, cotton, or a mixture of the two. In a mixture it is called a "union" fabric.

hydrophilic Water loving; having a high degree of moisture absorption or attraction.

hydrophobic Water-repelling; having a low degree of moisture absorption or attraction.

intimate blend Combining two or more different fiber types into a uniform mixture before the single yarn is spun.

Jacquard The original Jacquard attachment was developed and attached to a loom in order to provide for individual control of each warp end. This permitted the construction of highly complex and decorative woven fabrics. In addition to this use of the term today, the term is also used to identify complex designs in knitted fabrics.

jean A sturdy cotton fabric, softer and finer than *drill,* made in solid colors or stripes. It is used for sport blouses, work shirts, women's slacks, and children's play clothes.

jersey Elastic knitted fabric in a stockinette stitch. It was first made on the Island of Jersey off the English coast and used for fishermen's clothing. Jersey can be made from wool, cotton, rayon, nylon, other man-made fibers, or a combination of any of these. The term is frequently applied to *tricot*-knitted fabrics used for dresses.

jute A bast fiber widely used for fabrics made for such end uses as sacking, burlap, twine, and as backing fabric for tufted carpets.

kapok A natural cellulose fiber from seed pods. Kapok is used for life jackets, special stuffing for pillows, and in some mattresses. It is not spun into yarn form.

kersey A thick, heavy, pure wool and cotton *twill weave* similar to *melton.* It is well fulled, with a nap and a close-sheared surface. Kersey is used for uniforms and overcoats.

knit fabric   A fabric structure made by interlooping yarns. Knit fabrics may be warp or weft (filling) knitted.

lace   An open-work cloth with a design formed by a network of threads made by hand or on special lace machinery, with bobbins, needles, or hooks.

lamb's wool   Wool clipped from sheep less than eight months old.

lamé   A fabric woven with metal threads, usually gold or silver or aluminum, that form either the background or the pattern of the fabric.

lastrile   See *spandex*.

lawn   A lightweight, sheer, fine cotton or linen fabric, which can be given a soft or crisp finish. It is sized and calendered to produce a soft, lustrous appearance. Lawn is used for dresses, blouses, curtains, lingerie, and as a base for embroidered items.

leno weave   A structure in which pairs of *warp yarns* are twisted around each other between *filling yarns*. This technique gives firmness and durability to open-weave fabrics and inhibits yarn slippage.

linear polymer   A *polymer* formed by end-to-end linking of molecular units. The resulting polymer is very long and narrow. It is typical of fibrous forms.

linen   Yarns and fabrics made from fibers from the flax plant.

linen toweling   See *toweling*.

loft   The springiness or fluffiness of a fiber.

longcloth   A fine, soft cotton cloth woven of softly twisted yarns. It is similar to *nainsook* but slightly heavier, with a duller surface. Longcloth is so called because it was one of the first fabrics to be woven in long rolls. It is also a synonym for *muslin* sheeting of good quality. The fabric is used for underwear and linings.

loom   The machine used in making woven fabrics.

luster   The gloss, sheen, or shine of a fiber, yarn, or fabric.

macromolecule   A large molecule formed by hooking together many small molecular units. The term can be used synonymously with "polymolecule" or *polymer*.

madras   (1) A finely woven, soft, plain- or Jacquard-weave fabric with a stripe in the lengthwise direction and *Jacquard* or *dobby* patterns woven in the background. Some madras is made with woven checks and cords. It can be used for blouses, dresses, and shirts. (2) A fabric hand-woven in India from cotton yarns dyed with native vegetable colorings. The designs are usually rather large, bold plaids that soften in color as the dyes fade and bleed.

man-made fibers   Those fibers produced through chemical reactions controlled by people, as opposed to those fibers occurring naturally, such as cotton, wool, and silk.

marquisette   A light, strong, sheer, open-textured curtain fabric, often with dots woven into the surface. The thread count varies from 48×22 to 60×40.

matelassé   A soft double or compound fabric with a quilted appearance. The heavier type is used in draperies and upholstery, while crepe matelassé is popular in dresses, semiformal and formal suits and wraps, and trimmings.

melton   A thick, heavily felted or fulled wool fabric in a *twill* or *satin* weave, with a smooth, lustrous, napped surface. In less expensive meltons the *warp yarn* may be cotton instead of wool.

mercerization   A treatment applied to cotton yarn and/or fabric to improve the luster and increase the affinity of the fiber for dyes.

mesh fabrics   A general term for fabrics having large open areas between yarns. Mesh fabrics may be made by various techniques such as weaving, knitting, knotting, and lacemaking.

metallic fiber   A manufactured fiber composed of metal, plastic-coated metal, metal-coated plastic, or a core completely covered by metal.

micronaire fineness   The weight in micrograms of 1 inch (2.54 cm) of fiber.

mineral fibers   Inorganic fibers obtained from such sources as rock, ore, and glass.

modacrylic   A manufactured fiber in which the fiber-forming substance is any long-chain synthetic polymer composed of less than 85 percent but at least 35 percent by weight of acrylonitrile units.

mohair   Long, fine fiber (hair) from the Angora goat. See also *angora*.

moiré   Fabric with a wavy or watered effect.

moisture regain   The moisture in a material determined under prescribed conditions and expressed as a percentage of the weight of the moisture-free specimen.

molecular orientation   The degree to which fiber molecules are parallel to each other and to the longitudinal axis of the fiber.

moleskin A heavy sateen-weave fabric made on either a 5- or 8-shaft construction; uses heavy, soft filling yarns in order to provide a napped surface following finishing.

monk's cloth A heavy, loosely woven basket-weave fabric in solid colors or with stripes or plaids woven into the fabric. It is used chiefly for draperies and slipcovers.

monofilament yarn Yarn composed of only one fiber *filament.*

monomer A single unit or molecule from which *polymers* are formed.

mosquito netting A sheer fabric made in either gauze or leno weaves. Formerly made of cotton, today may be found of cotton or nylon fibers. Designed for use as a covering to prevent the entrance of mosquitos to the area covered.

mousseline de soie Literally, "muslin of silk"; silk organdy, a *plain-weave* silk chiffon-weight fabric with a slight stiffness.

multicomponent fabric A fabric in which at least two layers of material are sealed together by an adhesive or other processes.

multifilament yarn Yarn composed of several fiber *filaments.*

multilobal A fiber with a modified cross section exhibiting several lobes.

muslin A large group of *plain-weave* cotton fabrics ranging from lightweight to heavyweight. The sizing may also be light or heavy. Muslin can be solid colored or printed. It is used for dresses, shirts, sheets, and other domestic items.

nainsook A fine, soft cotton fabric in a *plain weave.* Better grades have a polished finish on one side. When it is highly polished, nainsook may be sold as polished cotton. In low-priced white goods *cambric, longcloth,* and nainsook are often identical before converting; the finishing process gives them their characteristic texture, but even so it is often difficult to distinguish one from the other. Nainsook is heavier and coarser than *lawn.* It is usually found in white, pastel colors, and prints and is used chiefly for infants' wear, lingerie, and blouses.

narrow fabric Any nonelastic woven fabric that is less than 12 inches (30.5 cm) in the *filling* direction (width). Narrow fabrics have a *selvage* on each side. Ribbon and seam binding are not included in narrow fabrics.

natural fibers Fibers obtained in usable form directly from animal, vegetable, or mineral origin.

net An open-structure fabric in which yarns are knotted to provide shape, form, and design.

ninon A smooth, transparent, closely woven *voile,* with the *warp yarns* grouped in pairs. It is available in plain or novelty weaves. Man-made fibers are generally used for glass curtains and dress fabrics.

nonthermoplastic Not capable of being softened by heat.

novelty yarns Yarns with such surface characteristics as uneven diameter, varied color, or other irregularities that produce special design effects.

novoloid A manufactured fiber containing at least 85 percent by weight of a cross-linked novolac.

nylon A manufactured fiber in which the fiber-forming substance is a long-chain synthetic polyamide in which less than 85 percent of the amide

$$\left(\begin{array}{c} -C-NH- \\ \| \\ O \end{array} \right)$$

linkages are attached directly to two aromatic rings.

nytril A manufactured fiber containing at least 85 percent of a long-chain polymer of vinylidene dinitrile ($-CH_2-C(CN)_2-$) where the vinylidene dinitrile content is no less than every other unit in the polymer chain. Nytril fibers are no longer manufactured in the United States.

olefin A manufactured fiber in which the fiber-forming substance is any long-chain synthetic polymer composed of at least 85 percent by weight of ethylene, propylene, or other olefin units, except amorphous (noncrystalline) polyolefins.

oleophilic Tending to absorb and retain oily materials.

oleophobic Tending to repel oily materials.

organdy A thin, transparent, stiff, wiry cotton *muslin* used for dresses, neckwear, and trimmings. Organdy, when chemically treated, keeps its crispness through many launderings and does not require restarching. It crushes readily but is easily pressed. Shadow organdy has a faint printed design in self-color.

organzine A yarn of two or more plies with a medium twist.

orientation See *molecular orientation.*

Osnaburg Named for the town in Germany

where it was first made, a coarse cotton or blended fiber fabric in a *plain weave* that resembles crash. It is finished for use in upholstery, slacks, and sportswear. It was originally used unbleached for grain and cement sacks.

ottoman A heavy corded silk or synthetic fabric with larger and rounder ribs than *faille,* used for coats, skirts, and trimmings. *Fillings* of the cloth are usually cotton or wool, and they should be completely covered by the silk or man-made fiber *warp.*

outing flannel A soft, lightweight, *plain-* or *twill-*weave fabric usually napped on both sides. Most outing flannels have colored yarn stripes. Outing flannel soils easily, and the nap washes and wears off. It is used chiefly for sleeping garments.

oxford cloth Soft, somewhat porous cotton shirting fabric given a silklike luster finish. A basket weave, usually of 2 × 1 construction, and available in plain white or colors; the fabric tends to soil easily because of the soft, bulky filling yarns. Oxford cloth is commonly used for shirts and blouses because it is soft and porous and therefore comfortable.

oxford shirting A cotton or blended fabric in a basket weave first made in Oxford, England, and used for shirts, blouses, and sportswear.

panné Usually applied to either satin or velvet and identifies a surface with an unusually high luster.

peau de soie A heavy but soft *satin* with a very fine cross rib and a low luster. The term is French for ''skin of silk.''

percale A medium-weight, *plain-weave* printed cotton, such as 80 × 80; a staple of dress goods. Percale sheets are high quality, with a count of at least 180 threads per square inch. Most percales are made of combed yarns with a count of 84 × 96 or 180 threads per inch. Some fine percale sheets count over 200 threads per inch, such as 96 × 104 or 96 × 108.

permanent press A term applied to textile products that have been treated so they retain their appearance following laundering.

picks See *filling yarns.*

pile A surface effect of raised yarn ends on fabric, accomplished by the introduction of yarn loops, cut or uncut, or other erect yarns ends.

pile weave A weave in which additional sets of yarns are interlaced during weaving to form the raised effect.

pilling The formation of tiny balls of fiber in the surface of a fabric.

piqué Strictly, a ribbed or corded cotton with wales running across the fabric. The term is often used in the trade to refer to Bedford cord or warp piqué, in which the cords run lengthwise.

plain weave One of the three basic weaves. In plain weave each filling yarn passes successively over and under each warp yarn with each row alternating.

plissé Usually a print cloth treated with chemicals that cause parts of the cloth to shrink, creating a permanently crinkled surface.

ply yarn A yarn in which two or more single strands are twisted together.

polyamide A synthetic polymer in which the simple compounds used in production are linked together by amide (—NH—CO—) linkages.

polyester A manufactured fiber in which the fiber-forming substance is any long-chain synthetic polymer composed of at least 85 percent by weight of an ester of a substituted aromatic carboxylic acid, including but not restricted to substituted terephthalate units and para substituted hydroxybenzoate units.

polyethylene An olefin fiber made of ethylene monomer units.

polymer A large molecule produced by linking together many *monomers.*

polymerization The conversion of monomers into large molecules or polymers.

polypropylene An olefin fiber made of propylene monomer units.

polyvinyl alcohol fiber See *vinal.*

pongee (1) A thin, natural tan-colored silk fabric originally made of Chinese *wild silk* with a knotty rough weave, named for the Chinese ''Pun-ki,'' meaning ''woven at home on one's own loom.'' It is used primarily for summer suits and dresses, and both plain fabrics and prints are used for decorative purposes. (2) A staple fine-combed cotton fabric finished with a high luster and used for underclothing. (3) A man-made fiber fabric simulating pongee.

poplin A tightly woven, high-count cotton with fine cross ribs formed by heavy *filling yarns* and fewer, finer *warp yarns.* Poplin has heavier ribs, heavier threads, and slightly lower count than broadcloth, ranging from 80 × 40 to 116 × 56.

printcloth A medium-weight, plain-weave fabric made of carded yarns. Yarn count may vary from 64 × 64 to 80 square; widths vary widely. Printcloths are converted into a wide variety of differently finished fabrics and printed with many different types of patterns.

printing A process for applying color patterns to the surface of yarns or fabrics.

protein fibers Fibers made up of amino acids in various configurations. May be natural, such as wool or silk, or man-made, such as the azlons.

pulled wool Wool pulled from the hide of a slaughtered animal.

punti di Roma knits A *double-knit fabric* combining the appearance of rib and *jersey* stitches. It involves interlock knitting for two rows, followed by one row knitted on dial needles only and then one row knitted on cylinder needles only.

quill A tube of wood, metal, or plastic on which the *filling yarn* is wound. The quill is placed in a shuttle to deliver the filling yarn during weaving on shuttle-type looms.

raw silk Silk that has not been degummed.

rayon A manufactured fiber composed of *regenerated cellulose* as well as manufactured fibers composed of regenerated cellulose in which substituents have replaced not more than 15 percent of the hydrogens of the hydroxyl groups.

reeling The process of winding silk *filaments* onto a wheel.

regenerated cellulose Material which begins as cellulose, is converted to some other form during some stage in the chemical processing, and, finally, reappears as cellulose during the final stage of manufacture.

reprocessed wool Wool fibers reclaimed from the scraps of fabric that have never been used.

residual shrinkage The shrinkage remaining in a fabric after final finishing and processing.

resiliency The ability of a fabric to return to its original shape after compressing, bending, or other deformation.

retting The removal, usually by soaking, of the outer woody portion of the flax plant to gain access to the fibers.

reused wool Wool fibers reclaimed from fabrics that have been worn or used.

ribbon Narrow fabric made by special weaving techniques in several widths and designated for trimming.

roving The process by which a sliver of many fibers is attenuated to between ¼ and ⅛ of its original size; also, the product of this operation.

rubber A manufactured fiber in which the fiber-forming substance is composed of natural or synthetic rubber.

sailcloth A very heavy, strong, *plain-weave* fabric made of cotton, linen, or jute. There are many qualities and weights. Sailcloth can be used for sportswear, slipcovers, curtains, and other heavy-duty items.

saran A manufactured fiber in which the fiber-forming substance is any long-chain synthetic polymer composed of at least 80 percent by weight of vinylidene dichloride units ($-CH_2-CCl_2-$).

sateen A cotton or spun-yarn fabric characterized by *floats* running in the *filling* direction. It is usually *mercerized* and used for linings, draperies, and comforters.

satin weave One of the three basic weaves. Satin weave fabrics are characterized by *floats* running in the *warp* direction in such a manner as to impart a gloss, luster, or shine to the fabric.

slipper satin A closely woven, very strong satin fabric made of silk or man-made fibers and frequently with brocade effects. Used in evening shoes, evening dresses, and wraps. It is an extremely heavy and strong satin construction.

saturation regain The moisture in a material at 95 or 100 percent relative humidity.

scroop A characteristic rustling or crunching sound acquired by silk that has been immersed in solutions of acetic or tartaric acid and dried without rinsing. It is probably caused by acid microcrystals in the fiber rubbing across each other.

scutching The separation of the outer covering of the flax stalk from the usable fibers.

seersucker A lightweight cotton or cotton blend with crinkled stripes woven in by setting some of the *warp yarns* tight and others slack.

selvage One of the long, finished edges of a bolt of fabric.

serge One of the oldest basic terms in textiles, it now implies any smooth face cloth made with a two-up-and-two-down twill weave. Frequently of worsted yarns; it is made in many weights and textures. The cloth is usually piece dyed. Worsted serge gives excellent service, holds the creases very well but develops a shine with wear because of the high twist in the yarns and the compactness of the weave. Today, serge may be made of fibers other than wool.

sericulture   The raising of silkworms and production of silk.

shantung   Originally, a hand-loomed *plain-weave* fabric made in China. Made of *wild silk,* the fabric had an irregular surface. Today the term "shantung" is applied to a plain-weave fabric with heavier, rougher yarns running in the crosswise direction of the fabric. These are single complex yarns of the slub type. The fabric can be made of cotton, silk, or man-made fibers.

sharkskin   (1) A cotton, linen, silk, or man-made fiber fabric with a sleek, hard-finished, crisp, and pebbly surface and a chalky luster. *Filament yarns,* when used, are twisted and woven tightly in either a *plain-weave* or a basket-weave construction, depending upon the effect desired. *Staple-fiber yarns* are handled in the same manner, except for wool. (2) A wool fabric characterized by its *twill weave.* The yarns in both *warp* and *filling* are alternated, white with a color, such as black, brown, or blue. The diagonal lines of the twill weave run from left to right; the colored yarns from right to left.

shed   The opening between *warp yarns* through which *filling yarns* are passed.

shoddy   See *reused wool.*

silk   A continuous-filament fiber formed by the silkworm or by larvae of certain other insects.

silk noil   Short ends of silk fibers used in making rough, textured, spun yarns or in blends with cotton or wool; sometimes called waste silk.

single-knit fabric   A weft-knitted fabric constructed with one set of needles.

single yarn   (1) A yarn composed of short *staple fibers* with sufficient twist to hold together. It is the simplest yarn structure. (2) A yarn composed of several *filaments* held together by sufficient twist. (3) Other single yarns may be made from a single filament, *monofilament* yarn, and from strips of material, such as paper, foil, and plastic sheets.

sisal   A bast fiber obtained from the leaves of the agave plant.

sliver   See *card sliver.*

spandex   A manufactured fiber in which the fiber-forming substance is a long-chain synthetic poly-

mer comprised of at least 85 percent of a segmented polyurethane.

specific gravity   The ratio of the mass of a material to the mass of an equal volume of water at 4°C. See also *density.*

spinning   The process or processes used in the manufacture of *yarns* and of *filament fibers.*

spinning quality   The ease with which fibers lend themselves to yarn-manufacturing processes; *cohesiveness.*

spun silk   Yarns made from short fibers of pierced cocoons or from short ends at the outside and inside edges of the cocoons.

spun yarns   Yarns composed of *staple fibers.*

staple fibers   Short fibers that are measured in inches or fractions of inches (or centimeters).

suede cloth   A woven, knitted, or formed fabric of cotton, man-made fibers, wool, or blends, finished to resemble suede leather. It is used in sports coats, gloves, lining, other items of apparel, and accessories.

surah   A soft, usually twilled fabric often of silk or man-made fibers, woven in plaids, stripes, or prints. It is used for ties, mufflers, blouses, and dresses.

swiss   See *dotted swiss.*

synthesized fibers   Fibers made from chemicals that were never fibrous in character.

synthetic fiber   A fiber made from chemicals that were never fibrous in form; more frequently referred to as "man-made synthesized fiber."

taffeta   A fine, *plain-weave* fabric, smooth on both sides, usually with a sheen on its surface. It is named for the Persian fabric "taftan." Taffeta may be a solid color or printed or woven so that the colors appear iridescent. It is often constructed with a fine rib; this fabric is correctly called *faille* taffeta.

tapestry   A fabric in which the pattern is woven with colored weft or *filling yarns.* It is used extensively for wall hangings and table covers.

tenacity   The tensile strength of a fiber, expressed as force per unit of linear density of an unstrained specimen. It is usually expressed in grams per *denier* or grams per *tex.*

tensile strength   The maximum tensile stress required to rupture a fiber, expressed as pounds per square inch or grams per square centimeter.

terrycloth   A heavy, absorbent cotton made with extra heavy *warp yarns* woven into loops on one or both sides.

tetrafluoroethylene A textile fiber made in either staple or filament form from tetrafluoroethylene *monomer* units. Called Teflon.

tex A unit for expressing linear density, equal to the weight in grams of 1000 meters (1 km) of yarn, filament, fiber, or other textile strand. The term "tex" is used as one system for identifying yarn number. See also *denier*.

textile Generally used to identify any product made from fibers of spinnable length. More specifically: (1) *Staple fibers* or *filaments* suitable for conversion into yarns and for the preparation of woven, knitted, or nonwoven fabric. (2) *Yarns* made from natural or man-made fiber. (3) Fabrics made from fibers and yarns. (4) End-use articles fabricated from fibers, yarns, and/or fabrics when the product retains the flexibility and drape of the original yarn or fabric.

textured yarns Yarns that develop stretch and/or bulk as a part of subsequent processing. The process imparts the desirable properties of spun *staple yarns* to *filament yarns*.

texturing The process of imparting crimp, loops, or other modifications to continuous *filament yarns*. Texturing produces yarns with increased cover, resiliency, abrasion resistance, warmth, insulation properties, and moisture absorption. It provides modified surface textures.

thermoplastic Tending to become soft and/or moldable upon application of heat.

thermosetting A procedure in which a substance is softened by heat, whereupon the substance undergoes chemical change, becomes firm, and assumes a completely different structure and different properties. The substance cannot be softened by reapplications of heat.

thread A strong *yarn*, usually *ply* or cord, of even surface especially designed for sewing or other needlework.

three-dimensional polymers A *polymer* formed when molecules unite in both length and width, producing a relatively rigid structure. This is typical of polymers used in finishing textiles.

ticking A heavy *twill* made with a colored yarn stripe in the *warp*. It is used for mattress covers, home furnishings, and sportswear.

tow A large strand (1 or more inches or 2.5 or more cm in diameter) of continuous man-made *filament fibers* extruded simultaneously through one large spinnerette. Tow has little or no twist and is collected in a loose, ropelike form. It is held together by *crimp*. Tow may be cut into *staple fiber* lengths and processed on regular spinning equipment or it can be processed on special tow conversion machinery directly into sliver or yarn.

toweling Any of several types of fabric intended for use as towels; specifically, fabric woven in long pieces and then cut to the desired sizes, as distinguished from cloth woven in towel lengths with borders or other decorations. Cotton or linen is generally used and the fabric is often relatively coarse in texture with low-twist yarns that are absorbent.

trade name A name given by a manufacturer or merchant to a product to distinguish it as one produced or sold by that manufacturer. It is called, more accurately, a trademark name and may be protected as a trademark.

trademark A word, letter, device, or symbol used in connection with merchandise and alluding distinctly to the origin or ownership of the product to which it is applied.

tram silk A low-twist *ply* silk yarn formed by combining two or three *single yarns*.

triacetate A man-made fiber produced from cellulose triacetate. See also *acetate*.

tricot The most common, and the simplest, warp-knit fabric. Tricot has fine *wales* on the face and ribs on the back that parallel the *courses*. It can be made plain or in patterns such as meshes or stripes.

trilobal A fiber with a modified cross section having three lobes.

tropical suiting A lightweight *plain-weave* suiting for men's and women's summer wear. It has various weaves and is made of a variety of fibers. If called "tropical worsted," it must be an all-wool *worsted* fabric.

tweed A term derived from the river Tweed in Scotland, where the fabrics were first woven. It is now used to describe a wide range of light to heavy, rough-textured, sturdy fabrics characterized by their mixed color effect. Tweeds can be made of *plain, twill,* or *herringbone* weave, with practically any fiber or mixture of fibers.

twill weave One of the three basic weaves. Yarns are interlaced in such a manner that dominant diagonal lines are observed. The weave is characterized by a series of *floats* staggered in a definite pattern in the *warp* direction.

tussah silk See *wild silk*.

unbalanced yarns Yarns in which there is sufficient twist to set up a torque effect, so that the yarn will untwist and retwist in the opposite direction.

velour A soft, closely woven, smooth fabric with a short, thick pile. It is named for the French word for velvet. Velour is often made of cotton, wool, or mohair.

velvet A fabric with a short, soft, thick, warp-pile surface, usually made of silk or man-made pile fiber with a cotton back. It is sometimes made of all silk or all cotton. The fabric is often woven double, face to face, and then, while still on the loom, it is cut apart by a small shuttle knife. There are several varieties of velvet, which differ in weight, closeness of pile, and transparency.

velveteen A filling pile fabric in which the pile is made by cutting an extra set of filling yarns which are woven into the fabric in a float construction and bound into the base fabric by the warp yarns. Differs from velvet in that velvet is a warp pile fabric, whereas velveteen is a filling pile.

venetian satin A type of warp-faced satin that is stronger than regular satin and heavier; each end floats over seven picks and interlaces with the eighth pick, producing a smooth surface with a slight twill-line effect to the right. It is tightly woven. Made of combed ply yarns and generally mercerized and schreinered for a high luster. Originally this was of all cotton, but today it is made of blends of cotton and other fibers such as polyester and of all rayon yarns.

vinal A manufactured fiber in which the fiber-forming substance is any long-chain synthetic polymer composed of at least 50 percent by weight of vinyl alcohol units ($-CH_2-CHOH-$), and in which the total of the vinyl alcohol units and any one or more of the various acetal units is at least 85 percent by weight of the fiber.

vinyon A manufactured fiber in which the fiber-forming substance is any long-chain synthetic polymer composed of at least 85 percent by weight of vinyl chloride units ($-CH_2-CHCl-$).

virgin wool New wool that is made into yarns and fabrics for the first time.

viscose rayon One type of rayon produced by xanthating cellulose and dissolving it in sodium hydroxide. The solution is extruded into an acid bath where the pure cellulose is regenerated and coagulated into filament form.

voile A sheer, transparent, soft, lightweight *plain-weave* fabric made of highly twisted yarns. It can be composed of wool, cotton, silk, or a man-made fiber. Voile is used for blouses, dresses, curtains, and similar items.

waffle cloth A fabric with a characteristic honeycomb weave. When made in cotton it is called waffle piqué. It is used for coatings, draperies, dresses, and toweling.

wale A column of loops that are parallel to the loop axis and to the long measurement of a knit fabric.

warp yarns Yarns that run parallel to the *selvage* or longer dimension of a fabric.

waste silk See *silk noil.*

weaving The method of forming fabrics by interlacing two or more sets of yarns, *warp* and *filling,* at right angles to each other.

weft yarns See *filling yarns.*

whipcord A *twill-weave* fabric similar to *gabardine* but with a more pronounced diagonal rib on the right side. It is so named because it simulates the lash of a whip. Cotton whipcords are often four-harness warp-twill weaves.

wickability The property of a fiber that allows moisture to move rapidly along the fiber surface and pass quickly through the fabric.

wild silk Silk produced by moths of species other than *Bombyx mori.* It is tan to brown in color and is coarser and more uneven than ordinary silk. It is usually called tussah silk.

wilton carpet Wilton carpeting or wilton rugs are a cut pile construction made with Jacquard designs. The pile yarns may be either worsted or woolen, whereas the base yarns may be of cotton. Worsted wilton is considered to be the best carpet made.

woof yarns See *filling yarns.*

wool A fine fiber (hair) obtained from the sheep. In labeling, the term ''wool'' may also be used to identify fibers from other fleece animals such as the Angora goat, the cashmere goat, camel, alpaca, llama, and vicuna.

worsted yarn Smooth-surfaced yarn spun from long-staple, evenly combed, and wool fibers.

woven fabric Fabric composed of at least two sets of yarns, one *warp* (longitudinal) and one *filling* (crosswise), interlaced at right angles to each other.

yarn A continuous strand of textile fibers, *staple* or *filament*, in a form suitable for knitting, weaving, or other method of intertwining to form a fabric. The term "yarn" may be applied to narrow strips of material used in textile construction.

zibeline A fabric made of wool, cotton, camel's hair, mohair, or man-made fibers. It is characterized by a long, sleek nap brushed, steamed, and pressed in one direction, thus hiding the underlying *satin weave*.

Index